DAVIS RICH DEWEY

AF873362

FINANCIAL HISTORY OF THE UNITED STATES

Elibron Classics
www.elibron.com

Elibron Classics series.

ISBN 1-4021-9737-3 (paperback)
ISBN 1-4212-9811-2 (hardcover)

This Elibron Classics Replica Edition is an unabridged facsimile of the edition published in 1922 by Logmans, Green and Co., New York.

AMERICAN CITIZEN SERIES

EDITED BY

ALBERT BUSHNELL HART, LL.D.

FINANCIAL HISTORY

OF

THE UNITED STATES

DAVIS RICH DEWEY, PH.D.

AMERICAN CITIZEN SERIES

EDITED BY ALBERT BUSHNELL HART, LL.D.

Outline of Practical Sociology; with Special Reference to American Conditions.

By CARROLL D. WRIGHT, President of Clark College. With Maps and Diagrams. [*New Edition preparing.*]

Actual Government as Applied under American Conditions.

By ALBERT BUSHNELL HART, LL.D., Eaton Professor of the Science of Government in Harvard University. With 6 Colored Maps and 11 other Illustrations and Diagrams. Crown 8vo.

Financial History of the United States.

By DAVIS R. DEWEY, PH.D., LL.D., Professor of Economics and Statistics in the Massachusetts Institute of Technology. With Diagrams. Crown 8vo.

Constitutional Law in the United States.

By EMLIN MCCLAIN, LL.D., sometime Lecturer on Constitutional Law at the State University of Iowa. Crown 8vo.

Principles of Economics; with Special Reference to American Conditions.

By EDWIN R. A. SELIGMAN, PH.D., LL.D., McVickar Professor of Political Economy in Columbia University. With 6 Colored and 22 other Diagrams. Crown 8vo.

Organized Democracy; An Introduction to the Study of American Politics.

By FREDERICK A. CLEVELAND, PH.D., LL.D. Crown 8vo.

Public Opinion and Popular Government.

By A. LAWRENCE LOWELL. President of Harvard University. Crown 8vo.

LONGMANS, GREEN, & CO.: NEW YORK

American Citizen Series

Financial History
of
The United States

BY

DAVIS RICH DEWEY, PH.D., LL.D.,
PROFESSOR OF ECONOMICS AND STATISTICS,
MASSACHUSETTS INSTITUTE OF TECHNOLOGY.

EIGHTH EDITION

LONGMANS, GREEN AND CO.
55 FIFTH AVENUE, NEW YORK
LONDON, BOMBAY, CALCUTTA, AND MADRAS
1922

First edition, February, 1903
Second edition, revised, November, 1903
Third edition, revised, July, 1907
Reprinted, August, 1909; August, 1911
Fourth edition, revised, August, 1912
Fifth edition, revised, January, 1915
Sixth edition, revised, January, 1918
Seventh edition, May, 1920
Eighth edition, revised, June, 1922

MADE IN THE UNITED STATES

TO THE SEMINARY

OF THE

DEPARTMENT OF HISTORY, POLITICS, AND ECONOMICS

OF JOHNS HOPKINS UNIVERSITY,

Of which the author was a member from 1883 to 1886. Under the guidance of Adams, Ely, and Jameson, we read and learned. The first has gone, leaving affectionate memories and organized activities of permanent usefulness; the others are still doing their work in a spirit of broad-minded sympathy and fine scholarship.

Preface.

THE attempt to compress into a volume of moderate size an account of Federal finance from the Colonial period down to the present time occasions perplexity. Some knowledge of politics and economics must be pre-supposed, but the exact measure it is difficult to estimate. In order to place readers as far as possible on a common basis, the reference lists which are scattered through the volume have been constructed on a generous plan. In no way, however, are these lists to be regarded as conditional to an understanding of the text; they are simply opportunities for a better preparation, or a further study of special topics.

In writing this work, I have kept two things constantly in mind: first, its proportions, or the general perspective; and second, the relations of financial legislation to democracy. It is easy in the light of accumulated experience to pass judgment on the errors of the past, but historical study, in my opinion, is more fruitful if the reader endeavors to interpret the past in accordance with the experience which was available at the time the occurrences took place. Past environment is the true test of past action. With this conviction, I have endeavored to refrain, possibly not with entire consistency, from emphasizing the mistakes of previous generations. A work on "American Finance" might well have a didactic purpose, but this is a history and not a treatise.

In determining the proportions of this volume, I have been obliged to pass by many incidents of keen interest; the omissions are necessarily far greater than the inclusions. The result is doubtless a loss of interest, but it is hoped that the gain from an orderly presentation of the essential facts may be a substantial compensation.

It is impossible to include by name all of those who have given friendly counsel, but I wish to thank in particular the editor of this series, Professor Hart, and Professor Henry B. Gardner, of Brown University. The former undertook a very considerate reading of the manuscript, and without the support of his knowledge of American history my task would have been much more difficult. To Professor Gardner I am under great indebtedness; his learning and sound judgment have constantly stood me in good stead, and strengthened a friendship of long standing. I also wish to make acknowledgment to Professor Bullock, who has done pioneer work for several periods of American finance; his investigations justify the hope that he will find opportunity to write a larger work on the finances of our country. I am in a special way indebted to my colleague, Professor Currier, to Mr. S. N. D. North, and to various officials of the Treasury Department.

MASSACHUSETTS INSTITUTE OF TECHNOLOGY,
BOSTON, *January*, 1903.

Since the original appearance of this volume, changes have been made in successive editions in order to bring the narrative down to date. The earlier writing has been amplified by two chapters, one of which is added for this edition in order to cover the financing of the war in 1917–1918, and the three succeeding years.

June, 1922.

SUGGESTIONS FOR STUDENTS, TEACHERS, AND READERS.

I. Introductory Reading: Political History and Biography.

It is hardly necessary to say that the student of American finance should be acquainted with the main outlines of the political history of the United States, and also have some general knowledge of that part of applied economics which deals with taxation and monetary questions. It is believed that a knowledge of American history as represented in the series, "Epochs of American History," will enable the reader to apply an intelligent judgment to the following narrative of fiscal events, but as a further help precise page references have been given in the several chapters to general historical works which show the relation of politics to financial affairs. With this end in view, as an introduction to more special reading, the following list of histories and biographies is also suggested. Of the larger histories, that by Schouler is probably the most helpful single work, as it extends over a long period, 1783–1861, and gives prominence to tariff and banking questions. Of the biographies, those of Lodge on *Hamilton*, Stevens on *Gallatin*, Schurz on *Clay*, Sumner on *Jackson*, Hart on *Chase*, and Burton on *Sherman*, are to be recommended. These and other works are noted below; the descriptive notes will enable the student to select the volumes in which he may be especially interested.

ADAMS, HENRY. *History of the United States of America* (during the administrations of Jefferson and Madison). (N. Y., 1889–1891. 9 vols.) — An authoritative history for the period covered. The index in Vol. IX is very full; see Bank of U. S.; Banks, State; Dallas, A. J.; Finances; Gallatin; Loans; Manufactures; Specie; Specie payments; Taxes; Treasury notes.

ADAMS, HENRY. *The Life of Albert Gallatin.* (Philadelphia, 1880.) — Of the greatest value for 1801–1813, pp. 267–492.

BLAINE, JAMES GILLESPIE. *Twenty Years of Congress, from Lincoln to Garfield.* (Norwich, Conn., 1884. 2 vols.) — Valuable as a record of political events. Extracts from many debates; Vol. I, chapters 18, 19, 22 treat of the finances of Civil War period; Vol. II, chapters 13 and 24 of post-bellum financial legislation.

BOUTWELL, GEORGE SEWALL. *Reminiscences of Sixty Years in Public Affairs.* (N. Y., 1902. 2 vols.) — Is interesting for side-lights on the establishment of the internal revenue system and on bond issues after the Civil War.

BURTON, THEODORE E. *John Sherman.* (Boston, 1906.) — More a financial narrative than a biography.

DALLAS, GEORGE MIFFLIN. *Life and Writings of A. J. Dallas.* (Philadelphia, 1871.)

GORDY, JOHN PANCOAST. *A History of Political Parties in the United States.* (N. Y., 1900–1904. 2 vols.) — Concise and valuable for Constitution, and Hamilton's policy; see Vol. I, chapters 2–9, 13; Vol. II, chapters 20, 25, 28.

HART, ALBERT BUSHNELL. *Salmon Portland Chase.* (Boston, etc., 1899.) — The best critical biography of Chase; see chapters 9 and 11 on finances of the Civil War, and chapter 15 on the Supreme Court decisions.

HOLST, HERMANN EDUARD VON. *The Constitutional and Political History of the United States.* Translated by John J. Lalor and others. (Chicago, 1877–1892. 7 vols. and an index vol.) — Devoted primarily to political aspects of slavery; consult, however, in index, Vol. IX, Bank; Banks; Commercial Crisis, 1837; ditto, 1857; Nullification; Public Lands; Sub-Treasury; Tariff.

LODGE, HENRY CABOT. *Alexander Hamilton.* (Boston, etc. 11th ed., 1895.) — An appreciative study by a political admirer.

MCCULLOCH, HUGH. *Men and Measures of Half a Century.* (N. Y., 1889.) — Though discursive and anecdotal, it throws much light on banking in the West before the Civil War, and on financial operations of the treasury at its close.

MCMASTER, JOHN BACH. *History of the People of the United States from the Revolution to the Civil War.* (N. Y., 1883–1913. 8 vols. published.) — The volumes published, covering the period 1783–1861, contain serviceable indexes and descriptive tables of contents; currency and tariff controversies are described.

MORSE, JOHN TORREY, Jr. *Life of Alexander Hamilton.* (Boston, 1876. 2 vols.) — A fuller biography than that of Lodge; sympathetic yet critical.

OBERHOLTZER, ELLIS P. *Jay Cooke, Financier of the Civil War.* (Phila., 1907. 2 vols.) — Describes methods of placing loans and the relations of the government to the national banks during the Civil War period and subsequently to 1872.

OBERHOLTZER, ELLIS P. *Robert Morris, Patriot and Financier.* (N. Y., 1903.) — Biography based on family papers. Consult chapter 3.

RHODES, JAMES FORD. *History of the United States from the Compromise of 1850.* (N. Y., 1892–1906. 7 vols.) — Covers the period, 1850–1877.

SHEPARD, EDWARD M. *Martin Van Buren.* (Boston, etc., 1888.) — Contains an excellent study of economic conditions, 1830–1840.

SHERMAN, JOHN. *Recollections of Forty Years, a Biography.* (The Werner Company, Chicago, N. Y., etc., 1895.) — As an account of the author's active participation in public finance, the memoirs are of great interest.

SCHOULER, JAMES. *History of the United States of America under the Constitution.* (Rev. ed., N. Y., 1913. 7 vols.) — Covers the period 1783–1877; a most serviceable account of political events; the descriptive tables of contents can be used to advantage.

SCHUCKERS, JACOB WILLIAM. *Life and Public Services of Salmon Portland Chase.* (N. Y., 1874.) — Contains extracts from documents and letters; a full biography, but not critical.

SCHURZ, CARL. *Life of Henry Clay.* (2 vols. 5th ed., Boston and N. Y., 1888.) — An excellent biography, but the tariff contests, 1820–1830, are not brought into prominence; see, however, Vol. II for the period 1833–1837.

STEVENS, JOHN AUSTIN. *Albert Gallatin.* (4th ed., Boston, 1886.) — The author was equipped by business training to treat of finance. See chapter 6 for period 1801–1812.

SUMNER, WILLIAM GRAHAM. *Alexander Hamilton.* (In "Makers of America" series, N. Y., 1890.) — A critical and almost harsh study of Hamilton; very valuable to the student of finance.

SUMNER, WILLIAM GRAHAM. *Andrew Jackson.* (Boston, etc. new ed., 1899.) — Shows wide reading in contemporary documents; treats of land, internal improvements, tariff, second U. S. Bank, and currency.

TYLER, SAMUEL. *Memoir of Roger Brooke Taney, Chief Justice of the Supreme Court of the United States.* (Baltimore, 1872. Rev. ed., 1876.)

II. Financial Histories

There are but few histories devoted exclusively to public finance; only one, indeed, that by Bolles, covers the general field over an extended period. The reader must therefore rely upon works on taxation, the tariff, coinage, and banking, and for special topics and episodes will often find the most satisfactory treatment in the political histories and biographies already referred to. The following volumes represent those which are most general in their treatment; of these the works of Bolles and Noyes are especially to be recommended; the narrative by Bolles stops with 1885, while the smaller work by Noyes is confined to the period 1865–1907. There is a great need of detailed works on the expenditures of the government and the various phases of treasury administration.

ADAMS, EPHRAIM D. *The Control of the Purse in the United States Government.* (Reprinted from the *Kansas University Quarterly*, April, 1894.) — An academic study of the debates in Congress on the interpretation of constitutional provisions relating to treasury management, loans, taxation, and money bills. Careful references are given.

BOLLES, ALBERT SIDNEY. *American Finance, with Chapters on Money and Banking.* (N. Y., 1901.) — Especially valuable on expenditures; treats also of State finance. A discussion of present conditions rather than historical.

BOLLES, ALBERT SIDNEY. *The Financial History of the United States.* (2d ed. N. Y., 1884–1886. 3 vols.) — Vol. I includes the period 1774–1789; II, 1789–1860; III, 1861–1885. The only single work which covers an extensive period; it represents research, and is closely restricted to questions of finance; no attempt is made to sketch in the political and social background, and the reader may be confused without preliminary reading. The author leans to protection, and takes the banker's point of view in questions of currency. The work is especially valuable for chapters on accounting and expenditures. Referred to as Bolles.

BOURNE, EDWARD GAYLORD. *The History of the Surplus Revenue of 1837.* (N. Y., etc., 1885.) — A brief, scholarly monograph with abundant references and bibliography. In addition to the historical account, it summarizes the earlier proposals of distribution of surplus funds in the treasury.

BRONSON, HENRY. *Historical Account of Connecticut Currency, Continental Money, and the Finances of the Revolution.* (In *New Haven Colony Hist. Soc. Papers*, Vol. I. New Haven, 1865.) — This is more than a local study; the author is drawn into a general review of the financial measures of the Revolutionary War. The essay is scholarly and the style vigorous.

BULLOCK, CHARLES JESSE. *Finances of the United States, 1775–1789, with Especial Reference to the Budget.* (Madison, 1895. Univ. of Wisconsin. *Bulletin, Economics,* etc., Vol. I, No. 2.) — The best monograph on the finances of the Revolutionary period, with bibliographies at the beginning of each chapter. Indispensable to the advanced student.

KEARNY, JOHN WATTS. *Sketch of American Finances, 1789–1835.* (N. Y., 1887.) — A brief study of 150 pages, clear and helpful in questions concerning the treatment of the debt. Little attention is given to taxation.

NOYES, ALEXANDER DANA. *Thirty Years of American Finance, 1865–1896.* (N. Y., etc., 1898.) — Treats the earlier period very briefly, but is of special value for 1878–1895. Relation of public finance to the money market is given prominence. This has been replaced by *Forty Years of American Finance* (1909), bringing the history down to 1907. The references to the earlier edition have been allowed to stand.

SCHUCKERS, JACOB WILLIAM. *Brief Account of the Finances and Paper Money of the Revolutionary War.* (Philadelphia, 1874.) — The style is somewhat rhetorical, and, while the writer has on the whole chosen sound authorities, the essay does not indicate a very wide research. Is an interesting account within a moderate space.

SCOTT, WILLIAM A. *The Repudiation of State Debts.* (N. Y., etc., 1893.) — Chapters 2–6 are historical, describing various acts of repudiation in twelve States. Of value as explaining some of the remote influences affecting federal credit, 1825–1850.

SPAULDING, ELBRIDGE GERRY. *History of the Legal Tender Paper Money issued during the Great Rebellion.* (Buffalo, 1869.) — The title is hardly accurate; the volume is largely a collection of documents, speeches, etc., relating to the legal tender acts.

SUMNER, WILLIAM GRAHAM. *The Financier and Finances of the American Revolution.* (N. Y., 1891. 2 vols.) — Contains a mine of valuable material, but is not clearly arranged.

SUMNER, WILLIAM GRAHAM. *A History of American Currency.* (N. Y., 1876.) — A series of topical notes designed for reference rather than consecutive reading.

WELLS, DAVID AMES. *Practical Economics.* (N. Y., etc., 1885.) — Treats of the silver question, tariff revision, and, most valuable of all, experience of the United States in taxing distilled spirits, subsequent to the Civil War.

III. Paper Money, Banking, and Loans.

The list of titles on particular questions of American finance could be made very extensive. The tariff and money have been at one time or another subjects of party struggle, and given rise to an interminable amount of controversial writing in pamphlets, governmental reports, magazine articles, speeches, and addresses. Much of this is of little value, and yet it has to be taken into account in order to understand the kind of reasoning which has appealed to American democracy, and which in the mass has powerfully affected the general trend of public action. With a full appreciation of the mischief which may result from indiscriminate reading, an endeavor has been made in the reference lists of the several chapters to present various points of view. The following selected list, however, is restricted to volumes which deal with facts rather than with theories; if it be urged that these volumes are too one-sided in their method of interpretation, the answer is that thus far the advocates of opposing theories have not devoted attention to historical exposition.

The reader must also bear in mind that this volume does not include a narrative of bank currency or of coinage. The limits of the work do not permit it, even if there were a logical reason for their inclusion. Fortunately, finance has a restricted definition which has been taken advantage of in outlining the proportions of this study. The boundaries of banking and coinage often touch upon the borders of finance, and the more frequent excursions the reader can make into this outlying territory, the larger will be his experience and the more penetrating his powers of interpreting matters relating to the public purse.

For facts regarding loans, the history by Bayley and the collection of *Laws*, edited by Dunbar, are of the highest importance; the first for the clear presentation of the statistics of loans, and the second for the statutory provisions governing their issue. On the more special topic of treasury notes the history of *United States Notes*, by Knox, easily stands first; for that of local banking the encyclopædic work of Sumner should be consulted, and for a critical appreciation of the national banking system the single chapter of Dunbar's work, in *Chapters on the Theory and History of Banking*, is suggested as the most useful. The more general work by White, on *Money and Banking*, and the *Report of the Monetary Commission*, prepared by Laughlin, also deserve special recognition. These two latter deal with the most recent developments.

ADAMS, HENRY CARTER. *Public Debts*. (N. Y., 1887.) — An essay in finance rather than a history; but there is frequent suggestive reference to American experience.

American Bankers' Association, 1875–1889. (N. Y., 1890. 2 vols.) — A series of annual reports; volumes subsequent to 1889 can be secured through the secretary of the association. The proceedings are also now published in the *Commercial and Financial Chronicle* (N. Y.). The addresses are presented, as might be expected, from the banker's point of view.

BAYLEY, RAFAEL A. *History of the National Loans of the United States from July 4, 1776, to June 30, 1880*. (In Vol. VII, 10th Census of the U. S., 1880, pp. 295–486; also published separately.) — References are to the paging in the Census volume. Describes the conditions under which each loan was made, with tables of annual issues and redemptions; a work of the highest value to the specialist. Referred to as Bayley.

BULLOCK, CHARLES JESSE. *Essays on the Monetary History of the United States*. (N. Y., etc., 1900.) — Part I. is a general survey of national experience with "cheap money," especially valuable for abundant references in foot-notes; Parts II. and III. are monographs on the paper currencies of North Carolina and New Hampshire. Referred to as Bullock.

CATTERALL, RALPH C. H. *The Second Bank of the United States*. (University of Chicago Press, Chicago, 1903.) — Valuable; based upon a study of the papers of Nicolas Biddle.

CLARKE, MATTHEW ST. CLAIR, and HALL, DAVID A. *Legislative and Documentary History of the Bank of the United States*. (Washington, 1832.) — A collection of reports and debates in Congress.

CLEVELAND, FREDERICK A. *The Bank and the Treasury*. (N. Y., 1905.) — Deals with plans for currency reform.

CONANT, CHARLES A. *A History of Modern Banks of Issue*. (N. Y., 1897; 4th ed., 1911.) — Chapters 13–15 treat of the Bank of the United States, State banking systems, and the national banking system.

DE KNIGHT, WILLIAM F. *History of the Currency of the Country and of the Loans of the United States from the Earliest Period to June 30, 1900*. (2d ed. Washington, 1900. pp. 277.) — Prepared under the direction of the Registrar of the Treasury. Not so clear as the work of Bayley, but covers a later period. Referred to as De Knight.

DUNBAR, CHARLES FRANKLIN. *Laws of the United States relating to Currency, Finance, and Banking from 1789 to 1891*.

(Boston, 1891.) — A necessary handbook for the student of finance; contains the important parts of our national legislation respecting currency, coinage, loans, and banking, carefully annotated and classified. Referred to as Dunbar.

DUNBAR, CHARLES FRANKLIN. *Chapters on the Theory and History of Banking.* (N. Y., etc., 1896.) — The clearest exposition of the theory of banking, with reference to American practice. Chapter 9 is devoted to the national banking system.

DUNBAR, CHARLES FRANKLIN. — *Economic Essays.* (N. Y., 1904.) — A collection of scholarly essays, with a few new papers on state banks and crises.

ELLIOT, JONATHAN, editor. *The Funding System of the United States and Great Britain.* (Washington, 1845.) — A valuable collection of public documents relating to the public debt, for the period 1775-1843. There is a serviceable index. This report constituted Document No. 15, H. R., 28th Cong., 1st Sess.

GOUGE, WILLIAM M. *Short History of Paper Money and Banking in the United States, including an Account of Provincial Continental Paper Money.* (Philadelphia, 1833.) — Part II. contains an historical treatment, and within a narrow compass a large amount of contemporary evidence in regard to the abuses of local banking.

HEPBURN, A. BARTOW. *History of Coinage and Currency in the United States.* (N. Y., 1903.) — Author was formerly comptroller of the currency. Contains bibliography, pp. 437-449; also laws.

KNOX, JOHN JAY. *History of Banking in the United States.* (N. Y., 1900.) — Only a portion of the work was prepared by Mr. Knox; the chapters are of unequal value, but contain much material otherwise inaccessible.

KNOX, JOHN JAY. *United States Notes.* (3d ed. N. Y., 1894.) — A model book, and not likely to be displaced; contains a history of all issues of paper money by the government. Of interest are the facsimiles and forms of treasury notes. In the appendix is the legal tender decision of 1884. Referred to as Knox.

LAUGHLIN, J. LAURENCE. *Report of the Monetary Commission of the Indianapolis Convention.* (Chicago, 1898.) — Of great value to the student. For historical treatment, see pp. 197-223 on the national banking system, and Part III. on demand obligations. Appendix contains copies of laws and valuable tables.

MITCHELL, WESLEY CLAIR. *A History of the Greenbacks.* (Chicago, 1903.) — An authoritative study of the history of the issues and the economic consequences of the legal-tender acts.

PHILLIPS, HENRY, Jr. *Historical Sketches of the Paper Currency of the American Colonies prior to the Adoption of the Federal Constitution.* (Roxbury, Mass., 1865–6. 2 vols.) — Represents a careful antiquarian research, and is the most detailed account in print. Contains bibliographies and lists of issues.

RICHARDSON, WILLIAM ADAMS. *Practical Information concerning the Public Debt of the United States, with the National Banking Laws.* (Washington, 1872.) — Of value for its technical information in regard to terms of bond issues.

SUMNER, WILLIAM GRAHAM. *History of Banking in the United States* (Vol. I. of *History of Banking in all the Leading Nations;* compiled by thirteen authors: *N. Y. Journal of Commerce*, 1896.) · Author has worked from first sources, and is severe in his criticism of early banking methods; there is a lack of recognition of social and political conditions. The work practically stops with 1863, as only a few pages are given to the national banking system.

UPTON, JACOB KENDRICK. *Money in Politics.* (Boston, 1884.) — Historical chapters from colonial period to 1884. Author was once Assistant Secretary of the Treasury; a useful compendium.

WHITE, HORACE. *Money and Banking illustrated by American History.* (Boston and London, 1902.) — One of the best books on the subject; opposed to legal tender paper money. Referred to as H. White. A fourth edition appeared in 1911; references are to the earlier edition which contains historical material omitted in the last.

WILDMAN, M. S. *Money Inflation in the United States.* (N. Y., 1905.) — A suggestive study of opinion and conditions underlying agitation for increased issues of bank notes and treasury notes.

IV. Coinage and Silver Question.

LAUGHLIN, J. LAURENCE. *The History of Bimetallism in the United States.* (4th ed. 1897.) — Is a standard work; contains valuable statistics and extracts from speeches. Author is a prominent gold monometallist.

LINDERMAN, HENRY RICHARD. *Money and Legal Tender in the United States.* (N. Y., 1877.) — Presents in brief form the laws relating to coinage, legal tender, and money standards; definitions of technical terms are clear and concise.

MUHLEMAN, M. L. *Monetary and Banking Systems.* (N. Y., 1908.) — Contains concise summaries and statistics in a convenient form.

RUSSELL, HENRY B. *International Monetary Conferences.* (N. Y., etc., 1898.) — Is not intended to advance any theory, but tells the story of the conferences and the intervening monetary events of importance.

TAUSSIG, FRANK W. *The Silver Situation in the United States.* (N. Y., 1893. Also published as Vol. VII, No. 1, of the *Publications of the American Economic Association*, Jan., 1892.) — A clear and brief monograph on the silver question from 1878 to 1892. The "argument for silver" is analyzed.

WATSON, DAVID K. *History of American Coinage.* (N. Y., etc., 1899.) — Is a history of legislation and legislative opinion rather than of the art of minting.

V. Tariff and Internal Revenue.

For information on the industrial results of taxation, and particularly of the tariff, the reader must seek elsewhere; this volume is confined to a view of taxation as a source of treasury supply. Fortunately, the relations of industry to the tariff have been emphasized in the standard history by Taussig, and this should be freely consulted at every stage of the narrative. Several of the volumes treat of the development of tariff arguments. For internal revenue the volume by Howe is the standard work.

ADAMS, HENRY CARTER. *Taxation in the United States, 1789–1816.* (*Johns Hopkins Univ. Studies*, II, Nos. 5, 6. Baltimore, 1884.) — A scholarly study, which has not been displaced.

ELLIOTT, ORRIN LESLIE. *The Tariff Controversy in the United States, 1789–1833, with a Summary of the Period before the Adoption of the Constitution.* (*Leland Stanford, Jr., University Monographs. History and Economics*, No. 1, Sept., 1892. Palo Alto, Cal.) — Generous extracts are made from the debates; devoted to opinion rather than to industrial results.

GROSVENOR, W. M. *Does Protection Protect?* (N. Y., 1871.) — A criticism of protection, based upon a statistical study of the growth of industries; valuable for its tables.

HILL, WILLIAM. *First Stages of the Tariff Policy of the United States.* (*Pub. American Economic Association*, Vol. VIII, No. 6. Baltimore, 1893.) — A thorough study of colonial tariffs and act of 1789; explains causes which affected public opinion.

HOWE, FRANK C. *Taxation and Taxes in the United States under the Internal Revenue System, 1791–1895.* (N. Y., etc., 1896.) — The only complete study of the subject, and designed for the special student.

LAUGHLIN, J. LAURENCE, and WILLIS, H. PARKER. *Reciprocity.* (N. Y., 1903.) — Valuable for tariff history since 1890. Full bibliography.

RABBENO, UGO. *The American Commercial Policy.* (2d ed. London, etc., 1895.) — A fair treatment of our commercial policy from colonial times.

STANWOOD, EDWARD. *American Tariff Controversies in the Nineteenth Century.* (N. Y., 1903. 2 vols.) — A valuable history. Referred to as Stanwood.

SUMNER, WILLIAM GRAHAM. *Lectures on the History of Protection in the United States.* (N. Y., 1884.) — Five lectures delivered before the International Free-trade Alliance; polemical as well as historical.

TARBELL, IDA. *The Tariff in Our Times.* (N. Y., 1911.) — A narrative history from 1860 to 1911; opposed to protection; not systematic, and to be used as supplementary reading to throw light upon efforts of special interests to secure protection.

TAUSSIG, FRANK W. *The Tariff History of the United States.* (5th ed. N. Y., etc., 1910.) — The best volume on the subject; although emphasis is placed upon the benefits of commercial freedom, there is an entire absence of controversial bias. Valuable for analysis of industrial results

THOMPSON, ROBERT ELLIS. *Protection to Home Industry.* (N. Y., 1886.) — Four lectures delivered at Harvard University. Protectionist point of view; controversial rather than historical.

PUBLIC DOCUMENTS ON THE TARIFF.

Customs Regulations of the United States prescribed for the Instruction and Guidance of Officers of Customs. (Treasury Document No. 2492. Washington, 1908.) — An exhaustive index of present administrative practice.

EVANS, WILLIAM W. *Imports and Duties 1894–1907.* (Washington, 1908.) — A compilation of statistics prepared under the direction of the Committee on Ways and Means.

Tariff Acts passed by the Congress of the United States from 1789 to 1897. ROBERT G. PROCTOR, compiler. (Washington, 1898.)

Tariff on Imports in the United States, etc., and the Free List, together with Comparative Tables of Present and Past Tariffs. Report No. 12, Senate, 48th Cong., 1st Sess. (Washington, 1884.) — Contains a full index of articles on which duties have been imposed, 1789–1884.

Treasury Decisions under Tariff, Internal Revenue, Immigration, Navigation Laws, etc. (Issued weekly by the Treasury Department. Washington, 1897- .)

YOUNG, EDWARD. *Special Report on the Customs-Tariff Legislation of the United States.* (Washington, 1874. Bureau of Statistics, Treasury Department.) — Contains brief synopses of debates, and abstracts of most important schedules in the earlier tariff acts; also votes by States on the several acts, with comparative statements of rates of duties.

VI. Treasury Administration.

There is great need of a comprehensive work on fiscal administration in all its branches. The work of Goss is satisfactory for a portion of the field, — customs administration; and those of Kinley and Phillips adequately treat of the custody of public funds and the relation of public funds to the money market. No one work, however, presents in a systematic form the powers and actual duties of the several treasury officials, the method of preparing the budget, the system of accounting, and the technical management of loans; on all these points the reader must in a large measure rely upon Bolles, whose work does not extend beyond 1885.

GOSS, JOHN DEAN. *The History of the Tariff Administration in the United States.* (*Studies in History and Economics, and Public Law of Columbia College*, Vol. I, No. 2. N. Y., 1891.) — Excellent monograph in brief compass on methods of entry, appraisement, classification, etc.

HOTCHKISS, WILLARD E. *The Judicial Work of the Comptroller of the Treasury.* (In *Cornell Studies in History and Political Science.* Ithaca, N. Y., 1911.) — A scholarly work. Treats of the history of the office; and describes the control over appropriations.

KINLEY, DAVID. *The History, Organization, and Influence of the Independent Treasury System of the United States.* (N. Y., etc., 1893.) — A scholarly work showing the relation of the independent treasury to business and crises. Author favors a reorganization of the banking system to replace the independent treasury. In 1910 this work was revised and published by the National Monetary Commission. (Sen. Doc., No. 587; 61 Cong., 2 Sess.)

MAYO, ROBERT. *The Treasury Department in its Various Fiscal Bureaus; their Origin, Organization, and Practical Operations.* (Washington, 1847.) — Is a compendium of technical forms, books, and duties of the officials; only historically of interest.

PHILLIPS, JOHN BURTON. *Method of Keeping the Public Money of the United States.* (In *Publications of the Michigan Political Science Association,* Vol. IV, No. 3. Ann Arbor, Dec., 1909.) — A careful study of actual practice, 1789–1900. Many references in foot-notes.

VII. Documents, Statistics, Sources, and Periodicals.

The amount of documentary material is very great. The most useful is the annual *Finance Report,* and with this series the reader should early acquaint himself. The examination of even a single volume, as for example, the latest, including the report of the Secretary of the Treasury, and the reports of the several bureaus will vitalize the subject as no amount of general reading will accomplish. Next in value are the *Statistical Abstract* and the *Monthly Summary of Commerce and Finance.*

MISCELLANEOUS DOCUMENTS.

Annals of Congress, 1789–1824. (Washington, 1834–1856. 42 vols.) — *Register of Debates in Congress, 1824–1837.* (Washington, 1825–1837. 29 vols.) — *The Congressional. Globe: containing Sketches of the Debates and Proceedings, 1833–1873.* (Washington, 1837–1873. 109 vols.) — *Congressional Record, 1873–* . The congressional debates are summarized in *Abridgment of Debates of Congress, 1789–1856,* by THOMAS H. BENTON. (N. Y., 1857–1861. 16 vols.) — For the general student this is by far the most useful collection for the earlier period.

American State Papers: Documents, Legislative and Executive, 1789–1828. (Washington, 1832. 5 vols.) — Is the chief source of documentary material for the earlier period, containing reports of Secretaries of the Treasury, reports of committees, memorials, and statistical tables.

Reports of the Secretary of the Treasury of the United States, 1789–1849. (Washington, 1837–1851. 6 vols.) — The standard collection of reports, and necessary for special inquiries. Each volume has an index: I, 1789–1814; II, 1815–1828; III, 1829–1836; IV, 1837–1844; V, 1845; VI, 1846–1849.

Report on the Finances. (Annual report of the Secretary of the Treasury, beginning with 1849, bound as a separate volume.) — This includes the reports of the several treasury bureaus, among which those of the Commissioner of Internal Revenue, Comptroller of the Currency, and Director of the Mint are of special value. (These three reports are also published separately with additional statistical tables.) The Finance Reports are of the first importance to the student of financial questions, and may be generally secured by application to the Treasury Department or through the citizen's congressman.

Statistical Abstract of the United States. (Published by the Bureau of Statistics, Department of Commerce and Labor. First issue in 1878.) — Of special interest are tables on receipts and expenditures; expense of collecting revenue; internal revenue and sources; money in treasury and in circulation; gold and silver coinage and ratio; national banks; merchandise, exports, and imports; pensions; and postal service.

Summary of Commerce and Finance. (Published monthly by the Bureau of Statistics, Department of Commerce and Labor, Washington.)

American Almanac and Repository of Useful Knowledge, 1830–1862. (Boston, 1830–1862. 33 vols.) — Contains statistics of commerce, expenditures, etc.

American Almanac and Treasury of Facts, Statistical, Financial, and Political, 1878–1889. Edited by A. R. Spofford. (N. Y., 1878–1889.) — A standard statistical compendium while published.

American Annual Cyclopedia and Register of Important Events, 1861–1874. (N. Y., 1862–1875. 14 vols.) — Since 1874 continued as *Appleton's Annual Encyclopedia.* The annual article on Finance is a useful summary. Consult also Index, 1861–1875, and 1876–1887. 2 vols.

American Yearbook. (N. Y., 1911– .) Published annually under the supervision of representatives of learned societies. See chapters on Public Finance and Banking.

Appropriations, New Offices, etc. Statement showing appropriations, salaries, contracts authorized, and chronological history of the regular appropriation bills, etc. (Treasury Department, Washington.) — Annual document.

Combined Statement of the Receipts and Expenditures of the United States. (Published annually by the Division of Bookkeeping and Warrants, Treasury Department.) — Shows receipts by States, and expenditures by each department.

Letter of the Secretary of the Treasury Transmitting Estimates of Appropriations. (Annual publication, Washington.)

Statement of Balances, Appropriations, and Expenditures of the Government. (Published annually by the Division of Bookkeeping and Warrants, Treasury Department.) — Shows unexpended balances, appropriations available, etc.

Statement of Appropriations and Expenditures for Public Buildings, Rivers, and Harbors, Forts, Arsenals, Armories, and other Public Works from 1789 to 1882. (Treasury Department Document, No. 373. Washington, 1882.)

UNOFFICIAL SOURCES.

HART, ALBERT BUSHNELL. *American History told by Contemporaries.* (N. Y., etc., 1897–1902. 4 vols.) — A compilation of sources. Referred to in this volume as Hart.

MACDONALD, WILLIAM. *Select Documents Illustrative of the History of the United States, 1776–1861.* (N. Y. and London, 1898.) — Of special value for documents on banking. Contains reprints of Hamilton's reports and of papers relating to the Bank controversy and Compromise Tariff.

MCPHERSON, EDWARD. *Political History of the United States during the Great Rebellion.* (Washington, 1864. 4th ed., 1882.) — *Political History of the United States during the Period of Reconstruction, 1865–1870.* (Washington, 1871. 3d ed., 1880.) — This work was continued for a few years by a series of *Handbooks of Politics*, published biennially. Contains copies of bills, votes, acts, judicial decisions, etc.

PITKIN, TIMOTHY. *A Statistical View of the Commerce of the United States of America.* (Enlarged ed., 1835. New Haven, 1817.) — References are to the first edition. Statistical tables are helpful.

SEYBERT, ADAM. *Statistical Annals.* (Philadelphia, 1818.) Embracing views of the population, commerce, fisheries, lands, post-office establishment, revenues, mint, military and naval establishments, expenditures, public debt, and sinking fund of the United States of America; founded on official documents, 1789–1818. — Statistical tables are clear and well arranged; of great aid to the special student.

THAYER, JAMES BRADLEY, editor. *Cases on Constitutional Law, with Notes.* (Cambridge, 1895. 2 vols.) — See especially Vol. II, chapter 7, on taxation; chapter 11, on money.

SPEECHES, ADDRESSES, AND COLLECTED WORKS.

BENTON, THOMAS HART. *Thirty Years' View from 1820 to 1850.* (N. Y. and Boston, 1854–1856. 2 vols.) — Contains many extracts from speeches, particularly on the U. S. Bank, surplus, and deposits.

CALHOUN, JOHN CALDWELL. *Works.* (Ed. by Richard K. Crallé. N. Y., 1853-1855. 6 vols.) — Vols. II-IV contain speeches in Congress treating of the currency, sub-treasury, surplus, tariff, and internal improvements.

CLAY, HENRY. *Works.* (Ed. with *Life* by Calvin Colton. N.Y., 1857. 6 vols.) — Contents, Vols. I-III, *Life and Times*, by Colton (1844. 2 vols. Rev. ed., 1856. 3 vols.); Vol. IV, *Private Correspondence* (1855); Vols. V-VI, *Speeches.* Also republished with introduction by Thomas B. Reed (N. Y., 1898). The life by Colton is eulogistic; a useful bibliography on Clay is given in Vol. I, pp. 34-38.

GALLATIN, ALBERT. *Writings*, ed. by Henry Adams. (Philadelphia, 1879. 3 vols.) — Vol. III is of most interest to the student of finance; contains the sketch of finances (1796), and the essays on banking (1830 and 1841). All of Gallatin's writings on financial questions are of the first importance.

GARFIELD, JAMES ABRAM. *Works*, ed. by B. A. Hinsdale. (Boston, 1882. 2 vols.) — Garfield's speeches are scholarly and show research; the editor's notes are helpful and include chronological summaries of legislation.

HAMILTON, ALEXANDER. *Complete Works*, ed. by Henry Cabot Lodge. (N.Y., 1885-1886. 9 vols.) — Vols. II-III are devoted to finance, and Vol. VIII contains the index.

RICHARDSON, JAMES DANIEL, editor. *A Compilation of the Messages and Papers of the Presidents, 1789-1897.* (Washington, 1896-1899. 10 vols.) — References have been freely made to the collection throughout this volume, under the title, *Messages and Papers.*

SHERMAN, JOHN. *Selected Speeches and Reports on Finance and Taxation from 1859 to 1878.* (N. Y., 1879.) — An aid to the special student.

TAUSSIG, FRANK W., editor. *State Papers and Speeches on the Tariff.* (Cambridge, 1892.) — Contains Hamilton's Report on Manufactures; Gallatin's Memorial of the Free-Trade Convention; Walker's Treasury Report of 1845; Clay and Webster on the Tariff of 1824.

WEBSTER, DANIEL. *Works.* (Boston, 1851. 6 vols.) — Vols. III-V are of immediate interest for finance, containing speeches in Congress, 1815-1850, treating of the currency, banking, surplus, deficits, tariff, and public lands.

WOODBURY, LEVI. *Writings, Political, Judicial, and Literary.* (Boston, 1852. 3 vols.) — Vol. I contains speeches on tariff legislation and banking questions, including the removal of deposits.

PERIODICALS.

Bankers' Magazine. Rhodes Journal of Banking and the Bankers' Magazine consolidated. (N. Y., 1846- .) — In July, 1895, the Bankers' Magazine and Statistical Register united with Rhodes Journal of Banking under the title of Rhodes Journal of Banking and the Bankers' Magazine consolidated. In January, 1896, the title of Bankers' Magazine was resumed with sub-title as above. The earlier volumes of this series are an indispensable aid, on account of special articles, documentary material, and monthly tables.

Bradstreet's. A Journal of Trade, Finance, and Public Economy. (Issued weekly. N. Y.) — Comment and editorials make a fairly complete record on public finance.

Bulletin of the National Association of Wool Manufacturers. Quarterly. (Boston, 1869- .) — Contains valuable papers illustrating the protectionist point of view.

Commercial and Financial Chronicle. (Published weekly. N. Y., 1865- .) — Editorials represent New York bankers' point of view on the relation of the treasury to the money market.

The Financial Review. (Issued annually by the publishers of the *Commercial and Financial Chronicle.* N. Y., 1873.) — Of special value is the annual retrospect of United States securities, course of debt, and prices of bonds.

The Journal of Commerce and Commercial Bulletin, consolidated 1893. *Journal of Commerce,* established, 1827; *Commercial Bulletin,* established, 1865. (N. Y.) — A valuable daily for information concerning public finance.

Niles' Weekly Register and Niles' National Register. (Baltimore, 1811–1848. 73 vols.) — Of great value for the first half of the last century.

Sound Currency. Monthly, formerly published by Committee on Sound Currency of Reform Club. (N. Y., 1894–1901. 8 vols.) — Many of the issues are reprints of special studies; lists of monetary literature are published; some of the more important issues published previous to 1896 were gathered into a volume known as the Sound Currency Red Book.

In addition to the above, valuable articles are found in the quarterlies devoted to political science and economics; —

American Economic Review. (Cambridge, Mass., 1911- .) — Published by the American Economic Association.

Annals of the American Academy of Political and Social Science. (Philadelphia, 1890– .)

The Journal of Political Economy. (Chicago, 1892– .)

Political Science Quarterly. (Boston, 1886– .)

The Quarterly Journal of Economics. (Boston, 1886– .) Issue for August, 1911, contains index of previous volumes.

The Yale Review. (New Haven, 1892–1911. 19 vols.)

VIII. Bibliographies and Finding Lists.

As a further aid to the reader the following special bibliographies are recommended. The list by Bogart and Rawles is of special value for the period 1789–1865, and with its aid the bibliographies in this volume can easily be made more comprehensive. The use of government documents is still a forbidding task, but the labor may be lightened by consulting in advance the *Aids* by Lane.

BOGART, ERNEST L., and RAWLES, WILLIAM A. *Trial Bibliography and Outline of Lectures on the Financial History of the United States*. (Oberlin, 1901. pp. 49.) — An excellent list selected with discrimination, with precise page references, extending through the Civil War.

BOWKER, RICHARD ROGERS, and ILES, GEORGE. *The Reader's Guide in Economic and Political Science*. (N. Y. and London, 1891.) — Bibliographical, with brief notes; see especially pp. 35–41 on money and banking; pp. 54–65 on protection, free trade, and tariff (p. 56, references to public documents); pp. 68–73 on public finance.

CHANNING, EDWARD, HART, ALBERT BUSHNELL, and TURNER, FREDERICK JACKSON. *Guide to the Study of American History*. (Boston, etc., 1912.) — A most useful handbook of references to political and economic topics allied to finance. For special references to financial subjects, see §§ 169, 177, 205, 237, 243, 252, 262, 271.

Comprehensive Index of the Publications of the United States Government, 1889–1893. (Washington, 1894.) — Compiler, JOHN G. AMES, was Superintendent of Documents in the Department of the Interior. While not a detailed topical index, it is indispensable to the student who wishes to consult congressional documents; see particularly, Silver, p. 392; Tariff, p. 416; Treasury Department, p. 427.

Catalogue of Public Documents of the Fifty-fourth Congress, First Session, and of all the Departments of the Government of the United States for the Period from July 1, 1895, to June 30, 1896. (Washington, 1898.) — Prepared under the supervision of the Superintendent of Documents, government printing-office. This index is more easily used than the foregoing; helpful cross-references are given. See in particular Finance, etc., pp. 220–221; National Banks, p. 419; Reciprocity, p. 535; Silver, pp. 578–579; Tariff, p. 613.

Catalogue of the Public Documents of the Fifty-fourth Congress, Second Session, etc., for the Period July 1, 1896 to June 30, 1897. (Washington, 1899.) — Consult topics as in foregoing volume.

Catalogue of the Documents of the Fifty-fifth Congress, etc., for the Period from July 1, 1897, to June 30, 1899. (Washington, 1901.) – See Bonds of the U. S., pp. 103–105; Currency, p. 232; Customs Service, p. 234. Consult other topics as in previous volumes. This is bound as *Document Catalogue 4*; for succeeding congresses similar volumes have appeared.

LANE, LUCIUS PAGE. *Aids to the Use of Government Publications.* (Boston, Vol. VII, No. 49, pp. 40–58. In *Quarterly Publications of the American Statistical Association*, March, 1900.) — Contains a select list of indexes of federal public documents.

LIBRARY OF CONGRESS. The Library of Congress in recent years has issued a series of bibliographies on public questions, among which are to be noted those relating to *First and Second Banks of the United States* (1908); *Banks and Banking* (1904); *Currency* (1908); *Monetary Question* (1913); *Reciprocity* (1910); *Wool, with special Reference to Tariff* (1911); *Sugar* (1910); *Taxation of Inheritances and Incomes* (1907); *Postal Savings Banks* (1908); and *Income Taxation* (1911).

MCKEE, T. H. *Index to the Reports of Committees.* (Washington, 1887. 2 vols.) — Author was clerk in the document room, U. S. Senate. See lists of reports of Senate committees on appropriations and finance; and of the House committees on appropriations, banking and currency, commerce (import duties); expenditures, manufactures, retrenchment, and ways and means,

POOLE, WILLIAM FREDERICK, and FLETCHER, WILLIAM ISAAC, and others. *Poole's Index to Periodical Literature, 1802–1881.* (Rev. ed. Boston, etc., 1893. 2 vols.) — *First Supplement, 1882–1886.* (Boston, etc., 1888.) — *Second Supplement, 1887–1891.* (Boston, etc., 1893.) — *Third Supplement, 1892–1896.* (Boston, etc., 1897.) — *Fourth Supplement, 1897–1901.* (Boston, etc., 1903.) — The standard guide to periodical literature; consult especially Bank of United States; Banks; Banking; Currency; Silver; Tariff; United States, Finances of. This work is continued by the *Readers' Guide to Periodical Literature*, published by H. W. Wilson Co. (N. Y.)

POORE, BEN PERLEY. *A Descriptive Catalogue of the Government Publications of the United States, Sept. 5, 1774, to March 4, 1881.* (Washington, 1885.) — Not very easily used, but the only index available for the period as a whole.

IX. Special Exercises and Investigation.

In no subject of applied economics is there more abundant opportunity for individual and special investigation than in that of American finance. As an example of immediate interest, it is suggested that the student read the daily treasury statement, which can be obtained by application to the Treasury Department, or may be found in the columns of the principal financial daily and weekly newspapers. The writer has secured useful results by assigning to the several members of a class the graphic representation of the principal facts found in the daily treasury statement, such as the amount of cash in the treasury, the amount of money in the national bank depositories to the credit of the treasurer of the United States, and the daily receipts and expenditures. The daily checking of these and similar tables leads to the development of a keen judgment not only as to what is occurring, but as to what may occur on the morrow.

As illustrating the range of practical exercises which quickly introduce the student to the consideration of current questions, a few subjects are suggested: —

1. The price of government securities as quoted in *Niles' Register*, the *Bankers' Magazine*, the *Commercial and Financial Chronicle*, or *Bradstreet's*, with reasons for fluctuations.
2. The chronological history of a loan bill, as derived from the *Annals of Congress*, the *Globe*, or *Record*.
3. The history of a loan, its issues and redemptions.
4. The deposit of government funds in national banks over a period of years, and the reasons for changes.
5. The history of the tariff duties on a single commodity, as tea, wool, salt, sugar; with this can be combined a study of import figures for the same commodity.
6. The classification of expenditures according to a logical scheme. The expenditures of the government have never been tabulated in a detailed and systematic way; and it is hoped that in the near future monographs may be written devoted to an historical account of the several branches of public ex-

penditures. As contributory to this larger work, much preliminary research can be done to advantage by the individual student.

7. The assignment of a speech of a senator or representative on some financial question, with the requirement that all facts be checked by reference to official documents.
8. The distribution of votes on a financial bill; this is of more value for the earlier period of our history, for since the Civil War votes on the tariff have been strictly drawn on party lines.
9. The preparation of bibliographies with special reference to government documents. No labor here is too slight; the reports of congressional committees are buried treasures, awaiting energetic pick and shovel.

CHARTS

Contents.

Financial History of the United States.

CHAPTER I.

COLONIAL FINANCE.

1. References.

BIBLIOGRAPHIES: Bogart and Rawles, 3–9; Channing and Hart, 284–285; 289 (Stamp Act); A. M. Davis, *Currency and Banking in the Province of Massachusetts Bay*, in *Pub. of Amer. Econ. Assn.*, Third Series, I, No. 4, ch. XXII; J. Winsor, *Narrative History of America*, V, 170–177; and monographs referred to below in *Johns Hopkins University Studies* and *Columbia College Studies*. The notes in C. J. Bullock, *Monetary History of United States*, furnish many references on money. Fac-simile cuts of paper money are found in Winsor and in Davis.

COMMODITIES AS MONEY: H. White, 10–22; S. W. Rosendale, *Wampum Currency*, in *Sound Currency*, III, No. 8 (March, 1896); C. J. Bullock, 7–12; W. B. Weeden, *Indian Money*, in *J. H. U. Studies*, II, 385–481.

COINAGE: Bullock, 12–28; D. K. Watson, *History of American Coinage*, 1–7; J. H. Hickox, *A Historical Account of American Coinage* (Albany, 1858, Plates); S. S. Crosby, *Early Coins of America* (Boston, 1875, Plates); C. H. Swan, Jr., *Spanish Silver Dollars in Massachusetts*, in *Sound Currency*, VI, 73–80; W. G. Sumner, *The Spanish Dollar and the Colonial Shilling*, in *Amer. Hist. Rev.* (July, 1898); W. G. Sumner, *Coin Shilling of Massachusetts Bay*, in *Yale Review*, VII, 247, 405.

PAPER MONEY: (i) CONTEMPORARY: W. Douglass, *Discourse concerning the Currencies of the British Plantations in America* (1740), reprinted and edited by C. J. Bullock, in *Stud. Amer. Econ. Assn.*, II, No. 5 (especially pp. 305–318); J. Wright, *The American Negotiator of the Various Currencies of the British Colonies in America* (1761); *South Carolina's First Paper Money* (1739), in *Sound Currency*, V, 34–45; B. Franklin, *Works* (Bigelow, ed.), I, 359–383; IV, 11–15, 79–94; A. B. Hart, *American History*, II, 251–254; A. M. Davis, *Tracts Relating to the Currency of the Massachusetts Bay.* (ii) GENERAL: G. Bancroft, *Plea for the Constitution*, 9–28; C. J. Bullock, 29–59; W. Gouge, *Money*, Part II, 1–25; J. J Knox, 1–8; F. A. Walker, *Money*, 305–326; H

White, 120–134; W. G. Sumner, *History of American Currency*, 1-43. (iii) SPECIAL: H. Phillips, *Historical Sketches of the Paper Currency of the American Colonies* (2 vols., 1865); F. F. McLeod, *Fiat Money and Currency Inflation in New England from 1620 to 1739*, in *Annals Amer. Acad. Pol. Sci.*, XII, 57–77 (Sept., 1898); H. Bronson, *Historical Account of Connecticut Currency*, in *Papers of New Haven Col. Hist. Soc.*, I (1865); J. G. Palfrey, *History of New England*, V, 96–109 (Massachusetts); A. M. Davis, *Currency and Banking in the Province of Massachusetts Bay*, in *Pub. of Amer. Econ. Assn.*, Third Series, I, No. 4 (Dec., 1900, Plates); C. H. J. Douglass, *Financial History of Massachusetts*, 117–135; S. S. Rider and B. R. Potter, *Some Account of the Bills of Credit or Paper Money of R. I.*, 1710–1786; H. White, *New York's Colonial Currency*, in *Sound Currency*, V, 50–64; C. J. Bullock, 207–259 (New Hampshire), 125–183 (North Carolina); C. W. Macfarlane, *Pennsylvania Paper Currency* in *Annals Amer. Acad. Pol. Sci.*, VIII, 50–126; P. A. Bruce, *Economic History of Virginia*, II, ch. 19; W. Z. Ripley, *Financial History of Virginia*, 108–144 (hard money), 145–166 (paper money).

COLONIAL BANKING: H. White, 248–258; A. M. Davis, *Currency and Banking in the Prov. of Mass. Bay;* Part II, *Banking*, in *Pub. of Amer. Econ. Assn.*, Third Series, II, No. 2 (May, 1901), particularly ch. 12; A. M. Davis, *A Connecticut Land Bank of the 18th Century* in *Quar. Jour. of Econ.*, XIII, 70.

TAXATION: *The Stamp Act*, 1765, in *American History Leaflets*, No. 21 (May, 1895); B. Franklin, *Works*, IV, 97-111; 288–299; V, 440–531; A. B. Hart, *American History*, II, 394–417; W. MacDonald, *Select Charters*, 272 (Sugar Act), 281 (Stamp Act), 322 (Revenue Act), 327 (Tea Act); C. C. Plehn, *Introduction to Public Finance*, 139–142; E. R. A. Seligman, *Income Tax in American Colonies and States*, in *Pol. Sci. Quar.*, X, 220–247; W. Hill, *Colonial Tariffs*, in *Quar. Jour. of Econ.*, VII, 78–100; O. L. Elliott, *The Tariff Controversy*, 5–66, in *Leland Stanford, Jr., Univ. Monographs Hist.*, No. 1; J. D. Goss, *History of Tariff Administration in the U. S.*, in *Col. Coll. Stud.*, I, No. 2, 10–23; W. C. Fisher, *American Trade Regulations before 1789*, in *Papers of Amer. Hist. Assn.*, III, 221; W. G. Sumner, *Alexander Hamilton*, 37–52 (taxation by England); F. R. Jones, *History of Taxation in Connecticut*, 1636–1776, in *J. H. U. Stud.*, XIV, No. 8; C. H. J. Douglass (as above), 13–95; J. C. Schwab, *History of New York Property Tax*, in *Pub. Amer. Econ. Assn.*, V, No. 5; E. L. Whitney, *Government of the Colony of S. C.*, in *J. H. U. Stud.*, XIII, 97–109; W. Z. Ripley (as above), 11–107; P. A. Bruce, *Economic History of Virginia;* H. L. Osgood, *New England Colonial Finance*, in *Pol. Sci. Quar.*, XIX, 80–106.

2. Scope of the Work.

The term finance, according to the precise academic definition of modern authorities, refers to the receipts and expenditures of an individual, company, or government. "The supply and application of state resources constitute the subject matter of public finance," is the definition given by Prof. Bastable; and successive American writers on this subject, Adams, Plehn, and Daniels, use the term in substantially the same sense. In the following narrative of American experience the expression "financial history" will be given a broader scope and will include also some consideration of the monetary system of the country, such as coinage and bank issues. This extension is made partly for convenience, since the two subjects of money and of finance in its narrowest interpretation are related in interest to the student of public affairs; and partly because it is impossible to explain the policy of the government of the United States, either as to expenditures or to income, without reference to the development of public opinion and experience in the management of its monetary operations.

In no country of the world has national finance been so quickly and so violently affected by political environment and current economic experience as in the United States. This influence has been due to many causes, — in part to the sudden break with the parent country in 1775, leaving animosities which grew into suspicion or contempt for European experience; in part to the abstract political philosophy which early obtained a strong hold upon the reasoning of political leaders in America and which led to a confidence in abstract ideas beyond practical possibilities; and in part to the newness of our economic life and the enormous scale on which the resources of the country have been developed. A complete and satisfactory treatment of the financial history of the United States might well involve, therefore, the bases of American political philosophy as expressed in constitutional law and judicial interpretation, and also a view of the material extension of the country as witnessed in the unparalleled growth of agriculture, manufactures, mining, transportation, and foreign commerce. Such an extended treatment is obviously impossible within the limits set for this work; but the reader should be alert to connect this narrative of financial measures with the underlying forces of political opinion and economic development.

The financial history of the present government of the United States has its roots in the methods, experiences, and political philosophy of the thirteen colonies. In part the revenue systems of those settlements were prescribed by external authorities or inspired by non-resident commercial interests; in part they were the expression of local needs, enunciated by freemen slowly learning to legislate for themselves. The colonies were established at different times and under different impulses, and it is consequently natural that they should have tried a variety of revenue measures, for the most part crude and yet on the whole not badly adapted to new and raw conditions of material life. Rarely, except in time of war, were the demands upon the colonial treasuries burdensome or excessive, and the adjustment of revenue to expenditure or of expenditure to revenue was easily made. Most of the colonies fell into the error of too abundant issues of paper money; at first, to meet special strains, and, later, in many instances to discharge ordinary obligations which should have been met by taxation; but this error was fostered by the argument that the community needed a greater supply of money both as loanable capital and as a medium of exchange,—an argument entirely distinct from budgetary requirements. With the revolt against England in the latter part of the eighteenth century there arose the necessity of some national system of finance to meet expenditures undertaken in a common cause, particularly in the support of the army. A national system had to be created not only out of the varied and crude financial experiences of the thirteen colonies, but also in a time of political confusion, when there was little opportunity for inquiry, deliberation, and careful maturing of plans. Financial disaster was the result. During the closing years of the Revolution and after the treaty of peace in 1783 rapid and critical experiments were tried, leading finally to a new constitution which laid the foundation of the present federal financial system of the United States. Introductory to the federal system of finance which will chiefly occupy this narrative, two chronological periods must therefore be considered: (1) the financial experiences of the colonies; and (2) the finances of the Revolution together with the transition experiments of the Confederacy.

In the treatment of colonial financial practice it will be impossible to consider each colony separately, either in fiscal organization or as to ways and means for getting revenue. The survey must serve simply to disclose the more important methods and fiscal instruments with which the people of the United States had become acquainted on their own soil during the years of preparation for their national independent career.

3. Economic Factors.

The economic life of the colonies was extremely simple, and yet was active in many different ways. The settlements were scattered over an extended seaboard and differed in climate and natural resources. They differed also in occupations; besides the plantations of sugar, tobacco, rice, and indigo in the South, and the smaller farms of tillage and pasturage in New England and the middle colonies, everywhere were fisheries, forests of timber and naval stores, and scattered outposts of hunters and trappers. In many ways these wide-spread communities were sufficient for the satisfaction of their own economic wants. With wonderful resourcefulness the people resorted to household manufactures covering an extended range of commodities, but the standards of life had been so far developed that each section called for supplies from abroad, such as English woollens, linens, ammunition, and household supplies. The people of New England engaged in the manufacture of clapboards, hoops, shingles, and framed timber, which they exported to the West Indies in exchange for sugar, rum, and molasses; in part these latter commodities were used at home and in part they were disposed of in other markets to help settle the indebtedness to England. But, more than all else, Northern settlers found their security against bankruptcy in the construction of ships and in the fisheries. Ships were exported to England; and fish were sent in colonial bottoms to Portugal, Spain, and Italy; cargoes were secured in these countries for England, and the profits of this freighting did much to settle the international balance of trade.

The colonies of New York, New Jersey, and Pennsylvania had much the same products as those in New England, with the exception of fish. Richer in soil and warmer in climate, they were able to raise large quantities of wheat and other grains, to manufacture them into flour, and easily to dispose of them in the West Indies. In payment the middle colonies likewise secured funds in bills of exchange for use in buying goods in England. The products of the Southern colonies were in immediate demand in the mother country, and hence the commerce of this section was more direct. It will thus be seen that for the economic prosperity of a large part of the settlements the trade of the West Indies was necessary; and as the struggle to gain this trade was keen the regulations prescribed by England were frequently disregarded.

This restrictive legislation, commonly called the navigation laws, began in 1660 by limiting the export market of colonial sugar, cotton, tobacco, indigo, ginger, and dyeing woods to the English dominions; but gradually other commodities, as rice, naval stores, and furs, were placed upon the "enumerated list," to the great embarrassment of colonial enterprise. So, too, the importation of European goods was restricted to British, that is, English or colonial built, shipping, laden in England, thus requiring all American vessels, if importing continental produce, to make an immediate clearing from England itself. From these harsh regulations modifications were made in permitting exportations of enumerated goods not only to the mother country, but also to that part of Europe lying to the south of Cape Finisterre, to certain parts of Africa, and to the West Indies in general. The frequent changes in the navigation policy of England, its interference with the natural course of trade to the prejudice of settlements struggling against odds, and the disrespect shown to law through constant evasion, must be taken into account in seeking for an explanation for a part of the later antagonism of the colonies to the mother country.[1]

Manufactures were but slightly developed outside of the household at any time before the Revolution. Labor was expensive, and more profitable when directed to other pursuits. There were a few fulling-mills, hat-making establishments, an occasional paper-mill, charcoal furnaces for pig iron, some forges for making bar iron, and slitting-mills. There was, however, enough manufacturing enterprise to arouse the fears of English manufacturers, and in a few but important instances to lead to repressive legislation in the field of manufactures, especially woollens, hats, and iron. In spite of all the laws calculated to reduce the colonists to industrial dependency, the settlements as a whole prospered, — as a matter of fact, the laws in many instances were not enforced with stringency. The higher custom-house officials, with the consent of the treasury, were permitted to live in England, and treated their offices as sinecures. Apparently the statesmen in control of English affairs recognized that it would be disastrous to the fortunes of the colonies to compel strict obedience, and under this policy of toleration there grew up a large illicit but permitted trade.

The white population of the colonies at about the middle of the eighteenth century amounted to a little over a million.

[1] Professor Ashley in a recent and exhaustive study concludes, that, with the exception of the molasses business, the great bulk of the American trade was strictly legal. It is a source of regret that I have not had the opportunity to make an examination of this subject in accordance with the evidence submitted.

One-third was in New England, a little more in the middle colonies, and about one-quarter in the settlements south of Pennsylvania. The annual value of the imports was about £900,000 just after the date referred to, but it greatly increased because of the shipments on account of the war with France; and the commercial interests of the colonists were brought much more prominently to the surface. The exports did not quite equal the imports in value according to the custom-house valuations, and this explains the constant drain of specie, and the agitation for issues of paper currency to supply commercial needs of exchange.

It is hardly necessary to add that there were no bankers in the colonies; such functions of banking as were then developed were carried on by merchants. The differentiation of commercial occupations had hardly begun; there were few if any joint-stock companies, and associated action on any large scale was unknown. The individual merchant, when opportunity arose and ambition led, was a factor, an exchange-agent and banker, a ship-owner, and, in general, undertook all the financial responsibilities which are now shared by several kinds of corporations under forms of restricted liability. The individual relied upon himself; he was careful, therefore, not to get into debt, because standing debt indicated a serious departure from right living, to be punished by imprisonment. Undoubtedly the harsh provisions of the debtor laws which were tenaciously maintained long after expanding industry justified the use of credit, had much to do with inspiring paper money issues, from which it was believed relief would come.

4. Expenditures.

Taxation is necessitated by public expenditure, and this in turn depends upon the stage of refinement of civic life which has been developed. The colonial governments were of a simple type. In the early days of settlement the support of the governor was probably the most burdensome single charge placed upon a colony. The salaries of the few executive assistants or heads of departments were small, and in many instances the governor and inferior officers were paid by fees, thus lessening the need of regular taxation. Occasionally there was additional expenditure for the support of a colonial agent in London. The legislative sessions were short, and the pay of members when allowed not large. The court-houses were often handsome but never large, and there was no need for a highly organized and expensive judiciary. In times of peace there was no local navy, not even in the ship-building colonies. The military burden was met for the most part by a system of locally organized militia, the expenses of which were assessed upon the individual members or upon the town or county. No expensive public works were undertaken, the demand being confined to bridges, highways, and a few public buildings. Nor had there been developed that class of expenditures, now so common, for the satisfaction of humanitarian and social impulses, as for the care of the sick, poor, insane, or criminals, except by the local units of administration. Only in case of an Indian war or conflict with France, the great rival of England on the North American continent, was any heavy demand made upon the colonial treasuries; hence taxation was light.

5. Taxation.

The colonists were acquainted with taxation under two different forms. The English government in accordance with its trade and navigation laws established a revenue or customs service which was entirely under its control, the officers being appointed by the Crown. The regulations and duties imposed under these laws were primarily designed to protect the commerce and manufactures of the mother country rather than to enrich the treasury, and the revenue thus collected at the custom houses was insignificant. Besides the imperial system of taxation, each colony had its own methods of raising revenue for local needs; and here may be found the greatest variety of taxes, including direct taxes upon persons and property, indirect taxes upon consumption through excise or internal duties, and a system of tariff and customs duties which some of the colonies established in addition to the system maintained by England. The administrative methods of the colonies were simple and in keeping with the immature development of commerce and industry. In some of the colonies there was no separate fiscal organization for the collection of taxes, the duty being entrusted to the judicial machinery, especially the sheriff.

The taxing systems of the colonies varied from each other according to the economic conditions of the several sections of the country; they have been conveniently classified by Seligman into three different types. In the democratic communities of New England we find the primitive poll tax and a tax on the gross produce of the land, which was finally expanded into a general property tax; to these was then added a faculty tax. In the Southern colonies with their class supremacy the land tax was naturally unpopular among the landholders, and taxes laid upon slaves found little favor because they also reached only the influential and ruling part of the community. Consequently taxation was mainly indirect through import and export duties. In the middle colonies conditions cannot be so easily classified either as democratic or aristocratic; the trading class with Dutch methods dominated, and this naturally favored the excise system which had been developed in Holland.

The New England preference for property and poll taxes was natural, for the early settlers of these colonies left England at a time when property and poll taxes were common in the form of tenths, fifteenths, and subsidies. For example, Massachusetts in 1646 enacted that a single tax should equal 20d. a poll and 1d. in a pound of property, in money or its equivalent; on this unit as a basis the single tax was doubled, trebled, etc., by the authorities as the occasion demanded,—a practice which recalls the doubling or trebling of the "fifteenth" in England. In King Philip's War the rate was raised to sixteen units; the average was, however, about four. Such a system of taxation was highly congenial in communities where general land ownership was normal and property was widely distributed. Negotiable securities were unknown. There were no large estates or division of settlers into classes widely differing from each other in fortune or social attainments; property was mainly in land, buildings, and cattle, contributing visible wealth known to all and consequently easy to assess. Business transactions were limited in amount, and of a direct or simple character. To tax the visible, tangible property was substantially to tax the entire accumulations of the community, and the varying value of land was not an obstacle, because as a rule the early land taxes were based on product rather than on value.

The poll tax was the complement of the property tax: each adult male in Massachusetts was valued at the same property sum, as for example, £20; and the poll tax was then levied at a penny or its multiple per pound, as in the case of the property tax. This system of poll reduplication would obviously work injustice to the poor, and under the second charter was discarded.

Closely identified with and supplementary to the property and poll taxes was the faculty or income tax; laborers, artisans, and tradesmen paid according to their incomes or earnings. In the Massachusetts law of November 4, 1646, it was ordered that "every laborer, artificer, and handicraftsman that usually take in summer time above 18d. by the day-wages or work by great, which by due valuation amounts to more than 18d. by the day shall pay per annum 3s. 4d. into the treasury over and beside the 20d. before mentioned." Men in other callings, as smiths, butchers, bakers, etc., should be "rated proportionable to the produce of the estates of other men;" and again by another act the classes above mentioned were taxed on the capitalized value of their wages. Other New England colonies followed Massachusetts in the taxation of profits; and later the faculty tax was introduced into Pennsylvania, Delaware, Maryland, and a few of the Southern colonies. The faculty tax of the period under consideration was not, however, a true income tax in the modern sense; individuals, like articles of personal property and plots of land, were arbitrarily assessed at fixed amounts according to the occupation followed, and in some cases the tax became antiquated and an unjust class-tax based upon certain assumed earnings.

Indirect taxation in Massachusetts was of less importance. Tonnage duties were here imposed, as in nearly all the colonies. Import duties were levied upon luxuries and in particular upon wines and liquors; and in the excise schedule wines and spirits were the principal articles selected. In 1737 an excise was placed upon coaches, chariots, chaises, and chairs; and a few years later for a brief period upon tea, coffee, arrack, snuff, and earthenware.

The Southern colonies made but little use of the property tax, but relied chiefly upon indirect taxation, supplemented at times by the poll tax. In Virginia, which may be taken as representative of the Southern group, attempts were made to tax real estate, but owing to the opposition of the planters and land-owning class, its development was slow. Though the poorer classes were strenuous in opposing the poll tax, it continued in force, but was gradually reinforced by the imposition of customs duties upon the imported liquors and slaves as well as upon the exports of tobacco. The burden of the poll tax and the discrimination thereby shown against the landless and smaller tenants was indeed one of the causes of Bacon's Rebellion in 1676. With the growth of negro slavery in the eighteenth century the poll tax also became unpopular with the wealthy planters, who were financially responsible for the amounts imposed upon their slaves. Still at the beginning of the French and Indian War of 1756, which created heavy burdens, the poll tax bore the charge of the campaign; and in 1763 it alone produced more than all the other taxes on land, tobacco, and slaves imported, together with the licenses, fees, and carriage duties. With the close of the French War there was a return to the old system of indirect taxation as far as was practicable, but the contest had left permanent fiscal results in the establishment of special taxes, as those on coaches, chariots, and fees from licensing and in suits at law.

In the colony of New York a more mixed system of taxation prevailed. While the early settlers were under Dutch rule and the colony was known as New Netherlands it was to be expected that Dutch fiscal methods would prevail. In her system of landed estates under powerful patroons who would oppose any direct tax upon land the New Netherlands resembled Virginia; but more than that, New Amsterdam, the principal city, was from the first pre-eminently a trading centre. In Holland indirect taxes were laid upon the important foreign commerce enjoyed in that day by this enterprising commonwealth, and excise duties were levied upon wine, beer, and liquor. These two forms of taxation, being the principal sources of revenue in the mother country, were speedily introduced by the colonial commercial company into the New Netherlands, and were also in harmony with the economic conditions of the settlement. Goods were imported from Holland to the island of Manhattan and thence distributed along the Hudson and throughout the interior. As New Amsterdam lay in the direct line of commerce between New England and the settlements of Virginia, it became the centre of an export trade, the chief articles of which were tobacco and furs, and especially beaver skins.

The excise taxation of the Netherlands also found a fruitful application in this colony, as there were numerous distilleries, breweries, and wine-presses. When the colony was transferred to English control in 1664, the new authorities, according to English precedent, made a beginning in the development of a direct property tax, and after the establishment of the colonial assembly in 1683 permanently incorporated it into the revenue system. The increasing freedom in land tenure and the agricultural settlement of the interior made the process more easy, so that in the latter part of the eighteenth century the method of taxation in New York was similar to that employed in New England. In addition to the property tax New York also continued import duties and excises; and the quit rents of the settlers which were still retained furnished a small supply of revenue for the colonial treasury.

6. Tariffs; Import and Export Duties.

In the rapid summarization of the sources of revenue in Massachusetts, Virginia, and New York mention has been made of import and export duties. In view of the part which customs revenue has played in the American fiscal system developed since 1789 some further description should be given to these taxes. The colonies had a long experience with trade tariffs. Nearly every assembly levied import duties for its own treasury in addition to those imposed by England in the execution of the navigation laws. The objects for which these duties were imposed varied as they do now: sometimes they were imposed to check the importation of articles, consumption of which was regarded as useless or injurious; sometimes as retaliatory weapons against rival colonies or European nations other than England; and sometimes for protection of home industries. In communities, however, which were largely self-sufficient in satisfying their economic wants, which constructed their own furniture and tools, spun and wove their own cloth, and limited their food to the products of their own farms, the volume of international exchange could not be large, and a system of duties on imported goods was necessarily restricted in its scope.

In the imposition of such taxes for non-revenue purposes there was no consistent or permanent policy developed, and generally distinctly protective acts were short-lived. An example of sumptuary legislation was the measure enacted in 1638 in Massachusetts ordering that "whosoever shall buy or receive out of any ship any fruit, spice, sugar, wine, strong water, or tobacco shall pay to the treasurer one-sixth part of the price or value thereof; and every person who shall buy or receive any of the said commodities with intent to retail the same to others shall pay the treasurer one-third part of the value or price thereof." Connecticut levied heavy duties upon the export of lumber in order to husband her supply of building materials. Maryland enacted discriminating duties against provisions and liquors brought in from Pennsylvania; and Virginia in return retaliated against Maryland by imposing fees upon the latter's shipping. For protecting home industries Massachusetts at one time imposed double rates on all commodities brought in by inhabitants of Rhode Island, Connecticut, and New Hampshire. There was an impost of 5s. per hogshead on all molasses and 60s. per hogshead on all rum imported into Massachusetts by foreigners, and also discrimination in favor of Massachusetts shipping. Pennsylvania in 1704 for protective purposes taxed the importation of hops. Indeed, tariff duties are too numerous to permit specification; apart from temporary and hastily devised acts, Professor William Hill classifies them under four heads: (1) tonnage duties or taxes on shipping; (2) export duties on tobacco; (3) import duties on slaves; (4) regular tariff schedules in which wines and liquors were the most important items.

Of all these taxes the most general were the tonnage duties, known also as castle duties or powder duties, the latter name arising from the fact that the ship's owner was obliged to turn over to the colonial government an amount of powder and shot according to the ship's burden; later these payments were commuted into cash. Although the primary purpose of the tonnage duty was revenue, to be specifically applied to national defence, its maintenance gave considerable protection to local shipping, since home vessels were frequently exempt from payment.

Duties on exports were common, generally levied only for revenue, and the range of commodities selected was wide. Virginia placed export duties on tobacco, skins, furs, wool, and iron; Connecticut, upon timber and staves; New Jersey, upon staves and many other products of the forests; Canada, upon skins and furs; South Carolina, upon leather, furs, skins, Indian slaves, and timber; Maryland, upon tobacco constantly, and at times upon furs, skins, beef, pork, bacon, iron, flour, wheat, and all European goods. The export duty on tobacco was naturally found only in the Southern colonies; in Maryland it was utilized for payments to the proprietor in support of the government and for colonial needs of a general character, while in Virginia it became one of the most important and regular elements of the revenue. Here the duty ranged from 2 to 10 shillings a hogshead of 500 lbs. The import tax on slaves also found its principal operation in the Southern colonies. Although the tax was levied in Pennsylvania, New York, and Massachusetts, and possibly other colonies, its proceeds were small, not only because few slaves were imported, but because the rates were low.

In the development of a general tariff schedule South Carolina went the farthest; a large number of articles were taxed and rates were higher than elsewhere. In 1703 a general tariff was enacted in which specific duties were placed upon liquors, provisions, and slaves, and an ad valorem rate of 3 per cent. upon all other commodities. During succeeding years until 1740 ad valorem duties were low, varying from 1 to 5 per cent., while the list of specific duties was continually enlarged until the end of the colonial period. In Massachusetts the tariff schedule was briefer and the rates imposed were still more insignificant; nevertheless tariff legislation was systematic, and the tariff law was regularly renewed from 1692 until 1774, — English goods, however, were not subject to duties after 1719. Specific duties were imposed on wine, rum, tobacco, sugar, molasses, and dye goods, and ad valorem duties on all other commodities at a rate at first of 1d. on 20s. worth in 1692, increased to 2d. in 1731, to 4d. in 1739, and continued at that rate until 1774. In New York the heavy duties imposed during Dutch rule and at the command of the Duke of York "had an influence in accustoming the colonists to tariff taxes, so that when they were allowed an assembly and permitted to make their own laws for raising revenue they collected most of it by duties on imports and exports." In the other colonies the import duties were hardly important enough to justify the name of tariff systems, and in some none can be found. Connecticut, Pennsylvania, Maryland, and North Carolina taxed only a few articles besides liquors, while Maryland imposed duties only for temporary purposes or for special objects rather than as a source of constant revenue.

From this confused mass of colonial tariff legislation a few points of permanent interest may be extracted. In the early tariffs specific duties were the exception, and low ad valorem duties varying from 1 to 5 per cent. were the general rule; but in the course of time there was a change toward specific duties, both to avoid fraud and to secure a more definite tax. The tariffs were enacted but for short periods, and in the bills of levy it was common to specify the object for which the revenue would be applied. As to whether duties were actually collected according to the laws enacted, Professor Hill is of the opinion that there was gross evasion, first because the open disregard of the English navigation laws must have had demoralizing results as to obedience of local law; and, secondly, because the returns of revenue from this source were so small, — in New York, for instance, the impost did not produce more than one-fifth of what was due.

7. Control of Appropriations.

Although the expenditures of the several colonies as a rule were not large, the provincial assemblies early showed a disposition, like the English House of Commons, to keep as firm a grasp as possible over appropriations, and their insistence led to continued contests with the governors. It was the wish of the Crown that the governors be granted permanent support, but the colonists almost invariably insisted upon limiting supplies for salary to one year, partly to prevent encroachment upon their liberties, partly to prevent misapplication of funds, and largely in order to preserve a useful weapon in controversies with the governor. The home government also intended that after supplies had been voted the signature of the governor alone should be necessary for warrants drawn on the public treasury, opportunity being given to the assembly only to inspect the accounts. Here again the colonists extended their claims; and some of the assemblies after passing bills involving appropriations determined that no payments should be made except upon a distinct vote of the legislature. They wished not only to vote supplies but to control disbursements and to audit the accounts. A few of the colonies went so far as to elect their own treasurers, entirely independent of the control of the governors, and thus they thrust the executive into the background in the management of the finances. So great was the dislike of executive control in matters involving taxation and expenditure that it was not uncommon, when special appropriations were made for extraordinary expenditures, to appoint special commissioners to supervise these particular accounts, in order that executive influence might be reduced to a minimum. This jealous fear of the provincial governor later had its fruit in the effort of the Continental Congress to manage the finances through committees and boards instead of intrusting them to a single head. Gerry of Massachusetts in his opposition to the establishment of a department of the treasury under a single secretary was simply maintaining the principle which had previously been so tenaciously upheld in his colony, that the treasurer should at all times be accountable to the assembly.

8. Money and Coinage.

The early colonists were poor and brought little ready money with them from Europe, nor did they have credit abroad. As no silver or gold mines were worked in the settlements, the only source of supply of the precious metals was through trade and shipping; that is, by exporting commodities to a greater value than were imported, or by acting as carriers for English commerce. The colonists were, however, in constant want of manufactured commodities and articles of luxury which could be obtained only on the continent, and consequently, even if the balance of trade in staples with England or the West Indies was favorable, the final settlement of indebtedness to America was more likely to be made in merchandise than in silver. The consequence was that the quick amount of a standard money medium did not keep pace with expanding industry and internal commerce. To meet the current need of instruments of commercial exchange, the colonists repeated most of the monetary experiments which had been previously made in other communities and tried some novelties of their own. The situation became the more complicated since the colonies were not forced by any controlling head to adopt uniform monetary legislation. Barter was resorted to in the earlier stages of settlement; then certain staple commodities were declared by law to be legal tender in payment of debts. Curious substitutes were employed, such as shells or wampum. Corn, cattle, peltry, furs were monetary media in New England; tobacco and rice in the South. The term bills of students at Harvard College were for many years met by the payment of produce, live stock, meat, and "occasionally with various articles raked up from the family closets of student debtors." One student, later president of the college, in 1649 settled his bill with "an old cow," and the accounts of the construction of the first college building include the entry, "Received a goat 30s. plantation of Watertown rate, which died."

Taxes were paid in commodities at rates of valuation considerably higher than the market, and storehouses in some colonies were maintained in which public property was deposited by tax-gatherers. As commodities acceptable for money payment were valued at rates above the market price, a discrimination was shown against silver, which tended to keep specie out of circulation. In the endeavor to retain the small supply of silver which came in through trade, the colonists frequently made another error in declaring current silver to be of legal value higher than the mint value as determined at the place of coinage. The course of trade was such that Spanish and Portuguese rather than English coins became the most common, and the coin principally in use was the Spanish silver dollar or piece of eight reals; but as if to increase the disorder, the colonists retained the English system of pounds, shillings, and pence, as their money of account. An accurate mathematical valuation made the "piece of eight" equal to 4s. 6d. of English money. If that ratio had been preserved there would have been no interference with the free circulation of the coin according to the natural flow of trade. At first, for purposes of convenience the customary rate at which the piece of eight circulated was made five shillings (an overvaluation of 11 per cent.), but in 1652, when a mint was established in Massachusetts, shillings and smaller coins were minted at a rate a little less than six shillings to a heavy piece of eight. In Virginia it was resolved to raise the value of the Spanish coin to six shillings, in the hope that specie might be attracted by favorable estimation. New York went still farther and in 1676 increased the valuation to six shillings and ninepence, and later in some of the colonies the valuation was placed as high as eight shillings, and in one or two instances even higher.

The valuation of money was thus differently regulated by statute in different colonies, and the confusion was the greater because of the circulation of light coins which drove out the heavy coins or good money. The colonists were not alone in their foolish attempts to legislate a valuation of coin other than as value by weight; they were simply imitating what had been previously tried in Europe. In spite of all these legislative efforts to attract specie it disappeared; in vain were laws passed in some colonies against the exportation of coin; in vain were Massachusetts searchers given extraordinary powers to examine outgoing vessels. In 1704 the English

Crown endeavored to rectify the evil by a general regulation of the value of Spanish money, and fixed the maximum rating of a piece of eight at six shillings currency. This gave rise to the term "proclamation" money, and rated silver coins at a third above their sterling value. Again a few years later Parliament attempted to clinch this proclamation by making it a felony to pay or receive the coins at above the specified rates. The spirit of this legislation was then defeated by the colonists, who passed laws fixing the price of silver at so much per ounce without reference to the proclamation, and who also turned to paper issues and banking schemes with greater readiness.

Massachusetts was the only colony which ever established a mint; placed under the operation and management of John Hull, its operations were confined to minting small silver pieces, familiarly known as pine-tree shillings. Vigorous attempts were made to force the managers to pay a portion of the profits to the government, but with little success, and in 1684 the mint was closed by order of the Crown. Attempts to establish mints in Virginia and Maryland were unsuccessful.

9. Bills of Credit.

Since there was a scarcity of circulating medium, caused by the constant drain of specie for export, it is not strange that projects for converting credit into wealth should have sprung up in the colonies, especially when we remember that in the mother country the same period witnessed numerous like schemes, some of them of large proportions. Several plans were devised during the seventeenth century for the establishment of banks or funds for the issue of currency, based upon the deposit or pledge of securities. The first important issues of paper money were, however, due to a somewhat different reason, — the fiscal requirements of an exhausted treasury. The experience of Massachusetts will serve as a useful illustration: In 1690 this commonwealth made an issue of £7000 of bills of credit, soon increased to £40,000, in order to pay the soldiers who engaged in the expedition against Port Royal and Quebec in the French War. This was an unexpected measure, for it had been anticipated that the cost of the attack would be met from the proceeds of the victory. The government of the colonies was passing through a crisis; its very legality was questioned, and it was utterly impracticable to raise in a few days as large a sum of money as would be necessary. This issue is thus described by Cotton Mather:

"The *General Assembly* first passed an Act, for the levying of such a sum of *Money* as was wanted . . . and this *Act* was a *Fund*, on which the *Credit* of such a Sum, should be rendered *passable* among the people. Hereupon, there was appointed an Able and Faithful *Committee* of Gentlemen, who printed from *Copper Plates*, a just Number of *Bills*, and Flourished, Indented, and Contrived them, in such a manner as to make it Impossible to Counterfeit any of them, without a speedy Discovery of the *Counterfeit;* besides which, they were all Signed by the Hands of *three* belonging to that Committee." . . . "The *public Debts* to the Sailors and Souldiers, now upon the point of *Mutiny* (for, *Arma Tenenti, Omnia dat, qui Justa negat!*) were in these *Bills* paid immediately."

The text of one of these Massachusetts notes was as follows: —

"This indented bill of ten shillings, due from the Massachusetts Colony to the Possessor, shall be in value equal to money, and shall be accordingly accepted by the Treasurer, and Receivers subordinate to him in all publick payments, and for any stock at any time in the Treasury. Boston in New England December the 10th, 1690. By order of the General Court."

These early emissions being payable in one year were practically due or exchequer bills in anticipation of taxes, and for some years were redeemed, though as promptly replaced by further anticipations. At first they depreciated, but they circulated at par for a time while the issues were limited in quantity and were indirectly declared to be legal tender, by giving them a premium of 5 per cent. over silver in the payment of taxes. The issues were enlarged and in 1704 the time of redemption was extended to two years, in 1709 to four years, in 1710 to five years, in 1711 to six years, and later to thirteen years. Delay became a habit and the continuance of these forced loans gradually weakened the willingness of the people to submit to taxation even for current expenditures, or to apportion with prudence taxes according to expenditures. Depreciation now set in and together with the introduction of bills of neighboring colonies drove silver out of circulation. The question of the issue of paper currencies finally developed a running dispute between the provincial legislature and the royal governors, who insisted upon adequate taxation to cancel these credit obligations.

In 1711 Massachusetts introduced a variation from the issue of bills based upon public credit and secured on the pledge of taxes, by an issue in the form of bills to certain Boston merchants, to enable them to secure supplies for a public undertaking. This method was repeated in 1714 on a more open and general scale, when £50,000 in public bills were issued and loaned on real estate security for five years at 5 per cent. interest, one-fifth to be paid back each year; and opportunity was given for a general subscription by the public. Under this scheme no provision had to be made for redemption by laying taxes, and another advantage was found in the interest which the public treasury would receive without any real outlay of capital. Similar issues of loan-bills took place in 1716, 1721, and 1728, making the total amount £260,000; these circulated side by side with the ordinary bills of credit.

In the issue of paper currency Massachusetts was quickly followed by New Hampshire, Rhode Island, Connecticut, New York, and New Jersey, — all these previous to 1711. South Carolina fell into line in 1712, Pennsylvania in 1723, Maryland in 1734, Delaware in 1739, Virginia in 1755, and

Georgia in 1760. Space cannot be given to the history of all these issues; they were monotonously alike in character, in origin, and in results. Ingenuity in devising variations of the main principle appears to have been exhausted. There were interest-bearing notes, some of which were legal tender, while others were not; there were non-interest-bearing notes, some of which were legal tender for future obligations but not for past debts; some were legal tender for all purposes, and others not legal tender between private persons, but receivable for all public payments. In some instances funds arising from certain sources of taxation were pledged for the redemption of the notes, in others not. In some cases they were payable on demand; in others, at some future time. Sometimes they were issued by committees, and sometimes by a specially designated official.

10. Loan Banks.

Reference has been made to the loan bills of Massachusetts as distinguished from bills of credit. A third form of paper money is the issue of the so-called "loan banks." Banking institutions of that period were exceedingly crude measured by the experience of modern private finance: even the mother country two hundred years ago had had but little experience in this field. A colonial bank was not at all like that of modern days, — a convenient institution for receiving deposits, making discounts, and negotiating drafts, — it was, as Francis A. Walker tersely defined it, "simply a batch of paper money," whether organized by private individuals or by public authority; the issuers never had permanent places of business, or special resources or corporate existence; indeed they rarely had any property to pledge as a basis of credit.

In Massachusetts, private banks to loan bills upon real estate, personal security, and merchandise were organized in the seventeenth century, but of their history little is known: they were certainly short-lived, and it is probable that the issue of government notes in 1690 checked the development of institutions of this character. In 1714 when a proposition was made "for a partnership to emit bills on security, to be supplemented by obtaining the signatures of citizens to an agreement to receive such bills in trade," opposition was shown to granting to a private company such valuable privileges and opportunities for profit, and consequently there was substituted a rival scheme for the establishment of a public bank which should emit bills on real-estate security. As always in such cases, some inadequate security was taken, and the finances of the colonial government suffered additional embarrassment. In 1733 the project for a private bank again engaged public attention, inspired in part by the excessive circulation of Rhode Island bills within Massachusetts; and a company of merchants issued £110,000 of notes redeemable in ten years in silver at 19 shillings per ounce, the security of the notes depending solely upon the solvency of the merchants. Inasmuch as silver rose rapidly in value after this issue, on account of further large colonial emissions of paper currency, the merchant notes went to a premium when compared with loan bills, and were soon hoarded.

The most notable private banking scheme in Massachusetts was projected in 1740; since a circulating medium was scarce, it was proposed to set up a bank on land security; and subscriptions were invited to a capital stock of £150,000, that is, people were requested to apply for loans in certain amounts in bills of the bank; the only cash payment required was 40 shillings in each £1000 subscribed, for the purposes of organization. "Each subscriber was to furnish satisfactory mortgage security for his loan, on which he was to pay interest at the rate of 3 per cent. per annum, and the principal was to be paid in twenty annual instalments of 5 per cent. each. These payments were to be made in 'manufactory notes,' as the notes of the company were called, or in hemp, flax, cordage, bar-iron, cast-iron, and certain other enumerated commodities." There was no agreement to redeem the notes, nor was there any real capital. As Mr. Davis, the learned historian of this institution, observes, "It is obvious that it was possible for the mortgage loans of the Land Bank to be paid off entirely in commodities, thus leaving the notes afloat without other security than was afforded by the partnership." The career of this bank, as well as that of its rival, the Silver Bank, was summarily cut short in 1741 by the application of the parliamentary "Bubble" Act, originally enacted in 1720 at the time of that financial craze in England which was promoted by the extravagant schemes of John Law. By far the larger part of these bills were redeemed, but, owing to the insolvency and dishonesty of some of the holders, the accounts were never satisfactorily settled. For more than twenty-five years there was litigation, legislation, and meetings of committees devoted to the consideration of this troublesome affair.

In Pennsylvania a public loan bank was managed with success and won the praise of English officials, who in general were not partial to issues of paper money. In 1722 the colony of Pennsylvania became industrially depressed because of previous unwise enterprises, and, in the words of Keith, "labored under great discouragement for want of a currency;" many were leaving Philadelphia; "the shop-keepers had no money to go to market, and the farmer's or planter's crop was then reduced to the lowest value; so that all the European goods imported, as well as the bread and flour or country produce, were bought up and engrossed at a low price, by a cabal of only four or five rich men, who retailed them again on credit at what rate they pleased, taking advantage of the people's necessities and circumstances; by which means they soon got the whole country into their debt, exacting bonds of everybody at 8 per cent., which was then the legal interest. This made such an universal clamor all over the province, that when the assembly met the latter end of the same year, they hastened to prepare a bill for establishing a paper currency; but instead of following the same method which had been hitherto used in the neighboring colonies, by taxing the people in order to raise an annual fund for sinking the paper, they invented a much more commodious and expedient way." They established a loan-office governed by four commissioners, who were empowered to issue and loan bills of very small denominations, the largest not exceeding 20 shillings; the security was to be land of double the value lent, together with a bond and judgment on the borrower's whole estate, with the condition that one-twelfth of the sum should be annually paid back with interest at 5 per cent. Not less than £20 nor more than £200 could be loaned to any one person, and the accounts were to be inspected by a committee of the assembly once in every six weeks.

"It is inconceivable to think what a prodigious good effect immediately ensued on all the affairs of that province; the shipping from the west of England, Scotland, and Ireland, which just before used to be detained five, six, and sometimes nine months in the country before they could get in the debts due to them and load, were now despatched in a month or six weeks at farthest. The poor middling people who had any lands or houses to pledge, borrowed from the loan-office, and paid off their usurious creditors. The few rich men who had before this given over all trade, except that of usury — were obliged to build ships, and launch out again into trade." In 1739 a similar fund was issued for sixteen years, and was equally well managed, receiving the commendation of Thomas Pownal. The reasons for the greater success of Pennsylvania was perhaps due to the wiser provisions for redemption, — in Massachusetts, for example, the period was either too short, as five years from 1714; or too long, with not so general a demand for payments by instalments; hence it was easy for borrowers to put off the day of settling their obligations, until they were financially involved. In Pennsylvania all the bills were issues against instalment mortgages running for sixteen years, and this colony was also careful not to issue excessive amounts, and imposed more adequate taxes for the support of the government.

11. English Legislation against Paper Currency.

The issue of paper money did not go unopposed. The depreciation was so great that every department of business and industry was affected, — in 1740 sterling exchange in Massachusetts was quoted at 550. The significance of this is clear when it is understood that at the rating of six New England shillings to the Spanish or Mexican dollar, 133⅓ shillings lawful money were equivalent to 100 shillings; sterling exchange at 550 meant therefore a depreciation of paper currency of about three-fourths; and in 1750, when exchange was 1100, a depreciation of nearly nine-tenths.

In Rhode Island the earlier bills were finally worth but little more than 4 per cent. of their face value. In New York and Pennsylvania results were not so serious, but in the Carolinas depreciation took away nine-tenths of the value of the bills. As the colonies made their issues independently of each other, there was much jealousy in regard to the circulation of bills of a neighboring government, and many colonial laws were enacted to prevent it. Under the familiar principle of Gresham's law, the poorly regulated bills of Rhode Island tended to displace the better protected bills of Massachusetts, even in Massachusetts.

Serious complications also arose because of the circulation of various issues of a colony at the same time. Old issues were abandoned in apparent despair of redemption and taken up at various discounts by new issues. Mr. Davis relates that in January, 1736–1737, the Massachusetts council approached the subject in a very serious mood and voted that "whereas his majesty's good subjects have for many years been great sufferers by the uncertain and sinking state of the bills of public credit, which difficulty doubtless more particularly moved this court in a very solemn manner to implore divine guidance and blessing in the present sessions: wherefore to comply with this obligation and profession, it seems necessary that this court shall do all that is possible to remedy this threatening mischief." The remedy adopted was the emission of bills of credit in a new form of value 1 to 3 of the old issue. Thus bills were known as old tenor and new tenor; and as the same downward remedy was easy, in Massachusetts we find various other substitute issues, as middle tenor, new tenor firsts, and new tenor seconds.

As a rule the issues of the colonies south of New England, with the exception of the Carolinas, were made in greater moderation, and the conditions of redemption were more carefully observed. Virginia did not emit bills until after the middle of the eighteenth century. The evil of depreciation was greatest in the New England colonies, partly because, being introduced there first, the bills had a longer career, and partly because of the more frequent establishment of loan banks of issue, private and public, which helped to confuse and demoralize public opinion in regard to the proper functions and limitations of paper currency. In Massachusetts, between 1702 and 1750 inclusive, £4,634,700 bills were issued, of which £2,814,900 were retired, leaving outstanding £1,819,800. The years 1732, 1739, and 1749 were the only years during the whole period in which no emissions were made. The English government showed its disapprobation of the reckless monetary issues by suppressing the Land Bank in Massachusetts in 1741; and finally in 1751 Parliament exercised its prerogative, and enacted a law forbidding any further issue of legal-tender bills of credit by the New England colonies, and in 1764 this earlier prohibition was extended to all the other colonies. The restriction, however, did not apply to treasury notes not legal tender, which were issued for very brief periods in anticipation of taxes. During this period some of the colonies endeavored to redeem their notes. Massachusetts, out of the funds voted by Parliament as payment for expenditures in King George's War, retired her currency at the rate of 7½ to 1; and Connecticut a little later at 8⅚ to 1.

The interference of the home government in prohibiting paper issues had more than immediate results. It provoked colonial opposition, was regarded as an unjustifiable interference with local liberties, and helped to develop the growing discontent with government by England. At the time the Land Bank of Massachusetts was suppressed a contemporary writer wrote that the temper of the people was irritated and inflamed to such a degree that they seemed ripe for tumult and disorder; two-thirds of the House of Representatives were bitter partisans or abettors of the Land Bank scheme; and while many in the colony recognized the possible evils of the project, the arbitrary extension of the Bubble Act, originally designed for England and Ireland, excited so general a feeling of hostility to English interference that any good from efforts in the way of educating the people to sounder ideas was largely lost. Franklin in 1766 told England that one of the reasons for the ill-feeling in America toward her authority was the prohibition of paper money. The restrictive act of England did not entirely suppress colonial paper money; under the exceptions prescribed, temporary treasury notes as well as the notes of loan banks which had not been suppressed continued to circulate; so that in 1774 it was estimated that $12,000,000 were in current use. Hence in the crisis of the Revolution the colonists could hardly be expected to turn away from paper currency.

The story of the colonial issues belongs perhaps more properly to the history of commerce or of money than to financial history, but this protracted and disturbing experience had much to do with creating in later times erroneous opinions concerning public finance. Accustomed to rely largely upon bills of credit, the colonists in some sections were averse to taxation, and the explanation of the disastrous financiering of the Revolutionary War is to be found in a study of the financial experiences and monetary abuses extending over all the settlements from the beginning of the eighteenth century.

12. Taxation by England.

Until 1765 England attempted to collect but little revenue from the colonies for her own imperial purposes, and that little had been secured through tonnage taxes, customs, and port dues, which had for their chief object the regulation of trade in accordance with the purposes of the Navigation Acts. Although the English government showed little disposition to enforce these laws, the colonies recognized the right of Parliament to regulate commerce, and if dues had been demanded on this score alone it is possible that open hostilities would have been long deferred. There might have been irritation and protests, but the abstract political privilege of England was acknowledged. As Rufus Choate said, "Even James Otis in that great argument of 1761, upon the subject of writs of assistance, which breathed (I may use the vivid expression of John Adams) 'the breath of life into America,' admitted, upon the ground of *necessity*, the power of England to pass her whole series of acts of trade 'as regulations of commerce,' while he utterly denied their validity as laws of revenue." Original evidence in regard to the attitude of the colonists may be found in a resolution put forth by the colonists in one of their declarations of rights: "But from the necessity of the case, and a regard for the mutual interests of both countries, we cheerfully consent to the operation of such acts of the British Parliament as are *bonâ fide* restrained to the regulation of our external commerce for the purpose of securing the commercial advantages of the whole empire to the mother-country and the commercial benefits of its respective members; excluding every idea of taxation, internal or external, for raising a revenue on the subjects in America without their consent."

In 1763 England determined to strengthen her military position against France; and, in order to prosecute war more vigorously and promptly than she had been able to do in the past, to quarter a permanent body of troops in America. For this purpose £300,000 were needed annually, and it was proposed by the English ministry that one-third of this sum should be assessed upon the colonies through stamp duties levied upon certain legal and commercial papers. This was an internal tax requiring for its collection special officials, and was a clear departure from the principle of levying duties for the restriction of trade, and it was also inquisitorial as compared with customs duties. The principle that taxation should depend upon consent of the payers had long been claimed as a fundamental right and had been incorporated in early legislation. Not only was the order given to enforce the commercial laws with vigor, but new import duties were placed upon molasses, coffee, and East India goods, white sugar and indigo from foreign colonies, Spanish and Portuguese wine, and wine from Madeira and the Azores. The radical change in policy of the home government aroused great opposition, and the agitation thus began swept away the theoretical reasoning which had previously distinguished between external and internal taxation, and led to hostility to all forms of taxation by England, whether by excise or customs duties. The maxim that there should be no taxation without representation became a part of the avowed current political philosophy.

The stamp tax was abandoned in 1766, but a year later the English ministry returned with renewed vigor to its policy of taxation, and imposed import duties upon glass, red and white lead, painters' colors, paper, and tea. It was estimated that the yield of the tax would be about £400,000. It was natural that the opposition to this measure should be great. The former protest had been effectual and there was reason to hope that popular agitation would once more gain a victory. As a result of the refusal to consume imported goods, the yield of the tax was only £16,000, of which more than £15,000 were spent for collections. In 1770 the duties were repealed, save upon tea. It was not long, however, before the final break with England came, for reasons in which taxation played only a part; nevertheless these measures led to a vigorous discussion of the fundamental principles of the right of taxation, a discussion which found its ultimate solution only in war.

CHAPTER II.

REVOLUTION AND THE CONFEDERACY, 1775–1788.

13. References.

Bibliographies: Channing and Hart, 319; Bogart and Rawles, 9–15; J. Winsor, *Narrative History of America*, VII, 81–82; C. J. Bullock, *Finances of the United States from 1775 to 1789*, at beginning of each chapter, and page 266.

General Reading: J. P. Gordy, *History of Political Parties*, I, chs. 2, 3, 4; A. B. Hart, III, 120–137; R. Hildreth, *History of the United States*, III (consult index under paper money, conventions financial, estimates, expenditures, requisitions, Morris, Robert); McMaster, I, 139–144, 187–193, 202–208, 266–270, 281–293, 331–361. *Proposals to Amend the Articles of Confederation* in *Amer. History Leaflets*, No. 28 (July, 1896); *Elliot's Debates*, I, 96 (address to States by Congress); 106 (reply to R. I.); V, 1–108 (consult index: loans, taxation, paper money); 109–122 (note by Madison).

Special Works: Bullock, as above (most valuable single study); W. G. Sumner, *Financier and Finances of the American Revolution;* Bolles, I; G. W. Greene, *Historical View of the American Revolution*, 137–172.

Paper Money: J. Elliot, *Funding System*, 6–16 (paper issues); C. J. Bullock, 60–78; H. White, 134–148; W. B. Holt in *Sound Currency*, V, 81–112; J. J. Knox, 9–12; F. A. Walker, *Money*, 326–336; Bolles, I, especially chs. 3, 9, 13; W. G. Sumner, *History of American Currency*, 43–54; De Knight, 12–17; M. S. Wildman, *Money Inflation*, 47–66.

Loans, domestic: Bolles, I, chs. 4–7, 18; foreign: Bolles, I, ch. 17; Morse, *Life of Benjamin Franklin*, 300–332; Franklin's *Works* (Bigelow, ed.), vol. VI–VIII; De Knight, 17–20, 29–32; Bayley, 299–316; McMaster, I, 227–230.

Taxation: *Federalist*, Nos. 30–36 (taxation); Bolles, I, ch. 14; G. T. Curtis, *Constitutional History of the U. S.*, 114–134, 162–167; J. Story, *Commentaries*, Bk. II, ch. 4, sect. 253–265; W. Hill, *Early Stages of Tariff Policy* in *Pub. Am. Econ. Assn.*, VIII, 38–107; M. E. Kelley, *Tariff Acts under the Confederation* in *Quar. Jour. of Econ.*, II, 473–481; G. Bancroft, *History of the Constitution;* T. Pitkin, *Statistical View*, 26–33 (ed. 1835); E. P. Oberholtzer, *Robert Morris*, 117–120.

Administrative Machinery: Bolles, I, 9–22, 109–116, 267–269, 305–308, 334–340; J. C. Guggenheimer, *Development of the Executive*

Departments in *Essays in the Constitutional History of the U. S.*, 122–137, 154–160.

BANK: Bolles, I, 273–275; J. Sparks, *Life of Gouverneur Morris*, I, 227–242; W. G. Sumner, *Alexander Hamilton*, 107–115; J. J. Knox, *History of Banking*, 25–32; W. G. Sumner, *Financier of the Revolution*, II, 25–35, 183–192.

14. Governmental Confusion.

The first Continental Congress, which met September 5, 1774, contented itself with public addresses. Open warfare did not begin until the following spring; at first the organization of the militia and the burden of its support were sustained by the several protesting colonies, and not until June, 1775, did Congress order the raising of an American Continental army. This was followed in September by legislation for fitting out a navy, and later by the establishment of a committee for foreign affairs; the supervision of the frontier Indians and the administration of the post-office were also added to the duties of Congress. For the carrying on of these various activities revenue was obviously needed, but the Continental Congress and such governmental machinery as existed had no compelling powers for the collection of funds. The government was a creature of emergency; the colonists were content to follow and obey their legislative body against a common enemy, England, but they recognized no authority which could coerce revenue from themselves. Associated in a struggle against what was termed unlawful taxation, the colonists showed no disposition to entrust the power of taxation to a body of delegates whose authority did not rest upon an organic constitution. The financial measures undertaken to carry on the struggle were consequently as revolutionary as the war itself. There could be no consistent policy; and what little system there was speedily broke down because of inherent defects. From the confused action of the time we may separate the following questions as of permanent and special interest to the student of finance: —

1. The issue of bills of credit.

2. The financial relations of Congress to the States and the system of requisitions.

3. The borrowing of funds both at home and abroad.

4. The ineffectual struggle to secure national taxation.

In the adjustment of the several methods of revenue to one another there was no well-defined plan; Congress did one month what it had vigorously opposed a month previously. In general, reliance was placed at the outset upon the issue of bills of credit; borrowing was then begun in a small measure, and, as the struggle continued, developed more extensively, particularly from Holland and France. Beginning with about 1778 many requisitions were systematically made upon the States, to be met by local taxes; and finally in the latter part of the war a change was made in the financial machinery of the administration by concentrating responsibility upon one person instead of distributing it in committees. With this change came the suggestion of a bank, which would extend the helping hand of private credit after public credit was paralyzed.

Owing to the troubled conditions under which the Continental Congress and the national government were established, to the fluctuating value of the depreciated paper currency which was issued in enormous amounts, and to the indefinite relations between Congress and the several States, — it is difficult to present exact statements of the receipts and expenditures of the government during the revolutionary period. From such data as are available the income of the continental treasury from 1775 to 1783 as measured in specie has been calculated as follows: —

Paper money	$37,800,000
Domestic loans	11,585,506
Foreign loans	7,830,517
Taxes	5,795,000
Miscellaneous receipts	2,852,802
Total income	$65,863,825
Outstanding certificates of indebtedness	$16,708,000

If the total cost of the war were sought, there should be added to the above sums the expenditures of the several States.

15. Issues of Bills of Credit; Continental Money.

Almost the first financial step of Congress after hostilities began was to vote an issue of paper money, and within a week of the battle of Bunker Hill, under date of June 22, 1775, authority was given for an issue of $2,000,000 of bills of credit based upon the credit of the States, with a careful apportionment of the amount each colony should redeem between 1779 and 1782. Between that date and November 29, 1779, a period of about four years and a half, forty of these emissions with a total issue of $241,552,780 were authorized, and there is a strong possibility that more was surreptitiously put out by the embarrassed treasury officials. At no time, however, was the amount above named in circulation, since from the beginning there was some small redemption; no more were printed after 1779, when Congress voted that the amount of bills in circulation should not exceed $200,000,000. Tabulated by years the number of issues and amounts authorized were as follows: —

	No. of resolves authorizing issues	Amounts
1775	3	$6,000,000
1776	4	19,000,000
1777	5	13,000,000
1778	14	63,500,300
1779	14	140,052,480
Total	40	$241,552,780

In addition to the continental issues the States put out $209,524,776 of paper notes. Of this sum more than one-half ($128,441,000) was issued by Virginia alone; $33,325,000 by North Carolina, and $33,458,926 by South Carolina; New

England and the Middle States in this crisis were more sparing with their issues.

The continental bills were of various denominations; in the first issue of 1775 it was voted that there should be 49,000 bills of one, two, three, four, five, six, seven, and eight dollars; in the next year Congress authorized a considerable amount of small bills in notes of fractional parts of a dollar, as two-thirds, one-half, one-third, and one-sixth. In later issues larger denominations were printed, running as high as sixty-five dollars. The first issues could not be supplied as rapidly as needed, and it was quickly found that the signing of the notes would take more time than members could possibly devote to the task; consequently twenty-eight gentlemen were named and compensated to be signers of bills, each bill being signed by two persons. Much disorder was introduced by the counterfeiting of notes both by English and Americans, and many efforts were made to prevent it, by altering plates, calling in certain issues, and requesting States to pass severe laws for the punishment of counterfeiters.

So far as declarations went Congress entered upon the printing of bills with abundant forethought; the pledge of the faith of Congress was early given, and a method of redemption was recommended. The first issue was put forth to meet the immediate emergency of a projected war; the subsequent issues were authorized as a last resort because of the failure of the States to contribute. It must constantly be borne in mind that there was no real national government; Congress was little more than a debating association made up of representatives of the several new States; legislation was practically limited to recommendations instead of the enacting of law; and when Congress voted recommendations it was assumed that the States would support by appropriate legislation the votes of their respective delegations. In the month following the first issue of bills of credit, Congress asked that each colony provide ways and means to sink its proportion of bills, and crudely apportioned the responsibility among the States according to population, including negroes.

It was suggested that the payments be made in four instalments, beginning with November 30, 1779, and that this could be brought about by the adoption of provisions that the notes be receivable by the colonial governments for State taxes, and then be transferred to Congress in payment of the amounts assigned to the several States. Again, upon the issue of $5,000,000, ordered May 9, 1776, Congress voted that the thirteen united colonies be pledged for its redemption at such periods and in such manner of appropriation as Congress shall hereafter direct. In a circular "Letter of Congress to the Inhabitants," in the autumn of 1779, solemn attention is directed to the fact that the people had pledged their faith for the redemption of the bills, not only collectively through their representatives, but individually. With no power of taxation, Congress could with little consistency pledge itself for redemption, but had to place the pledge upon the several States. This reliance was a vain hope, for the States, instead of rendering their proportionate shares, increased the difficulties by making note issues of their own.

Congress itself did not declare these continental notes to be legal tender, but called upon the States to devise the necessary legislation inflicting forfeitures and penalties upon those refusing to accept the bills. This recommendation was more acceptable than that of provision for redemption, and it was generally enacted by the several States that a refusal to accept the bills constituted an extinguishment of the debt. Closely allied with the enactment of State legal-tender laws to give support to the bills was the passage of resolutions in Congress in denunciation of all persons who refused to receive bills. On November 23, 1775, such disloyal action was brought to the attention of Congress, and a committee was appointed to consider the matter. A report was submitted, and it was resolved "That if any person shall hereafter be so lost to all virtue and regard for his country as to refuse . . . , such person shall be deemed an enemy of his country."

With similar ends in view was passed legislation to enforce the regulation of prices when depreciation of the bills became most marked; monopolizers and engrossers were severely denounced; and after seeking to punish by fine and imprisonment persons who should advance the price of commodities, the different States began to hold price conventions and to attempt to fix prices of labor and of commodities. The first of these assemblages was held at Providence in December, 1776, whereupon Congress recommended the plan to other States.

16. Depreciation of the Currency.

Since all the attempts to support the credit of the bills failed, depreciation set in early and was quickly accelerated. There is some dispute as to the exact date when the bills first fell from grace; according to Ramsay, the people at first received the currency willingly, and during the last months of 1776 the depreciation was slight and gradual; but when the amount of the issues exceeded $20,000,000, "there was a point both in time and quantity beyond which this congressional alchemy ceased to operate." In 1779 the depreciation became very marked, and during that year the values of the continental currency in specie on successive dates was as follows: —

1779	January 14,	8 to 1	1779	June 4,	20 to 1
	February 3,	10 " "		September 17,	24 " "
	April 2,	17 " "		October 14,	30 " "
	May 5,	24 " "		November 17,	38½ " "

Congress was exceedingly slow to recognize officially in the finance accounts that there was depreciation, but finally, on March 18, 1780, it confessed judgment and made provision for the acceptance of paper in the place of silver at the rate of 40 to 1. A tax of $15,000,000 a month for thirteen months was levied upon the States, to be paid in bills of the old emissions;

these in turn were to be destroyed and replaced by a new tenor or issue in an amount not exceeding one-twentieth of the face value of the old issue. Six-tenths of these bills were to be paid to the States and the rest retained for national purposes. The new bills were to be redeemable in specie in five years, to bear interest at 5 per cent., and to be receivable for taxes. Under this law $119,400,000 of notes were paid in by the States and destroyed; of the new tenor notes only $4,400,000 were actually issued.

Congress also attempted to give some order to the depreciation by resolving "that the value of the bills when loaned shall be ascertained by computing these on a progressive rate of depreciation commencing with September 1, 1777, and continuing to March 18, 1780, in geometrical progression and proportional to the time from period to period, assuming the depreciation at the several periods to be as follows:"[1]

On March 1, 1778,	1.75	for one Spanish milled dollar
On Sept. 1, 1778,	4	" " " "
On March 1, 1779,	18	" " " "
On March 18, 1780,	40	" " " "

Congress also at this time advised the States to repeal the punitive legislation directed against those who refused to receive the bills.

As to the actual sacrifice by the people measured in the commodities which they gave for the national paper currency which was issued, no exact statement is possible, but various estimates have been made of the specie value of the total issues: Jefferson placed it at $36,367,000, Hildreth at $70,000,000, Bronson at $53,000,000, and Bullock more recently makes an independent calculation and arrives at estimates varying from $37,800,000 to $41,000,000.

The old continental currency after 1780 depreciated more

[1] In this scale it was assumed that there was no depreciation until September 2, 1777. The table may be found in *Finance*, V, 766.

rapidly than ever. In January, 1781, it was valued at 100 to 1, and in May of that year, says Pelatiah Webster, "it ceased to pass as currency, but was afterwards bought and sold as an article of speculation, at very uncertain and desultory prices, from five hundred to one thousand to one." And another writer, Breck, says: "The annihilation was so complete that barber-shops were papered in jest with the bills; and the sailors, on returning from their cruise, being paid off in bundles of this worthless money, had suits of clothes made of it, and with characteristic light-heartedness turned their loss into a frolic by parading through the streets in decayed finery which in its better days had passed for thousands of dollars." The final and official fate of the Continental currency was not much more glorious. Under the funding act of 1790 small amounts of new tenor notes were received in subscription for stock; but the older notes were accepted only at the rate of 100 to 1, and of the $78,000,000 then estimated to be outstanding only about $6,000,000 were subscribed for stock. The remainder had probably been lost or destroyed.

17. Was Paper Money Necessary?

How far was the issue of these bills necessary for the maintenance of the independence of America? The experience of the United States in the issue of bills of credit has furnished the stock example to nearly every writer on the subject of money. No criticism has been too severe. "Paper money," said Pelatiah Webster, a contemporary of the Revolution, "polluted the equity of our laws, turned them into engines of oppression, corrupted the justice of our public administration, destroyed the fortunes of thousands who had confidence in it, enervated the trade, husbandry, and manufactures of our country, and went far to destroy the morality of our people." Later writers have arraigned the political leadership of the Revolution because Congress did not try taxation at the outset, urging that the colonists were accustomed to taxation, and were well able to bear it. It is said that the States at an early period of the war "when the fever was up" would have freely followed "recommendations" of Congress, and that it was only natural that the States should refuse the more vigorous method of taxation after Congress had exhibited a policy of weakness and error.

If we consider only what is possible among a people properly grounded in the principles of monetary science, the criticism against the issue of paper currency during the Revolution is justifiable; but the question is not what might conceivably have been done, but what could be done in America during the Revolution by fallible statesmen. The nation was engaged in a struggle for existence; at such a time the rules of monetary art, like the ordinary rules and methods of civil procedure, must give way to the prime necessity of using all the resources available. If the result is disastrous, war means a measure of disaster and loss! Whether the sacrifice could have been lessened by a refusal to issue these forced loans upon the people is a fair question for discussion, but cannot be settled simply by the accumulation of proof that the monetary system broke down. Besides the issue of treasury notes, there are at all times practically only two other policies open to a nation: borrowing by voluntary loans, and taxation. At the initiation of the struggle it could not be hoped that the colonies would be able to borrow abroad, and indeed, if it had not been for the hostile feeling of France to England, there is no reason to suppose that the new republic in the early stages of the struggle could have borrowed in Europe at all. As for borrowing at home, that implies an amount of free capital which did not exist in America at that time. The difficulties of laying adequate taxation under the existing plan of confederated government was equally great; for to grant such a power meant for the States to abdicate their privilege of self-taxation enjoyed as colonies and to give up their political independence on a money issue. The colonies, it must be recalled, had chafed under the restrictions placed by Parliament upon colonial issues, and it was natural that one of the first measures of popular protest should be a return to the issues of paper which England had denied them. Connecticut, Massachusetts, and Rhode Island, in May, 1775, a month before Congress acted, voted local issues, and in June three other colonies followed. Acting under an emergency it could not be expected that Congress would frame an independent policy which might antagonize its constituents; nor was this a time to eradicate financial delusions by a campaign of education. The responsibility therefore in a large degree must be thrown back upon the provincial assemblies.

The danger of the issues was recognized at the time by the leaders of public opinion; there was a substantial element of the population, particularly in the larger cities in the East, which stood aloof from the revolt against England, not so much out of opposition as because of the fear that independence would bring excessive issues of paper money with all its consequent derangement to business affairs. Popular opinion, however, was yet to be convinced that either States or nation or individuals must inevitably suffer; and allied with popular ignorance was the more conscious effort for relief, if not repudiation, on the part of debtors in the community, who hoped to find in an inflated currency an easier way to discharge obligations. The actual loss to the individual was in part disguised by the fact that the continental currency passed from hand to hand in daily transactions, and thus the depreciation was distributed. The revolutionary issues are not to be regarded as an isolated act, but as the culminating incident in a half century of financial experience; moreover, the issues were made in so wholesale a fashion, the responsibility of maintaining their credit was so largely divided, the tie between issue and redemption was so weak, that the lesson then learned is little applicable to modern conditions, and we cannot get much practical help for sound finance out of a general denunciation of the continental currency.

18. State Taxation and Requisitions.

In its attempts at taxation Congress was unsuccessful, for here again it had no independent power of securing revenue. The State might be asked to contribute fixed sums, but the request had no compelling power and was but feebly honored. Whether the States could have raised by direct methods of taxation sufficient supplies for current needs of war, is a question which it is impossible to decide. But it must be remembered that the taxing systems in local operation were of a simple character, designed only for small peace expenditures, and that their development in times of war, when there was a partial occupation of territory by the enemy, would have been extremely difficult. Even during the French and Indian Wars, the people in the richer and longer settled portions of the country were free from the harassing disturbances of military campaigns. To meet the extraordinary needs for national military purposes which were necessitated by revolt was a problem which the art of taxation as then developed in America was not prepared to solve. In the instructions which were prepared for Franklin in October, 1778, excuses were made for the neglect of taxation: it was argued that America had never been heavily taxed, nor for a continued length of time; and, since the contest was upon the very question of taxation, the laying of imposts, unless from the last necessity, would be madness.

What was accomplished by the mild method of requisitions, or assessment of taxes on States, may easily be described. Beginning with November, 1777, requisition followed requisition, varying in amounts and in times and methods of payment. Some of the amounts called for appear absurdly large, but they measure the inflated prices of the period, caused by the depreciated currency. The States, however, did not meet the demands even with paper currency; between November 22, 1777, and October 6, 1779, there were four requisitions calling for $95,000,000 in paper money, but the payments on these amounted to only $54,667,000. The three specie requisitions of August 26, 1780, $3,000,000; November 4, 1780, $1,642,-988; March 16, 1781, $6,000,000, amounting in all to $10,-642,988, yielded only $1,592,222. The productivity of the several requisitions in specie value until January 1, 1784, was as follows, according to the table prepared by Professor Bullock: —

Requisitions (4) Nov. 22, 1777, to Oct. 6, 1779 . .	$1,856,000
Specific requisition, 1780	881,000
Specie requisitions (3) before Oct., 1781	1,592,000
Specie requisitions Oct., 1781, to Jan., 1784 . . .	1,466,000
Total receipts, value in specie	$5,795,000[1]

In 1780 resort was had to a demand on the States for specific supplies of corn, beef, pork, rum, hay, etc., — a fiscal method recalling a stage of primitive economic organization. In furnishing these supplies there was much inefficiency and great waste. Some of these requisitions provided that they might be met by the payment of specie or new tenor bills, or commissary certificates, or partly in certificates of interest, known as indents. The system of requisitions proved of little importance until after the war was over; it could not succeed, for it lacked any well organized plan of assessment. As Professor Sumner says, "It was impossible to know how much each State ought to pay, and there was no adequate publication of the facts as to what each State had paid. Being in the dark as to facts, each State maintained that it had paid more than its share."

19. Domestic Loans.

The loans of the United States during the period 1776–1789 may be conveniently grouped under two headings, domestic and foreign. The borrowing of money by Congress, with the exception of a small loan in June, 1775, for the purchase of gunpowder, was not authorized until October 3, 1776, nearly

[1] This is exclusive of the requisitions of March 18, 1780, which were laid for the purpose of calling in the old paper, and which yielded no new net revenue.

a year and a half after the commencement of the Revolution. By that time bills of credit had been issued, and little was forthcoming in the way of taxes for the use of Congress; consequently authority was given for borrowing $5,000,000 at the rate of 4 per cent. For placing the loan, loan-offices were established in each State; lenders received indented certificates corresponding to the modern coupon bonds in denominations from $300 to $1000; commissioners, remunerated at the rate of one-eighth of one per cent. on the amounts received, were appointed by the State authorities, in order to allay local jealousy; and payment was promised in three years. The rate of interest offered was too low, and in the subsequent loans of January 14 and February 22, 1777, the rate was increased to 6 per cent. Again the results were not favorable: during the first year between October, 1776, and September, 1777, the amount received was only $3,787,000. About this time Congress was able to secure a loan from France, and it was determined to meet the interest on the domestic loan certificates by bills of exchange drawn upon the foreign fund in possession of the American envoys in Paris. This increased the credit of the home loan-offices, so that from September, 1777, until the offices were closed, $63,289,000 in paper was subscribed, of which the specie value was only $7,684,000, according to the scale of depreciation adopted by Congress in 1780.

After March 1, 1782, the interest was not met, and indents, or certificates of interest indebtedness, were issued; since these were receivable for taxes by the States, they were in part redeemed and cancelled by payment into the federal treasury on State account. In addition to the loan-office certificates, there were other forms of certificates, such as those issued by quartermasters, commissaries, and other purchasing agents. So urgent were the needs of the army, that throughout the war it was necessary to impress large quantities of supplies, particularly wagons, horses, and aids for transportation, in return for which certificates of value were given. These obligations were of a great variety and contracted without order or system, and the amount outstanding in 1790 was estimated by Hamilton at $16,708,000. Short-time and temporary loans to the amount of $1,272,842 were also obtained in 1782 and 1783 from the new Bank of North America.

20. Foreign Loans.

Funds were obtained either in loans or subsidies from the governments of France and Spain and from private bankers in Holland. The first assistance came from France in 1776 in the form of a subsidy through the agency of Beaumarchais, over whose accounts the United States afterwards had a protracted dispute; and a small subsidy was secured from the Spanish treasury. Through the importunities of Franklin, France also granted subsidies of 2,000,000 livres in 1777 and 6,000,000 livres in 1781. In all, these sums which may be regarded as gifts, amounted to $1,996,500. Between 1777 and 1783 the United States borrowed from France, $6,352,500; Holland, $1,304,000; Spain, $174,017, — making a total of $7,830,517.

By years the foreign loans were obtained as follows: —

	France	Spain	Holland
1777 . . .	$181,500		
1778 . . .	544,500		
1779 . . .	181,500		
1780 . . .	726,000		
1781 . . .	1,737,763	$128,804	
1782 . . .	1,892,237	45,213	$720,000
1783 . .	1,089,000		584,000
Total . . .	$6,352,500	$174,017	$1,304,000

Attempts were early made to obtain loans to be repaid in France, secured by the exportation of goods from America, particularly tobacco; but the danger of capture by English cruisers broke this policy. The earlier negotiations were clothed in secrecy for fear on the part of France and Spain of political complications with England; and the intercourse of the American agents and later of the envoys with the French officials reveals most pathetically the financial straits of the American government. Without warning the envoys were drawn upon by Congress, and only by repeated pleadings with the French government could they secure funds with which to honor the drafts. The French loans were granted for political reasons, and not until 1782 did there appear the first evidence of a national credit in Europe; John Adams then secured loans from bankers in Holland, the more welcome since after 1783 France withdrew her aid.

Congress first and last authorized loans far larger than could actually be secured, for the needs of the government were unceasing and repeated authorizations and applications had to be made. The foreign loans were either indefinite in length or ran for periods not over fifteen years; interest was 5 per cent., except on 10,000,000 livres of the French loans, which drew 4 per cent. Of the sums loaned by France little was actually received by the treasury in this country, as it was expended in France for supplies, but one instalment served a good purpose in paying the interest on domestic loans, and another was the specie foundation of the Bank of North America. The service of France to the United States is not, however, to be measured by the direct money payment, for it is estimated that she spent $6,000,000 for the French army and navy in the American cause.

The growing credit of the new republic is reflected in the favorable rate of interest, 5 per cent., demanded on the Dutch bankers' loans. By 1782 it was seen in Holland that victory was assured, and there was not only an intelligent appreciation of the immense resources of the country which could be applied to the extinction of the debt, but confidence in the political integrity of the new government.

21. Financial Provisions in the Articles of Confederation.

In 1781 the Articles of Confederation went into effect; this instrument for national government brought little succor to the treasury. The financial provisions were as follows: —

No State shall lay any imposts or duties which may interfere with any stipulations in treaties entered into by Congress.

All expenses for the common defence or general welfare shall be defrayed out of a common treasury supplied by the several States in proportion to the value of land and improvements; the taxes to be levied under the direction of the State authorities.

Power was given to Congress to ascertain the necessary sums of money to be raised, to appropriate the same, to borrow money or emit bills on the credit of the United States, transmitting every half year to the several States an account of the sums borrowed or emitted, these grants of power being subject to the assent of nine States as represented in Congress.

The omissions were more important than the actual provisions, though even the latter were too attenuated to breathe a healthy vitality into the administration of the finances. As a vigorous commentator expresses it, the Articles "gave to the confederation the power of contracting debts, and at the same time withheld the power of paying them. . . . It provided the mode in which its treasury should be supplied for the reimbursement of the public credit. But over the sources of that supply, it gave the government contracting the debt no power whatever. Thirteen independent legislatures granted or withheld the means according to their own convenience."

22. Effort to Secure a National Tax.

The ill success of Congress in securing revenue from the States led in the latter years of the war to a more determined effort to obtain a national tax. As just stated, under the Articles of Confederation adopted in 1781, the powers of taxation were explicitly restricted within a narrow compass, and, more than this, it was provided "that no treaty of commerce shall be made whereby the legislative power of the respective States shall be restrained from imposing such imposts and duties on foreigners as their own people are subjected to, or from prohibiting the exportation and importation of any species of goods or commodities whatsoever." This left the making of tariffs to the States. Though Congress could not coerce it hoped to persuade; following a suggestion of a price convention held at Hartford, it early in 1781 recommended a duty of 5 per cent. upon imports, excepting arms, ammunition, and clothing, or other articles imported for the United States or any State, also excepting wool cards and cotton cards, and wire for making them, and salt during the war. Inasmuch as unanimous consent was necessary for constitutional amendments, the attempt failed through the opposition of one State, Rhode Island, which asserted that the tax would bear more heavily upon commercial States, that its collection would necessitate officers irresponsible to the State, and that it would give power to Congress to collect money for its expenditures indefinitely and without accounting to the State. "She considered it the most precious jewel of sovereignty that no State be called upon to open its purse but by the authority of the State and by her own officers." Letters were addressed to Rhode Island in protest; a committee was sent to remonstrate and to convince, but the opposition was too strong. In the midst of these fruitless endeavors Morris in 1781 proposed in addition a land tax, a poll tax, and an excise on distilled liquors, from each of which it was estimated the yield would be $500,000, and the import duties were expected to produce $1,000,000 a year. This proposition was renewed in 1782, but came to naught, and the government was still powerless to collect revenue.

In 1783 the plan for a national tariff was revived in a constitutional amendment prepared by Congress, which provided for specific duties on certain classes of goods, namely, liquors, sugars, teas, coffees, cocoa, molasses, and pepper, and an ad valorem rate on all other goods. The tariff was to run for twenty-five years, and the revenue thus obtained was to be applied only to the payment of interest on the public debt, and in no way used for current expenditures. In order that State pride might be appealed to, and local apprehension of the dangers of a national system be lessened, the collection of duties was to be made by State officials. The appeal met with a slow response. As late as 1786, four States had failed to accept the measure, — New York, Georgia, Rhode Island, and Maryland. During the year the three latter gave way, but this time New York was refractory and brought failure to the plan.

The reluctance of some of the States to grant a national impost was also due to a commendable desire to secure commercial freedom without interference. During the war most of the local tariffs had been abandoned, owing to the interruptions of trade; later, when peace was re-established, many people, remembering the harassing restrictions of the Navigation Acts, which were associated with a government of tyranny, looked forward to opportunities of unfettered trade. As a historian of our early tariff history says, "Liberty was the watchword of the age. What Locke, Rousseau, and Voltaire had done to awaken a desire for political liberty and equality the Physiocrats and Adam Smith were doing for industrial and commercial freedom. Whether or no their teachings were widely known in America, the lawmakers of the time immediately after the Revolution certainly followed them in leaving commerce as free as possible; and in some instances they stated explicitly their adherence to the doctrine of free-trade and their respect for the advocates of that doctrine." In spite of these hopes, force of circumstances drove the new States into the contrary policy and the re-imposition of tariffs. Burdened with debts the new States felt the need of revenue from every possible source. The severity of the English trade laws was now realized more acutely than when as colonists they were accustomed to evade them, with the toleration of England. As an independent nation they were cut off commercially from all the advantages of the West India trade. A desire for retaliation was naturally awakened, and in some quarters the need of protection was openly avowed. Even Massachusetts, whose commercial interests were most important, in 1786 passed a law bearing the preamble, "And whereas it is the duty of every people blessed with a fruitful soil and a redundancy of raw materials to give all due encouragement to the agriculture and manufactures of their own country"; and the act specifically provided that more than fifty different commodities, if produced on foreign soil, should be declared contraband and prohibited from being brought into the State. Other States, including Pennsylvania and New York, acted in the same way. The deprivations caused by the long war had started many manufactures into life, and for their perpetuation protective support of tariffs was warmly urged.

23. Fiscal Machinery.

The administrative machinery in charge of the finances of the government underwent many changes during the period under consideration. For a long time Congress jealously kept in its own hands the executive control as well as legislation. In 1775 two treasurers were appointed to receive and pay out the public funds. Next a committee of claims was authorized, composed of thirteen congressional delegates, and this in turn was supplemented in February, 1776, by a standing committee of five members of Congress, whose business it was to superintend the officials engaged in financial affairs, and to attend to the emission of bills of credit. This treasury board, under which was the office of accounts with an auditor-general at its head, may be regarded as the germ of the later treasury department. In 1778 the entire system of book-keeping was remodelled; provision was made for the appointment of a comptroller, auditor, treasurer, and two chambers of accounts; accounts were examined and adjusted by the auditor and sent to one of the chambers of accounts for correction; they were then returned and examined a second time by the auditor, who had the final decision, save upon appeal to Congress. The account having been finally endorsed by the auditor, was forwarded to the comptroller, by whom drafts were issued on the treasurer. The next year the congressional treasury was set aside to make place for a new board of five, of which three commissioners should not be delegates in Congress.

The movement in all the executive service was toward concentration of authority, and in February, 1781, the treasury commission was abolished, and in its place was ordered the appointment of a superintendent of finance. For this position Robert Morris was chosen. A merchant and trader of Philadelphia, engaged in large affairs, his experience had made him a valuable member of the local assembly of Pennsylvania and of Congress; it also opened the way for charges of gain-seeking! John Adams wrote of him: "I think he has a masterly understanding, an open temper, and an honest heart; and if he does not always vote for what you and I would think proper, it is because he thinks that a large body of people remain who are not yet of his mind. He has vast designs in the mercantile way, and no doubt pursues mercantile ends which are always gain; but he is an excellent member of our body." On the face of it Morris was given large powers; he was authorized to examine the state of the public finances, report plans for getting revenue, direct the execution of the orders of Congress respecting revenues or expenditures, superintend and control the settlement of the public accounts, and perform other duties relating to his department. Some changes were also made in the accounting; to the comptroller was given the duties of the late auditor-general, retaining none of the functions possessed by the comptroller under the law of 1778; and a register was appointed for the first time.

Morris was clear as to the necessities of the time. On the one hand there must be retrenchment and economy, for which there was ample opportunity, because of the previous loose administration under a system of congressional committees which employed an excessive number of agents and sub-agents in buying and distributing supplies. What was of still more importance, Morris endeavored to collect the requisitions from the States, to create a national revenue and impost, and to place the revenue on a specie basis in order that some degree of stability might be introduced into the budget. He put new life into the loan policy and hoped to plant government credit on a more stable foundation, through the establishment of a bank aided by his personal credit. Because of his knowledge of mercantile affairs and banking connections abroad he knew how to bring about more orderly dealings in foreign exchange in the execution of the foreign loans; and his appreciation of the need of specie led to greater pressure upon the American envoys in foreign capitals to negotiate loans. The last investments from France were useful in founding a bank, and Morris took advantage of the improving credit of the United States as shown by the Dutch loans.

Yet Morris after all had little real power; he could not overcome the fundamental obstacles in the way of healthy finance; State pride, jealousy, and bickering withstood his appeals to the States to levy taxes. Early in 1783 he tendered his resignation, but was prevailed upon to continue in office until December, 1784. There is no doubt that difficulties were intentionally placed in his way because of the repugnance to giving powers of finance to a single person. Morris was charged with irregularities in his accounts and with speculation to his own advantage in government property; these charges he answered in detail, but his business relationships were so involved and his private interests so complicated with public affairs that it was difficult to maintain before the public a position of impartial devotion to public welfare.

24. Bank of North America.

The establishment of a financial institution or bank was early suggested as an important aid to the government in organizing facilities of credit The first experiment undertaken in July, 1780, known as the Bank of Pennsylvania, was, in the words of Morris, "nothing more than a patriotic subscription of continental money for the purpose of purchasing provisions for a starving army." The subscribers protected themselves by holding the bills drawn by Congress on the envoys abroad, as collateral security until the supplies were paid for. In the following year Morris submitted a plan in which a bank with real commercial functions should be incorporated; its special advantage to the government lay in the advancing of loans to the treasury in anticipation of expected resources. Congress consequently approved the recommendation and incorporated the Bank of North America with a permitted capitalization of $10,000,000. The amount actually subscribed was pitifully small; only by the greatest exertions could $70,000 be secured from private subscribers, and if the government had not made a subscription of $200,000 in specie, which opportunely arrived from France, the project would doubtless have failed. The bank then was practically founded upon government funds but managed by officials of its own selection. Small short-time loans from the funds subscribed were made by the bank to the government, and as the treasury made a special effort to repay these loans in preference to other claims the practical result was the maintenance of a convenient working balance which the government could depend upon for immediate necessities. The accounts of the bank with the treasury were as follows: —

	Amounts borrowed	Repayments
1782	$923,308	$865,394
1783	349,534	388,981
1784		18,467
Total	$1,272,842	$1,272,842

The bank paid in dividends to the United States $22,867, while the United States paid to the bank for interest on loans

$29,719. Besides direct loans to the government the bank was an aid in discounting the notes of individuals who held claims against the government, and, from the connection of the wealthy men in the management of the bank, inspired confidence in the abilities of the government itself to meet its obligations; it gave Morris additional opportunity to strengthen the credit of the government by his own private endorsement. The relations of the bank with the government ceased after peace was established, and the bank then fell into popular disfavor in Pennsylvania, as it was regarded as the representative of an oppressive money power. Finally in 1787 it secured a charter from Pennsylvania and as a local institution entered upon a long career.

25. Financial Collapse, 1783–1789.

The indebtedness of the national government apart from outstanding bills of credit at the beginning of 1784 was substantially as follows:

Foreign, including arrears of interest	$7,921,886
Loan Office certificates	11,585,000
Unliquidated certificates of indebtedness	16,708,000
Arrears of interest on domestic debt	3,109,000
Total	$39,323,886

The annual interest charges on this indebtedness were approximately $1,875,000, divided as follows: foreign, $375,000; domestic, $1,500,000. In addition to the above debt there were the bills of credit which had been practically repudiated, and the indebtedness of the States; the latter amounted to about $21,000,000, of which $18,271,787 was afterwards recognized as incurred strictly for war purposes and assumed in the federal debt in 1790.

At the close of the war a reduction in expenditures was expected but was not easily made. The pay of the soldiers during the war was inadequate because of the depreciation of the paper currency, and was often delayed beyond the limit of patience. Although the rank and file were in part appeased by bounty lands, the officers were not so easily satisfied, and on account of their position could more vigorously enforce their demands; accordingly in 1783 it was voted to allow to the officers a bonus of full pay for five years. But still there were no funds, and once more recourse was made to promises and certificates of indebtedness carrying interest. Government credit indeed sank so low that liquidated and certificated claims against it were worth less than fifteen cents on a dollar.

In brief, the expenditures valued in specie, from 1784 to 1789, were $4,432,279. In addition there were new unpaid accounts at the national treasury in September, 1789, of $189,906. The receipts for this period were:

Requisitions	$1,945,325
Foreign loans	2,296,000
Miscellaneous sums	338,568
Total	$4,579,893

The financial transactions for this period are summarized by Bullock as follows: "The principal of the domestic debt had been decreased $960,915 by the receipts from the public lands; while the arrears of interest had increased from $3,109,000 to $11,493,858 at the end of 1789, in spite of the fact that $2,371,000 of indents had been drawn in by taxes. The principal of the foreign debt had increased from $7,830,517 to $10,089,707, while the arrears of foreign interest had grown from $67,037 to $1,640,071 at the end of 1789."

During these years Holland proved a source of constant help; the foreign loans there placed, 1784–1789, were:

1784	$1,395,200
1785	53,600
1786	47,200
1787	129,200
1788	270,800
1789	400,000
Total	$2,296,000

Not only did the treasury continue embarrassed but there was much popular unrest, political and industrial, as is frequently the case after a long war. The issue of paper money by States was once more agitated, and seven of the States, including Rhode Island, New York, New Jersey, Pennsylvania, North Carolina, South Carolina, and Georgia, authorized new emissions. In Massachusetts a serious insurrection, headed by Daniel Shays, demanded the issue of credit money; and in the other colonies there were bitter contests between the party of inflation and its opponents. The reasons for distress, however, were not fundamental or necessarily long-enduring; it is a mistake to conclude that the country was drifting toward inevitable ruin because many people were in debt. In what way the country was suffering from the disturbances of war is set forth in the following striking passage from a contemporary student of finance and public economy, Tench Coxe:

"Among the principal causes of their unhappy situation were the inconsiderate spirit of adventure to this country, which pervaded almost every kingdom in Europe, and the prodigious credit there given to our merchants on the return of peace. To these may be added the high spirits and the golden dreams which naturally followed such a war, closed with so much honor and success. Triumphant over a great enemy, courted by the most powerful nations in the world, it was not in human nature that America should immediately comprehend her new situation. Really possessed of the means of future greatness, she anticipated the most distant benefits of the Revolution, and considered them as already in her hands. She formed the highest expectations, many of which, however, serious experience has taught her to relinquish, and now that the thoughtless adventures and imprudent credits from foreign countries take place no more, and time has been given for cool reflection, she can see her real situation and need not be discouraged."

At heart the country was economically sound, but the national financial system was weak, and in 1786 it broke down completely; further borrowing at home or abroad was almost impossible; requisitions were of slight avail; domestic creditors were throughly alarmed, and when the efforts to secure unanimous consent for a national tax failed, it was agreed that, if a federated republic were to continue, the government, particularly in its relations to finance and commerce, must be remodelled. Every keen-sighted statesman of the period recognized the necessity, although there was great variance of opinion as to the degree of readjustment. The dissatisfaction resulted in the Convention of 1787, which framed a new constitution.

CHAPTER III.

FINANCIAL PROVISIONS OF THE CONSTITUTION.

26. References.

J. Elliot, *Debates*, V; G. Bancroft, *History of the Constitution* (consult table of contents); G. T. Curtis, *Constitutional History of the U. S.*, I, chs. 26–27; R. Hildreth, *History of the United States*, III, 508–523; J. P. Gordy, *Political Parties*, I, ch. 7; L. H. Boutell, *Life of Roger Sherman*, ch. 8; J. Story, *Commentaries on the Constitution* (fifth ed., useful for references to judicial opinions), Bk. II, ch. 14 (taxes); chs. 15, 42 (loans); ch. 17 (coinage); ch. 25 (bank); ch. 26 (internal improvements); T. M. Cooley, *Principles of Constitutional Law* (third ed., references to judicial opinions), ch. iv, § 1, 2, 5, 6; T. M. Cooley, *Laws of Taxation* (second ed., 1886), 83–85, 90–99, 109–112; J. R. Tucker, *Constitution of the United States*, 457–508 (taxation); G. Bancroft, *Plea for the Constitution*, 42–52 (paper money); C. J. Bullock, 74–78 (paper money); J. J. Knox, 12–18 (paper money); C. J. Bullock, *Direct Taxes under the Constitution*, in *Pol. Sci. Quar.*, XV (1900), 217–239, 452–481; also in *Yale Review*, IX, 439–451; X, 6–29; E. J. James, *The Legal Tender Decisions*, in *Pub. Amer. Econ. Assn.*, III, 64–71 (also *Note*, p. 80); J. B. Thayer, in *Harvard Law Review*, I, 79; H. C. Adams, *Finance*, 113–116 (budget).

27. Financial Sections of the Constitution.

For the history of the drafting of the Constitution, the contending principles which clashed in the convention, and the compromises which were thereby forced, the reader must refer to special treatises. In brief there were two plans before the convention: the one, narrow in its scope, proposed to continue the general form of government established under the Articles of Confederation but to give Congress power to levy duties for revenue and to regulate commerce; the other was more far-reaching and looked to a fundamental change in the very principle of the federal organization by the substitution of centralized power for a confederacy. Apart from differences of opinion resulting from the study of political philosophy, different practical interests had to be reconciled, — the large States as against the small States; the States with a free population as against the States with slaves; and commercial States as against those with little or no foreign intercourse. Many of the conclusions reached were therefore the result of compromises rather than the expression of clear-cut and definite conviction as to the superior merit of the proposition involved.

Public finance in the Constitution, which became the fundamental law of the nation in 1789, is especially provided for in the clauses governing taxation, loans, coinage, appropriations, and accounts. The following articles deal explicitly with these subjects:

Taxation: "The Congress shall have power to lay and collect taxes, duties, imposts, and excises, to pay the debts and provide for the common defence and general welfare of the United States; but all duties, imposts, and excises shall be uniform throughout the United States." (Art. I, Sect. 8, § 1.)

"No capitation, or other direct, tax shall be laid, unless in proportion to the census or enumeration hereinbefore directed to be taken." (Art. I, Sect. 9, § 4.)

"No tax or duty shall be laid on articles exported from any State." (Art. I, Sect. 9, § 5.) "Nor shall vessels bound to or from one State be obliged to enter, clear, or pay duties in another." (§ 6.)

"No State shall, without the consent of the Congress, lay any imposts or duties on imports or exports, except what may be absolutely necessary for executing its inspection laws; and the net produce of all duties and imposts, laid by any State on imports or exports shall be for the use of the treasury of the United States; and all such laws shall be subject to the revision and control of the Congress. No State shall without the consent of Congress lay any duty of tonnage." (Art. I, Sect. 10, § 2.)

Initiative of Revenue Bills: "All bills for raising revenue shall originate in the House of Representatives; but the

Senate may propose or concur with amendments, as on other bills." (Art. I, Sect. 7, § 1.)

Loans: [The Congress shall have power] "to borrow money on the credit of the United States." (Art. I, Sect. 8, § 2.)

Coinage: [Congress shall have power] "to coin money, regulate the value thereof, and of foreign coin." (Art. I, Sect. 8, § 5.)

Indebtedness: "All debts contracted and engagements entered into before the adoption of this Constitution shall be as valid against the United States under this Constitution as under the Confederation." (Art. VI, Sect. 1.)

Appropriations: "No money shall be drawn from the treasury but in consequence of appropriations made by law." (Art. I, Sect. 9, § 6.)

[Congress shall have power] "to raise and support armies, but no appropriation of money to that use shall be for a longer term than two years." (Art. I, Sect. 8, § 12.)

Accounts: "A regular statement and account of the receipts and expenditures of all public money shall be published from time to time." (Art. I, Sect. 9, § 6.)

Restriction on States: "No State shall coin money; emit bills of credit; make anything but gold and silver coin a tender in payment of debts." (Art. I, Sect. 10.)

28. Taxation.

In taxation the grant of federal power was large, — so large as to be alarming to those who feared the rule of a central government. Convinced that the bestowal of power to secure revenue must be more generous than under the Articles of Confederation, it was agreed that taxes might be collected from the people without intervention of State or local officers. The limitations are: first, that all duties, imposts, and excises must be uniform throughout the United States; second, that direct taxes shall be in proportion to population; and, third, that no export duties shall be imposed by Congress or by States. The reason for the first limitation is clear; State jealousy demanded an explicit declaration that imports and excises should not vary to the benefit of one section over against another. All parts of the country were to be placed upon the same footing. Unsuccessful attempts have been made to interpret the word "uniform" as referring not only to territory but to individuals: so that for example in the imposition of an income tax no exceptions can be made in favor of small incomes, and no variations shall be admitted in the rate, but it has been well established that the right to tax includes the right to make individual exemptions or discriminations.

The second limitation, on apportionment of direct taxes, was adopted only after long and wearisome debate. The rule of the Articles of Confederation by which taxes were imposed upon the several States according to the ascertained value of the land with its buildings and improvements was an effort to apportion according to wealth; but none of the States ever made adequate assessment of the value of land, and apparently did not intend to do their duty in that respect. The defect had been quickly recognized, but when it was proposed to change to a basis of population a new complication arose, because part of the States were slave-holding. In the convention the difference of interest between States with many slaves and those with few or none was tangled with the question of the proper basis of representation in the House of Representatives. The South wished to keep any advantage of numbers and yet avoid any burden of taxation laid on a basis of population. A compromise was finally reached by which the North yielded on the question of representation, the South on that of taxation, and a half-way point was found in the so-called federal ratio by which slaves counted at three-fifths their number, both for representation and for direct taxes. The result was that slaves helped to increase the political power of the Southern States.

At one stage of the debate, in the hope of securing common action, it was proposed that all taxation including every branch of revenue, indirect as well as direct, should be apportioned by population. As was clearly shown, by such a restriction Congress would be embarrassed, if not completely blocked, in raising any revenue by import or other indirect taxes, and would thus be driven back to the intolerable system of requisitions upon the States; the amendment was consequently abandoned. As a fiscal device the system of taxes in proportion to numbers has slight justification; and the Constitution seems hardly to have considered the probable incidence of taxation thus crudely imposed. With a more even distribution of property, apportionment according to population might work with fairness; but property does not accumulate in any such proportion, and the principle would have worked grave injustice had taxes been frequently collected in this manner. Even Gouverneur Morris, who proposed the restriction, afterwards saw the disadvantages which might arise from it, and, before the convention adjourned, endeavored without success to remove the difficulty. The acceptance of this illogical method of distributing direct taxes was probably due to a belief that such taxes would rarely be levied, and the previous failure of requisitions — direct taxes under another name — had a powerful influence in persuading the unprejudiced to favor indirect taxes as a better means of supporting public credit.

The restriction that capitation and direct taxes should not be laid until a census was taken was inserted at the insistence of the Southern delegates, so as to prevent the immediate imposition of a tax which might bear unfairly upon slaveholders.

The denial of power to tax exports was the work of the important States of the seaboard, under the leadership of South Carolina. There were many leaders in the convention who rightly urged that the financial powers of the government would not be complete without the power to tax exports as well as imports; Washington, Madison, Wilson, Gouverneur Morris, and Dickinson all favored it, but the South especially stood in opposition. Tobacco, rice, and indigo, staple products of the Southern States, furnished nearly one-third of the exports; South Carolina declared that her exports in a single year were £600,000; and her delegates would not assent to the possibility of a system of taxation which might prove a discriminating burden upon the products of her soil. The protection of the commercial interests of the Southern States also appears in the limitation of the tax on slaves (who might be imported up to 1808) to a maximum of ten dollars for each person.

Notwithstanding the number of explicit constitutional limitations on taxation, the actual workings of the tax system have been much affected by what the Constitution does not say. Taxes must be laid and collected for "the common defense and general welfare," but it is difficult to define what is a public purpose. Since the federal tax laws seldom state the particular objects for which the revenue shall be used, it is useless to make constitutional objection to a particular tax, on the ground that it may furnish means for a later improper expenditure.

The definition of the term "direct tax" has proved troublesome; it is probable that the makers of the Constitution intended to limit its application to polls and land; yet, though the Supreme Court has had occasion to deliver several important decisions bearing upon this subject, no satisfactory interpretation has been reached. The question later becomes of great practical importance in determining the right of Congress to impose an income tax.

The constitutional restrictions on the States in regard to taxation were designed not only to strengthen the resources of the federal treasury, but also to fasten more firmly in the hands of the general government all the powers which might indirectly affect commerce; hence State tariffs either on imports or exports are expressly forbidden, because they disturb the uniformity of commercial regulations with foreign countries. This clause has shorn the revenue resources of the States more than was anticipated; for, though the States retain concurrent powers of taxation on all objects of taxation except imports, new conditions of commerce have given to the federal government a growing advantage. A century ago production and trade were limited to a narrow circle by lack of transportation; under the present conditions of commercial exchange, extending across a continent, the opportunity of the State to lay excise taxes either on manufactures or sales is seriously restricted, and thus this important source of revenue is practically monopolized by the general government. In like measure the constitutional provision in regard to federal control of interstate commerce necessarily checks the State in taxing goods brought from other States to be used within its own border. Again, the Constitution provides that the citizens of each State shall be entitled "to all the privileges and immunities of the citizens of the several States": this effectually prevents States from laying discriminating taxes upon the citizens of sister commonwealths. Corporations, however, are not regarded as citizens so far as this clause is concerned, and consequently their status is an exception to the rule of equal privileges.

The question of the initiation of revenue bills gave rise to one of the great compromises of the Constitution. It was agreed that the smaller States should have equal representation in the Senate on condition that the House, where the large States were the more powerful, possess the exclusive right to originate revenue bills. The wisdom of the clause was gravely questioned by many of the leading men in the convention; once it was thrown out of the draft; but it was again inserted as the *quid pro quo* for the exclusive right to the Senate to ratify treaties, to judge impeachments, and to confirm appointments. The limitation is not complete, inasmuch as the Senate can propose or concur with amendments as on other bills; and, as will be shown later, the Senate in practice has gone much farther in encroachments on the prerogative of the House. In limiting the initiative of revenue bills to the House of Representatives an analogy may be found in the English Parliamentary custom which provides that all money bills shall originate with the House of Commons. The term "to raise revenue," however, is not construed as including post-office bills, mint bills, or bills relating to the sale of public lands.

29. Borrowing; Bills of Credit.

The borrowing power of the national government is well-nigh complete; there is no limitation as to time, manner, place, amount, security, payment, or interest. A broad interpretation gives Congress the right to establish a bank, inasmuch as the credit of the government is thereby strengthened and its borrowing powers enlarged. During the Civil War the question was raised whether Congress was given the right to make a forced loan through the emissions of bills of credit. Full discussion of this point belongs to a later period; but so frequent and insistent has been the reference to the intentions of the fathers of the Constitution that it is necessary here to quote an extract from the debate on the proposition to strike out "and emit bills on the credit of the United States": —

Mr. Gouverneur Morris. — If the United States had credit, such bills would be unnecessary, if they had not, unjust and useless.

Mr. Madison. — Will it not be sufficient to prohibit the making them a tender? This will remove the temptation to emit them with unjust views. And promissory notes, in that shape, may in some emergencies be best.

Mr. Morris. — Striking out the words will leave room still for notes of a responsible minister, which will do all the good without the mischief. The moneyed interest will oppose the plan of government, if paper emissions be not prohibited.

Mr. Gorham was for striking out without inserting any prohibition. If the words stand, they may suggest and lead to the measure.

Mr. Mason had doubts on the subject. Congress, he thought, would not have the power unless it were expressed. Though he had a mortal hatred to paper money, yet, as he could not foresee all emergencies, he was unwilling to tie the hands of the legislature. He observed that the late war could not have been carried on had such a prohibition existed.

Mr. Gorham. — The power, as far as it will be necessary or safe, is involved in that of borrowing.

Mr. Mercer was a friend to paper money, though in the present state and temper of America he should neither propose nor approve of such a measure. He was consequently opposed to a prohibition of it altogether. It will stamp suspicion on the government to deny it a discretion on this point. It was impolitic, also, to excite the opposition of all those who were friends to paper money. The people of property would be sure to be on the side of the plan, and it was impolitic to purchase their further attachment with the loss of the opposite class of citizens.

Mr. Ellsworth thought this a favorable moment to shut and bar the door against paper money. The mischiefs of the various experiments which had been made were now fresh in the public mind, and had excited the disgust of all the respectable part of America. By withholding the power from the new government, more friends of influence would be gained to it than by almost anything else. Paper money can in no case be necessary. Give the government credit, and other resources will offer. The power may do harm, never good.

Mr. Randolph, notwithstanding his antipathy to paper money, could not agree to strike out the words, as he could not foresee all the occasions that might arise.

Mr. Wilson. — It will have a most salutary influence on the credit of the United States to remove the possibility of paper money. This expedient can never succeed whilst its mischiefs are remembered. And, as long as it can be resorted to, it will be a bar to other resources.

Mr. Butler remarked that paper was a legal tender in no country in Europe. He was urgent for disarming the government of such a power.

Mr. Mason was still averse to tying the hands of the legislature altogether. If there was no example in Europe, as just remarked, it might be observed, on the other side, that there was none in which the government was restrained on this head.

Mr. Read thought the words, if not struck out, would be as alarming as the mark of the beast in Revelation.

Mr. Langdon had rather reject the whole plan than retain the three words " and emit bills."

On the motion for striking out: New Hampshire, Massachusetts, Connecticut, Pennsylvania, Delaware, Virginia, North Carolina, South Carolina, Georgia, — aye, 9; New Jersey, Maryland, — no, 2.

Note by Mr. Madison. — This vote in the affirmative by Virginia was occasioned by the acquiescence of Mr. Madison, who became satisfied that striking out the words would not disable the government from the use of public notes, as far as they could be safe and proper, and would only cut off the pretext for a paper currency, and particularly for making the bills a tender, either for public or private debts.[1]

[1] *Madison Papers*, vol. iii., pp. 1343-1346.

The question was thus left in such a doubtful form that it is difficult now to decide whether the convention intended to deny absolutely to Congress the right to emit bills of credit under any circumstances whatever. Mr. Bancroft, an authority on the history of the Constitution, declares that the refusal is so clear that according to all rules by which public documents are interpreted the prohibition should not even be treated as questionable; he cites in proof the statement just quoted from the debates and makes a striking argument in support of this conclusion. A possible element of doubt is raised when it is remembered that the discussion in the convention was over the clause making a positive grant of power to Congress rather than over an express denial. Hamilton, who took a leading part in the agitation for a new Constitution, only three years later in 1790, appears to have felt that the prohibition was not literally complete. "The emitting of paper money by the authority of government is wisely prohibited to the individual States by the national Constitution; and the spirit of that prohibition ought not to be disregarded by the government of the United States. The wisdom of the Government will be shown in never trusting itself with the use of so seducing and dangerous an expedient." It is also difficult to believe that the issue of treasury notes in 1812, although not payable on demand or legal tender, would have been so easily accomplished if the framers of the Constitution who were still influential in public affairs had been confident in their conviction that the Constitution had absolutely taken away the right of emission of bills of credit. At any rate, the subsequent action of Congress from 1812 to 1860 in repeatedly authorizing bills of credit, and from 1862 to the present day in emitting legal tenders, affords a striking example of the ease with which the Constitution has been adjusted, if not strained, in order to meet real or fanciful emergencies.

Of more immediate importance at the time was the constitutional clause forbidding the States to emit bills of credit. It was first proposed that State issues should depend upon national consent, and fear was expressed that an absolute prohibition in the Constitution would arouse serious antagonism. The prohibition, however, was carried by eight States, Virginia alone voting in the negative and Maryland divided.

30. Coinage.

The question of coinage belongs more properly to a special treatise on money, but in recent years an interpretation has been given to the term which makes it necessary to refer briefly to its meaning. The word is generally applied to the making of gold, silver, or other metallic pieces of money. Advocates of government paper money, such as the Greenback Party, have defined "to coin" as "to make" or "to fabricate"; and hence assert that the clause in question gives the United States power specifically to issue and emit bills of credit as money. Since there was but little specie in the country in 1787, it is absurd to suppose — so the argument runs — that a power, the granting of which has for its very purpose the raising and supporting of an army, creating and maintaining a navy, etc., could be confined to the right of simply minting metallic coins. Two contemporary authorities have been cited: Franklin, who advocated the coinage of land into credit, and credit into coin called paper money; and Jefferson, who alluded to the use of treasury certificates as coining and striking money. Although the term may have been loosely used in colonial times, the federal courts for a long period in their interpretation restricted the right of coinage to metallic forms of money. In later years, in the endeavor to justify the legal-tender notes and to give the general government complete supremacy over the currency of the whole country, judicial authority has accepted the broader construction. Thus Justice Strong in *Shollenberger* v. *Brinton* said, "I cannot think it a latitudinarian construction of the Constitution to regard the phrase 'coin money and regulate its value' as synonymous with making money or supplying a currency. . . . If coining money and regulating its value means no more than putting a stamp on pieces of metal, and declaring what they are worth, it is no power over the currency, and there is no legalized currency. Stamping pieces of metal does not make them money. Coining money therefore, and regulating its value, means something more than making coins out of metallic substances. . . . When the Constitution was adopted the great thing sought in regard to the currency was uniformity of value. This could not be secured by local legislation. Hence the restrictions on the States, and the grant to the federal legislature without any express restriction. An exclusively metallic currency was not suited to the exigencies of a civilized and commercial age. It had proved inadequate during the Revolutionary War, and could not meet the wants of a rapidly extending trade." [1]

Again, from the power to regulate commerce ingenious efforts have been made to justify federal power over the currency. "Of all that goes to make up the sum," writes Hare, "or contributes to the successful prosecution of commerce, nothing is so important as the circulating medium." And Webster declared, "The regulation of money is not so much an inference from the commercial power conferred on Congress as it is a part of it. Money is one of the things without which in modern times we can form no idea of commerce."

The word "money" in connection with coinage has also been the subject of controversy, in that it includes both silver and gold. If this be the constitutional intention, it has been argued, quoting the words of Webster, "Neither Congress nor any other authority can legally demonetize either silver or gold. The command to Congress is to coin money, not to destroy it; to create legal-tender money for the use of the people; and the grant of authority to create money cannot be construed to mean authority to destroy money." Bimetallists and silver advocates in late discussions have made frequent reference to this interpretation.

[1] Justice Strong, 52 Pa., 67.

31. Appropriations.

While there may be ambiguities in the Constitution in regard to the getting of revenue, there has been still more perplexity in interpreting its meaning as to the spending of public revenues. No express checks were placed in the Constitution upon the methods of appropriations, except those already quoted. As to the range or scope of appropriations there have been two widely different schools of interpretation, depending in turn upon different convictions in regard to the powers entrusted to Congress by the Constitution. Congress is given power to "pay the debts and provide for the common defense and general welfare of the United States." Over the meaning of the latter clause there has been a searching and at times bitter controversy: on one side are the strict constructionists, who limit the power of Congress to those expressly enumerated; and, on the other, the broad constructionists, who justify congressional action over a wide range of activities in regard to which the Constitution is silent. Particularly has there been a struggle over the constitutionality of appropriations for education and internal improvements, but for a full discussion of these subjects the reader must be referred to treatises on the constitutional law of the United States. At one stage of the debate on the Constitution, it was determined to limit the right of initiating appropriation bills to the House of Representatives, as in the case of revenue bills, but no restriction appeared in the final draft.

In the general division of powers between the executive and legislative branches of the government there was a jealous safeguarding of democracy; the president as executive is given little power in the making of the budget; he is practically confined to drawing up formal estimates of receipts and expenditures, based upon existing legislation; and his responsibility and power end there, except that he retains the power of veto of revenue and appropriation bills. As this veto power must be applied to the bill as a whole, and not to individual items, the power over appropriation bills is rarely exercised for fear of crippling some important service of the government; and in the case of revenue bills it would not be exercised unless the executive and legislature were in radical opposition over the policy of framing a tariff.

32. Popular Objections to the Financial Powers.

When the draft of the Constitution was finally placed before the people for ratification, there was a most active discussion, at first in pamphlets, letters, and newspapers, and then in the State conventions. Dissenting critics found defects in every section. The substance of the opposition was that the new form of government would lead to centralized power, monarchy, and tyranny. In the first place attention was called to the fact that the condition of the country was not so bad as people supposed; State indebtedness had already been much reduced and there were indications of returning national credit; important aid was to be expected from the sale of the lands in the West; and it was loudly asserted that this satisfactory progress in the restoration of public credit would be stopped if a federal system were put in operation, entailing an increase in expenses.

The exclusive grant of import duties to Congress in particular was denounced as depriving the States of resources absolutely necessary for the integrity of their own individual credit, both for the support of internal government and the liquidation of the State debts. Most abhorrent of all was the grant of internal taxation to the federal government. Citizens were solemnly asked what would be their reflections when the tax-master thundered at their doors for the duty on that light which is the bounty of heaven, when a host of rapacious collectors invade the land, who will "wrest from you the hard product of your industry, turn out your children from their dwellings, perhaps commit your bodies to a jail." Well might a contemporary writer exclaim, "This is the mere frenzy of declaration, the ridiculous conjuration of spectres and hobgoblins." Nevertheless these fears were sincere; and their existence must be taken into account by the student of American finance. Less creditable was the desire on the part of the less well-to-do in the community, the unsuccessful in business and the debtor class, to perpetuate unsettled conditions in the hope that contracts and the payment of debts might not be too strictly enforced. "The same causes," observes Curtis, "which led individuals to take to legislation for irregular relief from the burden of their private contracts, led them also to regard public obligations with similar impatience." By vigorous pleading the cause of the Constitution triumphed, and in April, 1789, the new government was inaugurated.

CHAPTER IV.

ESTABLISHMENT OF A NATIONAL SYSTEM.

33. References.

BIBLIOGRAPHIES: Bogart and Rawles, 15-19; Channing and Hart, 331; W. MacDonald, *Select Documents*, 47, 61.

TARIFF: (i) SOURCES, *Hamilton's Report on Manufactures*, *American State Papers, Finance*, I, 123-146; also *Finance Reports*, I, 78-132; also *Works*, III; also W. MacDonald, *Select Documents*, 98-112; also *State Papers on the Tariff* (Taussig ed.), 1-107; E. Young, *Customs Tariff Legislation*, iv-xvi (debates and votes); *Statutes*, I, 24; *Annals of Congress*, 1789-1791, I, 106, et seq.; or *Benton's Abridgment*, I, 24-44, 57-65, 71-84. (ii) SPECIAL: Bolles, II, 73-102; O. L. Elliott, *The Tariff Controversy* (Leland Stanford, Jr., Univ. Pub.), 67-130 (summary of debates); U. Rabbeno, *American Commercial Policy*, 111-145; W. Hill, *Early Stages of the Tariff Policy*, in *Pub. Amer. Econ. Assn.*, VIII, 107-132; W. Hill, *Protective Purpose of the Tariff Act* of 1789, in *Journal of Political Economy*, II, 54-77; H. C. Adams, *Taxation in the U. S.* (J. H. U. Studies), 6-30; F. W. Taussig, ch. ii. (iii) GENERAL: H. C. Lodge, *Hamilton*, 108-116; W. G. Sumner, *Hamilton*, 172-183; J. T. Morse, *Life of Hamilton*, I, 357-369; McMaster, I, 544-550; Schouler, I, 86-92; R. Hildreth, IV, 65-101; J. G. Blaine, *Twenty Years in Congress*, I, 182-189; H. von Holst, *Constitutional History of the U. S.*, I, 94-97; Stanwood, I, 72-110.

DEBT: (i) SOURCES, *Hamilton's First Report on Public Credit* (Jan. 9, 1790), *American State Papers, Finance*, I, 15-37; also *Finance Reports*, I, 3-53; also *Annals of Congress*, 1789-1791, II, 2041-2074; also W. MacDonald, *Select Documents*, 46-58; also Elliot, *Funding System*, 23; also *Works* (ed. 1850), III, or (Lodge ed.) II; *Second Report* (Dec. 13, 1790), *American State Papers, Finance*, I, 64-67; also *Annals of Congress*, 1789-1791, II, 2074-2082; also W. MacDonald, *Select Documents*, 61-66. *Report of January*, 1795, in *American State Papers, Finance*, I, 320-346; also *Finance Reports*, I, 157-215; also J. Elliot, *Funding System*, 345. (ii) DEBATES: *Annals of Congress*, 1789-1791, I, 1131-1141 et seq., II; or *Benton's Abridgment*, I, 182-184, 190-201, 211-228. (iii) LOANS: Bayley, 299-316; *Statutes*, I, 138, 178; or Dunbar, 10-22. (iv) SPECIAL: A. Gallatin, *Writings*, III, 121-149; Bolles, II, 22-41; J. W. Kearny, *Sketch of American Finances*, 1-44; J. S. Landon, *Constitutional History of the U. S.*, 103-108; H. C. Adams, *Public Debt*, 161-166, 226; C. F. Dunbar, *Some Precedents followed by Hamilton*, in *Quar. Jour. Econ.*,

III, 32-45. (v) GENERAL: W. G. Sumner, *Hamilton*, 144-162; H. C. Lodge, *Hamilton*, 88-96, 117-131; J. T. Morse, *Life of Hamilton*, I, 287-332; J. P. Gordy, *Political Parties*, I, 118-129; R. Hildreth, IV, 152-173, 206-215; McMaster, I, 567-593; Schouler, I, 130-142.

TREASURY DEPARTMENT: *Annals of Congress*, 1789-1791, I, 400; or *Benton's Abridgment*, I, 90; *Statutes*, I, 65; or Dunbar, 7; Bolles, II, 3-21; H. C. Adams, *Finance*, 193-201; H. C. Lodge, *Hamilton*, 84-99; J. T. Morse, *Life of Hamilton*, I, 276-286; R. Hildreth, IV, 152-173, 206-215, 275; A. B. Hart, *Handbook of the History of the U. S.*, 100 (references, especially legal and constitutional).

34. Economic Conditions in 1789.

Before entering upon an account of the financial measures of the new government a brief estimate should be made of the economic conditions of the country. The population in 1790 was nearly 4,000,000, of which about one-sixth was colored, for the most part slaves. It was scattered as a fringe along the Atlantic seaboard from the south of Georgia to the north of Maine; in no latitude did it extend into the interior as far as 500 miles, — Albany was a frontier town and Pittsburgh a pioneer settlement. The population was still largely rural; there were but six cities of 7500 or more inhabitants, and the largest of these, New York, had only 33,000 people. Work and industry were the rule of life throughout the country. Agriculture busied nine families out of ten; land was cheap and bought on easy credit, for there were unlimited unsettled tracts stretching out to the West, partly in State lands, partly in the national domain. The value of property employed in agriculture was far greater than that devoted to manufactures or commerce. Excepting the slave plantations of the South, the farm-holdings were small, and the cultivation of each was carried on by members of the family with little hired labor. This developed throughout the North a general equality of political and social interests, if not of economic welfare.

Little change had come about in agricultural products since the colonial period. In the South, particularly in Georgia and the Carolinas, rice of a superior quality was raised in large quantities and formed an important export; the same

States also produced indigo for foreign shipment as well as for domestic use. Tobacco was a staple product throughout the South from the borders of Pennsylvania, and contributed a generous share of the exports. The wheat country extended from Virginia to the western end of New England, and American flour had an established reputation in the West Indies. Hemp and flax were raised in large quantities and formed the basis of important manufactures. Sheep for their wool, cattle, and dairy products also contributed to the prosperity of the farmer. The export of salt provisions was increasing. One of the most important economic resources was still the forests; the naval supplies, especially the tar, pitch, and turpentine of North Carolina, showed no exhaustion; and lumber and timber products were shipped from almost all the States. The clearing of the forests also yielded a by-product of pot and pearl ashes, the sale of which frequently tided the pioneer over the earlier months of privation.

Although agriculture was everywhere the principal occupation, the rapid expansion of settlement caused an increasing demand for mechanics to build the houses, barns, and workshops; and progress was making in some lines of manufactures. The growth of manufactures was especially marked after the establishment of peace; it is estimated that in 1787 the importation of manufactures into Massachusetts was only one-half what it was twenty years before. As soon as the restrictions of the colonial system were removed, the genius of the American people was displayed in every department of mechanical activity then known, — witness the concise description given by Hamilton in his memorable Report on Manufactures in 1791, as well as the equally authoritative papers of Tench Coxe, in which the capacities of the new republic are defended from the aspersions of English critics, who looked for an easy industrial subjugation, even if political supremacy were lost.

Hamilton's investigations showed that there were seventeen distinct branches of manufactures which were carried on as regular trades and which had attained a considerable degree of maturity. Naturally these industries were closely related to raw materials which the country then afforded. As examples may be mentioned the following: manufactures of leather, trunks, gloves, parchment, and glue; tanneries were numerous, and foreign competition was hardly to be feared. From iron came bar and sheet iron, rods and nails, stoves, household utensils, and implements of husbandry, some edged tools and hollow ware. There was an abundant supply of charcoal, and iron ore of almost every quality was abundant; one-half of the steel consumed in the United States was home-made. Of copper there were manufactures of wire, utensils for distillers, sugar refiners, and brewers, and articles for household use. Timber was the raw material of ships, an industry which had been carried to a high point of perfection; there were also manufactures of cabinet and coopers' wares. From grain came flour, and also the important products of ardent spirits and malt liquors; the rum distilleries of Massachusetts were dependent for their raw material upon the molasses of the West Indies, but in the Middle States stills were common for the distillation of the home grains and fruits; the largest part of the malt liquors consumed was the product of domestic breweries. From flax and hemp were produced cables, sail-cloth, cordage, and twine, and though the manufactures were not large, there was a promising beginning. Manufactures of paper were well advanced, and entirely "adequate to national supply." Different manufactories of glass were on foot, and among the extensive and prosperous domestic manufactures were those of refined sugars and chocolates. In addition there were manufactures of bricks and pottery, hats, oils of animals and seeds, tin-ware, carriages, snuff, starch, painters' colors, and gunpowder. The variety of these manufactures was no more striking than the resourcefulness in household manufacture; industry as a whole was in the handicraft stage; cloths of wool, cotton, and flax were thus produced in the greatest variety; and in some districts from two-thirds to four-fifths of all the clothing of the inhabitants was made in the home. Woollen manufactures were only beginning to take a place as a factory industry, while the establishment of cotton mills was not much more than a prophecy.

The means of internal communication were undeveloped. The Hudson River was navigable 180 miles from the ocean; the Delaware 160; and the Potomac 300 miles above the falls near Georgetown. A few short and narrow canals had been constructed. Roads were everywhere poor and transportation was slow. In 1790 there were but 75 post-offices; mails were infrequent, as, for example, but three per week between New York and Boston, requiring in the best of weather five days on the road. These impediments to travel and intercourse constituted an important element of friction which needs to be thoroughly appreciated as a partial explanation of the difficulty of imposing internal taxes which would be acceptable to the whole country.

The foreign trade can be described more definitely. The Americans had long enjoyed an economic advantage in the building of ships, and the enterprise of those engaged in the fisheries had developed a skilful and daring race of sailors. The country exported its surplus products of agriculture and forestry, and with the proceeds bought freely of luxuries and manufactures which were not available at home. The value of the exports at this time was about $20,000,000, and that of the imports probably about the same. Trade returns are, however, too incomplete to present a satisfactory analysis of foreign commerce, particularly of imports. As in the colonial period, exports to the West Indies provided funds with which to pay for imports from Europe.

A general survey of economic conditions must also take into account the growth of sectional interests. Slavery in the South was developing an economy of its own; New York and the New England cities were strongly inclined to commercial undertakings; Pennsylvania was awakening to the possibility of manufactures. These several interests were to furnish storm-centres in the debates and govern the discussion of economic questions.

35. Tariff Measures.

Before the new federal government was fairly organized it had to settle three fundamentally important financial questions: a revenue must be secured; machinery for the administration of the finances must be established; and provision must be made for the debt already accrued. Of these problems the most immediate was the provision for a revenue, and on April 8, 1789, evên before the inauguration of the president or the establishment of a treasury department, Madison laid the subject before the House of Representatives in the form of a proposition similar in most respects to the impost measure of 1783.

By common expectation taxation was to be first applied to foreign trade; the country was by its political training averse to internal taxation; local taxes fell largely on property; export taxes were prohibited; and direct taxes could not be laid until an enumeration of the population had been finished. The situation admitted of no delay; the spring importations would shortly reach port; and therefore Madison proposed "such articles of requisition only as are likely to occasion the least difficulty." The articles upon which specific duties were to be laid were eight in number: rum and spirituous liquors, molasses, wines, tea, pepper, sugar, cocoa, and coffee. The advantage which might have come from taxing the spring importations was, however, soon lost, through differences of opinion over details of the impost; then as ever afterwards it was difficult to reconcile taxation to the conflicting economic interests of different sections of the country.

Hopes were early expressed that the measure might be adequate to the situation of the country in its aid to agriculture, manufactures, and commerce; in other words, that taxation should have other than fiscal objects. It was urged that legislation should take into account changes of conditions since 1783, and special consideration was asked for certain industries. The result of divided counsels was a debate of seven weeks, devoted chiefly to the rates to be imposed upon molasses, distilled spirits, iron and steel, nails, candles, hemp, and cotton. The North advocated a high duty on rum, a prosperous manufacture which ought to be protected against Jamaica distilleries; while it objected to a high duty upon molasses, which was largely consumed as an article of food in New England and was also the raw material for the famous rum of that section. On the other hand, New England opposed high duties on hemp, because it would increase the cost of cordage, which was an essential material in shipbuilding, while those interested in Western lands wished to develop the growth of hemp. New England representatives were willing to encourage the manufacture of nails by a protective duty, and Pennsylvania championed the special needs of steel; but a Southern representative feared that agriculture would be depressed by high prices of farming tools. The interior and agricultural sections of the South vigorously opposed an impost on salt, as an unequal tax which, like an uniform poll tax, would discriminate against the poor, and would be particularly burdensome to the interior settlements with cattle needing a large supply of salt. In general the South strongly protested against the immense increase in rates proposed in protective amendments, and animadverted on the sectional character of a tariff which was designed to assist the producing manufacturers rather than the purchasing agriculturists. In the Senate there was a tendency to reduce the rates voted by the House; partly because the high duties would decrease the revenue; partly to prevent an incitement to smuggling.

The rates of duties as finally fixed by the act of July 4, 1789, provided for specific duties on over thirty kinds of commodities; for ad valorem rates varying from 7½ to 15 per cent. on a few specified articles, and for a 5 per cent. duty on all articles not enumerated. For example, iron was to pay 7½ per cent.; glass ware, China ware, and stone ware 10 per cent. Among the specific rates the most important were as follows: cocoa 1 ct. per lb.; coffee 2½ cts. per lb.;

molasses 2½ cts. per gallon; Jamaica spirits 10 cts. per gal.; all other spirits 8 cts. per gal.; brown sugar 1 ct. per lb.; refined sugar 3 cts. per lb.; tea from 6 to 20 cts. per lb.; salt 6 cts. per bu.; Madeira wine 18 cts. per gal.; other wine 10 cts. per gal.; tarred cordage 75 cts. per cwt.; untarred 90 cts. per cwt.; hemp 60 cts. per cwt.; nails 1 ct. per lb.; steel 56 cts. per cwt.; twine $2 per cwt. There were also specific duties on ale, beer, porter, cider, boots and shoes, candles, playing cards, woollen and cotton cards, cheese, coal, fish, indigo, iron chains and cables, malt, soap, manufactured tobacco and snuff. It is estimated that the average rate of duty under this tariff, reduced to an ad valorem basis, was 8½ per cent.

In the debate there was little fiscal generalization; Madison indeed was the only man to treat the subject broadly, and he preferred to confine the bill to the object of revenue. He held that if industry and labor be left to take their own course they will generally be directed to those objects which are the most productive. However, he stated some exceptions to the general rule of freedom: established manufactures ought not to be ruined; prohibition for sumptuary reasons might be allowed; and protective duties might be justified for purposes of embargo in time of war and for purposes of defence.

The first tariff act was limited to seven years; plainly Congress was not yet prepared to adopt a high tariff as a permanent system. Small changes and additions were enacted from time to time, but they were limited in duration; thus the tariff acts of 1790 and 1791 were to be continued until the special purposes for which they were enacted should be subserved; and the act of 1792 imposing a temporary addition of 2½ on the 5 per cent. ad valorem list was limited to two years, although afterwards prolonged until 1797.

Until 1821 no separation was made in the statistics of the value of imports between the amounts of dutiable and free goods, so that it is impossible to state the average rate of duty on the commodities which paid an import duty. The per cent. paid on the aggregate value of goods imported in the years 1791–1801 was as follows: —

Year	Per cent	Year	Per cent
1791	8⅛	1797	10
1792	11	1798	10½
1793	13½	1799	8½
1794	14	1800	8¼
1795	9	1801	9
1796	8½		

Besides the protective features the act of 1789 included important administrative details; such as the use of both specific and ad valorem duties, the granting of drawbacks on the exportation of goods imported, and the principle of discrimination against the shipping of foreign countries as a whole and against particular countries. Regard was shown to the trade with the East; the specific duties placed upon teas were doubled if the importation was made in foreign vessels; and on all other goods imported from China or India in foreign ships there was the higher ad valorem rate of 12 per cent. This principle of discrimination, though recognized in subsequent tariffs, was gradually abandoned, and any advantage thus derived was later sacrificed by the grant of reciprocal commercial privileges in treaties with foreign powers. On goods imported in vessels built or owned entirely in the United States there was a discount of 10 per cent. on the duties.

The original tariff measure included tonnage duties and in determining these there arose the question of foreign discrimination against American shipping, and of compelling proper treatment by levying specific rates upon vessels of those foreign nations which did not have trade relations with the United States. These questions were separated and disposed of in the tonnage act of July 20, 1789, which imposed a tax of 6 cents per ton upon American built and owned vessels, 30 cents upon vessels American built and foreign owned, and 50 cents upon foreign built and foreign owned shipping; in spite of great opposition this discrimination applied also to France.

Closely following the tariff measure was an act for regulating the collection of duties. In many of its details it followed the laws of New York, the State which had the largest amount of foreign trade during the period of the Confederacy. The country was divided into collection districts; ports of entry and delivery were enumerated; and provision was made for the appointment of collectors, naval officers, surveyors, weighers, measurers, gaugers, and inspectors. The administration of the customs during the early years was simple, and in place of a rigid system of forms governing every detail much was left to the discretion of the collectors. A few years later, in 1799, with experience as a guide, more elaborate legislation was enacted, carefully prescribing forms, bonds, schedules, and oaths.

36. Principle of Protection.

In the later fierce and partisan discussions over the first tariff the question has often arisen how far it was intended to operate in ways other than for revenue. The preamble undoubtedly expresses the principle of protection in the words, "Whereas it is necessary for the support of the government, for the discharge of the debts of the United States, and the encouragement and protection of manufactures that duties be laid," nevertheless there has been much dispute as to whether this first tariff was really protective in design.

The protectionist character of the first tariff is supported by Bolles, and more recently by Prof. William Hill, in a careful monograph on the "Early Stages of the United States Tariff Policy," who argues that "the encouragement and protection of manufactures was at least as important as any other motive in securing the passage of the act." The considerations which he advances appear to be conclusive. The legislation of the several States had been thoroughly protective; England by her measures for securing the monopoly of the carrying trade had so aroused and angered the Americans that the free trade ideas of the early Revolution had practically vanished; and the statements of the motives of those who took part in the congressional debates are explicit. Not only was Madison's revenue measure deliberately set aside for a system of protective duties, but individual members voiced the protective policy boldly, and local interests as in subsequent tariffs played a striking part in the struggle to adjust rates.

37. Establishment of the Treasury Department.

As soon as the revenue bill had been sent over to the Senate, the House immediately began to consider the establishment of a treasury department. There was still a lingering feeling that it was unsafe to intrust large financial responsibilities to one person, and the House long discussed whether the department should be under a commission or a single head. Gerry discoursed at length on the iniquity of the human race; inquired where a man could be found honest and capable enough to fill the office; and reminded his hearers of the ugly rumors that preceded Morris's retirement and led to the later abolition of the office of superintendent of finance. The inefficiency, however, of the treasury boards preceding the administration of Morris was as easily remembered, and the decision was fortunately in favor of a single secretary.

There was more discussion over the powers to be granted to the secretary. The bill as originally introduced authorized the secretary "to devise and *report* plans for the improvement and management of the revenue." In this phraseology the measure followed the words used by the Continental Congress in 1781 when it established the superintendency of finance, and in 1784 when it created the revenue board. Nevertheless, it was feared that the duty of reporting his plans would give the secretary undue influence in Congress, and that it would conflict with the constitutional provision that revenue bills should originate in the House of Representatives. Under the Constitution the House of Representatives was to exercise less power over the secretary of the treasury than Congress formerly had over the superintendent of finance and the revenue board, since the heads of departments must be appointed by the president, and were irremovable by Congress; it was therefore urged that caution should be exercised in putting powers into the hands of an irresponsible secretary.

The final enactment provided that there shall be a department of the treasury in which there shall be a secretary of the treasury, who shall be the head of the department. This secretary was to digest and prepare plans — the word "prepare" being a substitute for "report" — for the improvement and management of the revenue and the support of the public credit, to report budget estimates, to superintend the collection of revenue, to decide on forms of keeping accounts, and to execute the laws relating to the sale of public lands. This legislation further places the treasury department in a specially intimate relationship to Congress, independent of the president, by prescribing that a call for financial information be made directly to the treasury department without going through the president. The position of the secretary of the treasury was thus made anomalous; and Gallatin afterwards questioned whether this remarkable distinction, which is found to pervade the laws passed during the early years of Washington's administration, determining the power of the treasury department, was not introduced in order to give to Hamilton a department independent of every executive control. Hamilton indeed claimed the right of making reports and proposing reforms without being called upon for the same by Congress, but in practice his famous reports were preceded by specific calls.

The bill of 1789 also provided that the report of the secretary could be made to each branch of the legislature either in person or in writing as might be required. When the secretary of the treasury in 1790 announced his readiness to report on a plan for funding the public debt, the House of Representatives decided that the report should be made in writing, chiefly on the ground that only in that way could it be intelligently considered. Fear was again expressed of the personal influence of Hamilton.

Another important point is the confirmation in the statute of the intention of the Constitution to place the responsibility of the budget upon Congress instead of upon the executive as in European countries. The president or the secretary of the treasury may be called upon to assist, but the responsibility rests with Congress. To carry out this practice, in 1795 when the Republicans were in a majority in the House of Representatives under the leadership of Gallatin, it was further ordered that a standing committee on finance should be established. To this germ of the later ways and means committee were referred all reports from the treasury department, and all propositions relating to revenue; and to it was given the duty of reporting on the state of the public debt, revenue, and expenditures.

38. Internal Organization of the Treasury Department.

Besides providing for a secretary, the law authorized the appointment of a comptroller, auditor, treasurer, register, and an assistant to the secretary to be appointed by the secretary. All save the last are accounting officers and have no other functions. The number of comptrollers and auditors has been increased with the growth of the treasury business, but the titles, duties, and relations of the above officers have practically remained unchanged. In brief, the comptrollers are authorized to look into the propriety of the accounts, and also to countersign warrants drawn by the secretary of the treasury; the auditors are to see that the accounts are presented in proper clerical form; the register sees to it that the vouchers of bills are preserved; and the treasurer that no money leaves the safe-keeping of the government save on proper warrants. The system thus devised abounds in checks and safeguards no public money can be paid out except under an appropriation made by Congress; the executive, represented by the auditor and the comptroller, scrutinizes and endorses the account; a warrant must be signed by the secretary of the treasury, countersigned by the comptroller, and recorded by the register, and only then can the payment be made by the treasurer. In order to strengthen the checks, Madison proposed that the comptroller should have a tenure independent of the executive branch, a suggestion which has never been adopted. Although the system is clumsy, it is almost a perfect protection against payments from the treasury not authorized by law, or to persons other than the proper recipients. Upon the comptroller rests the responsibility of construing the text of statutes, and of withholding payments on the ground that there is no constitutional or statutory provision for them.

The president appointed Alexander Hamilton secretary of the treasury, September 11, 1789. Though only about thirty-five years of age, Hamilton's ability and experience fully justified the selection. While confidential secretary to Washington in the early years of the Revolution, he devoted considerable attention to the subjects of finance and trade; in 1781, he communicated to Robert Morris an elaborate plan for a bank, and in 1782 he was receiver of continental taxes in New York. To these special interests he added an experience as congressional delegate, lawyer, and pamphleteer. He had been especially emphatic and insistent in demanding national regulation of commerce for the collection of revenue. Although a revenue bill had been passed before his appointment, Hamilton was well in touch with the needs of the country and immediately displayed a most vigorous initiative. As secretary he prepared many reports, among which the five most important and comprehensive, both in grasp of principle and in practical results, are: Report on Public Credit, January 9, 1790; Report on a National Bank, December 5, 1790; Report on the Establishment of a Mint, May 1, 1791; Report on Manufactures, December 5, 1791; Second Report on

Public Credit, January 21, 1795. So great was his industry and power of statement that he was able to submit the first four of these documents within a period of less than two years.

39. Funding of the Debt.

These great reports show plainly that Hamilton from the first had in his mind a clearly conceived financial system, including additional revenue, the adjustment of the national debt, extinction of the State debts, a national coinage, and a national bank. The first question which he faced and settled was that of the national debt. The federal debt was by no means light; in addition to the loans contracted abroad, which have been discussed in the previous chapters, there was a mass of unfilled obligations to creditors at home. Hamilton promptly secured a request from the House to prepare a statement in regard to the debt and a plan for its settlement; and he had it ready January 9, 1790, as his Report on Public Credit. The foreign debt, which had been for the most part created by loans in definite amounts with precise conditions attached, could be stated with a fair degree of accuracy; and it does not appear that there were any serious differences of opinion in regard to the necessity of making prompt provision for its payment. "It is agreed," wrote Hamilton, "on all hands that that part of the debt which has been contracted abroad and is denominated the foreign debt ought to be provided for according to the precise terms of the contracts relating to it. The discussions which can arise, therefore, will have reference essentially to the domestic part of it, or to that which has been contracted for at home. It is to be regretted that there is not the same unanimity of sentiment on this part as on the other." This foreign debt, as calculated by Hamilton, amounted, including both principal and arrears of interest, to $11,710,000. Not only had the United States been delinquent in the payment of interest for periods varying from four to six years, but it had failed to pay the instalments of principal which began to be due in 1787.

The amount of the domestic debt was much more difficult to determine, as it consisted of a variety of credit obligations issued by different authorities at different times, bearing different rates of interest, with different guarantees of redemption. This was estimated by Hamilton as principal $27,383,000, accrued interest $13,030,000, and to this might be added $2,000,000 for unliquidated debt. The larger part of the domestic indebtedness was incurred during the Revolutionary War, with subsequent arrearages of interest; between 1783 and 1790 the principal had been slightly reduced by the sale of public lands, but the unpaid interest had gone on piling up, so that a third part of the domestic indebtedness in 1790 was represented by arrears of interest.

A portion of the credit obligations, although in the form of ordinary loans, had passed current in the community as a monetary medium, and in company with all the other outstanding promises of the government had depreciated in value. The important question then arose: On what basis should these obligations be paid? Should present holders of national certificates of indebtedness be paid the face value of the certificates which they might hold; or should they be paid face value plus the accrued interest; or should they be paid not the face value, but what they had paid for them. The present holder of a certificate might have taken for a personal debt of only $50 a bill dated 1783 for the face value of $100. Should the government pay $100, or $130, or $50 to him and $50 to the original holder? This question was exhaustively discussed by Hamilton in the "First Report on Public Credit," and the conclusion reached that present holders should be paid the full amount. Hamilton rejected the doctrine of discrimination; in the first place, because it was a breach of contract, and, secondly, a violation of the rights of a fair purchaser. The contract was that the people were to pay the sum expressed in the security to the first holder or his assignee; every buyer, therefore, stood exactly in the place of the holder, and having acquired that right by fair purchase his claim could not be disputed without manifest injustice. Those who parted with their securities from necessity might be hardly treated; but whatever claim of redress they might have should be brought to the government for settlement on independent grounds of equity.

The subject was taken up in the House of Representatives January 28, 1790, and resulted in a bitter debate. Popular feeling was strong in favor of discrimination, inasmuch as it was known that speculators had seized the opportunity of making profit by trading upon the ignorance of the people. Upon the publication of Hamilton's report, certificates went up to fifty cents on the dollar. A member of the House publicly declared that "Since this report has been read in this House, a spirit of havoc, speculation, and ruin has arisen, and been cherished by people who had access to the information the report contained, that would have made a Hastings blush to have been connected with, though long inured to preying on the vitals of his fellow-men. Three vessels, sir, have sailed within a fortnight from this port freighted with speculation; they are intended to purchase up the State and other securities in the hands of the uninformed though honest citizens of North Carolina, South Carolina, and Georgia. My soul rises indignant at the avaricious and immoral turpitude which so vile a conduct displays." William Maclay in his Diary, January 15, 1790, notes, "This day the budget, as it is called, was opened in the House of Representatives. An extraordinary rise of certificates has been remarked for some time past. This could not be accounted for, neither in Philadelphia or elsewhere. But the report from the treasury explained all." He remarks that he cannot call at a single house but traces of speculation in certificates appear, and one of his associates, Hawkins of North Carolina, told him that on his way to the capital he passed two expresses with very large sums of money on their way to North Carolina for purposes of speculation in certificates. Madison was ready with a compromise, and proposed that the present holders be offered the highest price in the market, the residue to go to the original lenders, — he thought it possible to identify the present holders through the presentation of certificates, and the original holders by the office records, — but even he could not devise a remedy for intermediate holders. In spite of opposition Hamilton's plan prevailed; all holders of certificates were to receive the face value of the government's promise with interest, the only exception being the still outstanding continental bills of credit, which were to be cancelled at only 100 for 1 in specie.

40. Assumption of State Debts.

A second and more burning question connected with the funding scheme was the assumption of the debts of the several thirteen States. The States when they entered the Union under the Constitution of 1789 brought with them a burden of indebtedness, largely the heritage of the common struggle for independence; and the question arose whether the general government should remove these burdens from the shoulders of the separate States, or the States should be left to pay their respective debts. Hamilton's argument in favor of an assumption was exhaustive: it would contribute to a more orderly, stable, and satisfactory arrangement of the national finances; the payment of public debt could be more conveniently and effectively made by one general plan than by different plans originating with different authorities; there was danger that the different States in order to secure their own local revenue would adopt different policies of taxation, which would introduce confusion and oppress industry; and as the States had been deprived of an important financial instrument by giving up import duties, the situation of the State creditors would be worse than that of the creditors of the Union unless the federal government came to the rescue. Behind these arguments lay Hamilton's policy of consolidating the interests of all the States in order to create political unity; and for this purpose a debt might indeed be regarded as a blessing.

The Southern States strenuously opposed assumption because their debts relative to population were much less than those of the North. They thought it wrong that they who had gone through the struggles of the Revolution and had settled their current financial burdens, whether by taxation or by repudiation with its attendant sacrifice to their own citizens, should be obliged to help pay the debts of the Northerners, who had relied more upon borrowing than upon taxation, and were now desirous of saddling their debts upon the South. Here again Hamilton was successful in carrying through his plan of assumption, but only through a bargain by which the South was granted the location of the federal capital in the territory set off from Virginia and Maryland.

The amount of stock which the States under the law could subscribe for and which was finally assumed is stated in the following table: —

State	Permitted by law	Actually assumed
New Hampshire	$300,000	$282,596
Massachusetts	4,000,000	3,981,733
Rhode Island	200,000	200,000
Connecticut	1,600,000	1,600,000
New York	1,200,000	1,183,717
New Jersey	800,000	695,203
Pennsylvania	2,200,000	777,983
Delaware	200,000	59,162
Maryland	800,000	517,491
Virginia	3,500,000	2,934,416
North Carolina	2,400,000	1,793,804
South Carolina	4,000,000	3,999,651
Georgia	300,000	246,030
Total	$21,500,000	$18,271,786

No subscriptions of certificates were received except those which had been issued for services or supplies during the war, and, as the foregoing table indicates, the allowance made by the act for most of the States was ample.

Hamilton has been vigorously criticised for thus adding to the national debt; it is plausibly argued that, if assumption were a matter of justice, the federal government should have taken into account the payments already made by the States in the reduction of their debts, or even have gone back and reckoned the requisitions honored or ignored by the several commonwealths. It is also argued that, if the funding had been delayed until an adjustment of accounts of the debtor and creditor States had been made, the obligations for which the United States could have been held responsible would have been reduced by $8,000,000. Hamilton's justification rested upon political expediency rather than upon a desire to make an exact financial balancing of claims. Not only was a prompt settlement of questions of dispute of greater immediate value than the careful adjustment of the several burdens, but Hamilton wished to gain the support of the capitalistic class, including the holders of State funds.

41. Character of the New Debt.

The funding act of August 4, 1790, under which the old indebtedness was provided for, authorized three different loans:

1. For the payment of the foreign debt the president was authorized to borrow a sum not exceeding $12,000,000, but nothing in the statute prevented an early redemption.

2. A loan to the full amount of the domestic debt was authorized, subscriptions to be received in any of the certificates of indebtedness which the government had previously issued during the Revolutionary War and the Confederation. No less than seven classes of obligations were defined by the statutes. These were as follows: —

(1) Those issued by the register of the treasury.

(2) Those issued by the commissioners of loans according to the act of Jan. 2, 1779, in exchange for bills of credit emitted May 20, 1777, and April 11, 1778.

(3) Those issued by commissioners to adjust the accounts of quartermasters and other supply officers.

(4) Those issued by commissioners to adjust accounts in different States.

(5) Those issued by the paymaster-general.

(6) Those issued for the payment of interest on loans, or indents.

(7) Bills of credit, at the rate of 100 to 1.

Subscribers to the principal of the new debt received two certificates, one for an amount equal to two-thirds of the subscription to bear 6 per cent interest; the other for the remaining third, beginning to bear interest after 1800. As the old indebtedness bore a uniform rate of 6 per cent. interest, this legislation practically meant a reduction, until 1801, to 4 per cent. Holders of old obligations were not obliged to convert; but, as it was probable that the market rate of interest would fall and the public credit would rise, it was expected that the government would speedily be in a position to extinguish the old debt, which was redeemable at pleasure, and thereby to terminate the interest. Conversion therefore appealed to the reason and interest of creditors rather than to their necessities. To clear off the arrears of interest, a 3 per cent. loan was authorized dating from 1791.

3. A third loan of $21,500,000 to take up the State indebtedness was proposed, subscriptions to be receivable in certificates previously issued by the several States for war purposes up to specified amounts. Here again there was a complicated provision for determining the rates of interest: each subscriber received three certificates, one for a sum equal to four-ninths of the subscribed sum with interest at 6 per cent.; another for two-ninths of the subscribed sum, to bear interest at 6 per cent. after 1800, and the third certificate for the remaining three-ninths, bearing an interest of 3 per cent. In the assumption of the debts incurred by the States it was necessary to adjust the accounts between the States and Congress which had accumulated during the Revolutionary period. Commissioners were appointed to determine how much money the States had advanced to the government and how much the government had advanced to the States, so far as such advances had accrued "for the general or particular defense during the war." The States which had balances placed to their credit were entitled to have them funded upon the same terms with the other part of the domestic debt.

The debt thus funded became at once stable and suitable for investment. The previous domestic debt was redeemable at pleasure; but the government agreed to limit the amount of redemption of the new debt in any one year to a specified amount. The government's creditors were so far forth better off; they were no longer subject to "the prevailing passions, prejudices, or intrigues of a majority of but a single branch of the government."[1] Quarterly, instead of annual, payments of interest were authorized, at thirteen different places instead of at one. The national revenues were pledged to the payment of interest on domestic stock, subject only to the requirements necessary for fulfilling the conditions of the foreign loan, which was always regarded as a prior claim; and the proceeds of the sales of land in the Western territory were also pledged for the discharge of the debt.

As a piece of fiscal workmanship the funding act was too complicated, since it created a variety of new stocks or bonds bearing varying rates of interest with varying terms of redemption. Hence it was difficult to picture clearly the fiscal conditions of the government year by year; and charges of treasury juggling with debt statements were common. A more excusable error in the plan as carried out lay in giving too long a life to the new obligations. A few years later in Jefferson's administration it was clear how much more advantageous to the treasury would have been the right to pay off at least a portion of the indebtedness at an earlier date. On the whole the funding was successfully carried out, for there was a prompt acceptance of the terms, and within a few years the old confused obligations almost disappeared, as may be seen from the subscriptions to the new stock of the United States:

1791	$31,797,481
1792	
1793	26,160,777
1794	5,096,678

[1] Kearny, p. 18.

CHAPTER V.

NEW FINANCIAL NEEDS, 1790–1801.

42. References.

BIBLIOGRAPHIES: Bogart and Rawles, 19–23; Channing and Hart, 332–333, 340.

BANK: (i) SOURCES: *Hamilton's Report* in *American State Papers, Finance*, I, 67–76; also *Finance Reports*, I, 54–77; also *Annals of Congress*, 1789–1791, II, 2082–2112; 1940 (debates); also W. MacDonald, *Select Documents*, 67–98 (including opinions of Jefferson and Hamilton); also Clarke and Hall, *Legislative History of the Bank*, 15–35, 37–87 (debates), 86–112 (cabinet opinions); *Benton's Abridgment*, I, 272 (debates); *Statutes*, I, 191 · or Dunbar, 22. (ii) SPECIAL: A. Seybert, *Statistical Annals* (1818) 518–521; L. C. Root, in *Sound Currency*, IV, No. 7 (April, 1897); Bolles, II, 127–141; W. G. Sumner, *History of Banking in the U. S.*, I, 22–57; *Accounts of the First Bank*, in *Quar. Jour. Econ.*, VI, 471–474; C. F. Dunbar, in *Quar. Jour. Econ.*, III, 54–58. (iii) GENERAL: C. A. Conant, *History of Modern Banking*, 288–294; H. White, 258–262; J. T. Morse, *Life of Hamilton*, I, 333–347; J. S. Landon, *Constitutional History of the U. S.*, 112–115; R. Hildreth, IV, 256–266; W. G. Sumner, *Hamilton*, 162–170.

COINAGE: (i) SOURCES: *Hamilton's Report on the Mint*, in *American State Papers, Finance*, I, 97–107; also *Finance Reports*, I, 133–156; also *Annals of Congress*, 1789–1791, II, 2112; also *Old South Leaflets*, No. 74; *Statutes*, I, 246; or Dunbar, 227; or *Report of Monetary Commission* (1898), 463; *Report of International Monetary Conference* (1878), 425–443 (plans of Morris and Jefferson). (ii) SPECIAL: D. K. Watson, *History of American Coinage*, 30–70; H. R. Linderman, *Money*, 15–27; J. L. Laughlin, *Bimetallism in the U. S.*, 13–24; Bolles, II, 156–174. (iii) GENERAL: McMaster, I, 190–199 (plans of Morris and Jefferson); J. T. Morse, *Life of Hamilton*, I, 351–356; H. C. Lodge, *Hamilton*, 106–108, 130.

EXCISE: (i) SOURCES: *American State Papers, Finance*, I, 64–67, 151–158, 348–350; *Annals of Congress*, 1789–1791, II, pp. 1890–1910 et seq. (debates); *Annals*, 1796–1797, 2791–2867 (report on opposition to excise); J. B. Thayer, *Cases on Constitutional Law*, II, 1315 (carriage case), or 1 *Curtis' Decisions*, 150; A. Gallatin, *Writings* (Adams ed.), III, 87–96. (ii) SPECIAL: A. Seybert, *Statistical Annals* (1818), 455–478; H. C. Adams, *Taxation in the U. S.*, 1789–1816 (J. H. U. Studies), II, 45–60; F. C. Howe, *Taxation under Internal Revenue System*, 12–38; Bolles, II, 103–126; C. F. Dunbar, *Direct Taxes of* 1861, in *Quar. Jour. of Econ.*, III,

436. (iii) GENERAL: Stevens, *Life of Gallatin*, 50–56, 69–99 (Whiskey Rebellion); H. C. Lodge, *Life of Hamilton*, 180–184; J. T. Morse, *Alexander Hamilton*, I, 348–351; II, 147–171; J. P. Gordy, *Political Parties*, I, 201–214; R. Hildreth, IV, 253–255; McMaster, II, 25–81, 41–43, 189–203.

DEBT AND SINKING FUND: *Statutes*, I, 281–433; or Dunbar, 32–35; Bolles, II, 56–65; J. Elliot, *Funding System*, *Annals of Congress*, 1795–1796, 1499 (debate over amount of indebtedness); E. A. Ross, *Sinking Funds*, in *Pub. Amer. Econ. Assn.*, VII; J. W. Kearny, *Sketch of American Finances*, 45–60.

EXPENDITURES: *American State Papers, Finance*, I, 661 (statistics), 755 (report on accounts); *Writings of Gallatin* (Adams ed.) III, 98–121; Bolles, II, 182–202 (foot-notes for references).

HAMILTON'S POLICY: *Annals of Congress*, 1791–1793, p. 899 et seq.; or *Benton's Abridgment*, I, 418–440 (debate in 1793 on official conduct); *Annals*, 1799–1801, p. 1273 (report of committee, May 18, 1800); Bolles, II, 175–181; C. F. Dunbar, *Quar. Jour. Econ.*, III, 32–59; E. C. Lunt, *Hamilton as a Political Economist*, in *Journal of Political Economy*, III, 289; J. T. Morse, *Life of Hamilton*, I, 370–425, II, 20–66; W. G. Sumner, *Hamilton*, 184–190.

43. First United States Bank.

Besides the questions of urgency, such as the provision of a revenue, the establishment of an effective administration of finance, and the satisfaction of the government's creditors, there were other financial problems which early engaged the attention of Congress. In part these were inspired by Hamilton, who had definite convictions on the proper relation of government to finance, and in part they were due to new and unforeseen demands on the treasury.

Hamilton was convinced that a national bank would be an important factor in the improvement of national credit. Little in the previous experience of the country gave encouragement to such a project. During the Revolutionary period several banking propositions had been discussed, and as a result in the decade 1780–1790 three institutions had been established, — the Bank of North America, originally chartered by Congress in 1781 at the suggestion of Robert Morris; the Bank of New York, organized in 1784; and the Massachusetts Bank. Hamilton had already shown his interest in the subject by co-operating in the founding of the Bank of New York, for which he drafted the articles of association. On December 13, 1790, within a few months of his induction into office, he presented an elaborate document in favor of a federal bank. After rapidly reviewing some precedents in the history of other countries he sums up the advantages which would be derived from such an institution: First, there would be an increase of actual capital by an enlargement of notes in circulation, by providing greater use of individual notes of hand, and by a gathering up of individual deposits; second, the bank would make it easier for the government to obtain loans; and, third, it would make it easier for the individual to pay his taxes to the government, since he would have a greater opportunity to borrow, and there would be an increase and quickening of the circulation of money. Hamilton enumerated and discussed the possible economic disadvantages, such as increase of usury; interference with other kinds of lending; temptation to overtrading; disturbance of the natural course of trade; fictitious credit to bankrupts; and banishment of gold and silver from the country. The report closed with an outline of a constitution of a bank. In the congressional debate which followed, the opposition dwelt less upon the commercial and fiscal merits and demerits of a bank than upon the charges that a bank would be a monopoly inconsistent with a free republic.

After the debate seemed about at an end, it was renewed with much vigor on the question of constitutionality. Madison recalled that the Constitutional Convention of 1787 had rejected the insertion of a power to Congress to grant charters of incorporation, and roundly attacked the whole idea, asserting that "It appeared on the whole that the power exercised by the bill was condemned by the silence of the Constitution; was condemned by the rule of interpretation arising out of the Constitution; was condemned by its tendency to destroy the main characteristics of the Constitution; was condemned by the expositions of the friends of the Constitution whilst depending before the people; was condemned by the apparent intentions of the parties which ratified the Constitution; was condemned by the explanatory amendments proposed by Congress themselves to the Constitution."

The bill passed the House by a sectional vote of 39 to 20; in the negative there was only one vote north of Maryland, and in the affirmative but three south of that State. Washington was in doubt as to approving the bill, and asked his cabinet advisers for written opinions on its constitutionality. Randolph, the attorney-general, and Jefferson, secretary of state, submitted adverse opinions, which were then presented to Hamilton for examination. Hamilton's opinion is one of his ablest papers; it not only solved the president's doubts, but it furnished an arsenal of argument to be drawn upon in the future for a generous interpretation of the Constitution.

The charter provided for a capital stock of $10,000,000, of which one-fifth was to be subscribed by the government; the remainder was open to public subscription, one-fourth to be paid in specie and three-fourths in government stock bearing 6 per cent. interest. The government subscription was to be borrowed from the bank, payable in ten annual instalments, or sooner if the government should think fit; the note issues of the bank were limited by the provision that all debts should not exceed the deposits by more than $10,000,000, and they were receivable for all payments to the United States; the establishment of branches was authorized according as the directors might deem proper; and periodical statements of the bank's condition might be called for by the secretary of the treasury. The charter was to run for twenty years, and in the mean time the government pledged itself to grant no other bank charter. Capital was secured without difficulty, and the central bank was opened at Philadelphia, December 12, 1791, followed by the establishment of eight branches, at Boston, New York, Baltimore, Washington, Norfolk, Charleston, Savannah, and New Orleans.

In a history of government finance the chief interest in the experience of the United States Bank lies in the assistance which the bank rendered to the government treasury. In the first place the bank lent the $2,000,000 contemplated in the charter, and speedily supplemented this aid by other loans made in anticipation of taxes. As revenue in these early years was uncertain, and expenditures increased out of proportion, the government had a valuable advantage; but unfortunately it proved difficult to discharge the obligation which had been so easily incurred, and by 1796 the debt to the bank had increased to $6,200,000. The bank then became insistent upon payment because of its own needs, and the government sold a portion of its stock in 1796–1797; as financial pressure still continued, by 1802 it parted with all its holdings. The sales showed a profit, yielding a premium of $671,860. In addition the government during its ownership received dividends of $1,101,720, or about 8⅜ per cent. annually. As compared with the payments made by the government to the bank for its loan, the original investment netted a handsome profit.

The second fiscal service which the bank rendered to the government was in caring for its funds. As the government depended for its revenue almost entirely upon customs duties, collected at ports extending along a seaboard of thousands of miles, it would have been difficult for the treasury department in the early years of its existence to have made the necessary transfers, and as yet there were but few local banking institutions which could have been chosen for depositories. The bank and its branches, however, did not have the exclusive privilege of government deposits. In 1811, even before rechartering was refused, at least eleven local banks were employed, of which eight were in the eastern section of the country; and the private depositories had the custody of one-third of the public deposits.

44. Mint and Coinage.

During the Revolutionary period metallic money remained in the confusion of the colonial period. Various foreign coins circulated side by side, as the English guinea, crown, and shilling; the French guinea, pistole, and crown; the Spanish pistole; and the johannes, half-johannes, and moidore; and unequal values were given in different parts of the Union to coins of the same intrinsic worth, thus affording opportunity for clipping and fraudulent change. Various units of account were employed in different sections of the country, which tended to obscure a clear understanding of the economic conditions of the several States. The Articles of Confederation when they went into effect in 1781 did not contribute much to remove the complications, for, though Congress had power to regulate the alloy and value of coins struck either by its authority or by that of the States, the right to coin money was still retained by the State.

Several reports had been made on the subject of coinage. The first was by Robert Morris, January 15, 1782; he advised that a money unit affixed to both metals would not be stable or certain; that the money unit should be attached to silver alone; and that no coin should be struck to correspond to the money unit selected. The unit, by a system of elaborate calculations, he fixed at $\frac{1}{1440}$ of a dollar, assigning as a merit of this particular fraction the fact that all the currencies of the several States except one were reducible to it without a remainder; and that consequently it could be adopted by any State without change in coin. To this Jefferson objected on the ground that the unit was altogether too small and would be inconvenient in commercial computations, and as a substitute he recommended a unit of the value of the Spanish milled dollar, with which the colonies had long been familiar; and indeed it was the unit in which the public debt and the continental currency were expressed. Jefferson also advised that the money unit be attached to both metals. Although resolutions and ordinances were passed by the Continental Congress in favor of a decimal system of coinage, no practical step beyond the coinage of a small amount of copper coins had been taken when the new government came into existence.

The country still relied upon foreign coins, as is well illustrated by the provision in the act of July 31, 1789, that duties were payable in the gold coins of England, France, Spain, and Portugal, or in other gold coins of equal fineness.

The subject of coinage was exhaustively considered by Hamilton in a report submitted to Congress in May, 1791, in which he stood for a unit expressed in both gold and silver. While gold was to be preferred to silver for certain reasons, he held that it was not safe to abridge the quantity of circulating medium by annulling the use of silver. He recommended that the mint ratio between gold and silver be 1 to 15, — a proportion corresponding to the bullion values at that time, — and proposed that the monetary unit consist of 24¾ grains of pure gold or 371¼ grains of pure silver, the amount of silver corresponding as nearly as could be determined with that of the Spanish dollar in actual circulation, "each answering to a dollar in the money of account." In accordance with this plan Hamilton recommended the coinage of ten dollar and one dollar gold pieces, one dollar and ten cent silver pieces, and one cent and one-half cent copper pieces. There is nothing whatever in Hamilton's report which countenances silver monometallism; gold as well as silver was recognized as an actual standard of value at the time, and Hamilton's efforts were directed to determining a ratio between gold and silver which should bring uniformity out of disorder occasioned by the silver coinage then current.

The Mint Act of April 2, 1792, substantially followed the suggestions of Hamilton, omitting, however, any provision for the coinage of a gold dollar. In view of the importance which has been given in later discussions of bimetallism to this initial coinage legislation, the following paragraphs of the law are significant:

"The money of account of the United States shall be expressed in dollars or units, dimes or tenths, cents or hundredths."

"There shall be from time to time struck and coined at the said mint coins of gold, silver, and copper, of the following denominations, values, and description, viz.: eagles — each to be of the value of ten dollars or units, and to contain two hundred and forty-seven grains and four-eighths of a grain of pure, or two hundred and seventy grains of standard, gold . . .; half-eagles — each . . . ; quarter-eagles — each . . . ; dollars or units — each to be of the value of a Spanish milled dollar as the same is now current, and to contain three hundred and seventy-one grains and four-sixteenths parts of a grain of pure, or four hundred and sixteen grains of standard, silver."

Because there was no distinct provision for the coinage of a gold dollar, it has been hastily concluded by advocates of silver coinage that the original unit of value was the silver dollar. The error has resulted from not observing that there are different kinds of units. The word unit as employed in the Mint Act refers to a unit of numbers, and not, as crudely interpreted, to a unit of value.

The act of 1792 has indeed been given greater prominence than it deserves, for the currency question at that time did not arouse much interest. There was more discussion in Congress over the expense of establishing and maintaining a mint than there was over the ratio or the choice of metals. The fierce debate was over the absorbing question whether the coins should be stamped with the figure of the head of the president for the time being or with that of the Goddess of Liberty. There was also fear of enlarging the civil establishment, and thus extending the power of the federal executive. The mint was established at Philadelphia, and at first was placed under the control of the secretary of state, but later, under the advice of Hamilton, it was transferred to the treasury department. Its operations were on a small scale, and there was complaint on one side that it was inefficient, and on the other that it was too expensive; consequently an attempt, which proved unsuccessful, was made to abolish the mint and entrust the coinage to private contractors.

45. Excise Tax on Whiskey.

The tariff bill of 1789 was passed before there could be a full knowledge of the exact needs of the government or of the productivity of a given schedule of duties, but it soon became evident that more revenue was required; and Hamilton promptly recommended both an extension of import duties and the imposition of excise duties. Congress was loath to vote internal taxes; the creation of new federal offices was unpopular, while the suggestion that whiskey should bear the important part in this new class of duties aroused intense antagonism. In some sections of the country whiskey was so common an article of daily consumption that its special taxation was regarded as a discriminating burden upon one of the necessities of life. Under these conditions it was argued that a tax upon spirits was in the nature of a poll tax. After the assumption of the State debts and the shouldering of the annual interest charge thereon the need of further revenue became imperative; and by the act of March 3, 1791, Congress adopted a portion of the recommendations which had been previously submitted by Hamilton. Under this law duties were laid as follows: upon spirits distilled from molasses, sugar, and other foreign materials, 11 to 30 cents a gallon; upon spirits distilled from domestic articles, as whiskey from grain, 9 to 25 cents a gallon. Administrative machinery to carry out the provisions of the act was also created.

The revenue collected under this act could not be applied to current expenses, but was to be devoted solely to the payment of the interest upon the general debt, and, if there were a surplus, it was to be applied to the payment of the principal of that debt. The anticipated opposition to these duties became so strong that reductions in some of the rates were made by an early amendment of the original act. To country producers was granted the important option of substituting for a tax based on actual product a license tax on the presumptive monthly capacity of the still. By this system manufacturers hastened to improve their stills in order to increase the output, so that the tax per gallon was reduced to about 3 cents, and later, according to an estimate in 1801, to three-fifths of a cent; thus the revenue fell far below reasonable estimates.

In spite of all these concessions the tax was regarded with hostility, particularly in the agricultural regions of the Middle and Southern States. It was asserted that the commercial and importing interests of New England disliked the tariff, but looked with complacency on an excise upon an industry in which they were not greatly concerned. The opposition was most marked on the frontier, where transportation was so difficult and expensive that the only way in which corn could be made productive in trade was by its manufacture into a form which would reduce its bulk. The indignation became wide-spread and intense, and finally in 1794 led to an armed organization in Southwestern Pennsylvania and to an open defiance of the excise officers. Troops were called out; the Whiskey Insurrection, as it was called, failed as an attempt to defy the national government, but it led to another threshing over of arguments on the wisdom of excise duties. The four main arguments against the tax have been summarized as follows: the taxes tended to contravene the principle of liberty; they injured morals by inducing false swearing; they were burdensome because of oppressive penalties; and they interfered unduly with the process of distilling. These objections were carefully met by Hamilton, but the tax was not popular, and above all it was not fruitful; its gross return in 1793 was $422,000, from which heavy deductions had to be made: the cost of collection in the same year was 16.5 per cent., and, if the drawbacks allowed be deducted, the net yield was only 76.5 per cent. of the gross receipts.

46. Other Excise Duties; Carriage Tax.

The unproductiveness of the excise simply led Hamilton and his successor to urge and secure an extension of the system to a wider range of commodities. An act of June 5,

1794, provided for taxes on carriages, on sales of certain liquors, on manufacture of snuff, refining of sugar, and on auction sales. On carriages the rates of duty varied according to a classification into coaches driven by box or postilion, chariots with or without panels, two-wheeled top carriages, and other two-wheeled carriages. Like the contemporary English excise law, the schedule of duties did not include wagons used in agriculture or for transportation of commodities.

The constitutionality of the act was questioned so far as it imposed a tax on carriages and gave rise to the important decision by the Supreme Court in 1796 in the case of *United States* v. *Hylton.* The point of contest was whether the tax upon carriages was direct; if so, it could be laid only by the rule of federal apportionment as prescribed by the Constitution. The decision of the Supreme Court denied this construction and gave a generous interpretation to the term "indirect duties," though an interpretation not in harmony with the definitions ordinarily used by modern writers on finance. The term "duty" was held to be only less comprehensive than the general term "tax." As in Great Britain, — whence the United States took the general ideas of taxes, — the words "duties," "imposts," "excises," "customs," etc., embrace taxes on stamps and tolls for passage, and are not confined to taxes on importations only. A tax on expense was regarded by the court as an indirect tax; and inasmuch as a carriage was a consumable commodity, and a tax on it was a tax on the expense of the owner, an annual tax on carriages was to be properly classed as an indirect tax. Furthermore, a tax on carriages could not be a direct tax, because apportionment would tend to gross and arbitrary differences in the contribution of each State. The court, without giving a judicial opinion on the exact distinction between direct and indirect taxes, was inclined to believe that the direct taxes contemplated by the Constitution were only two, — a capitation or poll tax, without regard to property, profession, or any other circumstance; and a tax on land.

Professor Dunbar points out that this earlier definition of a direct tax came from the Physiocrats, a school of economic writers who held that agriculture was the only productive employment, and that the net product from land, to be found in the hands of the landowner, is the only fund from which taxation can draw without impoverishing society. This naturally led to a classification of taxes as "direct" when laid immediately upon the landowner, and "indirect" when laid upon somebody else. With the interpretation of the Constitution given by the Supreme Court the text-writers on constitutional law and lawyers have been in general accord. Justice Story in his "Commentaries" observes that all taxes are divided into two classes, — those which are direct and those which are indirect, — and that under the former denomination are included taxes on land or real property, and under the latter taxes on consumption. The decision had more than a current significance, and its influence is to be noted later in the discussions upon the income tax.

Among the excise duties was a license tax of $5 upon retailers of wines and foreign liquors (June 5, 1794); a tax so light that it could not cause hardship, although the principle of uniform licenses naturally operated as a premium to large dealers. On the manufacture of snuff a tax of 8 cents a pound was laid June 5, 1794, but this did not prove productive; it was soon discovered that the money withdrawn from the treasury under the grant of drawbacks on the export of snuff exceeded the return from the tax itself, and this tax was consequently soon abandoned. Upon the manufacture of sugar a duty of 2 cents a pound was imposed, and as the domestic manufacture supplied nearly all that was consumed in the country the tax met the expectations of Congress. The tax on auction sales (June 9, 1794) was at the rate of 25 cents per $100 for sale of goods connected with husbandry and 50 cents per $100 upon other goods. The productiveness of this tax was largely determined by the degree of honesty in the auctioneers, and false accounts were not uncommon. As the needs of the government increased, a further extension of excise taxation was made July 6, 1797, by the imposition of duties upon legal transactions, to be collected through the sale of stamps, which were affixed to the legal documents concerned.

47. Direct Taxation.

As early as 1794 direct taxation was suggested, and in 1796 the secretary of the treasury was directed to prepare a scheme for that purpose. The principal motives assigned in its favor were the needs of the treasury, and the danger of relying so largely upon revenues derived from commerce, which was liable to disarrangement by European wars: there ought to be other supplies of revenue besides customs to fall back upon. The opposition insisted that direct taxation was irritating to the people, and should be used only in extreme cases; it was unequal, and consequently unjust.

The first direct tax was imposed by act of July 14, 1798, and the amount to be apportioned among the States was $2,000,000. It was laid upon all dwelling-houses and lands and on slaves between the ages of twelve and fifty. The assessment was curious and careless; upon houses the rate was progressive; for example, on houses valued between $100 and $500 the rate was two-tenths of one per cent, while on dwelling-houses valued at more than $30,000 the rate was one per cent. Upon every slave the tax was 50 cents. After deducting the sums thus assessed upon dwelling-houses and slaves, within the United States, from the sum apportioned to each State, the remainder was assessed upon the land according to a valuation of each piece at such a rate as would produce the given sum. The proportions of the $2,000,000 assessed was calculated to fall as follows: upon houses, $1,315,000; lands, $457,000; slaves, $228,000. The tax did not operate according to the estimates made before its passage; and payments were so tardily made that at the end of three years one-fifth of the tax still remained unpaid. In 1800 the receipts were $734,000, and in 1801 $534,000.

48. Summary of Receipts, 1789–1801.

On the whole the government made a successful beginning with taxation; notwithstanding the friction in the levy of the excise duties, the morbid apprehensions of 1787 were shown to be unwarranted. Even if economic development was backward, if the population was not compact enough, if opportunities for evasion were easy and the expense of collection great, there was no longer reason to fear that the excise duties would be a despotic invasion of a subject's liberties. Although the receipts were small, the fact that the government had made clear its power to levy the duties was a promise of future financial support. The direct tax proved to be a clumsy and an ineffective instrument of revenue; import duties, however, justified all the claims made for their serviceableness; they steadily increased, being more than twice as much in 1800 as in 1791, and there were no indications that they disturbed the normal course of industry or discriminated against any section or class. The receipts from sales of public lands did not at the time yield much revenue. By years the ordinary receipts of the government from 1791 to 1801 were as follows: —

Calendar year	Customs	Internal revenue [3]	Miscellaneous [2]	Total ordinary
1791[1]	$4,399,000		$10,000	$4,409,000
1792	3,443,000	$208,000	17,000	3,669,000
1793	4,255,000	338,000	59,000	4,652,000
1794	4,801,000	274,000	356,000	5,431,000
1795	5,588,000	338,000	188,000	6,114,000
1796	6,568,000	475,000	1,334,000	8,377,000
1797	7,550,000	575,000	561,000	8,688,000
1798	7,106,000	644,000	150,000	7,900,000
1799	6,610,000	779,000	157,000	7,546,000
1800	9,081,000	1,543,000 [3]	224,000	10,848,000
1801	10,751,000	1,582,000 [3]	602,000	12,935,000

[1] Practically two years.

[2] Including sales of public lands dividends on bank stock, and in 1796 and 1797 proceeds of sales of bank stock owned by government, and in 1801 sales of public stores, etc.

[3] Including direct tax in 1800 and 1801.

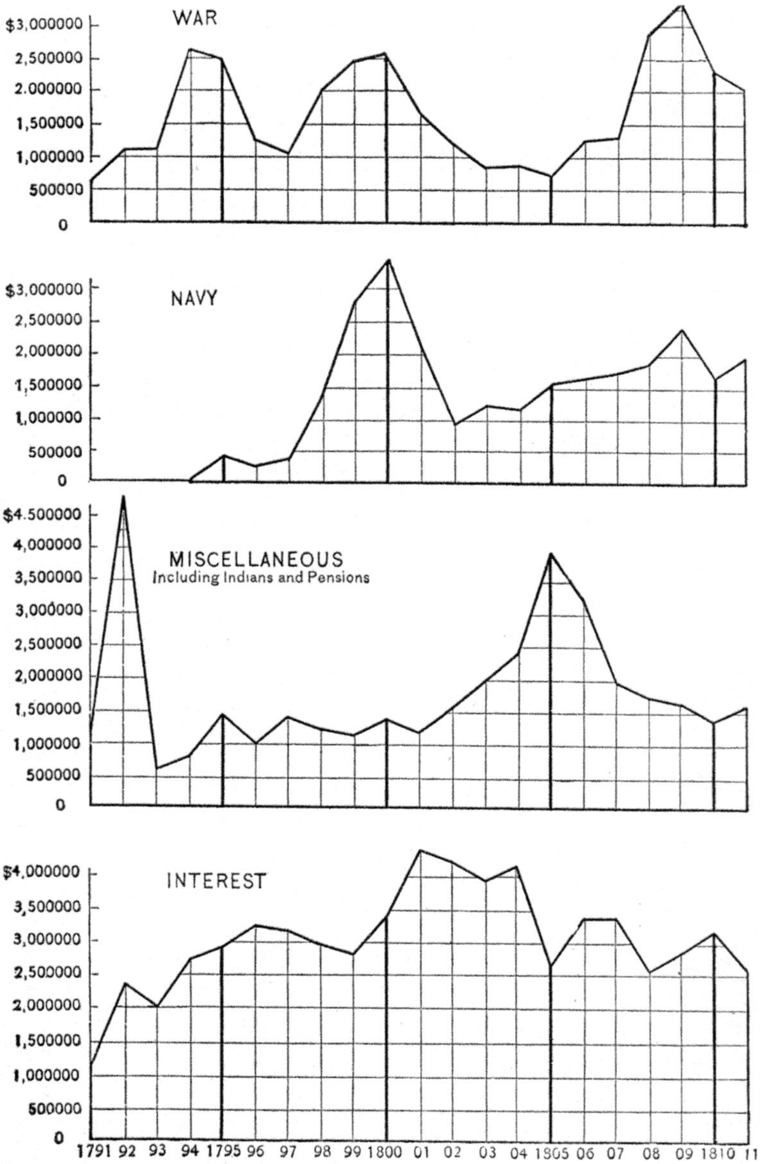

No. I.—ORDINARY EXPENDITURES, 1791–1811.

49. Expenditures, 1789–1801.

Expenditures exceeded anticipations during the period of the Federalist administration. Extraordinary demands continued to arise which absorbed the revenues, in spite of the enlarged resources from excise duties and advances in tariff rates. The Indian War which broke out in the Northwest in 1790 was succeeded by the Whiskey Insurrection in 1794, and by strained relations with England, which led to increased expenditures for the army, navy, and fortifications. Peace was made with Algiers in 1795 only by a heavy money payment. Then came the aggressions of France in 1797–1798, which called for a further expansion of the army and navy and the building of lighthouses and fortifications. As there was no decrease in the public indebtedness until 1802 the interest charge continued a heavy burden. The increase of these expenditures is illustrated in the following table: —

Calendar year	War	Navy	Interest on debt	Miscellaneous	Total
1791	$633,000		$1,178,000	$1,286,000	$3,097,000
1792	1,101,000		2,373,000	2,795,000	6,259,000
1793	1,130,000		2,097,000	618,000	3,846,000
1794	2,639,000	$61,000	2,752,000	844,000	6,297,000
1795	2,481,000	410,000	2,947,000	1,471,000	7,309,000
1796	1,260,000	274,000	3,239,000	1,016,000	5,790,000
1797	1,039,000	382,000	3,172,000	1,414,000	6,008,000
1798	2,009,000	1,381,000	2,955,000	1,260,000	7,607,000
1799	2,467,000	2,858,000	2,815,000	1,155,000	9,295,000
1800	2,561,000	3,448,000	3,402,000	1,401,000	10,813,000
1801	1,673,000	2,111,000	4,412,000	1,197,000	9,393,000

In the above table the column entitled "Miscellaneous" includes expenditures for Indians, pensions, foreign intercourse, and the civil list. According to the treasury classification only in one year, 1796, did expenditures for Indians amount to $100,000, and pensions rarely reached this sum. The "civil list" and "miscellaneous civil" varied from half a million to a million dollars. The exceptional outgo in 1792 is explained by the payment of $2,000,000 for subscription to the stock of the Bank of the United States and by certain adjustments in the settlement of debts apart from those given in the loan accounts.

The following table presents in a condensed form a comparison of the annual receipts, expenditures, and changes in debt in millions of dollars (amounts less than $100,000 indicated by*) :—

Taxes					Miscellaneous receipts	Total revenue	Expenditures	Surplus	Deficit
Year	Customs	Excise	Direct	Total					
1791	4.4			4.4	*	4.4	3.1	1.4	
1792	3.4	.2		3.7	*	3.7	8.2		4.5
1793	4.2	.3		4.6	*	4.6	3.8	.8	
1794	4.8	.3		5.1	.3	5.4	6.2		.8
1795	5.6	.3		5.9	.1	6.1	7.3		1.2
1796	6.5	.5		7.1	1.3	8.4	5.8	2.6	
1797	7.5	.6		8.1	.5	8.6	6.0	2.6	
1798	7.1	.6		7.8	.1	7.9	7.6	.3	
1799	6.6	.7		7.4	.1	7.5	9.2		1.7
1800	9.1	.8	.7	10.6	.2	10.8	10.8		
1801	10.7	1.0	.5	12.3	.6	12.9	9.3	3.6	

50. The Debt, 1789-1801.

Owing to the new, unanticipated financial burdens it was necessary for the government repeatedly to make small loans from the Bank of the United States in order to tide over immediate emergencies. In all this amounted to $10,376,000 during the years 1792–1798. A part of this embarrassing indebtedness was promptly discharged, but about one-third was not repaid until after 1801. Besides these temporary loans the government was obliged to secure authority for the issue of stock. In 1798 a loan was authorized to pay the builders of naval vessels, which finally amounted to $711,700; and in the same year a loan of $5,000,000 was authorized to make good deficiencies in the appropriations and for military purposes. In 1800 a loan for similar purposes was ordered, from which $1,481,700 was realized. The last two loans were limited in duration to fifteen years, and the treasury had to pay the exceptional rate of 8 per cent. because of public expectation of war and invasion.

By years the total amount of debt and its composition 1791–1801 was as follows in millions of dollars: —

	Old			New		
Year	Funded debt	Unfunded debt	Foreign, including conversions, under act of March 3, 1795	Time loans, 1798, 1800	Temporary	Total
1791	1.5	61.0	12.8			75.4
1792	9.7	52.9	14.5			77.2
1793	55.4	6.8	15.4		2.5	80.3
1794	55.7	5.9	14.3		2.4	78.4
1795	60.6	.9	14.7		4.5	80.7
1796	60.2	3.3	13.9	*	6.2	83.7
1797	59.7	3.1	14.0	*	5.1	82.0
1798	59.1	3.0	13.0	*	3.8	79.2
1799	58.4	2.9	12.9	*	3.8	78.4
1800	57.8	2.8	12.8	5.7	3.6	82.9
1801	57.0	2.8	12.4	7.2	3.4	83.0

* Less than $100,000.

51. Sinking Fund; Management of the Debt.

In the earlier years of financial reorganization the credit of the government was strengthened by the establishment of a sinking fund and the pledge of specific revenues for the payment of the debt and its interest. By the original funding act of August 4, 1790, the proceeds of the sales of public lands in the Western territory were pledged solely to the redemption of the debt. It was also enacted that certain surplus revenues then accruing might be used for the purchase of public stock in order to give the government an opportunity of free and prompt action in retiring indebtedness, as well as to influence the value of public stock through creating a demand. By the act of May 8, 1792, a regular sinking fund was established, to which were inviolably pledged the interest on so much of the debt as had been heretofore redeemed, and the surplus of all sums appropriated for the payment of interest on the debt.

A commission was authorized, consisting of the president of the senate, chief-justice, secretary of state, secretary of the treasury, and attorney-general, to make purchases for this fund and to render appropriate accounts. The fund, however, under this act did not grow rapidly, since the annual interest account of the sinking fund amounted to less than $40,000, and there was as yet no permanent appropriation out of the treasury. Another step in the arrangement for a sinking fund was taken by the act of March 3, 1795, which enlarged the powers of the commissioners and increased appropriations to the fund from the following sources: (1) such part of the duties, including import, tonnage, and excises on distilled spirits as, together with other income accruing to the fund, would be sufficient to make a beginning in 1796 of definite annual reimbursements of the 6 per cent. stock; (2) the surplus of the dividends on bank stock owned by the government in excess of the interest charge which the government paid to the bank on account of its loan; (3) this revenue to be supplemented from the regular revenue so as to begin annual payments on the bank loan and thus extinguish that debt by 1802. The fund was to be aided by the sales of public lands in Western territory; by payments made on account of debts due to the United States prior to the establishment of the government of 1789; and by surpluses unappropriated. The larger part of these supplies were of course contingent, and could not be relied upon for constant aid. The appropriations were, however, made permanent, to continue until the whole of the debt excepting the 3 per cent. stocks should be redeemed.

In the development of this sinking fund policy, Hamilton took the leading part; every step was practically inspired by him, and then and since controversy has arisen with regard to the accuracy of his reasoning. He is accused of introducing novel complications in the handling of the debt and provision for its payment, and also of adhering to the fallacy that a debt may be paid by the operation of compound interest applied to the portion of the debt redeemed. The latter charge has been carefully considered by Professor Dunbar, who concludes that neither Hamilton nor Pitt, by whom he was undoubtedly influenced, had any delusion as to the possibility of paying debt without money, or any notion that compound interest could be made to supply the place of an adequate revenue or even atone for its possible absence. Hamilton had good grounds for anticipating a surplus, and on this hope his advocacy of a sinking fund was really based.

52. The Administrations of Hamilton and Wolcott.

In spite, of the brilliancy of Hamilton's administration of the treasury department, he was subjected to savage criticism, inspired in part by the fact that he represented federalism in its most extreme form, and was consequently attacked on general principles by the supporters of State sovereignty, as a dangerous influence in the political development of the United States. A more specific criticism was due to the independent if not arbitrary methods followed in the management of the treasury. Hamilton never made it his business to send to Congress regular and systematic reports on the condition of the treasury, for he did not interpret that part of the act of 1789 which bore on the preparing and reporting of plans as imposing the initiative on him. Only two statements of the finances between 1789 and 1801 can be regarded as orderly and serviceable records of the progress and condition of the debt; and Gallatin in 1801 was the first secretary to render the finance report which is now annually submitted by the secretary of the treasury. Hamilton did not intend to deceive the people or to withhold information from Congress, but he was impatient of restraints and preferred to make reports in his own way and season. The complexity of accounts was also aggravated by the fact that in his time the appropriations were not made for specific objects but in lump. In 1789 the single appropriation bill in its thirteen lines contained but four items, — for civil expenses, for military expenses, for payment of the public debt, and for pensions. Until 1809 it was possible for the executive to transfer unexpended appropriations at will. Such loose methods provoked Gallatin to sharp criticism, which at first was regarded by Hamilton and his friends as a reflection upon the honesty of the treasury administration.

Notwithstanding these bitter attacks, Hamilton enjoyed the entire confidence of Washington and was defended by him; when accused in 1792 of extravagance and improper application of moneys expended, a congressional inquiry into the accounts of the treasury department found that no improper appropriation had been made, although there had been an application of some specific appropriations to objects other than those directed; but even these had been done with good judgment and in perfect integrity. Nevertheless, the opposition, led by Gallatin, persisted in finding fault with the debt statements, and, with some justice, protested that it was difficult to tell whether the debt was increasing or growing less. In 1795 Gallatin asserted that there had been an increase of $5,000,000 in the public debt; but a supporter of the administration claimed errors of more than $4,500,000 in the former's estimate; and so experienced an accountant as Gallatin's biographer, Stevens, declares that it is now impossible to determine the merits of the controversy.[1] A part of the misunderstanding was undoubtedly due to the book-keeping of the sinking fund, where there was so much complication, if not discrepancy, that an easy occasion was furnished to the critics of Hamilton. Repeated strictures on the insufficiency of the treasury statements finally led to the act of May 10, 1800, which provided: "That it shall be the duty of the secretary of the treasury to digest, prepare, and lay before Congress, at the commencement of every session, a report on the subject of finance, containing estimates of the public revenue and public expenditures, and plans for improving or increasing the revenues, from time to time, for the purpose of

[1] Stevens' *Gallatin*, p. 130.

giving information to Congress in adopting modes of raising the money requisite to meet the public expenditures."

After Hamilton's resignation in 1794, his understudy, Oliver Wolcott of Connecticut, was appointed secretary. He was justly regarded by the Republicans as the tool of his predecessor, and from 1795 was subjected to continued suspicion by those who were endeavoring to ruin Hamilton's past reputation. Wolcott resigned in 1800 and demanded an examination of his official conduct as secretary; the report of a committee of the House of Representatives was entirely to Wolcott's credit. During the few remaining months of Adams's administration, Samuel Dexter of Massachusetts served as secretary. As a whole the Federalist administration of the treasury is deserving of admiration: it put into operation a revenue system, varied in its scope, embracing customs duties, excise, and a direct tax; it formed a treasury administrative system on lines which have been substantially followed until the present day; it safely restored the credit of the government, and, if the debt had not been reduced as much as it had been hoped, the fault did not lie so much with the administration as with untoward and unexpected events. The finances were in a sound state, and the Federalists should receive some of the credit which is so fully granted to Gallatin's administration during the next ten years.

CHAPTER VI.

ECONOMIES AND WAR, 1801-1816.

53. References.

BIBLIOGRAPHIES: Bogart and Rawles, 23–28; Channing and Hart, 345.

ECONOMY, DEBT REDUCTION: *American State Papers, Finance*, I, 746 (report of committee of ways and means, April 9, 1802); or J. Elliot, *Funding System*, 460–469; *Statutes*, II, 167 (Act, April 29, 1802); or Dunbar, 49; Elliot, ditto, 553 (note on loans); Bayley, 339–341, 414; Bolles, II, 66–72, 203–216; J. W. Kearny, *Sketch of American Finances*, 56–68 (sinking fund); H. Adams, *Life of Gallatin*, 267–297, 348–355; E. A. Ross, *Sinking Funds*, in *Pub. Amer. Econ. Assn.*, VII, 63–68; H. C. Adams, *Public Debts*, 266–268; H. Adams, *History of U. S.*, I, 238–242, 251–255, 272; J. P. Gordy, *Political Parties in the U. S.*, I, 398–403, 414–417; J. A. Stevens, *Gallatin*, 185–212 (debt), 224–240 (revenue), 251–256 (accounts).

BANK: *American State Papers, Finance*, II, 351–418, 453, 463, 480, 516 (memorials, Gallatin's report, dividends, deposits); J. Elliot, *Funding System*, 513–517 (Gallatin's report); Clarke and Hall, *Documentary History of Bank*, 115–471; *Annals of Congress*, 1810–1811, p. 488, et seq.; or *Benton's Abridgment*, IV, 252, et seq.; Bolles, II, 145–152; A. Gallatin, *Works*, III, 328–334; H. Adams, *Life of Gallatin*, 426–430; H. Adams, *History of the U. S.*, III, 327–337, V, 207, 327, 337; H. White, 263–270; Schouler, II, 316–319; McMaster, III, 379–390.

WAR FINANCE: *American State Papers, Finance*, II, 374, 412, 441, 497, 523 (Gallatin reports); 538 (report of committee, Feb. 17, 1812); III, 1–19 (review by Dallas, Dec. 8, 1815); Gallatin, *Works*, I, 466; J. Elliot, *Funding System*, 534 (Gallatin's report on war loans, Jan. 10, 1812), also Gallatin, *Works*, I, 501–517, 642; Bolles, II, 219–224; H. C. Adams, *Public Debts*, 112–126; J. W. Kearny, *Sketch of American Finances*, 76–110; H. Adams, *Life of Gallatin*, 445–452; H. Adams, *History of U. S.*, VI, 156–175, 206–209, 438–448; VII, 44, 365–390; VIII, 239–262; J. A. Stevens, *Gallatin*, 212–224, 239–248; McMaster, IV, 208–218, 233–236.

LOANS AND TREASURY NOTES: *American State Papers, Finance*, II, 421, 564 (method of subscription), 569; *Statutes*, II, 694, 798; III, 144, 227; or Dunbar, 62–80; Bayley, 342–354; W. F. de Knight, 45–56; Bolles, 221–224; J. J. Knox, *United States Notes*, 21–39 (treasury notes).

INTERNAL REVENUE AND DIRECT TAXES: *American State Papers, Finance*, II, 627, 855; *Statutes*, III, 22, 39, 40, 42, 44, 77, 113, 137, 148, 159 (internal revenue); 53, 164, 255 (direct); F. C. Howe, *Taxation in the U. S. under Internal Revenue System*, 39–49; Bolles, II, 242–262; H. C. Adams, *Taxation in the U. S.* (J. H. U. Studies), II, 58–59; C. F. Dunbar, *Quar. Jour. Econ.*, III, 442–444; J. A. Stevens, *Gallatin*, 232–235, 243–245; H. Adams, *History of the U. S.*, IX, index under "taxes"; McMaster, III, 441–443.

54. Economies and Reduction of Taxation.

The year 1801 marks a great change in financial as in political ideals. The financial policy established by Jefferson's administration was prompted by two fundamental principles of Republican policy: first, the simplification of the civil service, not merely to reduce taxation but to decrease federal executive machinery and patronage; and, second, the abolition of excise duties, which in Republican party philosophy were still held to be inquisitorial and inconsistent with democratic freedom, particularly in time of peace. The application of these ideas might naturally, if there were no further disturbing factor, work out a harmonious result in the field of finance, since a reduction of expenditure would justify a reduction of taxation. For secretary of the treasury Gallatin was the logical choice; he was easily the leader among the Republicans in mastery of the principles of political economy, in skill in handling financial details, and in clearness of conviction and intensity of purpose. Like Hamilton of foreign birth, he had devoted himself to a public career; from 1790 to 1795 he was a member of the Pennsylvania legislature, and then entered Congress; in this body he served on the committee of ways and means. He had been unceasing in his demand for economy, for specific instead of general appropriations, for the extinction of the debt in preference to military and naval expenditures, and for a change in the form of the sinking fund.

The Republican party when in opposition had constantly attempted to retrench on the army and navy; in the troubled times of 1795 it desired to restore the army to the footing of 1792, and opposed naval appropriations, on the ground that a navy was prejudicial to commerce. When the power came no time was lost; the army was reduced to the peace establishment of 1796; the construction of several war vessels was stopped; and savings were made in the diplomatic and customs service. The net ordinary expenditures were thus brought down from nearly $7,500,000, exclusive of interest, for the fiscal year 1800, to less than $5,000,000 for the year 1801, and to an average of $4,000,000 during the next three years.

A reduction of taxation through the abolition of the excise duties was promptly undertaken, though Gallatin would have been glad to retain them longer. In March, 1802, John Randolph, the chairman of the committee of ways and means, upon assurance that economies of $600,000 could be made in the navy, recommended the repeal of these taxes, and declared that the whole system of internal duties was vexatious, oppressive, and obnoxious, hostile to the genius of a free people, and tended to multiply officers and increase the burdens of the people. The measure of repeal was quickly carried, April 6, 1802, and by this decisive stroke a net annual revenue of $600,000 was lost to the treasury, — of this about five-sixths was derived from the tax on distilled liquors. The Federalists urged that if there was to be a reduction of taxation it should not be on the luxury of distilled spirits, but in the import duties upon tea, coffee, sugar, and salt, the necessities of life; moreover, the excise revenue was a sure resource, while the fluctuations in foreign trade made the impost revenue uncertain; and it was inexpedient to destroy the administrative machinery organized for the collection of taxes, which had been brought into good working order through ten years of experience. On the other hand, statistics were presented to show the heavy cost of collecting internal revenue duties; 22,000 stills were scattered over the immense territory of the United States, and the licenses paid by 13,000 retailers produced but $65,000. There was but little possibility of materially lessening the expense of collection so long as the objects from which the revenue was drawn were so dispersed.

55. New Demands upon the Treasury.

It was not long before a special strain was placed upon the treasury by an agreement to pay $15,000,000 for the purchase of Louisiana. To meet this outlay Gallatin proposed the issue of $11,250,000 new 6 per cent. stock, redeemable after fifteen years in four annual instalments; $2,000,000 was to be paid cash down from the surplus in the treasury, and the remainder was to be met by a temporary loan. The purchase came at a fortunate time, since the customs in 1802 amounted to $12,400,000 as compared with $10,700,000 in 1801 and $9,100,000 in 1800. The country was taking advantage of the European war; its neutral commerce was expanding at an unprecedented rate; exports were large and prices high, customs revenue was pouring into the treasury, so that on January 1, 1803, there was a balance to the good of over $5,000,000. The success of the loan was more than had been anticipated. The abundant revenue on the one hand and the economies in expenditure on the other made it possible to effect the purchase from the sale of the new stock, and ready money, without recourse either to a temporary loan or to new taxes.

It soon become necessary to seek for further revenue because of war with Tripoli. Instead of restoring the excise duties the act of March 26, 1804, authorized an addition of 2½ per cent. on all imported articles which paid ad valorem duties, and an additional duty of 10 per cent. upon goods imported in foreign vessels. The proceeds of this act constituted a special fund known as the Mediterranean Fund, to be used for the protection of the commerce and the seamen of the United States against the Barbary Powers, and to be levied until a treaty had been made. In spite of Jefferson's avowed policy of peace in foreign relations, and Gallatin's persistent efforts to hold the navy department, as well as the war establishment, down to a policy of Republican economy and strict accountability, the administration was thus forced into extraordinary naval expenditures. Gallatin, however, did not propose that the demands of the navy should be lost in the general budget, but intended by making this a special fund based upon special taxes to keep before the public a clear apprehension of the burden it was carrying.

Another important interruption to Gallatin's plans of retrenchment and debt extinguishment took place in 1806, when Randolph proposed the repeal of the salt tax. The tax, though always unpopular, had been retained because of its productivity, since it then yielded more than a half million dollars per annum. Randolph had already shown his independence of the administration, and apparently was seeking opportunity to exhaust its patience; he complained that the government was inconsistent in not adhering to its loudly proclaimed policy of making expenditures according to specific appropriations, and he wished therefore to straiten and punish the treasury. The Federalists supported the repeal, possibly to embarrass the government, and many Republicans followed Randolph, not so much for the reason he assigned as because of the general unpopularity of the tax. The measure at first failed in the Senate, but in the course of the year the administration recognized the popularity of Randolph's proposition and submitted in advance a bill for the abolition of this duty, which was duly enacted March 3, 1807.

The next blow fell in 1807, when the misunderstandings with Europe on account of the establishment of the continental system, the issues of the English orders in council, the Berlin-Milan decrees, and the impressment of American seamen came to a head; and Jefferson reluctantly agreed to an increase of expenditures for national defence. While yielding to the growing demands upon the treasury, Jefferson further disturbed financial security by entering upon the alternate policies of non-importation of manufactured goods and of forbidding shipping to leave American ports. This commercial warfare soon upset the customs receipts. No financial disadvantages appeared in the returns for 1808; but in 1809 the customs fell from $16,300,000 to $7,200,000; expenditures for war increased from $1,300,000 in 1807 to $3,300,000 in 1809 and expenditures for the navy were larger by more than half a million dollars. The fortification of ports and harbors was hastened, gunboats were purchased, and the regular army enlarged.

In December, 1809, Gallatin was forced for the first time to confront a deficit in the budget, which was $1,300,000 short, exclusive of payments on account of the debt. Fortunately there was a handsome balance in the treasury from past savings, which could provide both for the deficit and current expenditures, as well as for debt requirements. Early in 1809 the Embargo Act was repealed, and commerce, although still burdened with a non-intercourse act, was resumed with great vigor. The customs in 1810 yielded $8,500,000 and in 1811 $13,300,000. Appropriations for the army and navy were again reduced, and thus the immediate financial danger was tided over. Still the causes of irritation toward England were at work; during the year 1811 the country drifted rapidly toward hostilities, and in June, 1812, war was formally declared.

56. Receipts and Expenditures, 1801-1811.

The ordinary receipts during the peace administration of the Republicans are concisely condensed as follows: —

Year	Customs	Other revenue	Total
1801	$10,750,000	$2,185,000	$12,935,000
1802	12,438,000	2,557,000	14,995,000
1803	10,479,000	585,000	11,064,000
1804	11,099,000	727,000	11,826,000
1805	12,936,000	624,000	13,560,000
1806	14,667,000	892,000	15,559,000
1807	15,846,000	552,000	16,398,000
1808	16,363,000	697,000	17,060,000
1809	7,258,000	515,000	7,773,000
1810	8,583,000	800,000	9,384,000
1811	13,313,000	1,109,000	14,422,000

The receipts under "Other" in the above table, in 1801 and 1802, were swollen by the income from internal revenue duties, the delayed direct tax, and the sale of bank stock. After 1803 the revenue from the sale of public lands began to be fruitful and is responsible for nearly all of the subsequent receipts in this column of the table.

Expenditures by years during the same period were as follows: —

Year	War	Navy	Interest on debt	Miscellaneous [1]	Total
1801	$1,673,000	$2,111,000	$4,412,000	$1,197,000	$9,393,000
1802	1,179,000	915,000	4,239,000	1,642,000	7,976,000
1803	822,000	1,215,000	3,949,000	1,965,000	7,952,000
1804	875,000	1,189,000	4,185,000	2,387,000	8,637,000
1805	713,000	1,597,000	2,657,000	4,846,000	9,014,000
1806	1,224,000	1,649,000	3,368,000	3,206,000	9,449,000
1807	1,288,000	1,722,000	3,369,000	1,973,000	8,354,000
1808	2,900,000	1,884,000	2,557,000	1,719,000	9,061,000
1809	3,345,000	2,427,000	2,886,000	1,641,000	10,280,000
1810	2,294,000	1,654,000	3,163,000	1,362,000	8,474,000
1811	2,032,000	1,965,000	2,585,000	1,594,000	8,178,000

[1] Including Indians and pensions.

The reasons for the fluctuations in the expenditures for war and navy have already been alluded to; the interest charge was lowered by the decrease in the principal of the public debt, interrupted by the Louisiana purchase; and the appropriations of large amounts for "foreign intercourse" in 1804–1806 account for the exceptional increase under "Miscellaneous" in those years.

57. Reduction of Debt; Sinking Fund.

During the peace administration of the Republicans there was a remarkable reduction in the debt; between 1801 and 1812 the debt was cut down by $38,000,000, and this in spite of the abandonment of the internal taxes and the salt duty, and the assumption of a large sum for the payment of Louisiana. The details of the operation are illustrated in the following table in millions of dollars: —

Year	Old Debt						Louisiana		Total
	Funded	Unfunded	Foreign, including conversions under act of 1795	Exchanged and converted	Previous time loans	Temporary	Debt	Assumed claims	
1801	57.0	2.8	12.4		7.2	3.4			83.0
1802	55.9	2.8	11.9		7.2	2.7			80.7
1803	54.7	2.7	10.7		7.2	1.4			77.0
1804	53.5	1.8	7.7		7.2	.9	11.2	3.7	86.4
1805	52.2	.9	6.0		7.2	.7	11.2	3.7	82.3
1806	50.8	*	4.2		7.2		11.2	2.0	75.7
1807	49.3	*	1.5		6.4		11.2	.5	69.2
1808	44.8	*	.4	2.7	5.6		11.2	.2	65.1
1809	37.4	*	.2	7.8	*		11.2	*	57.0
1810	36.1	*		5.6	*		11.2	*	53.1
1811	34.7	*		1.8	*		11.2	*	48.0
1812	33.2	*		.5	*		11.2	*	45.2

* Less than $100,000.

The foreign debt, including the stocks of 1795 which were issued as a substitute in place of a portion of this, and the costly loans of 1798 and 1800, were wiped out, and no further recourse was made to temporary loans.

Gallatin had little respect for a sinking fund. At best he thought it rendered the accounts complex and embarrassed the policy of debt extinction; in his opinion a better way was to apply the surplus of receipts over expenditures directly to the discharge of debts. In spite of this conviction, he did not feel prepared to abolish the sinking fund, which had been in operation for more than a decade and was supported by popular opinion because believed to be a substantial check on the treasury department. The purpose of his practical recommendations was to increase the permanent annual appropriations for the use of the fund to $7,300,000, and after the Louisiana purchase to $8,000,000. The significance of this legislation lay in Gallatin's perception that it was probable that there would be a surplus revenue over and above what was necessary to meet the demands of the sinking fund act of 1795, and this he desired to use for debt reduction beyond all possible claims which might be advanced from other quarters. He wished especially to leave no unused funds for the army and navy, with which he had little sympathy. Owing to the abundant revenue of the period, the payment of the debt went on with a rush, for which the good luck of the country is entitled to credit as much as any special wisdom of Jefferson and his advisers.

The financial experience of this period of peace is summed up in the following table in millions of dollars: —

Year	Taxes				Miscellaneous receipts	Total revenue	Expenditures	Surplus	Deficit
	Customs	Internal revenue	Direct tax	Total					
1801	10.7	1.0	.5	12.3	.6	12.9	9.3	3.6	
1802	12.4	.6	.2	13.2	1.7	14.9	7.9	7.0	
1803	10.4	.2		10.7	.3	11.0	7.9	3.1	
1804	11.0			11.2	.6	11.8	8.6	3.2	
1805	12.9			12.9	.6	13.5	9.0	4.5	
1806	14.6			14.6	.8	15.5	9.4	6.1	
1807	15.8			15.8	.5	16.3	8.3	8.0	
1808	16.3			16.3	.6	17.0	9.0	8.0	
1809	7.2			7.2	.5	7.7	10.2		2.5
1810	8.5			8.5	.8	9.3	8.4	.9	
1811	13.3			13.3	1.1	14.4	8.1	6.3	

58. End of the United States Bank.

The year 1811 marks not only the end of the peace administration but also the winding up of the United States Bank. In 1808 the directors of this institution memorialized Congress for a renewal of the charter, and the subject was referred to Gallatin, who made an elaborate report, March 2, 1809, in favor of the bank. He suggested some changes by which it might be more useful to the government, such as requiring the payment of interest on government deposits when in excess of $3,000,000, and the adoption of a regulation that the bank should loan to the government at any time a sum not to exceed 60 per cent. of its capital. Gallatin enumerated the advantages derived by the government from the bank, in its safe-keeping of the public deposits, in the collection of the revenues, in the transmission of public moneys, in the facilities granted to importers, and in loans that had been made to the government, in all amounting to $6,200,000. In Congress there was strong opposition to renewal of the charter; the numerous State banks established since 1790 had a diligent eye to their own interest. In 1790 there were but three such banks; in 1800 there were 28 with a capital of $21,300,000, and, in 1811, 88 with a capital of $42,600,000.

The United States Bank was also unpopular because of the large foreign holdings in the bank's stock, amounting to 18,000 shares out of a total of 25,000; this use of foreign capital was construed to be a large foreign tribute in dividends; and, though foreign stockholders could not vote, indirectly they could exert a "malignant influence." The extravagant character of this opposition was summed up by Senator Crawford in the following language: "The member who dares to give his opinion in favor of the renewal of the charter is instantly charged with being bribed by the agents of the bank, with being corrupt, with having trampled upon the rights and liberties of the people, with having sold the sovereignty of the United States to foreign capitalists, with being guilty of perjury by having violated the Constitution." The constitutionality of the bank was once more questioned, and the mere fact that Gallatin and his followers could find any merit at all in what was originally regarded as a federal invention only strengthened the purpose of some of the Republicans who held grudges against the administration.

In all the writings and speeches called forth by the contest there was little economic analysis or criticism; the bank was regarded as an undemocratic, political institution; or as an institution helpful in centralizing the forces of a weak government. The bill for renewal was finally lost in the Senate, February 20, 1811, by the deciding vote of the vice-president, George Clinton. It then became necessary for the government to turn to local banks for the custody of its funds. In 1812 twenty-one local institutions were employed, chiefly in the principal ports of entry, so that the collectors might have agents at command with whom the duty bonds of importers were placed for collection.

59. Inadequate Preparation for War.

When war was declared in June, 1812, although there had been several years of warning during which preparation might well have been undertaken, Congress was not ready with a financial policy adequate to meet the extraordinary demands. Little had been accomplished either in placing the army and navy upon a possible war footing or in devising fiscal resources against the gathering crisis. Gallatin had given some attention to the problem, realizing from the beginning of the strained relations that war with England was possible; but unfortunately in the various statements of his views during the period between 1807 and 1812 he wavered. Undoubtedly he felt the pressure of the unflagging antagonism of party opponents, who wished to discredit him with Jefferson, and he was encouraged by temporary revivals of better conditions in the treasury.

In 1807, when hostilities first appeared imminent, Gallatin outlined the financial principles which ought to be applied in case of war; he proposed that war expenditures should be met with loans, and that taxes should be increased only to provide for the annual expenses on a peace establishment, the interest on the existing debt, and the interest on any new loans. Gallatin arrived at this opinion on the theory that maritime war in the United States would deeply affect the resources of individuals, commercial profits would be curtailed, and the surplus of agricultural produce would fail to reach its accustomed foreign market; such losses and privations he was not willing to aggravate by taxes beyond what was strictly necessary. For the increased taxation which would be required Gallatin suggested a revival of the duty on salt, the continuance of the Mediterranean duties, and possibly a doubling of existing import duties. The excise duties, "however ineligible, will doubtless be cheerfully paid as war taxes if necessary."

In 1808 Gallatin took away much of the pith of his recommendations by declaring that in no event would he insist on internal taxes. He was rejoiced at the auspicious conditions for borrowing money; the high price of public stocks, the reduction of the public debt, the unimpaired credit of the general government, and the large amount of existing bank-stock in the United States left no doubt in his mind that necessary loans could be had on reasonable terms. In 1809 there was another change; not only was the war cloud still threatening, but there was an actual deficiency in the budget, hence Gallatin once more revived the possibility of internal duties in case the revenue were affected by war. For the present, however, he recommended only the continuation of the Mediterranean duties, unless a permanent increase in the military and naval establishments were contemplated.

A few months later, February 26, 1810, in response to a communication from the committee on ways and means, Gallatin again elaborated his views, placing the emphasis upon credit rather than on taxation, and thus developing the doctrine of war financiering which is associated with his name. As to the details of borrowing, he held that loans might be obtained from the holders of the old 6 per cent. stock, which was then falling due; from the banks that might in this way find a use for funds idle because commerce was blocked; and from individuals who would accept public lands as collateral security; lastly, he suggested the issue of treasury notes bearing interest and payable in one year. Loans, however, were to be relied upon for war, and war only, as it was inconsistent to borrow money to pay ordinary running expenses. "To meet these loans in the future we must depend on coming prosperity and the wisdom of successors; that is, favorable circumstances and rigid economy."

Congress easily accepted a waiting policy, and in March,

1811, authorized a loan of $5,000,000. It was not until December 9, 1811, that Gallatin clearly demanded internal revenue taxes. For this change of opinion he held Congress responsible: since he could no longer borrow from the United States Bank, the government was denied an important instrument of credit. A proposition for excise duties coming from a Republican secretary was an invitation for a party squabble; the committee on ways and means, in accordance with Gallatin's suggestion, reported a schedule of duties. A warm discussion took place, but it was hard to persuade Congress of the necessity; although a deficit was disclosed in the budget and it was generally agreed that war would take place, the proposition was defeated. It was late in the day to educate Congress to a strong policy of taxation, and that body showed its disregard for Gallatin's advice by authorizing, March 14, 1812, another loan amounting to $11,000,000.

In spite, then, of needs which were early apparent, Congress determinedly and definitely turned away from a policy of adequate taxation. War was declared in June, 1812; for immediate wants an issue of treasury notes to the amount of $5,000,000 was authorized June 30, and customs duties were doubled the following day. This latter act, however, gave but little financial comfort, since a large part of the country's commerce was with that nation which now became a public enemy; for a few months only vessels returning home paid the increased duties on their cargoes, and thereafter while the war lasted this source of revenue shrank to less than one-half of the returns in the previous decade.

With the recommendation made in December, 1811, Gallatin appears to have left the responsibility of laying excise duties once for all with Congress, for in his annual report at the end of 1812 after war was declared he refrained from renewing the recommendation. If therefore the government was poorly equipped with instruments of revenue, the responsibility lies only in part with Gallatin; he had wavered in his advocacy of internal duties, and yet in a final judgment of his abilities at this crisis due weight should be given to the cliques within the party which worked for his downfall and undoubtedly led him at this time to rely too much upon hope and credit, instead of vigorously and continuously insisting upon the needs of the present.

60. Treasury Administration, War Period.

A partial explanation of the failures in the administration of financial affairs during the war of 1812–1814 will be found in the political intrigues within the Republican party, and particularly in the factious elements found in Pennsylvania, Gallatin's own State. Gallatin clearly recognized the strength of this opposition, and, wearied with the contest, tendered his resignation early in 1811; he could not, however, be spared, and at the urgent request of Madison retained his post. His enemies, nevertheless, did not cease to break down his influence, so that finally in May, 1813, in the very midst of financial distress, Gallatin felt it wiser, if not to resign outright, at least to absent himself temporarily from political affairs at home. He consequently undertook a diplomatic mission and left the management of the treasury to William Jones, secretary of the navy.

This was an unfortunate arrangement, for the office needed a strong man, devoted solely to financial affairs; it was no time to drift. In February, 1814, Gallatin entered upon another diplomatic service and definitely resigned from the treasury. Madison then turned to Alexander J. Dallas of Pennsylvania, a lawyer, independent in party criticism, a conservative, and friend of Gallatin. For these reasons he was distasteful to the radical element in Pennsylvania, and was successfully opposed by the senators of that State. The appointment, after being declined by Richard Rush, comptroller in the treasury department, was offered to George W. Campbell of Tennessee. Although he represented the administration in the Senate, he brought no support and could not command the confidence of capitalists; he proved a failure and held office but a few months. Dallas was again nominated, and the opposition in the Senate being overcome by the stress of public affairs he was confirmed October 6, 1814. Dallas was an able man, but the evil had been done before his opportunity came; his chief work lay in restoring the currency through the re-establishment of a United States Bank.

61. War Loans.

As the war was sustained on public credit rather than by taxation, it is appropriate that the system of government loans should receive first consideration. The successive phases of the loan policy and their relation to other financial measures may be seen in the following chronological summary: —

1812, March 14	Six per cent loan, $11,000,000.
1812, June 12	War declared.
1812, June 30	Treasury notes, $5,000,000.
1812, July 1	Customs duties doubled.
1813, February 8	Loan, $16,000,000.
1813, February 25	Treasury notes, $5,000,000.
1813, July 22 and August 2	Internal revenue duties and direct tax.
1813, August 2	Loan, $7,500,000.
1814, March 4	Treasury notes, $10,000,000
1814, March 24	Loan, $25,000,000
1814, August	Suspension of specie payments.
1814, November 15	Loan, $3,000,000.
1814, December 15	Internal revenue duties increased
1814, December 24	Treaty of peace.
1814, December 26	Treasury notes, $10,500,000.
1815, January 18	New internal taxes.
1815, February 24	Treasury notes, $25,000,000.
1815, February 24	Seven per cent. loan.

As already indicated Congress, in March, 1812, three months before war was declared, authorized a loan of $11,000,000 to meet a probable deficit and the new expenditures for an enlargement of the army, the purchase of ordnance and equipment, the erection of fortifications, and the construction of ships. The loan bore 6 per cent. interest, and in accordance with the usual American policy none of it could be sold under par. In the preliminary debate some members severely questioned the wisdom of throwing upon the market so large an amount of stock, accompanied by no adequate provision for paying even the interest; and doubted whether sufficient moneyed capital available for loans really existed in the country at large. A considerable part of the banking capital rested upon credit instead of assets, and was of such a character that its holders were compelled to manage it with the utmost caution, and it was pointed out that in case of war much of the country's capital would be turned to manufactures, which would offer more tempting profits.

The government on the whole was successful in placing this first loan, but as further demands followed the real situation was revealed. Public credit began to fail; and in making the $16,000,000 loan of February 8, 1813, it became necessary to accept bids below par. It was with difficulty that the negotiations were carried out at all, and then only after a second opening of the subscription books and the acceptance of modifications dictated by subscribers. It was soon discovered that little financial support could be expected from the Eastern States, — largely because of the bitterness of the commercial interests, whose prosperity had long been endangered by Jefferson's policy of embargo, non-intercourse, and finally the declaration of war. The subscriptions, for example, to this loan were geographically as follows: —

States east of New York	$486,700
State of New York	5,720,000
Philadelphia	6,858,400
Baltimore and District of Columbia	2,393,900
State of Virginia	187,000
Charleston, S.C.	354,000
	$16,000,000

New England carried her opposition to the extreme point; of the $41,010,000 borrowed by the government exclusive of treasury notes and temporary loans up to the end of 1814, she contributed less than $3,000,000. The government also suffered in not being able to engage the co-operation of any strong banking institution, and the loss of the United States Bank was now distinctly felt.

The distress of the treasury was also manifest in the delayed grant to the executive of power to make special terms for loans. Up to this time government securities had not been sold at less than par, although in one instance it had been necessary to offer 8 per cent. interest to secure subscriptions. On August 2, 1813, however, a loan of $7,500,000 was authorized on condition that the stock be sold for not less than 88 per cent., and as affairs were temporarily in a somewhat more favorable condition, this loan was secured at an average rate of 88¼ per cent. The loans of the next year were negotiated under more disadvantageous terms, for in borrowing the first instalment of the $25,000,000 loan, under the act of March 24, 1814, the government abandoned its restrictions and was forced to agree that if more favorable terms were extended to any later subscribers equally advantageous terms be extended to previous purchasers. In this way it was made the interest of every holder of the first part of the loan to depress the price of government securities in order to secure further premiums from the treasury. Subscriptions were received at 12 per cent. discount; later at 20 per cent.; and still later, when subscriptions for a portion were accepted in State bank-notes worth but 65 per cent. in specie, the previous subscribers hastened to demand supplementary stock to the amount of the difference between the old and the new discount. At the close of the war, when public credit rose, the last war loan, authorized March 3, 1815, was more successfully negotiated at an average discount of little less than 5 per cent. The total loss to the government in disposing of its loans during the war period, 1812–1816, was enormous: in 1830 the committee of ways and means of the House estimated that for loans of over $80,000,000 the treasury received but $34,000,000 as measured in specie.

62. Issue of Treasury Notes.

Treasury notes were issued immediately after the declaration of war in the summer of 1812. Following a suggestion of Gallatin a bill was reported providing for a block which, together with the amount subscribed for the loan, should not exceed $11,000,000, to bear interest at 5⅖ per cent., equal to one and a half cents per day on one hundred dollars, to be retired in one year and to be receivable in all payments due the United States. The proposition did not go unprotested; the usual prophecy of depreciation and impaired credit was made. In favor it was urged that the proposed interest-bearing notes had many advantages over bank paper: they rested on the credit of the United States and were receivable for taxes and public dues; there was no resemblance between them and continental money, since when the latter was issued the national government had no compelling powers over the States for revenue; now its credit was sound and its power to raise revenue unquestioned. Though not secured by any specific fund set apart for their redemption, the entire duties and taxes of the year were indirectly pledged for this purpose, since the notes were receivable in payment of such duties and taxes. The measure passed the House by 85 to 41, and became law June 30, 1812.

If the issue of these notes had been stopped at this point they might well have been considered a kind of exchequer bills, or a temporary loan to anticipate future revenue, since the bills were payable in one year after issue, were interest-bearing, and receivable for public dues. Even the conservative Gallatin declared that this annual anticipation of revenue, though liable to abuse, facilitated both the collection of revenue and the making of loans if kept within strict bounds. On February 25, 1813, another issue of $5,000,000 was voted; not, however, without a further debate in which the possibility of ill was duly set forth. By another year not so much self-restraint was displayed, and in March, 1814,

$10,000,000 was authorized; and later in December, when the needs of the government became exceedingly pressing and loans were obtained only with a heavy discount, further legislation was enacted under which $8,318,000 was issued. New arguments were now discovered in favor of treasury notes: they were held more desirable than stock sold at a ruinous discount. Since many banks had suspended specie payments, and the country was in monetary disorder, United States treasury notes, receivable everywhere for dues and customs and guaranteed by the United States, might well be useful in providing a more stable currency. Even Dallas, the new secretary of the treasury, presented a report which approached an endorsement of the issue of legal-tender notes. Influenced by these considerations Congress passed an act, February 24, 1815, even when it was thought a treaty of peace had been signed, authorizing the issue of $25,000,000 treasury notes, — without, however, any legal-tender quality.

By this time opposition to the issue of such notes had been practically silenced; the barriers had been broken down, and if the war had continued it is likely that many of the abuses which had attended the issue during the Revolutionary War would have been repeated. The notes of the earlier issues were not intended to be currency, but in the last act no definite provision was made for redemption, and all notes issued of a denomination less than $100 bore no interest. The total amounts issued under the several acts were as follows: —

Act of June 30, 1812	$5,000,000
" " February 25, 1813	5,000,000
" " March 4, 1814	10,000,000
" " December 26, 1814	8,318,400
" " February 24, 1815, large notes	4,969,400
" " " " " small notes	3,392,994
	$36,680,794

Not all of these notes, however, were in circulation at one time, for the later issues in part were used to replace the earlier ones which were promptly redeemed. The amounts outstanding on January 1 each year were as follows: —

1813	$2,835,500
1814	4,907,300
1815	10,646,480
1816	17,619,625
1817	3,450,000

Since these were the first issues of anything like paper money by the United States under the Constitution the characteristics of the treasury notes deserve special notice: (1) Notes issued under the first two acts were in denominations of not less than $100; under the next two in denominations of not less than $20; and under the last from $3 upwards. (2) Notes issued under the first three acts were not originally fundable into stock, but were subsequently made so by the acts of December 26, 1814, and February 24, 1815. The notes of 1815 were made fundable by the act of issue. (3) Notes issued under the first four statutes were made payable in one year; under the last at no fixed date. (4) All save the small treasury notes, which were non-interest-bearing, bore interest at a rate of 5⅖ per cent. (5) None of the notes bore a formal promise to pay coin on demand, but all were in form of a receipt for all dues payable to the government. (6) None had any legal-tender qualities, though it is likely that such notes could have been issued had the war lasted a little longer. (7) The notes, with the exception of the later issues, were too large to get into general circulation. (8) The notes remained at par in specie until the banks generally suspended specie payments in August, 1814. (9) At the close of the war the notes remaining outstanding were rapidly funded into interest-bearing stock.

A comparison of the amounts borrowed by years 1812–1816, distinguishing between the long-term loans and treasury notes, with the net increase in debt each year according to Bayley's tables, is shown in the following table in millions of dollars: —

Year	Loans			Treasury Notes			Total		
	Issues	Redemptions	Increase	Issues	Redemptions	Increase	Issues	Redemptions	Increase
1812	12.7	5.6	7.1	2.8		2.8	15.5	5.6	9.9
1813	22.9	4.0	18.9	6.1		6.1	29.0	4.0	25.0
1814	18.3	1.7	16.6	8.3	5.8	2.4	26.6	7.5	19.1
1815	22.7	3.4	19.3	15.2	2.7	12.5	37.9	6.1	31.8
1816	7.8	3.0	4.8	4.2	9.7	5.5[1]	12.0	12.7	.7[1]

[1] Decrease.

63. Internal Revenue Taxes; Other Taxes.

One reason why Congress did not in 1812 enter upon internal taxation promptly and vigorously was the difficulty of framing the details of a new schedule of duties. Notwithstanding the urgency, a large part of the long discussion in the spring of 1812 over a bill to levy taxes on spirits was devoted to the inconsequential question whether the tax on distilled spirits should be levied upon the stills or should be a gallon tax. Although war was upon the country the settlement of this detail was regarded by some members as involving a momentous principle; in favor of a tax on stills it was urged that fewer offices would serve, oaths might be dispensed with, houses and cellars of distilleries would not be searched, and the firesides of the people would not be invaded by excise officers. On the other hand the proposed tax on stills would yield only $275,000, a sum altogether insignificant in view of immediate needs; it would equal hardly a cent a gallon as compared with 7.18 cents per gallon levied during the administration of Washington. The question of a whiskey excise was also complicated by the proposition to impose a tax upon land, and some Western merchants thought each of these would bear more hardly upon the people of that region, who were the least able to contribute. The evils of an excise system were depicted in vivid colors; nevertheless the West expressed its willingness to incur the responsibility of a tax on stills rather than to defeat the great work in which the nation was engaged. The House of Representatives could not bring itself to the passage of any measure at that time, and in June, 1812, postponed the whole subject by a vote of 72 to 46.

During the winter of 1812–1813 the question of internal revenue taxation was again raised, but time for consideration was then limited. The taunt by Mr. Cheves expressed the truth: "It was said last session that you would have time to lay internal revenue duties at this session, but I then said it was a mistake. You now find this to be the fact. By your indecision when the country was convinced they were necessary you have set the minds of the people against taxes. But, were it otherwise, you have not time now to lay them for the next year." In the summer of 1813 the president called Congress together for a special session, and the administration insisted upon the need of further taxation. A direct tax of $3,000,000 was immediately enacted to be assessed for the first time in 1814, and Congress laid duties on carriages, a duty on refined sugar, a license tax upon distillers of spirituous liquors, stamp duties, an auction tax, and a license tax upon retailers of wines and spirituous liquors. The duties imposed, however, were not high; outside of the direct taxes a revenue of only $2,000,000 was expected, and no advantage could be derived from the direct tax until the second year.

Congress was again assembled in special session in September, 1814, to replenish an exhausted treasury and to restore public credit. Existing internal duties were increased and duties rendered permanent as follows: (1) the direct tax was doubled to $6,000,000, to be assessed annually; (2) the duty on carriages was raised; (3) the tax on distillers of spirituous liquors was continued and a tax on distilled spirits was added; (4) duties on sales at auction and on licenses to retailers of wines and spirituous liquors and foreign merchandise were raised; (5) rates of postage were raised 50 per cent.; (6) in addition new duties were imposed on certain manufactured articles made in the United States and on certain articles in use, as household furniture and watches.

Although effective supplies were thus tardily granted and did not become available until the closing years of the war, they proved of welcome assistance in the restoration of the disordered finances. There was great delay in the collection of these duties, and for years after the repeal of the taxes returns into the treasury from this source find an entry in the budget. The amounts accruing and the duties actually received from the internal duties (as estimated in a report of the committee on ways and means, December 9, 1817) were as follows: —

Year	Accrued	Collected
1814	$3,262,197	$1,910,995
1815	6,242,504	4,976,530
1816	4,633,799	5,281,111
1817	3,002,000	3,000,000
Total	$17,140,500	$15,168,636

The annual cost of collection was high, varying from 7.8 to 4.8 per cent. The most productive of the excise duties were those on distilled spirits, the licenses for stills and retailers, and on auction sales. The system was not long enough in force to become effective in its administration or to afford the treasury officers definite data for reliable estimates. This latter difficulty was increased by the fact that there was too little general information at that time in regard to public resources or industrial conditions.

The three direct taxes imposed, with collections, were as follows: —

Year	Imposed	Collected
1814	$3,000,000	$2,219,497
1815	6,000,000	2,162,673
1816	3,000,000	4,253,635
1817		1,834,187

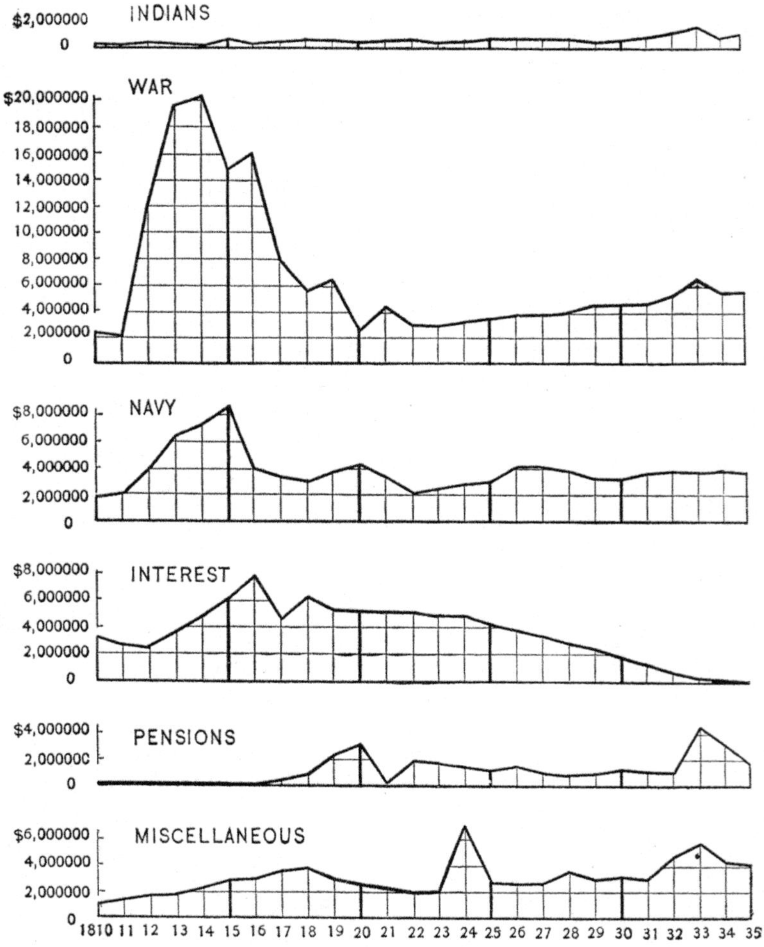

No. II. — ORDINARY EXPENDITURES, 1810–1835.

(Continuation of Chart No. 1, different scale.)

These taxes were apportioned among the States on the census of 1810, and the first act went so far as to apportion to each county in the several States the amount it should pay, thereby creating great inequalities. To avoid this evil the second act did not attempt to apportion the quotas among the counties, but left it to the States to equalize the burdens in the several collection districts. In view of the infrequent attempts throughout our history to levy a direct tax, it is suggestive to note that the several assessments made upon the States were met with a fair degree of exactitude and promptness. If there was an unequal incidence, there was little grumbling, thus showing a distinct advance from the disastrous policy of requisitions under the Confederacy.

As soon as the war was over prompt efforts were made to repeal the internal revenue duties. Dallas, who did not approve such a sweeping measure, declared that there was a sufficient scope for the operation of a permanent system of internal duties, and recommended at least the retention of the licenses on distilleries and retailers, the duty on refined sugar and the stamp duties. For the time being Congress followed this advice, but when President Monroe, in his first annual message in December, 1817, in deference to popular pressure recommended their repeal, a measure to that effect was quickly passed.

64. Expenditures and Receipts, 1812-1815.

Although the war was over early in 1815, the military and naval expenditures continued heavy throughout 1816; by years the expenditures, 1812–1815, were as follows: —

Year	War	Navy	Interest on debt	Miscellaneous[1]	Total
1812	$11,817,000	$3,959,000	$2,451,000	$2,052,000	**$20,280,000**
1813	19,652,000	6,446,000	3,599,000	1,983,000	**31,681,000**
1814	20,350,000	7,311,000	4,593,000	2,465,000	**34,720,000**
1815	14,794,000	8,660,000	5,990,000	3,499,000	**32,943,000**

[1] Including Indians and pensions.

The outgo during these four years was nearly as much as in the preceding twenty; the net results of this financial experience is seen in the following table in millions of dollars: —

Year	Taxes				Miscellaneous receipts	Total revenue	Expenditures	Deficits
	Customs	Internal revenue	Direct tax	Total				
1812	8.9			8.9	0.8	9.8	20.2	10.4
1813	13.2			13.2	1.1	14.3	31.6	17.3
1814	6.0	1.6	2.2	9.8	1.3	11.1	34.7	23.6
1815	7.3	4.7	2.1	14.1	1.5	15.6	32.9	17.3

A comparison of the deficits and increase of debt during this period shows an excess of over $13,000,000 of money borrowed above what was actually needed; as a result the treasury began the year 1816 with the largest balance to its credit since the organization of the government.

CHAPTER VII.

PROBLEMS OF REORGANIZATION AFTER WAR.

65. References.

BIBLIOGRAPHIES: Bogart and Rawles, 29–31; Channing and Hart, 356–359.

BANK AND CURRENCY REFORM: (i) SOURCES, *American State Papers, Finance*, II, 872 (Dallas, report on banking, Nov. 27, 1814); 891 (Madison's veto); III, 57–61 (plan of Dallas, Dec. 24, 1815); 306–391 (report on Bank, Jan. 16, 1819); Clarke and Hall, *Documentary History of the Bank*, 472–713, 781–795 (Marshall's opinion in *McCulloch* v. *Maryland*); *Messages of the Presidents* (Richardson ed.), I, 555 (Madison's veto); *Statutes*, III, 266; or Dunbar, 80; or W. MacDonald, *Select Documents*, 207; *Finance Reports*, II, 481–513 (Crawford's report on currency, Feb. 12, 1820; valuable); or *American State Papers, Finance*, III, 494; A. Gallatin, *Writings*, III, 282–287; H. Clay, *Speeches*, I, 74–80 (ed. 1857); J. C. Calhoun, *Works*, II, 153–162 (ed. 1853); D. Webster, *Works*, III, 35–59 (ed. 1851); J. B. Thayer, *Cases on Constitutional Law*, 271–285, 1340–1346. (ii) SPECIAL: Bolles, II, 278–283, 317–326, 359–374; L. C. Root in *Sound Currency*, IV, No. 17 (Sept., 1897); C. A. Conant, *History of Modern Banking*, 294–301; H. White, 271–281; W. Gouge, *History of Paper Money*, II, 55–121; W. G. Sumner, *History of Banking*, I, 63–190; R. C. H. Catterall, *The Second Bank of the United States*, 1–92 (foot-notes); W. G. Sumner, *American Currency*, 79–84 (disorders in 1819). (iii) GENERAL: W. G. Sumner, *Life of Jackson*, 231–235; J. A. Stevens, *Gallatin*, 270–275; H. Adams, *History of U. S.*, VIII, 249–251, 257–261; IX, 56, 82, 106–111, 116–118; McMaster, IV, 281–308 (local banks), 309–318 (organization of Bank), 484–490 (banking disorders), 495–505 (taxation of the Bank); Schouler, II, 447–449; III, 109–119 (difficulties in 1819).

RESUMPTION OF SPECIE PAYMENTS: *American State Papers, Finance*, IV, 132 (report of Dallas); *Statutes*, III, 343 (resolution, April 30, 1816), or Dunbar, 95; A. Gallatin, *Writings*, III, 287–293; Bolles, II, 318–322; H. Adams, *History of U. S.*, IX, 118–119, 128–132.

TARIFF OF 1816: *American State Papers, Finance*, III, 32–35, 52–54, 82–85 (memorials), 85–99, 103–107; E. Young, *Customs Tariff Legislation*, xxxvii–xl; *Statutes*, III, 310; Bolles, II, 284–293, 359–366; O. L. Elliott, *The Tariff Controversy*, 137–192; F. W. Taussig, *Tariff History*, 29–31,

40, 50; Calhoun, *Works*, II, 163-173; R. Hildreth, 582-588, 630; H. Adams, *History of U. S.*, IX, 111-116; McMaster, IV, 319-343; Stanwood, I, 134-162.

PAYMENT OF DEBT: *Finance Reports*, II, 251 (1823), 282 (1824), 316 (1825); *American State Papers, Finance*, III, 800 (report, April 15, 1822, retrenchment of expenditures); *Statutes*, III, 379 (sinking-fund act, March 3, 1817); or Dunbar, 97; Bolles, II, 303-316, 523-526; J. W. Kearny, *Sketch of American Finances*, III, 150; E. A. Ross, *Sinking Funds*, in *Pub. Amer. Econ. Assn.*, VII, 70-76.

LOANS: Bayley, 355-360; W. F. de Knight, 57-61.

66. Currency Disorder.

Upon the advent of peace the most important task was the re-establishment of the currency on a sound specie basis. When Congress refused to re-charter the United States Bank in 1811 the field was left free for State banking, and the opportunity was eagerly seized. Between 1811 and 1816 the number of these institutions rose from 88 to 246. Many were organized with almost no restrictions; at best there were serious defects, for there was little past experience to guide either the legislatures which had the power of incorporation or the bank managers; and there was no organized system of intelligence which would insure prompt publicity as to the condition of banks distributed over the wide area of country. War always brings a demand for new credit, and under this stimulus the notes of the banks were unduly expanded; the loose credit system of selling public lands in the West led to inflation; and this movement was hastened because after the suspension of specie payments in August, 1814, the government accepted State bank-notes in the payment of public dues, — hence the bank-note circulation increased from $45,000,000 in 1812 to $100,000,000 in 1817.

Besides meeting mercantile demands for credit, the banks found a tempting field for investment of their note issues in government loans. The banks were drawing interest on this stock; they used it for discounting purposes and they also profited by its gradual rise in the investment market. The result was embarrassing, for if, as sometimes happened, banks with small general resources took the loans of the government payable in twelve years and issued their own notes payable on demand, the banks had nothing but government stock to meet the notes when presented for payment, and this asset they were not always able to turn into cash. Coupled with the expansion of bank-note circulation was the withdrawal of a large amount of specie from the country; the dissolution of the United States Bank alone caused the export of $7,000,000 which had been invested by Europeans in its stock. The drain of specie was most marked from the banks of the Middle and Southern States, so that when Washington was captured by the British in 1814 all banking institutions except in New England, where more conservative methods prevailed, were forced to suspend specie payments. The disorder of the currency naturally disturbed the operations of the treasury; imports sought the ports where the currency was the most debased; and Philadelphia and Baltimore thus enjoyed a greater apparent prosperity than Boston. In the latter city it was necessary to make large disbursements, while the revenue receipts were diverted to the Southern ports. The direct loss to the government from poor or worthless bank-notes received during the four years, 1814–1817, amounted to over $5,000,000. The monetary derangement was so acute that the treasury department was obliged to keep four accounts with its depositories in four standards of value: cash or local currency; treasury notes bearing interest; treasury notes not bearing interest; and special deposits.

67. Establishment of the Second United States Bank.

An important part of the vigorous policy outlined by Dallas when he took charge of the treasury department in 1814 was the establishment of another United States Bank. For this there were two reasons: at first emphasis was placed upon the advantage which the bank would afford in supplying financial resources to an embarrassed treasury; and later it was held indispensable for the restoration of a national currency. Dallas appropriately recognized the services of a few of the

State banks during the war; but declared that "the charter restrictions of some of the banks, the mutual relation and dependence of the banks of the same State, and even of the banks of the different States, and the duty which the directors of each bank conceive they owe to their immediate constituents upon points of security or emolument, interpose an insuperable obstacle to any voluntary arrangement upon national considerations alone for the establishment of a national medium through the agency of the State banks." In Dallas' view a national bank could conciliate, aid, and lead State banks in the restoration of the currency to a specie basis; the government in turn would find its benefit in the rise of value of public securities and in increased confidence in the treasury notes.

Constitutional objections to a bank reappeared, but President Madison, Secretary Dallas, and the legislative leaders agreed in putting that argument aside and devoting attention to the financial and economic elements involved in the question at issue. For a time it was impossible for the advocates of a bank to agree on details which they could all support; hence a brief discussion of the various projects brought forward is desirable in order to illustrate the conflicting state of public opinion, although not one of them was finally adopted in its entirety. Three distinct and often conflicting purposes stood out in the debates: the need of a bank to give financial support to the government; the fear of governmental participation in banking; and the necessity of properly securing the note circulation, — ideas which were the key-notes of similar discussions during the next twenty-five years. Dallas originally proposed (in a report, October 17, 1814) a bank with a capital of $50,000,000; recognizing, however, that it would be impossible to secure so large a subscription in coin, he advised that of the $50,000,000 but $6,000,000 be subscribed in specie, and the remainder in government stock and treasury notes. Provision was made that the government should hold stock in the bank, and that the bank should lend $30,000,000 to the government; and in the bill reported in the House from the committee on ways and means, November 7, the president was given discretionary power to allow suspension of payment of specie by the bank. The chief purpose of this plan was to secure loans to the government; the capital of the bank was to consist largely of government credit in the shape of stock, and in return the bank was not absolutely bound down to pay on demand its obligations outstanding in the form of circulating notes.

Calhoun objected to a financial partnership of this character in which the government would borrow back its own credit, and in a second plan proposed that the government should use its own credit directly without the intervention of a bank, — that one-tenth of the capital should be in specie and the remainder in treasury notes to be thereafter issued; beyond this indirect relation the United States was to have no stock in the bank, no control over its operations, and no power to suspend specie payments. This plan would give support to treasury notes to the disadvantage of government stock, but as treasury notes by this time had many friends it was for the moment favored by the House. Dallas came out strong in opposition, because the fresh issue of treasury notes would gratuitously give an advantage to a single class of creditors and would tend to depreciate the value of the rest of the public debt; more than that he held that it would be extremely difficult to get $45,000,000 of treasury notes into circulation, either with or without depreciation. In later years Calhoun had to meet repeatedly the charge of inconsistency for his support at this time of a federal banking institution. His answer was always frank: he supported a national bank as an instrument of compulsion to force the local banks to resume specie payments; distrust of the State banks led him to waive for the time being his political philosophy.

In the course of the debate (December 29, 1814) Webster proposed still a third plan, — a bank with a capital of $30,000,000, with no obligation on the part of the bank to loan money to the government, with no permission to suspend specie payments, and with a penalty on a refusal by the bank to redeem its notes. In support of his measure Mr. Webster delivered an instructive speech: he thought that the advantages to result from a bank were overrated; for banks are not revenue; the foundations of revenue must be sunk deeper; and the principal good from a bank was in the future, not in the present. The bank proposed by Calhoun seemed to him most extraordinary and alarming; with a capital of $5,000,000 in specie and $45,000,000 in government notes, such an institution looked less like a bank than a paper-money department of the government: "the government is to grow rich because it is to borrow without the obligation of repaying, and it is to borrow of a bank which issues paper without liability to redeem it."

The first bill passed was along the lines suggested by Webster; the capital authorized was $30,000,000, of which the United States might subscribe $5,000,000 in government stock; of the private subscription of $25,000,000 one-half was to be in treasury notes, one-third in stock, and one-sixth in coin. No loan was to be made to the government exceeding $500,000; the bank could not purchase government indebtedness; and no permission was given to suspend specie payments. This bill did not meet the approval of Secretary Dallas, and was vetoed by President Madison, January 30, 1815, for the following reasons: the amount of the stock to be subscribed would not be sufficiently in favor of the public credit to cause any considerable or lasting elevation of the market price of government stock; the people would reap no adequate benefits, since the bank was free from all legal obligations to make loans to the government; and the bank as constituted would not provide a sufficient circulating medium, for it would be obliged to pay its notes in specie or be subject to loss of its charter. In brief, Madison's objection was that the bank as proposed would fail to provide a reliable circulating medium, or to furnish loans to the government in return for its franchise.

In December, 1815, Secretary Dallas again placed the subject before Congress, with some modification of his previous propositions: he now recommended a bank with a capital of but $35,000,000, to consist three-fourths of government stock (with no mention of treasury notes) and one-fourth of specie; instead of demanding that the bank make loans to the United States it was under obligation to pay a bonus to the government in return for the benefits of its charter; and, finally, he insisted that no opportunity should be given for a suspension of specie payments in case of emergency. In accordance with these principles a bill was introduced early in 1816. Calhoun gave his support, together with a violent attack upon State banks, which he accused of circulating $170,000,000 of bank-notes on not more than $15,000,000 of specie in their vaults. "The metallic currency has left our shores," said he; "we have treated it with indignity; it leaves us and seeks a new asylum on foreign shores." Smith of Maryland coincided with Calhoun that a bank was necessary but resented the attack upon the State institutions; during the war, he said, "they had been the pillars of the nation, now they were the caterpillars." John Randolph opposed the bill specifically and in general. A bank "would be an engine of irresistible power in the hands of any administration; it would be in politics and finance what the celebrated proposition of Archimedes was in physics, — a place, the fulcrum, from which at the will of the executive the whole nation could be hurled to destruction." "Every man present in the House or out of it, with some rare exceptions, was either a stockholder, president, cashier, clerk, or door-keeper, runner, engraver, paper-maker, or mechanic in some way or other to a bank." "It was as much swindling to issue notes with the intent not to pay as it was burglary to break open a house." "But a man might as well go to Constantinople to preach Christianity as to get up here and preach against banks." Clay, then speaker of the House, favored the bank, although formerly, when a member of the Senate, he had opposed the renewal of the charter of the first bank. In explanation he assigned his former opposition to three causes:

first, he had been instructed to oppose the charter by the legislature of his own State; secondly, the old bank had abused its powers in the interest of a political party; and, thirdly, he had previously doubted the constitutional authority of Congress to establish the bank. The situation in his opinion was changed in 1816, since it was now clear that such an institution was indispensable to treasury operations.

Finally, on March 14, 1816, the new bill, framed more in accordance with the ideas of the administration, was passed by the House by a vote of 80 to 71; of the minority 38 were Federalists and 31 were Republicans. The bill passed the Senate and was approved by the president April 10.

68. Career of the Bank, 1816-1819.

From the standpoint of note circulation the following provisions are of importance: circulation was limited to the total capital of the bank, $35,000,000; notes were payable in specie on demand, under a penalty of 12 per cent. per annum in case of failure; notes of denominations of less than five dollars were prohibited; and the notes were receivable in all payments to the United States. The relations of the bank to the government were twofold: the government subscribed $7,000,000 of the capital; and three-quarters of the remaining $28,000,000, or $21,000,000, was to be subscribed in the funded debt of the United States. Five of the twenty-five directors were appointed by the president. The bank was obliged to transfer the public funds of the government from place to place without commission; the deposit of the funds of the government was to be made with the bank, unless the secretary should otherwise direct, in which case the secretary of the treasury should lay before Congress the reasons for such action. In return for the privileges granted in the charter, the bank was obliged to pay $1,500,000 in three equal instalments to the United States, and finally the United States agreed to establish no other bank under federal charter except in the District of Columbia. Congress was given the power to inspect the books of the bank, and if there were reason to believe that the charter was violated to direct the president to issue a writ of scire facias whereby the bank should show cause why the charter should not be forfeited.

The enactment of the bank measure was quickly reinforced by the passage of a joint resolution providing that after February 20, 1817, all dues to the government should be paid in legal currency, treasury notes, notes of the bank of the United States, "and in notes of banks which are payable and paid on demand in the said currency of the United States." State banks were thus given about ten months to get their houses in order if they wished to secure a financial standing with the general government. This was a vigorous demand; the United States Bank had yet to be organized and many local institutions established in the Middle States were reluctant to reduce their loans and contract their circulation so as to rest on a specie basis. In midsummer, 1816, the banks of the Middle States held a convention and asked that the date of resumption be deferred, giving as a reason that the United States Bank could not be organized in the time assigned, and that they wished the aid of this institution in their efforts to resume. Dallas labored the harder to open the new bank on time; the stock was taken, directors elected, and an agent sent abroad to purchase bullion. In January, 1817, the bank was opened, and on February 20, the date originally set, the victory rested with the administration.

During the first year of its operations the bank was badly managed; for, instead of tactfully and vigorously taking the lead in restoring banking credit to a sound condition, the officers violated provisions in its charter and undertook through the numerous branches to oppress local banks. Although the charter provided for a subscription of $7,000,000 in specie, only $2,000,000 was paid in, and instead of the full complement of government stock $12,000,000 was subscribed in the personal notes of stockholders. Discounts were injudiciously if not illegally made on United States bank stock as collateral; stock jobbing was common; and, through inside arrangements made with bank officers, speculators borrowed money of the bank and bought shares simultaneously. Even the president and other officials of the bank speculated in its stock; and dividends were paid to stockholders who had not completed their subscriptions. Nor was the bank successful in restoring note circulation to a healthy state; although resumption was nominally made, specie continued at a slight premium. For this the bank possibly was only in part to blame; there was too little specie in the country and foreign trade was adverse. Instead of recognizing this difficulty the bank by sharp practice extended its own circulation beyond proper limits and also stirred up bitter feeling by endeavoring to control the circulation of note issues of local banks. Branches in the South and West loaned with great freedom, and as the notes issued on such loans were redeemable at any branch East or West the capital of the bank was unduly diverted to sections which did not enjoy commercial stability. It was not long before the bank saw the danger, and in August, 1818, it sent out orders to redeem no notes except at the office where issued; and in the hope of returning to safer ground it reduced its credits. This reversal of policy occurred at a time when commerce was struggling to recover itself from the inflation of the war period, and so sudden was it that instead of warding off it hastened the impending disaster; thus far the bank was not a success as an agency for improving the currency. Two years of reckless management culminated in the smash of the Baltimore branch with a loss of $3,000,000, and in January, 1819, a motion was introduced into Congress looking to a setting aside of the charter; nothing saved the bank from ruin but placing at the head of its affairs Langdon Cheves, a sound business man.

A conservative policy followed, which continued during the presidency of Cheves (1819–1823) and the earlier years of his successor, Biddle. The contraction which followed is made clear in the following figures of circulation and loans: —

Year	Circulation	Loans
1817	$1,911,000	$3,485,000
1818	8,339,000	41,181,000
1819	6,563,000	35,786,000
1820	3,589,000	31,401,000
1821	4,567,000	30,905,000
1822	5,578,000	28,061,000
1823	4,361,000	30,736,000

During its entire history the bank issued but little circulation in New England, and not until its later days any large amount in the Middle States. On account of this sectionalism in its operations the bank did not come into conflict with the strong local institutions of the East. In the South and West it exercised a strong financial guidance, which was greatly needed, but in doing this it occasioned jealousies and ill-will which counted to its disadvantage in the long run. The distribution of the bank's circulation in 1818, 1823, and 1832 is interesting to note: —

Section	Sept. 30, 1819	Jan. 2, 1823	April 4, 1832
New England	$518,000	$393,000	$901,000
Middle States	969,000	868,000	5,478,000
South	3,960,000	2,281,000	5,311,000
Southwest	670,000	744,000	5,637,000
West	817,000	45,000	5,131,000
Total	$6,934,000	$4,331,000	$22,458,000

69. Local Banks, 1815-1830.

It is difficult to form a clear impression of the progress of local banking previous to 1834 because of lack of complete official reports. The virtue of publicity in accounts of banking institutions was not generally recognized or insisted upon by law. Gallatin, whose essay on Banking and Currency written in 1831 is by far the most thorough discussion of the subject, refers "to the mystery with which it has been thought necessary" in several of the States "to conceal the operations of the banking institutions." This led not only to erroneous opinions on the part of the public, but gave free opportunity for mismanagement by bank officials. As far as records go the condition of banks in 1815, 1820, and 1829 was as follows in millions of dollars: —

Year	1815	1820			Nov. 1, 1829		
	State banks	State banks	U. S. Bank	Total	State banks	U. S. Bank	Total
Number	208	307			329		
Capital.	82.	102.1	35.0	137.1	110.1	35.0	145.1
Notes in circulation	45.5 to 100.	40.6	4.2	44.8	48.2	13.0	61.3
Deposits		31.2	4.7	35.9	40.7	14.7	55.5
Specie.	17.	16.6	3.1	19.8	14.9	7.1	22.1
Loans	150.		31.4		137.0	40.6	177.6

The character of the local institutions varied greatly, depending upon the available amount of surplus capital in different sections and the degree of past commercial experience of the communities in which they were established. Each State was working out for itself a system which presented with some degree of accuracy the current stage of economic thought and industrial development. No account of this can be given here, but in order to understand the contest which Jackson later waged against the United States Bank and the financial entanglements of 1837 a few aspects of local banking must be noticed. The two principal defects in local banking were the opportunities for over-issue of notes and the making of loans on improper security. Of note issues, substantially three systems were tried in different parts of the country: (1) issues based only upon the general assets of a particular bank; (2) issues protected by a general safety fund; and (3) issues based upon the credit and faith of the States. In New England circulation was generally based upon assets;

as early as 1809 Massachusetts laid a penalty of 2 per cent. a month on banks which failed to redeem their notes on demand, and in 1829 passed an act providing that all banks thereafter incorporated should be restricted in their note circulation to one and a fourth times the capital. In New England there was also developed what was known as the Suffolk system of redemption, under which the notes of New England banks uniformly circulated at par and were generally held in good repute. By this plan all the large city banks had to stand ready at all times to redeem, and the country banks in New England were compelled to establish redemption agencies in Boston; the Suffolk Bank in Boston was charged with the duty of bringing any delinquent to terms by collecting its notes as fast as they made their appearance in Boston and returning them to the place of issue for payment in specie.

In New York the system of banking on general assets was supplemented by the safety-fund system introduced in 1829, under which each bank was required to pay annually to the treasurer of the State a sum equal to one-half of one per cent. of its capital stock until the payments should amount to 3 per cent., the fund to be used for the redemption of the notes of any failed bank. These precautions were the exception; Southern and Western States were not so careful to prevent over-issues, and many country banks established in remote places succumbed to the temptation. All banks indeed throughout the country issued notes of $5, and many those of a lower denomination. Failures of banks were common and bill holders and depositors suffered much. As the United States Bank with its branches covered a wide range of territory, it naturally had frequent occasion to discriminate against suspicious issues, and thus not only brought down the violent opposition of reckless financial adventurers but gave cause for complaint by banks which were honestly endeavoring to satisfy the great demand for loans in regions poorly provided with capital.

70. United States Bank, 1823-1829.

The history of the United States Bank from 1823 to 1829 was on the whole uneventful. Cheves was succeeded as President in January, 1823, by Nicholas Biddle of Philadelphia, who was elected to represent "a young and progressive policy" as against an "old and conservative policy." His aim was to increase the circulation and yet avoid the dangers which nearly wrecked the bank between 1817 and 1819. This he accomplished through the freer use of domestic bills of exchange and the introduction of branch drafts. Under the charter provision only the president and the cashier of the parent bank could affix signatures to bills of branches. This restriction practically barred branch issues, as the officers could not sign more than 1500 notes a day, and it was calculated that on this basis four years would be required to furnish the volume needed. The bank, therefore, repeatedly endeavored to secure congressional authority to permit the officers of the branch banks to sign notes, but the efforts failed on the ground that a variety of signatures meant a variety of notes, causing an increase in the evils of irresponsible and inflated circulation which the establishment of the bank was in part intended to remedy. The branch draft devised by Biddle was obviously a method for doing the same thing by the issue of drafts for even sums of $5, $10, or $20, drawn by a branch upon the parent bank, payable to an officer of the bank and upon endorsement payable to bearer, thus acquiring some of the characteristics of circulation bank-notes. The inflation in circulation which resulted from Biddle's expansive policy is seen in the following table of yearly average circulation of the United States Bank: —

Year	Circulation	Year	Circulation
1823	$4,487,000	1829	$13,102,000
1824	5,791,000	1830	15,067,000
1825	8,825,000	1831	19,035,000
1826	9,635,000	1832	19,989,000
1827	9,780,000	1833	18,636,000
1828	11,067,000	1834	16,790,000

As to the bank's relations to the treasury department, there was little criticism after 1819 until Jackson's term as president. In the annual report for 1828 Secretary Rush made special reference to the great service of the bank; the $97,000,000 received in the treasury during the four years of Adams' administration had been applied to the various objects of expenditure without embarrassment or delay, and the credit for this result was largely ascribed to the bank. "In faithful obedience to the provisions of its charter, and aided by its branches, the bank had afforded the necessary facilities for transferring the public moneys from place to place."

71. Constitutionality of the Bank.

Such scruples as statesmen may have had over the constitutionality of a bank chartered by the federal government were soon rendered purposeless by a decision of the Supreme Court. In 1818 the legislature of Maryland imposed a stamp duty on the circulating notes of all banks or branches thereof located in the State and not chartered by the legislature. The Maryland branch of the United States Bank refused to pay this tax, and the State court sustained a suit against the cashier, McCulloch; therefore the case was carried to the United States Supreme Court, and decided in 1819 in the famous case of *McCulloch* v. *Maryland*. The opinion written by Chief-Justice Marshall is in harmony with the long line of decisions through which he elaborated the fundamental powers of the federal government. Against the constitutionality of the bank it had in general been argued that the power of Congress to incorporate a bank is not among those enumerated in the Constitution; that the inclusion of such a power had been expressly rejected by the convention which framed the Constitution, and that the enumerated powers could be carried into exercise without a bank. To the argument that a bank might facilitate the collection of taxes, and be justified under the general powers of Congress on the ground of fiscal convenience, the reply was made that the

Constitution allows only the means which are necessary, and not merely those which are convenient for effecting the enumerated powers. Even the merit of convenience was not granted by opposing critics, who declared that the local or State banks in existence were entirely competent to meet all the needs of the government in the collection of revenue.[1]

Marshall in his decision declared that the United States Bank was an instrument which was necessary and proper for carrying on the fiscal operations of the government. The sword and the purse, all the external relations, and no inconsiderable portion of the industry of the nation, are intrusted to the government; having such ample powers, on the due execution of which the happiness and prosperity of the nation so vitally depend, it must also be intrusted with ample means for their execution. "Throughout this vast republic, from the St. Croix to the Gulf of Mexico, from the Atlantic to the Pacific, revenue is to be collected and expended, armies are to be marched and supported. The exigencies of the nation may require that the treasure raised in the North should be transported to the South, that raised in the East conveyed to the West, or that this order should be reversed. Is that construction of the Constitution to be preferred which would render these operations difficult, hazardous, and expensive?" The Constitution, said Marshall, did not intend to create a dependence of the government of the Union on those of the States for the execution of the great powers assigned to it. The choice of means implies the right to choose a national bank in preference to State banks, and Congress alone can make the election. The branches of the bank proceeding from the same stock are equally constitutional with the parent bank.

The court was equally explicit and emphatic in expressing its conviction that a State could not tax the bank or one of its branches. "If the State may tax one instrument employed by the government in the execution of its powers, they may

[1] Story, *Commentaries*, Bk. III., ch. 25.

tax any and every other instrument. They may tax the mail; they may tax the mint; they may tax patent rights; they may tax the papers of the custom-house; they may tax judicial process; they may tax all the means employed by the government to an excess which would defeat all the ends of government." For this reason the law passed by the legislature of Maryland imposing a tax on the Bank of the United States was declared unconstitutional. This opinion did not preclude State taxation of real property of the bank within the State, nor the taxation of securities, held by citizens of Maryland, in common with other property of the same description throughout the State.[1] Interpreters of the Constitution belonging to the school of strict construction also note that in this case the court confined the authority of Congress to the establishment of a bank as a means of exercising the fiscal functions of the government, and that consequently the establishment of national banks, as in our present system, for the purpose of providing a currency, is an altogether different question and must be justified on other grounds.[2]

An effort to tax the United States Bank was also made in Ohio; the State imposed a tax of $50,000 on each of the two branches established at Cincinnati and Chillicothe, to go into effect September 15, 1819. The branches continued business, refused payment, and the local sheriff in behalf of the State seized $98,000 in money; the bank through the United States Circuit Court secured the arrest of the State officials involved, and on appeal the dispute was carried to the Supreme Court in the case known as *Osborn et al* v. *United States Bank* (1824). In the opinion then delivered Chief-Justice Marshall was still more explicit in resting the validity of his decision in the case of *McCulloch* v. *The State of Maryland*, on the principle that the bank was a public corporation created for public and national purposes. If the bank were founded

[1] Wheaton's *Reports*, pp. 316–437; Marshall's *Writings*, pp. 160–187.
[2] Tucker, *Constitution of the U. S.*, 1: 516–518.

upon contract between individuals, having private trade and private profit for its great and principal object, it certainly would be subject to the taxing power of the State, as any individual would be; and the casual circumstance of its being employed by the government in the transaction of its fiscal affairs would not exempt its private business from the operation of the taxing power. It was denied, however, that the bank was founded for any such limited private purpose, and the court enlarged upon the services rendered to the government.

72. Issues of Banks Owned by States.

Another interesting constitutional question arose during the period under review; viz., the constitutionality of bills issued by banks established in the name of a State. Institutions owned and managed by States were organized in the South and Southwest: were not the notes then issued, depending upon the faith of State governments, practically bills of credit expressly forbidden to States by the Constitution? This question came before the Supreme Court in 1824 in the case of *Bank of the United States* v. *The Planters' Bank of Georgia*, and in 1829 in *Bank of the Commonwealth of Kentucky* v. *Wister et al.* In these cases the local banks of Georgia and Kentucky, in which the State governments had invested, endeavored to shield themselves behind the Eleventh Amendment, and entered a plea of non-suability of a sovereign State. The force of this plea was admitted by the Supreme Court, provided the State as a sovereign was the sole owner of the bank-notes issued, but if this ground were taken the court in the latter case held that the notes issued by the bank would be bills of credit, and contrary to the provisions of the Constitution of the United States. The next year (1830), in the case of *Craig* v. *The State of Missouri* (4 Peters, 140), the Supreme Court in an opinion delivered by Marshall declared that certificates issued by State loan officers and receivable for taxes and salaries were unconstitutional. Decisions of this character helped to excite popular resentment in the South toward the United States Bank, which though a private institution came to be regarded as a federal bank, to which was granted the privilege of note issue denied to a local bank even though clothed with the power of State sovereignty.

73. Tariff of 1816.

In 1816 the customs revenue of the government was enormous, not only passing far beyond any previous returns, but standing at a figure not again reached until 1850. The imports, valued in 1814 at less than $13,000,000, rose to $147,000,000 in 1816. "The English manufacturers, to whose merchandise after years of commercial war an ample market finally opened, rushed as if to the attack of a fortress."[1] An increase in customs duties resulted beyond all anticipation; instead of $13,000,000 for 1816, as previously estimated by Dallas, $36,000,000 were turned into the treasury.

Signs were early apparent of an importation overwhelming and for manufactures possibly ruinous. In 1815, upon submitting the treaty of peace, Madison called attention to the unparalleled development of manufactures, and "anxiously recommended this source of national independence and wealth to the prompt and constant guardianship of Congress." A step further was taken when in his annual message in December, 1815, he affirmed the necessity of protection to enterprising citizens "whose interests are now at stake." Dallas was also promptly called upon to prepare a bill, which he subsequently submitted in an elaborate report, February 12, 1816, stating the principles upon which the measure was framed. Not only was revenue to be secured and its collection rendered equal and certain, but the interests of agriculture, manufactures, trade, and navigation must be conciliated. Articles of foreign importation were arranged by Dallas in three classes according to the degree of dependence upon foreign countries: in the first class were commodities which could be manufactured in sufficient supply at home, on which

[1] Rabbeno, *American Commercial Policy*, p. 153.

it was proposed to place duties high enough to shut out foreign competition; in the second, articles partially supplied at home, which were to be treated to less protection; and, in the third, articles not produced at home, and consequently subject purely to fiscal considerations.

A general tariff bill was introduced March 12, 1816, and enacted April 27; in effect it fell slightly short of the rates recommended by Dallas. Both the debate upon this measure and the provisions of the act are of especial importance in fiscal history. The new textile industries were threatened by English competition; hence a duty on woollen and cotton of 25 per cent. until June 30, 1819, and after that date of 20 per cent.; with respect to cottons it was further provided that all cotton cloths, the original cost of which was less than 25 cts. per square yard, should be deemed to have cost that sum, and pay duties accordingly. This was the introduction of the minimum principle, and its immediate object was the exclusion of coarse, low-priced cotton fabrics from the East Indies. The act also imposed a 30 per cent. ad valorem rate on certain other goods, as hats, cabinet wares, manufactured wood, carriages, leather and its manufactures, and paper. A specific duty of 3 cts. a pound was laid upon sugar.

So great were the changes in rates that it is often asserted that the tariff of 1816 is the beginning in the United States of the distinct application of the protective principle to domestic industry by means of customs duties. Even if this be not strictly true, the change in policy was so marked that this tariff is properly regarded as a turning-point in economic legislation. Duties in the early tariffs may have incidentally afforded protection; but in 1816 protection was adopted as a fundamental basis of the fiscal system and revenue was subordinated to industrial needs. A comparison of tariff rates on the most important commodities as adopted in the first tariff of 1789, the rates prevailing just before the War of 1812, the war rates, and those enacted in 1816, shows the progress toward restriction: —

	1789	Acts of 1804, 1807, 1808	Acts of 1812 to 1816	Act of April 27, 1816
Cotton manufactures . .	free	17½ per cent.	35 per cent.	25 per cent.
Glass manufactures . .	10 per cent.	22½ per cent.	45 per cent.	20 per cent.
Rolled or hammered iron	7½ per cent.	17½ per cent.	35 per cent.	30 per cent.
Leather	7½ per cent.	17½ per cent.	35 per cent.	30 per cent.
Molasses	2½ cts. gal.	5 cts. gal.	10 cts. gal.	5 cts. gal.
Sugar, brown	1 ct. lb.	2½ cts. lb.	5 cts. lb.	3 cts lb.
Boots, men's leather . .	50 cts. pair	75 cts. pair	$1.50 pair	$1.50 pair
Cabinet ware	7½ per cent.	15 per cent.	30 per cent.	30 per cent.
Candles, tallow . . .	2 cts. lb.	2 cts. lb.	4 cts. lb.	3 cts. lb.
Carriages	15 per cent.	22½ per cent.	45 per cent.	30 per cent.
Earthenware	10 per cent.	17½ per cent.	35 per cent.	20 per cent.
Fish, dried	50 cts. quintal	50 cts. quintal	$1.00 quintal	$1.00 quintal
Hats	7½ per cent.	17½ per cent.	35 per cent.	30 per cent.
Hemp, manufactured .	.60 cwt.	$1.00 cwt.	$2.00 cwt.	$1.50 cwt.
Linen	5 per cent.	15 per cent.	30 per cent.	35 per cent.
Nails	1 ct. lb.	2 cts. lb.	4 cts. lb.	3 cts. lb.
Paper, writing	7½ per cent.	15 per cent.	30 per cent.	30 per cent.
Salt	10 cts. bushel	free	20 cts. bushel	20 cts. bushel

The debate over the tariff bill of 1816 was the beginning of the discussion as to the relative advantages of a definite policy of free trade or protection, a discussion which has lasted to the present time. On the whole opposition to increased restriction was weak in 1816 because there was an unquestioned emergency; the distress of the textile industry was obvious and silenced objections which would otherwise have been more insistent. The tariff question, possibly for the last time, was treated in a broad and rational spirit; support for the bill came from all parts of the country. The vote in the House of Representatives by sections was as follows: —

	In favor	Opposed
New England . .	17	10
Middle States . . .	44	10
West (Ohio) . . .	4	. .
South and Southwest	23	34
Total	88	54

Even in South Carolina the vote in favor of the bill was 4 to 3. The time had not yet arrived for the enumeration of the extreme doctrines which were subsequently formulated by protectionists on the one hand and by free-traders on the other. The policy of "let alone" was recommended by a few, but the champions of the merchants and of commerce dwelt chiefly upon the unjust discriminations of tariffs, the evil social effects of manufacturing, and contrasted the delights of bucolic life; such radical opposition as Randolph's represented the individualism of a free lance rather than the convictions of any well-defined class. There was, however, plenty of discussion over the scale of rates, as indicating the measure of protection which Congress was willing to grant. New England, whose interests were still commercial, criticised rather than antagonized, and even Calhoun, who had not yet consecrated himself to the sectional profit of the agricultural South, championed the interests of manufactures as a part of the security of the country. "Neither agriculture, manufactures, nor commerce, taken separately, is the cause of wealth; it flows from the three combined and cannot exist without each."

The importance of the tariff question as it developed during the next fifteen years, from 1818 until the passage of the compromise tariff in 1833, justifies its consideration in a separate chapter; but since the revenues were fairly constant after 1821, in spite of frequent changes in rates of duty, and as the several tariff measures were founded on other considerations than those of meeting the needs of the treasury, it is possible to continue here with advantage a general sketch of the state of the treasury, the receipts, expenditures, and public indebtedness from 1817 until 1834 when the debt was extinguished.

The administration of the treasury department during the terms of Monroe and John Quincy Adams was in competent hands. William H. Crawford succeeded Dallas as secretary of the treasury in March, 1816, and held office until 1825. He is a good illustration of the political statesman managing the affairs of finance; his experience in public life had been long and varied; he had been senator from Georgia, minister to France, and secretary of war; in 1816 he was talked of for the presidency, but stepped aside for Monroe, thus gaining, it was supposed, a right to the succession. He was a conservative Democrat, of the Virginian type as opposed to the more radical Westerners; he had been a stanch supporter of the First United States Bank, and in 1816 labored earnestly for the establishment of its succession. Though not a great man, he gave careful attention to the duties of his office, particularly during the first part of his administration when currency disorders were so grave, and left behind him an interesting series of reports. In March, 1825, Richard Rush of Pennsylvania succeeded Crawford; he had been long engaged in public affairs, and in Madison's administration had received valuable training as comptroller of the treasury. Rush wrote much, and, being an ardent protectionist, embodied in his annual reports earnest disquisitions in favor of restrictive tariffs. He was also an early advocate of the warehousing system. During this period improvements were made in the collection and publication of commercial statistics, which were greatly needed for understanding the relation of tariff duties to trade. The first commerce and navigation report appeared in 1821.

74. Financial Embarrassments, 1816–1821.

The first few years of this period were exceptionally perplexing to the treasury because of the violent fluctuations in the revenue. On January 1, 1816, the total indebtedness of the United States amounted to $127,334,000. The outstanding treasury notes were speedily funded into stock, and as the abundant revenues of 1816 justified the policy of rapid extinction of debt, Congress ordered under the act of March 3, 1817, that from the proceeds of customs, tonnage, internal revenue duties, and sales of public lands, $10,000,000 should be annually appropriated to the sinking fund. As revenues were still large in 1817, $9,000,000 additional were appropriated to the sinking fund for that year; and it was further provided that any annual surplus income beyond $2,000,000 should be devoted to the purchase of government securities. Too much faith, however, had been placed in the future; the years 1816 and 1817 were unusual in their yield, and the wonderful prosperity did not continue. Excessive importations were checked as trade returned to its usual channels, and the normal state of the budget began to be apparent. The customs receipts grew smaller; but unfortunately the falling off did not occur until after the internal revenue duties had been repealed. Deficits then occurred; and the years 1818 to 1821 proved to be a period of perplexity and discouragement in the administration of the finances. The difficulties were also aggravated by the bad management of the bank to which reference has been made.

The year 1819 was marked by a crisis, the first of those industrial and commercial storms which have since recurred at fairly regular intervals in our history. Its causes were complex: in part the inability of the manufacturing industries to recover a stable footing after the abnormal growth occasioned by the embargo and the war, and in part a spirit of speculation developed by the several years of rapid commercial expansion and bad banking. Distress was severe throughout the country; many laborers were thrown out of employment; prices of exportable articles fell; and, in general, a readjustment of values was forced upon the country. Contraction of credits by the banks in their endeavor to obtain a specie basis in 1817 also contributed to diminish the credit facilities which the banks could afford to importers; the State banks reduced their note issues from $100,000,000 in 1817 to $45,000,000 in 1819. The condition of tne treasury department speedily became grave, and in the annual report of December, 1819, Crawford announced a deficit and demanded either a reduction in expenditures or an increase in revenue: in any event a loan was necessary to tide over immediate embarrassments, and the secretary even ventured to suggest a small temporary issue of non-interest-bearing treasury notes. In April, 1820, the House committee on ways and means, in a report on a loan bill, effectively set forth the needed remedies; while they hesitated to recommend a loan, they believed that powerful reasons existed working against a restoration of internal revenue and direct taxation in a period of profound tranquillity. Economy and retrenchment in government expenditures were needed, especially in view of the depression of commerce and navigation, the depreciation in the value of exports and of property of every description, and serious embarrassments in all branches of industry, which compelled economy and retrenchment in the expenditures of every citizen. The excess of expenditures over revenue was ascribed principally to the heavy payments in the redemption of the public debt; $32,000,000 of indebtedness had been redeemed since January 1, 1817. To tide over the difficulty, a loan of $3,000,000 was authorized by the act of May 15, 1820; two-thirds of this loan was redeemable at the pleasure of the government, and bore interest at 6 per cent.; the remainder ran for twelve years and bore 5 per cent. interest.

In spite of a reduction in ordinary expenditures the situation in 1821 was still more grave. This was in part caused by the fact that several millions of the public debt were due in that year. Another loan of $5,000,000 running for fourteen years at 5 per cent. was authorized March 3, and as there was at the moment a large amount of capital in the hands of owners who hesitated to invest in private enterprises, it was readily taken at a premium of from 5.1 to 8 per cent. Commerce and industry then began to revive, and there was no further necessity of resorting to deficit loans. The experience of the years 1818 to 1822 affords another illustration of the great difficulty of adjusting revenue to expenditures in a new and rapidly expanding nation, especially a nation which relied for its revenue chiefly on import duties. Changes in political or commercial relations result in excessive fluctuations of revenue; thus in 1808 the imports, under restricting legislation and other causes, fell off by over $80,000,000, while in 1816, in the transition from war to peace, imports increased by $134,000,000 and customs duties by nearly $30,000,000 in a single year. So too from 1818 to

1822 the variations due to commercial causes were almost as sudden as those incident to war; imports diminished from over $121,000,000 in 1818 to about $87,000,000 in 1819, and in 1821 to about one-half what they had been three years before. In two years of peace, free commerce, and the full operation of the United States Bank, the revenue from import duties shrank more than one third.

75. Receipts and Expenditures, 1816-1833.

Beginning with 1822 the treasury settled down to a long term of prosperity. With the exception of 1824, when an unusual payment was made on account of the Spanish claims, an annual surplus was turned in until the difficulties of the panic of 1837 disturbed commerce and finance. The receipts from customs were fairly constant in volume, and this, together with the steady growth in receipts from sales of public lands, wiped out the debt in 1835.

The ordinary receipts of the government 1816 to 1833 were as follows: —

Year	Customs	Public lands	Miscellaneous	Total
1816	$36,307,000	$1,718,000	$9.652,000	$47,677,000
1817	26,283,000	1,991,000	5.825,000	33,099.000
1818	17,176,000	2,606.000	1,803,000	21,585,000
1819	20,283,000	3,274,000	1,146,000	24,603,000
1820	15,005,000	1,635,000	1,000.000	17,840,000
1821	13,004,000	1,212,000	157,000	14,573,000
1822	17,589,000	1,803,000	840,000	20,232,000
1823	19,088,000	916,000	536,000	20,540,000
1824	17,878,000	984,000	519,000	19,381,000
1825	20,098,000	1,216,000	526,000	21,840,000
1826	23,341,000	1,393,000	526,000	25,260,000
1827	19,712,000	1,495,000	2,259,000	22,966,000
1828	23,205,000	1,018,000	540,000	24,763,000
1829	22,681,000	1,517,000	629,000	24,827,000
1830	21,922,000	2,329,000	593,000	24,844,000
1831	24,224,000	3,210,000	1,092,000	28,526,000
1832	28,465,000	2,623.000	779,000	31,867,000
1833	29,032,000	3,967,000	946,000	33,948,000

The large figures under "Miscellaneous," 1816-1820, are due to the inclusion of the delayed internal and direct taxes, as stated in the table, page 140; and in 1827 to receipts from Great Britain on account of property seized during the War of 1812, amounting to $1,205,000.

After 1821 expenditures for the military and naval establishments varied little from year to year; while not brought down to the level which prevailed before the war, the per capita burden was on the whole no greater. Pensions now for the first time became an important item in the budget; by the act of March 18, 1818, pensions were granted to all Revolutionary soldiers on the basis of service and poverty, discarding the previous qualification of disability. Fraudulent claims on a large scale followed, which led to an amendment of the law by requiring more rigid examination of an applicant's material welfare. Some beginning was made in appropriations for internal improvements, a topic which will be subsequently treated. The great decrease in total expenditures as seen in the following table was due to the reduction and final elimination of interest charges on the public debt.

Expenditures by years 1816 to 1833 were as follows: —

	War	Navy	Pensions	Interest on debt	Miscellaneous[1]	Total
1816	$16,012,000	$3,908,000	$189,000	$7,823,000	$3,264,000	$31,196,000
1817	8,004,000	3,314,000	297,000	4,536,000	3,838,000	19,990,000
1818	5,622,000	2,953,000	890,000	6,209,000	4,341,000	20,017,000
1819	6,506,000	3,847,000	2,415,000	5,211,000	3,530,000	21,511,000
1820	2,630,000	4,387,000	3,208,000	5,151,000	2,907,000	18,285,000
1821	4,461,000	3,319,000	242,000	5,126,000	2,700,000	15,849,000
1822	3,111,000	2,224,000	1,948,000	5,172,000	2,542,000	14,999,000
1823	3,096,000	2,503,000	1,780,000	4,922,000	2,402,000	14,706,000
1824	3,340,000	2,904,000	1,499,000	4,943,000	7,585,000	20,273,000
1825	3,659,000	3,049,000	1,308,000	4,366,000	3,472,000	15,856,000
1826	3,943,000	4,218,000	1,556,000	3,975,000	3,343,000	17,037,000
1827	3,948,000	4,263,000	976,000	3,486,000	3,463,000	16,139,000
1828	4,145,000	3,918,000	850,000	3,098,000	4,381,000	16,394,000
1829	4,724,000	3,308,000	949,000	2,542,000	3,658,000	15,183,000
1830	4,767,000	3,239,000	1,363,000	1,912,000	3,859,000	15,141,000
1831	4,841,000	3,856,000	1,170,000	1,373,000	3,995,000	15,237,000
1832	5,446,000	3,956,000	1,184,000	772,000	4,929,000	17,288,000
1833	6,704,000	3,901,000	4,589,000	303,000	6,518,000	23,017,000

[1] Including Indians.

A comparison of the receipts with expenditures and the resulting changes in the debt give the following table in millions of dollars: —

Year	Receipts			Expenditures	Surplus	Deficit
	Taxes	Other	Total			
1816	45.7	2.0	47.7	31.2	16.5	
1817	30.7	2.3	33.0	19.9	13.1	
1818	18.3	3.2	21.5	20.0	1.5	
1819	20.6	4.0	24.6	21.5	3.1	
1820	15.1	2.7	17.8	18.2		.4
1821	13.0	1.5	14.5	15.8		1.3
1822	17.7	2.5	20.2	14.9	5.3	
1823	19.1	1.4	20.5	14.7	5.8	
1824	17.9	1.4	19.3	20.2		.9
1825	20.1	1.7	21.8	15.8	6.0	
1826	23.3	.9	25.2	17.0	8.2	
1827	19.7	3.2	22.9	16.1	6.8	
1828	23.2	1.5	24.7	16.3	8.4	
1829	22.6	2.2	24.8	15.1	9.7	
1830	21.9	2.9	24.8	15.1	9.7	
1831	24.2	4.3	28.5	15.2	13.3	
1832	28.4	3.4	31.8	17.2	14.6	
1833	29.0	4.9	33.9	23.0	10.9	

76. Difficulties in Management of the Funded Debt.

After 1822 the principal difficulty in managing the debt was due to surpluses which constantly accrued and could not be conveniently used in liquidation of the public debt except by the purchase of government securities bought at a premium in the open market. As the war loans for 1812 to 1816 ran for twelve years, there was little opportunity for free application of surplus revenue to debt extinguishment. In 1826 $19,000,000 became due; in 1827 another large block fell in, — each much more than the sinking fund could discharge; in 1829 and 1830, however, no part of the public debt was to fall due. Policy suggested that the excess of debt which could not be discharged in 1826 and 1827 should be thrown in equal proportions upon those years in which nothing was payable. Three attempts consequently were made to refund the debt under provisions by which annual payments might be made and the interest charge lowered. None of these were successful because of the low rate of interest offered, the brief period before redemption, and the growing activity in commercial and manufacturing operations which afforded inducements to the investment of capital. Under the act of May 26, 1824, conversions were made into stock at 4½ per cent. interest; $4,454,000 redeemable in eight or nine years, and $5,000,000 redeemable any time after 1831. Other slight conversions, $1,539,000, were made under the act of March 3, 1825. So favorable were the finances that after 1825, in spite of the handicap incident to fixed loans, the debt was rapidly paid off.

In reorganizing the finances at the close of the war an important change was made in the arrangement of the sinking fund. When the annual payment was increased to $10,000,000 in 1817 there stood on the books of the treasury to the credit of the commissioners of the sinking fund nearly $34,000,000 stock of fourteen different descriptions and bearing seven different rates of interest; interest as it accrued was paid into the fund with no other effect than of adding to the labors of those who wished to understand the accounts of the government. It seemed best to simplify the operations of the fund, and therefore it was ordered that all certificates of public debt when redeemed should be destroyed. "In the redemption plan of 1817," says Ross, "the sinking fund reaches almost the extreme of simplicity. It is true the payment on behalf of the public debt still went to a separate account, and was payable in theory to a special board. But the cunning and complicated apparatus of Hamilton and the English financiers had been done away with. There was no fixed payment on account of the principal of the debt, no inviolable appropriation, no sinking fund composed of specific items of revenue, no contract with the creditors, no automatic purchasing machinery, no borrowing on behalf of the fund, no hoarding of paid-off debt, and no payment of interest thereon."[1]

[1] Ross, *Pub. of Amer. Econ. Assn.*, vol. 7, p. 384.

CHAPTER VIII.

TARIFF LEGISLATION, 1818-1833.

77. References.

BIBLIOGRAPHIES: Channing and Hart, 364, 370-372; W. MacDonald, *Select Documents*, 284 (1833).

TARIFF: (i) SOURCES, *American State Papers, Finance* III, 234-240 (Secretary Crawford, Jan 20, 1818), 440, 526, 563, 582, 594-660 (memorials, etc., 1820-1821); IV, 467, 482 (memorials, 1824); V, 656, et seq. (memorials, 1827-1828), 778-845 (report of Mallary, Jan. 31, 1828); *Finance Reports*, II, 223 (Crawford, 1822), 319-326 (Rush, 1825), 361-365 (Rush, 1826), 396-411 (Rush, 1827); III, 232 (McLane, 1831), 289-293 (McLane, 1832); *Annals of Congress*, 16th Cong., 2d Sess. (1820); 18th Cong., 1st Sess., Part II (1824); *Register of Debates*, 20th Cong., 1st Sess. (1828); 22d Cong., 2d Sess. (1833); or *Benton's Abridgment*, VI, 601-651 (1820); VII, 568 et seq.; VIII, 9-37 (1824); IX, 589 et seq.; X, 54-118 (1828); XI, 44-107 et seq. (1832); XII, 81-181 (1833); *Messages and Papers*, II, 106, 191 (Monroe); 413 (Adams); 449, 523, 597, (Jackson); *Statutes*, III, 460, 461 (1818); IV, 25 (1825); 270 (1828); 403, 413 (1830); 583, 629 (1833); E. Young, *Customs Tariff Legislation*, xli-l, (1824), l-lxviii (1828), lxxii (1832), lxxxiii (1833); W. MacDonald, *Select Documents*, 231-237 (protests of S. C. and Ga., 1828); H. Clay, *Speeches* (ed. 1857) I, 218-237 (1820), 254-294 (1824), 416-428, 437-486 (1832), 536-569 (1833); H. Clay in *American Orations*, III, 338-373 (1832); J. Madison, *Letters*, III, 430; IV, 232; J. C. Calhoun, *Works* (ed. 1853); II, 163-172; D. Webster, *Works*, III, 94-149 (1824), 228-237 (1828); T. H. Benton, *Thirty Years in the U. S. Senate*, I, 95-102 (1828), 265-275 (1832), 297-346 (1833); *Report of Committee of Citizens of Boston* (1828); A. Gallatin, *Free Trade Memorial*, in *State Papers and Speeches* (Taussig ed.), 108-210 (1831). (ii) SPECIAL: Bolles, II, 370-433; F. W. Taussig, *Tariff History*, 19-24, 31-36, 40-45, 50-67, 68-112 (additional references in foot-notes); O. L. Elliott, *The Tariff Controversy*, 215-268; U. Rabbeno, *American Commercial Policy*, 146-183; D. F. Houston, *Study of Nullification in S. C.* (1896), see "Tariff" in index; W. M. Grosvenor, *Does Protection Protect?* 125-131, 141-145, 176-201; S. B. Harding, *Minimum Principle in the Tariff of* 1828, in *Annals Amer. Acad. Pol. Sci.*, VI, 100-114; H. P. Winston, *Tariff and the Constitution*, in *Journal of Polit. Econ.*, V, 40-70 (valuable references). (iii) GENERAL: W. G. Sumner, *Jackson*, 194-206 (1816-1828); 207-223, 281-291 (nullification);

C. Schurz, *Henry Clay*, I, 213–221 (1824); 356–366; II, 1–22 (nullification); H. C. Lodge. *Webster*, 156–166 (position in 1828); H. von Holst, *Calhoun*, 66–78 (nullification); H. von Holst, *Constitutional History of the U. S.*, I, 402–408; J. Parton, *Life of Jackson*, III, 34–36 (1824), 433 et seq. (nullification); J. G. Blaine, *Twenty Years in Congress*, I, 189–192; H. Adams, *Life of Gallatin*, 640–642 (1832); McMaster, IV, 510–521 (1820); V, 229–267 (1820–1828); Schouler, III, 420–426 (1828); IV, 54–109 (1833); Stanwood, I, 160–409.

CUSTOMS ADMINISTRATION: *Finance Reports*, III, 11–16 (Ingham, 1829), 91–94 (1830); *Statutes*, I, 627; III, 433; IV, 270, 409; J. D. Goss, *History of Tariff Legislation* (Stud. Columbia Col., 1891), 27–47; Bolles, II, 478–499.

78. Struggle for Increased Protection; Tariff of 1824.

The principal financial question in the decade 1820–1830 relates to the frequent changes in the tariff, which finally reached an average of duties entirely unanticipated and disturbing in its results. The framing of the successive schedules, however, was hardly a fiscal process; any full treatment of tariff history during this period would require not only careful inquiry into the economic development of the country, but also a study of the growing sectional antagonism between the North and South and of underlying political theories. The tariff act of 1816 had hardly gone into effect before it was regarded as incomplete; for while protection had been granted to the textile industries, and especially to cotton manufactures, no acceptable provision had been made for the iron interest. American iron producers suffered competition on the one side from England, whose pig and rolled iron were manufactured at a lower cost of production on account of the almost universal use of coke; and on the other from the charcoal iron of Sweden and Russia, where forests were extensive and labor was cheap. By a special tariff act April 20, 1818, the duties on iron were raised, and at the same time the protective principle was further recognized by postponing the reduction of the duties on cotton and woollens until 1826.

Influenced by the industrial and financial distress of 1819, which caused unfavorable treasury balances, Secretary Crawford recommended in successive reports a change in the tariff for the purpose of increasing the revenue, and he distinctly voiced a protective note: "It is believed that the present is a favorable moment for affording effective protection to that increasing and important interest [i.e., cotton, woollen, and iron manufactures] if it can be done consistently with the general interest of the nation." It was urged that higher duties would bring foreign capital and labor to the United States, and incorporate them into the domestic resources of the Union. Manufacturers also called for more generous protection because of the fall of prices which took place with the resumption of specie payments, and also to meet the rush of imports from England at the close of the Continental Wars. In spite of this open encouragement by the administration the attempt in 1820 to raise duties was unsuccessful; the bill passed the House but was defeated in the Senate by one vote. The administration continued its recommendations for increase of duties, and this question along with that of internal improvements began to affect national parties and presidential campaigns. In 1824 a general revision was entered upon; further protection was granted to the manufacturers of wool, iron, hemp, lead, and glass; and duties were raised on silk, linens, cutlery, and spices. A specific duty was imposed upon raw wool, and wool-growers for the first time became an important factor in the framing of American tariffs. The principle of minimum value was extended from cotton to woollen goods; hemp manufactures were taxed 25 per cent.; and on cotton goods the minimum valuation was raised so as to protect certain finer grades of fabric.

The clashing of sectional interests was clearly apparent in the debate upon this measure. In general the bill was supported by a combination of the Western and Middle States, and opposed both by the planting interests of the South and by commercial interests in the East. By sections the vote in the House of Representatives was as follows: —

	In favor	Opposed
New England	15	23
Middle States	60	15
West	18	0
South	1	57
Southwest (Tennessee and Kentucky)	13	7
Total	107	102

Iron, wool, hemp, glass, and lead were allied against commerce. Kentucky desired protection for its dew-rotted hemp, which suffered from the competition of the water-rotted hemp of Russia; the Middle States and Ohio desired a higher tax on wool; Pennsylvania was firm for additional duties on iron. In New England the States of Maine, New Hampshire, and Massachusetts gave but 3 votes in favor to 22 in opposition. Webster at this time represented a commercial district of Boston, and his speeches well illustrate the attitude of the navigating and importing interests of a section of New England. A few years earlier, in 1820, in a speech at Faneuil Hall before a public meeting called to protest against an increase of duties, he declared, "I feel no desire to push capital into extensive manufactures faster than the general progress of our wealth and population propels it. I am not in haste to see Sheffields and Birminghams in America. It is the true policy of government to suffer the different pursuits of society to take their own course, and not to give excessive bounties or encouragements to one over another." And in 1824 his speech in Congress in favor of freedom of trade was exhaustive, and proved to be a troublesome stumbling-block when New England later changed to the protective principle. Owing to the protest of such leaders the act of 1824 fell far short of the protection proposed in the bill originally introduced. The woollen manufacturers complained of the inconsistent treatment of their staple; for the duty on raw wool had been increased more than that on the finished product, and the sheep flocks in the United States could not supply more than one-half of the wool needed. The duty on imported woollens, the cost of which exceeded 33⅓ cents per yard, was raised from 25 to 33⅓ per cent.; the tax on raw wool was increased from a level ad valorem rate of 15 per cent. to a progressively increasing duty of 30 per cent. on all wool costing over 10 cents per pound, and, this, it was estimated, destroyed at least 5 per cent. of the new duty on cloth. There is thus early seen an illustration of the difficulty — absolutely insoluble — of adjusting the interests of wool-growers and cloth manufacturers to their common satisfaction. Wool manufacturers complained also of the duties on the raw materials entering into their business, such as olive oil and castile soap, and when they looked abroad they saw new evils to contend with. England had reduced her duty on raw wool, giving to manufacturers of that country an advantage in foreign competition which they had not hitherto enjoyed.

The old abuse of undervaluation of imports was growing more serious, so that the schedule of ad valorem duties did not give the degree of protection which might have been expected. A large part, some say four-fifths, of the wool manufactures were imported by and on account of foreigners, a practice which afforded opportunity for extremely low valuations. The industrial crisis of 1825 in England also served to throw upon the American market a large amount of goods to be sold at bankrupt prices, and embarrassment was occasioned by over-expansion of industry after the long period of depression, which in many instances led to a ruinous domestic competition.

79. Tariff of 1828.

From 1824 there was unceasing agitation of the tariff, headed by the woollen manufacturers, who insisted upon higher duties. Massachusetts now took a prominent part in the discussion, and Webster's constituents imposed upon him the awkward duty of presenting to the House of Representatives resolutions passed by the legislature asking for further protection to woollens. In

January, 1827, the so-called Mallary bill was reported in harmony with these demands; it aimed particularly at a full establishment of the minimum principle; but, though it passed the House, it was lost in the Senate by the casting vote of the vice-president, Calhoun. The failure of the Mallary bill led to an important development in the contest for higher duties, in spite of the fact that business had regained its courage after the slight depression of 1825–1826, and that prosperity at the moment seemed wide-spread. The cotton industry had become more thoroughly established during this period; a beginning had been made in the exportation of cotton goods; and the cotton manufacturers were not eager for a revision of the tariff. The experience of seventy years has shown that claims for assistance from government cannot stand isolated upon their special merits, but that the demand of one interest starts up appeals from all. The agitation by the woollen industry consequently led to a general campaign for increased protection; in 1827 a convention of the friends of protection was held in Harrisburg, and a scheme for a thorough-going protective policy was set forth in a memorial to Congress and in an address to the people.

The enlargement of the plan of attack so as to include the whole circle of manufacturing interests led to unforeseen political complications and intrigues, which in turn resulted in a tariff act, approved as a whole by few if any of the intelligent advocates of the protective principle, and calculated to excite the intensest irritation on the part of sections and interests not directly benefited. Clay, Adams, and Jackson were all candidates for the presidency, and the tariff question was raised to such prominence in the contest that it became necessary for each to make a public statement of his position. As far as the record went there was little to choose; they were all protectionists; Clay and Adams were advocates and propagandists, and even Jackson in 1824, in a letter much talked about, had frankly stated his approval of "adequate and fair protection." He rang the changes on the home market idea and concluded that "it is time we should become a little more Americanized, and, instead of feeding the paupers and laborers of Europe, feed our own, or else in a short time by continuing our present policy we shall all be paupers ourselves." Jackson's friends apparently, however, thought it wise in 1828 to be more wary, and so clinch Jackson's election to the presidency; it would not do to alienate a possible following in the North, while in the Southern States with the growing hostility to protection no candidate openly avowing the newer protection as the guide of his political life could hope for success. Recourse was consequently had to political strategy, which it was hoped would prevent legislation and sufficiently befog public opinion to make it easy for Jackson's friends to win support both North and South.

The details of this intrigue are well worth recounting, for they illustrate the willingness of politicians during the second quarter of the century to sacrifice clear-cut conviction to political expediency. At the time no satisfactory explanation was given for the astonishing law of 1828, but later Calhoun publicly stated the facts as he understood them. The House committee on manufactures was so organized as to give control to the friends of Van Buren, who were supporting Jackson in the Middle and Western States. The plot was to report a bill protective in character but carrying such high duties on raw materials that it would be extremely burdensome to the manufacturers of New England; the dissatisfied elements were then expected to join with the South, which was opposed to protection in any form, and their combined effort could prevent the passage of any bill. Thus the prestige of Adams and Clay would be weakened and Jackson would not be committed. McDuffie on a later occasion confessed as to his motives in regard to the measure, "We saw that this system of protection was about to assume gigantic proportions and to devour the substance of the country, and we decided to put such ingredients in the chalice as would poison the monster and commend it to his own lips."

The first part of the program was successfully carried out; the Committee's bill recommended an increase not only on hammered and bar iron, but also on pig and rolled iron, concerning which even the Harrisburg protectionist convention had made no request. The duty on hemp, which was increased nominally in behalf of the Kentucky product, naturally added to the expense of rope-makers, shipbuilders, and shipowners, and the duty on wool was changed to a mixed specific and ad valorem duty, in order to make effective the taxation of the coarse and cheaper varieties of wool in the production of which American farmers took little interest. On coarse woollen goods, used largely by the slaves in the South, low duties were continued, but, what was more objectionable, the minimum valuation for the first time was applied to woollens. The Harrisburg convention recommended that all woollen goods between 40 cents and $2.50 a yard be valued at the higher sum; the committee, however, inserted a minimum point at $1.00; recommended doubling the duty on molasses, and struck out the customary drawback on exported rum which had been distilled from imported molasses. These provisions were obviously oppressive to many established industries in the North and Pennsylvania, and it was supposed that the burdens were made so heavy that a revolt would follow.

The plans miscarried; the bill was indeed made odious, but so strong was the protective sentiment that the measure found acceptance in each branch of Congress. Its predominating note was protection to the woollen manufacturers, and the measure is frequently referred to as the "Woollen Tariff." Raw wool also received further protection; under the act of 1824 it was taxed 30 per cent. ad valorem, while under this bill it was subject both to an ad valorem duty of 40 per cent. and to a specific duty of 4 cents a pound, — the first compound duty in the tariffs of the United States. With some exceptions all woollen cloths paid 45 per cent. ad valorem; all cloths costing not to exceed 50 cents were valued at that sum, cloths costing

50 cents to $1.00 were valued at $1.00, those costing $1.00 up to $2.50 were valued at $2.50, those between $2.50 and $4.00 as if worth $4.00, and those exceeding $4.00 in value were taxed 50 per cent. ad valorem. We have in this complicated schedule practically an extension of the minimum principle first applied to cottons in 1816. The insertion of a minimum at $1.00 was regarded by many protectionists as a traitorous blow at their system; it offered a great temptation to undervalue goods which cost above the $1.00 limit so as to secure the advantages of the lower rate, and the results quickly showed themselves in fraudulent undervaluations. In spite of the forcibly expressed disappointment of woollen manufacturers at that time the act of 1828 in later years came to hold a proud position in the hearts of protectionists.

The tariff act of 1828 represented the high-water mark of protective legislation before the Civil War; it was generally condemned, and derisively termed the "Black Tariff" and the "Tariff of Abominations." It also led to important political results in the development of nullification in South Carolina. As in 1824, so in 1828, the votes on the tariff do not throw much light on party opinion; support was sectional as well as factional, as is seen in the following distribution of the votes in the House of Representatives: —

	In favor	Opposed
New England	16	23
Middle States	57	11
West	17	1
South	3	50
Southwest (Tennessee and Kentucky)	12	9
Total	105	94

From the South there was strong opposition to the tariff, and yet in the Senate Benton of Missouri and R. M. Johnson of Kentucky voted in its favor. It also received the support of the Northern Democrats, Van Buren, Buchanan, and Silas

Wright. In the House the entire delegation of Kentucky, Clay's State, voted in favor, while Jackson's State, Tennessee, was unanimously against it. Massachusetts, which had vigorously engaged in manufacturing under the stimulus of the tariff of 1824, was now divided : its delegation in the House of Representatives voted almost solidly against it, while Webster in the Senate made a powerful speech in its support, and confessed his conversion to the protective doctrine under stress of circumstances; since New England had accepted the act of 1824, and had entered upon manufactures with an earnest purpose, the nation was bound to fulfil the hopes which had been extended.

80. Intense Opposition to the Tariff.

The act of 1828 rekindled in the Southern States an opposition to the protective policy. A contest was inevitable, for the industrial interests of the South and the rest of the country were profoundly different. The South with its natural advantages for the growing of cotton, rice, and tobacco, and with abundant rude slave labor, was devoted solely to the production of a few staple agricultural commodities, and witnessed with indifference if not with impatience the building up of diversified industries and manufacturing cities. Indifference and impatience were converted into open hostility as soon as it was felt that this development was at the expense of its own profit. By her natural resources the South was equipped for a magnificent development of manufactures. The two great raw materials cotton and iron belonged to her inheritance; she had abundant water-power and fuel; but the institution of slavery necessarily restricted the productive genius of the South and forced her industries into grooves from which there then seemed no escape. The interest of the South obviously lay in free trade with England, which was its principal customer for cotton, hemp, and tobacco; and it was ingeniously reasoned that a tax on imports was in incidence a tax on exports.

Politically the act of 1828 gave strength to the development of the nullification doctrine, or the right of an individual State to declare a federal law null and void within State limits. As early as 1825 the legislature of South Carolina had adopted resolutions declaring that protective duties were unconstitutional; in 1827 the destructive policy of nullification was proposed at a public dinner in that State; and after the passage of the law of 1828 tariff meetings were held in the more important towns of that State, and threats made that South Carolina would separate from the Union unless the new tariff laws were repealed. Calhoun then renounced without reservation the national views which had governed his vote in 1816 and as leader of the movement declared that the tariff act was unconstitutional and must be destroyed. Great were the hopes entertained that Jackson, a Southern planter and slaveholder, would feel sympathy with this anti-tariff protest; South Carolina earnestly supported him for the presidency, and for a time after the first burst of indignation awaited his declarations in hopeful anticipation.

Jackson proved to be lukewarm, and it was even suspected that he cared little to reduce the tariff but was rather in favor of distributing the surplus. Unsuccessful attempts were made to reduce the duties on woollens, cottons, iron, hemp, flax, molasses,. and indigo to the rates existing previous to 1824. The most that could be accomplished was the reduction of the duties on salt, molasses, coffee, and tea, May 20 and 29, 1830; but the lowering of rates on articles in which domestic manufacturers were not interested could hardly be regarded as a weakening of the protective policy. The protectionists moreover added to their triumphs by the passage of a bill providing that custom-house appraisals be made more stringent and effective. The high-tariff party was, however, in perplexity because impost duties were still so productive that the revenue ran into surpluses with the prospect of a speedy extinction of the debt. Hence Clay in 1830 introduced a resolution into the Senate providing that duties upon articles imported from foreign countries and not coming in competition with the industries of the United States ought to be forthwith abolished, except the duties on wines and silks; and that those ought to be reduced. In 1831 representative national meetings of the advocates of protection and of free trade were held, — the former in New York and the latter in the protectionist stronghold, Philadelphia. Each appealed to the people and to Congress in memorials which summarized the representative arguments of the day.

81. Tariff of 1832.

The "abominations" of the tariff of 1828 were recognized by many Northern manufacturers, and the demands for a modification of the tariff were not confined to the South nor to the supporters of free-trade doctrines, yet Clay stood forth to champion without essential abatement his perfected theory of the "American System." When John Quincy Adams, now a representative in the House, suggested the possible advantage of a conciliatory policy, Clay declared that the contest was in a large measure imaginary, and relying upon his power of argument he reintroduced in the Senate, January 9, 1832, his resolutions of 1830; and in speeches on four different days he elaborated a defence of the American System.

The issue was made specific by the introduction into the House of several tariff propositions. First there was the report of the committee on ways and means, of which George McDuffie was chairman, which may be regarded as representative of the demands of South Carolina; it recommended that duties be lowered to a general ad valorem duty of 12½ per cent. on all merchandise excepting on goods already free, or on which the duties were less than 12½ per cent. Specific duties were assailed by the committee on two grounds: first that they exacted the same money duty on articles of varying value; and secondly because a lowering of the cost of manufacture under a specific duty always meant an increase in the rate.

In this report also reappears the argument that duties on goods imported were practically paid by the producers, since the exports paid for the imports. Inasmuch as the exports were chiefly cotton, rice, and tobacco, it followed from this view that the burden of import duties rested on the South. A minority report signed by two members of this committee was chiefly devoted to the effect of the tariff on prices. A rival report submitted April 27, 1832, by Louis McLane, secretary of the treasury, may be regarded as the program of the administration; it proposed to reduce the average rate of duty from 44 to 27 per cent., to reduce the duty on wool to 5 per cent. and on woollens to 20 per cent., and to abolish the minimum system on woollens except as to the lowest qualities. Neither of the two propositions could rally a sufficient support, and John Quincy Adams, as chairman of the committee on manufactures, was invited to draw up a bill. Much against his will he complied in a systematic report, dealing with the whole question both from history and economic argument; and finally he submitted a scheme of protection with an elimination of the more exasperating features of the tariff of 1828.

In the end, out of this maze of conflicting opinions, emerged the tariff act of July 14, 1832, closely based on Adams's report. In substance the act abolished the system of minimum valuation; reduced the duties on hemp and iron, and admitted free flax and wool worth less than 8 cents a pound. As Taussig observes, "The protective system was put back in the main to where it had been in 1824. The result was to clear the tariff of the excrescences which had grown on it in 1828, and to put it in a form in which the protectionists could advocate its permanent retention." Certainly the reduction of duties was not based on any theory of free trade. Revenue was still to be derived chiefly from articles requiring protection, and so far forth Clay's fundamental principle was endorsed; indeed, the tax on woollens was raised, and for the first time woollen yarn was taxed. The philosophy of protection was also clearly enunciated in all its sections, and the spirit of nullification was aroused if anything to a higher pitch. By geographical divisions the vote in the House on the tariff of 1832 was as follows: —

	In favor	Opposed
New England States	17	17
Middle States . .	52	18
West	18	0
South	27	27
Southwest	18	3
Total	132	65

The vote in the South as a whole was equally divided, owing to the strong support which the measure received in Virginia and North Carolina; in South Carolina and Georgia the opposition was great.

82. Nullification; Compromise Tariff.

After Jackson attained the presidency he was guarded in his deliverances in regard to the tariff; in his successive annual messages he suggested certain changes, but he did not protest against the tariff of 1828 as many of his Southern supporters expected, nor did he defeat the tariff measure of 1832. After his second election in 1832 he dwelt more earnestly upon the necessity of a revision; but South Carolina did not wait for legislation, and on November 24, the very month of the election, passed a nullification ordinance providing "that the tariff law of 1828, and the amendment to the same of 1832, are null and void and no law, nor binding upon this State, its officers and citizens." It was also declared that no collection of the duties enjoined by that law should be permitted in the State of South Carolina after February 1, 1833; neither should an appeal from a South Carolina court to a Federal court be allowed in any case arising from this legislation; and all officers and jurors were to take an oath to abide by this provision; goods seized by custom-house officers could be replevined by State officers.

This summary action of South Carolina was quickly met by Jackson's ringing proclamation under date of December 10, 1832; Governor Hayne issued a proclamation in return, and Calhoun, in order to be free in his action, resigned the vice-presidency and was immediately elected senator. Although Jackson was decisive in his rebuke of nullification he showed a conciliatory spirit, and Secretary McLane submitted recommendations which were made the basis of a congressional measure known as the Verplanck Bill, and reported by the committee on ways and means, December 27. The proposed measure was sweeping in its provisions, and to protectionists appeared to be a radical change of policy endangering the manufacturing system as a whole. In the first place it proposed to reduce the annual revenue from $27,000,000 to $15,000,000; secondly, and more serious, duties were to be reduced at once, without giving to the manufacturers adequate time to adjust themselves. No doubt this bill would have satisfied the extremists of South Carolina, but to the supporters of the American system it signified an industrial disaster. In this emergency Clay appeared with a new bill known in history as the compromise tariff of 1833; at bottom it recognized the principle of a horizontal rate which the nullifiers of the South regarded as essential to revision, but it was to be so gradual in its effects as to give manufacturers time to adjust their business to the change.

Although the political necessity of a settlement along lines of concession was generally recognized, the measure was not easily passed. New England and the Middle States were committed too far to protection to be willing to yield, and the West divided about evenly. By sections the vote in the House was as follows: —

	In favor	Opposed
New England . . .	10	28
Middle States . . .	24	47
West	10	8
South and Southwest	75	2
Total	119	85

The act provided for a general reduction of all duties exceeding 20 per cent.; between 1834 and 1842 duties were to be reduced by a biennial excision of one-tenth per cent. of the excess percentage above 20 per cent.; and then in January and July, 1842, the remaining excess was to be struck off. The law also enlarged the free list; but on the other hand the tariff party by strenuous insistence provided for home valuation of goods imported after 1842, and secured the abolition after 1842 of the credit system for payment of duties.

Clay's motives in fathering the act of 1833 are complex and perhaps not wholly consistent; perhaps he realized that the opposition majority in the next Congress would probably overthrow the protective system, and that if there were to be a change it should be gradual instead of summary in its action, and consequently less injurious to capital which had been recently invested. He probably wished to prevent a serious break with South Carolina, which might give Jackson an opportunity to wield military power. Perhaps also, as has been suggested, he had no expectation that the uniform 20 per cent. rate would ever go into effect.

The position of other statesmen on this measure is deserving of passing comment. Webster strictly opposed this tariff, holding that the essence of the protective principle lay in discrimination between various classes of imports which would be made inoperative by accepting a horizontal regulation. Again, Webster held that it was not only unwise but unconstitutional for Congress to bind itself for a term of years; but, more than all, he was controlled by his hostility to the States-rights philosophy. He would not yield to the South while nullification was rampant; any compromise seemed to him a reflection upon the true constitutional principles of unity and sovereignty which he so valiantly upheld. To Calhoun the measure was acceptable, partly because he was persuaded of the futility of longer carrying on the struggle against Jackson, and partly because the bill contained at bottom the principle for which the South was contending.

The tariff of 1833 is of particular interest since it contemplated a gradual reduction of duties which might give time to the capital and labor of the country to adjust themselves to the change; even the first modification was not to go into effect until nine months after the passage of the act. Fiscal experts, however, have generally been sceptical over horizontal reductions of tariff duties, inasmuch as it is impossible to foresee what will be the incidence of taxation when rates are cut uniformly on commodities varying in their supply and use. A 30 per cent. rate, for example, may be prohibitory; while a reduction to a 20 per cent. rate may allow foreign goods to compete freely with the domestic product. It is difficult to estimate the merits of the compromise tariff act as a producer of revenue, since it never went into complete effect. The disturbances to commerce, banking, and general business extending from 1834 to 1838 were so violent and due to so many causes that it is impossible to disentangle the influence of the tariff.

The compromise tariff has one unique interest in legislation because it is one of the few measures designed to limit the freedom of future Congresses over the revenue. The act was repeatedly referred to as an inviolable promise, and Calhoun for example maintained this so earnestly that he was unwilling later to abolish the admittedly unequal and odious salt tax, for fear that any change whatever would in the future give the manufacturing interests an excuse to reopen the whole tariff controversy. The average rates of duty on dutiable goods beginning with 1821, the first year in which statistics permit such comparison, were as follows:—

Year	Per cent.	Year	Per cent.
1821	35.6	1832	33.8[2]
1822	31.7	1833	31.9[3]
1823	32.7	1834	32.6
1824	37.5[1]	1835	36.0
1825	37.1	1836	31.6
1826	34.6	1837	25.3
1827	41.3	1838	37.8
1828	39.3[1]	1839	29.9
1829	44.3	1840	30.4
1830	48.8	1841	32.2
1831	40.8	1842	23.1

[1] Tariff increase. [2] Tariff revision. [3] Compromise tariff.

83. Problems of Customs Administration.

The tariff act of 1833 planned important changes in the administrative collection of customs duties. The difficulty in securing a fair valuation of the goods imported was increasing year by year, and became more serious as soon as ad valorem rates instead of specific duties constituted a considerable part of the tariff schedules. Before 1816 the value of goods was sworn to by the person making the entry, on the basis of an accompanying invoice, but when protection was accepted in earnest the need of accurate valuations was more acutely felt; authority was consequently given in 1818 to the secretary of the treasury to make an appraisement of the goods in case there were a suspicion of a fraudulent valuation. Dishonest returns might be effected by false measurements; or by returning the average for the actual cost of goods in a mixed package; or by intentional undervaluations. Another irregularity, not necessarily dishonest, came from consignments of goods by foreign manufacturers to agents in America with invoices based upon manufacturers' costs but decidedly lower than the valuation placed upon similar goods purchased by Americans in foreign markets; the home manufacturer was thus placed at a disadvantage as compared with his foreign rival.

An aggravated form of this practice was developed in the so-called auction system, by means of which the surplus holdings of English manufacturers accumulated during the long war with France were consigned and dumped on the American market at ruinous prices. This system not only led to State legislation for the control and even suppression of auctions, but had much to do with intensifying the protective sentiment of that period. In the hope of reducing these evils a law was therefore enacted in 1823 substituting for the words "actual cost," in the oath required of the importer, the phrase "just and true valuation of the goods at their fair market value"; this change did not remove reasons for complaint, and later the discretionary power of the treasury department in ordering an appraisement was made mandatory in all cases where ad valorem rates were levied.

A further mark of dissatisfaction is the provision in the compromise tariff of 1833 that a home valuation of goods imported be adopted after June 30, 1842. The clause was inserted in order to include freight as a part of the cost, and thus to increase the protection. Owing to political changes caused later by Tyler's erratic administration, the principle was not given a trial, and later during the free-trade period inaugurated in 1846 it was so sharply criticised that the proposition was allowed to drop. The chief objection made to home valuation was that it would inevitably cause different valuations of the same goods at different ports, thus violating the spirit and the letter of the Constitution, which declares that "all duties, imposts, and excises shall be uniform throughout the United States," and that "no preference shall be given by any regulation of commerce or revenue to the ports of one State over those of another." With less reason it was held that the practice would give special opportunities for fraud, since importers by fictitious or speculative transactions might control the market value at their respective ports, and thus fix the basis of the duties to be paid.

Another and a permanent change incorporated into the

compromise tariff was the abolition of credits to importers. The losses to the government under the generous system of granting credits secured by bonds had been less than might have been expected; of $781,000,000 secured in duties in the period, 1789–1830, the loss was less than $6,000,000. Nevertheless there was possibility of large loss; and it was unbusiness-like and inconsistent with sound administration for the government indirectly to loan capital to a particular mercantile interest. A still more serious defect from a fiscal point of view was that the credit system interfered with a proper adjustment of expenditures to revenue; it made it well-nigh impossible to estimate with any degree of promptitude the effect of a new tariff or to take immediate advantage of a commercial revival and increased imports. After 1842, therefore, credits were abolished, and the change to cash payments was intended somewhat to stiffen the protective system and to compensate for the lower rates which the compromise tariff of 1833 prescribed after 1842.

84. Analysis of Tariff Reasoning.

From the enactment of the compromise act of 1833 until 1861 the only warm contest over the tariff was that in 1846. Before leaving the subject it is worth while briefly to state some of the arguments which had been developed in favor and in opposition to protection of industry by the government. In the early debates on this subject what may be termed the "national independence" argument was a favorite and was forcibly used in popular appeals to patriotic constituents. It was held disgraceful that the United States should depend upon foreign nations for any articles of consumption; that independence in industry must go hand in hand with independence in political life. Europe in those days was much farther off than it is to-day; and the inconvenience of obtaining supplies was incomparably greater than at the present time. Even Hamilton was somewhat influenced by the argument; President Washington set it forth in his inaugural address in

1789, when he advised his countrymen "to promote such manufactures as tend to render them independent of others for essentials, particularly military supplies," and again more definitely in the annual address in 1796; even if commodities should by a tariff cost more in time of peace, the security and independence thence arising would prove an ample compensation. Succeeding presidents referred to this advantage with equal approbation, as for example Madison in the annual messages of 1810 and 1815 and Monroe in those of 1817 and 1823; while Clay in 1820 endeavored to attract support for the American system by contemptuously referring to the United States as an English colony of commercial slaves.

The argument for the creation of a home market to consume the surplus products of the farmers was early advanced, as by Hamilton in his great report on manufactures; and later by President Madison in 1815 and President Monroe in 1817. Mathew Carey by practical illustration pointed out the great advantages which agriculture had derived from the vicinity of manufactures at Harmony, Providence, and Pittsburgh. Finally the argument was presented in a more precise form: when the peace of 1815 changed the course of trade it was urged that Europe could no longer consume the surplus agricultural produce of the United States, for the American powers of production were increasing in a ratio four times greater than the foreign power of consumption; and, even if foreign nations could consume the surplus products of the United States, they would prefer adherence to their own restrictive laws; therefore the United States must create a home market. Even Jackson preached this doctrine: "Draw from agriculture the superabundant labor; employ it in mechanism and manufactures,—thereby creating a home market for your breadstuffs and distributing labor to the most profitable account and benefit to the country."

Of later growth was the argument that a protective tariff cheapens prices. Hamilton considered this argument, and admitted that the immediate effect of protective duties may be an increase in price, but "it is universally true that the contrary is the ultimate effect with every successful manufacture." The argument, however, was never made prominent until a quarter of a century later. Matthew Carey, in 1824, asserted that the United States saved more in one year in the cheapness and quality of commodities, particularly of cotton goods, than was lost in the time spent in maturing their manufactures. Similar ideas were expressed by President John Quincy Adams in his annual message in 1828, and the argument was especially developed by the "Friends of Domestic Industry" in their statement of 1831: on some commodities, to be sure, the prices had been increased, but by no means to the extent of the duty, and on many articles of domestic use the tariff had reduced prices to the foreign standard. Clay placed great stress upon this consideration, claiming that the tariff of 1824 had lessened the price of protected commodities, and putting forth the doctrine that "the duty never becomes an integral part of the price, except in the instances where the demand and supply remain after the duty is imposed practically what they were before, or the demand is increased and the supply remains stationary."[1] The advocates of free trade on their part met this argument with the assertion that prices were naturally falling, owing to the introduction of labor-saving machinery, and attention was directed to the fact that raw materials entering into manufactures were falling in price while gold and silver were appreciating in value.

The protectionists also laid stress upon the protective systems of Europe and asserted that the United States must be governed by the policy of foreign competing nations. Clay emphatically insisted in 1820, in 1824, and in 1832 that the question of protectionism must be decided in the face of the fact that European nations maintained restrictive systems. "I too, am a friend to free trade, but it must be free trade of perfect reciprocity." The maxim of free trade is "truth

[1] *Works*, vol. ii, p. 401. Colton's *Life*, vol. ii, p. 240.

13

in the books of European political economy. It is error in the practical code of every European State." In 1824 he declared that "if all nations would modify their policy axioms perhaps it would be better for the common good of the whole," and again in 1832 he complained that other nations would not break down their bars.

The "young industries" argument was also made much of; in the earlier development of the protectionist system it was not supposed that the policy would necessarily be permanent. "No one," said Clay in 1840, "in the commencement of the protective policy, ever supposed that it was to be perpetual. We hoped and believed that temporary protection extended to our infant manufactures would bring them up, and enable them to withstand competition with those of Europe." In like manner at a later period Henry C. Carey, who did more than any other writer clearly to formulate the protectionist reasoning, stated that restrictive duties were but a means to an end; protection was needed to attain ultimate free trade.

At first the arguments against the protective principle were general and based on the idea that manufacturing industry was not so innocent an occupation as agriculture. It was argued that labor and capital would be forced into new and reluctant employments for which this country lacked skill and ingenuity, that the manufacturing system was adverse to the genius of the American government by its tendency to accumulation of large capital and corruption of public morals. In 1822 John Taylor of Virginia published "Tyranny Unmasked," devoted to the argument that the system of protective duties would end in tyranny and monarchy. Somewhat allied to this plea was the contention of Calhoun, who in the oft-quoted speech of 1816 noted that the most serious objection which he could discover in manufactures was the dependence it caused among the employed; and later he repeatedly dwelt upon the bad effect upon politics and morals caused by the struggles for legislative favor. There was "less patriotism and purity, and more faction, selfishness, and corruption."

A purely economic objection was that advanced by Southern opponents of the tariff, beginning with about 1830, in the development of the theory that import duties are in effect direct taxes upon exports; the South was taught that a protective tariff was a system of taxation practically levied upon the productions of cotton, rice, and tobacco, which formed the bulk of the exports. This theory is based upon the principle that exports pay for the imports, and that consequently whatever increases the price of imported articles must increase the amount of exports needed to pay for a given quantity of goods. The consideration of this argument in its various refinements cannot be undertaken here, its chief interest in this connection lying in the fact that the general political reasoning of the South in regard to the powers of the federal government was in this case reinforced by economic logic of a convincing character.

A standing objection to the protective system was its unconstitutionality. After the adoption of the first tariff in 1789 it was not much urged until 1820; but after that date, with growing sectionalism developed by the slavery question, with suspicions aroused by the successive federalizing decisions of the Supreme Court, and provoked by the definite propaganda of the American system by Clay and John Quincy Adams, the constitutional objection was dwelt upon at length; it appears freely in the tariff discussion of 1824, and in 1828 the anti-tariff men tried to secure a definite issue to bring before the courts by incorporating into the tariff act of that year the preamble of the act of 1789, which declared without equivocation that the protection of domestic manufactures was one of the purposes of the act. The high-tariff party, however, would not admit the amendment, and the nullifiers afterwards claimed that the opponents of protection had denied the opportunity of an obvious and adequate legal remedy through the courts. In the same spirit Professor Sumner writes that Congress "had unquestioned power to lay taxes. How could it be ascertained what the purpose of the majority of

Congress was, when they voted for a certain tax law? How could the constitutionality of a law be tried when it turned on the question of this purpose, which in the nature of the case was mixed and unavowed."[1] In 1831 an attempt was made in South Carolina to test the constitutionality of the tariff in the courts by refusing to satisfy bonds which had been given to secure duties, and by entering a plea of "no consideration" for the taxes levied. The United States District Court, however, declined to hear evidence upon this plea.[2]

Madison, so often called the father of the Constitution, in a letter of 1827 to Mr. Cabell of Virginia expressed a "confident opinion" of the full power of Congress to protect manufactures; the phrase "to regulate trade" he understood to include the power to encourage manufactures, because that had been the use of the phrase among all nations, and particularly in Great Britain, "whose commercial vocabulary is the parent of our own"; such was the use made of the power to regulate taxes by the States so long as they retained power over foreign trade; in giving the general regulation of commerce to the federal government the people supposed that they were giving authority to protect their own industry; and the exercise of that power by the first Congress seemed to Madison conclusive evidence that they believed that the Constitution granted it.

[1] Sumner, *Jackson*, p. 285.
[2] *Ibid*, p, 220.

CHAPTER IX.

ATTACK UPON THE BANK; THE SURPLUS.

1829–1837.

85. References.

BIBLIOGRAPHIES: Bogart and Rawles, 33–37; Channing and Hart, 374–375; A. B. Hart, *Handbook of History, Diplomacy, and Government*, 160–162 (internal improvements).

BANK: (i) SOURCES, *Messages and Papers*, II, 462 (1829); 529 (1830), 576–591 (veto, July 10, 1832); Clarke and Hall, *Documentary History of Bank*, 735–777 (report of committee, 1830); T. H. Benton, *Thirty Years*, I, chs. 56, 60, 63–68, 72, 75, 77; W. MacDonald, *Select Documents*, 261–268 (veto); A. Gallatin, *Writings*, III, 328–346; *Documents*, etc., in *American History Leaflets*, No. 24 (Nov., 1825). (ii) SPECIAL: R. C. H. Catterall, *Second Bank of the U. S.*, 164–313; W. G. Sumner, *History of Banking*, 183–224; W. G. Sumner, *Jackson*, 235–249, 259–276, 291–296, 337–342; Bolles, II, 334–338; H. White, 281–313, or in *Sound Currency*, IV, No. 18; R. S. Long, *Andrew Jackson and the National Bank*, in *Eng. Hist. Review*, XII, 85–89; C. A. Conant, *History of Modern Banking*, 302–309; J. J. Knox, *History of Banking*, 62–79. (iii) GENERAL: C. Schurz, *Clay*, I, 351–378; H. von Holst, *Constitutional History of the U. S.*, II, 31–52; T. Roosevelt, *Benton*, 114–142.

REMOVAL OF DEPOSITS: (i) SOURCES, *Messages and Papers*, III, 5–19 (cabinet paper, Sept. 18, 1833); *Finance Reports*, III, 337 (Taney on removal of deposits), 451 (report, April 15, 1834); 602 (list of depositories); *Benton's Abridgment*, XII, 191 et seq.; W. MacDonald, *Select Documents*, 289–295 (cabinet paper), 295–303, 317–323 (see bibliographical note); *Statutes*, V, 52 (regulation of deposits); D. Webster, *Works*, IV; T. H. Benton, *Thirty Years*, chs. 92–101. (ii) SPECIAL: J. B. Phillips, *Methods of Keeping the Public Money*, in *Pub. Michigan Pol. Sci. Assn.* (Dec., 1900), 49–66 (references to public documents); Bolles, II, 334–339. (iii) GENERAL: J. Parton, *Jackson*, III, 499–536; H. von Holst, *History of U. S.*, II, 53–70; W. G. Sumner, *Jackson*, 296–321; C. Schurz, *Clay*, II, 23–51.

COINAGE: *Statutes*, IV, 699; V, 136; or Dunbar, 234–236; *Report of Monetary Commission*, 497 (Act of 1834); T. H. Benton, *Thirty Years*, I, chs. 105, 108; D. K. Watson, *History of Coinage*, 78–115; J. L. Laughlin, *History of Bimetallism*, 52–74.

INTERNAL IMPROVEMENTS: SOURCES, *Messages and Papers*, I, 419, 418 (Jefferson), 584 (veto of Madison, 1817); II, 142 (veto of Monroe, 1822), 483–493 (Maysville veto, 1830), 508, 683; III, 118–123; also index, "Internal Improvements" in vol. X.; *American State Papers, Miscellaneous*, I, 724 (Gallatin's report, April 12, 1808), 910–916; H. Clay, *Speeches*, II; Benton, *Thirty Years*, I, 21–27 (1824), 167 (Maysville veto). GENERAL: H. von Holst, *Constitutional History of U. S.*, I, 388–396; H. Adams, *Life of Gallatin*, 350–352 (also index); J. A. Stevens, *Gallatin*, 298–301; C. Schurz, *Clay*, I, 40–47 (1806); D. C. Gilman, *Monroe*, 239–248; W. G. Sumner, *Jackson*, 191–194.

LAND: (i) SOURCES, *Messages and Papers*, II, 305 (1825), 391 (1827), 600 (1832); *Finance Reports*, II, 175, 492 (1820); also index, "Public Lands," vols. I, II, III; A. Seybert, *Statistical Annals*, 306–308 (statistics, 1817); T. H. Benton, *Thirty Years*, I, II (1821), 102–107; A. Gallatin, *Writings*, I, 297. (ii) SPECIAL: A. B. Hart, *Disposition of our Public Lands*, in *Quar. Jour. Econ.*, I, 169–183, 251–254; C. F. Emerick, *Government Loans to Farmers*, in *Pol. Sci. Quar.*, XIV, 444; S. Sato, *History of the Land Question*, in *J. H. U. Studies*, IV (1886), 121–158; Bolles, II, 545; H. Adams, *Finance*, 255–260. (iii) GENERAL: W. G. Sumner, *Jackson*, 184–191; J. A. Stevens, *Gallatin*, 245–248.

SURPLUS AND DISTRIBUTION: (i) SOURCES, *Messages and Papers*, II, 451 (1829), 514 (1830); III, 56–69 (veto, Dec. 4, 1833), 239–246 (1836), 260 (table); *Finance Reports*, III, 228 (1831), 476 (1834), 643–646 (1835), 686–690 (1836); *Statutes*, V, 55; or Dunbar, 115; T. H. Benton, *Thirty Years*, I, 275–279, 362–368, 556–568, 649–658, 702–712; Benton's *Abridgment*, XI, 446, 492 et seq.; XII, 24, 124; H. Clay, *Speeches*, II; D. Webster, *Works*, IV. (ii) SPECIAL: E. G. Bourne, *History of the Surplus Revenue of* 1837, pp. 169 (bibliography). J. J. Knox, *U. S. Notes*, 167–182, 190–192; Bolles, II, 547. (iii) GENERAL: C. Schurz, *Clay*, II, 118–123; W. G. Sumner, *Jackson*, 325–331; T. Roosevelt, *Benton*, 143–156.

86. Criticism of the Bank.

In the two preceding chapters certain phases of fiscal experience extending through Jackson's first presidential term have been considered, as for example the state of the budget and the development of the tariff. The evolution of these branches of administration was but little disturbed by the change from President Adams to President Jackson; the fate of other financial subjects of importance, as for example the control of government funds, was, however, profoundly affected at once by Jackson's accession to power, so that it is necessary to return to the beginning of his term of office. Brief mention should be made of Jackson's secretaries. His first secretary of the treasury was S. D. Ingham of Pennsylvania, a manufacturer and a member of the House of Representatives for many years; he was a devoted worker for Jackson, not above taking part in the "bargain and corruption" cry against Clay. Ingham's qualifications for the treasury are not apparent, but Jackson did not demand a high standard. Ingham fell from grace in the famous Mrs. Eaton affair, and retired in April, 1831. For some months the department was without a secretary. On August 8, 1831, Louis McLane of Delaware was appointed; he was a man of ability who had achieved distinction in diplomacy at London; he was inclined toward federalism and had supported the bank; and while secretary he assisted in the preparation of the tariff bill known as the Verplanck measure. Opposed to the removal of the deposits from the custody of the United States Bank he was transferred to the department of state, May, 1833, when William J. Duane took his place. Duane, as will be seen, was quickly followed by Taney, who in turn gave way, June 27, 1834, to Levi Woodbury of New Hampshire; the latter held office throughout the remainder of Jackson's administration and that of Van Buren.

Underneath the apparent great prosperity of the bank of the United States there were, as has been indicated, forces ready to be aroused into hostility. The conflict between the bank and some of the States in their effort to tax branches of the bank left memories which boded no good; and the check which the bank exercised over inflated note issues of local institutions, while recognized as one of the fundamental reasons for the establishment of the bank in 1816, made lasting enemies. There was still a deeper agency at work which led to the final overthrow of the bank, — the revival of Jeffersonian democracy, which was displayed in many interesting ways about the year 1830: monopolies must be put down and it was held high time for a return to the simpler principles of the fathers of political democracy. Into the various manifestations of this movement it is impossible here to enter, but this phase of public opinion needs to be reckoned with, in order to account for the rapid downfall of the bank which, as a financial institution, had been on the whole wisely managed since 1819.

Open hostility to the bank, as first disclosed in 1829, was apparently prompted by local intrigues in the hope of making political capital; in June, 1829, Senator Woodbury of New Hampshire brought complaints against Jeremiah Mason, manager of the Portsmouth branch, alleging that Mason was not altogether civil in his manners, and was partial to anti-Jackson men in making loans and collections. It is doubtful if this incident had much real significance; Jackson's election was really due to the rising tide of democracy and especially the democracy of the West and pioneer settlements; and his position towards the bank was indicated in his first message to Congress, December, 1829, in which he affirmed that both the constitutionality and the expediency of the law creating the bank were questionable, and accused the bank of not establishing a uniform and sound currency. In its place he would have a bank, as a branch of the treasury department, based upon public and private deposits without power to make loans or to purchase property. A bank of this character would not be able to operate on the hopes, fears, or interests of large masses of the community, and would thus be shorn of the influence which made the present bank formidable.

The president's reference to the bank was made the basis of inquiry in both Houses of Congress. The House Committee in its report of April 13, 1830, favorably discussed the bank from three points of view: first, its constitutionality; second, its expediency; and, third, — in accordance with the vague suggestion made by Jackson in his message, — the wisdom of founding a different institution upon the credit and revenues of the government. The argument in favor of the expediency of the bank was practically a currency argument; it set forth that the dispute was not between an issue of paper currency and metallic currency, but between a national paper currency and a local paper currency. Since Congress had no constitutional power to forbid the issue of paper money by State banks, local bank-notes would circulate, and it was not worth while to discuss the superior advantages of a specie currency. The question therefore arose: Is it not better to have a staple currency which by virtue of its uniformity of value will prevent local bank-notes from circulating far from the place of issue? And the committee was convinced that the United States Bank by its notes did actually furnish such a circulating medium, more satisfactory even than specie. If the current medium were confined to specie, a planter in Louisiana who wished to purchase merchandise in Philadelphia would be obliged to pay 1 per cent. for a bill of exchange on Louisiana, covering the transportation and insurance of the specie, — an expense of which one-half was saved through the issue of drafts. Again, the bank was shown to have performed with most scrupulous punctuality its stipulation to transfer free of expense the funds of the government to any point where they might be wanted.

The committee had no sympathy with a bank resting on the credit and revenues of the government as suggested by Jackson; only the discretion and prudence of the government could then be relied upon to limit excessive issues of bills, and this frail dependence would not prevent inflated issues comparable to the paper money of the Revolution. Such a fiscal institution would surely get into politics; it would lead to a corrupt use of political patronage; all holders of government notes would be government debtors; political parties would be divided upon the question of adopting a strict or a liberal policy toward these debtors; and there would be every temptation to rely upon issues of the bank rather than upon taxation to supply the government treasury. The Senate report was equally favorable to the bank, and bank stock, which had fallen from 125 to 116, rose to 130.

87. Unsuccessful Effort to Recharter.

The real war upon the bank was yet to begin. In 1831 Senator Benton introduced a resclution against rechartering the bank. He took logical and effective ground by demanding the use of gold currency in place of bank-notes, and his steady attack along this line year after year gained for him the title of "Old Bullion." His denunciation of branch drafts, as expressed in a speech delivered in 1832, was comprehensive: the currency of the bank was not signed by the president of the bank; the notes were not issued under the corporation seal; they were not drawn in the name of the corporation; they were not subject to the double limitation of time and amount as in case of credit; they were not limited to the minimum size of five dollars; they were not subject to the supervision of the secretary of the treasury; they were not subject to the prohibition against suspending specie payment; they were not subject to the penalty of double interest for delayed payment; they were not payable at the place where issued; they were not payable at other branches; they were transferable not by delivery but by endorsement; they were not receivable in payment of public dues; the directors were not liable for excessive issues, and finally the holder had no right to sue at the branch which issued the order: he could only go to Philadelphia and sue the director there; a right about equivalent to the privilege of going to Mecca to sue the successors of Mahomet for the bones of the Prophet.

Charges of this character were too academic to attract much popular attention, but Jackson's pertinacity and downright positiveness that the bank was unsound made an impression upon the politicians and the people. The unseasonable activity of the bank in its own behalf in every possible direction, in the press, in pamphlets, and in political campaigns, also aroused suspicion as to whether it might not be well for the people to bestir themselves and at least to inquire into the question. In January, 1832, a petition for recharter was introduced in Congress and was favorably reported upon by committees in the Senate and in the House. The opponents of the Bank promptly attempted to counteract any favorable impression which this endorsement might give by securing once more the appointment in the House of a special committee to investigate the bank. Three reports were the result: though the majority was now adverse, accusing the bank of practising usury, of the issue of branch drafts, of making gifts to roads and canals, and of building houses to rent or sell, most of the charges were regarded by the House as inconsequential, and the bill for rechartering was passed, receiving, as might have been expected, the veto of the president (July 10, 1832). Jackson's message presented with force and earnest conviction the dangers of a money monopoly: "Is there no danger to our liberty and independence in a bank that in its nature has so little to bind it to our country? The president of the bank has told us that most of the State banks exist by its forbearance. Should its influence become concentred, as it may under the operation of such an act as this, in the hands of a self-elected directory, whose interests are identified with those of the foreign stockholders, will there not be cause to tremble for the purity of our elections in peace, and for the independence of our country in war?" If it were wise, he continued, to establish such a monopoly, the government ought to receive a fair equivalent; the value of the monopoly was estimated as at least $17,000,000, which under the terms of the bill it was proposed to barter away for $3,000,000. Although Congress was unable to pass the measure over the president's veto, it rejected Jackson's other recommendation made a few months later that the government should sell all its bank stock, in order to disconnect itself from corporations and all business pursuits which might properly be regarded as belonging to individuals.

88. Removal of the Deposits.

To understand the next incident in the contest between Jackson and the bank demands a reference to the statutory relations of the government and the bank. Section 16 of the Bank Act of 1816 provided "that the deposits of the money of the United States shall be made in said bank or branches thereof, unless the secretary of the treasury shall at any time otherwise order and direct; in which case the secretary of the treasury shall immediately lay before Congress, if in session, and if not, immediately after the commencement of the next session, the reasons of such order or direction." In accordance with this provision most of the funds of the government had been deposited with the bank, and until Jackson stirred up trouble no one had suggested a different policy. The question of general control of the government over the bank was first distinctly raised in a correspondence in 1829 between Biddle and Ingham, secretary of the treasury, who simply reflected Jackson's views. Biddle met the criticism squarely; he not only denied the power of the secretary of the treasury to exercise any supervision over the choice of officers of the bank or their political opinions, but he also maintained that the bank was responsible only to Congress, and was carefully shielded by its charter from executive control. To this Ingham replied that the bank was organized for national purposes and for the common benefit of all. Apparently the controversy did not have any immediate practical significance, and for the time being this phase of the subject dropped from sight.

In December, 1832, Jackson, spurred on to further activity by his re-election, which he properly regarded as a popular endorsement of his position, called attention to certain transactions of the bank in dealing in government stock, as contrary to its charter, and suggested that possibly the funds of the government were not safe, and that at least an investigation should be made. Another inquiry was thereupon ordered; not only did the majority of the committee on ways and means report that the funds were secure, but a special agent of the treasury came to the same conclusion. A minority of the committee sided with Jackson, made a slighting reference to some of the assets of the bank, and brought to view once more the evil practice of the Western branches of the bank in issuing accommodation bills. The House adopted the majority report on March 2, 1833, by a vote of 109 to 46.

An unfortunate incident for the bank occurred at this juncture: the treasury drew through the bank for nearly a million dollars on account of a payment due from France under the treaty of July 4, 1831; the French treasury for political reasons in turn protested the draft, and the bank was involved in a troublesome settlement of the account. To Jackson this was another proof of the insolvency of the bank, and when Biddle, in the interest of maintaining an easy money market, advised in 1832 against the immediate paying off a large portion of the 3 per cent. debt largely held by foreigners, and agreed to continue the account of treasury funds which was available for this purpose as a deposit account at interest, Jackson was more than ever convinced that the bank counselled delay because it had spent the government's money. The president's remarks are thus quoted: "I tell you, sir, she 's broke. Mr. Biddle is a proud man and he never would have come on to Washington to ask me for a postponement if the bank had had the money. Never, sir. The bank 's broke, and Biddle knows it." The president, therefore, was little influenced by the vote of confidence in the bank by the House, and determined at all hazards to break off all relations between the bank and the government.

Before Jackson could carry out his plan of removal of the deposits he was obliged to run amuck of his own official advisers. McLane, who succeeded Ingham as secretary of the treasury, objected to removal except under authority of Congress, and gave way, June 1, 1833, to William J. Duane. Duane was also indisposed to act, and, though earnestly besought, refused to issue the order. Jackson persisted, and was fortunate in receiving able support and counsel from Taney, his attorney-general. Strengthened by the argument of Taney, Jackson in a cabinet meeting held in September, 1833, justified his position and explained at length his theory of the relations of the government to the public purse. According to the president the duty of superintending the operation of the executive departments of the government had been placed upon him by the Constitution and the suffrages of the American people; he was responsible for the performance of duty by the heads of departments; far be it from him, however, to expect or require that any member of the cabinet should, at his request, order, or dictation, do any act which he believed unlawful or which in his conscience he condemned. The president begged his cabinet to consider the proposed measure as his own, in the support of which he would require no one of them to make a sacrifice of opinion or principle. A measure so important to the American people could not be commenced too soon, and he therefore named October 1 as a period proper for the change of the deposits, or sooner, provided the necessary arrangements with the State banks could be made. Duane's obstinacy increased; he not only declined to issue the required order, but refused to resign. He was therefore dismissed September 23, and Taney, who had been the author of the elaborate paper which Jackson had presented at the cabinet meeting just referred to, was appointed to do the deed. Taney loyally accepted the responsibility, and on September 26 issued the order directing the deposit of public moneys henceforth in certain State banks. Strictly there was no direct removal of funds to other institutions, — the amount on deposit with the bank being quickly exhausted through drafts for the ordinary expenditures of the government.

Jackson's exposition of executive powers did not pass unchallenged; the opposition urged that the treasury department was an executive department with distinct duties from those devolved upon the president, and that Congress had designedly given a separate and individual power to the secretary in order to keep asunder the purse and the sword. More specifically it was argued that the president's powers in regard to the bank were limited by the charter of the bank to two: the appointment of the government directors, and the issuance of the writ scire facias whenever he believed the charter to have been violated. All other powers by the statute of 1816 were delegated to others; the weekly statements of the condition of the bank were made to the secretary of the treasury, and not to the president; and if any further regulations were necessary the appointment of a committee of investigation could be authorized.

Another argument was that no money could be drawn from the treasury except under authority of appropriations made by law, and that the removal of the deposits without congressional authority contravened this clause. In reply Benton argued that the bank charter provided that the bank should give the necessary facilities for transferring public funds. The secretary had signed transfer drafts to the amount of two millions and a quarter; and his legal right to withdraw funds by this process was as unquestionable as his right to remove the deposits under another clause. "The *transfer* is made by *draft*," said Benton; "a *payment* out of the treasury is made upon a *warrant;* and the difference between a transfer draft and a treasury warrant was a thing necessary to be known by every man who aspired to the office of illuminating a nation or even of understanding what he is talking about." John Quincy Adams, then in Congress, took middle ground, asserting that the secretary of the treasury simply had power to decide whether the deposits should be made in the bank, but that when once made he could not withdraw them except in accordance with appropriations made by law; the right to withdraw by ordinary payment until the deposit was exhausted was not, however, denied.

Taney's reasons for removal were stated at length in a document presented to the Senate, December 3, 1833; the weakness of this argument is that it is political rather than fiscal; he said that the charter of the bank was to expire in 1836, and as there were strong arguments against the wisdom of recharter, and the people in the presidential election of 1832 had endorsed Jackson's policy, there was no reason to suppose that future legislative action would be more favorable to the bank; it was consequently unwise to permit the deposits to remain until the close of the corporate existence of the bank. The funds must be removed sometime, and in view of the bank's determined attitude of hostility to the government it was the part of wisdom to act promptly.

With the prolonged and bitter contest between the president and his friends and the majority in the Senate, with the Senate's censure of the president and the effort to expunge the resolution from its journal, we are not here concerned. The bank was unsuccessful in its endeavor to secure a renewal of its corporate powers under a federal charter, and its interest as a fiscal institution of national importance ceased with 1836. In regard to the real merits of the question of recharter there is much to be said on each side. The strictly economic or fiscal elements of the controversy, however, are thrown in the background by the political character given to the contest. Jackson was undoubtedly driven to an aggressive policy by the fact that Clay forced his political followers to make the support of the bank a test of party loyalty in the election of 1832. The political methods used by Clay gave color to the charge that the bank was in truth a monster; President Biddle's memorial in 1832 asking for a renewal was ill worded; the tactics of the bank to secure a favorable consideration were calculated to arouse suspicion in the mind of a man like Jackson, who always prided himself on standing up for the rights of the plain people. Suspicion of the motives of the bank was certainly justified when it became known that between January, 1831, and May, 1832, the loans of the bank had been extended from $42,000,000 to $70,000,000. As in 1811, much was made of the fact that a considerable portion of the stock was owned by foreigners, and that the stock held in this country was in the control of a few citizens, chiefly of the richest class; that such a monopoly privilege ought not to be sold cheaply, and if sold at all, in the words of Jackson, it should "not be bestowed on the subjects of a foreign government nor upon a designated and favored class of men in our own country."

Clay was to a large degree responsible for the final issue, since, before the controversy became acute, intimations were made to Biddle that upon certain changes in the charter the renewal might be accepted by the president. Clay, however, counselled against modifications, and made the grave error of supposing that he could carry the presidential campaign in 1832 on this issue. Three elements of opposition were too strong for him: a personal following who wished to endorse Jackson, irrespective of any opinion on the bank question; a large party honestly opposed to a great centralized moneyed institution as dangerous to freedom; and a smaller but earnest body who opposed all bank-note issues of every sort. Of the strength of this opposition Clay was apparently not well advised; for the popular verdict in the election of 1832 was overwhelmingly in Jackson's favor, the latter receiving 219 electoral votes to 49 for Clay.

89. The Pet Banks.

The selection of State banks to hold the funds of the government was made with care, although there were many heated charges that the choice was made solely on political grounds; Jackson's "pets" became one of the catch-words of party campaigning. The conditions imposed upon the banks as a protection to the government were fairly stringent; collateral could be called for, if the secretary of the treasury deemed advisable, and must be given if the deposits exceeded one-half a bank's capital; weekly returns of the condition of the bank were required, and the bank must be open to examination at any time. Economical arrangements were also made as to the transfer of public moneys from one place to another, and for the sale of bills of exchange on London in the final settlement of the public indebtedness held abroad. The whole matter carefully defining the authority of the government and the obligations of the banks was finally covered by the act of

June 23, 1836, "regulating the deposits of public money." It was then laid down that any bank employed as a depository should credit as specie all sums deposited to the credit of the United States, and that no bank should be selected which did not redeem its notes in specie or which issued any note of a denomination less than five dollars. It was further provided that, if the deposit exceeded a fourth part of the bank's capital for at least three months, the bank should pay 2 per cent. interest on the excess deposit. Apparently the interests of the government were well safeguarded.

The number of banks with the deposits to the credit of the "treasurer" and "other officers" at successive dates was as follows: —

Date	Number of banks	Amounts
January 1, 1835	29	$10,323,000
December 1, 1835	33	24,724,000
November 1, 1836	89	49,378,000

90. Change in Coinage Ratio.

The attack made by Jackson upon the Second United States Bank and its notes issues, together with the demands of Benton for a larger use of specie and especially of gold, might, even if there had been no other forces at work, have thrust the question of metallic currency into prominence. For several years after the establishment of the mint in 1792 foreign coins remained legal tender, and the Spanish dollar and its divisions continued to form the bulk of the metallic circulation. After 1813 the great increase in paper circulation in the form of bank-notes tended to displace all forms of metal. The coinage at the mint was small; the ratio of 15 to 1, established in 1792 under the advice of Hamilton, proved to be an undervaluation of gold as established in the world's market and consequently no gold was brought to the mint; this led to an entire discontinuance of the coinage of gold eagles during the period 1805–1837, and in fact the only gold coinage between 1804 and 1834 was about nine million dollars in the form of half-eagles and a small amount of quarter-eagles at irregular intervals. The mint valuation of gold proved to be so low that even the smaller coins were rapidly exported. In the first ten years of the mint's operations a little over a million silver dollars were coined, but these too disappeared from circulation; upon inquiry it was learned that they were exchanged for Spanish dollars and left the country. The American dollar, though lighter than the Spanish, was brighter and more serviceable for certain kinds of foreign trade, and was therefore sought for by dealers, while Americans were desirous of taking the Spanish dollar because of its greater weight. President Jefferson consequently in 1806 ordered the discontinuance of the coinage of the silver dollar.

The embarrassments thus occasioned by the lack of an uniform domestic monetary medium were repeatedly brought to the attention of Congress, and various plans of remedy were proposed. A Senate committee in 1819 suggested the expediency of forbidding the export of domestic coins. Crawford, secretary of the treasury, proposed a change in the ratio of 1 to 15.75, and in 1823 made a further suggestion in favor of 1 to 16. Secretary Ingham in 1830 advised a single standard of silver; a Senate committee in the same year recommended a ratio of 1 to 15.9; and the House in the course of four years enriched monetary literature with four reports. The outcome of all this deliberation was the coinage act of June 28, 1834 (slightly amended in 1837), by which the weight of the gold dollar was reduced from 27 grains to $25\frac{8}{10}$ grains nine-tenths fine, thus establishing a ratio of approximately 1 to 16. This ratio in turn proved to be an undervaluation of silver and led to the withdrawal of silver dollars, so that after 1840 this coin was rarely seen in circulation and even the fractional coins tended to disappear. The absence of silver was a serious disadvantage to retail trade, and probably had much to do with supporting a demand for a larger supply of bank money. To keep the smaller coins in circulation the weight of the pieces less than one dollar was reduced in 1853, and they were converted into subsidiary coins.

91. Internal Improvements.

The question of federal aid for internal improvements assumed new importance during the administration of President Jackson. Ever since the first proposal of such expenditures about the beginning of the century there were grave misgivings on the part of many, due to constitutional objections, and this resulted in an uncertain policy. There were two questions involved: the respect which the national government owed a State, and the right of Congress to make direct appropriations in favor of internal improvements. The former question bore on the relations of a federal government to States, a tender subject during the period when States still imagined that they were clothed with some of the regalia of sovereignty; the second question was simply one aspect of the meaning of the "general welfare" clause of the Constitution, an enigma which never failed to provoke dispute.

The first federal grants for roads were prompted by the need of better means of communication in the territories; here the first doubt referred to was obviously not involved; the territories could not legislate for themselves, they were under the guardianship of Congress. From the time therefore that Congress made a small grant of land to a private individual in 1796 for the opening up of a road from Wheeling to Maysville, Kentucky, no objection was made to the constitutionality of such appropriations; as Benton observed in 1824, members of all political schools voted for such appropriations, "the strict constructionists generally inquiring if the road was limited to the territory, and voting for the bill if it was."

A second stream of expenditure originated in the legislation authorizing the admission of the State of Ohio, April 30, 1802, which provided that one-twentieth of the proceeds of the sales of public lands lying within Ohio, which might be sold by Congress, should be applied to the building of public roads from the navigable waters emptying into the Atlantic to the Ohio River, with the consent of the several States through which the road should pass; this 5 per cent. was then divided into two parts, three-fifths for the making of roads within the State and two-fifths for roads leading to the State: and here was the origin of the 2 per cent. and 3 per cent. funds established at the admission of many of the commonwealths. In many cases Congress by subsequent legislation transferred its share of the fund to the State on condition that the money be expended for internal improvements, — an obligation unfortunately not always kept. By an act of May 1, 1802, the secretary of the treasury was granted $6000 to open such roads in the Northwest Territory as would best serve to promote the sale of public lands. The most important step was taken in 1806, when (March 29) Congress entered upon the laying out of a road from the head-waters of the Potomac through Pennsylvania and Virginia to the State of Ohio in accordance with the conditions of the act of 1802 under which Ohio became a State. This was the inauguration of a great public work, and appropriations were made in succeeding years with hardly an objection; the act of 1802 was interpreted as a compact which placed appropriations for the Cumberland Road upon a different footing from other projects, and under this theory about $2,500,000 were expended on the work during the first quarter of the century. Other improvements were early undertaken, less ambitious, however, in their development, as roads from the Mississippi River to the Ohio and roads in the Indian country of the Southwest. Justification for these expenditures was easily found in military necessity.

Side by side with these small legislative undertakings was the discussion of the expediency of federal aid on a much more liberal scale. Jefferson in his second inaugural address, 1805, declared that any surplus of revenue might well "be applied in time of peace to rivers, canals, roads, arts, manufactures, education, and other great objects within each State." In 1806 he justified even more emphatically a national system on the ground that the interests of the States would be identified and their union cemented by new and indissoluble ties; suggesting, however, that a constitutional amendment might be necessary. Gallatin, ever anxious to reduce the debt, at first did not encourage the application of revenue to such improvements; but the surplus of 1807 set his imagination at work, and in a special report of that year he suggested a general scheme, and intimated that three or four million dollars might be available. Commercial disturbances occasioned by the European wars and the embargo put to flight any such extravagant hopes.

In 1816 Calhoun secured the appointment of a committee to inquire into the expediency of setting apart the bonus and profits from the bank of the United States as a fund for internal improvement; but the bill passed at the next session to carry out this plan was vetoed by Madison on constitutional grounds. Monroe likewise, though friendly to federal aid, was troubled by constitutional scruples, and in 1822 vetoed a bill appropriating money for the erection of toll-gates upon the Cumberland Road; this opposition, however, did not extend to appropriations for the repair of this road, or even to grants of aid to enterprises which were initiated under State authority. The stricter constructionists realized that their position was unpopular, and in the hope of finding a way out of the labyrinth Senator Van Buren in 1824 proposed a constitutional amendment giving Congress the power to construct roads and canals, and recommended that money appropriated be apportioned among the States according to population. Clay in the meantime was enlarging his reputation by eager championship of generous expenditures for internal improvement, and aroused a patriotic interest in his appeals for national arteries of communication as a means of military defence, for lack of which millions of dollars and precious blood had been lost on the Northwest frontier. President John Quincy Adams was equally devoted to the cause, and beginning with his presidency in 1825 appropriations for surveys and construction of roads and canals were increased, and even railroads were planned for. The prospect of an overflowing treasury within a few years naturally stimulated projects for expenditures. Committees and engineers planned works the probable cost of which it was estimated in 1830 would amount to $96,000,000.

A halt was made when Jackson became president; while senator five years before he had repeatedly voted in favor of internal improvement bills, as for surveys, roads in Florida, Arkansas, and in Missouri, already a State, and for subscriptions to at least two canal companies. Between 1825 and 1829 Jackson's political convictions underwent a change which brought him into closer harmony with the stricter constructionists; the change, however, was due to a sincere belief that democratic government was threatened by great moneyed interests rather than to fine-spun interpretations of the Constitution. On May 27, 1830, Jackson returned a bill appropriating money for the Maysville Road, basing his objection specifically in this case upon the purely local character of the work projected, which was entirely within the limits of one State. He was not then ready to express an opinion as to whether he would veto a bill appropriating money for construction of works which were national in character, but he did not consider it expedient for the national government at that time to embark in a general system; like Madison and Monroe he testified to the benefits of internal improvement but wished an amendment to the Constitution enlarging the powers of the government. Jackson followed this veto with another within a few days, returning a bill for a subscription to stock in the Washington Turnpike Company, and at the end of the session pocketed a general bill for improvement of harbors and the construction of light-houses on the ground that it contained items of local character. Jackson put his criticism on more popular ground a year later when he animadverted against the system of federal subscriptions to private incorporated enterprises because the power of the government over the stockholders would be dangerous to the liberties of the people and the relationship thus established would be used to influence elections. Jackson's opposition put an end for a time to further appropriations for internal improvements under separate bills, excepting expenditures for the improvement of harbors and the removal of obstructions in navigable rivers for the security of foreign commerce. Some appropriations, however, were got through by putting them in the form of riders so as to escape a veto.

Expenditures for roads and canals, 1802–1835, were as follows, arranged by five-year periods: —

1802–1805	$5,000
1806–1810	94,000
1811–1815	364,000
1816–1820	1,475,000
1821–1825	635,000
1826–1830	2,737,000
1831–1835	4,210,000

92. Sales of Public Lands.

At the close of the Revolutionary War the federal government came into possession of an enormous domain by the cessions of claims by Eastern States to Western lands. In its early phases the subject hardly enters into a financial history, because the hope which Washington and Jefferson confidently held, that the sale of land would extinguish the debt, proved a mistake. From 1785 to 1800 only a little cash was received, and but a small quantity of bonds. In 1800 a radical change was made in the land policy by creating many land-offices and by selling on credit, the time for payment being extended over a period of four years. The credit system led to incomplete payments with vexatious readjustments, and many pioneers, encouraged by the easy terms offered by the government, later found it extremely difficult to extinguish their indebtedness. Sales by the government were made more rapidly, but, on the other hand, many forfeitures took place, and in 1820 land buyers owed the government over $21,000,000. Petitions were presented to Congress year by year to relieve settlers who defaulted payments. Finally in 1820, after the panic of 1819 had brought the evils to a crisis, the credit system was abolished; but, as a partial compensation for a less liberal policy as to credits, the normal price of the land was reduced to $1.25 per acre.

Between 1810 and 1830 the annual proceeds from the sale of land ranged between one and two million dollars; but beginning with 1830 there was a considerable increase, until in 1834 the receipts were nearly $5,000,000; in 1835, $14,757,600; in 1836, $24,877,179; in 1837, $6,776,236. In 1836 for the first and last time the revenue from this source exceeded that from customs. Since these proceeds were not required for the necessary expenditures of the government various proposals were made for cutting off this element of revenue; one plan was to give the new Western States all the land within their respective borders, thus disregarding the conditions of use for common benefit made by the original States; others were unwilling to go so far but favored the distribution of a part of the proceeds of the sales to the newer States. Political and sectional interests were involved; the West naturally desired a liberal policy of sale or grant of land; and such a policy likewise fell in with the interests of the high-tariff party of the East, who feared that if the revenue became excessive the tariff must be lowered. Before any plan could be drafted to prevent the accumulation of funds the country had to face a larger question, the disposition of the surplus.

93. Surplus Revenue.

The possibility of a surplus revenue had been suggested early in the history of our government. Jefferson, in his inaugural address in 1805, foresaw that a policy of economy coupled with national prosperity might lead to an overflowing treasury, and, as already observed, advocated a constitutional amendment clearly authorizing the use of government funds for internal improvements, arts, and education. Though delayed by the War of 1812 the prophecy of 1805 became a reality in less than thirty years. The question of a surplus as a subject for legislation did not come up again until after the depression of 1819–1823; but in 1826, when the extinction of the debt appeared to be near, a bill was introduced into the Senate providing that five million dollars be taken annually for four years from the sinking fund, and be distributed among the different States, in aid of internal improvements and education. The bill went no farther than to occasion a brief debate in which it was pointed out that the chief object of such a measure was to perpetuate a protective system; and Jackson in his first message in 1829 seemed to take that view, for he recommended an apportionment of surplus funds among the several States inasmuch as no satisfactory adjustment of the tariff appeared possible. Jackson soon repented of this suggestion and advised a reduction of the tariff duties; and then in 1832 held that the lands should not be made a source of revenue, but sold at nominal cost to settlers. He argued that as the "adventurous and hardy population of the West" did not receive their proportionate share of enjoyments from expenditures by the government, and as the real value of the land was due to their labor, they should be treated with special consideration.

In 1831 the Legislature of Pennsylvania, true to its protectionist interests, passed a resolution in favor of distribution; and in 1832 Clay brought the question once more before Congress by proposing that the revenue from lands be apportioned among the several States. The measure was vetoed, and in 1834 a slight disturbance in business made it expedient not to attempt to deplete the treasury. A reduction in tariff duties, however, was no longer an available remedy, because the compromise tariff, enacted only after a long and bitter struggle, was held in special regard as a settlement almost sacred in character and not lightly to be touched.

94. Distribution of the Surplus.

In January, 1835, the national debt was paid off; the existence of a surplus was an assured fact, and a committee of the Senate estimated that it would amount to nine millions each year for the next eight years. What was to be done with it? Everybody knew that the surplus excited wild speculation, and many people were sure that the money thus drawn from the great commercial centres and stored in remote banks was loaned to the profit of those who proved their loyalty to the administration. Clay renewed his proposition, and introduced a bill authorizing that 10 per cent. of the net proceeds of the land sales should be left in the treasury and that the residue be distributed. The obvious objection to the distribution of the proceeds of land sales was that the public lands had been originally ceded to the federal government for the specific purpose of paying the debt created by the Revolutionary War; and that as an integral part of the national income it could not be alienated to any State in particular. Moreover, the Constitution required that all revenue should be appropriated for certain definite objects concerned with defence, protection, or the general welfare of the United States; distribution to the States would not be such an appropriation, and the bill specified no constitutional purpose to which the money must finally be applied by the States; nor could there be such a limitation, since Congress had no power to compel the States to apply the money to any specific object. Apart from legal objections, other arguments lay against Clay's measure: some people wished to have the money spent by the national government on fortifications, as a specially fit use of a fund which had accrued from the sale of the national domain; the most valuable inheritance that any nation ever possessed ought, it was said, to be reinvested in permanent works for the common benefit and security of the whole country.

Secretary Woodbury in 1834 even suggested that the government make "a temporary investment in some stocks sound and salable."

A distribution scheme pure and simple could not pass Congress, and so the basis of legislation was changed; the bill of 1836 proposed that the States be made the depositories of the surplus, which should be subject to the demands of the treasury. The constitutional objections to a regular distribution bill being thus removed, or rather obscured, the bill was passed June 23, 1836; it provided that the money in the treasury January 1, 1837, reserving the sum of $5,000,000, should be deposited with the several States in proportion to their respective representation in the Senate and House. In return for the deposits the secretary of the treasury received certificates which set forth the obligations of the States to pay the amount expressed to the United States or their assigns, and he was given power to sell or assign these certificates whenever necessary for want of other money in the treasury; and it was further provided that these certificates should bear an interest of 5 per cent. from the time of their sale or assignment, redeemable at the pleasure of the States. When January 1 came around it was found that under the terms of the act about $37,000,000 would be available for deposit; as will be seen, owing to financial difficulties in 1837, the government was unable to transfer the whole of this sum; in all about $28,000,000 was paid over.

As Edward G. Bourne, the historian of the surplus, observes, the act was a makeshift: it was not wholly satisfactory to the Whigs, who wanted unqualified distribution; some of the States of the free-trade South received their shares with protest, and only because if they refused, the North would get them; others regarded the money as but a slight alleviation of the iniquitous exactions of the tariff and yet not to be despised; while the administration saw no other practical way out of the dilemma.

In spite of the statutory provisions relating to the deposit of funds, and the fact that Secretary Woodbury in his report for

1836 referred to the disposition of the funds as temporary and discussed anew the investment of surplus funds, everybody understood that it was an outright gift; and to this day not a dollar has been called for. The idea of a *douceur* was so deeply rooted that it was subsequently claimed that the government could not withhold the final instalment, which was unpaid owing to the embarrassments arising in 1837; the act was alleged to have created a contract between the national government and the States, by which the $37,000,000 belonged to the States the moment the act was passed. Benton forcibly described the measure: "It is in name a deposit; in form a loan; in essential design a distribution. All this verbiage about a deposit is nothing but the device and contrivance of those who have been for years endeavoring to distribute the revenues, sometimes by the land bill, sometimes by direct propositions, and sometimes by proposed amendments to the Constitution." Clay told his constituents in Kentucky that he did not believe that a single member of either House believed that a single dollar would be recalled; Calhoun in 1841 said that he still regarded it as simply a deposit, but he thought it should never be withdrawn except in case of war. Governor Seward in his message of 1841 stated that it was well understood by Congress that the form of a deposit was adopted to save the bill from the veto of the federal executive. Notwithstanding these opinions the treasury has carried on its books the sum deposited as part of its cash balance, and to this day the money thus deposited stands on the books of the treasury as unavailable funds, $28,101,644.

In 1883 the State of Virginia made a claim upon the secretary of the treasury for the deposit of the fourth instalment, and appealed to the Supreme Court of the United States for a mandamus to compel the secretary of the treasury to deposit with the State an amount equal to the fourth instalment, namely $732,809. The court, however, held that the act of June 23, 1836, created no debt or legal obligation on the part of the government, but only made the States the depositories temporarily of a portion of the public revenue not needed, as it was then supposed, for the purposes of the United States.

The uses made of the funds distributed were various. Massachusetts distributed them among the towns: Boston used the money for current expenses; Salem built a town hall; Groton repaired a broken bridge. The State of Maine made a per capita distribution; some States used the money for internal improvements, while a few saved it and use its income to-day for educational and other purposes.

CHAPTER X.

PANIC OF 1837 AND RESTORATION OF CREDIT.

95. References.

BIBLIOGRAPHIES: Bogart and Rawles, 39–42; Channing and Hart, 381–383.

SPECIE CIRCULAR: W. MacDonald, *Select Documents*, 327–329; or Dunbar, 270–271; or *Messages and Papers*, X, 104; *Benton's Abridgment*, XIII, 57–67, 92–99, 162–190, 331–333; *Finance Reports*, III, 764; IV, 38–49; T. H. Benton, *Thirty Years*, I, 676–678; Bolles, II, 348–350.

PANIC OF 1837: *Messages and Papers*, III, 324–346 (special message, Sept. 4, 1837); *Finance Reports*, IV, 28–31, 233; *Statutes*, V, 201 (suspension of revenue deposits), 206 (relief of deposit banks); or Dunbar, 118–120; T. H. Benton, *Thirty Years*, II, 9–67; A. Gallatin, *Writings*, III, 390–406; H. von Holst, *Constitutional History of U. S.*, II, 173–216 (references in foot-notes); Bolles, II, 346–352; C. A. Conant, *History of Modern Banking*, 479–485; W. G. Sumner, *History of American Currency*, 132–161; J. B. Phillips, *Methods of Keeping the Public Money* (*Pub. Mich. Polit. Sci. Assn.*), 71–83; E. M. Shepard, *Van Buren*, 242–277; C. Schurz, *Clay*, II, 113–127; T. Roosevelt, *Benton*, 189–208; J. A. Stevens, *Gallatin*, 280–286; Schouler, IV, 257–279.

TREASURY NOTES AND LOANS: *Statutes*, V, 201, 614; or Dunbar, 118–132; *Benton's Abridgment*, XIII, 351–367, 479–520, 661–679; D. Webster, *Works*, IV, 324–370; Bayley, 361–364; De Knight, 62–68; J. J. Knox, *United States Notes*, 40–62.

INDEPENDENT TREASURY: *Finance Reports*, IV, 10–15 (Woodbury, Sept. 5, 1835), 192–198, 362–364 (1840), 444 (1841); *Benton's Abridgment*, XIII, 374 et seq.; *Statutes*, V, 385 (Act of 1840), 439 (repeal, 1841); T. H. Benton, *Thirty Years*, II, 124, 219–228; D. Webster, *Works*, IV, 402–499; D. Kinley, *Independent Treasury System*, 23–39; J. B. Phillips, *Methods of Keeping the Public Money*, 103–111; E. M. Shepard, *Van Buren*, 278–299; C. Schurz, *Clay*, II, 136–151, 202–210 (Tyler).

TARIFF OF 1842: *Finance Reports*, IV, 464–469; *Messages and Papers*, IV, 180, 183 (vetoes); *Benton's Abridgment*, XIV; *Statutes*, V, 548; T. H. Benton, *Thirty Years*, II, 307–317, 410–417; J. C. Calhoun, *Works*, IV, 199–200; E. Young, *Customs Tariff Legislation*, lxxxix; H. von Holst, *Constitutional History of the U. S.*, III, 451–464; Bolles, II, 434–448; F. W. Taussig, *Tariff History*, 112–114; C. Schurz, *Clay*, II, 198–227 (general politics); Schouler, IV, 406–412.

STRUGGLE FOR BANK: *Messages and Papers*, IV, 63–68 (veto, Aug. 16, 1841); 68–72 (veto, Sept. 9, 1841); *Finance Reports*, IV, 445–447 (1841); *Benton's Abridgment*, XIV, 309–324, 348–384; T. H. Benton, *Thirty*

Years, II, 317–356, 376–394; E. C. Mason, *The Veto Power* (*Harvard Hist. Monographs*, No. 1), 76, 145; Bolles, II, 353; T. Roosevelt, *Benton*, 239–259; Schouler, IV, 384–392.

EXPENDITURES: *Finance Reports*, IV, 186 (1838), 239–242 (1839); *Benton's Abridgment*, XIV, 128–133; T. H. Benton, *Thirty Years*, II, 198–202; Bolles, II, 539–589; Schouler, IV, 327.

REPUDIATION: W. A. Scott, *Repudiation of State Debts* (bibliography), W. G. Sumner, *History of American Currency*, 162; C. Schurz, *Clay*, II, 211; Schouler, IV, 419–420.

96. Speculative Prosperity.

The extraordinary plethora of the treasury at the time of the distribution act of 1836 seemed based upon the general prosperity of the nation; in order, therefore, to understand the significance of the panic of 1837 and the relations of the more important fiscal events of this period it is necessary to consider certain points connected with the general economic development of the country since 1820. It was a period of international peace and an era of great territorial and business expansion, leading as usually happens to an undue extension of credit and speculation. Banking disorders were for a time at least not serious, and manufacturing had recovered from the depression succeeding the War of 1812. There was little to distract or disturb the normal course of material enterprise. Each succeeding presidential message naturally referred to the continued prosperity of the country.

The central point in this development was land settlement complicated by land buying for future sale. The construction of the Erie Canal from 1817 to 1825 opened up the land all along the great lakes; between 1820 and 1840, Ohio increased in population from 581,295 to 1,519,467; Indiana from 147,178 to 685,866; Illinois from 55,162 to 476,183; and Michigan from 8,765 to 212,267. The fertile soil disclosed in these Western prairies compared with the rigors of agricultural life on the Atlantic seaboard excited the imagination and naturally led to exaggerated hopes.

The Erie Canal was but one of many highways to the interior; canals penetrated far up to the foot-hills of the

Alleghanies; the Cumberland Road was carrying thousands of emigrants; railroad construction began in 1830. It was an age of internal improvements and the possibilities of the future seemed unlimited. The too generous credit system of the government toward land purchasers, which has been already described, stimulated still further the feeling that the success of the future would make up for any imperfection in present achievement. As the market value of land frequently rose to much above the government selling-price there was an eager contest on the part of those who could borrow money, to buy for speedy sale at an advanced price or to hold the land for a future profit. Borrowers found ready accommodation at local banks, and with the loans thus secured made their purchases from the land receiver; the purchase-money in many instances was thereupon re-deposited by the government in the bank whence it came, where it once more served as a loan to another or even to the same land speculator. These local banks and the government surplus thus became involved in a common network of credits; banks were established to meet this temporary demand, so that the lender leaned upon the borrower. The administrative hostility to the United States Bank and the hope of securing government deposits also gave impetus to the development of local banks.

The bank expansion which took place under this stimulus is seen in the following table (amounts in millions of dollars):

Year	Number of banks	Capital	Circulation	Loans
1829	329	110.2	48.2	137.0
1834	506	200.0	94.8	324.1
1835	704	231.2	103.7	365.2
1836	713	251.9	140.3	457.5
1837	788	290.8	149.2	525.1
1838	829	317.6	116.1	485.6
1839	840	327.1	135.2	492.3
1840	901	358.4	107.0	462.9
1841	784	313.6	107.3	386.5
1842	692	260.2	83.7	324.0
1843	691	228.9	58.6	254.5
1844	696	210.9	75.2	264.9
1845	707	206.0	89.6	288.6

Land speculation was also helped by the fact that the government was no longer a borrower from the public after the payment of the public debt, either for long or temporary loans; hence a considerable amount of capital was set free for reinvestment; furthermore the surplus funds of the government deposited in local banks encouraged these institutions to make loans out of proportion to actual assets. Between 1830 and 1837 the imports of merchandise exceeded the exports by $140,000,000; and, instead of demanding the payment of this balance in specie, foreigners left substantially the whole amount invested in the United States, a fact evidenced by an excess of imports of specie over exports amounting to $44,700,000. "The foreigners," says Shepard in his "Van Buren," "therefore took pay for their goods not only in our raw materials, but in part also in our investments, or rather our speculations, and sent these vast quantities of money besides. So our good fortune fired the imaginations of even the dull Europeans. They helped to feed and clothe us that we might experiment with Aladdin's lamp." Foreigners invested in the new railroad industry and more particularly in the bonds issued by States and municipalities. This credit expansion was made the more easy because of improvements in communication between Europe and America. It is also probable that American capital was withdrawn from agriculture and directed into more speculative enterprises; the value of flour and grain imported into the United States as a rule was insignificant, while that exported after 1830 was on the average about six million dollars annually; in 1837, however, the exports of grain fell off nearly a million dollars while the imports of grain were increased more than four and a half million dollars.

Speculation was not confined to Western lands; there was equal recklessness over cotton plantations in the Southwest, particularly in Mississippi and Louisiana, and in the real estate of the cities which controlled the cotton trade; the demand for the raw staple was greatly increased by the growth of manufactures of cotton goods in this country and by favorable conditions in England. The result was a rapid advance in the price of cotton, and also in the cotton crop which in Tennessee, Alabama, Mississippi, Arkansas, Louisiana, and Florida increased from 536,000 bales in 1833 to 916,000 bales in 1837. In 1833 the price of cotton ranged between 11½ and 13½ cents a pound; in 1834 between 11⅓ and 13¼; in 1835 between 14 and 20. Southern cities looked forward to a continuance of the great prosperity; at Mobile for example the assessed valuation of real estate increased from $4,000,000 in 1834 to $27,000,000 in 1837, although the number of polls assessed in the latter year was less than in the former.

97. The Specie Circular.

On July 11, 1836, the treasury department issued what is termed the specie circular, an order that agents for the sale of public lands should take in payment only specie, and no longer receive the notes issued by banks. As the whole question of the character of moneys receivable by the United States for duties and other obligations became a subject of debate in 1837 this is a fitting place to review the previous policy of the government as to the medium which could lawfully be tendered for taxes owed and for lands bought. One of the earliest acts passed by the first Congress was that of July 31, 1789, expressly requiring all duties to be paid in gold and silver only. Hamilton gave a liberal construction to this act, and by a circular of September 22, 1789, ordered that the notes of the Bank of North America and the Bank of New York, payable either on demand or within thirty days, should be received in payment of duties as equivalent to gold or silver. This action was defended in a report of April 22, 1790, on the ground that the law had for its object the exclusion of payments in paper emissions of the several State banks; it was not intended to hinder the treasury from making such arrangements as its exigencies might dictate; it was not to prevent if necessary an anticipation of the duties by treasury drafts at the several custom houses, nor to prevent the receipt of the notes of a public bank issued on a specie fund. The charter of the First United States Bank, 1791, expressly provided that the notes of that institution should be so receivable. In regard to payments for public lands a statute of 1796 required that lands be paid for in "money"; the act of March 3, 1797, added "evidences of the public debt"; under the act of May 10, 1800, specie or evidences of the public debt were required; and in 1812 treasury notes were made acceptable. By a joint resolution approved April 30, 1816, which was still in governance in 1836, it was provided that all duties, taxes, debts, or sums of money accruing or becoming payable to the United States should be collected and paid in the legal currency of the United States, or treasury notes, or notes of the Bank of the United States, or in notes of banks which are payable and paid on demand in the legal currency of the United States.

In a treasury circular of April 6, 1835, all collecting and receiving officers were instructed not to receive any bank-notes in denominations of less than five dollars, and intimation was given that the restriction would soon be extended to denominations of less than ten dollars, and that banks which continued the circulation of such notes would not be selected for fiscal agents. Again in an act of April 14, 1836, it was ordered that the United States government should not pay out any bank-note of any denomination unless the same were payable on demand in gold or silver coin at the place where issued, "and which shall not be equivalent to specie at the place where offered, and convertible into gold or silver upon the spot, at the will of the holder." It will thus be seen that the action of the treasury department was not precipitate; its policy for at least a year had been toward restricting the volume of bank-notes and increasing the circulation of specie. In issuing the specie circular of July 11, 1836, Secretary Woodbury declared that the order had for its object the repression of alleged frauds, the lessening of opportunities on the part of speculators to secure a monopoly of public lands to the injury of actual settlers in the new States, and the discouragement of the extension of bank issues and bank credits; he also briefly referred to the need of protection to the treasury.

The lively opposition to the circular came in part from speculators and in part from people who desired to buy for actual settlement but who could borrow only notes of non-specie paying banks and hence could get no land; on the other hand the measure helped speculators, since they were the only ones who could obtain specie, and because the new limitation of sales of public lands practically restricted the available supply to that already bought. The opposition, however, was so great that on the assembling of Congress both Houses passed a bill to annul the circular; the bill was delayed until the end of the session, and as the president did not sign it there was no opportunity to pass it over his veto which bore the date of March 3, 1837, 11.45 P. M.

98. Panic of 1837; Suspension of Specie Payments.

The check placed upon land speculation by the issue of the specie circular cramped the operations of Western banks and the Eastern institutions which were closely connected with them; coming, moreover, at the period when the distribution of the surplus was to begin, the specie circular was tangled up with a complicated credit system, and immediately brought on the inevitable crash. The first of the four instalments for deposit with the States was called January 1, 1837, and as the amount was based on the representation of the several States in Congress it practically meant the transfer of $9,000,000 from one section to another, for a large part of the government deposits at that time were in banks in the less populous States. To bring about these readjustments required a contraction of loans in some sections in order to release the government funds, as Schurz in his life of Clay describes the situation: "Millions upon millions of dollars went on their travels North and South, East and West, being mere freight for the time being, while the business from which the money was withdrawn gasped for breath in its struggle with a fearfully stringent money market." The first instalment was practically all paid; the second instalment, called April 1, was coming in when on May 10, 1837, the banks of New York suspended specie payments, and on the next day they were followed by the banks in the other large Northern cities. This suspension temporarily involved the government, since its funds were in the custody of the banks.

The panic which overtook this country was by no means due wholly to mistakes in the country itself. In November, 1836, the failure of two banks in Ireland and Manchester was felt on the London Stock Exchange; the three large business houses known as the three W's, — Wilkes, Wilde, and Wiggin, — which had closest relations in the granting of credit to America, were in particular affected. Since the imports of the United States at this time largely exceeded the exports the balance was met not by settlements in specie, but by the sale of American securities of one sort or another and by the securing of credits abroad. When the shock was first felt in London English creditors found it necessary to call in their loans. The financial depression brought on an immediate fall in the price of cotton, and the banks in New Orleans which had made large loans on cotton as security had to contract their credits, and these difficulties in turn were reflected in New York.

Another important contributory factor leading to trouble was the failure of the American crops in the years 1835 and 1837, unfortunately continued in 1838. This lessened the purchasing power of the farmers and crippled the merchants. It is the old story: in the confidence of getting in their payments from the country large importers had given time notes to settle for the balance of trade, thus swelling the volume of commercial paper and over-stimulating the growth of credit institutions. High protectionists have also placed emphasis upon the lowering of duties by the tariff of 1833 as the cause of the subsequent disasters.

All of the causes, however, of this diseased state of commerce and business were not clearly seen at the time; people then and since have thought the whole trouble was the insistence of the government in demanding payment for public lands in a currency which would hold its value. At a meeting held in New York March, 1837, to consider the situation, Webster publicly expressed this opinion. It was hoped that the new president, Van Buren, might be induced to rescind the specie circular, and immediately after the delivery of Webster's speech a committee was appointed to go to Washington to labor with the president. The committee had a dismal tale to tell: the value of real estate in New York had in six months depreciated more than $40,000,000; in two months there had been more than 250 failures; there had been a decline of $20,000,000 in the value of the stocks of railroads and canals which centred in New York; the value of merchandise in warehouses had fallen 30 per cent.; and within a few weeks 20,000 persons had been discharged by their employers. The president was civil; or, as Benton expresses it, treated the gentlemen with exquisite politeness and promised them an early answer. His answer proved to be a refusal to alter the policy, and at this time no human power could possibly have averted the storm. The question was not of selling government land but of realizing at any sacrifice on land security in a time of depression of the deadest kind. In the midst of this confusion the third instalment of the surplus was due July 1, 1837; the government could do nothing more than to pay to the States the notes received from the banks irrespective of their quality; and the fourth instalment, due October 1, was never paid.

99. Distress of the Treasury.

Further details of the general crisis of 1837 must here be omitted, but the student of finance is particularly interested in the measure which the government took to protect its funds. President Van Buren would not yield to a demand to rescind the specie circular, on the ground that the voters of the country in electing him president had passed approvingly on Jackson's hard-money policy; he placed the responsibility on Congress, and called an extra session on September 4 to devise relief for the treasury. The elaborate message which Van Buren sent in reviewed the situation, briefly advised temporary measures of relief, and devoted chief attention to the necessity of establishing an independent treasury system through which the government might in the future care for its own funds. The existing disturbance was attributed to overaction in all departments of business. Stress was laid upon the enormous and rapid increase in banking capital and paper circulation between 1834 and 1836; the extension of credits to traders in the interior; the large investment in unproductive lands; the expenditure of immense sums in improvements which had proved to be ruinously improvident; and the rapid growth of luxurious habits. For immediate relief he proposed a temporary issue of treasury notes, and the withholding of the payment of the fourth instalment of the surplus, due in October. Upon these latter recommendations Congress acted promptly and favorably; and authority was given October 12 for the issue of treasury notes not exceeding $10,000,000. For business men there was also a little comfort; importers were given more time to pay their duty bonds; and the secretary of the treasury was authorized to withdraw public moneys from the deposit banks in a manner as gradual and convenient to these institutions as might be consistent with the pecuniary wants of the government; no further interest was to be demanded on the deposits, and defaulting banks might give bonds to pay in instalments the moneys due the United States. On January 1, 1840, $896,000 was still due the government by the banks.

Commercial distress was deep-seated and recovery was slow; not until the latter half of 1838 did banks generally resume specie payments; even then some of the banks were unable to live up to their professions, — the banks of Philadelphia for example suspended again October 9, 1839, and did not resume effectively until March, 1842; in this vacillating and discouraging policy they were followed by many others, particularly in Rhode Island, New Jersey, and the South and West. The circulation was contracted from $149,000,000 in 1837 to $83,000,000 in 1842; this of itself lowered prices, deprived some sections of a circulating medium, and contributed to commercial distress. These misfortunes blighted the revenues of the government; imports declined from $190,000,000 in 1836 to $141,000,000 in 1837 and $113,000,000 in 1838; customs duties fell off and the revenues from sales of public lands shrank to their earlier figures; as is shown in the table, page 246.

Unfortunately during this period of distress the treasury had to meet increased expenditures; the extraordinary gain in the revenue during the years 1835 and 1836, together with the extinction of the debt, tempted Congress to large outlays, from some of which the government could not immediately retreat. The construction of public works, the more zealous extinction of Indian titles, plans for a speedy removal of the aborigines beyond the Mississippi, improvements of the District of Columbia, and, above all, the expenses in the Florida War, raised expenditures of the government in 1837 and 1838 to about double what they were in 1834 and 1835. The difficulties were aggravated by extravagance and corruption in administrative departments in which high officials were involved.

The result of all this was a series of annual deficits: —

Year	Deficit	Surplus
1837	$12,300,000	
1838	7,500,000	
1839		$4,600,000
1840	4,900,000	
1841	9,600,000	
1842	5,200,000	
1843[1]	3,400,000	
Total	$42,900,000	$4,600,000

[1] Half year.

100. Issue of Treasury Notes and Loans.

As has been stated, Congress on October 12, 1837, in order to meet the immediate strain, issued treasury notes; the bills authorized were limited to denominations of not less than $50; they were redeemable in one year, bore interest and were receivable in payment of all debts to the United States including payment for land. The expectation that a further issue would not be necessary was disappointed; and Congress, ever hoping that long-term bonds would not be needed, yielded to a policy of reissues, from which it did not free itself until 1844. Between 1837 and 1843 treasury notes were issued under eight different acts, amounting to $47,002,900, of which about one-third represents reissues. All of the notes were issued at par, and bore interest varying from one mill per cent. to 6 per cent.; the limitation of denominations to $50 or over was continued in subsequent acts. There was strong opposition to this policy, on the ground that the supply of monetary medium was inadequate to the needs of commerce; on the other hand Benton, true to his hard-money convictions, endeavored to make the lowest denomination $100 instead of $50. In the issue of 1843 a much controverted change in the policy of redemption was introduced by the treasury department; it was announced that the one-year notes would be purchased by the treasury at par on presentation, at any time before the expiration of their term, but the House committee on ways and means, which was instructed to report upon this question, held that the system made the notes practically demand notes and was contrary to the Constitution.[1]

When the Whigs gained control in 1841 the policy of issuing treasury notes was supplemented by three acts for long-term loans; although no one of these was highly important in itself as a fiscal measure, they contain points of permanent financial interest. The first of these acts, July 21, 1841,

[1] Report No. 379, 28th Cong., 1st Session, House of Representatives

was designed to fund outstanding treasury notes, and to meet current needs of the treasury. The loan had only three years to run, and the law prohibited the sale of stock at less than par; although the rates of interest offered were 5⅖ to 6 per cent., capital was not attracted; of the $12,000,000 authorized $5,672,976, or less than half, was issued. An attempt to permit the sale of stock at the highest price (which might be less than par) also failed, as this was regarded as a reflection upon the dignity of the government.

The two later loans of April 15, 1842, and March 3, 1843, were more liberal both as to interest and term of maturity; the stock could be sold at less than par after it had been advertised a reasonable time; and the periods of redemption were extended to 20 and 10 years respectively; of the loan of 1842, $8,343,000 was sold at from 97½ to par, and of the loan of 1843, $7,004,000 was marketed at a premium. In neither case, however, was the yield satisfactory; capital was otherwise engaged at that period, and American financial policy did not as yet command general confidence; coupled with the tardy recovery from the disaster of 1837 was the widespread suspicion caused by repudiation on the part of many States and cities.

101. Independent Treasury.

The plan which Van Buren proposed in his message of September, 1837, for the care of the public moneys by public officers was by no means new; it is said that Jefferson once suggested to Dallas some such plan; Gouge, an office-holder at Washington, a writer on money and banking, is also one of the sponsors for the system; and as early as 1834 a bill on somewhat similar lines had been briefly considered in Congress. In the message of September, Van Buren argued at length that it was not designed by the Constitution that the government should assume the management of domestic or private exchange any more than it should provide for the transportation of merchandise; that the previous experiments in the employment of local banks for the care of government funds had proved unsatisfactory; that the early practice of employing banks was a measure of emergency rather than of sound policy; that the emergency no longer existed, for instead of a load of national debt there was a large surplus which the government should adequately protect. Moreover, the use of government funds by banks led to pernicious results in the expansion of credit, rashness of enterprise, and speculation; the remedy, therefore, was that the government should take care of its own funds, and return to the practice of requiring the payment of all dues in specie with no exception whatever in favor of bills of specie-paying banks.

A bill was introduced into the Senate, September 14, 1837, for the establishment of an independent treasury, but it appeared without any prohibition on the treasury to receive the bills of specie-paying banks. The president openly objected, and Calhoun also announced that he could not support the bill unless the principle of specie payment was included; he moved and secured in the Senate an amendment which was afterwards known as the specie clause; in this form the bill passed the Senate 26 to 20, but failed in the House 120 to 106. In the regular session of 1837–1838 the measure was reintroduced, and, although the specie clause was stricken out in the Senate before passage by that body, the amended bill could not command a majority in the lower house. A third time at the next session 1838–1839, the same bill was brought forward without the specie clause, and for a third time failed. The election in 1838, however, changed the character of the twenty-sixth Congress and resulted in the election of a majority in favor of the independent treasury, so that the bill was passed and approved by the president July 4, 1840. A compromise was accepted as to payments in specie, by providing that until June 30, 1843, a part of all sums due to the United States might be paid in other than legal currency; after that date only gold or silver was to be receivable.

The arguments against the measure during the prolonged discussions in Van Buren's administration were not especially illuminating; political rather than fiscal and commercial considerations were prominent; great stress was laid upon the danger of a government bank, managed by the treasury department, acting under the commands of the president of the United States. "Public funds," said Clay, "would be unsafe in the hands of public officers; the perilous union of the purse and the sword so justly dreaded by our British and Revolutionary ancestors would become absolute and complete; it might indeed be that the Senate of the United States would be obliged humbly to implore some future president to grant it money to pay the wages of its own doorkeeper." It was also urged that the sub-treasury system would subvert all the State banks; would embarrass business by withdrawing from circulation large sums of money; and the proposed substitution of a purely metallic currency would reduce all property in value by two-thirds. Clay denounced the policy as a selfish solicitude for the government and an evidence of a cold and heartless insensibility to the sufferings of a bleeding people! A widespread feeling of indignation descended on the administration because it did not propose to encourage local banking institutions by the deposit of government funds; and the friends of a United States Bank once more championed its cause.

102. Tariff of 1842.

The serious decrease of the revenue of the government caused by the panic of 1837 provided a favorable opportunity for the protectionists; it could be urged that the tariff duties were not only too low to afford adequate protection to business, but that they would not produce enough to support a treasury so embarrassed that it was compelled repeatedly to find relief in the issue of treasury notes. The claim was the more convincing in 1840 because under the provisions of the compromise tariff further reductions were to take place. Nevertheless it was deemed expedient by the Whig political managers not to force the question of the tariff too prominently before the people in the presidential campaign of 1840;

and so Harrison, of some military repute, was selected by the Whigs, instead of Clay, the logical candidate. Harrison was elected and the Whigs were ready with a program both as to a bank and the tariff. If Harrison had lived constructive legislation would have been quickly effected; Harrison died within a month, and was succeeded by Tyler, who had been taken by the Whigs as candidate for vice-president without careful consideration of his views on economic questions. Tyler was enough of a Whig to favor tariff duties, but obstinately stood aloof from his party in the settlement of details.

Notwithstanding the inadequacy of revenues for current expenditures, the Whigs were willing to sacrifice the income from sales of public lands by distribution to the States, a policy which would fortify the future contention of protectionists that high duties were needed to keep the treasury supplied, and which found many friends among those who wanted the States to engage in costly internal improvements. This did not satisfy Tyler; and in order to secure the president's approval of the distribution act in 1841 the party leaders were forced to include in the law a proviso that if at any time the duties under the compromise tariff were raised the distribution of revenue should be suspended. In this way the non-tariff party hoped to tie down its opponents by an automatic check. Such a restriction was highly objectionable to the Whigs under Clay's leadership, and in two tariff bills passed by Congress in 1842 the proviso for suspending distribution was practically disregarded. Tyler promptly interposed his vetoes; and not until a third bill was framed, with the former provisos as to land distribution left undisturbed, could the new tariff obtain the president's approval; this was brought about August 30, 1842.

The tariff act of 1842 was highly protective; duties were increased, but not uniformly, to the level of the tariff of 1832; the average on dutiable articles was 23.1 per cent. in 1842, 35.7 per cent. in 1843, 35.1 per cent. in 1844, and 32.5

per cent. in 1845. Specific duties wherever practicable were laid, and special consideration was given to iron; on some individual commodities the rates were extremely high, as is seen in the following list, the second column showing the ad valorem incidence of taxation based on prices prevailing in 1844: —

Commodity	Specific duty	Ad valorem per cent.
Cotton bagging	4 cts. per sq. yd.	53
Railroad iron	$25 per ton	77
Pig iron	$9 per ton	72
Rolled or hammered iron	2½ cts. per lb.	51
Cut nails	3 cts. per lb.	43
Window glass	2 to 6 cts. per sq. yd.	62 to 165
Refined sugar	6 cts. per lb.	100
Molasses	4½ mills per lb.	51
Salt	8 cts. per bushel	61

A change was made in the method of collecting customs duties as had been earlier contemplated in the act of 1833; hitherto credit had been granted to importers upon the giving of bonds for the payment of duties within a certain period. When capital was scarce and commercial industry not highly organized, as in the early part of the century, it was necessary for the government to be liberal in its treatment of importers; with the increase of government receipts, and the growing possibilities of loss through fraud or incapacity of officials, the conviction gained ground that the government should do business on a cash basis. The application of this principle to the payment of customs duties was heartily supported by protectionists, because of the added burden which would be placed upon the importing interest. The merchants opposed the change and in 1846 secured a modification through the establishment of a warehouse system.

103. Struggle for a New Bank.

The new system of an independent treasury was not destined to enjoy a long existence; as soon as the Whigs gained power they repealed the independent treasury law, August 13, 1841, and it is probable that if Harrison had lived a third United States Bank would have been established. Tyler, really a States-rights Democrat, and not in harmony with his party, in this as on the tariff proved a stumbling-block to constructive legislation. The opposition complained that undue haste was shown in the repeal: Benton asserted that experience though brief had proved the sub-treasury system to be the safest mode yet devised for collecting the revenues, since nothing but gold and silver were received; and that it was the cheapest way of keeping the moneys, as the salaries of the receivers were less than the cost of employing banks. The Whigs, however, were prompt to gather the fruits of victory, and the new system was summarily set aside.

It was not an easy matter to provide a substitute; Clay and some other of the leading Whigs knew very well what they wanted, — a bank, — but the difficulty was to arrange a plan which would meet the objections of Tyler, who was known to be strict in his interpretation of congressional powers as granted by the Constitution. In the hope of preventing any future embarrassment from this source Ewing, the secretary of the treasury, was called upon to propose a plan, and it was supposed that a measure framed by him would meet with the approval of the president. Ewing recommended the establishment of a fiscal bank, with a capital of $30,000,000, to be incorporated in the District of Columbia; branches to be established in different States, but only with the assent of the States concerned. Tyler had objected to the title of bank, and also questioned the right of Congress to grant charters to banking corporations without the permission of the States. This latter restriction, however, was particularly objectionable to Clay, and during the debate an amendment was inserted that such agreement should be assumed unless dissent were expressed by the legislature of the State concerned at its next session. The contest which now took place between the president and the Whig majority of Congress, from this time on through the remainder of Tyler's administration, is of little interest to the student of finance. On the one hand, the president showed indecision and proved obstinate on what would appear to be minor points; while on the other hand, Clay and his immediate followers appeared to care more about discrediting Tyler than about getting a practical bank.

A bill was passed along the line of Clay's amendments, and on August 16, 1841, was vetoed by the president on four grounds: (1) the bill provides for the creation of a bank to operate over the whole Union, and is therefore unconstitutional; (2) it is a bank of discount, and for the same reason unconstitutional; (3) it is not limited, as it properly should be, to the power of dealing in exchange; (4) the assent of the States is not sufficiently secured. In spite of the party animosities aroused by this veto which the Clay Whigs called treachery, a second attempt was made to incorporate a banking institution, and on this occasion it was announced that the president's scruples would be recognized. The bank was to be styled the "Fiscal Corporation of the United States." By this time, however, it was impossible to please the president. Lyon G. Tyler thus explains and defends his father's position: "The Fiscal Corporation had, in fact, scarcely more than a point of resemblance to the idea prominent in the president's mind. It pretended to deal exclusively in exchanges, but it justified, in fact, the most obnoxious system of discounts, by prescribing no limit to the premium in the purchase of bills, or to the time the bills might run, or to their renewability. It rested on no actual exchange basis; and the drawer in one place might become the acceptor in another, and *vice versa*. A bill drawn at Philadelphia on Camden, New Jersey, at New York on a border town in New Jersey, at Cincinnati on Newport in Kentucky, might, for anything in the bill to restrain it, become a mere matter of local accommodation. The bill copied certain essential features from Clay's edition of the Fiscal Bank bill. The secretary's project permitted discounting in the District, and on *principle* there was no objection to this. But Clay's bill, which publicly challenged the issue of power, interdicted all discounting in the District, and forced it upon the States. So the Fiscal Corporation."[1]

The second bill, on September 9, was vetoed like the first, and for substantially the same reasons. Benton disposed of it by declaring that it would be better to "call this corporosity the Meal Tub Bank. A cattish name would certainly suit it in one particular; for, like a cat, it has many lives. This bank has been killed several times, but here it is still, scratching, biting, and clawing. Jackson killed it in 1832; Tyler killed it last week. But this is only a beginning; seven times more the Fates must cut the threads of its hydra life before it will yield up the ghost."

Tyler in his annual message, December, 1841, next brought forward a plan of his own. He recommended a Board of Control with agencies at prominent commercial points for the safe-keeping and disbursement of the public moneys; and a substitution at the option of the public creditor, of treasury notes in lieu of gold and silver, provided that the issue of notes be limited to $15,000,000 unless by express sanction of Congress. The deposit of specie to a limited amount was to be permitted in exchange for certificates of deposits; and the institution was to have power to purchase and sell domestic bills and drafts. The plan as a whole was termed the Exchequer Bank. According to Lyon G. Tyler the measure had three principal objects in view: The safe-keeping of the government moneys; the furnishing a paper circulation, always equivalent to gold and silver and of universal credit; and a provision for supplying to some extent the means of a cheap and safe exchange in the commerce between the several States; and he then expounds the president's plan: "The measure avoided extremes on both sides. It did not attempt to collect a capital by means of private subscription for the general purposes of loans and discounts, and therefore did not propose to perform the ordinary functions of a bank. On the other hand, it did not confine the currency exclusively to a *specie* currency,

[1] *Letters and Times of the Tylers*, vol. ii, p. 87.

as the independent treasury did, or make no attempt to furnish the country with facilities of exchange. A board of control in the city of Washington and agencies in the States comprised the essential features of the system. The charge of the union of the 'sword and purse,' which had been brought against the independent treasury, was avoided by several very ingenious provisions. The president was forbidden to touch a dollar of the public money, by his own authority, or change its custody. The secretary of the treasury only could do so, to meet the occasion of the public service or by a public official act. . . . And finally, under rigorous provisions against discounting, operations in exchange were permitted to give life to the currency and facilities to the public. But the *sovereignty of the States* was especially considered in that section which forbade the agencies to transact any business of a private character against the laws of the States." [1]

This plan received the unqualified endorsement of Webster, who declared that "if the Whig Congress will take the measure and give it a fair trial for three years it will be admitted by the whole American people to have proved the most beneficial institution ever established, the Constitution only excepted." Congress, however, was under the sway of political passions, and the bill was defeated almost as quickly as introduced. No further attempt was made in constructive legislation until the Democrats returned to power; in the meantime State banks were once more employed as depositories, and whenever practicable collateral security was demanded for the deposits held by the banks.

104. State Repudiation.

The discredit of federal finance during the years 1837–1844 was sharpened by the financial collapse of several of the State governments. Encouraged by the expansion of industry and commercial enterprise which was witnessed in this country during the first half of the century, many States, particularly

[1] *Letters and Times of the Tylers*, vol. ii, pp. 132–133.

in the North, borrowed money to invest in internal improvements, such as railroads and canals, which would aid in developing their resources; in the South, and in a less degree the West, States borrowed largely in order to engage in State banking schemes, and in the West States borrowed for commercial enterprises. These undertakings in many cases proved either unremunerative or too expensive for the State to carry; and in some of the newer commonwealths particularly there was not an honest determination, even where there was the ability, to meet the maturing obligations of interest and principal.

Mississippi for example in 1838 invested $5,000,000 in a banking institution which through a combination of bad management and general business confusion ran through its assets; the governor of Mississippi, taking advantage of irregularities in the issue of the bonds by the legislature, recommended that they be repudiated, and on this issue a repudiative legislature was elected and endorsed the executive. Florida also sold territorial bonds for investment in a bank, and when the inability of this institution to pay interest became apparent it also disclaimed its obligations for technical reasons.

In several of the Northern States — Pennsylvania, Maryland, Michigan, Indiana, and Illinois — the financial strains were great, and fears for a time were expressed that State honor might be stained. The evils were intensified by the fact that foreigners had invested liberally in the securities which were now disowned, and it was extremely difficult for this class of investors to understand either their own legal rights or the constitutional position of the States repudiating or delaying. It could hardly be expected that they would discriminate between States, or would consider them as equal sovereigns in a federal union, not to be reached by the ordinary processes of law. They were consequently dismayed and angered to find that the national government had no power over the defaulting members. Originally, under Art. 3, Sect. 1, of the Constitution, the judicial power of the United States was given power in controversies between a State and citizens of another State, or between a State or the citizens thereof and foreign States, citizens, or subjects. In 1793, when the State of Georgia was brought into court by a citizen of another State, an agitation was promptly begun for an amendment of the Constitution in order to maintain the dignity of sovereign States. The result was the Eleventh Amendment, which reads, "The judicial power of the United States shall not be construed to extend to any suit in law or equity, commenced or prosecuted against one of the United States by citizens of another State, or by citizens or subjects of any foreign State."

In view of another clause in the Constitution, which forbids States to violate contracts into which they have entered, the position of constitutional law towards State contracts is extremely unsatisfactory. The State is forbidden to commit a wrong, but if it commit one no remedy is afforded. Not only did foreigners regard this situation as absurd and unjust, but many Americans shared in this opinion. It was consequently proposed in a report submitted to Congress in March, 1843, that the federal government should assume the debts of the States; it was plausibly argued that the greater part of the indebtedness had been contracted in aid of public works which were "calculated to strengthen the bonds of union, multiply the avenues of commerce, and augment the defences against foreign aggression." Although the measure was supported by high authority both from the standpoint of justice and of expediency, it was defeated. To this day the individual creditor is helpless except in certain cases where he may be able to bring suit against State officials. A few States, to their credit, have provided in their own law remedies against themselves in cases of repudiation. But because of open repudiation by some of the States, temporary difficulties of others, coupled with the insolvency of many large enterprises in which foreigners had invested, American credit about 1840 suffered greatly. It almost became a by-word of reproach during the next decade, and it was exceedingly fortunate that during this period the country was so prosperous that it was not obliged to invite new supplies of foreign capital.

105. Receipts and Expenditures, 1834–1846.

The effect of the tariff of 1842 was at first disappointing from a revenue standpoint; in the second year there was an improvement; and in 1844 the yield amounted to $26,000,000, a sum greater than had been received from this source in any one year since 1833. By years the ordinary receipts from all sources from 1834 to 1846 were as follows: —

Year	Customs	Public lands	Miscellaneous	Total
1834	$16,214,000	$4,857,000	$720,000	$21,791,000
1835	19,391,000	14,757,000	1,282,000	35,430,000
1836	23,409,000	24,877,000	2,540,000	50,826,000
1837	11,169,000	6,776,000	7,009,000	24,954,000
1838	16,158,000	3,730,000	6,414,000	26,302,000
1839	23,137,000	7,361,000	984,000	31,482,000
1840	13,499,000	3,411,000	2,570,000	19,480,000
1841	14,487,000	1,365,000	1,008,000	16,860,000
1842	18,187,000	1,335,000	454,000	19,976,000
1843[1]	7,046,000[1]	898,000[1]	287,000[1]	8,231,000[1]
1844	26,183,000	2,059,000	1,078,000	29,320,000
1845	27,528,000	2,077,000	365,000	29,970,000
1846	26,712,000	2,694,000	293,000	29,699,000

[1] Half year.

Expenditures during this period were as follows: —

Year	War	Navy	Indians	Pensions	Interest on debt	Miscellaneous	Total
1833	$6,704,000	$3,901,000	$1,802,000	$4,589,000	$303,000	$5,716,000	$23,018,000
1834	5,696,000	3,956,000	1,003,000	3,364,000	202,000	4,404,000	18,627,000
1835	5,759,000	3,864,000	1,706,000	1,954,000	57,000	4,229,000	17,573,000
1836	11,747,000	5,807,000	5,037,000	2,882,000		5,393,000	30,868,000
1837	13,682,000	6,646,000	4,348,000	2,672,000		9,893,000	37,244,000
1838	12,897,000	6,131,000	5,504,000	2,156,000	14,000	7,160,000	33,865,000
1839	8,916,000	6,182,000	2,528,000	3,142,000	399,000	5,725,000	26,896,000
1840	7,095,000	6,113,000	2,331,000	2,603,000	174,000	5,995,000	24,314,000
1841	8,801,000	6,001,000	2,514,000	2,388,000	284,000	6,490,000	26,482,000
1842	6,610,000	8,397,000	1,199,000	1,378,000	773,000	6,775,000	25,135,000
1843[1]	2,908,000[1]	3,727,000[1]	578,000[1]	839,000[1]	523,000[1]	3,202,000[1]	11,780,000[1]
1844	5,218,000	6,498,000	1,256,000	2,032,000	1,833,000	5,645,000	22,484,000
1845	5,746,000	6,297,000	1,539,000	2,400,000	1,040,000	5,911,000	22,954,000
1846	10,413,000	6,455,000	1,027,000	1,811,000	842,000	6,711,000	27,261,000

[1] Half year.

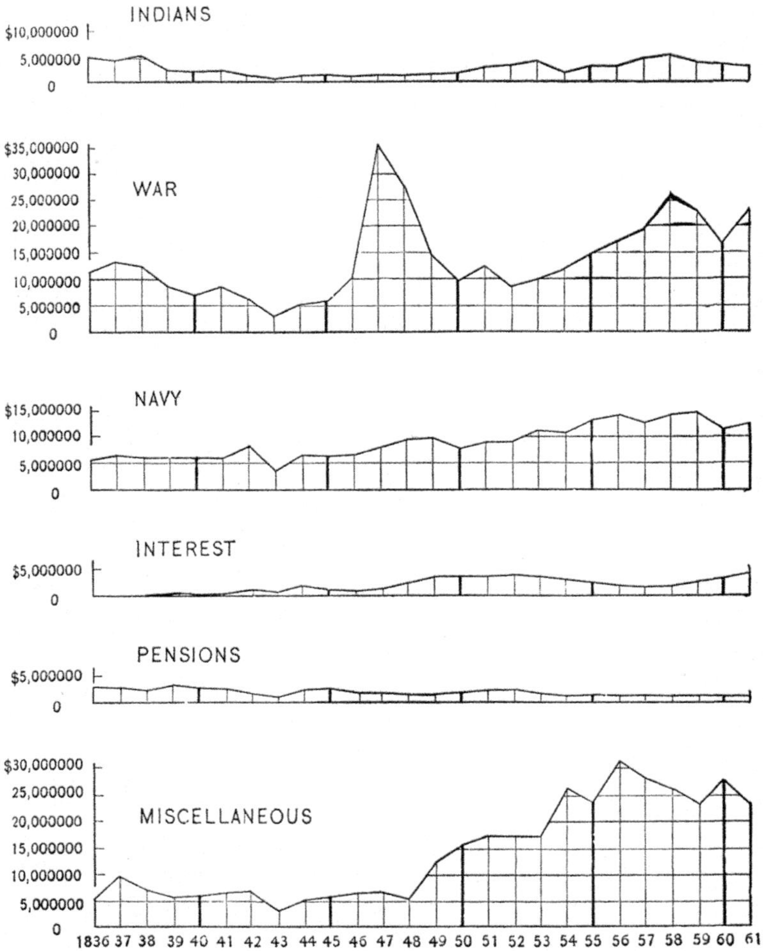

No. III. — ORDINARY EXPENDITURES, 1836–1861.

(Continuation of Chart No. 2, different scale.)

Reference has already been made to some of the causes responsible for increased expenditures in the years 1837–1838, but in addition the higher level of "miscellaneous" expenditures requires some explanation: the area of territory to receive the enjoyment of civil administration was being rapidly extended on account of the settlements in the West; new courts were established, and the judiciary was treated with more generosity by an increase in salary; reductions in the tariff made it necessary to increase the compensation of certain officers as an offset for loss of fees; there was an active construction of light-houses, custom-houses, and branch mints; and new roads were opened to the territories.

A comparison of receipts and expenditures is made in the following table in millions of dollars: —

Year	Receipts			Expenditures	Surplus	Deficit
	Taxes	Other	Total			
1834	16.2	5.5	21.7	18.6	3.1	
1835	19.3	16.1	35.4	17.5	17.9	
1836	23.4	27.4	50.8	30.8	20.0	
1837	11.1	13.8	24.9	37.2		12.3
1838	16.1	10.2	26.3	33.8		7.5
1839	23.1	8.3	31.4	26.8	4.6	
1840	13.4	6.0	19.4	24.3		4.9
1841	14.4	2.4	16.8	26.4		9.6
1842	18.1	1.8	19.9	25.1		5.2
1843[1]	7.0	1.2	8.2	11.7		3.5
1844	26.1	3.2	29.3	22.4	6.9	
1845	27.5	2.4	29.9	22.9	7.	
1846	26.7	2.9	29.6	27.2	2.4	

[1] Half year, January 1 to June 30, 1843.

CHAPTER XI.

TARIFF, INDEPENDENT TREASURY, AND STATE BANKS.

1846–1860.

106. References.

BIBLIOGRAPHIES: Bogart and Rawles, 41–42; Channing and Hart, 388–389.

TARIFF: *Messages and Papers,* IV, 403–406 (1845), 498–502, 647 (1846); V, 83–85 (1850), 123–126 (1851); *Finance Reports,* V, 4–16 (1845); VI, 6–14 (1846), 138–142 (1847), 283–291 (1848), 345 (report on warehousing system); 1853–1854, pp. 9–11; 1854–1855, pp. 12–16; 1856–1857, pp. 13–16; *Benton's Abridgment,* XV, 97–140, 565–631; *Statutes,* IX, 42 (1846), 55 (warehouse act, 1846); XI, 192; *State Papers and Speeches on the Tariff* (Taussig ed.), 214–251 (Walker's report); E. Young, *Customs Tariff Legislation,* xciii (1846), cvi (1857), cxiv (1861); D. Webster, *Works,* V, 161–243; Sherman's *Speeches,* 1–12 (Morrill tariff); Bolles, II, 449–461 (1846); 478–485 (warehouse system); F. W. Taussig, *History of the Tariff,* 114–154; J. G. Blaine, *Twenty Years,* I, 192–207; J. F. Rhodes, *History of the U. S.,* III, 28–59; Schouler, IV, 515–517; Stanwood, II, 69–83.

INDEPENDENT TREASURY: *Messages and Papers,* IV, 406–408 (1845), 502 (1846), 556, 648–649 (1848); *Finance Reports,* V, 17–21 (1846); VI, 6–8, 31–49 (regulations), 129–132 (1847); 1852–1853, pp. 14–15; 1853–1854, pp. 16; 255–275 (report by Gouge); 1856–1857, pp. 21–23; *Benton's Abridgment,* XV, 442–450, 631–636; *Statutes,* IX, 59; or Dunbar, 138; W. MacDonald, *Select Documents,* 358–365; D. Kinley, *Independent Treasury,* 40–65; J. B. Phillips, *Methods of Keeping the Public Money,* 117–130; Bolles, II, 352–358; *Bankers' Magazine,* IX, 625; X, 609; T. H. Benton, *Thirty Years,* II, 726.

FINANCES OF THE MEXICAN WAR: *Messages and Papers,* IV, 524–529, 553–556; *Finance Reports,* 1846–1848; *Statutes,* IX, 118, 217; Dunbar, 137, 142–148; Bayley, 364–367, 437; Bolles, II, 590–595; J. J. Knox, *United States Notes,* 63–69.

CRISIS OF 1857: *Messages and Papers,* V, 520; Bayley, 368; D. Kinley, *The Independent Treasury,* 176–180; W. G. Sumner, *History of American Currency,* 180–187; C. A. Conant, *History of Modern Banking,* 492–497; H. von Holst, *Constitutional History of the U. S.,* 1856–1859, 97–125; J. J. Knox, *United States Notes,* 70–76; Bolles, II, 599–602; Schouler, V, 419–420; C. F. Dunbar, *Economic Essays,* 266–293.

STATE BANKING: *Messages and Papers*, V, 437–441 (1857); *Finance Reports*, 1854–1855, pp. 22–23; 1855–1856, pp 29–31; W. G. Sumner, *History of Banking in the U. S.;* C. A. Conant, *History of Modern Banking*, 310–347; H. White, 313–398; C. J. Bullock, *Monetary History*, 82–93; L. C. Root, *N. Y. Bank Currency*, in *Sound Currency*, II, No. 5; *N. E. Bank Currency*, ditto, II, No. 13; C. F. Dunbar, *Economic Essays*, 314–329.

EXPENDITURES: *Messages and Papers*, V, 488–490 (1858), 524, 648 (1860); Bolles, II, 576–609.

107. Tariff of 1846.

The tariff of 1842 would have been more hotly contested had there not been a necessity for additional revenue. By 1844 good times had come again, and the tariff for the first time became a distinct party question, agitated in national conventions, set forth in platforms and made a feature in campaigns. Nevertheless in the contest of 1844 each of the parties was cautious and even ambiguous. The Democrats asserted that no one branch of industry should be fostered to the detriment of others, a doctrine which no Whig would deny; while the Whigs declared in favor of a tariff for revenue, discriminating with reference to protection, a doctrine which in the past had found general acceptance among Democrats. The Democratic ticket was aided by the selection of Dallas as candidate for the vice-presidency from protectionist Pennsylvania; and Polk, the head of the ticket, wrote a letter during the campaign in which he said: "I have heretofore sanctioned such honest discrimating duties as would produce the amount of revenue needed, and at the same time afford reasonable incidental protection merely, and not for revenue." Such hazy utterances helped to obscure the issue and to darken the mind of the average voter as to the real opinions or intentions of the party leaders; and, although Democratic success was not primarily due to their tariff policy, when they once more entered into power in 1845 they quickly attacked existing statutes. The financial situation was on the whole favorable for a radical experiment, since there was an excess of receipts in the treasury for 1845 and a further excess seemed likely in 1846. Robert J. Walker, secretary of the treasury appointed by President Polk, was an able man with positive convictions in regard to a revenue policy. He had worked out a theory of import duties which he promptly laid before Congress in December, 1845. His system embraced the following principles: —

1. No more money shall be collected than is necessary for the wants of the government economically administered.
2. No duty shall be imposed on any article above the lowest rate which will yield the largest amount of revenue.
3. Below such rate discrimination may be made descending in the scale of duties; or for imperative reasons the article may be placed in the free list.
4. The maximum duty shall be imposed on luxuries.
5. All minimums and all specific duties shall be abolished and ad valorem duties substituted.
6. The duties shall be so imposed as to operate as equally as possible throughout the Union.

Congress accepted nearly all of the plan but in one important particular fell short: no duties were placed on tea and coffee. These taxes had been dropped in 1832, and Congress did not dare in times of prosperity to risk popular disapproval and retax articles of such general use. By this omission an annual yield of $3,000,000 was lost, and Secretary Walker during the remainder of his term of office did his best to impress upon Congress the need of adopting his recommendation.

The vote in the House of Representatives by geographical sections on this tariff was as follows: —

States	In favor	Opposed
New England . . .	9	19
Middle States . . .	18	44
West and Northwest	29	10
South and Southwest	58	20
Total	114	93

Under the tariff act of July 30, 1846, articles of import were divided into various schedules designated by letters of the alphabet as follows: —

(A) Included brandy, spirits, etc., rate 100%.

(B) Included spices, preserved fruits and meats, cigars, snuff, and manufactured tobacco, rate 40%.

(C), (D), (E), and (F) Included the great bulk of commercial products, which were taxed 30%, 25%, 20%, and 15% respectively.

(G) Included books, building stone, diamonds, watches, rate 10%.

(H) Included various articles manufactured or in a low state of manufacture and used in existing industries, rate 5%.

(I) Included coffee and tea, copper ore, and a few other commodities, free from duty.

Aside from the free-trade basis of the tariff of 1846, or Walker tariff as it is frequently called, it is remarkable in its brevity,—less than 5000 words,—in its comprehensiveness, and in its condensation. It is also notable as the only tariff practically drafted by the executive. In spite of its free trade intent, protectionist principles appear in some sections; wool was taxed though a raw material, while coffee and tea were left free. Another feature of this tariff was the change from specific to ad valorem duties; it will be recalled that until 1816 both methods were in use, and there was no insistence upon either to the exclusion of the other; after 1816 the tendency was on the whole toward the substitution of specific duties wherever practicable, and by 1846 the reversal was complete. Theoretically the system is ideal; in practice it admits of grave injustice, and when a Whig secretary of the treasury, William E. Meredith, came into office in 1849 he easily secured testimony in regard to the inequalities of appraisement of goods at different ports and frauds from undervaluation: for example, the collector of customs at Boston complained that cord-wood from the provinces was entered at Boston at $1.50 per cord, at Gloucester $1.25 per cord, and at Portland and Bath $.75; and from New York came the story that when three parcels of cotton goods were sent as a test to as many different ports and entered by appraisement without invoices, the result was a difference of 25 per cent. between the highest and the lowest valuation.

The method of appraisement of goods was also changed by the act of 1846, and defined more precisely by an emendation of March 3, 1851; this provided that the valuation be based on the actual market value or wholesale price at the time of exportation to the United States, and that to this value be added the cost of the packing or covering, the commission of the broker who sold the goods, the export duties if there were any, wharf dues, and the cost of putting goods on board.

A further novelty for this country in customs administration was the establishment of a convenient system of government warehouses in which goods might lie with duty unpaid under the custody of the government for a certain length of time. In this way merchandise could be imported, landed, packed, repacked, assorted, and re-exported without so large an outlay of mercantile capital as would be necessary by prepayment of duties. The system quickly justified itself and has continued until the present time.

The average rates of duty on dutiable imports under the tariff of 1846 were as follows: —

Year	Per cent.	Year	Per cent.
1846	26.5	1852	26.
1847	22.5	1853	25.
1848	24.	1854	23.5
1849	23.	1855	23.
1850	25.2	1856	25.
1851	26		

108. The Independent Treasury Re-established.

The second important change carried through by the Democrats was the re-establishment of the sub-treasury system. In the long debate which took place few new arguments were added to those heard in the previous discussions of 1837–40. Again one side insisted that it was unsafe and unconstitutional for the government to "keep" its funds in the local banks, and again the other side emphasized the services rendered by the banks to the government. The measure as enacted in August, 1846, was so similar to that of 1840 as not to require further description; treasury notes, however, were added to gold and silver as receivable for public dues, and provision was made for the supply of vaults and safes in the new treasury building at Washington and at the mints and custom-houses; New York, Philadelphia, Washington, Charlestown, New Orleans, and St. Louis were the principal centres of deposit; four receivers-general and two keepers of mints, with the treasurer of the United States, were appointed public custodians. The new system began its career under difficulties; the opposition of the banks had to be faced, and no appropriations were voted for some of the offices created by the act. Inadequate provision was made for the care of funds of disbursing officers who were distributed throughout the country, and abuses arose because these officials sometimes kept public moneys or loaned them to their own profit. James Guthrie, who became secretary in 1853, remedied this by increasing the number of depositories and also by ordering that disbursing agents could pay through treasury drafts. The sub-treasury system appears to have been useful from the beginning and deserves credit for some of the success of the financiering during the Mexican War, but to what extent it was responsible for the prosperity of the national finances during the succeeding years it is hard to determine, for several commercial factors turned out favorable to the United States, as for example the heavy imports of specie in 1847 and the large production of gold after the Californian discoveries in 1848.

A careful personal examination of the several sub-treasuries and government depositories was made in 1855 by William M. Gouge; and he reported that in the twenty-three government depositories there was at the time one-half as much gold and silver as was held by the 1300 banks, and in some of them the safeguards against fire, thieves, and burglars were inferior to those provided by banks; still the only loss by robbery up to that time had been $10,000 at Pittsburgh. The accounts of the depositories he found accurate and uniform according to law, though there was some neglect as to official examination. The transfer of public funds from one place to another under the system was not so successful as had been hoped, because in some sections little specie was in circulation. With due allowance for these short-comings Gouge summed up the advantages of the system as follows: It created a new demand for specie; it limited the expansion of bank paper money; it avoided the derangement of business resulting from government association with banks; it prevented losses to the government; and it gave to the treasury a constant control of its funds. The advantage of this was seen in the panic of 1857, when the national government was able to meet every liability without embarrassment, while state governments with nominally filled treasuries were unable to pay their debts except in the depreciated currency of banks or by calling upon banks for specie through the redemption of notes, — a strain which simply added to the distress.

The real trial of the independent treasury system and its permanent effect on business and commercial crises could not be seen until after the Civil War; but in 1853 the accumulation of surplus funds in the treasury caused apprehension in commercial and financial circles. Relief was at the time afforded by the purchase of silver for new coinage authorized under the act of 1853 and also by the purchase of government stock. Even Secretary Guthrie, a most ardent defender of the independent treasury, or, as he termed it, "the constitutional treasury," admitted that the system might exercise a fatal control over the currency, banks, and trade by causing a stringency in the money market whenever receipts exceeded expenditures. The problem was simply an added argument for a more careful adjustment of revenue to expenditures. The good effects of the independent treasury system in the earlier part of its history do not necessarily prove its advantage under conditions widely different from those of a half century ago. If local banking had been wisely carried on during the first half of the nineteenth century it is not likely that the government would have undertaken or would have been intrusted with the varied and heavy responsibilities which it now bears. To escape the abuses and the disasters of ill-regulated banking the country adopted a system which is inelastic and ill adapted to present conditions, and which does not sufficiently take into account the growth of experience and skill in banking.

109. Finances of the Mexican War.

The Mexican War broke out in May, 1846, and was closed by the peace of February 2, 1848. A short and sharp contest, it caused no serious financial depression, and the debt created was simply and easily met. The expenditures of the war department during the three years April 1, 1846, to April 1, 1849, were $80,845,116, as compared with $21,991,123 in the three previous years; and the expenditures of the navy department for the period April 1, 1846, to October 1, 1848, were $18,758,900, as compared with $14,007,281 for the two and a half years before the war. These sums, making a total excess of $63,605,621, were met by loans in the form of treasury notes and government stock. In all a net indebtedness of $49,000,000 was created, but owing to the reissue of treasury notes and the conversion of treasury notes into stock the details of the several loans under the acts of July 22, 1846, January 20, 1847, and March 31, 1848, cannot be clearly presented in a narrow space. All of the loans were placed at par and a portion yielded a premium aggregating over a half million dollars. This success may well be compared with the financiering of the War of 1812, when loans in stock were sold with difficulty and at a discount and treasury notes were depreciated. The ease of the treasury was due not so much to a wiser intelligence as to the great increase in the wealth of the country and to the advance in government credit. Under one of the loan acts when subscriptions were invited for $18,000,000, bids were received for $57,723,000, almost all above par, and the assignment was made at rates from one-eighth of one per cent. to 2 per cent. above par. More significant than any other tribute to the credit of the government was the fact that the loan was subscribed for in specie — the first loan negotiated on this basis since the foundation of the government. The comment of the secretary of the treasury in his annual report of 1847 on this fortunate undertaking justifies quoting:

"The magnitude of the loan, the fluctuations below par of the previous stock and notes, the untried and to many alarming restraining operation of the constitutional treasury, the heavy expenditures of the war, and the requirement of all the payment from time to time in specie were deemed by many as insuperable obstacles to the negotiation of the whole of the loan at or above par. But under the salutary provisions of the constitutional treasury the credit of the government was in truth enhanced by receiving and disbursing nothing but coin; thus placing all its transactions upon a basis more sound and entitled to higher credit than when it held no specie, had no money in its own possession, and none even in the banks to pay its creditors but bank paper. Then, it was dependent upon the credit of the banks and was subjected to every fluctuation which affected their credit. Now, it stands upon the basis of specie, so as to be above all suspicion of discredit, whilst by its demand for coin for revenue payments it sustains not only its own credit but renders more safe the credit and currency and business of the whole Union."

An error of judgment was made in coupling so high a rate of interest as 6 per cent. with long terms of ten and twelve years before maturity, for on account of business prosperity the bonds quickly went to a premium, and their redemption when the government wished to pay its debts from the surpluses enjoyed in 1850–1856 was a costly operation.

110. Commercial Expansion.

The period from 1846 to 1857 was one of great industrial prosperity. Besides the war with Mexico, with its abnormal expenditures, business and public finance were affected by the discovery of gold in California, by the revolutionary disturbances on the Continent, by the famine in Ireland, and by the extension of railroads in the West. In 1845 the number of immigrants to this country was 114,000; in 1847, 225,000; and in each of the five years after 1849 it was more than 350,000. More immigrants, in fact, came between 1845 and 1855 than in the preceding twenty-five years. The statistics of railroad construction also tell a wonderful story; in 1846 there were about 5000 miles in operation; but after 1848 the annual gain in construction was over 1000 miles until we come to the war period of 1861. The famine in Ireland not only sent out thousands of laborers, it also created a great demand for American wheat and of course increased our purchasing power. An important change was also made in commercial conditions by the reduction and abolition of import duties in England which began in 1842. With the removal of these duties and the rapid extension of manufacturing industries in England there was a great increase in exports (principally cotton and food products) from the United States. The addition of the large territory ceded by Mexico increased importations and hence the revenue, and the extraordinary development in California had a stimulating influence upon the whole nation. The country possessed resources only partially developed, yet open to ready conquest through the application of railways and new machinery. It was indeed, as Secretary Walker with glowing optimism repeatedly affirmed in his annual reports, "a new commercial era."

111. Progress toward Lower Duties.

The wonderful revolution which was taking place in commerce and in industry makes it impossible to generalize from this experience as to the effect of import duties upon economic development; very likely prosperity would have followed under any system of revenue laws. The condition of the treasury grew more and more favorable as soon as the temporary burdens occasioned by the Mexican War were removed; between 1846 and 1851 the national debt was increased from $15,550,000 to $68,304,000 by war loans, but after the latter year the reduction was continuous until in 1857 the principal was $28,700,000. The receipts passed all expectations; the customs revenue was large; the new territory on the Pacific drained merchandise from the Atlantic ports, which "left a vacuum to be filled by fresh and larger importations of foreign dutiable goods." Again the sales of public lands yielded a large sum amounting in the three years 1854–1856 to over $28,000,000.

Although expenditures reached a much higher level than before the Mexican War there was a handsome surplus of receipts over expenditures to be applied to the debt, and it was early seen that as soon as the small debt was extinguished another surplus would arise. The Whig secretaries of the treasury in the Taylor-Fillmore administration, William E. Meredith and Thomas Corwin, true to their party convictions, endeavored to turn this experience to the benefit of the protectionist cause. Their efforts, however, made little impression, and so well satisfied was the country with its revenue system that during the ten years 1846–1856 the tariff question ceased to be an issue in politics. In the seven party platforms of 1848, 1852, and 1856 the only reference to the tariff was in that of the Whigs in 1852, when a mild reference was made to the wisdom of tariff discrimination by specific duties in encouragement of American industries. The attention of Congress during this period went chiefly to the slavery debates of 1847–1850, and to the Kansas-Nebraska Bill of 1854 and its consequences.

The country was drifting towards free trade, and there was even suggestion that all tariffs might be repealed and direct taxes and other receipts relied upon. James Guthrie, who became secretary of the treasury under President Pierce in 1855–1857, did not go so far as this, but he continually advised further reductions in the customs duties; his definite proposal was that all articles paying duties be divided into two classes, one paying 100 per cent. and the other 25 per cent., a grouping which would entirely remove the possibility of assimilating goods of one class to another in order to secure lower rates; he also advised that the free list be extended and was an early champion of the admission of raw materials used in manufactures free of duty. The tariff discussion during this period was practically concentrated upon two points: the effect of the tariff upon commerce and its effect upon labor. Walker and Guthrie, Walker in particular, eloquently set forth the necessity of making imports free if the country wished to export its surplus products and supported their contention by a mass of commercial and industrial statistics from the beginning of the century. Meredith and Corwin, on the other hand, dwelt upon the need of protection to American workmen who were subject to competition with the pauper or poorly paid labor of Europe, and they advanced equally ingenious tables of statistics to show that it would be far more profitable to sell these goods to a home market of manufacturers and artisans, and thus distribute the costs of transportation to railroads and canal companies at home rather than to foreign steamship companies.

112. Local Banking, 1837-1861.

An independent treasury system was really a protest against State banks as well as against a national bank; although there were signs here and there of a growing conservatism in bank management there was much to criticise. The rapid expansion and contraction of circulation which took place between 1837 and 1842 has already been referred to; between the latter date and 1861 the statistical changes in the principal items of the banking business were as follows (amounts in millions of dollars): —

Year	Number of banks	Capital	Loans	Deposits	Circulation	Specie
1843	691	228.9	254.5	56.2	58.6	33.5
1844	696	210.9	264.9	84.6	75.2	49.9
1845	707	206.0	288.6	88.0	89.6	44.2
1846	707	196.9	312.1	96.9	105.6	42.0
1847	715	203.1	310.3	91.8	105.5	35.1
1848	751	204.8	344.5	103.2	128.5	46.4
1849	782	207.3	332.3	91.2	114.7	43.6
1850	824	217.3	364.2	109.6	131.4	45.4
1851	879	227.8	413.7	129.0	155.2	48.7
1852						
1853	750	207.9	408.9	145.6	146.1	47.1
1854	1208	301.4	557.4	188.2	204.7	59.4
1855	1307	332.2	576.1	190.4	187.0	53.9
1856	1398	343.9	634.2	212.7	195.7	59.3
1857	1416	370.8	684.5	230.4	214.8	58.3
1858	1422	394.6	583.2	185.9	155.2	74.4
1859	1476	402.0	657.2	259.6	193.3	104.5
1860	1562	421.9	691.9	253.8	207.1	83.6
1861	1601	429.6	696.8	257.2	202.0	87.7

Where the States insisted on proper precautions the banks were good, sound, and commercially serviceable. In Massachusetts for example, in the period of commercial embarrassment between 1837 and 1844, 32 banks suspended, but the circulation of all but one was redeemed; from 1844 to 1855 only two banks failed, and all the note-holders were paid in full. In New York, where business conditions were not so settled, the results were less fortunate. Under the free banking system inaugurated in 1839 there were nearly 60 failures; but of these one-half were in the first five years. It was during this period that there was developed in this State the plan of basing issues upon deposits of approved securities, a plan which was subsequently utilized in the establishment of the present national banking system. In the Western States losses by bad banking were greater; in Indiana 51 of the free banks and private institutions failed between 1852 and 1857, with a serious loss to note-holders as well as to other creditors. On the other hand the State bank of Indiana, as well as that of Illinois, was conservatively managed and presents an interesting illustration of the possibility of sound local banking. A notable example of banking in its worst form may be found in the annals of Michigan; tricks were

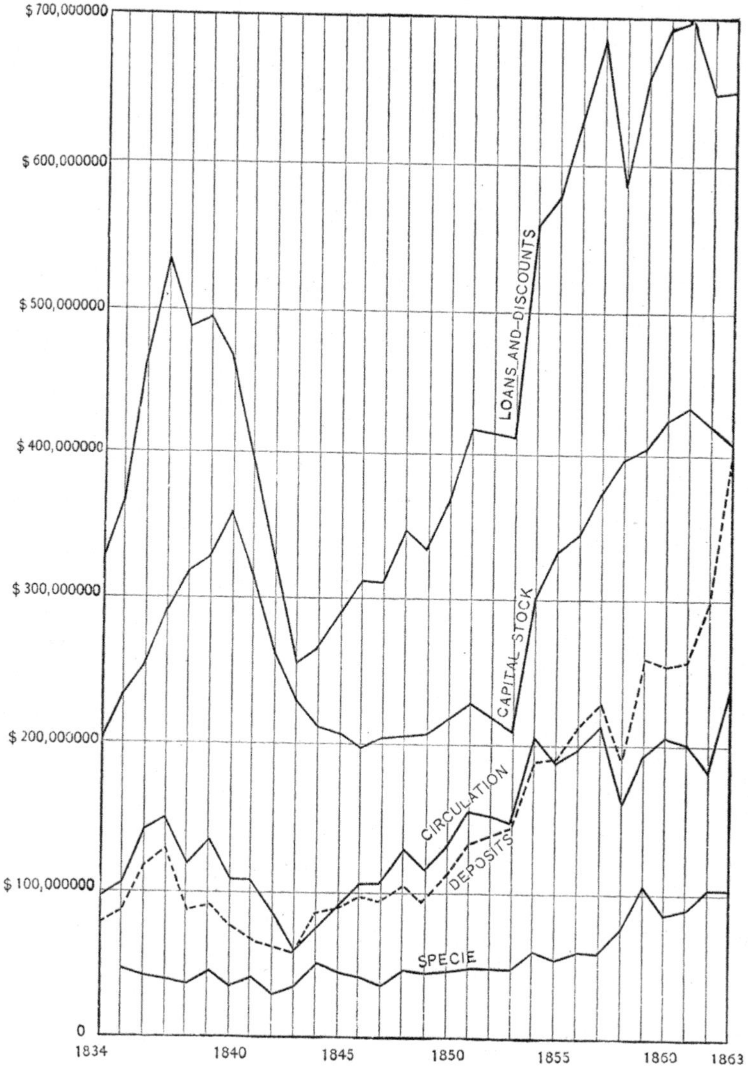

No. IV. — LOCAL BANK STATISTICS, 1834–1863.

employed to deceive the official bank commissioners as to the amount of specie on hand; the same boxes or bags of specie were quickly transferred from one institution to another, to perform a continuous service of reserve. In the words of the commissioners, "gold and silver flew about the country with the celerity of magic; its sound was heard in the depths of the forest, yet, like the wind, one knew not whence it came or whither it was going." In one instance it was found that the alleged box of specie showed a stratum of gold and silver but all beneath was nails and glass. With the best intentions it was hard to keep in order the Western banks in remote sections or on the frontier.

The question of the right of a State to establish under its own control a bank with power of note issue was finally decided by the Supreme Court under the influence of the stricter constructionists, led by Chief-Justice Taney, in favor of the States. The decisive case was that of *Briscoe* v. *The Commonwealth of Kentucky;* when first argued in 1834 two of the seven judges were absent and two of the remaining five were of the opinion that the notes issued by the bank of the Commonwealth were not bills of credit; hence a decision was withheld. In 1837 the court was complete and an opinion was rendered; Marshall's opinion was practically overruled, although the court made a sharp distinction between bills issued on the credit of a State and those issued by an institution in which the State may have become an exclusive stockholder, without, however, imparting to the bank any of the attributes of sovereignty. Five of the judges who concurred in this opinion, including Taney, were appointees of Jackson; Justice Story alone in a dissenting opinion maintained the arguments which Marshall had so powerfully elaborated during his long term as chief justice. Later, in the case of *Bank of Augusta* v. *Earle* (1839), the court held that the right to issue bank-notes was at common law an occupation open to all men, which the State might restrain if it saw fit, thus implying that the national government had no direct control.

In passing judgment upon the many defects and shortcomings of the varied systems of local banking it must be taken into account that any system would probably have broken down, for during the long period from 1815 to 1860 there was a reckless spirit of speculative enterprise always eager to find an outlet through the channels of credit. A practical defect in the banking of that period, aside from opportunities for irresponsible operations, was the lack of uniformity of note security, which resulted in great confusion in the ordinary currency. A country merchant might receive and pay out a thousand kinds of notes, some good, some doubtful, some presumably bad, and this condition grew worse as the circle of business activity was enlarged with the construction of railroads. The field of bad currency was thus made wider and a good system of banking had to suffer in public opinion because of competition with banks which had no character to maintain. This defect, as will be seen, was a forcible argument in 1863 in favor of establishing a national system.

113. Tariff of 1857; Panic.

The need of a reduction of revenue pressed with such urgency that a tariff measure was enacted March 3, 1857, lowering many of the duties and enlarging the free list. The schedules of 1846 were taken as a basis and the following principle was applied: upon articles enumerated in schedules A and B rates were reduced from 100 per cent. and 40 per cent. to 30 per cent.; on articles in schedule C from 30 per cent. to 24 per cent.; in schedule D from 25 per cent. to 19 per cent.; in schedule E from 20 per cent. to 15 per cent.; in schedule F from 15 per cent. to 12 per cent.; in schedule G from 10 per cent. to 8 per cent.; in schedule H from 5 per cent. to 4 per cent.; and on articles not specifically provided for from 20 per cent. to 15 per cent. In the application of this principle some exceptions were made; many drugs and dry stuffs, articles used in chemical arts, raw silk, tin, and wood were placed upon the free list or else transferred to lower rate schedules; cotton manufactures were favored by leaving the cotton duties nearly as high as established by the tariff of 1846. The average rates of duty on dutiable imports during the next four years was as follows: —

Year	Per cent.
1858	20
1859	19
1860	19
1861	18.1

The vote on this measure did not show a sharp party division. By geographical sections the vote in the House of Representatives was as follows: —

States	In favor	Opposed
New England . . .	18	9
Middle States . . .	24	28
West and Northwest	14	33
South and Southwest	60	2
California	2	0
Total	118	72

Hardly had the tariff of 1857 been enacted when a sharp commercial and banking panic came on, which for a period almost paralyzed manufactures; in August, 1857, the Ohio Life Insurance and Trust Company failed with large liabilities to Eastern institutions; a panic occurred in New York, followed by a suspension of specie payments. Important railroads reaching into undeveloped sections of the West went into bankruptcy, among them the Illinois Central, the New York and Erie, and the Michigan Central. The reason for the crisis of 1857 is still the subject of controversy: one alleged cause is the lowering of tariff duties in 1857; and some protectionists trace the collapse to the slow but poisonous workings of the tariff of 1846, — the argument being that the reduction of duties stimulated importations, which had to be paid for in specie, and that this drain of specie inevitably caused the panic.

This point of view is set forth by Mr. Blaine in his "Twenty Years of Congress":[1] "The protectionists therefore hold that the boasted prosperity of the country under the tariff of 1846 was abnormal in origin and in character. It depended upon a series of events exceptional at home and even more exceptional abroad, — events which by the doctrine of probabilities would not be repeated for centuries. When peace was restored in Europe, when foreign looms and forges were set going with renewed strength, when Russia resumed her export of wheat, and when at home the output of the gold mines suddenly decreased, the country was thrown into distress, followed by a panic and by long years of depression. The protectionists maintain that from 1846 to 1857 the United States would have enjoyed prosperity under any form of tariff, but that the moment the exceptional conditions in Europe and in America came to an end the country was plunged headlong into a disaster from which the conservative force of a protective tariff would in large part have saved it."

Other forces can be discovered in this period which were destined to bring disaster. There had been an exceedingly rapid industrial development, occasioned by railroad construction out of all proportion to immediate demands and by the stimulus of enormous additions to the monetary medium resulting from the new gold discoveries. Speculation was rampant and credit was once more strained to the utmost. The bank-note circulation which in 1843 was $58,000,000 amounted in 1857 to $214,000,000; and loans had increased from $254,000,000 to $684,000,000. It is too much to claim that this wide-spread shock was due to the tariff of 1857 which had been in operation but for a few months, or even to the tariff of 1846. To be sure imports had increased and there had been a heavy export of specie to pay for them, but

[1] I. 203.

at the same time the production of specie in the United States had been more than enough to cover this demand and to leave a generous amount in the country for domestic needs. It was certainly unfortunate that a reduction of revenue should have been made at a time when, as events proved, the government treasury was about to need special strengthening; but in connecting cause and effect it must be borne in mind that commercial depressions have for a century returned with an almost mathematical regularity, and that it is hardly reasonable to hold alone responsible a tariff which had apparently brought no disturbance during a period of ten years.

114. Morrill Tariff.

The year 1858 began a new series of treasury deficits and it was soon made clear that another revision of the revenue system was imperative in order to provide adequate supplies. The government was living hand-to-mouth, or as Morrill pithily expressed it, "was obliged to go to bed without its supper" every time the imports of the week fell short a million at the port of New York. Howell Cobb, the Democratic secretary of the treasury, and the Republicans in control of the House of Representatives were both agreed as to the need of the treasury, although they differed as to the method of relief. Secretary Cobb thought that the difficulty could best be met by raising rates in schedules C, D, F, G, and H to 25, 20, 15, 10, and 5 per cent. respectively, and by transferring certain articles from the lower to higher schedules; he denied the need of reviving the higher schedules of 40 and 100 per cent. in the tariff of 1846; and absolutely condemned any proposal of home valuation. No attention was paid to Cobb's recommendation and the country drifted on from one deficit to another. In the four years of Pierce's administration, 1853–57, the national income averaged over $68,000,000 annually; but in 1858 it dropped to $46,500,000; and in the three years 1858–60 deficits accumulated to the amount of

$50,000,000. At the same time current appropriations were increased; and it was repeatedly necessary to resort to the issue of short-term treasury notes and also of bonds. Only a small amount of time-loans was placed on account of the low rate of interest, 5 per cent., which the bond bore, and because of the provision in the law against selling at less than par.

In the winter of 1859–60 the Republicans had a plurality in the House of Representatives, and Justin S. Morrill, a Republican member from Vermont, introduced a tariff bill on which much labor had been spent. Morrill was a protectionist by conviction, but realized there was no chance of passing a protectionist measure. His bill was moderate; in his own words: "No prohibitory duties have been aimed at; but to place our people upon a level of fair competition with the rest of the world is thought to be no more than reasonable. Most of the highest duties fixed upon have been so fixed more with a view to revenue than protection." The most important change proposed was a return to specific duties on many commodities which were subject to undervaluation and fraudulent entry, as illustrated by the following examples:—

Commodity	1846	1857	1861
Carpets, valued $1.25 per sq. yd. . .	30 per cent.	24 per cent.	40 cts. per sq. yd.
Tarred cordage	25 per cent.	19 per cent.	2½ cts. per lb.
Cotton bagging	20 per cent.	15 per cent.	1⅝ cts. per lb.
Raw wool, valued 18 to 24 cts. per lb.	30 per cent.	24 per cent.	3 cts. per lb.

Where ad valorem rates were continued a return was generally made to the duties of 1846. The bill passed the House, May 10, 1860, by a vote of 105 to 64. This success together with the protectionist plank in the Republican national platform adopted a few weeks later was undoubtedly a factor which won Pennsylvania from the Democracy and elected Lincoln president in November. The measure passed the

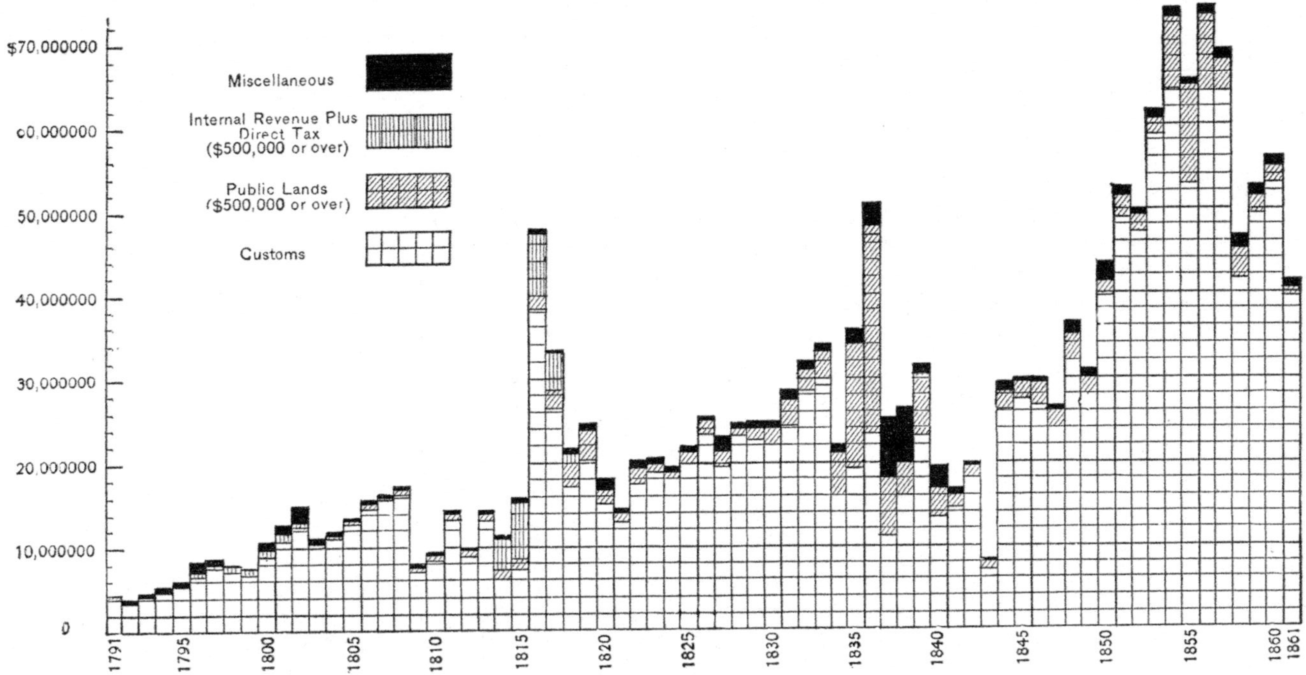

No. V.—ORDINARY RECEIPTS, 1791–1861.

(For continuation, see Chart No. 17.)

Senate the following winter, after secession had removed many members, and became law March 2, 1861.

115. Receipts and Expenditures, 1846–1861.

In following the course of receipts and expenditures summarized in the statistical tables of the treasury more than usual caution must be exercised for the period 1846–1861 because of changes in the system of accounts. By years receipts were as follows: —

Year	Customs	Public lands	Miscellaneous	Total
1846	$26,712,000	$2,694,000	$293,000	$29,699,000
1847	23,747,000	2,498,000	222,000	26,467,000
1848	31,757,000	3,328,000	543,000	35,628,000
1849	28,346,000	1,688,000	687,000	30,721,000
1850	39,668,000	1,859,000	2,065,000	43,592,000
1851	49,017,000	2,352,000	1,186,000	52,555,000
1852	47,339,000	2,043,000	464,000	49,846,000
1853	58,931,000	1,667,000	989,000	61,587,000
1854	64,224,000	8,470,000	1,106,000	73,800,000
1855	53,025,000	11,497,000	828,000	65,350,000
1856	64,022,000	8,917,000	1,117,000	74,056,000
1857	63,875,000	3,829,000	1,261,000	68,965,000
1858	41,789,000	3,513,000	1,353,000	46,655,000
1859	49,565,000	1,756,000	1,456,000	52,777,000
1860	53,187,000	1,778,000	1,089,000	56,054,000
1861	39,582,000	870,000	1,024,000	41,476,000

Expenditures were as follows: —

Year	War	Navy	Indians	Pensions	Interest on debt	Miscellaneous	Total
1846	$10,413,000	$6,455,000	$1,027,000	$1,811,000	$842,000	$6,711,000	$27,261,000
1847	35,840,000	7,900,000	1,430,000	1,744,000	1,119,000	6,885,000	54,920,000
1848	27,688,000	9,408,000	1,252,000	1,227,000	2,390,000	5,650,000	47,618,000
1849	14,558,000	9,786,000	1,374,000	1,328,000	3,565,000	12,885,000	43,499,000
1850	9,687,000	7,904,000	1,663,000	1,866,000	3,782,000	16,043,000	40,948,000
1851	12,161,000	8,880,000	2,829,000	2,293,000	3,696,000	17,888,000	47,751,000
1852	8,521,000	8,918,000	3,043,000	2,401,000	4,000,000	17,504,000	44,390,000
1853	9,910,000	11,067,000	3,880,000	1,756,000	3,665,000	17,463,000	47,743,000
1854	11,722,000	10,790,000	1,550,000	1,232,000	3,070,000	26,672,000	55,038,000
1855	14,648,000	13,327,000	2,772,000	1,477,000	2,314,000	24,090,000	58,630,000
1856	16,963,000	14,074,000	2,644,000	1,296,000	1,953,000	31,794,000	68,726,000
1857	19,159,000	12,651,000	4,354,000	1,310,000	1,593,000	28,565,000	67,634,000
1858	25,679,000	14,053,000	4,978,000	1,219,000	1,652,000	26,400,000	73,982,000
1859	23,154,000	14,690,000	3,490,000	1,222,000	2,637,000	23,797,000	68,993,000
1860	16,472,000	11,514,000	2,991,000	1,100,000	3,144,000	27,977,000	63,201,000
1861	23,001,000	12,387,000	2,865,000	1,034,000	4,034,000	23,327,000	66,650,000

By the act of March 3, 1849, the expense of collecting customs revenue was charged to miscellaneous expenditures instead of debited to accruing customs revenue. This alone added $2,000,000 annually to the expenditures account. Repayments to importers on excess collections swell the budget. New expenditures for meeting postal deficiencies, and for defraying the cost of mail services for Congress and the public departments were authorized under the several acts of March 3, 1847, March 3, 1851, and March 3, 1853, and charged up under "Miscellaneous." Miscellaneous expenditures greatly increased through payments to Mexico and liquidations of Mexican claims under the treaty of 1848, amounting between 1849 and 1858 to over $32,000,000. During this period public improvements, particularly the construction of public buildings and light-houses, were undertaken on a generous scale: the former were necessary in order to provide depositories for the funds of the government, and the latter were demanded by the vigorous and expanding commerce. Expenditures for the several classes of internal improvements from 1831 to 1860 were as follows: —

Year	Public buildings	Rivers and harbors	Roads and canals	Light-houses etc.
1831–35	$752,000	$3,058,000	$4,208,000	$1,535,000
1836–40	1,534,000	4,206,000	3,370,000	2,597,000
1841–45	845,000	1,113,000	596,000	1,772,000
1846–50	1,324,000	352,000	714,000	3,108,000
1851–55	4,603,000	2,334,000	939,000	5,562,000
1856–60	10,037,000	1,373,000	2,507,000	7,931,000

Expenditures for rivers, harbors, roads, and canals as here tabulated are included under "War" in the second table on page 267, while expenditures for public buildings and light-houses are to be found under "Miscellaneous."

A comparison of income and outgo is made in the following table in millions of dollars: —

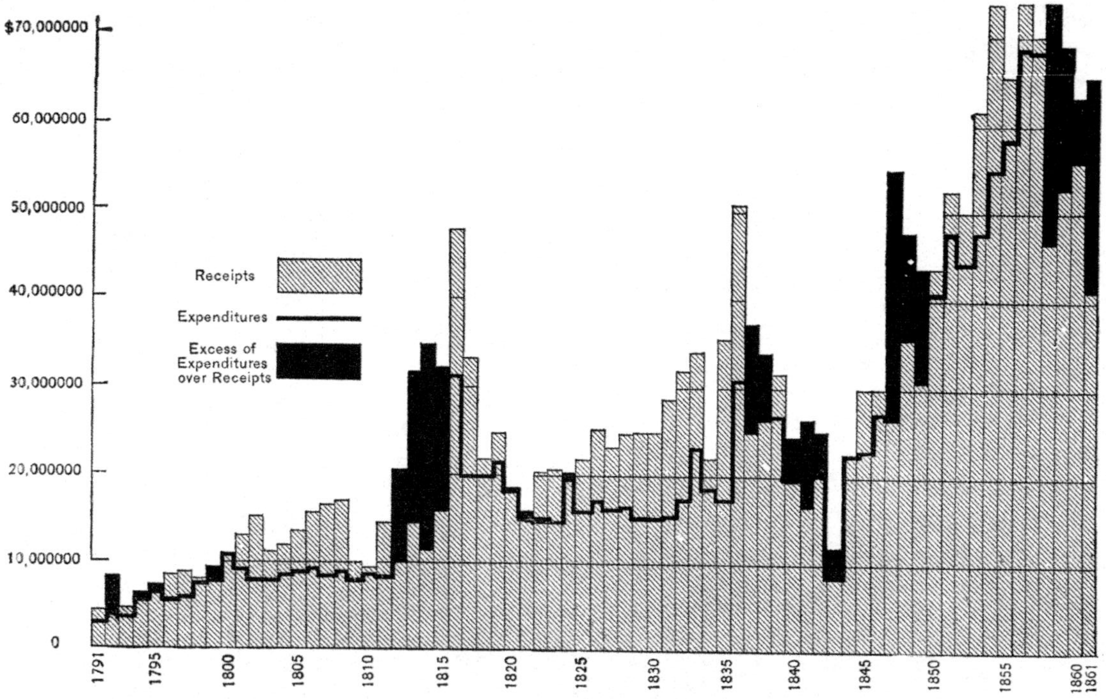

No. VI.—ORDINARY RECEIPTS AND EXPENDITURES, 1791–1861.

(For continuation, see Chart No. 18.)

Year	Receipts			Expenditures	Surplus	Deficit
	Taxes	Other	Total			
1846	26.7	2.9	29.6	27.2	2.4	
1847	23.7	2.7	26.4	54.9		28.5
1848	31.7	3.9	35.6	47.6		12.0
1849	28.3	2.4	30.7	43.4		12.7
1850	39.6	3.9	43.5	40.9	2.6	
1851	49.0	3.5	52.5	47.7	4.8	
1852	47.3	2.5	49.8	44.3	5.5	
1853	58.9	2.6	61.5	47.7	13.8	
1854	64.2	9.6	73.8	55.0	18.8	
1855	53.0	12.3	65.3	58.6	6.7	
1856	64.0	10.0	74.0	68.7	5.3	
1857	63.8	5.1	68.9	67.6	1.3	
1858	41.7	4.9	46.6	73.9		27.3
1859	49.5	3.2	52.7	68.9		16.2
1860	53.1	2.9	56.0	63.2		7.2
1861	39.5	1.9	41.4	66.6		25.2

Of the secretaries of the treasury after Walker, James Guthrie deserves special mention. No great administrative act is associated with his name; his reputation rests rather in the traditions of the treasury department and in his official reports which deal with questions now rarely raised in public controversy. He clearly realized the significance of the growth of government business, which is reflected in the preceding tables, and that this demanded a careful revision of departmental methods. This was the more necessary on account of the construction of new custom houses and branch mints, and the re-organization of the treasury department due to the transfer of the land office and of certain supervisory responsibilities relating to the expenditures of the United States courts, to the interior department established in 1849. Guthrie prescribed new forms of accounting, insisted upon a prompt settling of accounts, enlarged the scope of statistical returns, and placed the independent treasury system upon a business basis. New depositories were established for disbursing officers, and the accounts of officials which were in arrears in March, 1853, to the enormous sum of $132,000,000 were reduced by December, 1855, to

$25,000,000. Guthrie recognized the dangers of extravagant appropriations, and during the period of treasury prosperity preceding the panic of 1857, exercised a firm control, as far as his power extended, to keep the finances in a sound condition.

CHAPTER XII.

CIVIL WAR; LEGAL TENDERS.

116. References.

BIBLIOGRAPHIES; Bogart and Rawles, 43-45; Channing and Hart, 419-420.

FINANCIAL SITUATION IN 1861: *Statutes*, XII, 259 (Act of July 17, 1861); *Finance Report*, 1860-1861; *Bankers' Magazine*, XVI (1861-1862), 161-170 (loan of August), 290-293, 509; XVII, 135-150 (loan committee); J. Sherman, *Recollections*, I, 251-258; J. G. Blaine, *Twenty Years*, I, 396-408; *Bolles*, III, 20-42; S. W. McCall, *Stevens*, 139-151.

SUSPENSION OF SPECIE PAYMENTS: *Finance Report*, 1862, pp. 7-8; W. C. Mitchell, *Suspension of Specie Payments*, in *Jour. of Pol. Econ.*, VII, 289-326 (exhaustive study); Bolles, III, 34-40, 139-140; A. B. Hart, *Chase*, 230-234; W. G. Sumner, *History of American Currency*, 194-197; W. G. Sumner, *History of Banking*, 458-461; H. White, 150-152.

LEGAL TENDER NOTES: (i) SOURCES, *Finance Report*, 1861, pp. 17-20; 1862, pp. 12-16; 1863, p. 17; *Statutes*, XII, 345, 532, 709; or Dunbar, 163, 167, 173; E. McPherson, *History of the Rebellion*, 357; *Sound Currency*, III (Jan. 15, 1896), No. 4 (extracts of congressional debates); Bayley, 369-385, 445-457; W. F. de Knight, 77-99; E. G. Spaulding, *History of Legal Tender Paper Money* (1869; extracts from documents, etc.); C. Sumner, *Works*, VI, 319-345; J. Sherman, *Speeches*, 23-32; J. Sherman, *Recollections*, I, 268-283; J. G. Blaine, *Twenty Years*, I, 409-427. (ii) SPECIAL, W. C. Mitchell, *Greenbacks and the Cost of the Civil War*, in *Jour. Pol. Econ.*, V (1897), 117-156 (most thorough study of effects); also in *Report of Monetary Commission* (1898), 445-479; H. Adams, *Historical Essays*, 281-317; J. J. Knox, *United States Notes*, 122-147; Bolles, III, 43-86, 130-158; H. White, 149-165; *Report of Monetary Commission* (1898), 399-416, 502-508 (statutes); W. G. Sumner, *American Currency*, 197-209; J. K. Upton, *Money and Politics* (1884), 67-110; C. J. Bullock, *Monetary History*, 96-99 (references); F. A. Walker, *Money*, 369-372; H. C. Adams, *Public Debts*, 145-146, 166; J. L. Laughlin, *Mill's Political Economy*, 358 (fluctuations in value); F. P. Powers, *Greenbacks in War*, in *Pol. Sci. Quar.*, II, 79-90; S. Newcomb, *Critical Examination of our War Policy* (1865); A. B. Hart, *Chase*, 245-252; S. W. McCall, *Stevens*, 152-173; J. F. Rhodes, *History of United States*, III, 559-572 (references); IV, 237.

TREASURY NOTES: Dunbar, 158–196; Bayley, 370–383, 445–460; W. F. de Knight, 79–98; W. C. Mitchell, in *Jour. Pol. Econ.*, X (1902), 544–530 (demand notes; valuable references), 550–559 (fractional), 566–570 (treasury notes); R. M. Breckenridge, *Demand Notes of* 1861, in *Sound Currency*, V (1898), No. 20 (foot-notes); Bolles, III, 5–8, 29–30, 61, 84–85, 114, 126–128, 251.

GOLD SALES: *Statutes*, XIII, 132; or Dunbar, 191–193; J. A. Garfield, *Works*, I, 35–41; Bolles, III, 142–147; H. White, 174–190; J. K. Upton, *Money and Politics*, 176–193; A. B. Hart, *Chase*, 284–289.

117. The Situation in 1860.

The result of the elections of November, 1860, gave a severe shock to public and private credit; Southern banks withdrew large amounts of money on deposit in Northern banks; loans were contracted; and by the middle of the month the panic was complete. The government resorted to another treasury note issue under the act of December 17, 1860, but so low was the public credit and so disturbed the public mind that to float the notes at par it was necessary to pay from 10 to 12 per cent. interest on the larger part. With the beginning of the year 1861, although secession was becoming an accomplished fact, the appointment of John A. Dix as secretary of the treasury in place of Howell Cobb, with other changes in the cabinet, restored some measure of confidence in public credit. More vigorous efforts followed. By the act of February 8, 1861, a 6 per cent. loan was authorized with no restrictions as to sale at par, and this was reinforced by a new tax measure, the Morrill tariff. Nevertheless, when the new administration of Lincoln entered upon its difficult task on March 4, it found the treasury practically empty, the administrative departments disorganized, customs receipts almost at a standstill, the debt increasing, and government credit ebbing away. Nor could there be any thorough-going plans for the future, because nobody could clearly foresee the turn of political affairs.

The unsatisfactory condition of the treasury in 1860 is the more striking because the nation in that year was in excellent economic and material condition. The depression of 1857 was but temporary in its industrial effects; the development of railroad construction and shipping was speedily resumed; crops were abundant and prices remunerative. The cotton crop in 1860 reached 4,675,770 bales, nearly a million bales more than in any previous year; great gains had been made in the crops of wheat, corn, and other cereals; the production of anthracite coal in Pennsylvania was nearly 800,000 tons greater than in any preceding year; the output of pig iron was 913,000 tons, or 130,000 more than the average of the six preceding years; exports, including the precious metals, had reached the highest point then known, $400,000,000 (of which $316,000,000 was domestic merchandise), or $43,000,000 more than in any other previous year. The consuming powers of the people had never been so high, as was proved in particular by the unprecedented demand for sugar and tea; there was but little pauperism, and wealth on the whole was evenly distributed. 179,000 immigrants landed in 1860, or 58,000 in excess of the preceding year. The tonnage of American shipping was greater than ever before or since, and two-thirds of our imports and exports were carried in vessels having an American register.

In this wonderful material expansion and prosperity the Northern States had the advantage. Of the total population of 31,444,321, returned by the census of 1860, two-thirds were in the States which remained in the Union in 1861. The value of the real and personal property of the whole country was estimated at $16,159,000,000, of which $10,957,000,000 was credited to the northern group, and in the southern share was included $2,000,000,000 for slave property. The wealth produced in 1859 was valued at $3,736,000,000, of which $2,818,000,000 was in the North. There were a thousand million acres of unoccupied public lands north and west of the slave region, a source of potential wealth to the struggling government: as Secretary Chase said, "There are other mines than those of gold and silver; every acre of the fertile soil is a mine, and every acre is open to the fruitful contact of labor by the Homestead Act." The gold-bearing region of the Western States with comparatively insignificant exceptions was still the property of the nation; and the annual product of gold and silver was nearly $100,000,000. The contribution of Southern ports to the total import duties had been but $7,000,000, or 14 per cent. of the ordinary annual income from customs, and it was estimated that of the imports the South consumed less than half of its proportion according to population. The North was also fortunate in possessing the principal share of the manufacturing industries of the country.

118. Appointment of Chase.

The political storm burst on the country with startling rapidity: the South Carolina Ordinance of Secession came December 20, 1860; the Southern Confederacy was formed February 4, 1861; the civil war began with the firing on Fort Sumter, April 12; and the president called for troops April 15. During the four years of war that followed, one of the most serious concerns of the government was its public finance. For secretary of the treasury President Lincoln chose Salmon P. Chase of Ohio. Chase was a lawyer who had been senator from Ohio and governor of that State, and his long experience in the field of politics made him a rival candidate to Lincoln in the Republican Convention of 1860. His experience in public finance was small and his previous political career had never called for a thorough consideration of the problems of the treasury. The appointment, however, was not very different from the usual practice of successive administrations which made political leadership the principal reason in selecting a secretary of the treasury. Chase was reluctant to accept the appointment. "I sought to avoid it," he writes, "and would now gladly decline it if I might. I find it impossible to do so, however, without seeming to shirk cares and labor for the common good, which cannot be honorably shunned." A criticism of Chase's appointment or of his administration of the finances must take into full account the political traditions which had thus far governed cabinet selections; and it must also be remembered that neither Lincoln nor his cabinet officers appreciated the enormous and unprecedented strain which was to be placed upon the treasury department. Even when the difficulties were realized, everybody supposed that they would be of short duration. To accuse Lincoln of gross error of judgment, or Chase of rash willingness to undertake duties for which he had not complete preparation, is to judge them by events which they could not foresee.

Any attempt to estimate the success of Chase as a minister of war finance must also keep in view the legislative personalities through whom he had to work. The chairman of the House committee on ways and means, Thaddeus Stevens, was a man of great force, but untrained in matters of taxation and loans, and in disposition dogmatic, arbitrary, and impatient. Although he delegated the preparation of details to Justin S. Morrill, chairman of a sub-committee on taxation, and to Elbridge G. Spaulding, chairman of a sub-committee on loans and currency, he exercised a great influence in the framing of financial policies. Morrill had little opportunity in the early years of the war to exhibit his practical good sense in questions of the development of revenue; and in the framing of tax bills, where the plain necessity was a large revenue, he was hampered by strong protectionist sympathies. Spaulding's experience had been limited to the treasuryship of the State of New York and the management of a local bank in Buffalo, and there is no evidence that he was competent to deal with great national measures. In the Senate, Fessenden, the chairman of the committee on finance, was an able lawyer, but confessed his inexperience on many subjects with which he had to deal. Since 1845 there had been little to arouse public opinion or to train statesmen in questions of finance. Amid universal prosperity the tariff changes of 1846 and 1857 had not provoked prolonged discussion; and the attention of Congress had been chiefly turned to the question of slavery.

119. Revenue Measures, July, 1861

When Chase entered upon his work the public debt was $74,985,000, of which about $18,000,000 had been incurred since the beginning of the secession movement. The available funds in the treasury were but $1,716,000; and until Congress met for new legislation Chase was obliged to rely upon previous loan acts, of which the treasury had not yet fully availed itself. The result was not encouraging. Only a small amount of bonds was sold and these at a discount, and the few millions of treasury notes issued were entirely inadequate. When Congress met in special session, July 4, 1861, Chase was ready to propose financial measures on a more comprehensive scale. He estimated that the sum needed for the next year would not fall far short of $320,000,000 itemized as follows: —

Appropriations for former years yet unpaid . . .	$20,121,000
" already made for 1862	59,589,000
" required by new exigencies . . .	217,169,000
" to pay treasury notes becoming due	12,640,000
" to pay interest on public debt . .	9,000,000

To provide for the ordinary expenditures, for the interest on the public debt to be created, and for a sinking fund to extinguish the debt, Chase recommended that $80,000,000 be raised by taxation; the extraordinary expenses were to be met by loans. He urged no great development in the existing tax system; partly because the possibilities of the tariff act of March, 1861, had not yet been put to satisfactory test, and partly because he did not apprehend that the struggle would continue for more than a few months. He did, however, recommend that duties be levied on tea and coffee, then admitted free, and on sugar which was lightly taxed; from these sources he thought that $20,000,000 might be derived; and that a slight increase on the general list of dutiable articles would also add $7,000,000 to a tariff of which the ordinary productivity might be estimated at $30,000,000. With miscellaneous revenue he counted on a total of $60,000,000 a year; whether the remaining $20,000,000 should be raised by taxation, and whether by direct taxes or internal revenue duties, Chase was in doubt; and with deliberately expressed deference he left the selection of the particular sort of taxation to Congress.

On the proposed loan of $240,000,000 Chase suggested a high rate of interest, 7.3 per cent. on short-term treasury notes, or 7 per cent. on long-term bonds, to be sold at not less than par; for immediate needs he favored an issue of treasury notes in smaller denominations bearing a lower rate of interest. "The greatest care will, however, be requisite to prevent a degradation of such issues into an irredeemable paper currency, than which no more certainly fatal expedient for impoverishing the masses and discrediting the government of any country can well be devised." Congress quickly accepted the secretary's plan and in loan bills of July 17 and August 5, 1861, empowered the secretary to borrow not exceeding $250,000,000 in three-year 7.3 per cent. treasury notes or in twenty-year bonds not exceeding 7 per cent. The secretary was also authorized, in lieu of a portion of the above loan, to exchange for coin or pay for salaries or other dues of the United States non-interest-bearing treasury notes not exceeding $50,000,000, of a denomination less than $50 but not less than $5, payable on demand and receivable for all public dues; or notes bearing interest at 3.65 per cent., fundable into treasury notes of denominations over $50, and payable in one year. Unfortunately Congress did not respond so energetically to the recommendations made as to taxation; a few amendments of the tariff were enacted along the general lines suggested by Chase, but the rates in some instances were less than he desired. A direct tax and an income tax were also imposed, but were not to be effective until after periods of eight and ten months respectively. No more finance legislation was possible until the following winter; and the administration was left poorly equipped with resources for the contest now entered upon. Abundance of credit had been granted, but the revenue provided was insufficient to maintain this above suspicion and still more insufficient for the daily needs of the treasury.

120. Placing the Loan of $150,000,000.

In accordance with the provisions of the above-mentioned act the secretary undertook to borrow $150,000,000 by the issue of 7.3 per cent. three-year notes. In view of the difficulties encountered by the treasury department in placing small loans during the previous winter of 1860–1861 this operation might well seem hopeless; but three changes in conditions had occurred which affected the disposition of capitalists with funds to invest. In the first place a definite policy had been adopted; loan and tax bills had gone hand in hand; and, in the light available to the most acute political observers of the time, ample provision had been made for the demands of a contest which it was confidently believed would be over in a few months. Secondly, a more liberal rate of interest was authorized, which tended to attract capital deprived by political disturbance of its ordinary commercial use. Thirdly, the spirit of loyalty was being aroused to the recognition of the need of financial as well as military support of the government; business men more intelligently realized the dependence of commercial interests on the stability of the government. Thus it was possible in one operation to borrow and transfer from the people to the government more wealth than had as yet ever stood as the principal of the public debt.

Representatives of the banking institutions of Boston, New York, Philadelphia, after consultation with the secretary, "agreed to unite as associates in financial support to the government," to subscribe to an immediate loan of $50,000,000, and to promise to take two further instalments of $50,000,000 each. The securities issued were to be in the form of three-year 7.3 per cent. treasury notes. The task of the banks was not an easy one, for the institutions undertaking the negotiations possessed a capital of only $120,000,000, and their coin assets amounted to only $63,000,000; but it was agreed that the banks should be the medium of popular subscriptions through which the burden was to be transferred to private lenders. The inherent difficulty of carrying out the plan was great; and it was increased by differences as to the meaning of the agreement between the government and banks. In order to prevent the removal of a large volume of money from the channels of business, the banks desired that the funds which they loaned to the government should remain in their custody until checked out by the government to meet current disbursements. This meant, of course, that the banks would be permitted to use their notes in the payment of treasury checks. Under the sub-treasury act only coin was receivable by the treasury, but the existing public distrust had caused hoarding, and there was a relatively small amount of specie then available in the country; hence the transfer of so large a sum as $150,000,000 in gold was regarded by many experts as impracticable. It was indeed asserted that the act of August 5, 1861 (amending the loan act of July 17), in allowing "the secretary of the treasury to deposit any of the moneys obtained on any of the loans now authorized by law, to the credit of the treasurer of the United States, in such solvent specie-paying banks as he may select," was intended to give the secretary elastic powers to receive bank bills or book credit in place of coin. James Gallatin, representing some New York banks, declared "that this provision was particularly intended to authorize drafts for disbursements against the deposits created by the taking of loans." The secretary, however, strictly construed the sub-treasury bill and insisted that the banks should make their settlements in specie.

Another ground of remonstrance by bankers was Chase's free use of his power to issue demand notes; these notes were legal tender for the payment of public dues, and if they went largely into circulation the banks would naturally receive less gold in their daily business transactions, and thus would be less able to fulfil their loan agreement with the government. Some bankers asserted that the secretary had promised not to use this power. At first the notes were issued with moderation, but in November the secretary gave way to what he considered the imperative claims of the treasury and put out notes freely, on the ground that Congress had ordered appropriations beyond those estimated in the summer, and that the revenues from imports did not come up to the estimates; he saw no other relief. In spite of the differences of opinion, banks for a time continued to co-operate with the treasury department in carrying out the original agreement for the purchase of bonds.

When Congress met in December, 1861, the secretary in his regular annual report was obliged to revise the estimates of July, and to ask Congress for further means; he now estimated that taxation would yield less than was originally expected, and that appropriations would be larger by $214,000,000. Once more the secretary attempted to apply his principle of a proper balance between taxation and loans without a radical increase in taxes. He recommended a slight increase in customs duties, a readjustment of the direct taxes so that the loyal States should pay all of the $20,000,000; and the imposition of slight internal revenue duties, which, including the income tax, would yield $30,000,000. The secretary, like many other statesmen, still entertained the hope that the war might be brought to an auspicious termination before midsummer.

In connection with a request for authority to make further loans of $200,000,000 the secretary advanced his first proposals for a national banking system. He believed that the time had come when Congress should exercise its authority over the credit circulation of the country. He thought his plan would give the following advantages: (1) uniformity of circulation, in place of a bank-note circulation dependent on the laws of 34 States and 1600 private corporations; (2) an increased security to the Union, because of a common interest created by the disposition of national securities as a basis of circulation; (3) the safest currency the country had ever enjoyed. Little emphasis was laid on the special demand for United States stock as a basis of bank circulation, but this advantage evidently was a strong reason for making the recommendation. Chase did not refer to the recent controversy with the banks, nor did he specially discuss the issue of the demand notes; on the general question of government paper currency he did call attention to the inconveniences and hazards of the issue of United States notes, possibly ending in the "immeasurable evils of dishonest public faith and national bankruptcy."

121. Suspension of Specie Payments.

Although the secretary did not officially take notice of the growing embarrassments of the banks, bankers found them very serious; and on December 30, under the lead of the New York City banks, specie payments were suspended throughout the country; and this action was speedily followed by the government. This sudden and eventful shock to private and public credit has been the subject of much controversy. Chase declared that suspension was inevitable, because of unexpected military reverses, increased expenditures, and diminished confidence in public securities; and in this conclusion Republican leaders of the time acquiesced; they denied that the issue of demand notes in any way caused suspension, since only $33,460,000 was in circulation at the date of suspension, and up to that day every note presented for payment had been promptly redeemed in coin.

On the other hand the bankers declared that the two reasons for suspension were first, the pressures on banks because they were not allowed to retain the government deposits received in the loan operations until they were actually needed; and second, the banks were expected by their customers to receive the government demand notes for deposit, and permit them to be drawn against in coin; and such a burden the banks affirmed was too heavy to carry. They therefore laid upon Chase the responsibility for the suspension of specie payments: first, because he forced the banks to transfer the principal of the loans to the government without giving them the advantage of retaining the funds temporarily on deposit; and, secondly, because the banks were obliged to sustain the credit of the demand notes as well as the bank-notes. It has even been declared that the banks were sacrificed on the altars of their own patriotism, and that Chase had a wild idea of locking up the funds thus secured until needed for expenditure, so as to make a broader field for the circulation of United States demand notes.[1]

A fair judgment on this important question will be aided by carefully considering the legislation which bears on the subject. In 1861 the law provided: (1) that the sub-treasury should receive and pay out only coin or government notes; (2) that the treasury could deposit with such specie-paying banks as might be selected any of the moneys obtained from the new loans. Mr. Horace White believes that the act of August 5, 1861, "suspended the operation of the sub-treasury act so as to allow the secretary to deposit public money in solvent specie-paying banks and to withdraw it at his own convenience and pleasure for the payment of public debts. In short, he was permitted to handle the proceeds of the three loans in whatsoever way he pleased." Possibly it may have been the intention in framing the law of August 5 to permit the banks to pay in notes as well as to receive deposits from the government, but it is not clearly expressed, and in the opinion of some, as for instance John Sherman, the secretary could hardly have acted other than he did without laying himself open to the charge of ignoring the law.[2] Against this opinion it may at least be admitted, without attempting to locate the blame, that the first material mistake in the management of the war finances occurred when the

[1] *Cong. Rec.*, Feb. 9, 1895, p. 2200.

[2] John Sherman, *Recollections*, vol. i, p. 269.

government declined to use the bank check and the clearing-house.

The real explanation of the financial crisis of December, 1861, is not to be found either in errors of the treasury or in the selfishness of the banks, but in the condition of public feeling and a lack of confidence in the success of the war. The credit of the government was undoubtedly injured by the failure of Chase to recommend or of Congress to enact a far-reaching system of taxation, and the recent Trent affair caused an apprehension of international difficulty with England. Because there was little indication that the credit of the government was to be supported by vigorous taxation, the banks were handicapped in their efforts to sell bonds to investors. Depositors were also withdrawing funds from the banks for hoarding, so that the specie reserve was slipping away. On January 1, 1862, the banks had but $87,000,000 of specie to meet $459,000,000 of indebtedness. It would have been impossible to go through a war on the basis of a currency system so inadequate.

The demand notes not only irritated the banks, they also held an important relation in subsequent discussion to the legal tenders and the agitation for fiat money. After the suspension of specie payments these notes which were receivable for all public dues, circulated at a premium over State bank-notes and also over the treasury notes or greenbacks, which were issued in the following year but were not made receivable for customs. Hence it has been argued that the greenback circulation issued in 1862 might have been kept at par with gold if it, too, had been made receivable for all payments to the government, as well as given a legal-tender quality for settling private debts. The depreciation of the greenback is thus ascribed to the fact that it was not given the fullest credence and honor by the fiat of the government. The premium for the demand notes was, however, not due solely to their receivability in payment of duties; other causes had influence, such as the joint effect of the limitation upon their quantity and the prohibition of reissue.

122. Issue of Legal-Tender Notes.

The recommendations of Secretary Chase in his report of December, 1861, were referred to the committee on ways and means, and by it to a sub-committee of which E. G. Spaulding of New York was chairman; in due time the sub-committee prepared a bill which resulted in the act of February 25, 1862, one of the landmarks in the history of American finance. Its main provisions are as follows: (1) the issue of $150,000,000 of legal-tender United States notes (including the demand notes already authorized, in denominations of not less than $5); (2) the issue of $500,000,000 of bonds (familiarly known as five-twenties, redeemable after five years and payable in twenty years) bearing 6 per cent. interest, to be sold at market value for coin or treasury notes; (3) the issue of certificates of deposit bearing 5 per cent. interest, in exchange for United States notes left on deposit not less than thirty days, and to an amount not exceeding $25,000,000, payable after ten days' notice; (4) the creation of a sinking-fund.

No more striking illustration of the unsympathetic relations of a cabinet minister with the legislative branch can be found in the range of fiscal history; the act does not so much as mention the national banking system advocated by the secretary, but it does authorize legal-tender notes, which the secretary had not suggested and to which he was at heart opposed. The suspension of specie payments which occurred after the submission of the secretary's report had in a measure changed the situation; but, with all allowances possible, the history of the legal-tender act is a remarkable commentary upon the methods of financial legislation at this period. The account of Spaulding, chairman of the sub-committee, is that he applied to Chase for details on a new system of bank currency; inasmuch as the secretary did not promptly respond with a bill, he himself began the preparation of a measure such as he thought the treasury department desired, but while engaged upon it came to the conclusion that it could not be made available quickly enough to meet the crisis. "A system of national banks could not be organized and put in effective force for more than a year, and in the mean time the State banks would be in a condition of suspension, without coin or the possibility of obtaining it, and we need effective money." He saw that no tax legislation could be promptly effective; hence he drafted a section authorizing legal-tender notes, which was later, on January 7, 1862, submitted to Congress as a separate bill.

At first great opposition appeared throughout the country; the metropolitan press, with two exceptions, denounced it, and committees representing the State banks hastened to Washington to set forth their objections and to propose another project involving an increase in taxation, an issue of non-legal-tender two-year treasury notes, the use of banks as depositories of public funds, and the sale of bonds without limitation as to price. The bankers' plan, however, ran counter to popular convictions; it was virtually an abandonment of the sub-treasury system, against which there was no longer opposition; and it was a plan of carrying on the operations of the government by banks over which Congress had no control and which could issue money without limit so far as national laws affected it. It was furthermore shown that in the loyal States the bank circulation of January 1, 1862, was only $132,000,000; that this was diffused throughout the country and was not sufficient for the purpose of negotiating the loans which were required; and finally that there was popular opposition to selling bonds below par. Nor did the bankers' scheme appeal to the leaders of the political party which had breathed deep of the spirit of national sovereignty. Banks were referred to as "usurers" and "note-shavers;" "shinning" by the government through Wall street was strongly condemned; and the government was advised to "nerve up." "Why, then, go into the streets at all to borrow money?" "I prefer to assert the power and dignity of the government by the issue of its own notes." "To render the government financially more independent, it is necessary to make the United States notes a legal tender."

The debate opened January 28. Originally Mr. Spaulding's bill proposed the issue of only $100,000,000 of legal-tender notes, but the idea once planted grew with rapidity. Chase was reluctant to accept the measure, but day by day as the immediate needs of the country became more pressing and legislation lingered his opposition faded away. Nevertheless the measure did not pass the House without earnest protests, based both upon the unconstitutionality of the measure and upon the economic disasters it would entail. "If it be a war measure," said Morrill, "it is a measure which will be of greater advantage to the enemy. I would as soon provide Chinese wooden guns for the army as paper money alone for the army. It will be a breach of public faith. It will injure creditors; it will increase prices; it will increase many fold the cost of the war." This view was supported in many quarters and the government was assured that those who had sent their sons to the conflict would even more willingly lend their credit.

In the Senate the bill was supported by Senator Sherman in a speech the burden of which may stand as typical of the current argument: he said that every organ of financial opinion in the country was agreed as to the necessity of a legal-tender clause if the issue of demand notes was authorized; its necessity had been declared by the secretary of the treasury, the Chambers of Commerce of New York, Boston, and Philadelphia, the Committee of Public Safety of New York, and in fact by almost every recognized organ of financial opinion in the country; $100,000,000 was immediately due to the army and $250,000,000 was due by July 1; the banks had exhausted their capital in making loans; money could not be borrowed except at great sacrifice; there was no money to buy bonds; gold and silver had ceased to circulate; legal-tender currency was necessary to aid in making further loans; without the legal-tender clause the notes proposed to be issued would fall dead upon the money market; with it the notes will be the life-blood of the business of the country; the issue of $150,000,000 cannot do harm; it is only a mere temporary expedient. "As a member of this body, I am armed with high powers for a holy purpose, and I am authorized — nay, required — to vote for the laws necessary and proper for executing these high powers, and to accomplish that purpose. This is not the time when I would limit these powers. Rather than yield to revolutionary force I would use revolutionary force." If soldiers were to be compelled to take these notes as money, every one else should be compelled to take them. Sherman's main argument was that of necessity — necessity to meet the immediate obligations of government; necessity to give currency to treasury notes; necessity to provide money which would in turn purchase bonds; he was willing to leave the question of constitutionality to the courts.

The bill passed the House by a vote of 93 to 59; in the Senate it was considerably modified. The House provision that the treasury notes should be receivable for taxes, debts, and demands of all kinds due to the United States and all debts and demands owing by the United States was amended by requiring that duties on imports should be paid in coin, and that the interest on the bonds to be sold should be payable in coin. The Senate also added the sections authorizing the sale of bonds, the issue of certificates of deposit, and the establishment of a sinking fund. "These amendments," says Senator Sherman,[1] "were considered of prime importance. It was felt that the duty on imported goods should not be lessened by any depreciation of our local currency. Such importations were based upon coin value, and the tax levied upon them was properly required to be paid in coin. This security of coin payment would enable the government to sell the bonds at a far higher rate than they would have commanded without it; and tended also to limit the depreciation

[1] *Recollections*, vol. i, p. 275.

of United States notes," which were convertible into bonds. The majority in the Senate was overwhelming, the vote being 30 to 7.

The act says nothing as to time of repayment of the legal-tender notes and makes no pledge against further issue. A most important clause permitted the conversion of the legal-tender notes into five-twenty bonds; for it was argued that holders of notes would instinctively desire to exchange them for interest-bearing bonds; and upon reissue by the government they could be again exchanged for bonds. According to Stevens, this process would operate with such magic that the $500,000,000 of bonds authorized would be subscribed before the government could use the funds; $150,000,000 of paper notes would do the work of $500,000,000 in bonds!

The first step was soon repeated; in little more than three months, because of the inability of the government to borrow on the terms authorized, and the tardy effect of new taxes, Secretary Chase asked for another issue of legal tenders, a part of which should be in denominations of less than five dollars. Congress quickly assented by the act of July 11, 1862, providing for the issue of another $150,000,000, of which $35,000,000 should be in denominations less than five dollars but not less than one dollar. On January 17, 1863, a third issue of $100,000,000 was authorized, increased March 3 to $150,000,000, all of which might be in denominations of one dollar or over. By this time opposition had practically disappeared in Congress, for in the House the last bill passed to its third reading on the same day that it was presented, and in the Senate concurrence was secured on the following day by a vote of 38 to 2. Provision was made for the reissue of the new notes but not for their conversion into bonds; and the right of conversion for previous issues was to cease on July 1, 1863. Of the $450,000,000 authorized under the three acts named, $431,000,000 was actually outstanding on June 30, 1864. This was the end of emissions of non-interest legal-tender notes; these issues were supplemented by fractional currency and by interest-bearing notes running for a brief period, both of which classes were endowed with the legal-tender quality.

No subject in American finance has been more controverted than the exact degree of Secretary Chase's responsibility for the issue of legal tenders. That Mr. Chase was no friend of paper money is easily proven; by private experience, political training, and conviction he shared in a distrust of the local banking associations. When entering upon the duties of governor of Ohio in 1856, he referred to all mere paper-money systems as pregnant with fraud, justly incurring universal reproach. In his report of July, 1861, he recognized in plain language the danger in the issue of demand notes; he made no suggestion of legal tenders in his report of December, 1861; and it was with great reluctance that he accepted the plan formulated during the next few weeks by Spaulding's sub-committee. Chase was governed by "public exigency." On January 22 he regretted "exceedingly that it is found necessary to resort to the measure of making fundable notes of the United States a legal tender"; on January 29 it was his "anxious wish to avoid the necessity of such legislation"; if, however, United States notes be issued, "discriminations should if possible be prevented; and the provision making the notes a legal tender in a great measure at least prevents it, by putting all citizens in this respect on the same level, both of rights and duties"; and on February 5 he insisted that "it is very important that the bill should go through to-day, and through the Senate this week. The public exigencies do not admit of delay." He probably did not expect that the notes would remain in permanent circulation, since they were made convertible into the five-twenty bonds. Further proof of his innate dislike of the system may be found in his successive annual reports urging a limitation on the issues, and finally in the notable decision delivered in 1869, when as chief justice he declared that the legal-tender clause was unconstitutional.

The critics of Chase, however, assert that if he was so reluctant to issue notes, his political and moral responsibility was so much the greater; that his opposition to legal tenders was weak-hearted; an able financier should not have accepted with reluctance a proposition which he thought alarming, but should have aggressively fought it to the end. A bolder opponent of legal-tender paper money if pressed too hard by an impatient Congress would at least have used every agency in his power to avoid a second issue: he would have insisted on more taxation, and the selling of bonds for what they would bring; he would for the time being have smothered his antagonism to local banks, and accepted the conclusion that a great struggle for national preservation and national credit was not the time for reforming the paper currency by bringing forward a scheme of national banking.

To such an arraignment an answer may be found in a passage of the report of Fessenden, the successor of Chase, in December, 1864: "It is, in the secretary's judgment, not only difficult but impossible to apply fixed rules to a condition of affairs constantly changing, or to meet contingencies which no human reason can foresee by a steady application of general laws, especially in a government and with a people where public opinion is the controlling element, and that opinion is not under the direction of those who may happen to administer public affairs. Accordingly it has been seen that the attempt to conduct financial operations on so immense a scale, upon a strict specie basis, soon proved impracticable."

123. Convertibility of the Greenback.

The details of the loans and taxation during the war may be postponed to another chapter, but it is advisable here to carry the history of the legal tenders down to the end of the war, and to describe some of the economic results of the system. In the first place, it is to be observed that the first two issues of legal-tender notes were fundable within five years at the option of the holder into 6 per cent. gold bonds; this privilege was an indirect method of redeeming the notes by turning them into the most valuable and best protected form of government indebtedness founded on a specie support. Within a year, however, Chase objected to the option thus given to the holder of the note on the ground that it restricted the treasury in the sale of bonds. Obviously it would be impossible to sell bonds bearing a lower rate of interest, as he believed he could, so long as 6 per cent. bonds could be had through the funding of legal-tender notes. In view of his objections the act of March 3, 1863, made no provision for conversion of the third series of legal tenders, and even changed the contract expressed in the previous issues by requiring that the right to exchange notes already issued for bonds should be exercised before July 1 of that year. The note-holders made little protest and the serious results of this shifting of conditions were not recognized until afterwards. Spaulding, who took so important a part in the original legal-tender legislation, regarded this change of policy as the greatest mistake of the war; for legal-tender notes were a forced loan from the people to the government, and the former were protected as long as the lender had the option of promptly converting the notes into a loan at a fair rate of interest. After the act of March 3, 1863, the previous standard of value as measured in bonds was destroyed, and this led to an advance in the price of gold expressed in commodities and services. Senator Sherman in 1876 declared that this alteration was a most fatal step, and for his part in acquiescing in and voting for it he felt more regret than for any other act of his official life. Although the supporters of the administration maintained that there was no right which could not be barred by a statute of limitation, it was justly held that the credit of the government had suffered by this paltering with the public faith; and Chase so far recognized the obligation as to allow the exchange to continue until the beginning of the year 1864.

The most serious effect of this suspension of convertibility was seen at the close of the war; under the original conditions the legal-tender notes would have eventually returned to the treasury to be exchanged for gold-bearing bonds, and contraction of the currency would have proceeded according to economic law, instead of being subjected to the rigid formulæ of statutes, or to the vacillating policy of an administrative secretary. On the other hand, after the credit of the government so advanced that the bonds rose in market value above par in greenbacks, the government got the advantage of sales at a premium or the equal advantage of placing bonds at a lower rate of interest; this advantage, however, could not compensate for the indirect disadvantages of the greenbacks in weakening the assets of the treasury, nor for the subsequent unsteadiness of the standard of values.

124. Depreciation of the Greenback.

The economic results of the successive issues of the legal-tender United States notes, accompanied by enormous issues of short-term treasury notes which circulated almost as money, make a chapter of monetary history and experience too long for this work. The difficulty of clear comprehension is increased by the rapid expansion during the same period of local bank circulation, which added to the inflation. The two most distinct consequences to the government were: the rise of prices of commodities, and the fluctuating premium on gold. The first greatly increased the cost of the war, and the second seriously disturbed the operations of the treasury, which was especially interested in stable quotations of specie because on the one side it received gold for customs and on the other hand it paid it out in interest on its bonds.

The depreciation of the currency, measured in gold, is seen in the following table, which gives by months, 1862–1865, the average gold price of one hundred dollars in currency in the New York market: —

Month	1862	1863	1864	1865
January	$98	$69	$64	$46
February	97	62	63	49
March	98	65	61	57
April	98	66	58	67
May	97	67	57	74
June	94	69	47	71
July	87	77	39	70
August	87	79	39	70
September	84	74	45	69
October	78	68	48	69
November	76	68	43	68
December	76	66	44	68

The other index of depreciation is found in the general rise of prices; this cannot be attributed alone to the issue of paper currency; other factors were at work, such as increased taxation and the insatiable consumption of provisions and materials of war. We cannot take the premium on gold as measuring the difference between actual prices and the prices which would have existed if the country had remained on a gold basis, for the premium varied sharply from day to day, according to the progress of the war, the movements of foreign trade, or the manipulations of speculators; while the changes in prices moved sluggishly. When allowance is made for all the special factors there was an undoubted rise in general prices which can only be accounted for by the existence of a large volume of depreciated currency. The total effect of paper issues in increasing the cost of the war has been estimated at between $528,000,000 and $600,000,000; even this large amount is small when compared with the burdens which inflated prices placed upon the people in the ordinary relations of trade and industry.

True to the general law that wages of labor do not respond to economic forces as promptly as prices of commodities, statistical inquiry shows that the depreciated value of the money medium during the Civil War was not reflected in an equal measure by an increase of money wages. The relative course of prices and money wages has been computed in the "Aldrich Report" as follows: —

Year	Prices	Money wages
1860	100.0	100.0
1861	100.6	100.8
1862	117.8	102.9
1863	148.6	110.5
1864	190.5	125.6
1865	216.8	143.1

As the purchasing power of earnings was greatly diminished a heavy load was placed upon the laborers of the country. The government was the largest employer of labor in workmen, clerks and soldiers; but the government rarely makes changes in its salaries or pay, and hence did not feel the full effect of the increase in wages which took place in the individual field of labor. Of course government officials complained because the increased cost of living was out of proportion to income; and some of the best trained and most competent employees left the public service. The wages of soldiers, from the beginning of the war, long remained at $13 a month, although prices had about doubled by 1864. The distress indeed became so great that Congress on May 1, 1864, advanced the pay to $16 per month in currency. This was no great relief, since after the increase prices continued to rise. Artisans were forced to make similar sacrifices; the depreciated currency in its final consequences affected every wealth producer.

125. Gold Premium.

Another important consequence of the suspension of specie payments was the fluctuating premium on gold caused by the demand for specie as a commercial commodity. Gold was required in large quantities for three purposes: by the government for the payment of interest on bond issues; by importers to pay customs duties; and by bankers to settle balances due abroad. The stock of gold in the country in 1861 was not large, and was speedily lessened by the extension of paper issues and by unfavorable balances of trade, due to the sale of American securities by foreign holders and the decline of important exports. During 1862 the fluctuations in the quotations of gold in paper currency ranged between 102 and 132; in 1863 between 125 and 160; and in 1864 between 155 and 285. The political and economic factors which occasioned these varied changes were many and have been exhaustively treated by Mr. Wesley C. Mitchell in a recent study. Among the most striking of these influences he mentions the following:

First, the increase in the amount of greenbacks as, for example, reflected in the rapid rise of premium after July 11, 1862, the date of the second legal-tender act; secondly, the condition of the treasury as disclosed from time to time by the secretary's reports; thirdly, the credit of the government from week to week as shown in the quotations of its bonds; fourthly, changes in the personnel of the government, either in the treasury department or in Congress through political elections; fifthly, the state of the foreign relations of the country; sixthly, the war news and the fluctuation between hope and discouragement consequent upon military success or defeat. At the time, however, the relation between these several factors and the premium on gold was not clearly apprehended either by the treasury department or by Congress.

Purely speculative influences also played an important part in the variations of the premium. In order to provide a market for the purchase and sale of gold, an exchange was opened in New York, and the legitimate dealings executed there were quickly supplemented by the gambling of speculators, who found in the rapid fluctuations the elements of chance which always claims its followers. So open was this trading, virtually in the public credit, that it constituted in the minds of many a public scandal. It became an accepted belief that the evil of fluctuation was due to the "unpatriotic criminal efforts of speculators and probably of secret enemies to raise the price of gold regardless of the injury inflicted upon the country." "Gold gamblers as a class," said one senator, "were disloyal men in sympathy with the South."

It was indeed charged that some of the banks had assisted in this trading by making loans based on speculative values of special deposits of gold.[1]

Various methods were consequently enacted to check and even to stop this form of trading. For example, a tax was placed (March 3, 1863) upon time-sales of gold; and loans upon coin for security for more than its par value were prohibited. Chase also experimented with selling exchange upon London at a rate below the market, but this proved inoperative. Finally June 17, 1864, a "gold bill" to prevent wagers in the price of gold was enacted with the approval if not at the prompting of Secretary Chase. This act declared unlawful any contract to purchase or sell gold to be delivered on any day subsequent to the making of the contract; it also forbade the purchase or the sale of foreign exchange to be delivered at any time beyond ten days subsequent to the making of such contract; or the making of any contract for the sale and delivery of any gold coin or bullion of which the person making such contract was not at the time of making it in actual possession. The predicted failure of such drastic legislation was soon realized. The fluctuations in the premium on gold during the next few days defied all calculations, varying as follows: —

June	18,	95	to	95¼
"	20,	98	"	98½
"	21,	99½	"	108
"	22,	105	"	135
"	23,	105	"	125
"	24,	110	"	117
"	25,	112	"	120
"	27,	130	"	140
"	28,	130	"	140
"	29,	140	"	150
"	30,	140	"	151
July	1,	125	"	185
"	2,	130	"	150
"	5,	140	"	149

[1] Bolles, vol. iii, p. 142.

The situation in New York became intolerable; protests rushed upon Congress; and the law was repealed July 2, in fifteen days after its passage From this time on, in spite of rapid fluctuations, the range of depreciation was held in check; no more non-interest-bearing legal tenders were issued beyond the $450,000,000 authorized under the three laws referred to on page 288, and the military successes which occurred during the summer of 1864 presaged the speedy end of the war.

CHAPTER XIII.

LOANS, TAXATION, AND BANKING OF THE CIVIL WAR.

126. References.

BIBLIOGRAPHIES: Bogart and Rawles, 47–49.

LOANS: *Finance Report*, 1861, pp. 7–10; 1862, pp. 24–25; 1863, pp. 13–18; 1864, pp. 19–22; *Statutes*, XII, 259, 313, 345, 352, 709; XIII, 13, 218, 425, 468; or Dunbar, 160–198; Bayley, 370–383, 446–462; W. F. de Knight, 81–99; J. Sherman, *Recollections*, I, 299–302; J. W. Schuckers, *Life of Chase*, 338–355, 406–417; H. C. Adams, *Finance*, 537–542; or *Public Debts*, 126–133, 167; D. Kinley, *Independent Treasury System*, 101–111; A. B. Hart, *Chase*, 236–245; E. A. Ross, *Sinking Funds*, in *Pub. Amer. Econ. Assn.*, VII, 389; H. Adams, *Historical Essays*, 288–300; H. McCulloch, *Men and Measures*, 184; J. J. Knox, *United States Notes*, 97 (price of bonds); E. P. Oberholtzer, *Jay Cooke*, I, 212–325; 538–658.

TAXATION: *Finance Report*, 1863, pp. 3, 62–78 (internal revenue); 1864, p. 14; 1865, pp. 27–31; 1883, pp. 163–165 (direct tax); *Statutes*, XII, 294; XIII, 223, 432, 469; E. Young, *Customs Tariff Legislation*, cxxi–cxlii; *Report of Revenue Commission*, 1865–1866 (Well's etc.), pp. 13–16, 18–37, 44–48, 161–167; G. S. Boutwell, *Reminiscences*, I, 303–315; J. Sherman, *Recollections*, 302–309, 329–332; J. Sherman, *Speeches*, 299–306, 317 (income tax); J. W. Schuckers, *Life of Chase*, 312–316, 332–337; F. C. Howe, *Taxation under Internal Revenue System*, 50–190, 82–90 (direct tax); J. G. Blaine, *Twenty Years*, I, 429–434; F. W. Taussig, *History of the Tariff*, 160–170; Bolles, III, 63, 159–196, 398–405 (internal revenue); W. M. Daniels, *Public Finance*, 136–143 (tax on spirits); C. F. Dunbar, *The Direct Tax in* 1861, in *Quar. Jour. Econ.*, III, 444–451; J. A. Hill, *The Civil War Income Tax*, in *Quar. Jour. Econ.*, VIII, 416, 491; S. W. McCall, *Stevens*, 174–181; Stanwood, II, 109–138.

NATIONAL BANKING SYSTEM: *Finance Report*, 1861, pp. 18–20; 1862, pp. 17–21; 1863, pp. 20–21, 49–58; 1864, pp. 46–55; *Statutes*, XII, 665; XIII, 99, 484; or Dunbar, 171; J. W. Million, *Debate on National Bank Act of* 1863, in *Jour. Pol. Econ.*, II (1894), 251, 280 (references to *Congressional Globe*); E. McPherson, *Political History of the Rebellion*, 356–573; J. Sherman, *Speeches*, 32–79; J. Sherman, *Recollections*, I, 284–299; J. G. Blaine, *Twenty Years*, I, 470–487; J. J. Knox, *History of Banking*, 96–101, 220–269 (includes summary of debate); H. McCulloch, *Men and Measures*, 165–170; J. W. Schuckers, *Life of Chase*, 282–311;

Report of Monetary Commission (1898), 197–203, 505, 508, 511 (statutes); Bolles, III, 197–226; W. G. Sumner, *History of Banking*, I, 457–464; C. F. Dunbar, *History and Theory of Banking*, 132–141; C. A. Conant, *History of Modern Banking*, 348–366; H. White, 406–414; J. K. Upton, *Money and Politics*, 111–126; W. C. Mitchell, in *Jour. Pol. Econ.*, X (1902), 539–543 (State bank-note circulation); A. B. Hart, *Chase*, 274–284.

COST OF THE WAR: Bolles, III, 241–248; H. C. Adams, *Public Debts*, 127–133.

127. Taxation in 1861-1862.

The weakest element in the financiering of the Civil War was the delay in applying effective taxation. During the four fiscal years 1862–1865 the net receipts from taxes and loans (including treasury notes) were as follows: —

	Customs	Internal revenue and income tax	Total taxes[1]	Loans including treasury notes[2]
1861–62	$49,056,397		$50,851,729	$433,663,538
1862–63	69,059,642	$37,640,787	108,185,534	596,203,071
1863–64	102,316,152	109,741,134	212,532,936	719,476,032
1864–65	84,928,260	209,464,215	295,593,048	872,574,145
Total	$305,360,451	$356,846,136	$667,163,247	$2,621,916,786

From this it will be observed that during 1861-62 the ratio of loans to taxes was as $8.52 to $1; in 1862–63, as $5.51 to $1; in 1863–64, as $3.38 to $1; and in 1864–65, as $2.95 to $1.

It is easy after the war to blame the government for its procrastination and lack of vigor in laying taxes, but in 1861 and in the early part of 1862 the way did not appear clear. The blunder of delay was due in part to the fact that a new tariff had just been enacted; it is probable if there had been a clear realization of the enormous demands

[1] Including $4,956,657 in payments on a direct tax.

[2] Obtained by subtracting "expenditures on account of loans" from "receipts on account of loans" as given in the "Finance Reports," premiums in each case being added in. The results differ slightly from those obtained by taking issues and redemptions of public debt as given by Bayley, and summarized on page 308.

which would soon threaten the treasury, that the Morrill tariff measure would have been thoroughly recast before passage even at the expense of protection; there was, however, no such misgiving, and the law of March 2, 1861, was enacted, as framed in the peaceful days of the spring of 1860. For similar reasons the tariff act of August 5, 1861, touched only a small part of the schedules, increasing the rates on sugar, tea, coffee, and several other food products, not native to the United States; on hemp, hides, rubber, silk, lead, salt, soda, brandy, spices, and a few other articles. The act of December 24, 1861, was limited to raising the duties on sugar, tea, and coffee. This tardiness was not due to the unwillingness of the people to be taxed; there was no disposition to shirk the burdens of increased taxation; on the contrary, as stated by Senator Fessenden, the country was impatient to contribute; it had been calling for a tax bill that should raise revenue equal to the demands of the time; and so Representative Morrill referred, as early as January, 1862, to the necessity of assuring the country that whatever the army was doing, the committee on ways and means had not "hutted" nor gone into winter quarters.

In the development of a tax system appropriate to the events and conditions of the war, Chase took no leadership. At the outset, in July, 1861, he laid down certain propositions as to what constituted adequate revenue; but he believed that the war demanded no extraordinary taxation beyond what was necessary to pay the interest on the new loans created, and to extinguish annually a small amount of the new debt. In December, 1861, the taxation which Chase recommended was not intended to yield more than a fractional part of that expected from the loans, and he even advised against any radical change of the Morrill tariff, on the ground that the manufacturing interests ought to have a further trial of the system; he did ask, however, for internal revenue duties.

In January, 1862, Congress adopted a more determined

policy and announced its purpose to enact a revenue measure which would yield $150,000,000 annually. The plans included the development of an internal revenue system and the increase of customs duties. Of excise duties the country had had no experience for more than a generation, and conditions had greatly changed since 1815: the country was not homogeneous; over its broad surface were scattered the most diverse interests; population in some portions was dense, in others very sparse. In some States the people were without exception engaged in agriculture; in others there were important classes occupied in manufactures and commerce. It was therefore inevitable that an excise measure, when applied to so great a variety of subjects as it was absolutely necessary to include in order to yield an abundant revenue, should create some marked inequalities.

The guiding principle of the internal revenue measure of July 1, 1862, was the imposition of moderate duties upon a large number of objects rather than heavy duties upon a few. It included rates upon luxuries represented by spirits, ales, beer, and tobacco; licenses upon occupations; duties upon manufactures or products, upon auction sales, carriages, yachts, billiard tables, and plate; upon slaughtered cattle, hogs, and sheep; upon railroads, steamboats, and ferry boats, railroad bonds, banking institutions, and insurance companies; upon salaries and pay of officers in the service of the United States; upon advertisements, income, and legacies; and an extended list of stamp duties. The universality of this measure has been concisely described by Wells: "Wherever you find an article, a product, a trade, a profession, or a source of income, tax it."

Coincident with the enactment of this measure was the passage of a tariff bill (July 14, 1862); for the revision of import duties was absolutely required in view of the new duties placed by the internal revenue act upon domestic manufactures and industries. It was necessary "to make proper reparation, otherwise we shall have destroyed the goose that lays the golden egg." The protective features then added were simply designed to compensate temporarily for the internal duties. While the measure afforded in some instances more protection to the home manufacturer, it did not materially modify the provisions of the Morrill tariff of 1861.

128. Increase of Taxes.

In the secretary's report for 1862 there is no discussion whatever of taxation, although an internal revenue measure had been enacted by Congress which was more far-reaching than anything as yet suggested by Chase, and in 1863 the subject was dismissed with a short paragraph, in which attention is approvingly called to the recommendation of the commissioner of internal revenue, that excise receipts be increased to $150,000,000. The returns of the internal revenue measure of 1862 proved most disappointing: instead of the estimated $85,456,000 from internal revenue duties for the fiscal year 1862–1863, the returns were but $37,640,000. While this was a serious miscalculation, it was largely due to the unsettled conditions of business as well as to the necessity of establishing at short notice an entirely new branch of treasury administration for the collection of duties.

Although the revenue from customs duties more nearly approached the estimates, foreign trade was seriously affected by the energetic movements of the Confederate navy, and the proceeds of the new schedules were inadequate to the financial strain. A second expansion of the revenue policy was made in 1864, more far-reaching in its objects than that undertaken in 1862; but it was from the internal revenue law that the chief source of strength was derived. These duties were so increased in June, 1864, that their yield became twice as large as that from customs. Industry and commerce speedily adjusted themselves to the new conditions with the result that the taxes afforded a revenue of $109,741,000 in 1863–1864, and in the succeeding year of $209,464,000.[1] The general

[1] Although a new act was passed in 1864, the revenue of 1864–1865 was largely due to the old schedules of the first internal revenue act.

character of this excise act has been well summarized by Howe:

"In general the bill followed the lines outlined by earlier legislation, although a general increase in rates was made. Thus the duty upon spirits which had been 20 and 60 cents under the earlier laws, was increased to $1.50 and $2.00 per gallon under the new; upon smoking tobacco the tax was more than doubled, while the tax upon cigars was advanced from a maximum rate of $3.50 per thousand to a maximum rate of $40.00 per thousand. In a like manner, although not to such an extravagant extent, license taxes were increased, while specific duties upon many manufactured products were doubled. The general ad valorem rate was increased from 3 to 5 per cent. upon most articles included in the former schedule, while numerous new sources of revenue were ferreted out and taxed. Nothing was omitted, from the raw product to the finished commodity. Often an article received a half-dozen additions ere it reached the consumer. And not only were all the constituent elements which entered into an article taxed, as the bolts, rivets, castings, trimmings, and the like, of an engine, but the engine when completed was subject to an additional ad valorem duty upon its value; while all repairs which increased the value of an article 10 per cent. were rendered dutiable at a like rate."

The tariff act of June 30, 1864, like its predecessor of 1862, was necessary because of the increased excise duties placed upon manufactures; but it went further in the direction of protection, and did much to bring the customs schedules up to that level to which the country has since been accustomed. The average rate on dutiable commodities was increased from 37.2 per cent. under the act of 1862 to 47 per cent. A study of the measure does not yield much for guidance in finance. It was pushed through Congress with little debate; revenue was imperative; the industrial conditions of the country were in a rapid flux due to the abnormal and violent changes in price caused by the currency expansion;

and there was little opportunity to examine and no adequate expert opinion available to criticise details. This act of 1864 later became of interest because until 1883 it remained the basis and controlling principle of tariff legislation.

A few examples illustrate the character of the increases between 1861 and 1864: —

	Morrill tariff, March, 1861	Tariff of July 14, 1862	Tariff of June 30, 1864
Pig iron	$6 per ton	$6 per ton	$9 per ton
Iron rods	$20 per ton	$25 per ton	1½ cents per lb.
Steel in ingots valued less than 7 cents per lb.	1¼ cents per lb.	1¾ cents per lb.	2¼ cents per lb.
Salt	4 cents per bush.	18 cents per cwt.	18 cents per cwt.
Silks	30 per cent.	40 per cent.	50 per cent.
Wool, valued 18 to 24 cents per pound	3 cents per lb.	3 cents per lb.	6 cents per lb.
Wool, valued 24 to 32 cents per lb.	9 cents per lb.	9 cents per lb.	10 cents per lb. and 10 per cent.
Woollen manufactures not otherwise specified	12 cents per lb. and 25 per cent	18 cents per lb. and 30 per cent.	24 cents per lb. and 40 per cent.

The willingness if not indeed the open zeal of the people for taxation continued noteworthy. A foreign minister remarked to Seward that he was learning something new about the strength of popular government. "I was not surprised," he said, "to see your young men rushing enthusiastically to fight for their flag. I have seen that in other countries. But I have never before seen a country where the people were clamorous for taxation." David A. Wells, a careful observer of financial and industrial affairs during the war, has well said that such was the fervor of patriotism and determination to push the war to a successful issue that the people rejoiced in taxation: "The country was rich, and its accumulated resources had not for nearly two generations been in any degree drawn upon by the national government for extraordinary taxation." The revenue receipts in the latter months of the war were almost beyond belief. In the fiscal year 1865–1866 the tax receipts were nearly $500,000,000, as much as in the eight years preceding the war; nor was there any serious attempt to evade taxation. This acquiescence in the revenue policy of the nation was partly due to the material prosperity of those portions of the country which escaped the immediate ravages of war. Prices were rising rapidly, and this with the enormous demand for agricultural and manufactured products for the army gave for the time being an unexampled stimulus to the farmer and manufacturer.

129. Income Tax.

A convincing illustration of the willingness of the people to submit to revenue exactions was seen in the cordial acceptance of the income tax. In times of peace this duty, novel to the federal budget, would have met with instant condemnation; but under the circumstances its imposition and payment was held to be a patriotic duty. The first tax on incomes was authorized August 5, 1861, at a rate of 3 per cent. on the excess of all incomes above $800 per annum. This was increased in 1862, and again in 1865, until incomes between $600 and $5000 were taxed at 5 per cent., and above $5000 at 10 per cent. As the immediate war necessities became less pressing, the limit of exemption was advanced to $1000, and in 1867 to $2000; in 1872 the tax was abolished. The number of persons assessed with the total amounts received from this form of duty throughout the period of its imposition was as follows: —

	Number of persons	Amount collected
1863		$2,741,000
1864		20,294,000
1865		32,050,000
1866	460,170	72,982,000
1867	266,135	66,014,000
1868	254,617	41,455,000
1869	272,843	34,791,000
1870	276,661	37,775,000
1871	74,775	19,162,000
1872	72,949	14,436,000
1873		5,062,000

This clearly shows that the tax as a whole was very productive, amounting during the entire period to $347,000,000. Owing to delays in establishing the system, its assistance was not so powerfully felt during the years of actual warfare; but in the subsequent reorganization of the finances this revenue was of great help.

130. Loan Act of February, 1862.

As has been indicated, the loan operations of 1861 were temporary, with the exception of $50,000,000 in twenty-year 6 per cent. bonds; but in February, 1862, along with the legal-tender notes, provision also was made for a large 6 per cent. loan, popularly known as the five-twenty bond issue. From this time on loans followed each other with great rapidity, and with a perplexing variation in terms and conditions, which embarrasses an orderly presentation of the government financiering. And when to loans are added the issue of treasury notes and certificates of deposit the disorder becomes still more bewildering. The subject is rendered clearer by noting that the various forms of indebtedness may be grouped under four general classes as follows: —

	Rate of interest	Length of loan
A. Long-term bonds:		
1. Loans of July and August, 1861	6	20 years
2. Five-twenties of 1862 . . .	6	5–20 years
3. Loan of 1863	6	17 years
4. Ten-forties of 1864	5	10–40 years
5. Five-twenties of June, 1864 .	6	5–20 years
6. Navy pension fund	3	Indefinite
B. Short-term loans:		
7. Treasury notes of 1861 . . .	6	{ 60 days { 2 years
8. Seven-thirties of 1861 . . .	7 3/10	3 years
9. One-year notes of 1863 . . .	5	1 year
10. Two-year notes of 1863 . . .	5	2 years
11. Compound-interest notes . .	6 compound	3 years
12. Seven-thirties of 1864 and 1865	7 3/10	3 years
C. Non-interest notes:		
13. Old demand notes	None	Indefinite
14. Legal-tender notes	"	"
15. Fractional currency	"	"
D. Temporary indebtedness:		
16. Temporary loans	4, 5, 6	"
17. Certificates of indebtedness .	6	1 year

Issues and redemptions and conversions of some of the short-term forms of indebtedness were going on at the same time. In order to measure the growth of the annual indebtedness the redemptions must be subtracted from the issues for each year. This is done in the table on page 308, derived from data published in "Bayley's Report."

The loan act of February 25, 1862, authorized the issue of $500,000,000 of bonds redeemable after five and payable twenty years from date, bearing 6 per cent. interest. The bonds could be sold "at the market value" for either coin or treasury notes. This act proved to be of little immediate assistance, for previous to December, 1862, only $23,750,000 of the issue were sold. The reasons for the failure are not far to seek. Chase interpreted market value as at least equivalent to par value, and would not sell bonds below par; according to the treasury department these conditions made the negotiations of the bonds on a large scale practically impossible, for it was reasoned that no one would buy any considerable amount except with the idea of selling again at a profit; and, as bonds would not go above par because of the free convertibility of treasury notes into these securities at that rate, there was practically no reason for speculative purchases on the part of buyers. Chase was sharply criticised for his peculiar construction of the term "market value," which other financiers consider to mean not par value, nor value at a specified time or place, but the "going" price. The criticism is justified; the market value was the price the securities would bring when offered in the market; and the treasury could have sold a large amount of bonds at any time if it had placed them in the market, and sold them for what they would bring. Other reasons assigned for the slow sale of the bonds were the lack of currency, the high profits of commercial undertakings, the low rate of interest, and the indefinite time of payment, the bonds being neither for a long nor a short term. Again, the earlier issue of seven-thirty notes of 1861 bore a more favorable rate of interest to

Loan.	1861–1862				1862–1863				1863–1864				1864–1865				1861–1865			
	Issued	Redeemed	Net increase	Net decrease	Issued	Redeemed	Net increase	Net decrease	Issued	Redeemed	Net increase	Net decrease	Issued	Redeemed	Net increase	Net decrease	Issued	Redeemed	Net increase	Net decrease
Oregon war debt	1.0		1.0														1.0		1.0	
Loan of 1842						2.6		2.6										2.6		2.6
Texan indemnity										1.0		1.0		1.6		1.6		2.6		2.6
Loan of July and August, 1861	50.0		50.0						30.6		30.6		108.6		108.6		189.2		189.2	
Five-twenties of 1862	13.8		13.8		175.0		175.0		321.6		321.6		4.3		4.3		514.7		514.7	
Loan of 1863									42.1		42.1		32.2		32.2		74.3		74.3	
Ten-forties of 1864									73.3		73.3		99.6		99.6		172.9		172.9	
Five-twenties of June, 1864													90.7		90.7		90.7		90.7	
Navy pension fund													7.0		7.0		7.0		7.0	
Total	**64.8**		**64.8**		**175.0**	**2.6**	**172.4**		**467.6**	**1.0**	**466.6**		**342.4**	**1.6**	**340.8**		**1049.8**	**5.2**	**1044.6**	
Treasury notes of 1857		2.5		2.5														2.5		2.5
" " " 1860		10.0		10.0														10.0		10.0
" " " 1861	26.9	30.7		3.8		2.1		2.1		1.9		1.9					26.9	34.7		7.8
Seven-thirties " 1861	122.7		122.7		17.3	.1	17.2			.7		.7		138.4		138.4	140.0	139.2	.8	
One-year notes " 1863									44.5		44.5			38.5		38.5	44.5	38.5	6.0	
Two-year " " 1863									166.5	13.6	152.9			114.0		114.0	166.5	127.6	38.9	
Compound-interest notes									17.3	2.3	15.0		180.2	1.5	178.7		197.5	3.8	193.7	
Seven-thirties, 1864-65													671.2		671.2		671.2		671.2	
Total	**149.6**	**43.2**	**106.4**		**17.3**	**2.2**	**15.1**		**228.3**	**18.5**	**209.8**		**851.4**	**292.4**	**559.0**		**1246.6**	**356.3**	**890.3**	
Old-demand notes	60.0		60.0			56.2		56.2		2.9		2.9		.4		.4	60.0	59.5	.5	
Legal-tender notes	98.6		98.6		291.3	2.1	289.2		86.4	42.6	43.8		4.2	4.3		.1	480.5	49.0	431.5	
Fractional currency					20.2		20.2		8.2	5.5	2.7		14.6	11.4	3.2		43.0	16.9	26.1	
Total	**158.6**		**158.6**		**311.5**	**58.3**	**253.2**		**94.6**	**51.0**	**43.6**		**18.8**	**16.1**	**2.7**		**583.5**	**125.4**	**458.1**	
Temporary loans	66.4	8.5	57.9		115.2	67.5	47.7		169.2	197.3		28.1	131.4	118.5	12.9		482.2	391.8	90.4	
Certificates of indebtedness	49.9		49.9		157.5	50.4	107.1		169.2	165.1	4.1		131.0	174.8		43.8	507.6	390.3	117.3	
Total	**116.3**	**8.5**	**107.8**		**272.7**	**117.9**	**154.8**		**338.4**	**362.4**		**24.0**	**262.4**	**293.3**		**30.9**	**989.8**	**782.1**	**207.7**	
Grand total	489.3	51.7	437.6		776.5	181.0	595.5		1128.9	432.9	696.0		1475.0	603.4	871.6		3869.7	1269.0	2600.7	

investors, and so long as this was on the market it handicapped the new 6 per cent. loan.

131. Temporary Indebtedness.

The fiscal year 1862–1863 covers the darkest period of financial credit. The army suffered unexpected reverses during the summer of 1862; the proceeds of taxation were not large, bonds did not sell, and to tide over difficulties Chase had recourse to more novel forms of indebtedness, each of which constituted a slight measure of relief. Temporary loans were secured, for which certificates of deposit bearing 5 per cent. interest were granted; and the offers of such loans proved so large that the first limit of $25,000,000 imposed by the act of February 25, 1862, was on March 17 extended to $50,000,000, on July 11 to $100,000,000, and finally, June 30, 1864, to $150,000,000. These certificates were in special demand by banks, being used in settling clearing-house balances; $50,000,000 of the legal-tender notes, authorized July 11, 1862, were set apart as a reserve for the reimbursement of these certificates.

Another measure to meet temporary needs was the act of March 1, 1862, authorizing the issue of certificates of indebtedness to such public creditors as were willing to receive them in exchange for audited accounts. These certificates were payable in one year (or earlier at the option of the government), bore interest at 6 per cent. and were issued in sums not less than $1000 in amount; they entered into the currency until enough interest accumulated to make it an object to capitalists to hold them as an investment.

During the year 1862, on account of the premium on the precious metals, silver coins, including the small change, went out of circulation, greatly to the embarrassment of retail trade. Recourse was had to notes and tokens of municipal corporations and mercantile houses; and the Congress, July 17, 1862, authorized the use of postage and other stamps. This inconvenient medium was in turn replaced, March 3, 1863, by small notes known as fractional currency, in denominations running as low as three cents; eventually $50,000,000 of this non-interest currency was authorized: at the time of issue it was an effective addition to the resources of the treasury.

132. Loan Act of March 3, 1863.

When Congress met in December, 1862, it was confronted by a deficit of $276,900,000. Especially serious were the unpaid requisitions amounting to $46,400,000. It was at this hour of depression that Congress, January 17, 1863, ordered the third issue of United States notes; this was followed by invigorating measures, as the national currency act of February 25 and a new loan act of March 3. The latter measure gave opportunity for a great variety of credit operations; it provided for the issue of one-year, two-year, and compound-interest notes, and for the sale of 6 per cent. bonds payable in not less than ten nor more than forty years. Although $900,000,000 of this latter issue were authorized but $75,000,000 were sold, since new and successful efforts were made to dispose of the five-twenties authorized the year previous. Chase attributed the successful turn in bond-selling to the removal of the restrictions upon the negotiation of bonds prescribed in the act of February 25, 1862. The section providing for sale of bonds at "market value," which Chase interpreted as par value, was repealed; and, as has been stated, the opportunity to convert United States notes into bonds was limited to July 1. It is probable that the depreciation of the convertible greenback had much to do with stimulating bond sales; for when gold was at a high premium the true interest earned by a gold-bearing security doubled and sometimes trebled the nominal rate written in the bond. Chase, indeed, has been accused of endeavoring to inflate the currency in order to hasten conversion. His own words on a later occasion were: "The bonds do not seem to be readily taken as yet by the people. It required the printing and paying out of $400,000,000 of greenbacks before the five-twenty 6 per cent. bonds could be floated easily at par, and it will probably require the circulating paper issues of the government, now amounting to about $625,000,000, to be increased to $650,000,000 or $700,000,000 before the people will be induced to take 5 per cent. bonds in order to get rid of the surplus circulation that may accumulate in their hands, that cannot be more profitably invested in other modes." The real reasons for success in selling bonds at this crisis was the passage of the national banking act in February, 1863, the adoption of a different method of selling bonds direct to the people, and the increasing confidence in victory by the army.

In selling these bonds the systematic attempt of agents to make a wide distribution gave gratifying evidence of the feasibility of a popular loan. An experienced banker, Jay Cooke, was employed as general agent, receiving a commission of three-eighths of one per cent. on all sales (one-half of one per cent. on the first $10,000,000). He in turn engaged twenty-five hundred sub-agents in a large number of towns and cities, and made every effort to present the attractions of bond investment. A pamphlet was published by this active broker, who styled himself "General Subscription Agent of the Government Loan," in which a national debt is portrayed as a national blessing: the country was told that the generation fighting the war should not be called upon to pay for it, but should rely upon borrowing. The popular interest thus excited operated very powerfully in enlarging the subscriptions and as a result of this energetic campaign Chase was able to report, in December, 1863, the sale of nearly $400,000,000 of five-twenty bonds. This plan of selling bonds through a system of agencies outside of the immediate control of the government met with bitter criticism on the ground that it afforded opportunities to speculators and syndicates, and was abandoned by Chase in the negotiation of the next loan.

133. Short-Time Notes.

The loan act of March, 1863, also provided for the issue of short-time notes bearing 5 per cent. interest; they were legal tender for face value and convertible, principal and interest, into United States notes; it was not, however, intended that they should circulate as currency, but be held by investors. In the fiscal year 1863–1864, one-year notes of this character were sold through the associated banks of New York, Philadelphia, and Boston, aggregating $44,520,000; and two-year notes to the amount of $166,480,000. Experience soon proved that these notes had undesirable qualities. At the request of the banks, coupons were attached to the notes, with the troublesome limitation that they should not be cut off except by an officer of the government. This condition naturally made the notes unsuitable for popular investment, but they were largely taken by banks for reserve purposes; these in turn set free their own paper currency, and in proportion increased the evils of an inflated monetary medium. When the interest became due the coupons were cut and the banks sent the notes once more into circulation. "It was evident," says Mr. Chase, "that the periodical payments of interest would periodically make the notes simple legal tender, and so increase from time to time the volume of currency and expose the government and the business community to the evil of recurring inflation and contraction." Consequently, when a temporary loan had to be negotiated in the succeeding year, preference was given to the compound-interest treasury notes at a higher rate of interest.

134. Financial Situation in 1864.

When Chase made his third annual report to Congress in December, 1863, the finances were in a more favorable condition: the national banking act had been passed; taxation began to be productive; the successes of the Union armies at Gettysburg and Vicksburg in July, 1863, increased confidence;

the premium on gold went down to 23½; and there was a rapid subscription for the five-twenty bonds. The receipts, as stated in the report, during the fiscal year 1862–1863, were $124,443,000 from ordinary sources, and the enormous sum of $590,266,000 from loans; and the expenditures were $714,709,000. The debt, July 1, 1863, was $1,098,793,000, of which more than one-half had accumulated in the year then ending. Although the customs produced all that had been hoped for, $69,000,000, the internal revenue taxes (as already stated) proved a disappointment. Little change, however, was proposed in the sources of revenue; to meet the estimate of $755,000,000 for total expenditures in 1863–1864, Chase relied on ordinary receipts of $161,500,000, and further loans of $594,000,000; some additional increase of internal revenue duties was recommended, so that the yield from this source might be at least $150,000,000.

In compliance with a request of the secretary that he be given still greater freedom in negotiating loans, Congress, by a new loan act of March 3, 1864, provided for an issue of $200,000,000 of bonds bearing interest at not over 6 per cent. and redeemable at a period between five and forty years at the pleasure of the government. The government placed the minimum period of redemption at ten years, thus giving to the loan the popular name of ten-forties. For reasons not clearly apparent, Chase determined to lower the rate of interest on this loan from 6 to 5 per cent. The result was disastrous, for the market quotations of government bonds at the time were not so high as to justify expectation that the public would absorb a large amount at a lower rate of interest. Bond-buying nearly ceased. The total amount sold under the act of March 3, 1864, up to the end of the fiscal year, June 30, 1864, was only $73,337,000; and at the same time the expense of the war was increasing.

The treasury was once more forced to fall back upon short loans including one-year and two-year notes, compound-interest notes, and certificates of indebtedness. The ingenuity of Secretary Chase in devising short-term loans, under the discretionary powers of the acts of 1863 and 1864, is well illustrated in the three-year compound-interest notes, with a minimum denomination of $10, which were legal tender for their face value; at maturity each $100 note was worth $119.40. As the rate of interest was high, — 6 per cent. compound, — and as like other treasury notes they were exempt from taxation, they were sought by investors. At first the right to issue compound-interest notes was but sparingly exercised; and it has been asserted that the treasury erred in not putting out a much larger volume of this currency in small denominations, as low even as $10. The critic however must recognize that the small denominations would have gone into general circulation to reinforce the greenback circulation, which was especially responsible for the premium on gold. On the other hand the notes of denominations of $50 and upwards were absorbed by banks for reserve, where they displaced and drove into circulation greenbacks bearing no interest, thus increasing the currency inflation.

135. Administration of Secretary Fessenden.

On June 29, 1864, Chase resigned his secretaryship. He had been irritated over appointments to important positions in the treasury; he was also influenced in some degree by the discouraging aspect of the finances caused by the decline in bond sales; he was possibly embarrassed by the unexpected consequences of the passage of the Gold Bill of June 17, which has been previously described; and probably he expected to be recalled. Much against his will, Senator Fessenden of Maine was appointed successor to Mr. Chase. As chairman of the finance committee of the Senate he had taken a leading part in framing measures relating to revenue and appropriations. An Eastern lawyer, he did not carry into office a hostile suspicion of the banking interest; and, although he had been originally an opponent of the legal-tender bill, he afterwards admitted that there was under the circumstances no other resource than government paper.

The financial situation confronting Fessenden was one of embarrassment, particularly to a conservative financier. The cash balance in the treasury on July 1, 1864, was only $18,842,000; the customs duties for 1864–1865, estimated at $70,271,000, would not long pay the interest on the public debt, then estimated at $91,800,000; $161,796,000 of certificates of indebtedness were outstanding, for the payment of which there was a continuous pressure; a considerable portion, $110,000,000, of the seven-thirties of 1861 fell due in August and October; there were unpaid requisitions amounting to $71,814,000; pay to the soldiers was in arrears; and an immediate increase in the army had been ordered, which would further increase the daily expenses of the war from $2,250,000 to $3,000,000.

Fessenden continued in office only until March 3, 1865; but during this brief period he displayed courage and vigor. Although opposed to further short loans or note issues which tended to swell the paper currency, he found that the banks were not willing to take long loans on terms acceptable to the treasury. He consequently issued proposals for a great national loan under the act of June 30, 1864, authorizing $200,000,000 in the form of notes payable in three years with interest at 7.3 per cent., and for this purpose he employed once more the services of Jay Cooke and his sub-agencies. In the latter half of 1864 $110,800,000 of the seven-thirties were sold, and in 1865 $718,000,000, — the amount originally authorized being increased $600,000,000 by the act of March 3, 1865. Of the very first issue $20,000,000 went to the "gallant soldiers, who not only received them with alacrity but expressed their satisfaction at being able to aid their country by loaning money to the government." These temporary loans not only bore an exceptional rate of interest, but carried the valuable privilege of conversion into five-twenty 6 per cent. bonds. As for long-term loans, Fessenden took no chances; in place of the 5 per cents. which Chase attempted to market he returned to the 6 per cent. five-twenty and ten-forty bonds.

Fessenden undertook the retirement of the 5 per cent. coupon treasury notes which had proved so troublesome because alternately withdrawn and rushed into circulation, and he substituted 6 per cent. compound-interest notes, the popularity of which had been tested by Chase, and which were absorbed in large amounts. By these issues and conversions, as well as by the more determined military policy of 1864, the confidence of investors was strengthened.

136. Summary of Loans.

The loans of the Civil War period were summarized on page 306 under four general headings: long-term loans, interest-bearing notes, non-interest-bearing notes, and temporary loans. The use made of these several varieties during the successive years of the war is compared in the following table, which gives the net annual increase and decrease for each group in millions of dollars: —

Kind of loan	1861–1862	1862–1863	1863–1864	1864–1865	1861–1865
A. Long-term loans . . .	64.8	172.4	466.6	340.8	1044.6
B. Interest-bearing notes .	106.4	15.1	209.8	559.0	890.3
C. Non-interest-bearing notes	158.6	253.2	43.6	2.7	458.1
D. Temporary loans . . .	107.8	154.8	24.0[1]	30.9[1]	207.7
Total	437.6	595.5	696.0	871.6	2600.7

[1] Decrease.

At first reliance was placed on the short-term loan, a policy which introduced a distinct element of weakness. The proportions of long-term and short-term indebtedness by years were as follows: —

	Long term	Short term
1861–1862	15 per cent.	85 per cent.
1862–1863	29 " "	71 " "
1863–1864	67 " "	33 " "
1864–1865	39 " "	61 " "
1862–1865	40 " "	60 " "

Instead of incurring liabilities which would run for ten, twenty, thirty, or even forty years' time, the country was flooded, especially in the earlier years of the war, with short-time paper, which served in many instances the purposes of currency, expanded prices, and increased the speculation and extravagance always incident to war. Temporary obligations falling due in the midst of civil conflict were a source of double vexation to the treasury department, which was obliged to conduct a series of refunding operations, and at the same time to go into the money market to borrow ever-increasing sums for a war which apparently would never end.

137. Loan Policy of Chase.

In his policy for the negotiation of loans, Chase kept four objects steadily in view: (1) moderate interest; (2) general distribution; (3) future controllability; (4) incidental utility. Each may conveniently be discussed in turn.

(1) Moderate interest. Chase felt much satisfaction in the continuous decrease in the rate of interest. The first loans were negotiated at 7.30 per cent.; the next at 7; then at 6; and finally 5 per cent. was offered; while the indebtedness represented by United States notes and fractional currency bore no interest. To carry out the policy of low interest, and to stand by an unwillingness to sell bonds below par, Chase refused to borrow except on his own arbitrary terms. While unable, or perhaps unwilling, to establish a productive tax system at short notice, the treasury placed

bars across its own path, and left to itself no other recourse than the issue of treasury notes and short-term loans. The prejudice against the sale of bonds by the government on terms fixed by the commercial conditions of the money market early manifested itself in the financial history of the United States and has been referred to in a previous chapter. It rests on the same basis as the persistent political agitation against banks from the beginning of our government, and the deep-seated belief that there can be no harmony of interests between the public and the money lenders and brokers. Congressional debates during the Civil War furnish plenty of illustrations of this antagonism; banks were "sharps" and "harpies"; "out of the blood of their sinking country" banks are enabled to coin the gains of their infamy; brokers and jobbers and money changers are pitted over against the people of the United States. How far responsibility for insistence on a low rate of interest is to be distributed between Secretary Chase and other party leaders it is difficult to determine. Chase, however, did not hesitate to take great credit for this element of war financiering.

A signal blunder was made in substituting a 5 per cent. for a 6 per cent. bond. The actual results on the national credit were not anticipated; so long as the legal-tender notes were convertible into 6 per cent. bonds, in spite of military reverses and national discouragement, the premium on gold was kept within comparatively narrow limits. With the issue of the new bonds at a low rate of interest the subscriptions fell off by one-half; but more than that, as pointed out by Amasa Walker, "by issuing the new bonds at 5 per cent. instead of 6 the secretary virtually depreciated his own currency by the difference, because it required $1.20 in greenbacks to purchase an equal income or interest on 5 per cent. which $1.00 would purchase on bonds bearing interest at 6. Consequently the price of gold was raised 20 per cent., and of course the prices of all the government must purchase to carry on the war." It was this error which gave new encouragement to the secretary to issue more short-time notes, legal tender for their face value, in order to induce purchase of 5 per cent. bonds, and this in turn of course occasioned a further rise in the premium on gold.

(2) General distribution. A second object of Chase was the "general distribution" of the bonds: he wished the obligations of the government to be held far and wide, and pointed with satisfaction to the results of the popular subscriptions for bonds through the agency established by Jay Cooke in 1863–1864; in a single district in Ohio there were six thousand bondholders. Although he abandoned this method in the sale of the ten-forties because of the calumnies to which he was subjected, he "had determined to return to it and disregard slander and slanderers." When Fessenden undertook his great loaning operation he re-engaged Cooke and his agents, as he believed with great advantage. The method of appeal to the public for subscriptions instead of bargaining with the banks met on the whole with popular approval, and was again in accord with the underlying hostility to the large moneyed interests of the great cities.

(3) Future controllability. Chase was strongly opposed to long loans; it was his leading purpose, he says, to introduce into the financial methods of the treasury the principle of controllability. "He could never consent that the people should be subjected to the money-lenders, but insisted that the money-lenders should rather be subjected to the people." [1] It was with reluctance that at the outbreak of the war he acquiesced in the apparent necessity of negotiating twenty-year bonds; and in the issue of five-twenties and ten-forties, and the development of a system of temporary loans as the one-year and two-year treasury notes, certificates of indebtedness payable in one year, and certificates of deposit, he soon developed a policy more in harmony with his own convictions. In this way Chase was convinced that when peace was established the government would be able to

[1] Schucker's *Life of Chase*, p. 408.

fund the debt at a moderate rate of interest and to provide for payment at such periods as then seemed most advantageous. Within limits this policy has merit, but a reservation to the government of the right to extinguish bonds after five years must be paid for by the sale of bonds to investors at a lower price. This sort of time limitation also gave the impression to foreigners who were unacquainted with novel restrictions of this kind that "the funded debt was of a vague and dubious character."

It has been suggested that the short-term notes were in reality exchequer notes, and that in their issue the treasury department followed respectable precedents, as for example that of the British government. Our policy differed from that of Great Britain, however, in two respects: no earnest and persistent effort was made to limit the floating indebtedness by attracting its conversion into long-term bonds; and a large part of the treasury notes were made a legal tender.

(4) Incidental utility. In order to secure indirect advantages to business, Chase advocated the receipt of temporary loans in the form of deposits, reimbursable by the treasurer after a few days' notice, so that any stringency of the market might be alleviated. The advantage of this was seen in 1864, when during a pressure for current funds the treasury department quickly paid out over $50,000,000 of these deposits. Chase found advantage also in the wide diffusion of the debt, by which national unity and strength were secured; and finally he discovered "national good growing from the bitterness of debt" in the new basis of a national banking currency.

138. Arguments in Favor of a National Banking System.

Chase's first recommendation of a national banking system in 1861 has been noted; though not then acted upon the idea was not allowed to disappear. Chase had long been convinced of the evils of paper currency issued by local institutions; in his inaugural address as governor of Ohio in 1856 he not only announced that it was constitutional for Congress to prohibit local bank circulation, but he spoke favorably of free issues based upon ample securities. In 1862 when Chase again brought forward the plan, and made a more detailed study of the factors involved, the project met with greater public favor. The charter of banks resting upon national authority, and not upon a State, appealed to the growing feeling of nationalism in all departments of political action; it appealed also to those who were jealous of the power of private corporations; it appealed to those who wished to relieve the government from distressing bargains, and who hoped the government would thus gain the ascendancy in the control of capital; and finally it appealed to those who feared that further issues of United States notes would ultimately ruin both the government and private credit. Indeed, the national banking plan now found favor with many State banks and private bankers who had previously denounced any such scheme.

From the beginning of the public discussion to the thorough-going Bank Act of 1864 the arguments for the substitution of a national banking currency in place of notes issued by the State banks cover a wide range and furnish a useful picture of State banking in its later development. First there was the argument that a national system would furnish an uniform circulation. On January 1, 1862, there were in the United States 1496 banks that issued circulating notes, possessing an aggregate capital of $420,000,000 and carrying a circulation of $184,000,000. "They were established under the laws of twenty-nine different States; they were granted different privileges, subjected to different restrictions, and their circulation was based on a great variety of securities, of different qualities and quantities. In some States the bill-holder was secured by the daily redemption of notes in the principal city; in others by the pledge of State stocks; and in others by coin reserves. There were State banks with branches, independent banks, free banks, banks organized under a general law, and banks with special charters." In New York there were banks incorporated by special act, individual banks, and banks organized under the free banking law; in Louisiana there were chartered banks and free banks; in Ohio, independent banks, free banks, and a State bank with numerous branches; in Indiana a State bank with branches, and free banks; in Massachusetts, banks under special charters, and banks organized under a general law. In some States there were boards of bank commissioners who made frequent and thorough examinations, while in others no such boards existed or existed only in name; in a few States the public was informed as to the condition of the banks by the publication of periodical statements, but as a rule publicity was not insisted upon.

In November, 1862, the circulation in the loyal States was $167,000,000. In only nine of the States did the law require the circulation to be secured by State bonds, and the State securities pledged for the notes were only $40,000,000, leaving over $120,000,000 provided for by other assets, sometimes by none. All told, about 7000 different kinds of notes circulated, to say nothing of successful counterfeits. Over 3000 varieties of altered notes were afloat, 1700 varieties of spurious notes, and over 800 varieties of imitations, making more than 5500 varieties of fraudulent notes; and "the dead weight of all the losses occasioned by them fell at last upon the people who were not expert in such matters." In 1862 only 253 banks issued notes which had not been altered or imitated.

The desire for a national currency to put an end to these irregularities was probably stronger than any other consideration for arousing the popular interest in the establishment of a national banking system. It was this feeling which led to a reluctant acquiescence in the exemption of the capital, circulation, and deposits of national banks from taxation. It was the day of sacrifices; public good demanded the giving up of State banks as agents of currency and as a source of local taxation; it was held right that the national currency should be accorded privileges equal to those of the national bonded securities. On the other hand the danger of monopoly was recognized, and many wished to reserve the right of taxation to States and towns, so that the system might be destroyed, if necessary, after the crisis was over. If the country had been at peace it is doubtful indeed if the measure could have been passed.

A second argument against the State banks was found in the redundancy of the circulation, particularly after the issue of United States notes in 1862; and the blame for the general disorder of the currency was laid by many upon the bank-note circulation rather than upon the government notes. It was on this ground that Secretary Chase made a special arraignment of the banks in his report of December, 1862. While not believing that the volume of currency of the country was greatly in excess of legitimate demands, he admitted some redundancy and consequent depreciation, and attributed it to the banks. The increase in the circulation of State bank-notes in the Union States, in one year, 1862, from $130,000,000 to $167,000,000 was in his opinion due to no public necessity; and he held that the banks ought not to have been allowed to expand their issues during the suspension of specie payments. Bankers, he complained, did not even suggest a practical limit to the increase of circulation, and in this respect they showed a marked difference in policy from the government, which restricted the issue of treasury notes, made its bills convertible into United States bonds, and required that the interest on the bonds should be payable in coin.

This criticism made by Chase was admitted by many experts. In October, 1862, the Bankers' Magazine expressed a fear that the banking movement of that year had been unwise. There had been an "unfortunate rush for profit through the enlarged volume of circulation and loans, an inflation more rapid than ever occurred before in this country." Circulation had increased in New Hampshire 27 per cent.; in

Philadelphia 138 per cent.; in Providence 86 per cent.; in six months the bank circulation of New York City had increased 69 per cent.; in Massachusetts 20 per cent.; in Baltimore 32 per cent.; in Newark, N. J., 42 per cent.; and in the interior of New York nearly 11 per cent. By others the banks were accused of absorbing the government notes as fast as they were issued and of putting out their own notes in substitution, and then at their convenience converting the notes into bonds on which they enjoyed interest. "It is a struggle on the part of the banking institutions of the country to bleed the government of the United States to the tune of 6 per cent. on every dollar which it is necessary for the government to use in carrying on this struggle for our independence and our life."

A third defect in the State banks was found in their unequal distribution. At that time the relation of credit institutions to accumulated capital and volume of enterprise was but vaguely apprehended, if indeed it was recognized at all. In New England the circulation of the banks was about $50,000,000, while in Ohio, with three-quarters as large a population, it was but $9,000,000. Such sectional inequality was held by many to be dangerous and undemocratic.

State bank issues had also been characterized by violent contractions and expansions of the currency; this has already been referred to in previous chapters, but its renewed importance at this time justifies a brief review in illustration: in three years ending with 1818 the currency had been reduced from $110,000,000 to $45,000,000; in 1834 there was $95,000,000 in circulation; in 1837 the volume had risen to $149,000,000, and before the end of the year it fell to $116,000,000. In 1841 there was $107,000,000; at the end of 1842, only $59,000,000. In 1857 it had reached $215,000,000, its highest point of inflation before the war; and on the first of January, 1858, it had sunk to $155,000,000. This periodic inflation and withdrawal of currency was generally regarded as an evil; there was little appreciation of the excellent commercial functions of elastic bank-note issues for satisfying the needs of exchange as they fluctuate from day to day.

Again, the issue of notes by local banks was regarded as incompatible with the advantages to be derived by the government from the issue of treasury notes. At the outset the State banks had attempted to discredit the demand notes; and after the suspension of specie payments they used the legal-tender notes to redeem their own circulation, selling at a premium the gold which they otherwise would have been obliged to hold for this purpose. This gave the banks a freer opportunity to expand their own currency, and indirectly served to diminish the demand for the treasury notes of the government. Of less importance was the conviction not yet extinct that State banks could not constitutionally issue paper money; if objection was made that banks chartered by federal authority would have no more constitutional basis, an ingenious reply was made that national banks do not "issue" notes, but only use such as are furnished them in such quantities and under such restrictions as are prescribed by Congress.

In addition to these evils of the currency a potent reason for the establishment of the national banking system was the support to be afforded to public credit and national union. Chase thought that at least $250,000,000 of bonds would be required for deposit as security for circulation, — a constant demand which would secure steadiness in the price of the bonds. National institutions would also be convenient for the deposit of public moneys, since the government would possess an ultimate control over these funds, which was not possible in State institutions; and particularly would this be the case in the deposit of receipts accruing under the internal revenue act. In referring to the law which permitted the payment of internal revenue duties in legal-tender paper of the government, Blaine writes that no provision "could have operated so powerfully for a system of national banks. The people were subjected to annoyance and often to expense in exchanging the notes of their local banks for the government medium. The tax collectors could not intrust the funds in their hands to State banks except at their own risk. The fact that the bills of State banks were not receivable for taxes tended constantly to bring them into disrepute. The system of internal taxes now reached the interior and the people were made daily witnesses to the fact that the government would not trust a dollar of its money in the vaults of a State bank." [1]

Of importance in the development of public conviction in favor of a national system was the plea that the commercial interests of existing institutions might be reconciled with those of the whole people; that a national system was "recommended by the firm anchorage it will supply to the union of the States." Indeed a few advocates extravagantly declared that if the system had existed in 1860 secession would have been impossible.

139. National Banking Act of 1863.

The act to provide a national currency secured by a pledge of United States stocks and to provide for the circulation and redemption thereof was approved February 25, 1863. The system provided that a banking association upon depositing bonds with the treasurer of the United States could receive circulating notes to the amount of 90 per cent. of the current market value of the bonds deposited (not exceeding, however, 90 per cent. of the par value). The amount of notes to be issued was originally limited to $300,000,000, to be apportioned to banks in the different States according to population and existing banking conditions and necessities. The notes were receivable for all government dues except duties on imports, and were payable by the government except for its indebtedness and for interest on its bonds; otherwise the notes were legal

[1] Blaine, *Twenty Years*, i, 473.

tender only between the national banks. Each bank was required to redeem its circulation at its own counter. The system was to be supervised by a bureau of currency in the treasury department.

After the passage of the first act (1863) the system developed but slowly. The banks organized were for the most part in the Western States of Ohio, Indiana, and Illinois, due to the greater need of circulation in that section. On October 1, 1863, 66 banks had deposited less than $4,000,000 of United States bonds; a year later there were 584 with a circulation of $65,000,000. As the original banking act was defective in many particulars it was largely recast by the law of June 3, 1864. Provision was then made for redemption of circulation of all banks at agencies in certain principal cities; the amount of capital necessary for establishing a bank was increased, together with stricter provisions in regard to the paying in of capital; more convenient provision was made for the conversion of the State banks into national associations; and the banking business was given a status somewhat more independent of the treasury department than at first designed; of special importance was the modification of the independent treasury act in giving the secretary of the treasury power to select banks to be depositories of public money, except receipts from customs, on deposit of United States bonds as security. Provision was also made for taxing the national banks by the federal government, for in the few months which had already elapsed since the introduction of the system there had risen a clamor that the banks were evading taxation altogether, inasmuch as there was some question whether States under the decision of *Maryland* v. *McCulloch* (1819) would have the right to tax. Consequently in the act of 1864 Congress placed federal taxes upon the capital, deposits, and circulation of banks, and gave authority to States to tax the shares of banks.

The advantage of a currency uniform throughout the country speedily converted many who at first disapproved of the national banking system. Among these was Fessenden, who frankly acknowledged his change of mind and declared that the plan was based upon sound principles, and that its full benefit could not be realized "as long as any system at war with the great objects sought to be attained continued to exist unchecked and uncontrolled"; he consequently recommended in December, 1864, that discriminating legislation be enacted at the earliest possible moment to induce the withdrawal of all local circulation. Congress agreed, and in the act of March 3, 1865, ordered the taxation of State bank issues 10 per cent. annually, beginning with July 1, 1866. This forced local notes into retirement.

The founding a banking currency upon national government securities had many advantages; first of all, it not only created a special demand for bonds, but enlisted a strong and active financial interest in the general welfare of the government's credit. In the second place, by driving State bank issues out of existence through heavy taxation, it tended to create a demand for United States legal tenders and other treasury issues for meeting the ordinary operations of trade and exchange. Lastly, the assistance of the national banks in floating the loans of the government was of the greatest importance. A more remote effect of this legislation was its influence in shaping both popular discussions and congressional action upon government paper currency as a rival system to bank paper. The full measure of these results, however, was not felt while the war was actually in progress. The banks which were chartered during this period had already, as State institutions, invested their funds largely in government bonds, being attracted by the high rate of interest as measured in paper money; and too much weight must not be given to the new banking system as an instrument of war finance. It was not until the war was over, when the State bank issues felt the heavy hand of taxation, that the national system took complete possession of the field.

140. Receipts and Expenditures, 1861-1865.

The ordinary receipts of the treasury from taxation during the period of the Civil War have already been presented in a table on page 299. The proceeds from sales of public lands dwindle to insignificance, but under "Miscellaneous," as indicated in the table on page 330, there was an important increase in 1864 due to the sale of captured property and prizes, premium on sales of gold coin, and commutation money. Expenditures, 1862–1865, were as follows: —

	War	Navy	Miscellaneous[1]	Interest on debt	Total
1862	$389,173,000	$42,640,000	$24,564,000	$13,190,000	$469,569,000
1863	603,314,000	63,261,000	27,428,000	24,729,000	718,733,000
1864	690,391,000	85,705,000	35,186,000	53,685,000	864,968,000
1865	1,030,690,000	122,617,000	64,395,000	77,395,000	1,295,099,000

[1] Including Indians and Pensions.

An examination of these figures gives an approximate estimate of the cost of the war. In four years the expenditures for "war" amounted to $2,713,568,000 compared with $88,306,000 in the preceding four years (1858–1861); and for the "navy" to $314,223,000 compared with $52,644,000 in the previous term. To these totals must be added the interest charges on the debt created during the period. The expenditures during the four years of conflict, however, are but a portion of the account; several years elapsed before the expenditures for war and navy were brought down to a normal basis, and in the last year of the war, pensions began to swell the yearly cost of the government. In 1879 an estimate was made of the expenditures growing out of the war down to that date, showing the enormous sum of $6,190,000,000. A complete estimate would include a large amount of State expenditure which finds no record in the books of the national treasury.

A comparison of receipts and expenditures is shown in the following table in millions of dollars: —

Year	Receipts			Expenditures	Deficit
	Taxes	Miscellaneous[1]	Total		
1862	$50.8	$1.1	$51.9	$469.6	$417.7
1863	108.1	3.9	112.0	718.7	606.7
1864	212.5	30.8	243.3	865.0	621.7
1865	295.6	26.4	322.0	1295.1	973.1

[1] Including sales of public land.

CHAPTER XIV.

FUNDING OF THE INDEBTEDNESS.

141. References.

CONTRACTION OF THE CURRENCY: *Finance Report*, 1865, pp. 11–14; 1866, pp. 8–10; 1867, pp. v–xiv; 1868, pp. iii–vii; 1869, pp. xiii–xiv; *Statutes*, XIV, 31; XV, 34; or Dunbar, 199–201; J. Sherman, *Speeches*, 88–96; J. Sherman, *Recollections*, I, 373–388, 433–435; W. D. Kelley, *Speeches*, 210–238 (Jan. 18, 1868); J. A. Garfield, *Works*, I, 183–201 (March 16, 1866), 284–312 (May 15, 1868); H. McCulloch, *Addresses and Speeches*, 48–53 (Oct. 11, 1865); H. McCulloch, *Men and Measures*, 210–213; J. G. Blaine, *Twenty Years*, II, 317–330; *Bankers' Magazine*, XXI, 674–688 (G. Walker), 859–862; XXII, 5–8 (McCulloch), 161–170 (A. Walker), 351–356; XXIII, 698–713 (speeches of Senators Morton and Sherman); Bolles, III, 263–281; A. D. Noyes, *Thirty Years of American Finance*, 9–17; *Report of Monetary Commission* (1898), 416–423; W. G. Sumner, *History of American Currency*, 211–214; J. K. Upton, *Money and Politics*, 127–145.

FUNDING OF THE DEBT: *Finance Report*, 1865, pp. 21–26; 1868, pp. xxxix–xliii; 1869, pp. xvi–xviii; 1870, p. vi; 1871, pp. xvii, 255–259; *Statutes*, XVI, 272 (funding, July 14, 1870); or Dunbar, 205; J. Sherman, *Speeches*, 97–120 (May 22, 1866), 156–178 (Feb. 27, 1868), 239–283 (Feb. 28, 1870); G. S. Boutwell, *Reminiscences*, II, 141–145, 183–202; J. Sherman, *Recollections*, I, 435–440, 451–458; H. McCulloch, *Men and Measures*, 243–257; E. McPherson, *History of Reconstruction*, 597–604 (funding act of 1870); Bayley, 387–390, 464; W. F. de Knight, 103–108; J. G. Blaine, *Twenty Years*, II, 556–559; Bolles, III, 305–336; H. C. Adams, *Public Debts*, 226, 231–236; J. S. Gibbons, *Public Debt of the U. S.*, 1–38.

TAXATION OF BONDS: *Finance Report*, 1865, p. 26; 1867, p. xxx; J. A. Garfield, *Works*, I, 327–355 (July 15, 1868), 356–363 (July 23, 1868); J. Sherman, *Speeches*, 150–152; J. B. Thayer, *Cases on Constitutional Law*, II, 1357–1363; Bolles, III, 323–326; J. N. Pomeroy, *Constitutional Law*, 249–253 (ed. 1886); J. I. C. Hare, *American Constitutional Law* (1889), I, 258.

PAYMENT OF DEBT IN SPECIE: *Finance Report*, 1867, pp. xxii–xxviii; *Statutes*, XV, 1; J. A. Garfield, *Works*, I, 439–442 (March 3, 1869); J. Sherman, *Speeches*, 142–150 (Dec. 17, 1867), 159–170 (Feb. 27, 1868), 203–206 (Feb. 27, 1869); J. Sherman, *Recollections*, I, 440; Bolles, III, 315–320; E. L. Pierce, *Memoir of Charles Sumner*, IV, 353–355.

SINKING FUND: *Finance Report*, 1869, xiii; 1875, ix; 1876, ix; 1884 xx; Bolles, III, 314; E. A. Ross, *Sinking Funds*, in *Pub. Amer. Econ. Assn.*, VII, 289-392.

142. Character of the Public Debt in 1865.

The return of peace brought with it the necessity for a radical reorganization of the finances. "In the midst of the war, when the blood of the nation was up," as Garfield eloquently remarked; "when patriotism was aroused; when the last man and the last dollar were offered a willing sacrifice,—it was comparatively easy to pass financial bills and raise millions of money. But now when we gather up all of our pledges and promises of four terrible years, and redeem them out of the solid resources of the people in time of peace, the problem is far more difficult." The immediate tasks before the government were three: funding the debt into a more convenient form; revision of the tax system to accord with the debt policy; and the restoration of the standard of value by the resumption of specie payments. A fourth and embarrassing question was the order in which these problems should be settled.

The public debt reached its highest point September 1, 1865, when it stood at $2,846,000,000, less $88,000,000 in the treasury, leaving a net debt of $2,758,000,000. Of this vast indebtedness less than one-half was funded; $433,160,000 was in United States legal-tender notes, $26,344,000 in fractional currency, and the remainder consisted of various forms of short time paper or temporary securities, a large part of which was due before 1868, and a considerable amount was maturing daily. For example a temporary loan of $107,000,000 was payable at ten days' notice on the part of the holder; there were $830,000,000 seven-thirty notes; compound-interest notes amounted to $217,700,000; and certificates of indebtedness to $85,000,000. On June 30, 1866, the interest-bearing debt consisted of loans bearing five different rates of interest and maturing at nineteen different periods of time.

On a part of the loans the interest was payable in coin, and on part in currency. Of the 6 per cent. bonds and notes there were twelve different kinds; of the 5 per cent. loans five different issues; and of the seven-thirty notes at least five, some convertible at the option of the government and some at the option of the holder. Bonds of some issues were exchangeable for others. A large portion of the five-twenty bonds caused uneasiness to investors, because of a contingency clause by which the government might redeem them within five years of date of issue, that is, in 1867. Of the total debt only one-ninth ran in any contingency longer than two years. "Eight-ninths of it consisted of transient forms issued under laws made up to a great extent of incomprehensible verbiage giving unlimited direction over the mass to one man and expressing in the aggregate nearly one hundred contingencies of duration, option, conversion, extension, renewal, etc." It was indeed difficult, as Senator Sherman remarked, for the people of the United States to understand any save two or three of the loans, and none but a successful investor engaged in the sale and purchase of stock could tell the various differences in value of the several securities, and the reasons therefor.

143. Funding or Contraction.

The political conditions at this critical period were not favorable to the settlement of any great public question, owing to the bitter estrangement of President Johnson from the party leaders in Congress. Fortunately, however, this dissension did not mar the administration of the treasury, for Johnson paid little attention to financial questions. Hugh McCulloch, who succeeded Fessenden as secretary of the treasury in March, 1865, was trained for the position; he had been a successful banker in Indiana, and as comptroller of the currency had increased his reputation by the good judgment shown in establishing the national banking system. He possibly regarded fiscal subjects too partially from the standpoint of a conservative banker; on the other hand his western associations stood him in good stead. The financial committees of Congress were also under the leadership of strong men; Fessenden had returned to the Senate and was once more chairman of the committee on finance; in the House, Justin S. Morrill was chairman of the committee on ways and means.

Although, in the opinion of many experts, funding of the floating debt, and particularly the certificates of indebtedness, was the first if not the only immediate duty of the government, McCulloch placed emphasis upon the necessity of a speedy resumption of specie payments, and declared that this could be effected only by a reduction of the volume of currency; he consequently asked for wide discretionary powers to sell bonds for the purpose of retiring the notes.

In a thorough review of the finances in December, 1865, McCulloch declared that the legal-tender acts were to be regarded as war measures; that the statute making the notes a legal tender for all debts, public and private, was under ordinary circumstances not within the scope of the duties or of the powers of Congress; and that while he did not recommend the repeal of their legal-tender provisions, he was convinced they ought not to remain in force one day longer than would be necessary to enable the people to return to the use of constitutional currency. The issue of greenbacks as lawful money was a measure, expedient, doubtless, and necessary in a great emergency, but, as the emergency no longer existed, the notes should be speedily retired. McCulloch therefore asked that the compound-interest notes which were legal tender for their face value, should cease to be legal tender from the date of their maturity; and that authority be given not only to fund the temporary loan and the certificates of indebtedness, but also to sell bonds for the retirement of the compound-interest notes and the United States notes.

At first it appeared that this view would meet with general approval. The House of Representatives, December 18, 1865, passed a resolution, with only six dissenting votes, expressing its cordial concurrence as to the necessity of a contraction of the currency with a view to as early a resumption of specie payments as the various interests of this country would permit, "and we hereby pledge co-operative action to this end as speedily as possible." The resolution soon proved not to reflect the real sentiment of the people; for before many months a determined effort was making to revolutionize the traditional monetary sytem of the country. Without discussing all the propositions brought forward in this long controversy over resumption during the decade following the war, the narrative may be rendered clearer by a brief statement of the various theories of credit money set forth in the debates of the time.

144. Theories of Resumption.

The first group of writers and speakers insisted upon an immediate or at least a speedy return to specie payments, without waiting for contraction of the notes, or indeed for any legislative action. In this class, for example, were Ex-Secretary Chase and the New York *Tribune*, which during months together heralded the cry, "The way to resume is to resume." Senator Sumner in 1868 looked forward to resumption in eight months; he argued less from economic laws than from moral force, confidence, and the announced fixed purpose of the government to consummate the work.

A second class, in which were found many eastern bankers, advised the speedy accumulation of a gold reserve in order to raise the value of greenbacks to a gold standard. The weakness of this plan was the difficulty of getting the gold. The trade balance was against the United States, and any effort to purchase the required amount of gold from abroad through the sale of bonds would, it was reasoned, derange commerce. The plan was also declared to be uneconomical, since it locked up in an idle hoard a mass of specie which served no purpose other than to protect the treasury certificates circulating in their place. If either were to be condemned to idleness, why not retire the paper money altogether, and leave the gold free to do the ordinary work of exchange? The advocates of establishing a gold reserve, however, gradually gained ground and finally won in the next decade, largely because this plan did not necessitate any decrease in the volume of paper currency.

A third class believed that resumption could best be obtained by the retirement or contraction of paper currency. In this class there were many groups: some favoring contraction in one way and some in another. The extreme form of the theory was represented by Mr. David A. Wells in the so-called "cremation process": "I would have it enjoined upon the secretary of the treasury to destroy by burning on a given day of every week, commencing at the earliest practical moment, a certain amount of the legal-tender notes, fixing the minimum at not less than $500,000 per week, or at the rate of $26,000,000 per annum. This process once entered upon and continued, the gradual appreciation of the greenback to par with gold, and the ultimate equalization of the two, would not be a question of fact but simply of time. What specific amount of contraction of the legal tender would be necessary no one can tell with certainty." Another somewhat similar method, known as the graduated scale or English plan, proposed to redeem United States notes in gold outright at a fixed scale of say 90 per cent. of their face value. The objection was the humiliation of the government going into the markets of the world to buy its own notes at a discount.

A fourth class included those who did not believe in immediate action, but stood for inactivity: it was possible that contraction might not be needed to attain resumption; and finance ought to wait while industry readjusted itself to the needs of peace. This class believed that resumption depended upon commercial rather than upon legislative conditions, and talked hopefully of "growing up to specie payments." As fast as the great West was opened up by the Pacific railways, commercial needs and mining enterprises would absorb the full amount of existing currency, and the outgo of gold would be checked by a favorable balance of trade with foreign countries. It was shown that the stock of gold was small in the United States; and so long as the export of specie was larger than the annual production of the gold mines, the case was regarded as hopeless. Senator Sherman thus contrasts the advantage of a waiting policy with the contraction policy of McCulloch: "Both of us were in favor of specie payments, he by contraction and I by the gradual advancement of the credit and value of our currency to the specie standard. With him specie payments was the primary object; with me it was a secondary object, to follow the advancing credit of the government. Each of us was in favor of the payment of the interest of bonds in coin and the principal when due in coin. A large proportion of national securities was payable in lawful money or United States notes. He, by contraction, would have made this payment more difficult, while I, by retaining the notes in existence would induce the holders of currency certificates to convert them into coin obligations bearing a lower rate of interest."

Still another class, at first small but soon gathering a large following, opposed contraction outright and advocated a freer use of paper money. The inflationist view is well illustrated by the following extracts from a speech made in Congress in 1868: "I am distinctly in favor of expansion. Our currency, as well as everything else, must keep pace with our growth as a nation. My plan is to increase our circulation until it will be commensurate with the increase of our country in every other particular. . . . Expansion is the natural law of currency, and a healthy growth as a nation. . . . Reduce the currency — the means of the people — and in my opinion you are fast finding the road to universal bankruptcy. For my part I would issue as many greenbacks as the country can carry,— how great that amount may be I will not pretend to say." According to this view resumption was both unnecessary and undesirable. Greenbacks were to be substituted for all bank-notes and the interest-bearing bonds were to be retired with fresh issues of government money. The holders of such opinions in the course of a few years found common ground in a new political organization, the Greenback Party.

145. Arguments against Contraction.

So important was the question of the paper currency after the war that it is worth while to state further in detail the arguments against contraction: (1) The argument of private interest. Prices would be reduced with injurious effects upon trade, possibly resulting in a panic. Even admitting that the note issues of the war were redundant, contraction would only make matters worse; for values and business had adjusted themselves to an expanding currency without interruption, and reverse steps could not be safely undertaken without affecting debts and credit contracts, which constitute a large part of property rights. The government and the debtor class would both have to pay in a dearer currency than that in which their debts were contracted; as money decreases, prices shrink, but debts remain constant at their face value.

(2) Arguments of governmental interest. Contraction would reduce the public revenues through a distressed condition of commerce and industry, affecting employment, consumption, and import of commodities. The public credit would be endangered by checking the funding of the short-term interest-bearing securities into bonds redeemable within a brief period at the pleasure of the government and bearing a low rate of interest; only when currency is plentiful and cheap would there be any object in exchanging it for bonds. "The very abundance of the currency," said Sherman, "obviously enables us to fund the debt at a low rate of interest; and as the debt was contracted upon an inflated currency it is just and right that upon that same currency it should be funded in its present form." Stress was also laid upon the

advantage of a loan in the form of legal-tender notes, upon which no interest was paid.

(3) Argument of business interest. Contraction would embarrass the banks if it did not force many of them into liquidation: they would be compelled to sell the government securities in which their deposits were invested and also to curtail credits. Further, contraction would lower the rate of foreign exchange, and thus reduce exports and increase imports. The resumptionists maintained, in direct opposition to this argument, that the inflation of irredeemable paper money must infallibly raise prices so as to diminish exports and increase imports. Again the inflationists argued that more currency, rather than less, was needed, because of the immense area of the country to be developed under peace; the Southern States had been drained of a monetary medium, and the supply in the West was deficient; with the recuperation of the South, the new employment of discharged soldiers, and the development of the resources of the country, the increase of population would create new uses for money.

(4) Argument against the banks. Another line of argument was that the banks had as much to do as any action of the federal government with the depreciation in the value of paper money, and that it was a serious question whether the government could afford to resign the privilege of issue to other agencies. The circulation of the national banks, it was urged, was expanding to the detriment of government notes, and consequently, if there was to be contraction, a beginning should be made with the retirement of the national bank-notes rather than with the treasury notes. By a curious slant of mind the advocates of more paper money insisted that the national bank circulation of $300,000,000 was not needed: "It is so much over and above what the country can use to advantage. Its existence does infinite mischief, and while it continues must effectually prevent any return to specie payments."

146. Funding Act of April 12, 1866.

The first legislative step taken by Congress toward a general reorganization of the debt was the act of April 12, 1866, embodying two important features: first, power to convert temporary and short-time interest-bearing securities into long-term bonds already authorized under previous bond acts; secondly, a slight contraction of the United States notes. Under the first provision McCulloch proceeded at once to convert the temporary interest-bearing obligations into 6 per cent. five-twenty bonds, and made such rapid progress that in two years the volume of this species of indebtedness had been decreased $900,000,000. The temporary loans and certificates of indebtedness were also wiped off the books of the treasury department. An examination of the table on the opposite page clearly shows the changes in the several loans.

In dealing with the United States legal tenders, Congress was cautious and carefully held the secretary in check; a grudging authority was given to retire $10,000,000 of greenbacks within six months, and not more than $4,000,000 in any one month thereafter. Whether the method of a gradual and discretionary retirement of legal tenders was a wise solution or not, it placed a heavy burden of unpopularity upon the secretary of the treasury: if currency was scarce the secretary was blamed, and if it was redundant he was charged with inflating prices. The question of resumption was thus kept unsettled; the country remained in uncertainty as to the date of a return to specie payments; and this encouraged speculation in business affairs. It would have been better to provide for the note-holder as well as for the bond-holder by giving a right to convert the greenbacks into bonds, thus lifting the notes by gradual advance of public credit to par with gold. Certainly a great opportunity was lost, for public sentiment in the winter of 1866 would have sustained a more rapid contraction; the country at large was expecting it, and the deed might have been accomplished if Congress had had enough courage.

	1865	1866	1867	1868	1869	1870	1871	1872	1873	1874	1875	1876	1877	1878	1879
Seven-thirty notes of 1861	139.2	139.3	139.3	139.3	139.3										
One-year, two-year, compound-interest, and seven-thirty notes of 1864 and 1865	907.7	965.3	611.0	65.3	3.1	3.0									
Temporary loan	89.7	120.2	20.2	13.8											
Certificates of indebtedness	115.8	26.4													
United States notes	432.7	400.6	371.8	356.0	356.0	356.0	356.0	357.5	356.0	382.0	375.8	369.8	359.8	346.7	346.7
Fractional currency	15.1	20.0	22.8	27.7	27.5	39.9	40.6	40.9	44.8	45.9	42.1	34.4	20.4	16.5	
Three per cent. certificates				50.0	52.1	45.5	31.9	12.2							
Sixes of 1861	50.0	50.0	50.0	50.0	50.0	189.3	189.3	189.3	189.3	189.3	189.3	189.3	189.3	189.3	189.3
Five-twenties of 1862	514.8	514.8	514.8	514.8	514.8	499.7	463.7	279.5	263.6	169.5	65.3	1.0			
Loan of 1863	75.0	75.0	75.0	75.0	75.0	75.0	75.0	75.0	75.0	75.0	75.0	75.0	75.0	75.0	75.0
Ten-forties of 1864	172.7	171.2	171.4	194.6	194.6	194.6	194.6	194.6	194.6	194.6	194.6	194.6	194.6	194.6	138.4
Five-twenties of 1864	91.8	100.0	125.6	125.6	125.6	112.2	88.6	75.1	68.8	59.0	59.0	1.9			
Five-twenties of 1865; consols of 1865, 1867, 1868		103.5	482.3	913.5	958.4	869.3	777.9	737.4	715.7	703.3	703.3	701.5	586.1	458.9	63.0
Funded 5 per cent. 1881							59.7	200.0	200.0	315.8	412.3	516.9	508.4	508.4	490.4
Funded 4½ per cent. of 1891													140.0	204.0	250.0[1]
Funded 4 per cent. of 1907														98.9	667.0[2]
All others	78.1	97.1	108.0	110.7	160.2	95.8	75.9	91.7	126.7	117.3	115.6	96.0	131.7	163.9	129.8
Total	2682.6	2783.4	2692.2	2636.3	2656.6	2480.3	2353.2	2253.2	2234.5	2251.7	2232.3	2180.4	2205.3	2256.2	2349.6

[1] Including $65,000,000 issued for purchase of gold for resumption.

[2] Including $30,500,000 issued for purchase of gold for resumption.

The authorized measure of contraction gave but slight satisfaction to Secretary McCulloch; but he publicly expressed a hopeful outcome and predicted that resumption might be brought about by July 1, 1868. Conditions were against him: in 1866 there was a poor grain crop, frauds in the revenue, a disastrous panic in England which required a withdrawal of capital from America, and unexpected expenses on account of Indian hostilities and military governments in the Southern States. Besides these difficulties the secretary had to meet an aggressive and growing opposition in Congress. This opposition was an early symptom of deep-seated dissatisfaction throughout the country, a dissatisfaction incident to the difficult years of readjustment to peace conditions. Discontent was strongest in the agricultural sections, where farmers had incurred indebtedness on the long-time credits. Mortgages running for three, five, or even ten years were not uncommon. Farmers in the East were encouraged to larger enterprises by the high prices of agricultural products existing at the close of the war; new settlers were lured westward by the glowing descriptions circulated by railroads which with marvellous energy were completing their network of systems in the middle West and even stretching out feelers into the immense domain across the Mississippi toward the Pacific. Thousands of war veterans, hardened to adventure and reluctant to turn back to the quiet life of the East, pushed to the frontier for the making of homes. Wages of labor, in mechanical and mining industries, were forced to a high level. Many of these new ventures were doomed to disappointment; and, as is inevitably the case when economic disturbances are wide-spread and uniform in character, the blame was placed upon the government, and from it relief was invoked. A complete list of the financial propositions put forth at the period is beyond enumeration in a work of this character; chief among those proposals are to be noted the following: —

(1) Increase of government currency.
(2) Payment of bonds in currency instead of in coin.
(3) Taxation of United States securities.
(4) Suppression of national bank currency.

The first of these three controversies must be discussed before describing the funding act of 1870; the fourth, concurrent with the others, will be referred to in a subsequent chapter.

147. Abandonment of Contraction.

Within a few months after the passage of the contraction act an agitation was under way to prevent any further withdrawal of notes. The difficulties engendered by the English panic in May, 1866, furnished effective arguments. McCulloch and the contractionists were driven to the defensive and with difficulty prevented inflation. In the House a bill was passed authorizing the redemption of compound-interest notes by a new issue of non-interest legal-tender notes not exceeding $100,000,000. Influenced by the hostility displayed in the votes upon this and similar measures, by anxious foreboding of coming financial troubles, by the task of funding the interest-bearing notes, as well as by the unfortunate economic conditions already referred to, McCulloch deemed it wise not to persist in the discretionary use of the powers granted by the law of 1866 authorizing the retirement of notes. Nevertheless the secretary was not discouraged; in December, 1867, he admitted the impossibility of resumption in the following July, but he hoped that with good crops and no unfavorable legislation it might be accomplished a year later. McCulloch's hopefulness, however, counted for little as against the general uneasiness of the country, and he could not prevent the enactment of a measure by large majorities in both branches of Congress, February 4, 1868, suspending any further reduction of the currency. By this act the policy of gradual contraction was condemned.

During the two years in which contraction was carried on,

$44,000,000 in greenbacks were retired, but many asserted that the full measure of actual contraction included also the withdrawal of the compound-interest notes; Sherman for example maintained that the active circulation was lessened by $140,000,000; Sumner placed the reduction at $160,000,000. During the earlier years of the issue of interest-bearing notes, temporary securities had to some extent swollen the volume of currency, but later, when peace was restored, they were held almost exclusively by banks for purposes of investment, and it is very doubtful whether they should be regarded as part of the circulating medium. Notwithstanding these considerations the public generally agreed with Sherman and Sumner, and the contractionists were obliged to carry the responsibility for disturbances which were really incident to the refunding of temporary indebtedness.

148. Payment of Bonds in Currency.

Another assault upon national credit was made in the demand that bonds should be redeemed in paper money instead of in coin, unless there was an express stipulation to the contrary in the authorization of the particular loan. If we leave out of account the sensitive character of government credit, the complication of international fiscal relations, the need of government provision for future credits, there might appear to be some reason in the plea that the five-twenty bonds be paid in greenbacks. The facts in regard to the several issues of bonds were substantially as follows:

In the loan acts of July and August, 1861, no mention whatever was made in regard to the medium of payment, but this was before the suspension of specie payments or issue of legal-tender notes. The law of February 25, 1862, expressly appropriated coin received in customs duties "to the payment in coin of the interest on the bonds and notes of the United States," and also to the annual "purchase or payment of 1 per cent. of the entire debt." The act of March 3, 1863, under which $75,000,000 of 6 per cent. bonds were issued, expressly provides that such bonds shall be payable, principal and interest "in coin." The act of March 3, 1864, under which the ten-forty 5 per cents. were issued, contained a similar provision. The act of June 30, 1864, under which $125,561,300 five-twenty 6 per cent. bonds were issued, contained no coin provision as to the principal but did provide that the interest be paid in coin. The act of March 3, 1865, under which $203,327,250 five-twenties and $332,998,950 of consols of 1865 were sold, was also silent as to principal but provided for coin payment of interest. Under this act additional loans were made, known as consols of 1867, and consols of 1868.

It is thus seen that large bond issues were negotiated under laws which were silent as to the currency in which the principal should be paid. There was obscurity in regard to the medium of payment at the normal time of redemption; and the paper redemptionists particularly relied upon the circumstances under which the act of 1862 was passed. This act provided for the issue of legal-tender notes which were convertible into bonds, and also provided that these notes should be a legal tender in payment of all debts, public and private within the United States, except duties on imports and interest of bonds. It was therefore argued that since the laws issuing the legal-tender notes provided that such notes be received in payment of all claims against the United States of any kind whatsoever except interest on bonds; and since no explicit exception was made as to their use in the payment of the principal of the bonds, it was obviously intended that greenbacks should be used for the redemption of the bonds. Some indeed contended that the omission of any express provision, except as to interest, was an intentional reserve on the part of the government, to be free to avail itself of the privilege of redeeming the bonds in currency during the suspension of specie payments; and that with this end in view the bonds were practically made payable at the option of the government at the expiration of five years from date of issue in whatever might then be the legal tender of the country. The government, it was urged, should have the opportunity of taking up its obligations in the same depreciated paper for which it issued them, and of re-negotiating its loans under the circumstances of improved credit.

An illustration of a prevalent feeling as to the payment of debt is found in President Johnson's message of 1868, when he suggests that, inasmuch as the holders of government securities had received upon their bonds a larger amount than their original investment as measured by gold, it would be just that the 6 per cent. interest then paid should be applied to the reduction of the principal of the debt, thus liquidating the entire amount in sixteen years and eight months; public creditors ought to be satisfied with a fair and liberal compensation for the use of their capital. "The lessons of the past admonish the lender that it is not well to be over-anxious in exacting from the borrower rigid compliance with the letter of the bond."

Apart from the phraseology of the statutes it appears that during the early years of the war the possibility of the payment of bonds in other than coin was hardly raised. According to the explicit statement of Garfield in 1868, when the original five-twenty bond bill was before the House in 1862, all who referred to the subject stated that the principal of these bonds was payable in gold, and coin payment was the understanding of every member of the committee of ways and means. It was only because of an occasional doubt then expressed that it was considered necessary "from abundant caution" to make a definite promise in the ten-forty act of 1863. Chase, who undertook the negotiation of bonds, had advertised that the principal as well as interest would be paid in coin, and the government did not correct this non-statutory notice. It thus became practically an unwritten law to pay the obligations of the United States in coin.

Secretary McCulloch contended that the credit of the five-twenties issued under the act of March 3, 1865, would be improved by an express declaration of Congress that coin should be paid: faith and public honor demanded that the contracts of the government be complied with in the spirit in which they were made. Even without further legislative sanction by Congress, neither Chase nor McCulloch ever exercised any option; the six per cents. which matured in January, 1863, were paid in gold, and under date of November 15, 1866, McCulloch announced that the five-twenty bonds of 1862 would either be called in at the expiration of five years from that date and paid in coin, or would be permitted to run until the government was prepared to pay them in coin. Apart from these technical considerations there was a still more vital objection to payment in depreciated currency; when the legal tenders were issued it was supposed that they would be but temporary and would be promptly redeemed at the close of the war, and the possibility of using them for bond payment had hardly occurred to any one. Until therefore the government discharged its greenback obligations by raising them in value to gold, it was dishonorable to force a currency payment upon the bondholder.

Notwithstanding the established policy of the government and the general understanding of the investing public, a persistent agitation to secure payment in currency gained many adherents in 1868. This time the argument took on more extravagant forms: it was urged that the bondholders had taken advantage of the national distress; that the currency of the ploughholder was equally good for the bondholder; that the people were sorely burdened; that the bonds did not specify in what special currency they were to be paid; that it would therefore be "right" to pay them in lawful money of the United States, and that if we looked in the dictionary under the word "lawful" and under the word "money" we would find that lawful money meant greenbacks; that anyhow, no matter what it meant, the people would never consent to pay the bonds in coin, and that the bondholder had better make the best terms he could while compromise was still possible. Said Thaddeus Stevens: "I want to say that if this loan was to be paid according to the intimation of the gentleman from Illinois, — if I knew that any party in the country would go for paying in coin that which is payable in money, thus enhancing it one-half, — if I knew there was such a platform and such a determination this day on the part of my party, I would vote for the other side, Frank Blair and all. I would vote for no such swindle upon the tax-payers of this country; I would vote for no such speculation in favor of the large bondholders, the millionaires, who took advantage of our folly in granting them coin payment of interest."

This interpretation of the obligations of the government found its principal support in the interior and Middle Western States. Ohio championed the proposition so warmly that it was popularly known as "The Ohio idea." Its opponents derisively dubbed it the "rag baby." Each of the political parties was affected and for a time the bondholder was in peril. Even Senator Sherman, whose career on the whole stood for sound and trustworthy finance, supported a bill to compel holders of the disputed 6 per-cent. five-twenty bonds to accept a 5 per cent. security specifically payable in gold, and advised its adoption as a prevention of a worse measure.

This doctrine of bond payment by currency instead of by coin was incorporated into the platform of the national Democratic Party in 1868, although it did not gain endorsement from all elements in the party. The confusion is seen in the fact that Horatio Seymour of New York, who was not in accord with the financial plank of the platform, was selected for presidential candidate. The Republican party in its national convention denounced the plan, and yet several Republican State conventions showed sympathy with the idea. Not only did Butler of Massachusetts accept it, but some Republican leaders, as Morton of Indiana and Sherman of Ohio, compromised by declaring that the government had the right to redeem the principal of the debt in existing currency but did not have the right to make a new issue of currency for that purpose.

The Republicans won in the election of 1868; in 1869 President Grant proceeded promptly to redeem the declarations of his party. In unmistakable words in his inaugural address he declared that the national honor must be protected by paying every dollar of government indebtedness in gold, unless it was otherwise stipulated in the contract. The first measure passed in his administration, on March 18, 1869, pledged the faith of the United States to the payment in coin or its equivalent of all the obligations of the United States, except when other provision had been made in the law authorizing the issue. The apprehension of investors was relieved, and refunding at lower rates of interest was greatly facilitated; although in 1870 another wave of restlessness spread over the country, marked in Congress by the introduction of nearly fifty bills expressing every shade of financial opinion, government credit was not seriously affected.

Thus far the question of payment of bonds has been discussed from the standpoint of justice to the bondholder, and of advantage to the credit of the government by not standing on the letter of the statute. It has been asked whether the government, at the time of issue, might not have expressly stated, in terms so clear there could be no misunderstanding, that in redeeming the bonds it would pay either in its own notes or specie. As one critic states it, "Should not greenbacks have been sufficiently good for all purposes, for the soldier as well as for the capitalist, for the porter as well as for the manufacturer?" The answer is clear: The government would have failed to secure credit on a paper basis; it needed the best security it could offer; and for a time that appeared none too good. While the method followed undoubtedly placed a heavy load upon the people and resulted in the enriching of a special class so fortunate as to possess at the time funds for investment, the other method of supporting the finances entirely on promises must have resulted in even greater embarrassment than was actually experienced.

149. Taxation of Bonds.

The value of the obligations of the government was attacked in still another way by the demand that bonds should be subjected to local taxation. The judicial history of this subject is of interest, the earlier decisions of the Civil War period resting upon the opinion delivered by Chief Justice Marshall in the case of *Weston* v. *Charlestown*, in 1829. The question then before the court was whether the stock issued for loans made to the government of the United States is liable to be taxed by States and corporations. The court denied such power, and Marshall again placed on record the reasoning so powerfully expressed in his decision in the case of *McCulloch* v. *State of Maryland*, in regard to the necessity of protecting the national government in the free and unhindered exercise of all its powers. In the case of *Bank of Commerce* v. *New York City* (1862) the court decided that the capital stock of a State bank invested in stock of the United States was exempt from local taxation imposed by the city of New York; and again in 1864 in the Bank Tax case, after the State of New York had passed a statute taxing banks in that State whose capital was invested in bonds of the United States "on a valuation equal to the amount of this capital stock paid in or secured to be paid in," the court decided that no distinction could be made between "capital at valuation" and "the property in which the capital had been invested," thus denying the power of the State to tax indirectly the government securities. After the revision of the national banking act, June 3, 1864, the question assumed a slightly different form, for Congress expressly gave the States power to tax shares of stock in a national bank, provided that the tax so imposed did not exceed the rate imposed upon the shares of banks organized under State authority. This permission, however, still left private bondholders in a favored position and created dissatisfaction.

The earlier attempts to tax bonds did not spring from antagonism to bondholders as such, but from a desire to compel the owners of property bound up in national securities to contribute some share to local burdens. Gradually emphasis was laid upon the fact that the bondholder had bought the bonds at specially favorable rates; that they received an exceptional rate of interest; that as interest was payable in gold commanding a premium which in itself yielded a large profit, they were a favored class; that their property was not actively employed in the production of wealth; and in short that they constituted that national banking interest which came to be generally regarded as a privileged institution. Many bondholders indeed during the Civil War acknowledged that taxation of bonds would be wise not only on grounds of justice, but also for the public good because it would remove irritation.

Finally as the attack upon the financial policy grew more and more bitter, charges were freely made as to unfair class divisions and burdens. The great body of the people were pictured as working with their own hands through all the weary days of the year, while the owners of idle capital, favorites of fortune and special legislation, like the lilies, toiled not, and yet surpassed kings in the splendor of their habits and luxuries. The farmer and mechanic toiled at home to meet the exactions of the tax gatherer, while those whose hands were unstained with labor shaped the legislation of the country for the purpose of private gain and individual monopoly. Amid the roar of cannon and deluge of blood the capitalists trafficked for a profit of one hundred per cent.; over against this selfishness stood the patriotism of the soldier and the anguish of weeping firesides. So with taxation: contrast the exactions from the workers with the policy which exempts one-tenth of the property of the United States, — property that cost less by one-half than any other to obtain, which yields double the interest elsewhere derived, and which is owned by those who live in palaces.

In opposition to such views insistence was laid upon the sanctity of contract; the bondholders were public-spirited men who had contributed their property in the days of the country's distress; the large proportion of the bonds were held by investors with small means; a large block of bonds was held abroad, and it was absurd to attempt to tax the subjects of Great Britain, France, or Germany. Explanations of this character did not appeal to all; possibly it would have been wiser at the time of issuing bonds to have placed them on the same basis as other property. The exemption certainly made an invidious distinction and contributed much to the difficulties of financial legislation. This feeling grew in strength after the war was over, when it was no longer necessary to bolster up the credit of the government by extraordinary means.

150. The Refunding Act of 1870.

McCulloch retired from the treasury department in March, 1869, and was succeeded by George S. Boutwell of Massachusetts. Boutwell had long been in public service, including the office of bank commissioner of Massachusetts and commissioner of internal revenue, and since 1863 he had been a representative. Experienced and well-informed on financial questions, he made it his chief object to fund the public debt at a lower rate of interest. He was convinced that so long as the flow of gold was adverse there could be no effective resumption; his preference for funding received popular support because there was a widespread sentiment that the payment of 6 per cent. interest was discreditable to the reputation of the United States, inasmuch as European nations, with their complicated relations and expensive forms of government, were borrowing money at a lower rate; it was absurd to continue a war rate of interest in times of peace! It was also urged that the high rate of interest offered by the government operated unjustly upon industry in attracting capital away from real estate and industrial enterprises.

The time for refunding seemed favorable: the party in power was the party under which the debt had been incurred;

the act of 1869 had strengthened the public credit, and about $1,600,000,000 of five-twenty bonds were already or soon would be redeemable at the pleasure of the government. In his first report, December, 1869, Boutwell presented a detailed plan of funding the debt and suggested a rate of interest of 4½ per cent. This was followed by the important legislation embraced in the acts of July 14, 1870, and January 20, 1871, authorizing the issue of $500,000,000 bonds at 5 per cent., redeemable after ten years; $300,000,000 at 4½ per cent., redeemable after fifteen years; and $1,000,000,000 at 4 per cent., redeemable after thirty years, all to be paid in coin and exempt from national as well as local taxation; none to be sold at less than par in gold.

The bill as originally reported by the finance committee of the Senate provided that the longest bond should be redeemable within twenty years, thus adopting the American policy of early convertibility; stress was laid upon the doctrine that there should be no permanent national debt, and that the first and most urgent duty in time of peace was to discharge promptly the obligations incurred in time of war. Thus the Louisiana debt of 1803 was reimbursable within fifteen years; the war loans of 1812–1815 within twelve years; down to the Civil War no loan ever ran beyond twenty years; and Chase had compelled the right of optional payment within five or ten years at the utmost. The House of Representatives, however, in order to give the bonds greater acceptability to capitalists insisted that the 4 per cent. bonds should run for thirty years. Securities were thus created which unexpectedly went within no long period to a premium of more than 25 per cent. and afterwards when there was a large and growing surplus in the treasury it was difficult to retire the debt. Long before the bonds matured the government could borrow at a rate as low as 2½ per cent.

This legislation together with the supplementary acts of December 17, 1873, January 14, 1875, and March 3, 1875, shaped the character of the debt for the next quarter of a century. It settled once for all the question of taxation of bonds, and placed public credit upon a solid foundation. In one particular, however, it was ambiguous and opened the way to a new controversy. The funding act of 1870 uses the term "coin" and not gold. In 1870 silver was at a premium with gold in the bullion market; in later years as will be seen the silver advocates asserted that it was honorable to redeem the bonded indebtedness in silver dollars as well as in gold. Inasmuch as the word "coin" after discussion was deliberately substituted for "gold," there was point in their contention, so far as their argument rests upon purely technical considerations, whatever may be the judgment of a deeper appreciation of the fundamental forces which control public credit.

To many people the attempt to carry the public debt at less than 5 per cent. appeared foolish; even Senator Sherman thought that the proposed reduction of the rate of interest to 4 per cent. was practically the defeat of the measure. For a few years during the unsettled conditions of commerce, industry, and finance, this prediction on the whole seemed justified, for conversion was slow. The five-twenties of 1862 were first attacked, but the work of converting them into the 5 per cent. bonds due in 1881 was not finished until 1876; attention was then turned to the later five-twenties of 1865, 1867, and 1868. By this time the rate of interest had fallen and it was possible to complete the funding in 1879; fortunately no limitations as to the time of refunding were placed in the act. The changes are seen in the table, page 341.

151. Sale of Bonds Abroad.

In connection with the refunding scheme an interesting attempt was made by the treasury department to sell government bonds by direct negotiation abroad. During the Civil War earnest efforts had been made to borrow from foreigners, but there had been little encouragement for a steady market. Mr. R. J. Walker, formerly secretary of the treasury under Polk, was sent by Chase as a special revenue agent to Europe, and found strong distrust of the financial credit of our government. So bitter, indeed, was the hostility of Louis Napoleon and Lord Palmerston that United States stocks could find no place either on the London or Paris stock exchange, although the Confederate loan was quoted in Europe at nearly par in gold. To this political hostility was added a growing suspicion of American credit due to the successive issues of treasury notes. Even in Holland there were doubts of the financial good sense, if not of the good faith, of the American government. While the war lasted, therefore, but little foreign capital was transferred to the United States; but when peace was established European funds were rapidly turned westward and government bonds were sold abroad in large quantities until the agitation began for the payment of bonds in currency instead of gold.

In the minds of many people in the United States there was a strong prejudice against borrowing money abroad, because it was derogatory to the American people to appeal to other peoples for aid. In an early debate after peace was restored, Mr. Kelley, a representative from Pennsylvania, opposed a foreign loan, because, after sustaining a war without resorting to the degradation of borrowing abroad, the United States should not ask foreigners to loan money at 5 per cent. in order to redeem a non-interest-bearing loan. In particular he denounced the proposed issues of bonds payable in France, Germany, England, or elsewhere, in francs, florins, or pounds, "a proposition that would call a flush to the cheeks of the directors of an embarrassed railroad company." More serious objections were urged against foreign loans: that the profit represented by the margin between paper and gold ought to be secured by Americans; that foreign loans would drain the whole country of gold and silver, which would have to be paid out in interest to aliens and absentees; that bonds would be returned when foreigners desired to realize a profit; and thus the United States would be exposed to the vicissitudes of foreign markets.

It was hoped that the explicit declarations in favor of a coin redemption, as stated in the declaration of March, 1869, and renewed in the funding act of 1870, would remove the doubts of foreigners so that European capital would be attracted in a much larger volume for investment in the new securities, and thus secure absolutely the success of refunding. Possibly this might have occurred but for untoward events. A financial disturbance was occasioned in Europe by the Franco-Prussian War of 1870–1871, which created an unexpected demand for funds abroad. In the United States also the process of refunding was checked by the panic of 1873, and under these circumstances no bonds were sold until 1877 at a lower interest than 5 per cent.

152. Sinking Fund.

In the reduction of the debt the machinery of a sinking fund was once more brought into play. The act of February 25, 1862, authorizing the issue of the first legal-tender notes and the sale of five-twenty bonds, pledged that the coin paid for duties on imports, after satisfying all interest requirements of the public debt, should be applied to the annual purchase or payment of 1 per cent. of the entire debt of the United States. The interest on the amount purchased was also to be used for the benefit of the fund thus created. During the war no attempt was made to fulfil this pledge, as the government was continually borrowing and adding to its total indebtedness; and when peace was restored the provision was not regarded as binding; McCulloch in his annual reports makes no reference to it.

Although the form of the promises was neglected, the spirit was carried out, since McCulloch followed Gallatin's example of an earlier day by cancelling indebtedness outright from whatever surplus revenues were available. Secretary Boutwell, with more precise respect, inaugurated the policy of annual purchase of bonds, entered in a separate account as a "sinking fund." The funding act of 1870 no longer made it necessary to keep the bonds purchased in a separate fund, but directed that they be cancelled and destroyed; the principle of reduction by annual purchase, however, was left untouched. After the panic of 1873, with the consequent lessening of government income, the treasury department followed a halting policy. Some of the secretaries were more impressed than others with the sacredness of providing annually for the sinking fund, but found themselves hampered either by deficient revenues or by the objections to buying bonds at a premium. Bristow regarded the sinking fund as an object second only to the payment of interest on the public debt, and yet could not execute this trust. Ingenious explanations were consequently devised to show that the government was keeping faith when it did not keep its promises: the law providing for the sinking fund was not to be taken too literally: "the coin paid for duties on imported goods" was not actually "set apart as a special fund"; it was rather a pledge by Congress that it would provide revenues enough not only to pay the expenses of the government, but also to redeem 1 per cent. of the debt; the sinking fund was simply a representation of the balance of revenues over expenditures. Secretary Morrill, the successor of Bristow, in 1876 made an elaborate calculation to show that if the whole period be taken, beginning with 1862 and ending in 1876, the debt was reduced $223,144,000 more than was actually demanded by the sinking-fund requirements. Again the necessary preparations in 1877–1878 for specie resumption through the sale of bonds for the purchase of gold checked a literal compliance with the law. It was manifestly absurd for the government to sell bonds for gold and at the same time buy bonds for the sinking fund.

In the discussion of the struggling and halting efforts to place the finances of the government upon a sound and permanent basis after the war was over we must not hold a gloomy view of the condition of the country. To be sure there were agencies adverse to national development, such as irredeemable paper currency, and unequal and heavy taxation. The condition of the laboring class possibly was not so good as in 1860, for wages had not increased in proportion to the cost of living. The task of industrial readjustment imposed heavy strains, and in places the pressure created suffering; but in spite of these difficulties the material factors of industrial prosperity remained sound and vigorous, and the country quickly resumed the wonderful march of progress witnessed in the decade before the war. Immigration was large, and there was a generous increase in the products of industry. An official report in 1869 declared that within five years more cotton spindles had been put in motion, more iron furnaces erected, more iron smelted, more bars rolled, more steel made, more coal and copper mined, more lumber sawn and hewn, more houses and shops constructed, more manufactories of different kinds started, and more petroleum collected, refined, and exported, than during any equal period in the history of the country, — and that this increase had been at a more rapid rate than the growth of population. The natural resources of the country and opportunities for productive enterprise made it possible for the country to press forward by leaps which no mistakes of taxation, monetary issue, or treasury borrowing could withstand.

CHAPTER XV.

GREENBACKS AND RESUMPTION.

153. References.

CONSTITUTIONALITY OF LEGAL-TENDER NOTES: *Opinions* in 8 *Wallace*, 603-639 (1869); 12 *Wallace*, 457 (1872); 110 *U. S.*, 421 (1884); also in J. B. Thayer, *Cases on Constitutional Law*, II, 2222 (1869), 2237 (1872), 2255 (1884); also in *Bankers' Magazine*, XXIV, 712-737 (1869); XXVI, 832-895 (1872); also J. J. Knox, *United States Notes*, 156-166, 193-229 (1884); also E. McPherson, *Handbook*, 1872, pp. 53-62 (1872); G. Bancroft, *Plea for the Constitution* (1884); also in *Sound Currency*, V, No. 11; S. F. Miller, *Lectures on the U. S. Constitution*, 530; J. B. Thayer, in *Harvard Law Review*, I, 79; A. B. Hart, *Life of Chase*, 389-414; Bolles, III, 251-262 (references, p. 257); E. J. James, *Considerations on the Legal Tender Decisions*, in *Pub. Amer. Econ. Assn.*, III (1888), 49-80 (references, p. 80); J. H. Chamberlain, *Legal Tender Decisions*, in *Amer. Law Review*, XVIII, 410; T. H. Talbot, ditto, 618; H. H. Neill, *Legal Tender Questions*, in *Pol. Sci. Quar.*, I (1886), 250-258; B. T. DeWitt, *Are Legal-Tender Notes ex post Facto?* in *Pol. Sci. Quar.*, XV, 105-111; W. C. Ford, *Legal Tender Decision*, in *Princeton Review*, Sept., 1884, 123-132; J. K. Upton, *Money and Politics*, 157-170; H. White, 231-234; A. B. Hepburn, *History of Coinage*, 259-273.

PANIC OF 1873: *Messages and Papers*, VII, 243-247 (Grant, 1873), 268-271 (inflation veto), 285-287 (1874); *Finance Report*, 1875, pp. xi-xxi; J. Sherman, *Recollections*, I, 488-506; J. G. Blaine, *Twenty Years*, II, 556-566; E. McPherson, *Handbook of Politics*, 1874, pp. 134-155; Bolles, III, 283-290; H. White, *Fortnightly Review*, XXVI, 810; C. A. Conant, *History of Modern Banking*, 509-512; A. D. Noyes, *Thirty Years of American Finance*, 18-20; D. Kinley, *Independent Treasury System*, 181-190; V. B. Denslow, *Principles of Political Economy*, 390-395; E. Atkinson, *Journal of Political Economy*, I, 117-119 (inflation veto):

RESUMPTION OF SPECIE PAYMENTS: *Messages and Papers*, VII, 348 (Grant, 1875); *Finance Report*, 1867, v; 1868, vii; 1874, x-xviii; 1875, xii-xxii; 1876, xii-xviii; 1877, xi-xvi; 1878, viii-xvii; 1879, ix-xii; 1880, xii-xv; *Specie Resumption and Refunding of the National Debt*, in *Executive Documents*, 46th Cong., 2nd Sess., XVII (1879-1880); *Statutes*, XVIII, 296; XX, 87; or Dunbar, 214, 217; E. McPherson, *Handbook of Politics*, 1876, pp. 120-127; 1878, pp. 143-152 (attempts to repeal); J. Sherman,

Recollections, I, 507–549, 565–602; II, 636–660, 686–700; J. A. Garfield, *Works*, II, 490–527 (attempt to repeal), 175–185, 246–274, 609–627 (Jan. 2, 1879); W. D. Foulke, *Life of Oliver P. Morton*, II, 74–102, 317–338, 355–363; Bolles, III, 282–304; *Report of Monetary Commission* (1898), 425–436; A. D. Noyes, *Thirty Years of American Finance*, 21–56; J. K. Upton, *Money and Politics*, 146–156; C. F. Adams, *Currency Debate of 1873*, in *No. American Review*, CXIX, 111–165; H. White, *Present Phases of the Currency Question*, in *International Review*, IV (1877), 730; V (1878), 833–847.

GREENBACK PARTY: E. McPherson, *Handbook of Politics*, 1876, pp. 224–233; *Atlantic Monthly*, XLII, 521–530; E. N. Dingley, *Life of Nelson Dingley, Jr.* (1902), 134–146, 149–156, Alexander Johnson, in *Lalor's Encyclopedia*, II, 418–419; G. Walker, *Banker's Magazine*, XXXIII (1878), 248–252; C. J. Bullock, *Monetary History*, 105–109; M. S. Wildman, *Money Inflation*, 139–172.

154. Volume of Treasury Notes.

It is now necessary to return to the fortunes of government note circulation. The repeal of the contraction policy in 1868 left the volume of legal-tender notes in uncertainty. The act of June 30, 1864, declared that the total amount of United States notes should never exceed $400,000,000; and in 1866 a gradual reduction began, soon checked by the law of 1868. When Congress suspended further contraction the amount stood at $356,000,000; the $44,000,000 of balance was generally regarded, at least by those who looked forward to an early return of specie payments, as a reserve issue to be used only in case of emergency, when revenues fell below expenditures, or possibly as a redemption fund for the fractional currency, which amounted to about $50,000,000. In October, 1871, however, Secretary Boutwell issued $1,500,000 of these notes, and in the next year $4,637,000. This action, though giving satisfaction to advocates of a larger supply of currency and to stock-exchange speculators who clearly recognized that speculation flourished best under a regime of a fluctuating supply of currency, was sharply criticised both by those who believed that contraction was the true road to resumption, as well as by those who felt that changes in the volume of currency should not be left to the uncontrolled judgment of any one official. Although the treasury department made no public explanation or defence, it was considered expedient to retire the recent issues.

The subject did not rest, for the panic of 1873 again aroused a clamor for money. Secretary Richardson, who succeeded Boutwell, yielded under the plea of a great emergency, and between March 7, 1873, and January 15, 1874, issued $26,000,000, of legal tenders, above the $356,000,000, making the total $382,000,000. These issues were put into circulation by the purchase of bonds. Congress, either because it thought there was some doubt as to the secretary's power and preferred to assume responsibility, or because it wished to inflate the currency beyond the limit reached by Secretary Richardson, passed a bill in April, 1874, for the permanent increase of the currency to $400,000,000.

The significance of this proposition is clear: it not only was an indemnity act for an emergency issue, but it practically authorized an increase of currency in times of peace, thus constituting a precedent for any future Congress to enlarge the volume at will. Grant vetoed the bill in a memorable message, April 22, 1874, which may be regarded as the turning point in the agitation for an increased volume of treasury legal-tender notes; the president declared that the theory of increased circulation was a departure from true principles of finance, national interest, national obligation to creditors, congressional promises, party pledges on the part of both political parties, and of his own personal views and promises made in every annual message sent by him to Congress, and in each inaugural address. "I am not a believer in any artificial method of making paper money equal to coin, when the coin is not owned or held ready to redeem the promises to pay, for paper money is nothing more than promises to pay, and is valuable exactly in proportion to the amount of coin that it can be converted into."

Notwithstanding the reference to his previous convictions, Grant's veto came as a surprise to the public at large. Only a few months earlier he had stated that in view of the relative contraction in currency, due to the increase of manufactures and industries, he did not believe that there was too much money even for the dullest part of the year. Under such circumstances the party of monetary reform was greatly encourage by his later decisive utterance. The victory, however, was not complete, for under cover of the act of June 20, 1874, affecting the distribution of national bank currency, a section was smuggled in, declaring that the amount of United States notes outstanding should not exceed $382,000,000. This, however, was soon followed by the resumption act of January 14, 1875, looking forward to a final reduction in the volume to $300,000,000.

155. Constitutionality of Legal-Tender Notes.

For some time after the issue of the greenbacks there was uncertainty as to the legal-tender attribute of the treasury notes, and questions quickly arose which required settlement in the State and federal courts. The trend of the decisions of the Supreme Court from the first was toward a limitation of the notes: in *Lane County* v. *Oregon* (1868) it was held that the notes were not legal tender for State taxes; in *The Bank* v. *Supervisors* (1868) that they were obligations or securities, and consequently exempt from taxation; and in *Bronson* v. *Rodes* (1868) that they were not legal tender in the settlement of contracts specifically calling for the payment of specie. Finally the more direct question of constitutionality was passed upon by the Supreme Court in 1869 in the case of *Hepburn* v. *Griswold.* In 1860 a Mrs. Hepburn in a promissory note agreed to pay Griswold on February 20, 1862, $11,250. At each of the above dates the only lawful money was gold and silver coin. Mrs. Hepburn failed to pay the note at maturity, and upon a suit brought in Kentucky, March, 1864, tendered payment in United States notes which had been issued February 25, 1862, that is, five days after the maturity of the note. The tender was refused. An appeal was carried to the United States Supreme Court, and a decision rendered in December, 1869. The opinion by a fateful stroke of fortune was delivered by Chief-Justice Chase, in whose administration as secretary of the treasury the notes had been first issued. The legal-tender quality was denied; yet the whole question was not covered, because the case involved only the tender of notes in settlement of contracts entered on previous to the first legal-tender act; and Chase, in the declaratory portions of the opinion, was careful to limit the application of the decision to such contracts. Nevertheless the court clearly indicated its conviction on the question of the constitutionality of notes tendered in the settlement of current contracts, for it practically asserted that the legal-tender clause was not only improper but unnecessary. "Amid the tumult of the late Civil War — the time was not favorable to considerate reflection upon the constitutional limits of legislative or executive authority. If power was assumed from patriotic motives, the assumption found ready justification in patriotic hearts. Many who doubted yielded their doubts; many who did not doubt were silent. Some who were strongly averse to making government notes a legal tender felt themselves constrained to acquiesce in the views of the advocates of the measure. Not a few who then insisted upon its necessity, or acquiesced in that view, have, since the return of peace, and under the influence of the calmer time, reconsidered their conclusions, and now concur in those which we have just announced." Three justices concurred with Chase in the majority opinion, while a dissenting opinion was rendered by Justice Miller in which two of his associates joined, thus dividing the court, four to three.

The decision was unpopular. The close division of the court, when it was not complete, was an irritating factor, to say nothing of the disturbance to business if gold payments were to be enforced. A second case, *Knox* v. *Lee*, consequently came before the court, but before the decision was rendered in May, 1871, the membership of the court was changed by the addition of two members, one to fill a vacancy, and the other through a statute enlarging the court from seven to eight. Inasmuch as on this occasion the decision of 1869 was reversed, there have been charges that the court was packed in order to bring about the reversal. The evidence on this point has been carefully examined by Professor Hart in his biography of Chase, and the charges of collusion clearly shown to be unfounded. That the new justices would be in general accord with the administration was to be expected; there was, however, no previous understanding of their views on the particular question of legal tenders, and no instructions to bring about a reversal of the earlier decision. Nevertheless, it must be admitted that there was a strong popular expectation that as soon as the court was reorganized, a reversal of the opinion would be made. This is seen in the fact that the first decision did not lead to a reduction in the premium on gold; and the exceptional methods adopted by the court in order to bring another case quickly before it for adjudgment showed unusual feeling and pressure.

In the opinion on the case of 1871 (filed in 1872), the court held that a broad interpretation must be given to the Constitution, for it could not be expected that this document would completely enumerate all the powers of government with details and specifications; the powers of Congress must be regarded as related to each other, and means for a common end. Among the non-enumerated powers, there certainly must be included the power of self-preservation, and no reasonable construction of the Constitution could deny to a government the right to employ freely every means not prohibited, or necessary for its preservation. And in carrying out its purpose Congress is entitled to a choice of means which are in fact conducive to the exercise of a power granted by the Constitution. Marshall's words in the decision *McCulloch* v. *Maryland* are cited as convincing and conclusive. Let the end be legitimate, let it be within the scope of the

Constitution, and all means which are appropriate, which are plainly adapted to that end, which are not prohibited, but are consistent with the letter and spirit of the Constitution, are constitutional.

There were two main questions for the court to consider: Were the legal-tender acts inappropriate means for the execution of any or all of the powers of the government? and were they prohibited by the Constitution? As to the first question the emergency was great when the legal-tender acts were passed: the endurance of the government had been tried to the utmost. "Something revived the drooping faith of the people; something brought immediately to the government's aid the resources of the nation, and something enabled the successful prosecution of the war and the preservation of the national life. What was it, if not the legal-tender enactments?" As to whether other means might not have been effective, that was not for the courts to decide; the degree of appropriateness of given laws is for the legislature and not for the judiciary to determine.

On the second point the court held that the making of the treasury notes a legal tender was not forbidden either by the letter or by the spirit of the Constitution. Although certain express powers are given to Congress in regard to money, it cannot be inferred, as the Constitution has been in general construed, that all other powers are by implication forbidden. Since the States are expressly prohibited from declaring what shall be money, or from regulating its value, whatever power exists over the currency is vested in Congress. Considering that there is no express prohibition upon Congress in this matter, and that paper money was almost exclusively in use in the States as the medium of exchange, it must be presumed that the framers of the Constitution did realize that emergencies might arise when the precious metals would prove inadequate to the necessities of the government.

Nor could it be argued that the legal-tender acts are unconstitutional because they directly impaired the obligation of contracts, that is, of contracts made previous to the passage of the act. In contracts for payment of money, it did not mean money at the time when the contract was made, nor gold or silver, nor money of equal intrinsic value in the market; the obligation was to pay that which is recognized as money when the payment is to be made. "Every contract for the payment of money simply, is necessarily subject to the constitutional power of the government over the currency, whatever that power may be, and the obligation of the parties is therefore assumed with reference to that power." More than this, Congress does have the power to impair contracts indirectly by rendering them fruitless or partly fruitless, as in bankrupt laws, declaration of war, and embargoes. No obligation of a contract can extend to the defeat of legitimate government authority.

In conclusion, it was observed that the legal-tender acts did not attempt to make paper a standard of value: their validity does not rest upon the assertion that this emission is coinage, or any regulation of the value of money; or that Congress may make money out of anything which has no value. "What we do assert is, that Congress has power to enact that the government's promises to pay money shall be, for the time being, equivalent in value to the representation of value determined by the coinage acts or to multiples thereof."

156. Issues in Times of Peace.

This decision settled the question of constitutionality of legal-tender issues in times of war, but it left uncertainty as to the powers of government over currency during peace. The judicial decision on this point was made by the Supreme Court in 1884 in the case of *Juilliard* v. *Greenman*; the question before it was the constitutionality of that provision of the law of 1878 which required that all legal-tender notes redeemed at the treasury be reissued, kept in circulation, and continue to retain their legal-tender quality. The court decided in favor of the constitutionality of such reissues, by a generous interpretation of the doctrine of implied powers, in support of which the reasoning of Marshall, in the case *McCulloch* v. *Maryland*, is again reviewed at length. As preliminary to the main conclusion, it is shown that Congress has the power to pay the debts of the United States; that, in pursuance of this, all means which are appropriate, and not prohibited, are constitutional; that not too much weight should be given to the debates and votes of the constitutional convention of 1787, for there is no proof of any general consensus of opinion in the convention upon this subject; that the power to borrow money includes the power to issue obligations in any appropriate form, and, if desired, in a form adapted to circulation from hand to hand in the ordinary transactions of commerce and trade; that the issue of legal-tender notes is incident to the right of coinage; and finally that Congress has power to provide a currency for the whole country. As a consequence, Congress "may issue the obligations in such form and impose upon them such qualities as currency for the purchase of merchandise and the payment of debts as accord with the usage of sovereign governments"; and it is for Congress, the legislature of a sovereign nation, to declare whether, because of an inadequacy of the supply of gold and silver coin, it is wise to resort to legal-tender paper issues.

The decision reopened the controversy; this was largely academic; Bancroft the historian made a passionate protest in a pamphlet entitled: "A Plea for the Constitution of the United States of America, Wounded in the House of its Guardians"; but popular judgment on the whole was favorable. Lawyers and constitutional commentators were slowly coming to the conclusion that the interpretation of the Constitution must rest upon a broader basis than that of the debates of 1787; and the people at large were satisfied that there was to be no disturbance in the conditions to which they had been long accustomed.

157. Sale of Gold.

Closely related to the question of contraction was the policy to be followed in disposing of the gold which flowed into the treasury in the payment of import duties. The treatment of this surplus gold was, as previously described, a perplexing problem during the latter years of the war when the amount locked up in the vaults of the United States treasury was a considerable part of all the gold of the country, and was more than was needed for payment of interest on the public debt. Great pressure was brought upon the treasury to part with gold in one way or another to make the coin available for commerce. The treasury accumulation of coin, together with the rapid and violent fluctuations in the value of gold, became especially prominent in 1864. To return gold into general circulation, three ways were proposed: one by anticipating the payment of interest on the debt, a second by the purchase of bonds for the sinking fund, and a third by sale of specie. The first was thought ineffective, since the procedure would be too slow to have any appreciable effect upon the gold market; the second was considered absurd, in view of the fact that the government was then borrowing $2,000,000 a day to meet current expenses. In March, 1864, a joint resolution was adopted, involving the use of all three methods, authorizing the secretary of the treasury to anticipate the payment of interest and to dispose of any gold in the treasury not necessary for the payment of interest on the public debt, provided the obligation to create the sinking fund be not impaired.

McCulloch in his treasury policy regarded a steady market in gold as of more importance than the saving of a few millions of dollars in interest through refunding measures. He maintained that the treasury should use its powers to prevent speculative combinations in gold, and thus promote the steadiness of the money market, advance the currency toward a true standard of value, and prevent financial disturbance. This policy of continuous sale of gold met a double opposition: on the one hand, from those who believed that gold must be amassed in the treasury to effect a speedy resumption of specie payments; on the other, from those who argued that an advance in the market price of gold was desirable in order to prevent bondholders, especially foreigners who had purchased American securities with paper money at a great discount as compared with gold, from realizing any advantage which would result by returning and reselling these securities for money of greater worth.

For several years gold was sold by the treasury department at private sale, but in 1868, the practice was introduced of selling gold by auction to the highest bidder. Wall Street promptly protested, on the ground that the gold market was put into the control of speculators, to the great disadvantage of commercial buyers of gold for legitimate trade purposes. The commercial trading in gold as a commodity naturally centred in New York City, the largest importing market in the United States, where the dealings were so constant and enormous that the gold-room, situated next to the Stock Exchange, was a recognized institution in the financial life of New York, and the quotations there established were sharply watched by business men throughout the country. As the supply of gold outside of the government treasury was quite limited, it finally occurred to Jay Gould and James Fisk, two of the most daring speculators developed by post-bellum conditions, to endeavor to corner the gold supply. Their financial venture came to a crisis in September, 1869, in the early days of Grant's administration, when Boutwell was secretary of the treasury. Complete success could be attained only by preventing any unusual sale of gold by the treasury department; hence for months, as was afterwards learned, those connected with the project found means to impress upon the administration the wisdom of keeping up the price of gold during the autumn, in order to assist the West in moving its crops, since a high premium on gold was supposed to make the farmers' grain worth so much the more. In a few days the premium on gold was run up from 130 to 162; at this juncture Secretary Boutwell ordered the sale of gold, and the price then fell to 135, but in these few hours of rapid fluctuations many were irretrievably ruined. In the annals of Wall Street no day is more notorious than this Black Friday, September 23, 1869, and the unfortunate connection of the government with the affair helped to inflame the unreasoning hostility of the agricultural districts in the interior to all financial measures emanating from the larger cities of the East.

158. Panic of 1873.

In 1873 occurred a panic which affected every operation of finance and commerce. It was more than a panic; it was the beginning of a long period of financial and industrial depression, in many ways the logical outcome of ill-adjusted production and inflated credit. Remarkable changes in industry and commercial organization were coincident with an enormous expansion of railway construction: during the years 1860–1867 the annual increase in railways averaged but 1311 miles; in 1869 it rose to 4953; in 1870, to 5690; in 1871, to 7670; and in 1872, to 6167 miles,—a total of over 25,000 miles in four years. The process involved a sinking of capital far beyond what was immediately productive, and the opening of vast areas of wheat-growing country, revolutionized the price of grain, and disturbed the status of the farmer. The same expansion took place in Russia and South America; and this accession of new sources of world supplies on a large scale, together with the readjustments in trade due to the Suez Canal, gave to industrial development sudden twists and turnings quite beyond calculation. The rapid and unprecedented construction of railways in turn created a demand for iron, which led to over-investment in this industry. There appeared to be no end to possible opportunities and profits in the industrial world, and new securities were created on a large scale, while prices of all commodities were unduly inflated.

Another important factor in bringing economic organization to a standstill was a change in the international trade relations. The United States had incurred a heavy foreign indebtedness, having borrowed abroad between 1861 and 1868, on her national, state, railway, and other securities, an amount estimated at $1,500,000,000. In return for this credit the United States incurred an annual interest charge estimated in 1868 at $80,000,000; in addition payments made by American travellers abroad and for freights in foreign vessels brought the total annual tribute, in addition to payments for ordinary imports, up to $129,000,000. The natural resources for making this payment were curtailed by the war; the export of cotton practically ceased for several years; after peace was established, exports of merchandise increased, but not in the same proportion as the rise in imports. This is seen in the following table prepared by Wells and Cairnes, where a comparison is made of imports and exports before the war with the five years succeeding: —

	Imports (less re-exports)	Domestic exports (including specie)
1858	$251,700,000	$293,700,000
1859	317,800,000	335,800,000
1860	335,200,000	373,100,000
1868	351,200,000	352,700,000
1869	412,200,000	318,000,000
1870	431,900,000	420,500,000
1871	513,100,000	513,000,000
1872	617,600,000	501,100,000
Annual average of last 5 years	$465,200,000	$421,060,000

For a time the adverse balance was settled by the transfer of government bonds to foreign account, and these securities were as good as gold in settling the international balance of trade. An end came to the supply of bonds on terms which would satisfy the foreign investors, and it became necessary to draw specie; this disturbed the domestic money market. It is easy now to diagnose the evils and dangers, but in 1873 there was little anticipation of disaster, and consequently no proper preparation by conservative financial interests. When the crisis came, the treasury was so involved and so connected with private finance, that tremendous pressure was brought upon the government to relieve by its fiscal aid evils occasioned by the bad judgment of the business world. Fortunately the receipts of the treasury were so large at this time that even a serious depression did not greatly embarrass the government in providing for current supplies.

The secretary of the treasury was easily prevailed upon to issue (March, 1873–January, 1874) $26,000,000 of legal-tender notes in the purchase of bonds in order to relieve a stringent money market; and when Congress met in December, 1873, demands for government action took every form known to finance. So great was the impetus to the activity of expansionists and greenbackers, that for a brief period any positive action looking toward resumption seemed indefinitely postponed. Only by the veto of President Grant, which has been referred to, was actual inflation checked.

159. Resumption Act of 1875.

The political consequences of the panic were seen in the autumn of 1874, when the congressional elections, for the first time since 1860, went against the Republican party. Under the pressure of political necessity, inspired in part by the vigorous tone of Grant's veto and by the positive demands of Bristow who succeeded Richardson as secretary of the treasury, a bill was enacted for the resumption of specie payments by the expiring Congress, January 14, 1875, while the Republicans still held power to rally to its support sufficient votes for its passage. The measure was loaded with a variety of provisions: (1) A system of free banking which will be discussed; (2) the retirement of greenbacks equal to 80 per cent. of the amount of new national bank-notes issued, until the greenback circulation should be reduced to $300,000,000, after which no further reduction of the greenbacks was to take place. It was argued that this check would prevent either expansion or contraction of the currency, as nearly 20 per cent. of the notes were already held as bank reserves; (3) the withdrawal of paper fractional currency and the substitution of silver coin; (4) removal of the charge for coinage of gold; (5) resumption of specie payments on January 1, 1879: for this purpose the treasury was authorized to use the surplus specie in the treasury; and, if necessary, to sell bonds, of the classes authorized under the act of July 14, 1870, in order to obtain additional gold. The legal-tender quality of both greenbacks and national bank-notes remained unchanged.

Like most compromises, the measure aroused little enthusiasm: as a matter of fact, the premium on gold went higher in 1875 than in 1874, and in 1876 was as high as in 1871 or 1872. The act, save for fixing a distant date for resumption, contained but little definite provision for pressing the country on in its progress toward specie payments. It was regarded by some indeed as distinctly an inflation measure: the day of resumption was so remote that no inflationist need feel anxiety, and there was plenty of opportunity for more paper currency under the provision of free banking. The measure was purposely left vague, and by command of the party caucus there was practically no discussion of the bill in the Senate. If there had been strong conviction of the necessity of resumption, and a serious desire to effect it, a simple bill could have been passed, authorizing the retirement of treasury notes by conversion into bonds; but when an attempt was made to secure an explicit declaration that the measure did not permit the future reissue of the legal-tender notes which might be returned to the treasury, Senator Sherman frankly declared that this question, as well as others, was not definitely settled in the bill, and that it was wiser to leave to the future questions that divide and distract, and for the present hold to the main purpose of accomplishing the great work of resumption.

The most serious practical defect in the law, as afterwards stated by Sherman who finally had the responsibility of carrying the measure into effect, lay in the withholding of power from the secretary to sell bonds directly for United States notes; the treasury was obliged to sell bonds for coin, and as coin did not enter into general circulation, the treasury could not sell bonds at first hand to the people. It was necessary to carry on negotiations with the bankers, and this operation gave rise to attacks upon the government for entering into dealings with syndicates and money brokers. An error of a different sort was to make the retirement of United States notes dependent upon the issue of new bank-notes. From the standpoint of resumption the two processes had no relation whatever to each other; the retirement of a part of the government notes undoubtedly advanced the residue toward par in coin, but the volume to be retired should have been determined by considerations independent of national bank issues.

160. Resumption Accomplished.

The act remained practically inoperative so far as the proposition for immediate resumption was concerned. Secretary Bristow in 1875–1876 did not favor the policy of accumulating gold in a reserve, as he deprecated the loss of interest on the specie so withdrawn; and he feared the serious opposition of the financial world, particularly of Germany, which was at that time abandoning silver for gold monometallism. Political activity was again aroused to prevent contraction. The Democrats in their national platform of 1876 declared the resumption clause to be "a hindrance to a speedy return to specie payments," and this view was supported by a considerable number of Republicans. The views of the Greenback party will receive separate consideration.

When Hayes became president, March, 1877, John Sherman of Ohio was appointed secretary of the treasury. Sherman had served continuously in Congress since 1855, first as member of the House until 1861, and then as senator; in 1867 he succeeded Fessenden to the chairmanship of the committee on finance; his ability was unquestioned; he had shown exceptional facility in handling financial details, understood the money market thoroughly, and was a shrewd judge of men. Although his record on financial questions was marred by inconsistencies, as, for example, a change of opinion on the refunding measures, he had the confidence of eastern capitalists and of those who were working for an early resumption of specie payments. He had held an important part in framing the resumption act, and immediately upon taking office undertook more decided measures to carry it out. Sherman relied almost solely upon building up a gold reserve through the sale of bonds for coin. From Congress he realized that he would get no added support; rather there was danger that he would be prevented from doing anything at all, for in 1877 the inflationists were in control of both Houses of Congress, and again made a determined effort to repeal the resumption act. Such a measure was passed by the House of Representatives and failed in the Senate only through disagreement on details. The monetary system was also threatened with the free coinage of silver. Surrounded by embarrassments it was inevitable that Sherman should find difficulty in selling bonds: European financiers, alarmed by the greenback and silver coinage agitations, movements to be subsequently described, expected American finances to be deranged, and returned a considerable block of bonds which competed with the new issue. In spite of all obstacles, Sherman persisted in the policy of gold accumulation. He concluded that 40 per cent. of the notes was the smallest safe reserve of gold; on this basis $138,000,000 in coin was necessary. On January 1, 1879, the treasury had gathered together $133,000,000 of coin over and above all matured liabilities. To do this $95,500,000 of bonds were sold, the balance being met from surplus revenue. Slowly but gradually the value of the notes approached parity with gold, and on December 17, 1878, a fortnight before the date set, paper currency was quoted at par.

The following table shows the average annual value in gold of $100 in currency during the entire period of suspension:

Fiscal year	Value	Fiscal year	Value
1863	$72.9	1871	$88.7
1864	64.0	1872	89.4
1865	49.5	1873	87.3
1866	71.2	1874	89.3
1867	70.9	1875	88.4
1868	71.5	1876	87.8
1869	72.7	1877	92.7
1870	81.1	1878	97.5

In carrying through resumption, Sherman showed firmness and tact. He was careful not to antagonize too sharply the elements of both parties which favored silver coinage; though he disliked the silver bill of 1878, he accepted it and declared that it should be given a fair trial. When the bankers stated that they would throw the burden of the resumption of bank-notes, as well as of United States notes, upon the government, he professed no concern, remarking that such action would be suicide to the banks; that the government could withdraw all of its own deposits in banks, and present all bank-notes held or received, for instant redemption. The banks, in his opinion, would find no profit in presenting treasury notes for coin in order to embarrass the government; legal-tender notes were used by the banks for reserve; and these, being interested in keeping a strong reserve for which greenbacks were available, would find it more to their advantage to aid the government by making employment for the treasury notes.

To this day there is uncertainty and division of opinion as to what were the real forces that accomplished resumption, and the means by which it was afterwards maintained. Many have attributed the achievement solely to Secretary Sherman's financial wisdom and skill, and to the fact that as soon as it was seen that he was in earnest, public confidence co-operated to a successful issue. Without in any way questioning Sherman's administrative ability, we must recognize as a powerful

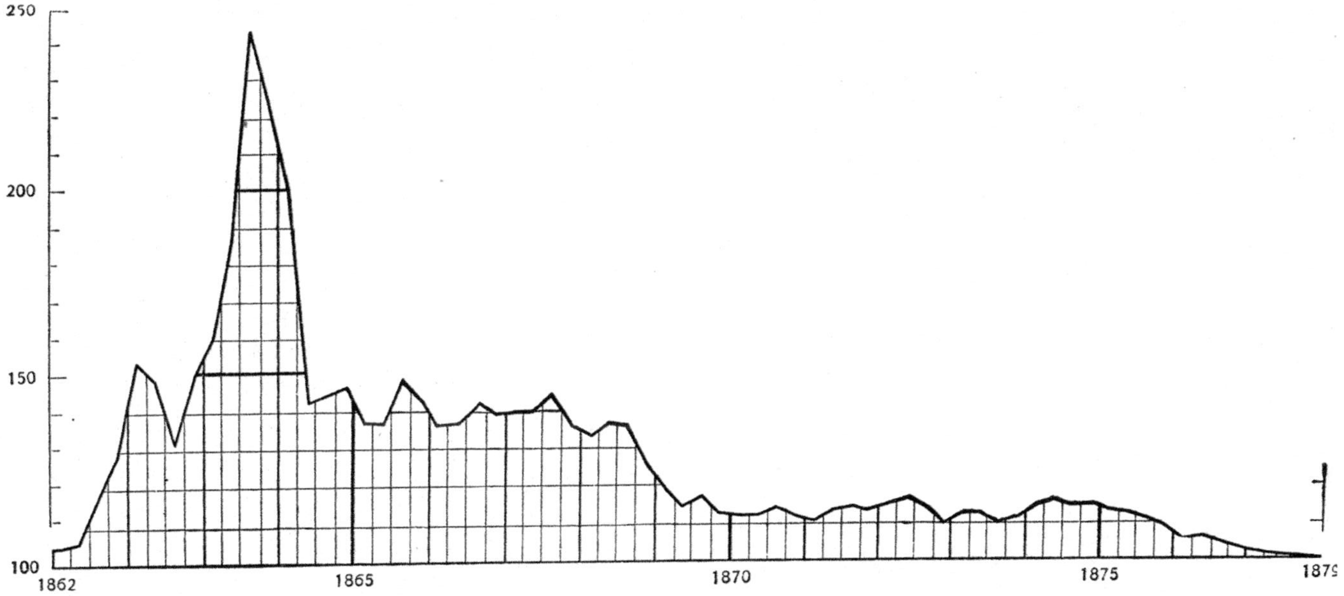

No. VII.—PREMIUM ON GOLD, 1862–1879.

(Measured in paper money.)

factor in effecting resumption, and in maintaining it during the early years of trial, the favorable commercial position of the United States. The tide of trade turned about 1878, and the United States at last was selling to foreign countries more than it was buying. Commerce came to the rescue of finance. Owing to the fall in prices following the depression of 1873, and the increasing demand of Europe for our cotton and food, intensified in 1879 and 1880 by the shortage in European crops, our exports more than doubled between 1872 and 1881, the increase from 1877 to 1881 being over 50 per cent. Such conditions were evidently favorable to the importation and retention of gold; and coupled with this happy turn in market conditions, was the fall of prices occasioned by resumption itself, which in turn was a powerful magnet for attracting gold back to this country.

In the actual carrying out of resumption, it is to be observed that there was no contraction whatever in the paper currency: no destruction of treasury notes took place; very little paper money was presented for gold, and whatever came in was paid out again by the treasury for immediate use. Under the original resumption act of 1875, authority was given for the cancellation of $82,000,000 legal tenders (dependent upon issue of new bank-notes), which would have reduced the total volume to $300,000,000. Some contended that under the resumption act of 1875 there could be no reissue of the greenbacks when once received into the treasury. The inflationist successes of 1877–1878 settled this uncertainty once for all, since Congress, May 31, 1878, ordered that there be no further destruction of greenbacks. The amount then outstanding was $346,681,000, a slight reduction from the $382,000,000 outstanding in January, 1875. As the law has never been changed, this volume of legal-tender circulation is still current. It was also enacted in 1878 that all notes when received into the treasury shall be "reissued and paid out again and kept in circulation," and the constitutional doubts as to the right to do this was, as has been seen, removed by the Supreme Court in the decision of 1884. The burden of redemption in gold was thus made perpetual, although no automatic process was devised which would promise an ever-ready stock of gold for exchange. Fortunately, on account of the commercial prosperity which was reflected in large treasury surpluses, the burden of keeping up the gold reserve was lightly felt during the next ten years. When, however, a new supply of treasury notes was added by the act of 1890, without any added provision for the gold reserve, and revenues showed a deficit instead of a surplus, the weakness of the arrangement was disclosed.

161. Greenback Party.

The question of legal tender should not be dismissed without some further account of the greenback philosophy and its advocacy by political parties. In 1876 dissatisfaction with the financial policy of the government was so bitter that it crystallized in a separate political organization known as the Greenback or National party, and later as the Greenback Labor party; a consideration of the views of this organization throws light upon the success of the free silver agitation. The propositions advocated by the Greenback party, as we have seen, were by no means new: inflationists are in evidence from the beginning of financial reconstruction; at one time or another, when party lines were not firmly drawn on financial questions, they exercised influence within each of the great political organizations. Unable, however, to force these parties to accept their views without reservation, many voters in 1876 abandoned their allegiance in order to form a new organization; nevertheless, this secession and party reconstruction did not mean that each of the older parties was purged of the doctrines of government fiat money and payment of bondholders in greenbacks. There still remained such a latitude of opinion that, on all questions touching monetary policy or the treatment of public debt, Greenbackers were likely to find a sympathetic support among Republicans and Democrats. It was during this period that the term "soft" currency was invented. The significance of the term is not very precise, but it included the doctrines of all then opposed to specie or hard money as the basis of the monetary system.

The specific demands of the Greenback party in 1876 were as follows: (1) Repeal of the act for the resumption of specie payments; (2) Issue of legal-tender notes convertible into obligations bearing interest not exceeding one cent per day on each $100; (3) Suppression of bank-notes; (4) No gold bonds for sale in foreign markets.

The underlying idea in the greenback philosophy, an idea which still finds much popular acceptance, is that the issue of currency is a function of the government, a sovereign right which ought not to be delegated to corporations. Such a view appealed to the spirit of nationalism and democracy, and naturally and quickly led to the full acceptance of the principle of "fiat money." This phrase in its extreme form signified a money that was not dependent for its value on the material of which it was made, that was not redeemable in any other money, and that had its origin, force, sanction, and value in the mandate of the government. The value of currency was held to depend not upon its convertibility, but upon its purchasing power. Bonds were based upon the credit of the United States and thus had value; why not follow the same reasoning and policy as to paper money?

The next step was to deny that there was any such thing as money of the world; money is national, not international; it is made money by law, and whatever the law makes money is money. "The only money capable of perfection would be one manufactured out of a material costing substantially nothing, redeemable in nothing else, inasmuch as the redemption of money is its destruction, non-exportable, deriving its existence from the will of the government, authenticated by an official stamp, and regulated as to its value by limiting the quantity."

Much was made of a non-exportable currency. The dollar, it was said, should have at all times a certain fixed and stable value below which it cannot go; it should be issued by the government alone, in the exercise of its high prerogative and constitutional powers; it should be stamped on convenient material of the least possible intrinsic value, so that neither wear nor destruction will occasion any loss to the government; it should be made of such material that it would never be exported; when issued, it should never be redeemed; and it was solemnly declared that there was no more reason why the dollar, the unit of values, should be redeemed, than that the yard-stick, the unit of length, should be redeemed. The dollar so issued should possess a value, a little greater than that of the gold dollar, in order that it might be fundable into a 3.65 per cent. bond. Its real value rested through the sovereign act of government, upon the wealth, the power, and the prosperity of the country. The note *was* a dollar and not simply an obligation. It was vehemently denied that the greenback was only "a promise" of the government! Every promise made by it had been scrupulously observed; the so-called promise on the United States notes to pay dollars was neither on demand nor at any fixed time. "Its value or purchasing power rested upon nothing except the laws of Congress making it receivable for certain classes of national taxes, and a tender for private debts, and the general consent of the people." "The degree of its purchasing value was determined by the quantity in circulation. Opinion as to the probability of its redemption in coin, neither created its value, nor fixed the magnitude of its value."

According to the greenbacker logic, resumption in 1879 was effected not by the retirement of greenbacks, or the creation of a gold reserve backed up by fortunate trade conditions, but by the word of the secretary of the treasury ordering the acceptance of greenbacks at par at the custom-houses in payment of the duties. "At once these greenbacks were made equal to gold. The greenback, meeting all the demands for money equally as well as gold, had the same worth as gold, and the premium on gold at once disappeared."

The speakers and newspapers in the greenback cause were

fierce in their denunciation of the so-called money interests; to them the American people were opposed, if not enslaved by the bondholding interests. These interests, rendered skilful and wise by years of dealings in the old world and new, were accused of successfully laboring for two objects: the perpetuation of the bond, and the increase of the value of the currency in which all payments on interest or principal of the bonds were to be made. The American people should not be "hewers of wood and drawers of water" to foreigners; it would gladly take at par all bonds that the government found necessary to sell, provided they were payable at the option of the holder and bore interest at 3.65 per cent. or lower. Finally the system of funding was held responsible for perpetuating an enormous, non-taxable, interest-bearing debt. It was reasoned that the bonds support the banks, the banks foster the public debt, and the funding measures deprived the people during twenty to thirty years, of their lawful right to pay the bonds, — a crime against the laborer and tax-payer. Recent legislation was cited in evidence: the first step in this campaign of oppression by bond-holders, it was said, was the act of March 18, 1869, which by one stroke doubled the property of bondholders by compelling the payment of all bonds in coin; the second blow was struck in extending the bonds by the refunding act of July 14, 1870; and the plot was carried to complete success in the laws excluding silver from coinage. It was thus reasoned that all of the banking, coinage, and bond legislation since the Civil War had been a part of a well-defined scheme to defraud the public.

In 1876 the Greenback party polled less than one hundred thousand votes (81,740); in 1878, at the congressional election, it secured the support of more than 1,000,000 voters; in 1880, 308,578; in 1884, with Butler as the presidential candidate, 175,370. This was the last presidential election in which the Greenback party figured. For a time its financial demands were enunciated by the Labor party, and later were put into the platform of the Populists or People's party.

Although the advocates of greenbacks never acquired responsible party power, they gained several decisive victories which have left permanent results. Chief among these may be mentioned the stopping of contraction in 1868, and in 1878, the repeal of the cancellation of notes which was authorized by the resumption act.

CHAPTER XVI.

BANKING AND TAXATION, 1866-1879.

162. References.

BANKING: *Finance Report*, 1873, pp. 76–98; 1875, pp. 202–205 (profits), 223-227 (taxation); 1877, pp. 168–176 (taxation); 1878, pp. 156–166; 1879, pp. 123–125 (profits), 144–150 (taxation of bonds); 1881, p. 188 (profits); Bolles, III, 341–365; J. A. Garfield, *Works*, I, 543–571 (June 7, 1870), 571–593 (June 15 and 29, 1870); C. A. Conant, *History of Modern Banking*, 265–270; *Report of Monetary Commission* (1898), pp. 200–218; C. F. Dunbar, *Theory and History of Banking*, 141–143; J. J. Knox, *History of Banking*, 101–151; C F. Dunbar, *Economic Essays*, 346–364.

TAXATION: *Finance Report*, 1871, p. viii; 1874, pp. xxiii–xxvii (customs); 1875, pp. xxxiv–xxxvii; 154–159 (whiskey frauds); 1877, p. 120 (frauds); 1878, pp. 61–64 (tax on tobacco); *Report of U. S. Revenue Commission*, 1865–1866 (Pub. Doc. 1866, p. 483); Bolles, III, 398–444 (internal revenue), 445–488 (tariff); J. A. Garfield, *Works*, I, 205-216 (tariff bill of 1866), 383–390 (Jan. 19, 1869), 520–543 (tariff bill of 1870); II, 551–571 (1878), 637–655 (1879); F. H. Hurd, in *American Orations*, III, 374–405 (Feb. 18, 1881); W. McKinley, *Speeches and Addresses* (ed. 1894); 1–22 (Apr. 15, 1878); W. D. Kelley, *Speeches*, 9–84 (Jan. 31, 1866), 322–391 (June 1, 1868); J. Sherman, *Speeches*, 121–137 (Jan. 23, 1867), 284–306 (May 23, 1870), 336–355 (March 15, 1872); E. Young, *Customs Tariff Legislation*, cxlii–clxxviii; F. A. Walker, *Discussions in Economics and Statistics*, I, 27–68 (1870); F. W. Taussig, *History of the Tariff*, 171–229 (references in foot-notes); F C. Howe, *Taxation Under Internal Revenue System*, 197–204, 214–222; D. A. Wells, *Practical Economics*, 152–234 (distilled spirits; industrial effects and frauds).

163. Bank-Note Circulation.

The two preceding chapters have been devoted almost exclusively to questions relating to the debt, the struggle over issues of government paper money, and the resumption of specie payments; there are three other subjects which require special consideration to bring the narrative during the period of readjustment, 1865–1879, into an orderly presentation: these are the development of the national banking system, the reduction of taxation, and silver coinage. If it be objected that precedence should be given to the subject of taxation, the answer is that while revenue is at the basis of national vitality, its treatment during these years received the barest consideration.

When the war closed the bank-note circulation was about evenly divided between State and national bank bills. The application in 1866 of the 10 per cent. tax upon all local issues finally drove such institutions as wished to enjoy note circulation to reorganize under federal charters; and from this date controversies over banking were added to the other perplexities of Congress. Such subjects as the redemption of notes and the proper adjustment of bank reserves to deposits, do not properly concern national finance; but some other phases of the banking problem are of interest to the government in its fiscal capacity; among these may be mentioned the growth of bank-note circulation as related to the whole question of currency, the amount of United States bonds held by banks, the distribution of the circulation, the deposit of public moneys in national banks, the power of federal supervision over bank issues, and the taxation of banks. In treating these subjects it is impossible to avoid an occasional reference to monetary controversies which have been previously discussed.

Between 1864 and 1879 the number of banks, their capital, circulation, and bonds held to secure circulation, were as follows, in milions of dollars: —

	No. of banks	Capital	Circulation	Bonds held to secure circulation
1864	508	$86.8	$45.3	
1865	1513	393.2	171.3	
1866	1644	415.5	280.3	$331.8
1867	1642	420.1	293.9	338.6
1868	1643	420.6	295.8	340.5
1869	1617	426.4	293.6	339.5
1870	1615	430.4	291.8	340.9
1871	1767	458.3	315.5	364.5
1872	1919	479.6	333.5	382.0
1873	1976	491.1	339.1	388.3
1874	2004	493.8	333.2	383.3
1875	2088	504.8	318.4	370.3
1876	2089	499.8	291.5	337.2
1877	2080	479.5	291.9	336.8
1878	2053	466.1	301.9	347.6
1879	2048	454.1	313.8	357.3

In 1866 the national bank circulation was $280,000,000, well within the limit of the $300,000,000 which had been set in the original bank act. The law intended that one-half of the circulation should be apportioned among the different States according to population; but in the earlier acts formulating the system, there were certain changes and contradictions, so that when this principle of apportionment was applied, it was found that banks in the older sections of the country, particularly in New England, had gained more than their share of notes. For example, in 1869, Massachusetts held more than one-sixth of the circulation, and that State, with her neighbors, Rhode Island, Connecticut, and New York, enjoyed more than one-half of the entire amount. This was regarded as unfair to the West and the South. The deficiency of bank-note circulation was especially marked in the South which naturally had been in no position to avail itself of the privileges offered by the banking act in the early days of its development. Wisdom, if not justice, demanded that a fresh opportunity be given this section, since it was good national policy that the South be rapidly reunited to the North in a common industrial prosperity and in reciprocal financial interests. Some went so far as to urge that if there were to be inequalities, the population of the Western States should have more circulation *per capita* than that of the Eastern States; the latter with its dense population could easily use checks and drafts, but in the West the laborers and mechanics were forced to carry currency in their pockets.

A readjustment of bank-note circulation was generally favored, but it was difficult to accomplish: either to increase above the $300,000,000 limit, or to secure equalization by withdrawal of circulation from banks which had more than their share, had its embarrassments. It was impracticable, within a short time to withdraw circulation which had been assigned; there was moreover objection to an increase in the total volume, both from inflationists who believed that the expansion of banking currency would destroy any excuse for further issues of government legal-tenders, and from contractionists, who were convinced that expansion of paper currency of any sort, whether banking or government, tended to put off the day of specie payments.

The question was temporarily adjusted by the funding act of July 12, 1870; among its provisions was authority for an increase of $54,000,000 in bank-note circulation (making a total of $354,000,000) to go to those sections where there was a deficiency, to be followed when this amount had been taken out, by the withdrawal of $25,000,000 from those States having an excess, and the assignment of this to States having less than their proportion. The support of the anti-inflationists was secured by the retirement of an equal amount of the three per cent. certificates, which were in use for bank reserves and clearing-house exchanges. This made but little change in the total volume of notes, and the method of reapportionment was so clumsy that distribution was not modified. Opportunity to take out new circulation was but tardily taken advantage of, — between the passage of the act and Nov. 1, 1871, there was issued $24,773,000; in 1872, $16,220,000; and in 1873, $7,357,000. The South and West slightly increased their circulation, but showed no great eagerness, for the high rate of commercial interest which prevailed in these sections did not stimulate investment in bonds for the purpose of circulation. In 1874 the excess and deficiency of circulation, upon the basis of the law of 1870, for different sections was as follows: —

	Excess	Deficiency
New England	$69,905,000	
Middle States	7,861,000	
Southern and Southwestern		$52,354,000
Western		21,033,000
Pacific States and Territories		7,587,000

The total circulation in 1874 was but $333,000,000, leaving a margin which could have been apportioned, if desired, to States having a deficiency. So sluggish were the South and

West that there was justification in the charge made by the anti-inflationists that the clamor for more currency was insincere. Grant, in the veto message of 1874, admitted that at first he was disposed to give great weight to the argument of unequal distribution of banking capital in the country, but when he reflected that there was a considerable amount of circulation authorized by existing law which had not been taken out, he did not believe that it was yet time to consider the question of "more currency." As the full amount of circulation permitted by the law of 1870 was not taken out, it was unnecessary to withdraw notes from banks having an excess. All questions of volume, equalization, or distribution, however, were set aside by the resumption act of 1875, which provided for the issue of bank-notes to any amount, subject to the general provision of the banking act as to purchase and deposit of bonds.

164. Relations of the Banks to the Government.

Under the permissive authority given by the national banking act to the secretary of the treasury to use national banks as depositories of public money, except receipts from customs, these institutions performed a useful service. During the fifteen years, 1863–1878, the receipts of public money by the depository banks were over $220,000,000 annually; at the end of this time only $255,000 stood on the books of the department as unavailable on account of failure of any of the banks, and for a portion of this sum the treasury had security. Upon all balances deposited to the credit of public disbursing officers the banks paid a duty of one-half of one per cent. Between 1864 and 1878 the balance of the treasury with banks on June 30 each year was as follows:

1864	$39,977,000	1872	$7,778,000
1865	36,066,000	1873	62,185,000
1866	34,298,000	1874	7,790,000
1867	26,183,000	1875	11,914,000
1868	23,302,000	1876	7,871,000
1869	8,875,000	1877	7,556,000
1870	8,484,000	1878	6,938,000
1871	7,197,000	1879	7,183,000

Any doubts which existed as to the constitutional powers of the federal government to supervise banking issues were settled in 1869 by the Supreme Court in the case of *Veazie Bank* v. *Fenno.* The taxation of State bank-notes was held constitutional, not merely because it was an instrument for suppressing a circulation which came into competition with notes issued by the government, but because it was a right of Congress to provide a currency for the whole country, either in coin, treasury notes, or national bank-notes. There was no question of the power of the government to emit bills of credit, to make them receivable in payment of debts to itself, and to make this currency uniform in value and description, as well as convenient and useful for circulation; as an instrument to this end, the court upheld the power of Congress to tax other issues. This right had been previously denied by many Democrats, especially by those who held to the stricter interpretation of the Constitution, and adhered to limited powers of the federal government. On the other hand, so great a Democratic authority as Gallatin had earlier, in his "Considerations on the Currency," written in 1831, anticipated the position of the court in observing that Congress had power to lay stamp duties on notes, and had exclusive control over the monetary system.

National banks during this period were subject to three federal taxes: one per cent. upon the average amounts of circulatory notes outstanding; one-half of one per cent. upon the average amount of deposits; and one-half of one per cent. upon the average amount of capital stock not invested in United States bonds. In addition to these taxes banks in many States were subject to State taxation which frequently made the total burden quite heavy; for example, in 1874 the national banks with a capitalization of $494,000,000, paid in United States taxes $7,256,000 and in State taxes $9,620,000, making a total of $16,876,000 or 3½ per cent. on the capital. The federal taxes yielded the following sums in millions of dollars: —

	Circulation	Deposits	Capital	Total
1865	$0.7	$1.1	$0.1	$2.0
1866	2.1	2.6	0.4	5.1
1867	2.9	2.7	0.3	5.8
1868	2.9	2.6	0.3	5.8
1869	3.0	2.6	0.3	5.9
1870	2.9	2.6	0.4	5.9
1871	3.0	2.8	0.4	6.2
1872	3.1	3.1	0.4	6.7
1873	3.4	3.2	0.5	7.0
1874	3.4	3.2	0.5	7.1
1875	3.3	3.5	0.5	7.3
1876	3.1	3.5	0.6	7.2
1877	2.9	3.4	0.7	7.0
1878	2.9	3.3	0.6	6.8
1879	3.0	3.3	0.4	6.7

165. Antagonism to the National Banking System.

With this brief outline of the principal facts concerning the growth of national banking, it is possible now to consider the long and bitter controversy over the very existence of the system which was intimately connected with the whole question of sound government finance. The reluctance to reduce the volume of government treasury notes has already been described; in dealing with the issues of national banks, congressional policy was still more inconsistent: there was both distrust and caprice, and there can be no understanding of banking legislation or even of fiscal policy during the next quarter of a century without a keen appreciation of this suspicion and even the hatred which existed in some sections.

The indictment was something like this: under the national banking system, a few men in every town or city had been able to build up handsome fortunes; if the banking system were to continue under national control, it must be made more free; otherwise abolish all bank paper and substitute United States currency, — the people's money. Government money was superior to that of banks; treasury notes shared in the triumphs of victory; it was the fashion to glorify the "battle-scarred" and "blood-stained" greenbacks; why not rely upon them rather than upon the credit of private institutions. The banking system was accused of costing the nation too much, and of being dangerous to the liberties of the people; it controlled elections, and sent its stockholders to Congress. As the future of national banks depended upon public indebtedness, its interests and the nation's interests clashed. Again, as the people knew that the ultimate redemption of bank-notes was secured by the deposit of government securities, and by the maintenance of a reserve for which greenbacks were available, they would unquestionably prefer that which secures to that which requires to be secured; the substance was more solid than the shadow. The redundancy of currency was attributed, not to greenbacks, but to the prevailing and traditional vice in the banking system of piling up credits on credits by banking on deposits. Inasmuch as banks could influence the volume of money, it was regarded as a grave wrong for the government to delegate to this subordinate and irresponsible agency an absolute dominion over industry and commerce, and over prices and wages, by inflating or contracting the currency. Opinions of this sort were too frequently associated with a rapidly developing distrust of the money interests of the city by the country region; and distrust of the richer plenty of the East by the West with its scattered population and small supply of capital.

The argument against the banks which had the most influence was that of excessive profits: it was insisted that the banks received a "double profit," in interest on the bonds deposited, and in interest on the loan of notes which the banks received for the bonds. Again and again it was proved that the profit was not so much as critics asserted, since the banks were burdened by State taxes, by the several federal taxes upon circulation, capital, and deposits, and by restrictions as to the maintenance of reserve and redemption funds. It was also shown that although banking circulation was generally if not eagerly taken up after the passage of the act of 1865, many banks limited their investment in bonds to one-third of their capital, the minimum allowed by law, and some even neglected to call for the notes attaching to the minimum deposit. Again, after bonds went to a premium, their purchase for deposit as security enforced a new burden and risk on the banks. Another point of attack was the government deposits in banks. Even conservative writers, like Professor Bowen of Harvard, assailed the policy because it gave to the secretary of the treasury independent authority to make his own selection of depositories, and thus revived the worst features of the exploded pet banks.

The popular opposition to the expansion of the national banking system was reinforced by the jealousy which prevailed in certain administrative bureaus of the treasury department. John Jay Knox, comptroller of the currency, in commenting upon the restrictions placed upon the free development of the banking system by the act of June 20, 1874, observes that certain officials in the treasury department were in favor of perpetuating the legal-tender notes. After noting that the tendency of all government bureaus is to magnify their own importance, he writes that "the position of the National Banking Bureau in the treasury department was at the commencement very strong. With Secretaries Chase, Fessenden, and McCulloch the legal-tender note was but a temporary expedient, while the national bank currency was to be the permanent money of the country. With Boutwell and Richardson the importance of the legal-tender note as a financial factor in increasing the power of the secretary began to gain on the national bank-note. This tendency began to be felt in the subordinate offices. . . . In fact, there were from a very early day two factions in the treasury department, the legal-tender faction and the national bank faction. The former, whenever they had the opportunity, did what they could to prevent the retirement of legal-tender notes and the substitution therefor of national bank currency."

166. Revision of Internal Revenue System.

The tax legislation of the war period proved enormously productive, but it also revealed many incongruous and contradictory provisions which needed remedy as soon as possible. During the war, tariff questions were subordinated to those of revenue, and in the first years of peace there was no sharp line of party loyalty drawn upon that question, and a variety of views was tolerated within the party; not until 1880 was the tariff made a supreme party issue. Congress in 1865 recognized the difficulty of tax revision amid the pressure of other measures connected with reconstruction, and delegated the preparatory work of inquiry to a commission composed of David A. Wells, Stephen Colwell, and S. S. Hayes. The reports of this commission are of high value in throwing light not only upon questions connected with the incidence of taxation, but also upon the condition of trade and industry at the close of the war. In presenting its first report, in January, 1866, the commission commented on the difficulty of making a satisfactory inquiry because statistical data were lacking or imperfect. Budget estimates were unreliable, in the face of unexpected events of war, frequent alterations in the tariff, and defects in the internal revenue system. When advances in rates were made, the increase was anticipated by importers, manufacturers, and dealers, and it was therefore hard to test the capacity of any tax as a source of revenue. For example, at least a year's supply of distilled spirits was manufactured and stored away before the operation of the tax of July 1, 1864; and about two years' supply of spices was imported before the increased duties on that commodity went into effect. The difficulty of estimating revenue in advance was also aggravated by the inflated and fluctuating values of all commodities, occasioned by the rapidly increasing volume of paper money.

The commission condemned the existing system of internal revenue, particularly on the ground of its diffuseness; frequent duplication of taxes caused undue enhancement of prices, which, in turn, tended to decrease exports and consumption, and thus to threaten the existence of many branches of industry. Commodities were taxed not only during manufacture, but also upon sale, so that from 8 to 20 per cent. of the value of nearly every finished industrial product went into the treasury. On cotton fabrics, the tax ranged from 9 to 14 cents a pound; while on fine sugars it was equal to all the value created by the labor employed. For the mechanical production of a book, twelve to fifteen separate taxes were levied: upon each constituent part of the book, as paper, cloth, leather, boards, thread, glue, gold-leaf, and type material, amounting in each case to from 3 to 5 per cent., while the finished article paid its tax of 5 per cent. In some cases the tax was altogether too high to secure the maximum of revenue; distilled spirits, for example, were taxed in 1865, $2.00 as compared with 20 cents a gallon in 1863. The stimulus thus given to fraud was seen when the tax was reduced, July 20, 1868, from $2.00 to 50 cents; the revenue leaped from $18,655,000 in 1868 to over $55,000,000 in 1870. Another serious defect was the lack of equalization and adjustment between the tariff and the excise; on some commodities the burden placed upon domestic manufactures was heavier than that from import duties, a condition which, if prolonged, would necessarily destroy the home industry.

In general, the commission proposed the speedy reduction or abolition of taxes which tended to check development, the retention of all those which, like the income tax, fell chiefly upon realized wealth, and the concentration of duties upon a few commodities. The advantage of freedom in trade was dwelt upon: "Freedom from multitudinous taxes, espionage, and vexations; freedom from needless official impositions and intrusions; freedom from the hourly provocations of each individual in the nation to concealments, evasion, and falsehoods." The recommendations of the commission were only in part respected. While there was a general willingness to abolish the internal revenue duties, every attempt at radical lowering of the tariff duties met a successful protest. Many protectionists easily arrived at the conviction that war rates on imports made a good permanent peace policy.

The sequence of the most important internal revenue acts was as follows: the act of July 13, 1866, repealed the tax on coal and pig iron, and lowered the duties on manufactures, products, and gross receipts of corporations, etc., taking off at one blow $45,000,000. The act of March 2, 1867, reduced the rate on cotton, and repealed duties on a considerable number of manufactured products; exempted incomes up to $1,000, and repealed the gross receipts tax on advertisements and toll roads. The act of February 3, 1868, repealed the tax on cotton; the act of March 31, 1868, finally removed all taxes upon goods, wares, and manufactures except those on gas, illuminating oils, tobacco, liquors, banks, and articles upon which the tax was collected by means of stamps; the act of July 30, 1868, reduced the tax upon distilled spirits from $2.00 to 50 cents per gallon; and the act of July 14, 1870, brought the system of internal revenue taxation down to the level at which it was maintained until 1883. The taxes left were those on spirits, tobacco, fermented liquor, adhesive stamps, banks and bankers, and a small amount on manufactures and products.

In general, "all taxes which discriminated against prudence and economy, as the taxes upon repairs; against knowledge, as the taxes upon books, paper, and printing; against capital and thrift, as the differential income tax; against the transportation of freight by boat or vehicles, and against the great leading raw materials, as coal and pig iron, cotton, sugar, and petroleum," were quickly swept away, leaving taxes which might be regarded in the light of luxuries, "involving an entirely voluntary assessment on the part of the consumer." The special licenses, stamp, corporation, and income taxes were continued, but later in 1870, when the debt had been largely funded, and the receipts from customs, and distilled and malt liquors and tobacco showed a large increase, nearly all the license taxes except those on brewers, distillers, and dealers in liquor and tobacco, were repealed. The income tax was continued until 1872 with the rate reduced to 2 1-2 per cent. upon incomes in excess of $2,000.

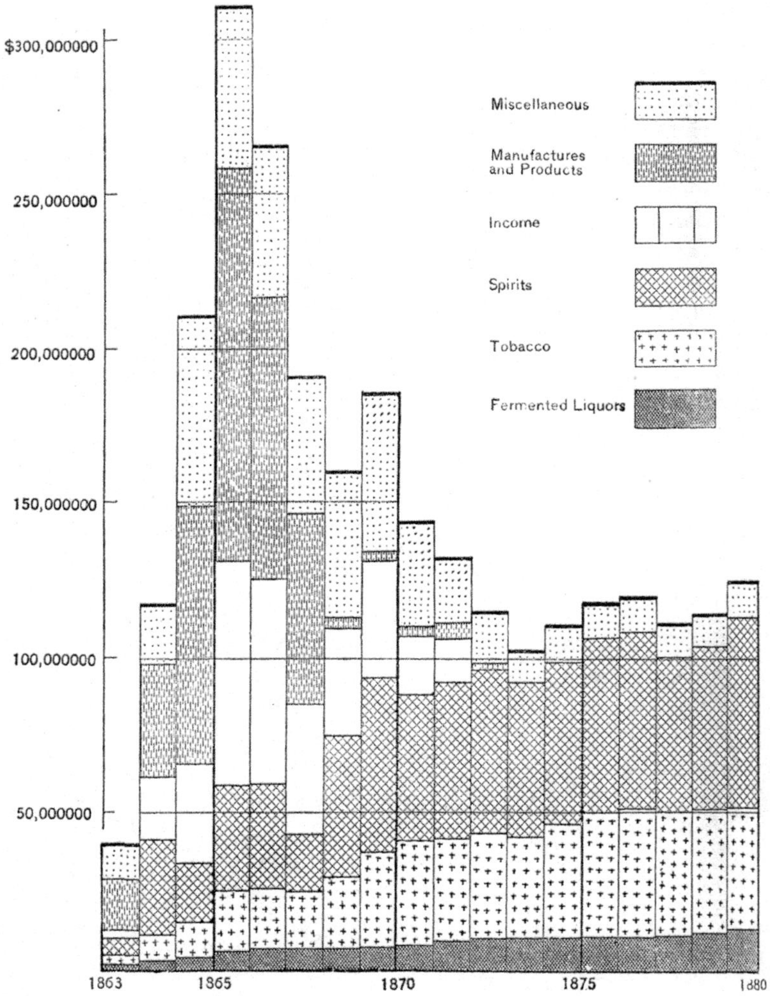

No. IX. — RECEIPTS FROM INTERNAL REVENUE, 1863–1880.

(For continuation, see Chart No. 11.)

The receipts from the principal sources of internal revenue, 1866–1880, were as follows in millions of dollars: —

	Distilled spirits	Fermented liquor, including licenses	Tobacco, including licenses	Manufactures [1]	Banks and bankers	Gross receipts [2]	Special licenses	Adhesive stamps	Income	Total [3]
1866	33.3	5.2	16.5	127.2	3.5	11.3	14.1	15.0	73.0	310.9
1867	33.5	6.1	19.8	91.5	2.0	7.4	13.6	16.1	66.0	265.9
1868	18.7	6.0	18.7	61.6	1.9	6.3	11.9	14.9	41.5	191.2
1869	45.0	6.1	23.4	3.3	2.2	6.3	9.9	16.4	34.8	160.0
1870	55.6	6.3	31.4	3.0	3.0	6.9	11.0	16.5	37.8	185.2
1871	46.3	7.4	33.6		3.6	2.8	5.0	15.3	19.2	144.0
1872	49.5	8.3	33.7		4.6			16.2	14.4	131.8
1873	52.1	9.3	34.4		3.8			7.7	5.1	114.1
1874	49.4	9.3	33.2		3.4			6.1		102.6
1875	52.1	9.1	37.3		4.1			6.6		110.5
1876	56.4	9.6	39.8		4.0			6.5		117.2
1877	57.5	9.5	41.1		3.8			6.5		119.0
1878	50.4	9.9	40.1		3.5			6.4		111.1
1879	52.6	10.7	40.1		3.2			6.7		113.9
1880	61.2	12.8	38.9		3.3			7.7		124.5

[1] Products of iron, wood, glass, paper, cotton, wool, leather, oil, gas, minerals, etc.
[2] Advertisements, transportation companies, insurance companies, theatres, etc.
[3] Total includes some small receipts not given in previous columns.

This table is evidence of the stability of internal revenue taxes. The violent change in the receipts from distilled spirits in 1868 was due to special circumstances, as frauds and the expectation that the taxes would be lowered, which checked the withdrawal of spirits stored in bond; once the rate was adhered to the proceeds were fairly uniform. The same is true in a greater degree of duties on fermented liquors and tobacco. In the operations of the internal revenue system of this period there are two points of interest: taxes were repealed in as disorderly a way as they were originally imposed; there was no careful adjustment in revision; first one bit was carved off and then another; in the second place the business community was not morally robust enough to accept in times of peace the high duties which prevailed even after the wholesale reductions and repeals of 1870. The story of the administration of the taxes upon distilled spirits is discreditable; it reflected upon the honor of the civil service engaged in this branch, and it furnishes an illustration of the demoralization of influential manufacturers who tried by corruption to escape payment of duties. It became a scandal during Grant's second term, and only by the most determined efforts of Secretary Bristow were the intrigues and frauds brought to light.

167. Tariff Changes.

In the revision of tariff duties the whole question of protection of domestic industries was once more raised. Opposition came both from vested interests which had flourished under the artificial aids given by the high war tariffs and also from those who believed in restriction and protection as permanent elements of national policy. The conflict of opinion within the Republican party delayed action: on the one hand Representative Morrill, chairman of the committee on ways and means, failed in 1866 to pass a highly protective measure; on the other hand the tariff measure framed in 1867 by Mr. Wells and endorsed by Secretary McCulloch, which reduced and rearranged duties, was defeated. Actual legislation was confined to the act of March 2, 1867, increasing the duties on wool, and the act of February 24, 1869, which applied to one commodity, copper. The annually increasing revenue, however, made some sort of general revision a necessity; dissatisfaction was especially marked in the West, where many Republicans with protectionist convictions insisted that public opinion called for a reduction. Garfield for example warned the House of Representatives that unless the protectionists recognized the signs of the times they would before long be compelled to submit to a violent reduction made without discrimination. Even Sherman declared that Congress might "as well dismiss to future generations extreme ideas of free trade and protection, which are alike inconsistent with a revenue system." The strength of the protectionist sentiment throughout the country, however, was not appreciated; if waning it was certainly reinforced by the industrial depression after 1873; for in times of business failure, the country is little likely to weaken its financial props, no matter what the argument of final advantage. In the agricultural communities of the East and Middle States, Greeley's New York "Tribune," with his weekly plea for high protection, had great influence. Greeley in a conversation with Garfield remarked, "If I had my way, if I were king of the country, I would put a duty of $100 a ton on pig iron, and a proportionate duty on everything else that can be produced in America. The result would be that our people would be obliged to supply their own wants, manufactures would spring up, competition would finally reduce prices, and we would live wholly within ourselves." In Congress this extreme view was championed by William D. Kelley of Pennsylvania, whose persistent support of duties on iron secured for him the popular title of "Pig Iron Kelley."

The tariff duties were in part reduced by the act of July 14, 1870. A comprehensive bill was originally proposed, but the debate was so prolonged and the disagreements so complicated that finally, in order to secure any legislation whatever, portions of the tariff measure were added to an internal revenue bill which went through. It was a half-hearted measure, reducing duties on articles in which the domestic industry had little interest, such as tea, coffee, wine, sugar, molasses, and spices. A reduction on pig iron was offset by an increase on steel rails and a few other articles.

Again in 1872 another attempt was made to secure reduction; in the West there was a strong and growing sentiment among Republicans in favor of lowering duties. Farmers in that section began to grumble; and an additional argument was the plethora of the treasury beyond the requirements of the sinking fund. Two measures were introduced, one in the House and one in the Senate; the House bill was the more radical, but still accepted protectionism as a valid principle; the Senate measure proposed simply a 10 per cent. horizontal reduction. The Senate bill was finally accepted as a compromise. In addition the revenue duties on tea and coffee were abolished and some special reductions were made, as in the case of salt and coal; while the free list of raw materials entering into manufacture was slightly extended. The reduction of 1872 was hasty and ill-advised and too much influenced by abnormal importations of 1871–1872. The loss of duties on tea and coffee alone cut off an annual income of about $20,000,000. After the panic of 1873 revenue fell; the iron and steel industry in particular is most sensitive to industrial disorder, and duties from commodities belonging to this group shrank to but a fractional part of former returns, as will be seen by referring to the following table (in millions of dollars): —

	Sugar, molasses, etc.	Coffee	Tea	Spirits and wines	Tobacco	Iron and steel manufactures	Wool and manufactures of	Cotton manufactures	Silk manufactures	Flax and manufactures of	Total[1]
1869	35.1	11.5	9.8	7.2	2.9	13.8	25.6	8.2	12.7	5.7	180.0
1870	40.7	12.7	10.2	8.0	3.7	15.1	26.1	9.2	13.9	5.7	194.5
1871	32.6	11.0	8.3	8.4	4.8	18.7	33.6	10.8	18.0	6.5	206.3
1872	31.0	7.2	5.1	8.6	5.5	21.9	42.0	12.3	20.3	7.3	216.4
1873	32.0			8.7	6.3	18.2	38.5	11.6	17.3	7.2	188.1
1874	34.9			8.0	6.2	10.9	32.3	9.0	14.2	6.2	163.1
1875	37.2			6.9	4.3	6.8	30.9	8.0	14.0	6.2	157.2
1876	41.9			6.1	4.7	4.7	25.3	6.6	13.9	5.4	148.1
1877	37.1			5.6	4.4	3.8	20.3	6.5	12.8	5.3	131.0
1878	38.8			5.0	4.6	3.3	19.9	6.6	12.2	5.2	130.2
1879	40.3			5.2	4.3	3.7	18.8	10.0	14.0	5.4	137.3
1880	42.2			6.0	4.7	19.2	29.2	10.8	18.6	6.0	186.5

1 The totals in this column include miscellaneous classes which have been omitted.

As customs receipts fell in two years, from $216,000,000 in 1872 to $163,000,000, caused by the reduction of duties and the embarrassments of the panic of 1873, the 10 per cent. horizontal reduction was repealed in 1875. This practically completed the tariff legislation until the general act of 1883.

168. Receipts and Expenditures, 1866–1879.

The total receipts for the years 1866–1879 are shown in the following table: —

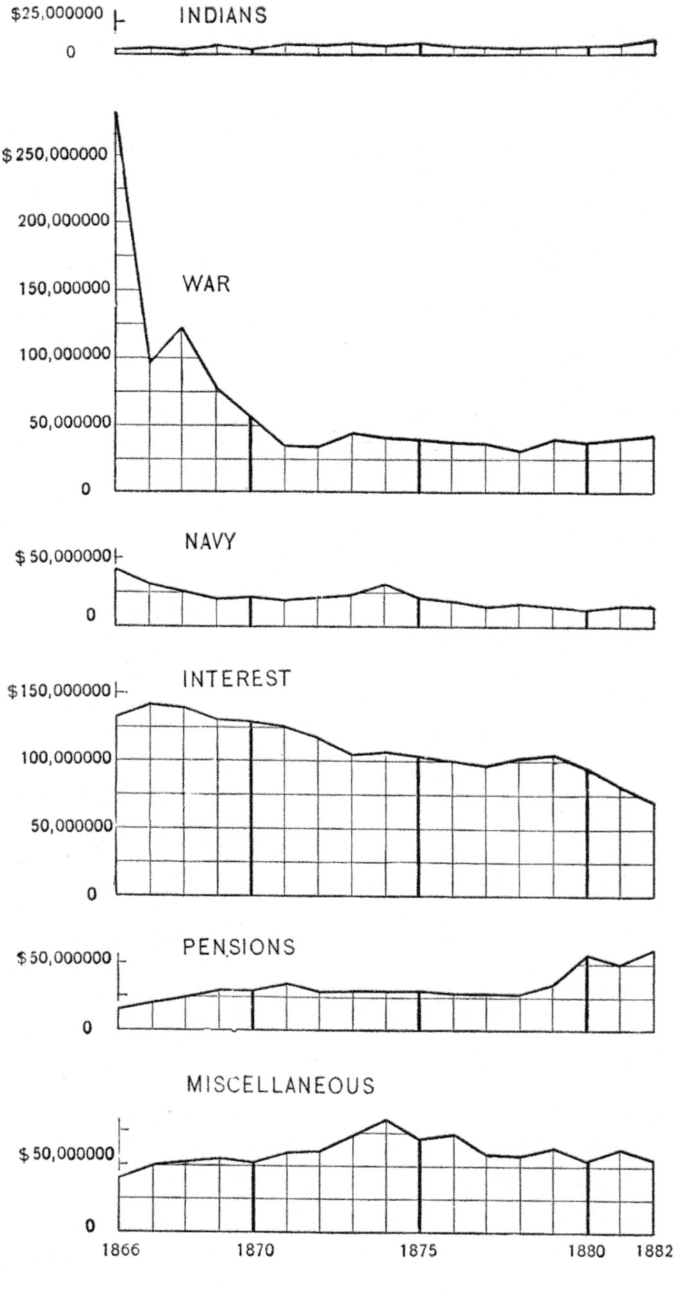

No. VIII. — ORDINARY EXPENDITURES, 1866–1882.

(Continuation of Chart No. 3, different scale.)

	Customs	Internal revenue	Other	Total net ordinary
1866	$179,046,000	$309,226,000	$31,667,000	$519,949,000
1867	176,417,000	266,027,000	20,402,000	462,846 000
1868	164,464,000	191,087,000	20,883,000	376,434,000
1869	180,048,000	158,356,000	18,784,000	357,188,000
1870	194,538,000	184,899,000	16,522,000	395,959 000
1871	206,270,000	143,098,000	25,063,000	374,431,000
1872	216,370,000	130,642,000	17,682,000	364,694,000
1873	188,089,000	113,729,000	20,359,000	322,177,000
1874	163,103,000	102,409,000	34,429,000	299,941,000
1875	157,167,000	110,007,000	16,846,000	284,020,000
1876	148,071,000	116,700,000	25,295,000	290,066,000
1877	130,956,000	118,630,000	31,414,000	281,000,000
1878	130,170,000	110,581,000	16,695,000	257,446,000
1879	137,250,000	113,561,000	21,511,000	272,322,000

The miscellaneous receipts under "other" in the above table require some explanation. The sales of public land yielded from $1,000,000 to $4,000,000 annually; the tax on circulation and deposits on national banks was nearly constant, approximately $7,000,000; the premium on sales of gold yielded several millions; fees, — including consular, letters patent, steamboats and land, — proceeds of sales of government property, fines and penalties, and repayment of interest by Pacific Railway Companies account for most of the balance. In 1874 the award of the Geneva tribunal, $15,500,000 is credited to the treasury.

Expenditures for the principal objects of government during the years 1866–1879 were as follows: —

	War	Navy	Pensions	Interest on debt	Indians	Miscellaneous	Total
1866	$283,154,000	$43,285,000	$15,605,000	$133,067,000	$3,295,000	$40,613,000	$519,022,000
1867	95,224,000	31,034,000	20,936,000	143,781,000	4,642,000	51,110,000	346,729,000
1868	123,246,000	25,775,000	23,782,000	140,424,000	4,100,000	53,009 000	370,339,000
1869	78,501,000	20,000,000	28,476,000	130,694,000	7,042,000	56,474,000	321,190,000
1870	57,655,000	21,780,000	28,340,000	129,235,000	3,407,000	53,237,000	293,657,000
1871	35,799,000	19,431,000	34,443,000	125,576,000	7,426,000	60,481,000	283,160,000
1872	35,372,000	21,249,000	28,533,000	117,357,000	7,061,000	60,984,000	270,559,000
1873	46,323,000	23,526,000	29,359,000	104,750,000	7,951,000	73,328,000	285,239,000
1874	42,313,000	30,932,000	29,038,000	107,119,000	6,692,000	85,141,000	301,239,000
1875	41,120,000	21,497,000	29,456,000	103,093,000	8,384,000	71,070,000	274,623,000
1876	38,070,000	18,963,000	28,257,000	100,243,000	5,966,000	73,599,000	265,101,000
1877	37,082,000	14,959,000	27,963,000	97,124,000	5,277,000	58,926,000	241,334,000
1878	32,154,000	17,365,000	27,137,000	102,500,000	4,629,000	53,177,000	236,964,000
1879	40,425,000	15,125,000	35,121,000	105,327,000	5,206,000	65,741,000	266,948,000

We have now reached a period when the amounts involved in the classification of the expenditures as returned in the summary tables of the "Finance Reports" are so crude that a more minute analysis of the figures is necessary in order to give even a slight comprehension of the meaning of the enormous outlay of the government. Particularly is this true of the columns entitled "War" and "Miscellaneous." Unfortunately the reports of the treasury department do not furnish any detailed tabulations for the period in question, and as there is no uniformity in the tables of expense given from year to year a table of only approximate completeness can be compiled. For example the title "War" is misleading; expenditures under this item include outlay for the support of the army, ordnance, signal service, forts, and fortifications, suppressing Indian hostilities, bounties, reimbursements to States for raising volunteers, claims of loyal citizens for supplies, and, most alien of all, improvements of rivers and harbors. During this period the annual amounts expended for rivers and harbors were as follows in millions of dollars: —

1866	.3	1874	5.7
1867	1.2	1875	6.4
1868	3.5	1876	5.7
1869	3.5	1877	4.7
1870	3.5	1878	3.8
1871	4.4	1879	8.3
1872	5.0	1880	8.1
1873	6.3	1881	9.1

The general title "Miscellaneous" covers up expenditures of the most varied character, and in order to illustrate the growth of the governmental activity after the Civil War and the variety of objects supported from the national treasury, the following detailed table for a few items is given in millions of dollars: —

MISCELLANEOUS EXPENDITURES.

	Civil list	Foreign inter-course	Expenses of col-lecting customs	Expenses of col-lecting internal revenue	Postal defi-ciency	Mint	Light-houses	Public build-ings	Total [4]
1866	12.3	1.3	5.4	5.8		.7	1.4	.3	40.6
1867	15.6	1.5	5.7	7.9	2.6	.9	2.2	1.1	51.1
1868	12.0	1.4	7.6	8.7		.7	2.6	1.4	53.0
1869	12.4	8.4 [1]	5.4	7.2	2.5	.8	1.9	1.5	56.5
1870	19.0	1.5	6.2	7.2	2.8	1.1	2.6	2.2	53.2
1871	18.8	1.6	6.6	7.1	3.7	1.0	2.7	2.8	60.4
1872	16.2	1.8	7.0	5.7	3.6	.8	3.1	4.0	61.0
1873	19.3	1.6	7.1	5.3	4.8	.7	2.9	6.8	73.3
1874	17.6	1.5	7.3	4.6	4.2	1.2	2.5	7.2	85.1 [5]
1875	17.3	3.2 [2]	7.0	4.3	6.5	1.2	2.9	8.6	71.1
1876	17.2	1.4	6.7	3.9	4.5	1.4	2.7	4.7	73.6
1677	15.8	1.2	6.5	3.6	5.7	1.2	2.4	5.1	58.9
1878	16.6	1.2	5.8	3.3	5.6	1.0	2.2	2.9	58.2
1879	16.4	6.8 [3]	5.5	3.5	5.3	1.0	2.3	3.4	63.7

[1] Including $7,200,000 payment for Alaska.

[2] Including $1,900,000 British claims.

[3] Including $5,500,000 award to Great Britain by Fisheries Commission.

[4] Total includes other items in addition to those given in previous columns. This table is only approximately correct, the figures being selected from the accounts at the end of the report of the secretary of the treasury.

[5] Including award of Geneva Tribunal, $15,500,000, investment account.

The following table compares the total receipts and expenditures, 1866–1879, in millions of dollars: —

	Receipts			Expendi-tures	Surplus	Deficit
	Taxes	Other	Total			
1866	490.2	29.7	519.9	519.0	.9	
1867	446.6	16.2	462.8	346.7	116.1	
1868	357.3	19.1	376.4	370.3	6.1	
1869	339.2	18.0	357.2	321.2	36.0	
1870	379.7	16.3	396.0	293.7	102.3	
187.	349.9	24.5	374.4	283.2	91.2	
1872	347.0	17.7	364.7	270.6	94.1	
1873	302.1	20.1	322.2	285.2	37.0	
1874	265.5	34.4	299.9	301.2		1.3
1875	267.2	16.8	284.0	274.6	9.4	
1876	264.9	25.2	290.1	265.1	25.0	
1877	249.6	31.4	281.0	241.3	39.7	
1878	240.7	16.7	257.4	237.0	20.4	
1879	250.8	21.5	272.3	266.9	5.4	

CHAPTER XVII.

SILVER AND BANKING, 1873-1890.

169. References.

SILVER, 1873-1879: *Messages and Papers*, VII, 463-464 (1877), 486-488 (Hayes' veto, 1878), 616-617 (1880); *Finance Report*, 1877, pp. xvi-xxv; 1878, pp. xiv-xvii; 1880, pp. xviii-xxii; *Report of Monetary Commission of* 1876, 87-131 (evil effects of demonetization; J. A. Garfield, *Works*, II, 329-353 (1876-1880); J. Sherman, *Recollections*, I, 459-470; II, 603-635 (Bland Act); J. G. Blaine, *Twenty Years*, II, 602-611; J. J. Knox, *United States Notes*, 149-155; J. L. Laughlin, *History of Bimetallism*, 92-105 (act of 1873), 209-243 (act of 1878); D. K. Watson, *History of Coinage*, 135-160 (act of 1873), 168-178 (act of 1878); Bolles, III, 373-397; A. D. Noyes, *Thirty Years of American Finance*, 35-42; F. W. Taussig, *Silver Situation*, 1-19 (act of 1878); H. White, 213-223 (act of 1873); C. J. Bullock, *Monetary History*, 110-114 (references to *Congressional Record*); *Report of Monetary Commission* (1898), 138-145; J. K. Upton, *Money and Politics*, 197-226; H. B. Russell, *International Monetary Conferences*, 150-192; J. T. Cleary, *The "Crime" of* 1873, in *Sound Currency*, III, No. 13; F. A. Walker, *Discussions in Economics and Statistics*, I, 177-191; M. S. Wildman, *Money Inflation*, 173-215.

SILVER, 1880-1889: *Messages and Papers*, VIII, 243 (1884); 342-346 (Cleveland, 1885); *Finance Report*, 1881, pp. xiv-xv; 1884, pp. xxix-xxxiv; 1885, pp. xvi-xxxiv (Secretary Manning); 1886, xix-xxxix; 1889, lx-lxxxiv (Secretary Windom); F. W. Taussig, *The Silver Situation*, 19-48; J. L. Laughlin, *History of Bimetallism*, 243-254; A. D. Noyes, *Thirty Years of American Finance*, 75-82, 96-99, 103-112, 138-145; H. White, *The Silver Situation*, in *Quar. Jour. Econ.*, IV (1890), 397-407; W. C. Ford, *Silver or Legal Tender Notes*, in *Pol. Sci. Quar.*, IV (1889), 615-627; G. S. Coe, *Bank Notes and the Silver Danger*, *Bankers' Magazine*, XXXVIII, 367; R. P. Bland, *Restoration of Silver*, in *Forum*, II (1887), 243; *Shall Silver be Demonetized?* in *No. Amer. Rev.*, vol. 140 (1885), 485; vol. 141, p. 491 (discussion); W. M. Stewart, *Contraction of the Currency*, in *No. Amer. Rev.*, vol. 146 (1888), 327; D. A. Voorhees, *Plea for Silver Coinage*, in *No. Amer. Rev.*, vol. 153, p. 524; Consult under "Silver" in *Poole's Index*, *First Supplement* (1882-1887), p. 403; vol. III (1887-1892), p. 393; A. B. Hepburn, *History of Coinage*, 297-319.

170. Demonetization of Silver.

The long record of agitation, debate, and legislation on silver belongs more strictly to monetary history, but since the treasury was forced to support a coinage of inferior bullion value at a parity with gold, it demands a careful consideration from students of American governmental finance. During the Civil War and for some years afterwards, there was practically no public discussion in this country as to the use of silver as a monetary medium. Silver was slightly undervalued at the mint and never except in insignificant amounts had been coined into dollars; only as minor coin did it appear in circulation. In 1866 a revision of all the laws relating to mintage and coinage was suggested in order to provide a code or compendium which would more clearly correspond to existing technical and commercial needs; and in 1869 a committee composed of Knox, comptroller of the currency, and Linderman, director of the mint, was appointed to consider the subject; the following year a report was submitted which among other provisions recommended that the silver dollar be dropped from the list of coins. In view of the prolonged dispute over demonetization the paragraph in the report concerning the silver dollar is in part reprinted: —

"The coinage of the silver dollar piece, . . . is discontinued in the proposed bill. . . . The present gold dollar piece is made the dollar unit in the proposed bill, and the silver dollar piece is discontinued. If, however, such a coin is authorized, it should be issued only as a commercial dollar, not as a standard unit of account, and of the exact value of the Mexican dollar, which is the favorite for circulation in China and Japan and other oriental countries."

The bill as a whole was a "mint" bill, designed to correct ambiguities in the law of coinage; and there is no evidence that it was intended to reorganize the monetary system. The silver dollar was not and had not been in general circulation for years. The first bill to carry out general revision, which was introduced in April, 1870, did, however, provide for the coinage of a silver dollar, limited in legal tender to five dollars in any one payment. It failed through lack of consideration in the House after passage in the Senate; a second effort succeeded, and a bill revising and amending the laws relative to the mint, assay offices, and coinage of the United States passed the House May 27, 1872, by a vote of 110 to 113, and the Senate, January 17, 1873, with no dissenting votes. In this act the only mention made of any silver dollar was one of 420 grains designed to meet the special trade in the Orient. At the time the omission of the standard silver dollar of 412½ grains occasioned no comment, but in the subsequent fierce and partisan discussions there has been a persistent endeavor to prove that the act of 1873 was the result of a conspiracy on the part of Eastern bankers and legislators to demonetize silver without the general knowledge of the public. So determined has been this effort to discredit the act that the episode has been frequently referred to by supporters of silver as the "Crime of 1873."

There is no space to enter at length upon the evidence surrounding the passage of this act, but it is believed that the most careful investigation on the part of the inquirer accustomed to the use of public documents will not disclose any intention of deceit. There was no prolonged debate over the demonetization of silver, for at the time there was little interest either in Congress or out of Congress in the fortunes of the silver dollar. The evidence connected with this legislative episode has been examined at length by Professor Laughlin in "History of Bimetallism in the United States," and by Mr. Horace White in his "Money and Banking," and, if their conclusions be regarded as influenced by a long and continued advocacy of gold monometallism, the reader is referred to the candid statements of General Walker, who certainly had no sympathy with efforts to limit the world's supply of metallic money. The latter says, "Now, as one who has read a good deal on both sides on this subject, I do not believe that any fraud was committed or intended. . . . Our public men had had almost no training in economics of finance. Very few people knew what the monetary system of the country was. . . . . Few Congressmen outside of the committee knew that any vital change was impending. The measure passed through the usual course."[1] While Mr. Walker discredits the allegation of fraud and of sinister motives he affirms that there was a "grievance," inasmuch as the promoters of the measure did not call attention sharply to the changes proposed by the measure and make sure that its bearings were fully comprehended. This, however, raises the whole question of the merits of bimetallism, a subject beyond the province of the present narrative.

A striking illustration of the ignorance of this law, where it would be least expected, is seen in a letter of President Grant, October 6, 1873, several months after the passage of the act. In discussing the panic, its causes and methods of relief, he expressed a "wonder that silver is not already coming into the market to supply the deficiency of the circulating medium. . . . I want to see the hoarding of something that has a standard of value the world over. Silver has this, and if we once get back to that our strides toward a higher appreciation of our currency will be rapid."

171. Struggle for Free Coinage; Bland Act

It was not long before the omission was brought to general notice, through a variety of causes which were assailing the whole structure of national finance. The panic of 1873 with the continued after depression aroused to new activity all who were convinced that relief depended upon fresh supplies of government money; the veto of the inflation bill by President Grant, however, checked any possible increase of treasury notes. The demonetization of silver and the adoption of a gold standard by Germany in 1871,

[1] Walker, *Discussions in Economics and Statistics*, vol. i, p. 183.

the limitation of coinage of full legal-tender silver by the countries of the Latin Union in 1874, coupled with the discovery of silver mines of large yield in this country, quickly unsettled the price of silver; it was natural, therefore, that both those who were interested in silver as a salable commodity and those who were earnestly convinced of the need of an enlarged money supply should join hands in the protest against the demonetization of silver.

The drop in the market price of silver is shown in the following table: —

	Price of silver per ounce in London, in pence	Ratio of gold to silver
1840	$60\frac{3}{8}$	15.61
1850	$60\frac{1}{16}$	15.70
1860	$61\frac{11}{16}$	15.29
1870	$60\frac{9}{16}$	15.57
1871	$60\frac{1}{2}$	15.57
1872	$60\frac{5}{16}$	15.63
1873	$59\frac{1}{4}$	15.92
1874	$58\frac{5}{16}$	16.17
1875	$56\frac{7}{8}$	16.58
1876	$52\frac{3}{4}$	17.87
1877	$54\frac{13}{16}$	17.22
1878	$52\frac{9}{16}$	17.94
1879	$51\frac{1}{4}$	18.39
1880	$52\frac{1}{4}$	18.04
1885	$48\frac{5}{8}$	19.39
1890	$47\frac{11}{16}$	19.77
1895	$29\frac{7}{8}$	31.57

After a resolute agitation a bill introduced by Mr. Bland of Missouri, July 25, 1876, providing for free and unlimited coinage of silver, passed the House of Representatives November 5, 1877, by a vote of 163 to 34. The Senate, however, under the leadership of Senator Allison, changed the bill by limiting the volume of coinage, and in this form the measure was enacted; it restored the full legal-tender character of the

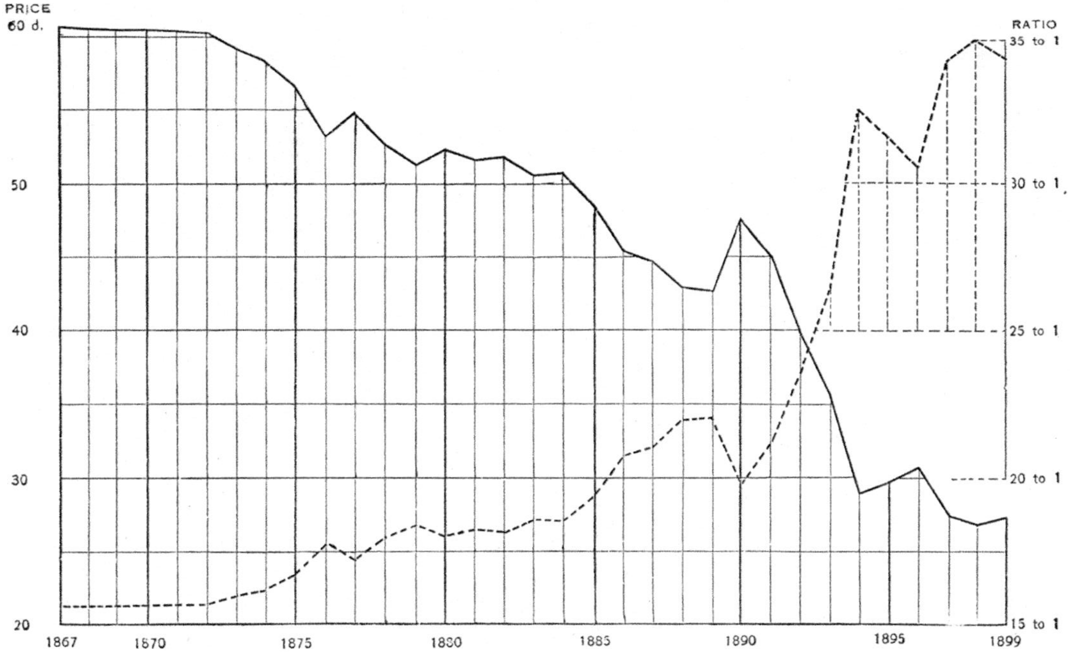

No. X. — SILVER, 1867–1899.

Price of Bar Silver ———
(in London, per ounce sterling, 0.925 fine.)
Ratio of Gold to Silver - - - -

silver dollar and authorized the secretary of the treasury to purchase silver bullion at the market price, not less than $2,000,000 nor more than $4,000,000 worth per month, and coin the same into dollars. Provision was also made for the issue of silver certificates upon deposit of silver dollars, in denominations not less than ten dollars. The vote in the Senate was 48 to 21. President Hayes vetoed the measure, but the silver sentiment in each House was strong enough to pass the bill over his veto. This act demanded the expenditure of at least $24,000,000 per annum in the purchase of a commodity which was falling in value in the world's markets, and which ultimately might be constituted a lien upon the gold assets of the treasury.

172. Coinage under the Bland Act.

The Bland-Allison Act continued in operation until 1890, and during the twelve years of its existence was the occasion of the coinage of 378,166,000 silver dollars. By years the coinage and issue of silver certificates were as follows in millions of dollars: —

July 1	Silver dollars issued to date	Silver certificates issued
1878	8.6	1.9
1879	35.8	2.5
1880	63.7	12.4
1881	91.4	51.2
1882	119.1	66.1
1883	147.3	88.6
1884	175.4	120.9
1885	203.9	139.9
1886	233.7	116.0
1887	267.0	145.5
1888	299.7	229.5
1889	333.5	262.6
1890	369.4	301.5

The purchase value of the silver in this coinage was $308,279,000, yielding a seigniorage of nearly $70,000,000 which was turned into the treasury. From the beginning it was difficult to keep the silver dollars in circulation. The New York banks at the outset, November 12, 1878, placed their stamp of disapproval upon them by adopting a rule prohibiting the payment of balances between banks belonging to the clearing-house, in silver, either in coin or certificates. As Congress by the act of August 12, 1882, attempted reprisal by refusing an extension of charter to any bank that should continue membership in a clearing-house refusing silver, the banks gave way, but they were then accused of boycotting silver under a tacit agreement.

Nor did the coin find favor with the public at large. The people were not accustomed to use coins of heavy weight, and under the original act no provision was made for the issue of silver certificates in denominations of less than ten dollars. The government labored actively to get the dollars into circulation; it not only required disbursing officers to use silver dollars in payment for salaries and other current obligations, but also offered to place the silver in the hands of the people throughout the country without expense for transportation. Notwithstanding these endeavors, Secretary Sherman in 1880 represented that it was difficult to maintain in circulation more than 35 per cent. of the amount coined. When received by creditors the coins were quickly deposited in local banks, and by them transferred to city institutions, until they finally found refuge in the sub-treasuries of the government. In the hope of making the silver money more acceptable to the public, Congress in 1886 authorized the issue of silver certificates in smaller denominations, of $1, $2, and $5, and the treasury department, by hoarding as far as practicable legal-tender notes of small denominations, created a demand for small bills which it met with silver certificates. A reduction of $126,000,000 in bank-note circulation during the years 1886–1890 also helped to provide an outlet for silver, and at the same time gave point to the contention of the silver advocates that without the use of silver the volume of monetary medium was deficient.

173. Unsuccessful Efforts to stop Coinage.

From time to time the controversy blazed up anew. The treasury department felt the combined burden of providing for the continued purchase of silver, of coining it into dollars, and of maintaining a gold standard; and endeavored either through the message of the president or the report of the secretary to impress upon the public its convictions. McCulloch, in 1884 for a second time secretary of the treasury, disclosed the executive apprehension by announcing that unless the coinage of silver dollars was suspended, there was danger that silver, and not gold, would become the metallic standard. In 1885 Secretary Manning, Cleveland's finance minister (1885–1889), devoted the larger part of his annual report to currency reform; the latter warned Congress that the hoarding of gold had already begun; that the ceaseless stream of silver threatened to overflow the land and cause fear and uncertainty; and in conclusion recommended the suspension of compulsory coinage.

The legislative branch of the government paid little heed to these executive appeals; in the country at large there was industrial unrest, and in some sections undoubted distress. All commercial ills were still widely supposed to be due to an insufficient volume of money. The greenback advocacy gave way in a measure to the agitation for the coinage of silver, with no limitation whatever as to amount. A commercial and financial panic in 1884 with its subsequent depression furnished the complainants with abundant illustration. There had been administrative mismanagement of important railway companies, an excessive construction of railways, and a wasteful investment of capital in non-paying enterprises. Iron and steel industries were consequently seriously affected, and this in turn extended the circle of disturbance. Many mines were shut down, and for a time there was a large "army" of the unemployed.

While general conditions did not become so bad as in 1873,

the discouragement was marked, because the reasons for commercial disaster were not so easily seen. After a partial recovery in 1885 there was an unusual outbreak of strikes, boycotts, lockouts, and labor disturbances in 1886–1887; labor organization proceeded rapidly and the Knights of Labor for a brief period gained great power. An improvement of agricultural conditions in Europe after 1880 lessened the demand for American produce, and tended to lower the price of the surplus exported. The Western farmer attributed his evils in part to the railroads and in part to the demonetization of silver. "Granger" railway legislation to control rates was consequently sought in State legislation, and unlimited coinage of silver in Congress. International bimetallists of repute and authority attributed the bitter experience of trade and industry of May, 1884, "to the wanton mischief perpetrated by Germany between 1871 and 1875" in demonetizing silver.

Senators and representatives of both the great parties from Western farming and mining States could not be turned from persistent efforts to increase the volume of money; in season and out of season they attempted to attach to every bill which had the remotest connection with government finance some proposition which would either secure an increase of treasury notes or add to the coinage of silver. The strength of their sentiment was seen in 1886, when a free-coinage bill was defeated in the House of Representatives by a majority of only 37. Although the extreme silver party failed to carry out its projects, its opponents equally failed to stop compulsory coinage. The advocates of silver also made strenuous efforts to force the treasury department to pay out silver indiscriminately in order to force the government on to a silver basis, but were defeated by Secretary Manning, who stanchly declared that he would not pay silver except when silver was asked for.

174. Continued Opposition to National Banks.

The elements which supported an enlarged issue of paper money or the unlimited coinage of silver kept alive antagonism to the national banks and opposed all legislation tending to relieve the difficulties which the system was then laboring under. While ever ready to point to the decline of bank-note circulation as an illustration of the evil in the monetary system which demanded rectification, they were unwilling to allow expansion through banking corporations. The banks could expect no favors. Popular denunciation of banks was rabid. Bankers were represented as meeting in annual conventions, "eating bonbons, and drinking wine, and passing resolutions" hostile to public interest; men were supposed to go into the banking business for selfish interests alone, thus supplanting the government which had a heart and sympathy for humanity; the banks were said to defy the law by loaning money to Western farmers on mortgages, and also in exacting extortionate rates of interest. The banking interest was typified as the supreme leader in the active opposition to an expanding monetary supply. The banks were constantly made to hear about their earlier hostility to the greenback financiering of the Civil War; attention was directed to their attempt to retire the greenback circulation, and to their antagonism to the Bland Act by refusing to accept silver dollars. They were charged with trying to create a panic in 1881 by withdrawing $19,000,000 of currency in order to frighten Congress which passed a bill, vetoed by the president, to make the conditions of note issue less profitable; and also with working in the same year to prevent the refunding of the debt, then maturing, at a lower rate of interest.

175. Decline in Bank Circulation.

The commercial reasons for the reduction of the national bank-note issues are not far to seek; the government in paying off its debt limited the supply of bonds which could be bought by the banks, and at the same time there was an increasing demand for government securities by individuals, trustees, and financial corporations for investment. In this way the bonds advanced to so high a premium that it was unprofitable for the banks to retain them even with the accompanying privilege of circulation. This is well illustrated in the accompanying chart. The steady shrinkage of circulation which took place, beginning with the year 1880, is seen in the following table: —

July 1	Volume of national bank-notes	July 1	Volume of national bank-notes
1880	$344,505,000	1886	$311,699,000
1881	355,042,000	1887	279,217,000
1882	358,742,000	1888	252,368,000
1883	356,073,000	1889	211,378,000
1884	339,499,000	1890	185,970,000
1885	318,576,000	1891	167,927,000

Repeated but unsuccessful efforts were made in behalf of the banks to secure laws less onerous to circulation. Among the measures proposed was an increase of notes to the face value of the bonds deposited, the plan finally adopted in 1900, or to 90 per cent. of the market value of the bonds as measured by their average market value for the six months previous; the acceptance of bonds of the District of Columbia, guaranteed by the United States; repeal of the tax on circulation; funding of the high-rate bonds into a new issue bearing a lower rate of interest and running for a longer period of time; substitution of some other security, as State, county, or municipal bonds for United States bonds as a basis for circulation; permission to banks to issue circulation upon their general credit, without the deposit of specific securities but protected by a general safety fund, as in the old New York system. The proposition which found general approval among those friendly to the banking interest was to refund the public indebtedness into a long low-rate bond. This was recommended by the comptroller of the currency in 1882 and 1883, and bills to that effect were advocated in Congress; the defect in the plan was the postponement of the payment of the debt. Suggestions were made that the national banking system be continued without the feature of note circulation, since the advantage of federal banks of deposit and discount was well worth retaining. So strong and persistent, however, was the opposition to any favors whatever to banks that no remedial legislation was obtained, and the banks were obliged to accommodate themselves to laws antiquated and out of relation to the marvellous commercial and industrial expansion of the country.

CHAPTER XVIII.

SURPLUS REVENUE AND TAXATION, 1880-1890.

176. References.

TARIFF LEGISLATION, 1880-1889: *Messages and Papers*, VIII, 580-591 (Cleveland, 1887); *Finance Report*, 1881, pp. xviii-xxi; 1882, pp. xxiv-xxxiii; 1883, pp. xliv-lii; 1884, pp. xv-xvii: 1886, pp. xlvii-lviii; *Report of the Tariff Commission*, 1882, I, 1-35; 50th Cong. 1st Sess. (1888), *Senate Report*, No. 2332 (Aldrich), pp. 89, 91-101 (minority); *House Report*, No. 1496, pp. 102-111 (Mills); E. McPherson, *Handbook of Politics*, 1884, pp. 18-77, 135-138; 1886, pp. 149-156; 1888, pp. 51-55, 146-166; 1890, pp. 169-189, 223-244; J. Sherman, *Recollections*, II, 841-855 (1883), 1004-1010; W. McKinley, *Speeches and Addresses*, 70-123 (Tariff Commission, 1883), 131-159 (Morrison bill), 250-262 (1888), 277-289 (minority report on Mills bill, 1888); F. W. Taussig, *History of the Tariff*, 230-250 (1883); A. D. Noyes, *Thirty Years of American Finance*, 92-96; *The National Revenues* (ed. A. Shaw, 1888), 32-41, 78-123, 217-226; O. H. Perry, *Proposed Tariff Legislation since* 1883, in *Quar. Jour. Econ.*, II (1887), 69-78; *The Tariff Literature in the Campaign*, in *Quar. Jour. Econ.*, III (1889), 212-217; Stanwood, II, 202-241; D. R. Dewey, *National Problems*, 57-75.

INTERNAL REVENUE: *Finance Report*, 1881, pp. xx, 64; 1882, pp. 69-73; 1883, l-lii; 1886, lv-lvi; 1887, xxix-xxxi; F. C. Howe, *Taxation under the Internal Revenue System*, 165, 221-223; R. M. Smith, in *The National Revenues* (ed. A. Shaw, 1888), 68-77.

SURPLUS: *Messages and Papers*, VIII, 48, 134 (1882); 178 (1883); 508-511 (1886); 580-583, 786-788 (1888); *Finance Report*, 1883, pp. xxx-xxxiii; 1886, xl-xliv; 1887, xxv-xxxiii; E. McPherson, *Handbook of Politics*, 1886, pp. 225-229; H. C. Adams, *Surplus Financiering*, in *The National Revenues*, 45-55; A. D. Noyes, *Thirty Years of American Finance*, 87-88, 123-126; W. McKinley, *Speeches and Addresses*, 203-211 (1886), 263-270 (1888); C. F. Randolph, *Surplus Revenue*, in *Pol. Sci. Quar.*, III (1888), 226-246; *Poole's Index*, vol. III (1882-1887), consult "surplus," p. 416.

EXPENDITURES: *Messages and Papers*, VIII, 120-122 (river and harbor veto of Arthur, 1882), 137, 201, 246, 677, 837-843 (direct tax veto, 1889); A. D. Noyes, *Thirty Years of American Finance*, 89; E. McPherson, *Handbook of Politics*, 1888, pp. 173-174 (refunding direct tax); 1890, pp. 18-21 (ditto); W. H. Glasson, *History of Military Pension Legislation in the U. S.*, 70-119.

177. Surplus Revenue.

In 1882 there was a large balance of treasury receipts over expenditures, and a prospect of similar good fortune in the future. The secretary of the treasury with some humor observed that times had changed since the law of 1789 establishing the treasury department, which made it the duty of the secretary to prepare plans for the *improvement* of the revenue: "What now perplexes the secretary is not wherefrom he may get revenue and enough for the pressing needs of the government, but whereby he shall turn back into the flow of business the more than enough for those needs, that has been drawn from the people." A reduction in the internal revenue duties, together with a change in trade conditions marked by the panic of 1884 and reflected in customs receipts, somewhat cut down income, while more liberal expenditures by Congress put off for a brief period the need of decisive action to prevent a surplus. In 1886 a substantial surplus reappeared, and proved to be the beginning of a series of favorable annual balances; as in 1837, nearly half a century earlier, the problem of surplus financiering was too much for the statesmanship of Congress.

In 1882 the Republicans were still in power and the propositions of Mr. Folger, Republican secretary of the treasury, have special significance; he recognized the evil of large receipts and small disbursements, so far as it affected the business of the country; and he deprecated taking the collections of the government out of the money markets in sums and at dates which have little or no agreement with the natural movement of money. He agreed that the locking up of no inconsiderable proportion of the currency could not fail to embarrass trade. Apparently the only available method of disbursing this excess of assets was by payment of the debt; but the remedy seemed unwise in view of the ruling premiums on the bonds and the restrictions regulating the official call of bonds. At all events the secretary thought that if Congress wished him to make purchases of bonds at a premium, it should assume the responsibility more explicitly by law.

Secretary Folger also discussed the possibility of relief by the deposit of public moneys in national banks, but held it unwise to amend the laws so as to release any of the customs receipts to the custody of these institutions, since this revenue was to a great extent pledged to the payment of the interest and principal of the bonds, and the government ought prudently to take heed of possible financial disturbance and disaster. Only two other means of disposing of the surplus occurred to the secretary: one was to parcel out the surplus among the several States of the Union; the other to complete the terms of the distribution act of 1836 by paying to the States the amounts due in the fourth instalment; neither of these propositions received any countenance. In his opinion the only radical cure was in the reduction of taxation; there should be a repeal of all the internal duties except those on spirits, fermented liquors, tobacco, and bank circulation, and a general reduction of customs duties on nearly all articles in the tariff. This recommendation was responded to by the half-hearted revision of 1883.

When the surplus again became embarrassing in 1886 the Democrats were in power. The premium on the bonds was higher than ever, and Secretary Manning emphatically condemned any policy which would give the proceeds of taxation to bondholders in premiums by anticipated purchases, nor did he expect Congress to throw upon him such a thriftless task. He also frowned upon relief through extravagant appropriations, or by the accumulation of a treasury hoard. His positive recommendations were reduction of taxation and retirement of the greenbacks; that is, of the unfunded debt of $346,000,000. These views were emphatically endorsed by President Cleveland, but did not receive the undivided support of the Democratic party and thus came to nothing. In 1888 the Democratic platform simply called for tariff revision and the reduction of extravagant taxation. The Republicans in their platform of that year "would effect all needed reduction of the national revenue by repealing the taxes on tobacco, which are an annoyance and burden to agriculture, and the tax upon spirits used in the arts and for mechanical purposes, and by such revision of the tariff laws as will tend to check imports of such articles as are produced by our people." According to this program, if further relief were needed, the entire repeal of all internal revenue taxes was preferable to the surrender of any part of the protective system.

Having briefly sketched the general background, the following phases of the whole problem of surplus revenue which excited public attention in the decade 1880–1890 may now be considered in detail: (1) deposits of public moneys in banks; (2) reduction of taxes; (3) increased appropriations; (4) purchase of bonds and debt reduction.

178. Deposit of Funds in National Banks.

As has been stated, the original national bank act of 1863, so modified the independent treasury act, as to permit national banks, when designated by the secretary of the treasury, to be depositories of certain public moneys upon pledging with the treasury a security in United States bonds. The total government balances in banks varied as receipts fluctuated, and as the several secretaries pursued different policies. In Cleveland's administration from 1885 to 1889, the deposits were increased as a means of relief, so as to make the surplus revenues commercially available; and in 1888 they reached $61,000,000. Cleveland did not consider this an ideal method of disposing of government funds, and submitted to it only as a temporary expedient to meet an urgent necessity. Critics taunted the treasury department with virtual partnership with the banks. Mr. Windom, who became secretary of the treasury in 1889, representing a Republican administration, changed this policy, and announced that he should reduce the deposits as rapidly as possible "leaving only such amounts as are necessary for the business transactions of the government. The national bank depositories have been, and are, useful auxiliaries to the sub-treasury system, but the deposit of public funds therewith to an amount largely in excess of the needs of the public service is wholly unjustifiable. Such a policy is contrary to the spirit of the act of August 6, 1846, which contemplates a sub-treasury independent of the banks." Among his objections were: a temptation to favoritism; the dependence of the treasury upon the banks on account of the difficult and delicate task of withdrawing the deposits; the injustice of granting to banks the free use of money, and at the same time paying to those parties interest on their bonds pledged as security; and finally, and most important of all, interference with business whenever it was necessary to withdraw the deposits. This indictment does not represent the permanent attitude of the Republican party, for in the later administration of President McKinley the banks were again intrusted with generous deposits.

179. Reduction of Internal Revenue Duties.

So long as revenues were heaped up in the treasury beyond immediate needs either for current expenditures or for the sinking-fund requirements, it was natural that there should be a growing demand for a reduction of taxation. It was urged with strong effect that the citizens of that day had already paid their share of the cost of the war, and that the remaining portion should be transferred to another generation. Many of those who under ordinary circumstances would have gladly continued taxation in order to effect a rapid extinguishment of the national debt, objected strenuously to its payment if it was necessary to offer premiums to the fortunate holders of government obligations. This reluctance was easily turned into bitter opposition by those who were openly hostile to the national banking system; they were convinced that bondholders and bank directors were synonymous terms, and that the banking and trust institutions which had bonds in large quantities were endeavoring to drive a hard bargain with the government. It is not unlikely, however, that banking and financial interests were content that the debt should remain stationary, in order that there might be no withdrawal of bonds which furnish the very basis of the banking system.

Reduction of taxation could be brought about either by changes in the internal revenue or in the customs schedules. The former appeared the more attractive field for immediate action, inasmuch as internal revenue taxes were popularly regarded as war duties, to be abandoned as soon as practicable in times of peace, and their modification would not affect unfavorably vested manufacturing interests as much as would changes in the tariff. Extreme protectionists wished the abolition of all internal revenue duties; Kelley argued with great elaborateness that their maintenance was a wanton exaction, costing in its administration $5,000,000 annually and requiring the services of more than four thousand people; that it created a lobby and bred political corruption; that it produced monopolies and was unequal in its incidence. A compromise was effected. There was a general agreement that certain odds and ends of excise might be sacrificed, as follows: —

Friction matches	$3,272,000
Patent medicines, perfumery, etc.	1,978,000
Bank checks	2,318,000
Bank deposits	4,008,000
Savings-bank deposits	88,000
Bank capital	1,138,000
Savings-bank capital	15,000
Total	$12,817,000

In addition the national banks paid into the treasury $5,959,000, of which $5,521,000 was on deposits, and the remainder on capital.

The tax on bank checks was declared to be irritating and hampering in its nature; the tax on matches was on a household article of hourly and necessary consumption by all classes;

the tax on savings-bank deposits was a tax on thrift; the tax on patent medicines and perfumeries was vexatious because levied on innumerable articles; and the taxes on the capital and deposits of banks were not needed. The tax on national bank circulation was regarded in a different light, as a tax on a franchise of profit to a favored grantee.

The act of March 3, 1883, abolished the above taxes and reduced the duties on tobacco by one-half. The loss in the total revenue was not so great as anticipated, as there was a constant gain from the duties on spirits and fermented liquors. In 1890 a further reduction of 25 per cent. was made upon snuff, chewing and smoking tobacco, and the special license taxes upon the sale of tobacco were repealed. The changes which took place are seen in the following table in millions of dollars: —

Internal Revenue by Sources, 1880–1890

	Spirits	Fermented liquors	Tobacco	Oleo-margarin	Banks and bankers	Adhe-sive stamps	Total
1880	61.2	12.8	38.9		3.4	7.7	124.0
1881	67.2	13.7	42.9		3.8	7.9	135.3
1882	69.9	16.2	47.4		5.3	8.1	146.5
1883	74.4	16.9	42.1		3.7	7.7	144.7
1884	76.9	18.1	26.1				121.6
1885	67.5	18.2	26.4				112.5
1886	69.1	19.7	27.9				116.8
1887	65.8	21.9	30.1	0.7			118.8
1888	69.3	23.3	30.7	0.9			124.3
1889	74.3	23.7	31.9	0.9			130.9
1890	81.7	26.0	34.0	0.8			142.6

180. Tariff Revision.

A general reduction of customs duties was not so easily effected. A revision of the tariff was necessary in order to meet the changed conditions of trade; and popular favor greeted the suggestion that a commission be appointed, made up of leading representatives in manufactures, agriculture, and commerce, to frame a tariff. The proposition was supported

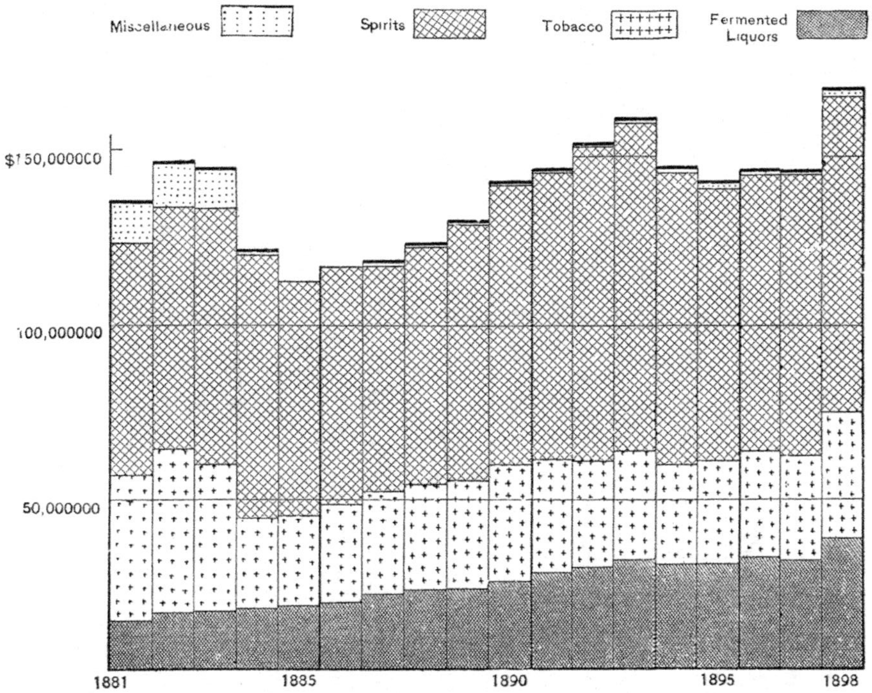

No. XI.—RECEIPTS FROM INTERNAL REVENUE, 1881–1898.

(Continuation of Chart No. 9.)

to Taussig, "duties were advanced on protected articles of which importations continued in considerable volume. The advance was by no means universal, being affected, as our tariff legislation so often has been, by the haphazard manner in which the details of the measure were finally settled. But it was made in so large a number of important cases as to give the act a distinctive protectionist flavor."

The act did not receive general commendation even from protectionist supporters of the Republican party. Secretary Folger in 1883 referred to it slightingly and suggested the need of further reduction of taxes. John Sherman is outspoken in his criticism of the act of 1883, and the comment he makes in describing the forces at work in the passage of the measure may well serve as typical of conditions too often attending tariff legislation.

"When the bill was reported to the Senate it was met with two kinds of opposition, — one, the blind party opposition of free-traders, the other, the conflict of selfish and local interests, mainly on the part of manufacturers, who regarded all articles which they purchased as raw material, on which they wished the lowest possible rate of duty or none at all, and their work as the finished article, on which they wished the highest rate of duty. . . . The Democratic Senators with a few exceptions voted steadily and blindly for any reduction of duty proposed, but they alone could not carry their amendments, and only did so when reinforced by Republican Senators, who, influenced by local interests, could reduce any duty at their pleasure. In this way, often by a majority of one, amendments were adopted that destroyed the harmony of the bill. . . . This local and selfish appeal was the great defect of the bill."[1] Senator Sherman always regretted that he did not defeat the bill, by voting with the Democrats against the adoption of the conference report, for it barely passed 32 to 30. It was only because of the propriety and necessity of a reduction of internal revenue taxes included in the same bill that he felt

[1] *Recollections*, vol. ii, p. 851.

justified in supporting the measure on its final passage. The complaint of selfishness and illogical vote is interesting as coming from a Senator who knew something about local considerations. Defeated in his endeavors to protect wool at a high level in the interest of his Ohio constituents, Sherman was himself willing to seek revenge by sacrificing compensatory duties on worsteds, and thus by his own action co-operate to mar the harmony of the bill.

181. Unsuccessful Democratic Tariff Measures.

The tariff of 1883 did not settle the problem of taxation: if it was in order for Secretary Folger to suggest the possibility of another early revision, the Democratic party, traditionally opposed to protection, was sure to continue the agitation for lower duties. During the next five years the Democrats were strong enough to secure the consideration of two general tariff bills, but failed to enact new legislation. The "Morrison horizontal" bill of 1884 proposed an average reduction of 20 per cent. in import duties, with important additions to the free list. The principle of the bill never gained a warm support; it was not a scientific method of constructing a tariff, and its uniform levelling might cause unexpected injury and introduce new inequalities as troublesome as those already said to exist. Within the Democratic party a protectionist wing, led by Randall of Pennsylvania, harassed the tariff reformers, and ultimately, by voting with the Republicans, defeated the measure; of the 151 negative votes in the House on the Morrison bill 41 were Democratic.

In 1885 a Democratic administration was inaugurated and both the president and Secretary Manning advocated a radical overhauling of the tariff. The administration's repeated and vigorous demands tended to unite the Democratic party on this question and to eliminate those not willing to yield individual interests to party conviction. In December, 1887, President Cleveland startled not only the country but his party by confining his entire message to the existing surplus and the need of tax reform. He spoke decisively, if not over passionately, of the diffusiveness of the tariff system; the uselessness of many of the duties, and the trifling service of others, and referred to the tariff as illogical and inequitable. "Our progress towards a wise conclusion will not be improved by dwelling upon the theories of protection or free trade. It is a *condition* which confronts us, not a theory." With special stress he advocated free raw materials. The critics of the president held the message to be not a plea for reforming a defective tariff, or for lopping off excrescences or incongruities, but a free-trade document designed to destroy the protective system. The Republican majority in the Senate prepared a new and strong protectionist tariff measure as a counter-challenge. Under severe pressure the Democratic House passed the Mills bill with only four dissenting votes in the party.

The Republican taunt that the Democrats were not sincere in their arraignment of the tariff had some ground; the Democrats had been in control of the House of Representatives from 1875 to 1881 and from 1883 to 1888, and yet had never agreed on well-defined opinions in regard to import duties. After the Civil War the platforms of the Democratic party lacked clear and positive convictions as to a tariff policy. In 1868 the party demanded a tariff for revenue which would afford incidental protection to domestic manufactures; in 1876 and 1880, that custom-house taxation shall be only for revenue; in 1884, that any change of law must at every step be regardful of the labor and capital involved in industries; and in 1888 they repeated the same proposition. The Democratic party during this period seemed concerned with the details of schedules rather than with fundamental principles, and consequently the issue did not arouse any popular enthusiasm in political campaigns. Even the reform message of Cleveland was delayed until the latter part of his term, and the continued clashing within the Democratic party was well illustrated in the closing days of the Cleveland administration.

After the Mills bill was brought forward Randall proposed a protectionist tariff bill for the reduction of revenue by $95,000,000, of which $75,000,000 would come from cuts in the internal revenue; and later with the aid of more than a score of Democrats he secured the reference of a bill for the abolition of all taxes on tobacco to the committee of appropriations, of which he was chairman, thus turning it away from the committee on ways and means, to which it more properly belonged.

The Republican party was now united. From the first, it had on the whole legislated consistently in favor of protection to domestic industries, although only gradually did it accept this doctrine as a supreme test of party allegiance. In the platforms of 1872, 1876, and 1880, it cautiously declared that the import duties should be so adjusted as to aid in securing remunerative wages to labor, and to protect the industries, prosperity, and growth of the whole country; in 1884 it more frankly demanded that import duties should not be for revenue only, but should afford security to our diversified industries and "protection" to the rights and wages of the laborer; in 1888 it was more uncompromisingly in favor of the American system of protection. It was on this issue that the presidential campaign of 1888 was definitely fought out. The Republicans won the presidency, and in 1889, when the new House of Representatives was organized, prepared to carry out their pledges in the construction of a new tariff, designed at the same time to reduce revenue and afford protection.

The customs receipts, grouped according to some of their principal sources, will be found in the Appendix. There were no marked fluctuations during this decade except a slight decline caused by the depression of 1884.

The total receipts, 1880–1890, from all sources were as follows: —

	Customs revenue	Internal revenue	Other	Total net ordinary
1880	$186,522,000	$124,009,000	$22,995,000	$333,526,000
1881	198,159,000	135,264,000	27,359,000	360,782,000
1882	220,410,000	146,497,000	36,618,000	403,525,000
1883	214,706,000	144,720,000	38,861,000	398,287,000
1884	195,067,000	121,586,000	31,866,000	348,519,000
1885	181,471,000	112,498,000	29,721,000	323,690,000
1886	192,905,000	116,805,000	26,729,000	336,439,000
1887	217,286,000	118,823,000	35,294,000	371,403,000
1888	219,091,000	124,296,000	35,879,000	379 266,000
1889	223,832,000	130,881,000	32,337,000	387,050,000
1890	229,668,000	142,606,000	30,806,000	403,080,000

182. Increased Expenditures.

The existence of large surplus funds in the treasury gave rise to many propositions for increased expenditures. Some of these were undoubtedly urged solely for selfish and partisan ends or as an easy way of temporizing with the revenue question. A few argued that money was lying dead in the treasury and that it was a duty for Congress to put this dead money into circulation; even distribution was again proposed. Other projects, however, were advocated in good faith in the belief that the government, with the enlarged sense of nationality developed by the results of the Civil War, now had opportunities and even duties to perform for fuller enjoyment of its expanding life. Among the measures requiring greater expenditures were successive river and harbor bills. Although these improvements did not receive all that was asked for, generous provision was made in comparison with previous appropriations. In 1882 President Arthur vetoed a river and harbor bill authorizing the expenditure of $18,743,875, on the ground that the amount called for was extravagant and because appropriations were made for purposes not for the common defence or general welfare and which did not promote commerce between the States; and this attitude for a brief period held appropriations in check. Expenditures by years for rivers and harbors were as follows in millions of dollars: —

Expenditures for Rivers and Harbors			
1880	8.0	1886	4.1
1881	8.5	1887	7.8
1882	11.4	1888	7.0
1883	13.6	1889	11.2
1884	8.2	1890	11.7
1885	10.5		

The defence of the sea-coast was also pressed on the ground that existing guns, forts, and ships were worthless. While the United States, wearied with war, had devoted its energies to internal transportation and to the payment of the war debt, other nations had been experimenting with coast defences, projectiles, explosives, armies, and new types of vessels. Large sums were claimed for the restoration of the merchant marine by bounties and subsidies, and for the construction of government public buildings to take the place of those rented. Further relief was asked for the veterans of the Union army, and a pension bill was pushed, granting pensions to soldiers and sailors who had served in the Civil War, if they were no longer able to support themselves; although vetoed by Cleveland in 1887, it attracted a large and popular support. Through several sessions of Congress debates were devoted to more rapid surveys of public lands, irrigation of the Western deserts, the construction of the Nicaraguan canal, and the so-called Blair educational bill providing for the distribution of large funds to the several States for educational purposes. A bill was also passed in 1889, but vetoed by Cleveland, providing for the repayment of the direct tax collected under the act of 1861. This alone would have relieved the treasury of at least $15,000,000, or if the percentage allowed for collecting the tax be included, of over $17,000,000.

The political philosophy which inspired these generous plans is well summed up in an appeal made by Senator Dolph of Oregon in the course of a debate in 1887: "In short, if we were to take our hands off the increasing surplus in the treasury, and stop bemoaning the prosperity of the country and trying to make the people dissatisfied with the alleged burden of taxation which they do not feel; and devote our energies to the development of the great resources which the Almighty has placed in our hands, to increasing the products of our manufactories, of our shops, of our mines, and of our forests; and to cheapen transportation by the improvement of our rivers and harbors and restoring our foreign commerce, we would act more wisely than we do."

Only a few of the projects just outlined secured final approval in Congress. The most notable increase in expenditure was for pensions; before 1880, the largest expenditure for this purpose in any one year had been but $35,000,000, — after that it was never less than $50,000,000; and in 1886 the beginning of a steady upward climb was made, reaching $106,936,813 in 1890 and $159,357,558 in 1893. Some slight increase was made for the navy beginning in 1889, but the more liberal expenditures for this branch of the public service did not swell the budget until the next decade.

The total expenditures by years, 1880–1890, were as follows: —

	War	Navy	Indians	Pensions	Interest on public debt	Miscellaneous	Total
1880	$38,116,000	$13,536,000	$5,945,000	$56,777,000	$95,757,000	$54,713,000	$264,847,000
1881	40,466,000	15,686,000	6,514,000	50,059,000	82,508,000	64,416,000	259,650,000
1882	43,570,000	15,032,000	9,736,000	61,345,000	71,077,000	57,219,000	257,981,000
1883	48,911,000	15,283,000	7,362,000	66,012,000	59,160,000	68,678,000	265,408,000
1884	39,429,000	17,292,000	6,475,000	55,429,000	54,578,000	70,920,000	244,125,000
1885	42,670,000	16,021,000	6,552,000	56,102,000	51,386,000	87,494,000	260,226,000
1886	34,324,000	13,907,000	6,099,000	63,404,000	50,580,000	74,166,000	242,482,000
1887	38,561,000	15,141,000	6,194,000	75,029,000	47,741,000	85,264,000	267,931 000
1888	38,522,000	16,926,000	6,249,000	80,288,000	44,715,000	72,952,000	259,653,000
1889	44,435,000	21,378,000	6,892,000	87,624,000	41,001,000	80,664,000	281,996,000
1890	44,582,000	22,006,000	6,708,000	106,936,000	36,099,000	81,403,000	297,736,000

The principal items included under "Miscellaneous" are tabulated in a table to be found in the Appendix.

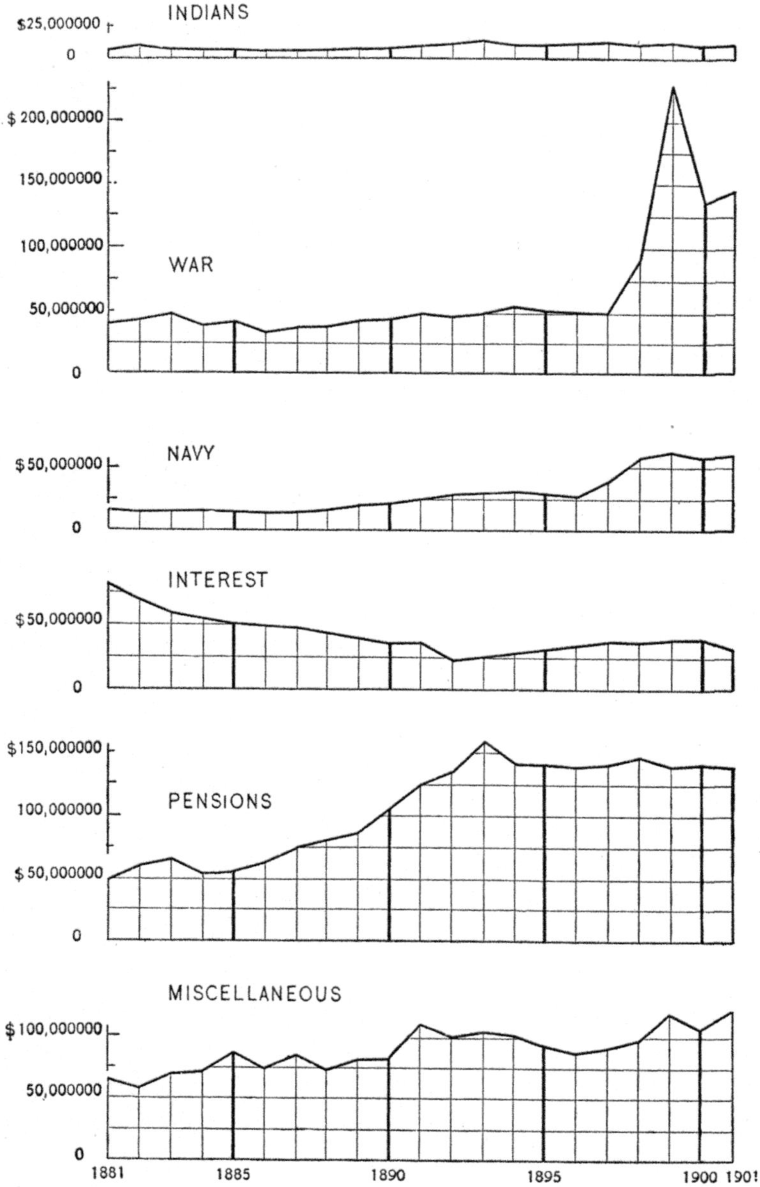

No. XII. — ORDINARY EXPENDITURES, 1881–1901.

(Continuation of Chart No. 8, same scale.)

A comparison of receipts and expenditures, with the surpluses annually accruing, is shown as follows in millions of dollars: —

	Receipts			Expenditures	Surplus
	Taxes	Other	Total		
1880	310.5	23.0	333.5	264.8	68.7
1881	333.4	27.4	360.8	259.6	101.2
1882	367.1	36.4	403.5	257.9	145.6
1883	359.5	38.8	398.3	265.4	132.9
1884	316.7	31.8	348.5	244.1	104.4
1885	293.9	29.8	323.7	260.2	63 5
1886	309.8	26.6	336.4	242.5	93.9
1887	336.1	35.3	371.4	267.9	103.5
1888	343.4	35.9	379.3	259.6	119.7
1889	354.7	32.4	387.1	282.0	105.1
1890	372.3	30.8	403.1	297.7	105.4

183. Treasury Purchase of Bonds.

It has already been stated that the funding act of 1870 tied up a large portion of the public indebtedness in a 4 per cent. thirty-year bond. Owing to the financial disturbances occasioned by the Franco-Prussian War and the panic of 1873, the placing of these bonds was not effected until 1877, which made the new issue irredeemable before 1907, save through purchase in the open market. The 4½ per cent. fifteen-year bonds issued in 1876, were not redeemable until 1891. When the surplus appeared in 1882 there was no immediate embarrassment, as over $400,000,000 of 3 per cent. and 3½ per cent. bonds, temporarily issued in exchange for the 5 per cent. bonds which came due in 1881, were redeemable at the pleasure of the government; three successive surpluses of equal amounts would cancel the outstanding debt. In 1886 this opportunity for relief was exhausted; practically all the bonds subject to redemption at the option of the government had been cancelled, and Secretary Fairchild in 1887 questioned whether he had power under the law to buy bonds beyond the sinking-fund requirements. The dispute turned on a clause in an appropriation act of March 3, 1881, empowering the secretary of the treasury to apply the surplus money in the treasury to the purchase and cancellation of bonds; the administration construed this as a power which lapsed with this particular appropriation bill, and it placed the responsibility upon the legislative branch by asking for definite authority. This was not granted, and the secretary at first refused to purchase bonds in excess of the requirements of the sinking fund; and to buy even this latter amount involved difficulty. At best the purchase of bonds depended upon the frame of mind of bondholders; and every proposition to purchase appreciated the price of securities, while the subsequent higgling over terms necessary to protect the interests of the government kept alive the commercial suspense as to whether the money market at a given time would be relieved. A striking instance of this bargaining took place in the summer of 1887, when the secretary called for offers; 4½ per cent. bonds ran up from 109 to 111, and most of the tenders were above 110. The next week bondholders recognized the stand taken by the treasury, and lowered their demands to 110, but no acceptances were made higher than 109½. This firmness again led to offers varying from 106½ to 109.

The cost of redemption of public indebtedness is seen in the following table giving the prices of the two principal issues of bonds during the period 1880–1890 (fractions discarded): —

Year	Four and one-half per cents. of 1891	Four per cents. of 1907
1880	106–112	103–113
1881	111–116	112–118
1882	112–116	117–121
1883	112–115	118–125
1884	110–114	118–124
1885	112–113	121–124
1886	110–114	123–129
1887	107–110	124–129
1888	106–109	125–130
1889	104–109	126–129
1890	102–105	122–126

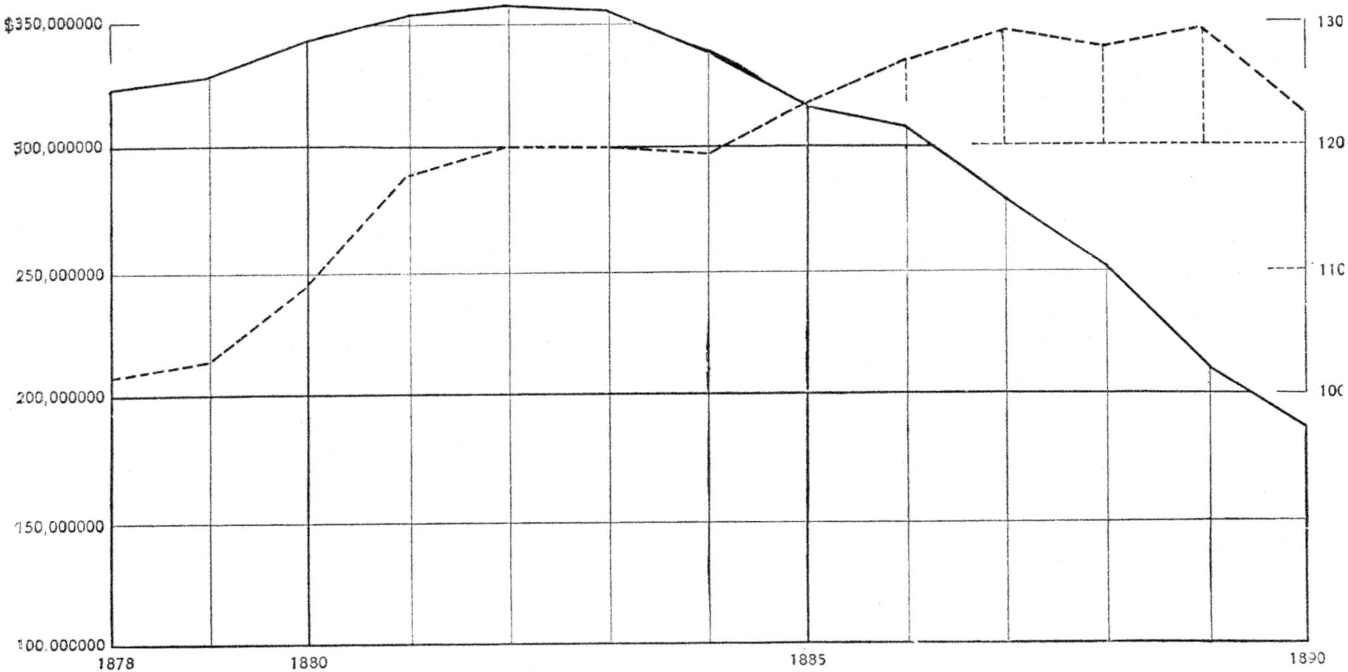

No. XIII. — BANK CIRCULATION, 1878–1890.

National Bank-note Circulation ———

Price of Four Per cent. Bonds - - - - - - - -

In 1888 the secretary stated that many offerings of bonds had been declined because the price was thought to be too high, but finally almost all the bonds offered were bought at some price. In that year $94,000,000 of bonds were secured at a cost of $112,000,000. The purchases continued through 1889 and 1890, the treasury changing its terms of purchase as the market warranted. Although the several secretaries of the treasury during this era of abundant revenues preferred reduction of taxation to the payment of the debt under the onerous conditions imposed, they found consolation in reckonings which showed a final saving to the people by the stoppage of interest payment on debt cancelled. For example, Secretary Windom in 1890 calculated that as a result of purchase and redemption of bonds, the reduction in the annual interest charge amounted to nearly $9,000,000, and the total saving of interest to $51,576,000. On the other hand, as explained by a previous secretary, Fairchild, the people lost the use in business of the money devoted to the purchase of bonds taken from them, by continued high taxation; so far as this use of money in business was more important than its use when saved by the cancellation of bonds, the people lost by the transaction. In all, the net public indebtedness was reduced from $1,996,000,000 in 1879 to $891,000,000 in 1890, — a debt extinguishment without parallel in the history of any nation. For the treasury it meant a reduction of interest on the debt from $105,000,000 in 1879 to $36,000,000 in 1890.

184. The Public Debt, 1880-1890.

The annual changes in the character of the debt are shown in detail in the table on the following page. The old war loans disappeared and the 5 per cent. loan created under the funding act of 1870, which fell due in 1881 and continued on indefinite terms for a few years at 3½ and 3 per cent. interest, was extinguished in 1887. With the introduction of certificate forms of money, as of gold certificates in

	1880	1881	1882	1883	1884	1885	1886	1887	1888	1889	1890
Loan of 1861 — sixes.	157.3	140.5	22.1[1]								
Loan of 1863 . . .	63.2	55.1	47.8								
Ten-forties of 1864	2.7										
Five per cents. of 1881	484.9	442.1	1.2								
Four and one-half per cents. of 1891	250.0	250 0	250.0	250.0	250.0	250.0	250.0	250.0	222.2	139.6	109.0
Four per cents. of 1907	737.5	737.2	738.9	737.6	737.7	737.7	737.8	737.8	714.2	676.1	602.2
Funded loan of 1881; continued 3½ per cents . .			401.5	35.1							
Loan of 1882; 3 per cents. indefinite				304.2	224.6	195.4	151.4	23.7			
Legal-tender notes	346.7	346.7	346.7	346.7	346.7	346.7	346.7	346.7	346.7	346.7	346.7
Silver certificates	12.4	51.2	66.1	88.6	119.8	139.9	116.0	145.5	229.5	262.6	301.5
Gold certificates .	8.0	5.8	5.0	82.4	98.6	140.3	131.2	121.5	142.0	152.0	157.5
Certificates of deposit	14.5	11.9	13.3	13.4	12.4	29.8	18 5	9.1	14.7	17.0	12.3
Other loans . . .	47.2	28.5	25.7	26.2	40.7	24.2	23.5	23.3	23.6	25.1	22.9
Total	2120.4	2069.0	1918.3	1884.2	1830.5	1864 0[2]	1775.1[2]	1657.6[2]	1692.9[2]	1619.1[2]	1552 1[2]
Cash in treasury	201.1	249.4	243.3	345.4	392.0	488.6	493.0	482.4	629.9	643.1	661.3
Debt less cash . .	1919.3	1819.7	1675.0	1538.8	1438.5	1375.4	1282.1	1175.2	1063.0	975.9	890.8

[1] Continued at 3½ per cent. indefinite; see loans of 1882.

[2] Exclusive of Pacific Railway bonds.

1863, currency certificates in 1872, and silver certificates in 1878, the public debt tables become misleading unless carefully analyzed. Against certificates the treasury carries correspondingly large amounts of cash; and the true liabilities of the treasury are determined by subtracting from the total indebtedness the item "cash in the treasury," which includes the gold, silver, or United States notes held in pledge for the certificates.

CHAPTER XIX.

SILVER AND THE TARIFF, 1890–1897.

185. References.

SILVER LEGISLATION: *Messages and Papers*, IX, 40–41 (1889), 113–114 (1890), 193–195 (1891), 401–405 (Cleveland, special message, Aug. 8, 1893), 444, 483–489, 653–655 (1895); *Finance Report*, 1889, pp. lx–lxxxiv (Windom's recommendation); 1890, pp. xlvii–l; F. W. Taussig, *The Silver Situation*, 48–71 (act of 1890); A. D. Noyes, *Thirty Years of American Finance*, 138–152 (act of 1890); D. K. Watson, *History of American Coinage*, 179–191 (Sherman act of 1890), 192–201 (repeal); *Report of Monetary Commission*, (1898), 259–265 (act of 1890), 266–280 (repeal); J. Sherman, *Recollections*, II, 1061–1071 (act of 1890), 1175–1200 (repeal); R. F. Hoxie, *Debate of* 1890, in *Jour. Pol. Econ.*, I, 535–587; D. R. Dewey, *National Problems*, chs. 5, 14 and 16.

FREE COINAGE: W. H. Harvey, *Coin's Financial School* (Chicago, 1894); R. P. Bland, in *No. Amer. Rev.*, CLI (1890), 344–353; D. W. Voorhees, *ditto*, CLIII (1891), 524–535; W. M. Stewart, *ditto*, CLIV (1892), 552–561; R. P. Bland, *ditto*, CLVIII (1894), 554–562; W. J. Bryan, *ditto*, CLXIII (1896), 703–710; A. J. Warner, *Arena*, VIII (1893), 547; W. M. Stewart, *Forum*, XI (1891), 429–437; R. P. Bland, *ditto*, XIII (1892), 45–52; W. H. Harvey, *ditto*, XIX (1895), 405–409.

OPPOSITION TO FREE COINAGE: F. W. Taussig, *The Silver Situation in the U. S.*, in *Quar. Jour. Econ.*, IV (1890), 291–315; H. White, *ditto*, 397–407; F. A. Walker, *Jour. Pol. Econ.*, I, 163–178; J. Sherman, *Bankers' Magazine*, XLV (1891), 608–617; J. J. Knox, *ditto*, 617–622; W. P. St. John, *ditto*, 887–898; J. Seligman, in *No. Amer. Rev.*, CLII (1891), 204–208; E. O. Leech, *ditto*, 299–310; E. O. Leech, *ditto*, CLVII (1893), 42–51; J. H. Eckels, *ditto*, 129–239; *Forum*, XI (1891), 10–18; XII (1891), 472–476, 611–613, 772–782; XIII (1892), 34–44, 281–294, 439–450.

GOLD RESERVE: *Messages and Papers*, IX, 561–565 (Jan., 1895), 642–651 (Dec., 1895); *Finance Report*, 1891, pp. 10–15 (report of treasurer); 1892, pp. xxviii–xxix, 9–19; 1893, pp. 9–13; 1894, pp. lxviii–lxxv, 5–11; 1895, pp. lxvi–lxxxii; 1896, pp. lxxi–lxxviii, 6–7; *Report of Monetary Commission* (1898), 430–444; A. D. Noyes, *Thirty Years of American Finance*, 150–181; W. C. Ford, *Movement of Gold and Foreign Exchanges*, 1894–1895, in *Yale Review*, IV (1895), 128; also in *Sound Currency*, II, No. 22; F. Fetter, in *Pol. Sci. Quar.*, XI (1896), 237–247; F. W. Taussig,

Treasury Condition in 1894–1896, in *Quar. Jour. Econ.*, XIII (1899), 204–218.

Panic of 1893: *Report of Monetary Commission* (1898), 219–223; A. D. Noyes, *Thirty Years of American Finance*, 182–206; or in *Pol. Sci. Quar.*, IX (1894), 12–30; C. A. Conant, *History of Modern Banking*, 524–554; J. D. Warner, *Currency Famine of* 1893, in *Sound Currency*, II, No. 6 (copies of clearing-house certificates, etc.).

Sale of Bonds: *Messages and Papers*, IX, 567–568 (Feb. 8, 1895); *Finance Report*, 1893, pp. lxix–lxxiv; 1894, p. xxxiii; 1895, pp. lxix–lxxii; *Investigation of the Sale of Bonds*, Pub. Doc., 54th Cong., 2d sess., Sen. Doc., 187 (1896), p. 332; A. D. Noyes, *Thirty Years of American Finance*, 207–223, 234–254; A. D. Noyes, *The Late Bond Syndicate Contract*, in *Pol. Sci. Quar.*, X, 1895, 573–602; C. A. Conant, *History of Modern Banking*, 544–551; B. Ives, *Government and the Bond Syndicate*, in *Yale Review*, IV, 10–22.

Banking and Currency: *Messages and Papers*, IX, 554–556 (1894); *Finance Report*, 1894, pp. lxxviii–lxxxi (Carlisle), 393–398 (Eckels); 1895, pp. lxxxii–lxxxv (Carlisle), 376–378 (Eckels); 1896, pp. 498–506 (Eckels); A. L. Ripley, *Two Plans for Currency Reform*, in *Yale Review*, VII (1898), 50–71; J. L. Laughlin, *Baltimore Plan of Bank Issues*, in *Jour. Pol. Econ.*, III (1894), 101–105; *Report of Monetary Commission* (1898), 20–75, 231–236, 260–276; J. F. Johnson, *Report of Monetary Commission*, in *Annals Amer. Acad.*, XI, 191–224; F. A. Cleveland, *Report of Monetary Commission*, in *Annals Amer. Acad.*, XIII, 31–56; C. A. Conant, *History of Modern Banking*, 377–385; C. N. Fowler, *Financial and Currency Reform*, in *Forum*, XXII (1897), 713; H. White, *Money and Banking* (revised ed.), 417–456.

Tariff: *Messages and Papers*, IX, 121–122 (1890), 191–193 (1891), 309–311 (1892), 552 (1894), 741–743 (1896); *Finance Report*, 1889, pp. xxx–xxxii; F. W. Taussig, *History of the Tariff*, 251–283 (tariff of 1890), 284–320 (tariff of 1894); William Hill, *Comparison of Votes on McKinley and Wilson Bills*, in *Jour. Pol. Econ.*, II, 290; J. Sherman, *Recollections*, II, 1201–1208 (tariff of 1894); A. D. Noyes, *Thirty Years of American Finance*, 223–233; Stanwood, II, 243–358; D. R. Dewey, *National Problems*, 174–187.

Income Tax: *Finance Report*, 1895, pp. 481–483; J. M. Gould and G. F. Tucker, *Federal Income Tax Explained* (1894); F. C. Howe, *U. S. under the Internal Revenue System*, 233–252; W. M. Daniels, *Public Finance*, 196–206; George Tunnell, *Legislative History of the Second Income Tax*, in *Jour. Pol. Econ.*, III (1895), 311–337; E. R. A. Seligman, *The Income Tax* (1911), 493–589; C. F. Dunbar, in *Quar. Jour. Econ.*, IX, 26–46; A. C. Miller, in *Jour. Pol. Econ.*, III, 255; J. K. Beach, *Income Tax Decision*, in *Yale Review*, V, 58–75; C. G. Tiedman, *Constitutionality of the Income Tax* in *Annals of Amer. Acad.* VI, 268–279; A. Abbott, *Bankers' Magazine*, L (1894), 185; *Poole's Index*, IV, 277–278.

SUGAR BOUNTY: *Finance Report*, 1892, pp. 454–470; 1893, p. 643; 1894, p. 706; 1895, pp. 478–481; 1897, p. 611; H. C. Beach, in *Amer. Law Review*, XXIX, 801.

RECIPROCITY: *Messages and Papers*, IX, 123 (1890), 141 (treaty with Brazil), 148 (Cuba), 152 (Dominican Republic), et seq.; F. W. Taussig, in *Quar. Jour. Econ.*, VII (1892), 26–39; W. L. Wilson, *Forum*, XIV (1892), 255–264.

186. Silver Act of 1890.

In 1890 the subject of silver coinage came up in an unexpected form, and for eight years was the most serious financial and political problem. No special prominence had been given to this question in the presidential campaign of 1888. Mr. Windom, secretary of the treasury, however, in his first report, December, 1889, surprised the country with a novel plan for the utilization of silver; even the president declared that he had "been able to give only a hasty examination to the plan, owing to the fact that it had been so recently formulated." Windom had formerly served as secretary of the treasury for a few months under Garfield and afterward as senator from Minnesota; he was generally recognized as a shrewd politician, familiar with the temper of the West on the currency question. Six Northwestern States had recently been created, and as the silver sentiment was very strong in these new communities, the advocates of free coinage of silver gained a disproportionate strength in the Senate; and, though the senators from these States were Republican on leading party issues, they were willing to hold up general legislation in order to secure a currency to their minds; it was even understood that no tariff bill could be passed without concessions to the silver party.

Windom's detailed discussion of the silver question is a useful compendium of the arguments for silver coinage advanced by various classes of bimetallists. The solutions proposed are summarized as follows:

1. A ratio between gold and silver fixed by international agreement; the mints of the leading nations of the world to be open to the free coinage of both metals.

2. Continuance of the policy of the Bland Act of 1878.

3. Increase of the purchases and coinage of silver to the maximum of $4,000,000 per month authorized by that law.

4. Free coinage of standard silver dollars.

5. Coinage of silver dollars containing a dollar's worth of bullion.

6. Issue of certificates to depositors of silver bullion at the rate of one dollar per 412½ grains of standard silver.

All of these propositions were dismissed by Windom either as impracticable, inadvisable, or inferior in weight to his own plan. In brief, he recommended the issue of treasury notes against the deposit of silver bullion, at the market price of the silver when deposited; the notes to be redeemable in either gold or in silver at the current market rate at the time of payment. As this plan was not accepted, it is unnecessary to discuss it further. The bill which finally passed, July 14, 1890, authorized the secretary of the treasury to purchase 4,500,000 ounces of silver bullion each month and to issue in payment thereof treasury notes of full legal tender. The essential differences between this act and that of 1878 were: increase in the monthly purchase of silver; treasury notes to be full instead of partial legal tender, as in the case of the silver certificates; redemption of treasury notes either in gold or silver coin at the discretion of the secretary. After July 1, 1891, standard silver dollars were to be coined only when necessary for the redemption of the notes.

On the whole, the measure provided for the purchase of all the American product of silver, but did not admit unlimited coinage. In order to reassure those who feared that such large purchases would result in depreciation of the standard, the act declared that it was the established policy of the United States to maintain the two metals on a parity with each other. This was afterwards interpreted by the treasury as "a virtual promise that the notes shall always be redeemed in gold or its exact equivalent." Although an increase of silver purchases is apparently required by the Sherman Act as compared with the Bland Act, this would not necessarily follow; for by the act of 1890 the annual additions to the currency would grow less if the price of silver fell, while by the Bland Act the annual additions grew larger as the price of silver fell. For substituting the measurement of purchases by ounces instead of by dollars, Senator Sherman has the credit, and its importance becomes obvious in view of the subsequent fall in the value of silver.

187. McKinley Tariff of 1890.

Closely following the silver-purchasing law was the enactment of a new tariff, October 1, 1890, in order to fulfil the election promises of the Republican party in 1888. The Senate bill of 1888 was brought forward and served as the basis of the measure which was reported. As Mr. McKinley of Ohio was chairman of the House committee on ways and means, the act according to custom is popularly known by his name. The title of the long and detailed act reads: "An act to reduce the revenue and equalize duties on imports, and for other purposes." The justification of any such characterization lay in the repeal of the raw sugar duties; in the reduction of duties on steel rails, iron, and steel plates, and on structural iron and steel; and in an increase of the free list embracing a number of articles of no great commercial importance. Throughout the debate the protectionist philosophy was developed to a point hitherto unknown in tariff discussion. Restrictive duties were no longer regarded as a temporary stage in the arduous journey toward industrial freedom, but a principle which ought to be permanently adopted. Protection was affirmed in increased duties upon wool, woollen goods, — particularly the finer grades, — and dress goods; upon the finer cottons, lawns, laces, and embroideries; upon linens, silk laces, and plush goods; upon cutlery and tin-plate; and upon barley, hemp, and flax. In some cases the duties were practically prohibitory, and so far forth the revenue was certainly reduced. The minimum principle was extended beyond the experiment of 1828; for cotton stockings, velvets, and plushes, boiler and plate iron, pen-knives, shotguns, and pistols, and table cutlery, classes were established based upon values; and on all goods of the same class the same specific duty was laid. The administrative regulations for collecting the customs were made more stringent by another act in the same session.

Two new principles were introduced by the McKinley Act: one was the grant of a bounty of two cents a pound for fourteen years on the production of sugar within the United States; and the other, the recognition of commercial reciprocity. The president was empowered to levy duties by proclamation on sugar, molasses, tea, coffee, and hides, if he considered that any country, exporting these commodities to the United States, imposed duties upon agricultural or other produce of the United States, which in view of the free admission of sugar, molasses, tea, coffee, and hides into the United States, he might deem to be reciprocally unjust and unreasonable. This policy was especially designed to apply to Central and Southern American countries, and was adopted largely through Mr. Blaine's influence as a part of a wider measure of Pan-American commercial union. By this method the executive branch of the government was relieved from submitting to the Senate special reciprocity treaties. Under this act commercial agreements relating to reciprocal trade were made with Brazil, the Dominican Republic, Spain (for Cuba and Puerto Rico), Guatemala, Salvador, the German Empire, Great Britain (for certain West Indian colonies and British Guiana), Nicaragua, Honduras, and Austria-Hungary. During the debate the reciprocity provision was opposed by some excellent constitutional lawyers within the Republican party, on the ground that Congress could not delegate its taxing power to the president. It is held, however, that the president did not under this act receive legislative power, but simply the right to determine the particular time when certain legislation should go into effect.

The grant of a federal bounty also raised constitutional objections, more particularly after the Democrats came back into power in 1893. In 1895 the comptroller of the treasury refused to pay the sugar bounty levied while the law was in operation, on the ground that such a grant was unconstitutional, but this contention was not sustained by the Supreme Court. Again, when the bounty provision was dropped in the Wilson Tariff of 1894, it was held that under the act of 1890 a contract had been made with citizens who had invested their capital in the beet-root industry, on the supposition that it would be protected for fourteen years; this objection proved of little avail, and the sugar-beet growers found themselves as liable as other industries to the uncertainties of tariff legislation.

188. The Gold Reserve and its Decline.

The enactment of these two important measures, the Sherman Silver-purchasing Act and the Tariff Act, within a few weeks of each other, makes it hard to analyze the financial situation; nor can the effects of either act be traced to their proper cause. The revenues declined more than was anticipated and commercial disturbances caused an increased exportation of gold which led to the presentation of treasury notes for redemption in gold: the net assets of the government were reduced; and the quality of the assets was changed. Almost without warning the condition of the treasury gold reserve assumed the highest importance, and its ups and downs were daily watched for and discussed with feverish interest by bankers and moneyed interests.

By the resumption act of 1875 the secretary of the treasury had authority to accumulate gold in order to resume specie payments, but no provision was made by law for a definite gold reserve of a precise amount. No attention had been paid to the earlier recommendations of Secretary Sherman from 1877 to 1881 that the resumption fund be specifically defined and set apart; the so-called reserve was simply the balance of the gold in the treasury, and not a distinct account. It was not, as sometimes stated, a fund sacredly pledged to redeem the legal tenders; in reality it was only a part of the "available cash." Consequently the proportion and character of the reserve depended only on the practice of the treasury from time to time. Two considerations finally determined in the minds of the public what the size of the redemption fund ought to be: under the resumption act no part of the face value of the bonds sold for redemption purposes (amounting to $95,500,000) could be applied to current appropriations; and Secretary Sherman in his recommendations preliminary to resumption suggested a minimum reserve of at least $100,000,000. An indirect recognition of a gold reserve is found in an act of 1882, providing for an issue of gold certificates, which declared that such issue should be suspended whenever the gold coin and bullion in the treasury reserved for the redemption of the United States notes fell below $100,000,000. Some held that a separation of the treasury moneys into two funds, one for redemption and another for current disbursements, might be made simply by administrative act without the mandate of Congress; but when Secretary Manning in Cleveland's administration tried to make the distinction, he was forced to abandon it, and the question slipped along without attracting much attention; nevertheless, by tradition public sentiment adopted $100,000,000 as the line of demarcation between safety and danger.

Later, when the silver question became more pressing, it was argued that there was no authority for making up this fund out of gold alone; that the word coin in the resumption act included silver. Another line of argument was that the maintenance of a reserve composed of gold alone had cost the government immense sums through holding for years $100,000,000 of "dead" money; and it was further urged that the law of 1878 requiring the reissue of legal-tender notes was practically a suspension of the resumption act of 1875, as far as the redemption of the new notes was concerned. The legal status of the reserve was, however, of little concern as long as the amount of available gold in the treasury was so large that nobody apprehended another suspension of specie payments.

For fourteen years, 1878–1892, only an insignificant amount of gold was paid out by the treasury in the redemption of legal-tender notes; the total amount of gold in the treasury increased almost steadily and continuously from $140,000,000 on January 1, 1879, to $300,000,000 in 1891. In 1890 the new issue of treasury notes, together with a change in commercial conditions, placed heavy burdens upon the reserve, the rapid diminution of which is shown in the following figures: —

Date	Net gold reserve
June 30, 1890	$190,232,405
" " 1891	117,667,723
" " 1892	114,342,367
" " 1893	95,485,413
" " 1894	64,873,025

The reasons for the fall in the gold reserve are too various and complicated to be treated here: the failure of the great English banking-house of Baring Brothers in 1890 brought about a considerable withdrawal of English capital invested in the United States; and an unhealthy and inflated industrial development in this country was stimulated by the new tariff. To outward appearances the country was very prosperous; expenditures were large, imports increased, and a failure of the crops in Europe in 1891 enlarged our grain exports. For a brief season only, were the natural effects of the Sherman law delayed; Europe soon recovered, American exports fell, and in the six months ending June 30, 1893, the balance of trade against the United States was $68,800,000. The tariff of 1890 was followed by diminished customs receipts. The revenue from customs was as follows: —

1890	$229,668,000
1891	219,522,000
1892	177,452,000
1893	203,355,000
1894	131,818,000

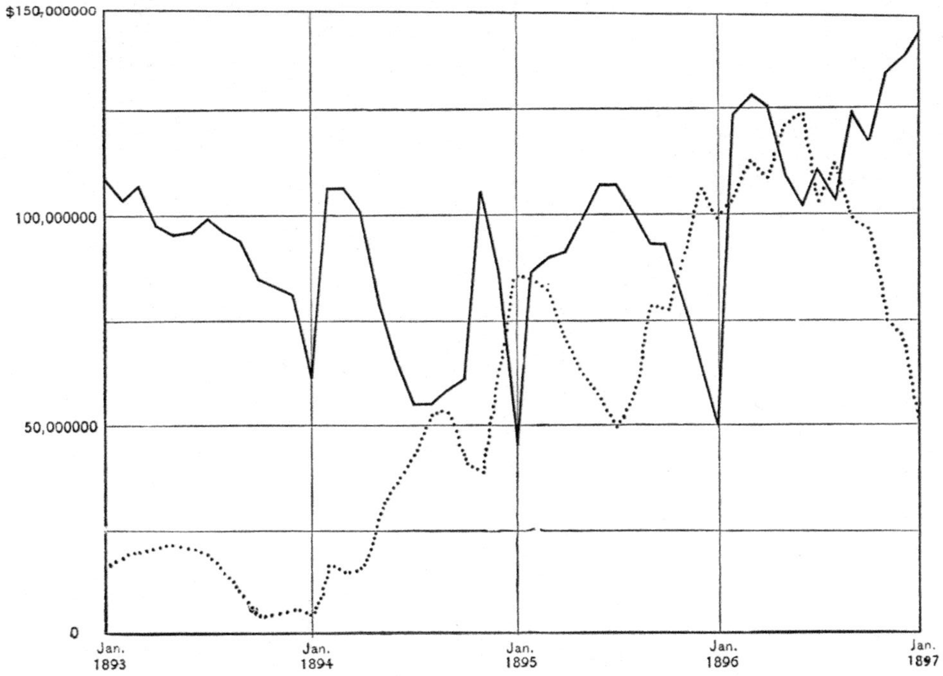

No. XIV. — NET GOLD IN TREASURY, 1893–1897.

Net gold in treasury, solid line.
Net legal tender notes in treasury, dotted line.

Fortunately the internal revenue receipts maintained their customary level with something to spare; but increased appropriations, due largely to the passage of a dependent pension bill in 1890, cut deep into the funds of the treasury. In 1890 the surplus was $105,344,000; in 1891, $37,239,000; in 1892, $9,914,000; in 1893, $2,341,000; but in 1894 appeared a deficit amounting to $69,803,000. The treasury had been weakened by the reluctance of Secretary Windom to deposit government funds in national bank depositories, and by his preference to rely entirely upon the purchase of bonds for getting money back into circulation. In the earlier years of Harrison's administration, bonds were purchased freely, — too generously in view of the impending strain upon the resources of the treasury.

Another element of concern was due to the change in the kind of money received by the government in the payment of revenue. Before the passage of the Sherman Act nine-tenths or more of the customs receipts at the New York custom-house were paid in gold and gold certificates; in the summer of 1891 the proportion of gold and gold certificates fell as low as 12 per cent., and in September, 1892, to less than 4 per cent. The use of United States notes and treasury notes of 1890 correspondingly increased. The startling changes which took place in the quality of the receipts from customs at New York are shown in detail (page 444) for the two years 1891 and 1892 by reducing the amounts to percentages.

The reason for this substitution of notes for gold was partly due to a reversal in treasury practice. For many years it had been the custom of the sub-treasury in New York to settle its clearing-house balances almost exclusively in gold or gold certificates. For example, in the fiscal year 1889–1890 the sub-treasury paid gold balances to the banks of nearly $230,000,000, and in the next year $212,000,000. The banks were thus daily supplied with gold which they in turn could furnish to their customers either for custom purposes or export deliveries. In August, 1890, the treasury began the policy of using

Quality of Receipts from Customs at New York, 1891-1892

1891	Gold coin	United States notes	Treasury notes	Gold certificates	Silver certificates
January	.1	4.1	5.2	88.5	2.1
February	.1	5.0	7.3	81.0	6.6
March	.2	6.0	12.4	64.9	16.5
April	.2	7.2	25.6	47.0	20.0
May	.2	15.0	30.2	27.8	26.8
June	.2	44.6	28.9	12.3	14.0
July	.2	49.0	27.4	14.9	8.5
August	.2	50.5	31.5	12.6	5.2
September	.1	55.3	28.4	11.7	4.4
October	.2	44.0	31.6	19.8	4.4
November	.1	31.3	22.3	43.5	2.8
December	.1	14.8	16.7	65.3	3.1
1892					
January	.1	15.0	14.5	66.1	4.3
February	.1	36.2	28.6	25.8	9.3
March	.1	42.5	33.0	18.7	5.7
April	.2	46.4	31.6	14.9	6.9
May	.1	40.6	36.4	9.9	13.0
June	.2	26.8	49.1	8.0	15.9
July	.1	28.4	42.2	13.8	15.5
August		25.6	51.9	12.1	10.4
September		45.8	39.7	3.6	10.9
October	.1	51.9	35.0	6.6	6.4
November	.1	52.8	33.0	7.8	6.3
December		46.4	40.0	4.4	9.2

the new treasury notes in the settlement of New York balances, and in the year ending June, 1891, Secretary Foster, apparently convinced of the need of a larger gold reserve to support the credit of treasury notes, increased the use of the older United States notes and held on to the gold reserve. The unexpected result was that the banks, deprived of their usual supply of gold for trade purposes, sought for it at the treasury by the presentation of government notes.

189. Panic of 1893; Repeal of Silver Purchases.

In March, 1893, Cleveland for a second time entered upon the presidency. He demanded as the first condition of relief the suspension of silver purchases. The silver advocates, however, were still powerful in both parties, and President Cleveland was at a disadvantage in not having the undivided support of his own party. Even the position of Secretary Carlisle was

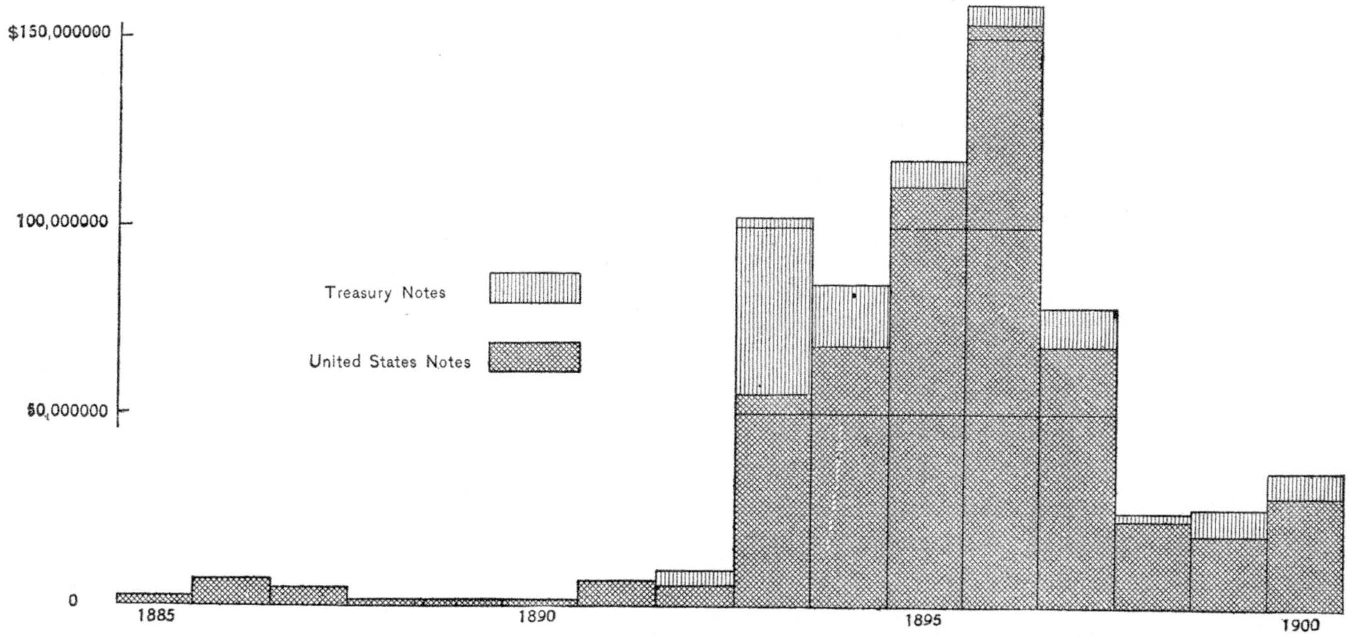

No. XV. — TREASURY NOTES REDEEMED IN GOLD, 1885–1900.

doubted: it was publicly declared that he stood ready, if expediency demanded it, to redeem the treasury notes of 1890 in silver instead of gold, and, while standing upon the letter of the law which demanded their redemption in *coin*, practically to cut asunder the parity of gold and silver which had thus far been maintained. Although the president attempted by a specific declaration to make clear the harmonious purpose of the administration that redemption would continue in gold, public apprehension would not be allayed. Whatever might be the wishes of the administration, it was feared that it would not have power to carry them out; particularly when it was announced in April, 1893, that the gold reserve had been drawn down to $96,000,000 by redeeming the treasury notes of 1890.

At this juncture of financial and commercial difficulties, in June, 1893, the British government closed the mints in India to the free coinage of silver. The price of silver bullion fell promptly and rapidly, and, while such a decline might on another occasion have produced no immediately serious consequences to the treasury, it came at a moment when public opinion, at least in the Eastern States, was aroused to a belief that the entire financial problem was associated with the coinage of silver; and it thus furnished one of the contributory forces which drove the commercial community into a state of panic.

It was not until June 30, 1893, when the panic was well under way, that a special session of Congress was called for August 7; only by the most strenuous efforts could an adequate support, composed of elements in both political parties, be rallied to uphold the president's insistence that purchases of silver by the government should cease. The House quickly acquiesced, and on August 21, by a vote of 239 to 108, passed a bill for the repeal of the purchasing clause; but the Senate was stubborn, and not until October 30 could a favorable vote, 43 to 32, be secured. So far as the treasury was concerned, the mischief had been done; although the government was relieved from further purchase of silver which increased the volume of obligations to be supported by gold, the old burdens still were sufficiently heavy, in connection with the low state of commerce and industry, to exhaust its immediate revenues. Thus on December 1, 1893, the actual net balance in the treasury above the gold reserve, pledged funds and agency accounts was only $11,038,448. Trade and industry had been disorganized; the panic of 1893 extended into every department of industrial life. In December, 1893, the comptroller of the currency announced the failure during the year of 158 national banks, 172 State banks, 177 private banks, 47 savings banks, 13 loan and trust companies, and 6 mortgage companies. Some of these institutions afterwards resumed business, but the permanent damage was great. The fright of depositors was general and the shrinkage in deposits enormous; bank clearings were the lowest since 1885; clearing-house loan certificates were once more resorted to, this time on a much larger scale than ever before, and extended to cities throughout the country.

The production of coal, both anthracite and bituminous, fell off; the output of pig-iron, which had been about 9,157,000 tons in 1892, fell to 6,657,000 tons in 1894; new railway construction almost ceased; in 1894 there were 156 railways, operating a mileage of nearly 39,000 miles, in the hands of receivers; among these were three great railway systems,— the Erie, Northern Pacific, and Union Pacific. The total capitalization in the hands of receivers was about $2,500,000,000, or one-fourth of the railway capital of the country. The earnings of railroads and the dividends paid to stockholders were seriously affected; securities fell to one-half and even one-quarter their former value; commercial failures increased from 10,344 in 1892, with liabilities of $114,000,000, to 15,242 in 1893, with liabilities of $346,000,000. The problem of the unemployed became general; special committees were organized in nearly all of the large cities to provide food, and in many places relief work by public bodies was instituted. In the spring of 1894 general want and distress led to labor strikes and riots, as in Chicago, and even to more abnormal outbreaks, as seen by the march of Coxey's army of unemployed from Ohio to Washington. The distress was increased by the failure of the corn crop in 1894; the demand for wheat in Europe fell off and wheat was sold on the Western farm for less than fifty cents a bushel.

190. Sale of Bonds for Gold.

Under these adverse conditions it was inevitable that the revenues of the government should continue to decline. In the six months, January to June, 1893, the excess of expenditures over receipts was $4,198,000, and during the fiscal year ending June 30, 1894, this excess increased to $69,803,000. It was even necessary to encroach upon the gold reserve for current expenses, and for months this fund was far less than caution and prudence demanded. When the integrity of the gold reserve was first assailed, both Secretary Foster, in the closing months of Harrison's administration, and Secretary Carlisle, at the beginning of Cleveland's term, endeavored, with some success, to tide over emergencies by appealing to the banks to exchange gold for legal tenders. The banks recognized that the instability of government credit seriously affected the value of all securities in which they were interested; and in February, 1893, they handed over to the treasury about $6,000,000 in gold, and in March and April about $25,000,000 more. The expedient was not enough to stop the continued drain upon the treasury. At the very moment that the government was relieved of notes through the exchange of gold by the banks, other notes were presented to the treasury for redemption, largely to draw gold for exportation in the settlement of trade balances. The decline of revenue, the presentation of notes for redemption in gold, and the proportion of the flow of gold to foreign countries as compared with the domestic supply through mining, is shown by years in the following table: —

Fiscal year ending June 30	Excess of revenue over expenditures	Excess of expenditures over revenue	Legal-tender notes presented for redemption	Excess of exports of gold over imports	Gold product of United States
1889	$105,053,000		$730,000	$49,667,000	$32,800,000
1890	105,344,000		732,000	4,331,000	32,845,000
1891	37,240,000		5,986,000	68,130,000	33,175,000
1892	9,914,000		9,126,000	496,000	33,000,000
1893	2,342,000		102,100,000	87,506,000	36,000,000
1894		$69,803,000	84,842,000	4,528,000	39,500,000
				$214,660,000	$207,320,000

The only way to protect the fund of gold reserve under the circumstances was borrowing,—that is, the sale of bonds for gold,—yet some people who were opposed to the overthrow of the gold standard consistently urged that borrowing be postponed until the last moment, so as to add as little as possible to the resources available for purchases of silver. Some of the gold party would even have permitted the drain to go on to the end, notwithstanding the inevitable evils, in the belief that the country could be convinced of its errors in no other way.

Eventually, to prevent a suspension of specie payments in gold, the treasury department made successive issues of bonds for the purchase of gold. These issues are very interesting to the student of finance. No administration wishes to add to public indebtedness in times of peace; and Secretary Carlisle had scruples against selling bonds, except with the authority of the Congress then sitting; hence the issue of bonds was put off to the last possible moment. The only existing authority for selling bonds was the resumption act of 1875; this provided only for ten-year 5 per cent., fifteen-year 4½, and thirty-year 4 per cent. bonds, all of which would command a premium so high as to diminish their attractiveness as an investment, and, taken in connection with the length of time which they ran, to hamper the treasury in purchasing or refunding the debt when the crisis was over. The administration asked for the issue of low-rate bonds, but Congress, inspired in part by free silver arguments, and in part by political intrigues to discredit the administration, paid no attention to the recommendation of the secretary. Finally, in January, 1894, without special legislation, but under the ancient authority of the resumption act, $50,000,000 of 5 per cent. ten-year bonds were sold, yielding $58,660,917; and again in November an equal amount of bonds with like conditions were marketed, yielding $58,538,500. The sale of the first issue was on the whole creditable, considering that at about the same time the president was obliged to veto a bill providing for coining the silver seigniorage, and that an effort had been made in the courts to enjoin the secretary of the treasury from selling bonds under the law of 1875.

In each case the sale of bonds called for subscriptions in gold, but the new supplies were quickly exhausted by fresh redemption of notes. The fluctuations in the volume of gold in the treasury as a consequence of the bond sales is seen in the following figures:

Date	Gold in treasury
January 31, 1894	$65,650,000
February 10, "	104,119,000 *Bond issue*
November 20, "	59,054,000
" 30, "	105,424,000 *Bond issue*
February 9, 1895	41,393,000

The endless chain appeared to be in full and unceasing operation; not only was gold being withdrawn for export but also for individual hoarding, in fear of an impending suspension of gold payments. The treasury finally recognized the futility of selling bonds for gold, most of which was drawn out of the treasury itself, by the presentation of legal-tender notes for redemption. A new device was tried: in February, 1895, the secretary of the treasury entered into a contract with certain bankers, for the purchase of 3,500,000 ounces of standard gold at the price of $17.80441 per ounce, to be paid for by the delivery of United States bonds having thirty years to run and bearing 4 per cent. interest; not less than one-half of this gold was to be procured abroad, and the parties with whom the contract was made stipulated that they would "as far as lies in their power exert all financial influence and make all legitimate efforts to protect the treasury of the United States against the withdrawals of gold, pending the complete performance of this contract." An ounce of standard gold was worth $18.60465, and the difference between that sum and the contract price represented the premium received by the government on the bonds, making the price at which the bonds were accepted $104.4946. A condition was affixed to the contract, by which, in case congressional authority could be secured, a 3 per cent. *gold* bond might be substituted, and for this the syndicate agreed to pay a higher price.

In view of the unfavorable terms of the bargain imposed by this contract, the administration hoped that Congress would promptly act and authorize the issue of the lower and more remunerative bond. Faithful in its adherence to silver, Congress could not be swerved; it defeated the bill authorizing the sale of a low-rate gold bond, and then engaged in an angry debate denouncing the executive for his subserviency to the gold standard banking interests in entering into a contract not only disgraceful but illegal. In reply it could be shown that the New York sub-treasury was within forty-eight hours of gold exhaustion.

191. Legality of the Bond Issues.

A prolonged debate followed over the powers of the executive, involving a discussion of section 3700 of the Revised Statutes, originally passed in 1862, which authorized the secretary of the treasury "to purchase coin with any of the bonds or notes of the United States authorized by law, at such rates and upon such terms as he may deem most advantageous to the public interest;" of the funding act of 1870, which detailed the kinds of bonds that could be issued in funding, and which forbade any increase of indebtedness through the issue of bonds for funding purposes; and in particular of the resumption act of 1875.

The opposition laid great stress upon the wording of this last measure which gave to the secretary of the treasury power "to prepare and provide for the redemption" of the legal-tender notes through the use of surplus reserves and the sale of bonds. No authority, it was declared, was given to *maintain* redemption; no permanent powers were thus bestowed upon the executive. Cannot the people through their Congress be trusted to meet their obligations, whether current or plighted, for the redemption of paper money? It was held contrary to the spirit of the Constitution that the executive department should be able of its own discretion to create debt, burden the people with interest charges, and thus necessitate taxation without legislative sanction. Such a practice was entirely inconsistent with the fundamental principles of popular government, for by it the executive could set aside the wish of the legislature and dispense altogether with the aid of Congress in raising money.

Again it was urged that the issue of bonds for redemption purposes was limited by the amount of legal tender in circulation in 1875. At that time no provision was made for the reissue of the notes; the possibility of an endless chain was not suggested. Authority for a fixed volume of circulation ($346,000,000) and for the reissue of notes was not granted until 1878; was it probable, therefore, that the act of 1875 in its provision for sale of bonds could have contemplated the use made during the years 1894–1896? In that case could not the secretary of the treasury issue bonds as many times as the legal-tender notes were passed over the counters of the treasury? Under no circumstances, it was reasoned, was there authority to sell bonds to redeem the treasury notes of 1890, for at best the power under the act of 1875 was limited to the earlier greenbacks.

All this discussion, however, was really off the main contention which was that there was a surplus on hand for redemption if the secretary would only use silver; not only was there the free silver in the treasury, there were also potential funds in the "coinage of the seigniorage," and in the coinage of the silver purchased and stored under the act of 1890. Here was a reserve, a locked-up surplus of nearly three hundred million dollars; how absurd, said the silverite, to declare that the treasury needed replenishing by borrowing! Why should silver be dishonored by not issuing it for redemption purposes? Moreover, this dishonor was wholly without warrant, for the act of 1890 expressly stated that it was "the established policy of the United States to maintain the two metals on a parity," and the act of 1893 repealing coinage further "declared that the efforts of the government should be steadily directed to the establishment of such a safe system of bimetallism as will maintain at all times the equal power of every dollar coined or issued by the United States in the markets in the payment of debts." By parity, it was urged, was meant something more than redeemability; equality was its true significance; "parity" is when "one is as strong and as tall as the other, and is able to bear as much burden as the other." There could be no parity as long as the government's creditor was given an option in the selection of the metal in which payment could be made.

Extremists went so far as to declare that the panic of 1893 was brought about by a well-defined conspiracy of bankers "to bring the government to its knees and bully the people into submission to their terms." It was stated and apparently believed that capitalists, not finding profitable investment in railroads, mines, and manufactures, desired further issue of bonds in order that they might "invest their surplus in the muscle, blood, and sweat of the American people, and fix that investment far beyond the power of emancipation."

The reply to these arguments was the swift and positive assertion that by existing law the secretary was under obligation to borrow money to protect the credit of the nation, and that the powers granted under the act of 1875 were continuous until repealed. There was a contract morally binding upon the government and possibly legally binding, to pay gold to the holder of every legal-tender note, and for this purpose the government should if necessary sell bonds. A refusal to pay gold on demand would send it to a premium and thus destroy the parity which had been stipulated in the act of 1890. As for using silver for redemption, that practically involved the whole question of the free coinage of silver, — a question which should be settled on its own merits, and not forced upon the country indirectly by depriving the executive of borrowing powers previously granted.

In addition to the criticism upon the general question of the issue of bonds, the contract with the syndicate is of special interest for two reasons: first, because it was a notable example of the assumption of administrative obligations by private bankers, in promising to protect for a definite period the gold fund of the government; in the second place, it was an attempt on a large scale to import gold and prevent its exportation through the manipulation of the foreign exchange market. The government on its side was forced to onerous conditions, yet thought it wise to make the arrangements secretly, or at least through agents selected without competition.

The history of this negotiation and the difficulties attending the control of the international movement of gold in the face of adverse commercial conditions lie outside of this narrative; here it is only necessary to state that at first the syndicate was successful, because of some slight improvement in trade, but later it practically failed to control the price of exchange. It once more became cheaper for merchants to ship gold than to purchase bills, and gold continued to be withdrawn from the treasury. On December 3, 1895, the gold reserve stood at $79,333,000, and after the commercial apprehension caused by President Cleveland's Venezuelan message a fortnight later, the reserve was still further reduced. Once more the administration resorted to a bond sale, and again the action was preceded by a special message from the president to Congress asking for a grant of authority to issue gold bonds instead of coin bonds, and also for the retirement of the legal-tender notes which continued in an endless chain their journey to the treasury, and drove off gold to the commercial market. As Congress still refused to act, the treasury resorted to a fourth issue of $100,000,000 4 per cent. bonds. The treasury now carefully avoided any appearance of dealing through a syndicate and publicly advertised for offers, with the encouraging result of 4640 bids, amounting to $684,262,850. 781 different bids were accepted and the premium yielded about $11,000,000. The relief obtained by the treasury, however, was meagre, for it is estimated that $40,000,000 of the bonds were purchased with gold withdrawn from the treasury by the redemption of notes. This was the government's penalty for its endeavor to separate itself from all dealings with a banking syndicate.

In spite of this sale of bonds the reserve remained near the traditional danger line. In July, 1896, it fell to $90,000,000 because of hoarding due to popular apprehension as to the success of the silver movement in the November presidential election. Fearful that a new bond issue might strengthen the claims of the silver advocates, bankers and dealers in foreign exchange voluntarily combined to support the treasury by exchanging gold for notes. The effort succeeded, and the reserve was placed in safety. After the elections in November gold came out from its hiding-places, and was turned into the treasury in large amounts. Business and revenue improved and the difficulties of the treasury department were tided over.

Many Republicans held the earnest conviction that the issue of bonds would not have been necessary if the revenue had been sufficient. Not only had industry and commerce been unsettled by the tariff act of 1894, but the operations of the endless chain must certainly continue, it was held, until there was a generous income in excess of expenditures, whereby a considerable part of the credit currency might be covered into the treasury and thus lessen the possible claims for redemption. The administration emphatically replied that at no time when bonds were issued was there intention of paying the expenses of the government with their proceeds, and that the treasury department had no authority whatever to issue bonds for such purposes. President Cleveland was insistent that on each occasion of a bond issue there were sufficient funds in the treasury to meet the ordinary expenditures of the government. The proceeds of the bonds sold for the maintenance of the national credit were, however, turned into the general fund of the treasury, and consequently, though not originally designed for that purpose, employed to meet indiscriminately all demands made upon the government, whether for redemption of notes or the payment of debts. The tables in the next chapter show that there was a series of deficits beginning with 1894, but the deficit by no means equalled the amounts of bonds sold.

192. The Gorman-Wilson Tariff.

When the Democrats returned to power in March, 1893, it was with the distinct understanding that the tariff should be revised. Between 1890 and the election of 1892 the McKinley tariff was held responsible for the general increase of prices and aroused a strong and immediate revulsion of popular feeling. Within a month after the passage of the McKinley tariff act the Democrats swept the country in the congressional elections of November, 1890. As the Republicans retained the Senate, no revenue legislation got even as far as the president. The tariff issue was again uppermost in 1892, for the financial difficulties of the treasury had not yet been clearly revealed to the public. Relying upon the arguments of increased prices and the dangerous power of trusts, which were denounced as creatures of the tariff, the Democrats gained complete victory. Although conditions greatly changed in the year between the election and the assembling of the new Congress in December, 1893, the Democratic party leaders determined to carry out their pre-election pledges.

Discipline within the party, however, had been weakened by dissensions created by the continued struggle over the repeal of the silver-purchase act, and the Democratic majority in the Senate was small, so that the proposed legislation required not only determination, but also very considerable compromise.

The House measure as it first appeared under the leadership of Mr. William L. Wilson, while of necessity a concession to the adjustment of business under the protection policy, was a step in the direction of freer trade. In the Senate the bill was changed, under the guidance of Senator Gorman, until the protective elements fairly outweighed any principle of reform. The so-called Wilson Tariff Bill, passed August 27, 1894, was therefore by no means satisfactory to those who sincerely believed in tariff reform; the dissatisfaction of President Cleveland was such that he refused to sign the bill and allowed it to become a law by passive neglect. In a letter to Representative Catchings he complained that "Senators have stolen and worn the livery of Democratic tariff reform in the service of Republican protection." The details of this tariff, which continued in force less than three years, are for the most part of little present interest; rates were modified here and there, and the free list was extended so as to include wool, and duties were reimposed on sugar. But these revisions of schedules do not disclose the application of any uniform or consistent principle. Reciprocity was practically abandoned.

The tariff act of 1894 reintroduced an income tax, providing that a tax of 2 per cent. be levied on all incomes above $4000. Besides the usual arguments that such a tax was inquisitorial, created perjury, was undemocratic and unconstitutional, a more serious objection was brought, that it made a discrimination against the well-to-do and was a demagogic bid for the support of the poorer classes. Obviously with such a high limit of exemption and low rate of taxation the total proceeds from a revenue point of view could not be great. The adoption of a limit of exemption at $4000 was largely due to the strenuous efforts of the Populist party. Almost the entire support of the measure came from the South and West; from New England, Pennsylvania, and New York there were but five votes in the House of Representatives in its favor.

The income tax provision was brought before the Supreme Court in its October term, 1894, on the ground of unconstitutionality, in the case *Pollock* v. *Farmers' Loan and Trust Co.* (157 U. S. 429). Four questions were involved: first, whether a tax on the income of real estate is a direct tax within the meaning of the Constitution, and therefore unconstitutional unless imposed by the rule of apportionment; second, whether a tax on income of personal estate is a direct tax; third, whether the act infringed the rule of uniformity; fourth, whether the tax imposed upon income from State and municipal bonds is constitutional. The court unfortunately showed uncertainty as to its conviction. In an opinion rendered April 8, 1895, the court held that the tax on rent or income from land was a direct tax, and therefore unconstitutional unless apportioned; it was evenly divided as to whether a tax on income derived from other sources, as trade or money at interest, was direct, and consequently declined to declare that part of the law unconstitutional. This left the issue in a most unsatisfactory form, and a re-hearing was arranged for May 6. As a result of re-argument one of the justices changed his opinion, and in the second decision, delivered May 20 (158 U. S. 601), the court decided against the constitutionality of the measure on all four points.

This practically reverses the decision of the Supreme Court in 1880, in the case of *Springer* v. *United States* (102 U. S. 586), involving the question of the constitutionality of the income tax of the Civil War. The court at that time closely followed precedent and, adopting the definitions accepted in *Hylton* v. *United States*, according to which the only direct taxes within the meaning of the Constitution are capitation taxes and taxes on real estate, declared that the income tax complained of was within the category of an excise or duty. In 1895 there was a much more elaborate if not ingenious discussion, both by the counsel and the court, not only of the legal and historical precedents, but also of the definitions current in economic literature. In the public discussion and in some of the court opinions the question was treated not so much from fiscal expediency as from the standpoint of fundamental principles of liberty and right government. On the one side were those who were convinced that wealth should be taxed as such; on the other, those who saw the beginning of a class oppression of property interests. It was also charged that the measure was sectional in its aim; by putting the limit of exemption as high as $4000, the South and West would largely escape the burdens of the tax. Since the decision of the court was adverse, further discussion of a federal income tax becomes largely academic: possibly an income tax can be framed which would avoid the constitutional objections; if so, a revival of the tax is likely.

The inconsistencies of the tariff of 1894 were recognized by many Democrats. Defeated in the effort to make a consistent general revision, several so-called "pop-gun" bills passed the House: bills to place raw materials, as coal, iron, and sugar, on the free list. They all failed in the Senate. Such a policy was harassing to commercial interests and tended to the unsettlement of business affairs. The result was a lack of confidence in the financial ability of the Democratic party; a popular feeling sprang up that even the tariff of 1894 favored the trusts, now looming into power; and the failure of the income tax provisions to stand judicial review led to charges that some of the Democratic leaders were insincere.

193. Currency Measures.

When the tariff bill of 1894 was disposed of, the attention of Congress was once more concentrated upon the credit currency, and again the greatest variety of views found expression. At one extreme were those who attributed the financial ills to the over-issue of government notes, and who insisted that the remedy lay, if not in the absolute destruction of such issues, at least in their temporary withdrawal or suppression by some indirect process, so that the treasury might not be plagued by the demand for redemption. President Cleveland was of this class; and his secretary of the treasury, Mr. Carlisle, was finally converted to the same view. In harmony with the idea was the proposition of Mr. Gage, then a banker in Chicago, that $200,000,000 in bonds should be issued for subscription in treasury notes, which were then to be cancelled, on the ground that "the government must be taken out of the note-issuing business." It was maintained that the desperate endeavor to uphold the redeemability of treasury notes resulted in a large increase of federal indebtedness, and that it would be far better to purchase and cancel notes outright with that outlay; all the notes of 1890 and a portion of the greenbacks might then be destroyed.

Absolute cancellation was in general regarded as too radical, and Secretary Carlisle voiced the common opinion that the United States legal-tender paper had become so incorporated into the currency system and constituted so large a part of the active circulation that it could not be absolutely withdrawn without producing disturbance both in the fiscal operations of the government and in the business of the people. Mr. Carlisle consequently devised a plan for the eradication of legal tenders without cancellation; this was that banks should deposit in place of bonds United States notes (including treasury notes of 1890) to the amount of 30 per cent. upon the circulation applied for. If all the national and State banks in existence should take out circulation to the full amount proposed, this regulation, it was calculated, would tie up or "put under bushel" $225,000,000 of treasury notes. Mr. Eckels, the comptroller of the currency, went a little farther and proposed the deposit of as much as 50 per cent. of government notes as a pledge of bank circulation.

Other proposals brought before Congress, while recognizing the desirability of relieving the government from the embarrassments of redemption, did not place so much emphasis upon contraction of government currency, but looked especially to greater elasticity of the banking currency. The Baltimore plan (so called because endorsed by the American Bankers' Association meeting held at Baltimore) did away altogether with the deposit of bonds for the security of notes; circulation was based upon capital; emergency circulation was allowed under special restrictions of taxation; and the security of the note-holder was protected through a guaranty or safety fund, as in the former New York State banking system and present Canadian banking law. None of these bills were enacted; the defects of government note and bank note circulation could command little serious consideration in Congress as long as party passion was so fierce over the silver question.

194. Struggle for Free Coinage.

Apart from and antagonistic to all these schemes of banking reform stood the supporters of free silver. To their minds the way to currency reform was clear and unconfused with questions of reserve, safety funds, elasticity of issue, or redemption; the evil lay in an inadequate money medium, and had little to do with banking or treasury finance. They held that industry was depressed because of the continued mint discrimination against silver, and that it was folly to discuss banking systems and revenue bills until this fundamental defect was remedied.

The doctrine that the forces controlling the flow of specie were universal in their operation was impatiently cast aside; the interests of Europe and the United States were regarded as radically different. By the lowering of prices of agricultural produce since 1891, the debtor farmer found an ever-increasing difficulty in the payment of interest charges, and the foreclosure of city and farm mortgages throughout the West seemed evidence of general distress. Sober-minded representatives arraigned existing conditions: chains of slavery laid upon labor; privileged classes more strongly intrenched; silver stricken down as a co-laborer with gold. When told that the treasury was in difficulty, they called attention to the silver cash balance in the treasury. "What afflicts the country is a surplus and not a want of revenue," they said; money was impounded in the treasury. The industrial depression after 1893 made many converts to this idea, and the continued low price of wheat convinced the great agricultural West irrespective of party that its property interests were dependent upon the restoration of silver; the issue was distinctly presented to the people in the elections of 1896. The platform and the presidential candidate of the Democrats were clear and outspoken. "We demand the free and unlimited coinage of both gold and silver at the present legal ratio of 16 to 1 without waiting for the aid or consent of any other nations." This demand, which was first enunciated in a national platform of the Greenbackers in 1880 and kept alive by the Farmers' Alliance and People's party, was now accepted without reservation by one of the old historic parties. The Republicans on the other hand declared that they were "opposed to the free coinage of silver except by international agreement with the leading commercial nations of the world, which we pledge ourselves to promote." Seeing that the existing gold standard would be preserved by the Republicans till that unlikely event, an influential body of delegates, under the lead of Senator Teller, seceded from the Republican convention, and gave subsequent support to the Democratic candidates. This defection from the Republicans was in turn offset by the inactivity of many Eastern Democrats, who had no sympathy either with the Democratic platform or its candidate; this led to the nomination of an independent Democratic ticket on a gold platform. The Populists also entered vigorously into the campaign. Although advocating in their platform irredeemable paper money and the redemption of the public debt in this currency, for the moment they united in the support of Mr. Bryan for the presidency.

Undoubtedly other questions than that of free coinage

of silver influenced the minds of voters, such as Democratic criticism of the judiciary for the income tax decision, but the struggle centred on the money question. An effort was made by Mr. Bryan to rest the campaign on the deepest passions of human life: "In this contest brother has been arrayed against brother, father against son. The warmest ties of love, acquaintance, and association have been disregarded; old leaders have been cast aside when they refused to give expression to the sentiments of those whom they would lead, and new leaders have sprung up to give direction to the cause of truth." Few new arguments were presented, but the activity in meetings and political literature was unprecedented. The silver advocates made use of a very effective medium of argument by issuing millions of copies of pamphlets, as "Coin's Financial School," in which well-known business men in favor of the gold standard were represented as nonplussed and staggered by the simple conversational instruction of a guileless boy teacher. Public interest had never been so aroused over a financial question since Jackson's war on the bank. For a short time business almost came to a standstill because financial and commercial interests felt that the possible adoption of free coinage would make revolutionary changes in prices and contracts.

The elections were in favor of the Republicans, and hence of the gold standard. The continuance of a Republican majority in the House of Representatives, however, did not insure immediate positive action on the money question, for on this point even some of the Republicans who had stood by the party were not in accord with their own platform, and soon it became understood that upon any House bill on the currency the Senate would affix an amendment providing "for the free and unlimited coinage of silver at the ratio of 16 to 1 without the aid or consent of any other nation." This position was tenaciously held by the Senate from 1894 to 1900.

CHAPTER XX.

TARIFF, WAR, AND CURRENCY ACT.

195. References.

GOLD RESERVE: *Finance Report*, 1897, p. 7; 1898, p. 10; 1900, pp. 14-15. L. J. Gage, *Condition and Prospects of the Treasury*, in *No. Amer. Rev.*, vol. 168 (1899), pp. 641-653.

LOANS: *Finance Report*, 1898, pp. xciii-xcvii (Spanish war loan); 1900, pp. lxxviii-lxxxi, 528; F. A. Vanderlip, *War Loan*, in *Forum*, XXVI (1898), 27-36; C. C. Plehn, *Introduction to Public Finance* (3d ed., 1909), 451-465.

THE CURRENCY: *Finance Report*, 1897, pp. lxxii-lxxxi (Secretary Gage), 337-336 (comptroller); 1898, pp. xcvii-civ; 1899, pp. lxxxviii-xcvi, F. M. Taylor, *Quar. Jour. Econ.*, XII (1898), 307-342 (excellent bibliography, p. 342); *Report of Monetary Commission* (1898); C. N. Fowler, *Forum*, XXII (1897), 713-721; R. M. Breckenridge, *Comptroller's Objections to Currency Reform*, in *Jour. Pol. Econ.*, VII, 253-267; *Economic Studies*, IV (Feb., 1899), 31-44; J. L. Laughlin, *Withdrawal of the Treasury Notes of* 1890, in *Jour. Pol. Econ.*, VI (1898), 248-249.

TARIFF: F. W. Taussig, *History of the Tariff*, 321-360; J. L. Laughlin and H. P. Willis, *Reciprocity* (1903), 270-413; C. A. Conant, in *Review of Reviews*, XVI (1897), 167-174; R. P. Porter, in *No. Amer. Rev.*, vol. 164 (1897), 576-584; J. Nimmo, Jr., *Forum*, XXIV (1897), 159-172 (transit trade); H. W. Wiley, *Tariff on Sugar*, in *Forum*, XXIV (1898). 689-697; Stanwood, II, 360-390.

CURRENCY ACT OF 1900: *Finance Report*, 1900, pp. xxxi-xxxiv, 473-477; F. W. Taussig, *Quar. Jour. Econ.*, XIV (1900), 394-415, 450 (text); J. L. Laughlin, *Recent Monetary Legislation*, in *Jour. Pol. Econ.*, VIII (1900), 289-302; C. A. Conant, *Refunding Law in Operation*, in *Review of Reviews*, XXI (1900), 711-716; J. F. Johnson, *Banker's Journal* (Chicago), VII (1901), 53-63; J. F. Johnson, *Pol. Sci. Quar.*, XV (1900), 482-507; R. P. Falkner, *Currency Law of* 1900, in *Annals Amer. Acad.*, XVI (1900), 33-49; F. A. Vanderlip, *Forum*, XXIX (1900), 129-138; A. B. Hepburn, *History of Coinage*, 395-414.

196. Dingley Tariff, 1897.

Although the industrial outlook had begun to brighten when the Republicans assumed control in March, 1897, the condition of the national treasury was unsatisfactory. After 1893 the annual deficits were as follows: —

1893–1894	$69,800,000
1894–1895	42,800,000
1895–1896	25,200,000
1896–1897	18,000,000

To the Republican leaders there could be but one cause, the inadequacy of the tariff of 1894, and there could be but one remedy, — another revision under Republican guidance and responsibility. Little respect was given to the plea that as long as the currency was unsound, no tariff could bring much comfort; nor was any respect paid to the claim that the tariff was not the principal issue in the elections of 1896. Promptly after inauguration in March, 1897, President McKinley called an extra session of Congress to consider the need of further revenue. A bill was reported from the committee on ways and means under the chairmanship of Mr. Dingley, and after a brief consideration in the House, a more leisurely discussion in the Senate, and conference between the two Houses, resulting in the usual compromise, it became a law, July 24, 1897. The measure was thoroughly protective in its provisions, but when it is remembered that the Wilson tariff of 1894 was also of the same general character, an analysis of the new tariff will not disclose many points of interest. On some commodities the duties of 1890 were restored; on others compromises between the rates of 1890 and 1894 were accepted, and in a few instances the lower rates of the Wilson tariff were allowed to stand. Duties were re-imposed on wool, increased on flax, cotton bagging, woollens, silks, and linens, and on certain manufactures of iron and steel. On coal there was a compromise; on iron and steel, duties were left practically unchanged. On sugar, which plays a more important part from a fiscal point of view, there was a radical revision; in place of the ad valorem rate of 40 per cent. on raw sugar, the duty was increased and made specific. The policy of free raw sugar adopted by the Republican party in 1890 was definitely abandoned, for the need of revenue was urgent, and the slowly developing beet sugar industry demanded protection.

The principle of reciprocity authorized by the McKinley tariff was again incorporated into the tariff system, but was to be brought into operation by treaties executed by the Senate, instead of by executive proclamation as provided in the act of 1890. The declared policy of the Republican party is that these treaties shall in no way infringe upon the principle of protection, but shall be "so directed as to open our markets on favorable terms for what we do not ourselves produce in return for free foreign markets." To make a treaty which will not in some degree modify the protective policy is a problem; and there are those who confidently expect that this country will gradually arrive at a greater measure of free trade through reciprocity.

Although the congressional debates on the Dingley tariff were devoted largely to pictures of the industrial prostration due to previous relaxation of the protective principle, the majority keenly appreciated the needs of the treasury and gave more than usual attention to making it productive of revenue. The real merits of the Dingley bill on this point were obscured by the war with Spain in 1898, which interrupted commerce and business, and compelled recourse to internal revenue legislation. In fact it is hard to analyze the productivity of the several tariffs of 1890, 1894, and 1897, partly because the currency contest depressed business, and partly because there was never time enough to determine the real effect of the several measures. Industry cannot accommodate itself at a moment's notice to changes of tariff schedules, and in each case the time was too brief to allow a safe generalization on the fiscal merits of the several measures.

197. Spanish War Finance.

The course of financial reorganization was interrupted early in 1898 by the war with Spain. The action of the treasury and of Congress in this crisis was alike commendable: as soon as the possibility of war became apparent, Congress unanimously appropriated $50,000,000 for national defence, to be expended without restriction by the president. The loan act was supplemented by the war revenue bill of June 13, 1898. The recent tariff measure was not disturbed, and reliance was placed almost wholly upon new internal revenue duties. Nearly all of the taxes on tobacco and fermented liquors were doubled; but no change was made in the duties on spirits, thus leaving a fruitful source of revenue in reserve for future emergency. Special taxes were laid upon banks, brokers, proprietors of theatres, bowling alleys, billiard and pool rooms, and amusement places in general. Stamp taxes were imposed upon a great variety of commercial transactions, involving the use of documents, as the issue or sale of corporation securities; upon bank checks, bills of exchange, drafts, etc.; upon express and freight receipts, telephone and telegraph messages, insurance policies and many other business operations in daily use. Duties collected through the use of stamps, were laid upon patent and proprietary medicines and toilet articles, chewing gum and wines; and an excise tax was imposed upon firms engaged in refining sugar or petroleum. A novelty in federal finance was a tax on legacies, ranging from three-quarters of 1 per cent. on direct heirs to 5 per cent. on distant relations and strangers, with a progressive increase in the rates as the estates increased in size, to a maximum of 15 per cent. The productivity of the new taxes is seen in the following condensed table: —

	1898	1899	1900	1901
Distilled spirits	$92,500,000	$99,200,000	$109,800,000	$116,000,000
Manufactured tobacco .	36,200,000	52,400,000	59,300,000	62,400,000
Fermented liquors . . .	39,500,000	68,600,000	73,500,000	75,600,000
Inheritance taxes . . .		1,200,000	2,800,000	5,200,000
Stamp and business taxes (Schedules A and B) .		43,800,000	40,900,000	39,200,000
Miscellaneous	2,600,000	8,200,000	9,000,000	8,000,000
Total	$170,800,000	$273,400,000	$295,300,000	$306,800,000

Under the authority to borrow, conferred by the act of June 13, 1898, $200,000,000 of 3 per cent. bonds were sold. Any doubt whether a bond bearing so low a rate of interest could be advantageously placed under the existing sensitive conditions of trade and finance disappeared as soon as the treasury invited subscriptions. A popular loan was effectively secured by issuing the bonds in denominations as low as $20, and in giving priority in the allotment to subscribers for the lowest amounts. In all there were 232,224 subscriptions for $500 and less, accompanied by a full payment for the bonds; and 88,002 bids for larger amounts. The total subscription amounted to $1,400,000,000. The success of this loan was due partly to sentiment, as a patriotic desire to share in the financial support of the war; and partly to the self-interest of the national banks, which were eager to obtain additional bonds to secure circulation. The "popular loan," however, was floated at a probable sacrifice of about $5,000,000 which would have come as a premium from competitive bidding; and the theory that "the dissemination of government securities among the people would attach the holders thereof by closer bonds of sympathy to the government," was weakened by the rapid sale of bonds at a small profit by the original subscribers. Within a few months the original holdings of about 116,000 subscribers passed into the possession of a comparatively few persons and corporations.

The cost of the war is not easily estimated. The actual expenditure during the four months of hostilities was not large, but the ultimate outlays have made an enormous difference in the nation's budget. During the four preceding years of peace, 1894–1897, the expenditures for the army were $206,000,000 and for the navy, $122,000,000, a total of $328,000,000; while during the succeeding years, 1898–1901, the expenditures for the army reached $603,000,000 and the navy $238,000,000, making a total of $842,000,000. A portion of this expense is to be charged to the campaign in China and the restoration of peace in the Philippines, operations which are consequent upon the Spanish War. The permanent result has been a higher level of expenditures for military and naval purposes, as well as a higher per capita tax for all federal purposes. New pensions made an increasing draft on the treasury.

198. Currency Act of 1900.

The war was quickly over, and although new and difficult problems of colonial administration engaged the attention of the country, the need of reforming the currency and banking was not forgotten. At first the outlook was discouraging: early in 1898 the Senate passed a resolution that government bonds were payable in standard silver dollars at the option of the government with no violation of public faith; and shortly afterward the silver element in the Senate forced the incorporation of a silver coinage provision (section 34) into the war revenue act, directing the secretary of the treasury to coin into standard silver dollars, to an amount not less than $1,500,000 each month, all of the silver bullion in the treasury, purchased in accordance with the act of 1890. The advocates of reform, however, were not idle. Outside of Congress, a group of men known as the Indianapolis Monetary Commission had been organized in 1897 through the action of a convention of representatives of chambers of commerce and boards of trade, particularly of the Middle West. This commission made a preliminary report in December, 1897, and in January, 1898, a bill embodying its proposals was introduced into the House of Representatives by Mr. Overstreet of Indiana. This plan provided for gold to be the sole standard of value; the stoppage of the coinage of silver dollars; a division in the treasury department between the funds received and used for current expenditures, and those used for issue and redemption of treasury notes; the retirement of the demand obligations of the government; and a radical change in the national banking system. The activity of this commission, and the thoroughness of its report, established a centre of persistent and aggressive influence in Congress and set before reformers a reasonable goal. The improvement in industrial conditions was encouraging; foreign commerce was expanding enormously, and new records, both of imports and exports, were reached. Harvests were generous and manufacturers were behindhand with their orders. The revenues of the government were abundant, in spite of the war with Spain, and there was little complaint of the new taxes. The world's annual product of gold exceeded all previous figures and removed any reasonable apprehension of scarcity of gold; hence the argument for bimetallism lost practical weight.

The struggle for currency reform was still prolonged, but on March 14, 1900, a gold standard or currency law was enacted. The important provisions of the law are three: First, gold is declared to be the standard, and it is made the duty of the secretary of the treasury to maintain at parity with gold all other forms of money: this parity is not to rest on a mere declaration; fiscal machinery is provided by means of which, within certain limits, the redemption of government notes in gold may be automatically continued without special legislation. Second, the circulation of national banks is made more profitable, and opportunity is given for the extension of the banking system to smaller towns and institutions; and third, authority was given for the refunding of a large portion of the public debt at a low rate of interest. The measure was a compromise, for the silver advocates in the Senate still had to be reckoned with, and even the reformers were not agreed on all points. In view of the approaching presidential campaign in which silver was again to be the supreme issue, it is probable that the act went as far as conditions would warrant.

199. Redemption of Treasury Notes.

Two changes were introduced to secure the better maintenance of the gold standard and an unquestioned redemption of credit notes; the gold reserve was enlarged so as to stand at the outset at $150,000,000; and authority was given for the sale of short-term bonds whenever in the future the ordinary receipts of gold should not be adequate to maintain the reserve at a level of at least $100,000,000. That there may be no doubt as to the resources of the treasury, the reserve is made a specific and separate account in treasury book-keeping, so that it is now possible to distinguish between the general fund of the treasury and that set aside for the redemption of credit money.

The machinery for maintaining the current integrity of the reserve is effective, though clumsy. If there be no gold available in the general fund the notes which are presented for redemption must be retained until the gold reserve is made good, so that the sum total of gold and notes may equal $150,000,000; if the volume of gold should then fall below $100,000,000, the gold reserve is to be restored by the sale of one-year three per cent. bonds. Under the conditions of this complicated and roundabout method, it is clear that though the gold reserve may be drawn down from $150,000,000 to $100,000,000, $50,000,000 of notes will be locked up in the reserve fund and withdrawn from circulation; and the operations of the endless chain will so far forth be weakened. At the time of the passage of the act, the sum of the United States notes and the treasury notes of 1890 was $437,000,000, and the reserve of $150,000,000 was therefore equal to 34 per cent. During the period 1879–1890, the reserve of $100,000,000 to protect $346,000,000 of United States notes was equal to 29 per cent.; and in 1893 when $153,000,000 of the new treasury notes had swollen the credit money to a grand total of $500,000,000, the reserve amounted to but 20 per cent.

Although the act of 1900 increases the reserve, the obligation to maintain silver at a parity with gold has increased the burden which, under certain contingencies, the gold reserve may be called upon to support. As yet, however, the prosperity of the government has been so great that there is no apprehension of difficulty from this source, and the possibility of danger in the future is lessened on account of changes in the character of the paper issues. Whenever treasury notes of 1890 are redeemed, silver dollars only will be issued in their place: silver certificates take the place of United States notes hitherto issued in denominations of less than ten dollars, and according to the act not more than one-third of the outstanding notes of a national bank are to be in denominations of five dollars. These provisions will tend to enlarge the use of silver and silver certificates in retail trade; and so broad is the territory of trade and so constant the demand for small bills, that it will be difficult to gather together quickly a dangerous amount of silver or its certificates for exchange into gold at the government counter.

200. Refunding.

The refunding provisions of the act of 1900 authorized the secretary of the treasury to refund into new thirty-year two per cent. gold bonds the outstanding three per cents. of 1908 (Spanish war loan), the four per cents. due in 1907, and the five per cents. due in 1904, a total of $839,000,000. In taking up bonds not yet due, no higher price was paid than a capital value on the basis of a two and a half per cent. return; the new two per cents. were issued at par, but only in exchange for the old bonds refunded, as they fell due or as holders agreed to surrender them; and authority was given to the secretary of the treasury to pay in money the premium on the old bonds refunded.

The success of a voluntary refunding scheme in anticipation of the term fixed in the bond always depends on the inducements to bondholders to make the exchange. In this instance there was a small compensatory premium in cash and an indirect but ingenious incentive was devised to interest banks in the success of the scheme; banks which accepted new for old bonds as a deposit to secure circulation, were relieved of one-half of the tax on circulation, and this in addition to the advantage of prolonging the note circulation by the possession of long-time bonds instead of those subject to a speedy surrender brought the banks into an active co-operation.

The gain to the government is not so clear or complete: to be sure a more permanent provision was made for the indebtedness which fell due within seven years of the act; and there was a considerable saving in the interest charges. In return for these advantages, the government has hampered itself with conditions in the payment of its debt which will prove troublesome when there is a succession of treasury surpluses; and the saving in interest is largely offset by the premiums paid by the government on bonds not due. It was calculated in 1900, that the substitution of $850,000,000 of two per cents., on the terms proposed, would give to the government a net profit of about $23,000,000. Between the passage of the act and December 31, 1900, $445,940,750 of bonds were so funded; the premium paid was $43,582,000, and the saving of interest was $54,548,000. If no reckoning be made of the circulation tax surrendered, the net saving to the treasury on the exchange mentioned, amounts to $10,966,000. Certainly the opportunity for payment of the debt was too long deferred, as was subsequently illustrated in purchases of bonds at high premiums. It is fair to conclude that the funding scheme was intended rather to relieve the difficulties of banking than to offer the best possible management of the finances over a long series of years.

The changes in the character of the debt, 1891–1901, are shown in the table on page 474.

201. Receipts and Expenditures, 1891-1901.

The ordinary receipts during the years 1899–1901 were beyond all expectation, the customs and internal revenue each being in excess of the amount for any three previous consecutive years. The ease with which these enormous sums were paid is a striking illustration of the growth of the country in a single generation. The internal revenue amounted to $876,000,000 as compared with $785,000,000 in the earlier

	1891	1892	1893	1894	1895	1896	1897	1898	1899	1900	1901
Four and one-half per cent. of 1891: refunding and redemption	$50.9	$1.2									
Four per cent. loans of 1907; refunding and redemption	559.6	559.6	$559.6	$559.6	$559.6	$559.6	$559.6	$559.6	$559.6	$355.5	$257.4
Funded loan of 1891 continued at 2 per cent.		25.4	25.4	25.4	25.4	25.4	25.4	25.4	25.4	22.0	
Loan of 1904: 5 per cent.				50.0	100.0	100.0	100.0	100.0	100.0	47.7	21.9
Loan of 1925: 4 per cent					31.2	162.3	162.3	162.3	162.3	162.3	162.3
Spanish war loan, 1908–18: 3 per cent.									198.7	128.8	99.6
Consols of 1930: 2 per cent.										307.1	446.0
Legal-tender notes	346.7	346.7	346.7	346.7	346.7	346.7	346.7	346.7	346.7	346.7	346.7
Gold certificates	152.5	156.6	94.0	66.4	48.5	42.8	38.8	37.4	34.3	227.8	289.0
Silver certificates	314.7	331.6	331.0	337.1	328.9	342.6	375.5	398.6	406.1	416.0	435.0
Certificates of deposit	22.8	30.3	12.4	59.2	55.8	32.0	61.8	26.6	21.3	3.7	
Treasury notes of 1890	50.2	101.7	147.2	152.6	146.1	129.7	114.9	101.2	93.5	76.0	47.8
National bank-notes (redemption account)	40.0	26.8	20.7	26.4	25.4	20.1	24.5	30.5	35.8	35.1	29.4
Others	8.6	8.6	9.0	8.8	8.5	8.6	8.3	8.2	8.3	8.3	8.2
Total[1]	$1546.0	$1588.5	$1546.0	$1632.2	$1676.1	$1769.8	$1817.7	$1796.5	$1992.0	$2137.0	$2143.3
Cash in treasury	694.0	747.0	707.0	732.9	774.4	814.5	831.0	769.4	836.6	1029.2	1098.6
Debt less cash	$852.0	$841.5	$839.0	$899.3	$901.7	$955.3	$986.7	$1027.1	$1155.3	$1107.7	$1044.7

[1] Exclusive of Pacific Railroad bonds.

years 1865–1867, when industry and business were burdened with every variety of excise which could be devised; while the later taxes occasioned annoyance and in some instances friction, there was little sense of sacrifice on the part of the public. In 1901 the Spanish war taxes were partially repealed, and by the act of April 12, 1902, entirely removed. By years the receipts from 1891 to 1901 were as follows: —

	Customs	Internal Revenue	Other	Total net ordinary
1891	$219,522,000	$145,686,000	$27,404,000	$392,612,000
1892	177,452,000	153,971,000	23,514,000	354,937,000
1893	203,355,000	161,027,000	21,437,000	385,819,000
1894	131,818,000	147,111,000	18,793,000	297,722,000
1895	152,158,000	143,421,000	17,811,000	313,390,000
1896	160,021,000	146,762,000	20,193,000	326,976,000
1897	176,554,000	146,688,000	24,479,000	347,721,000
1898	149,575,000	170,900,000	84,846,000 [1]	405,321,000
1899	206,128,000	273,437,000	36,395,000	515,960,000
1900	233,164,000	295,327,000	38,749,000	567,240,000
1901	238,585,000	307,150,000	41,920,000	587,685,000

[1] $64,000,000 received from sale of Kansas Pacific Railroad and Union Pacific Railroad.

Expenditures by years, 1891–1901, were as follows: —

	War	Navy	Pensions	Interest on debt	Indians	Miscellaneous	Total
1891	$48,720,000	$26,113,000	$124,415,000	$37,547,000	$8,527,000	$110,048,000	$355,372,000
1892	46,895,000	29,174,000	134,583,000	23,378,000	11,150,000	99,841,000	345,023,000
1893	49,641,000	30,136,000	159,357,000	27,264,000	13,345,000	103,732,000	383,477,000
1894	54,567,000	31,701,000	141,177,000	27,841,000	10,293,000	101,943,000	367,524,000
1895	51,804,000	28,797,000	141,395,000	30,978,000	9,939,754	93,279,000	356,195,000
1896	50,830,000	27,147,000	139,434,000	35,385,000	12,165,000	87,216,000	354,179,000
1897	48,950,000	34,561,000	141,053,000	37,791,000	13,016,000	90,401,000	365,774,000
1898	91,992,000	58,823,000	147,452,000	37,585,000	10,994,000	96,520,000	443,368,000
1899	229,841,000	63,942,000	139,394,000	39,896,000	12,805,000	119,191,000	605,071,000
1900	134,774,000	55,953,000	140,877,000	40,160,000	10,175,000	105,773,000	487,713,000
1901	144,615,000	60,506,000	139,323,000	32,342,000	10,896,000	122,282,000	509,966,000

Some of the principal expenditures under "Miscellaneous" are presented in a table in the Appendix. Within the term of a single Congress, expenditures amounted to a billion of dollars, and a comparison of the principal items for 1901 and 1891

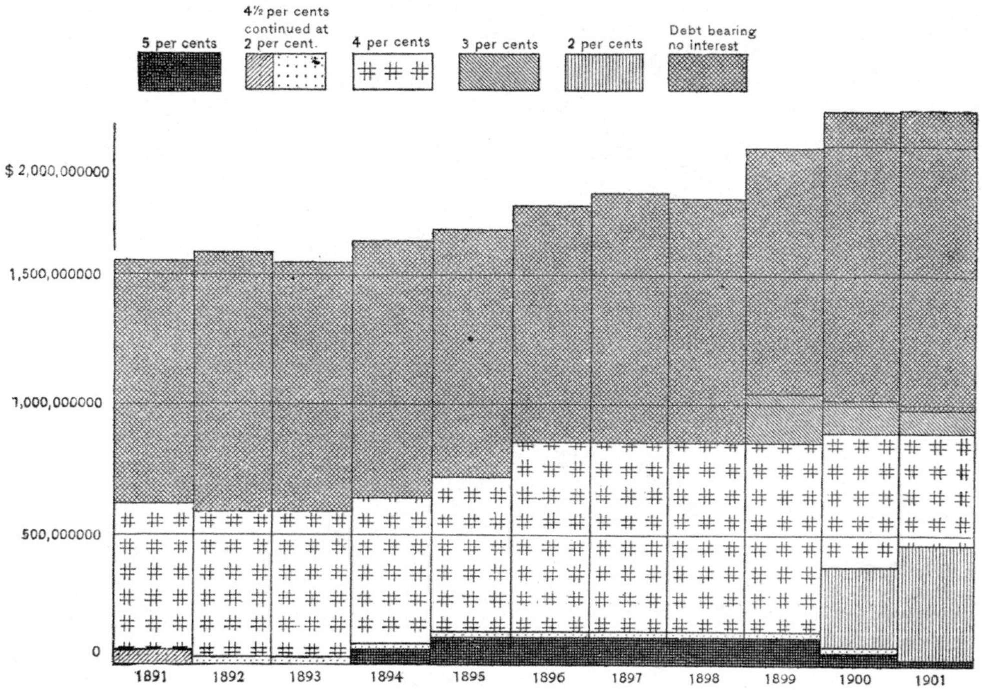

No. XVI. — COMPOSITION OF PUBLIC DEBT, 1891–1901.

(Gross debt, including certificates.)

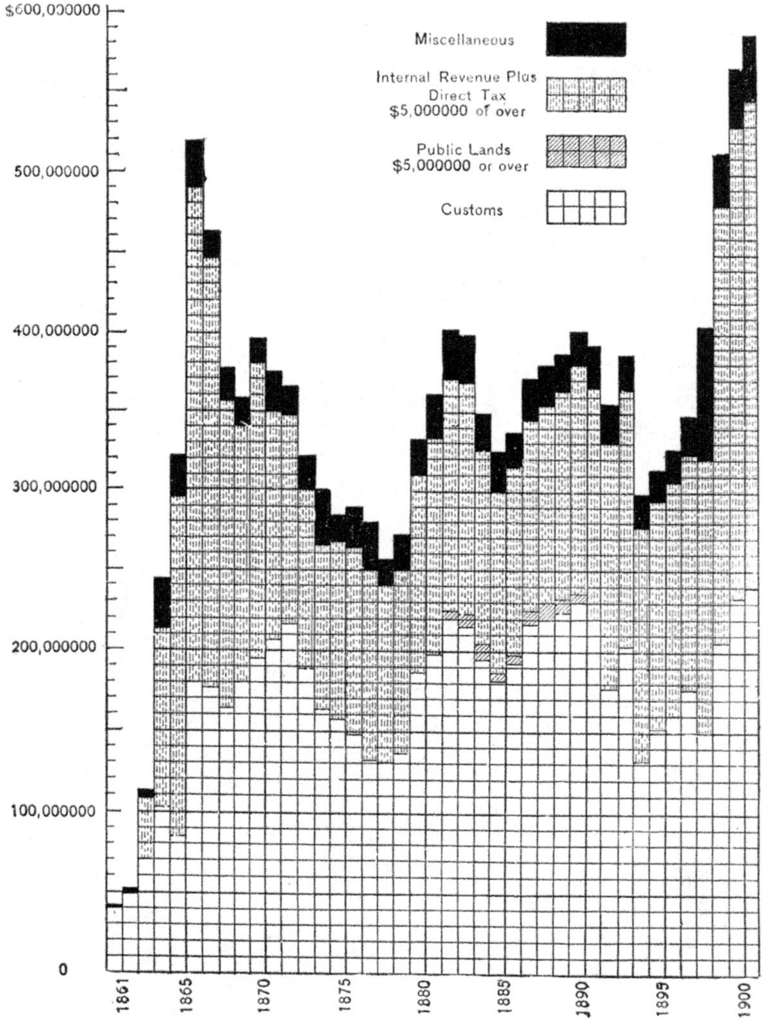

No. XVII. — ORDINARY RECEIPTS, 1861–1901.

(Continuation of Chart No. 5, different scale.)

shows that this was largely due to the demands of the military and naval establishments and pensions.

A comparison of ordinary receipts and expenditures is shown in the following table in millions of dollars: —

	Receipts			Expenditures	Surplus	Deficit
	Taxes	Other	Total			
1890	372.3	30.8	403.1	297.7	105.4	
1891	365.2	27.4	392.6	355.4	37.2	
1892	331.4	23.5	354.9	345.0	9.9	
1893	364.4	21.5	385.8	383.5	2.3	
1894	278.9	18.8	297.7	367.5		69.8
1895	295.6	17.8	313.4	356.2		42.8
1896	306.8	20.2	327.0	352.2		25.2
1897	323.2	24.5	347.7	365.8		18.1
1898	320.5	84.9	405.3	443.4		38.1
1899	479.6	36.4	516.0	605.1		89.1
1900	528.5	38.8	567.2	487.7	79.5	
1901	545.8	41.9	587.7	510.0	77.7	

CHAPTER XXI.

FINANCIERING UNDER EXPANSION.

202. References.

BANKING AND CURRENCY: A. D. Noyes, *Forty Years of American Finance*, 355–380; E. C. Robbins, *Selected Articles on a Central Bank of the U. S.* (1910; bibliography, 5–14); V. Morawetz, *The Banking and Currency Problem of the United States* (1909; opposed to a central bank); O. M. W. Sprague, *Banking Reforms in the U. S.* (1911; reprint of articles in *Quar. Jour. Econ.*, 1909–1910; critical of plans for a central bank); C. N. Fowler, *Seventeen Talks on the Banking Question* (1913); H. White, *Money and Banking* (fifth ed., 1914), 401–536; J. F. Johnson, *Money and Currency* (revised ed., 1914), 366–407; A. P. Andrew, *Substitutes for Cash in the Panic of 1907*, in *Quar. Jour. Econ.*, XXII (1908), 497–516; A. P. Andrew, *The Currency Legislation of 1908*, in *Quar. Jour. Econ.*, XXII (1908), 666–667; A. D. Noyes, *A Year after the Panic of 1907*, in *Quar. Jour. Econ.*, XXIII (1909), 185–212; T. Cooke, W. A. Scott and O. M. W. Sprague, *The Aldrich Plan*, in *Amer. Econ. Rev.*, I (1911), 234–271; P. Warburg and O. M. W. Sprague, *Central Bank*, in *Pub. Am. Econ. Assoc.*, Third Series, X (1909), 338–376; W. C. Mitchell, *The Publications of the National Monetary Commission*, in *Quar. Jour. Econ.*, XXV (1911), 563–593; *The Reform of the Currency*, in *Proc. Acad. Pol. Sci. of N. Y.*, I, No. 2 (1911), 197–493; IV (1913), No. 1; E. W. Kemmerer, *The U. S. Postal Bank*, in *Pol. Sci. Quar.*, XXVI (1911), 462–499; E. W. Kemmerer, *Six Years of Postal Savings in the U. S.*, in *Amer. Econ. Rev.*, VII (1917), 46–90; H. P. Willis, *The Federal Reserve Act*, in *Amer. Econ. Rev.*, IV (1914), 1–24; T. Conway and E. M. Patterson, *The Operation of the New Bank Act* (1914); O. M. W. Sprague, *The Federal Reserve Act of 1913*, in *Quar. Jour. Econ.*, XXVIII (1914), 213–254; H. P. Willis, *What the Federal Reserve System Has Done*, in *Amer. Econ. Rev.*, VII (1917), 269–288.

PAYNE-ALDRICH TARIFF: *Tariff Hearings Sixtieth Congress, 1908–1909* (9 vols.; index in vol. 9); F. W. Taussig, *Tariff History of the U. S.* (1910), 361–408; G. M. Fisk, *The Payne-Aldrich Tariff*, in *Pol. Sci. Quar.*, XXV (1910), 35–68; M. T. Copeland, *The Duties on Cotton Goods in the Tariff Act of 1909*, in *Quar. Jour. Econ.*, XXIV (1910), 422–428; Ida Tarbell, *The Tariff in Our Times* (1911); H. C. Emery,

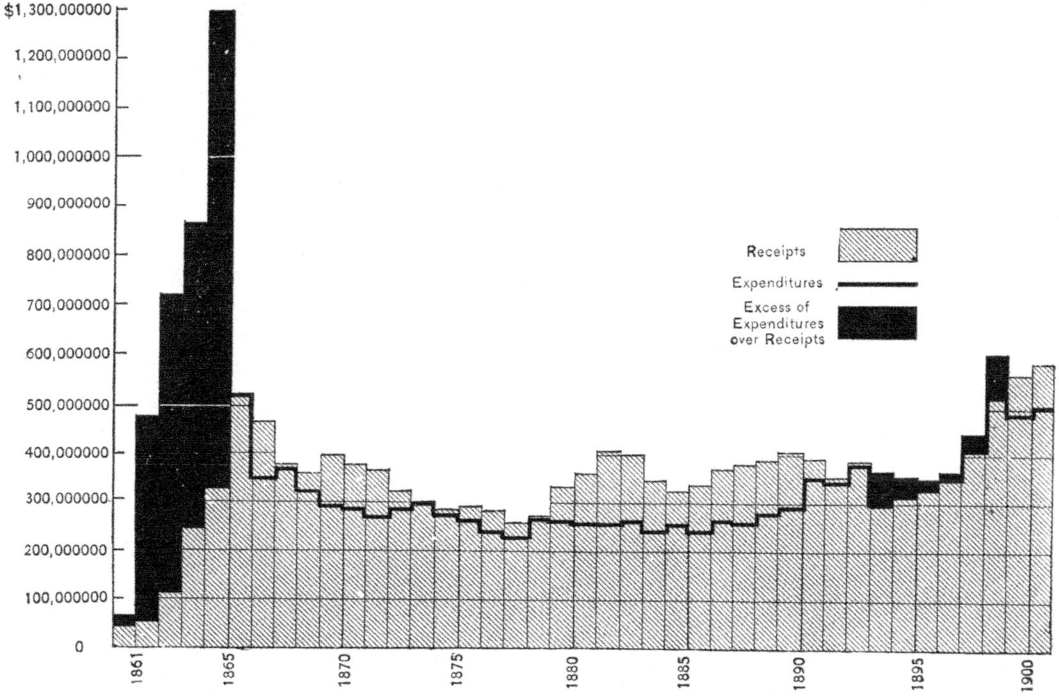

No. XVIII. — ORDINARY RECEIPTS AND EXPENDITURES, 1861–1901.

(Continuation of Chart No. 6, different scale.)

The Best Way to Work for Tariff Revision, in *Papers and Discussions of Amer. Econ. Assoc.*, Apr., 1909, 287–300; H. P. Willis, *The Tariff of 1909*, in *Jour. Pol. Econ.*, XVII (1909), 589–619; XVIII (1910), 1–33, 173–196.

Reciprocity: B. H. Hibbard, *Reciprocity and the Farmer*, in *Amer. Econ. Rev.*, I (1911), 221–233; E. V. D. Robinson, *Reciprocity and the Farmer*, in *Jour. Pol. Econ.*, XIX (1911), 550–566; H. P. Willis, *International Aspects of Reciprocity*, in *Jour. Pol. Econ.*, XIX (1911), 527–541; F. W. Taussig, *Sugar; A Lesson on Reciprocity and the Tariff*, in *Atlantic Mo.*, CI (1908), 334–344.

Underwood Tariff: F. W. Taussig, *Tariff Hist. of U. S.* (sixth ed., 1914), 409–449; C. C. Williamson in *Amer. Year Book 1913*, 349–354; W. S. Culbertson, *The Tariff Board and Wool Legislation*, in *Amer. Econ. Rev.*, III (1913), 59–84; H. P. Willis, *The Tariff of 1913*, in *Jour. Pol. Econ.*, XXII (1914), 213–238; *House Report*, No. 5, 63d Cong., 1st Sess.

Income Tax and Corporation Tax: E. R. A. Seligman, *The Income Tax* (1911), 590–676; M. H. Robinson, *The Federal Corporation Tax*, in *Amer. Econ. Rev*, I (1911), 691–723; K. K. Kennan, *Income Taxation* (1910), 273–286 (corporation tax); 287–306 (income tax amendment); A. W. Machen, Jr., *A Treatise on the Federal Tax Law of 1909* (1910); E. M. Phelps, *Selected Articles on the Income Tax* (1911); R. G. Blakey, *The New Income Tax*, in *Amer. Econ. Rev.*, IV (1914), 25–46; E. R. A. Seligman, *The Federal Income Tax* (1914), in *Pol. Sci. Quar.*, XXIX (1914), 1–27.

Revenue Act of 1916: R. G. Blakey, *The New Revenue Act*, in *Amer. Econ. Rev.*, VI (1916), 837–850.

203. Treasury Relief of the Money Market.

Commercial confidence and prosperity which began in 1897 continued, but the great expansion of business, and the necessities of corporate finance, placed at times a severe strain upon the money market. Revenue, moreover, exceeded expenditures and the problem of surplus financiering once more perplexed the Treasury. Between 1899 and 1903 there were four years of uninterrupted surplus. In 1901 the Spanish war taxes were partially repealed, and in 1902 entirely removed. Notwithstanding this repeal the income from internal revenue was far greater in 1903 than in 1898, and in 1902 the Treasury balance was greater than in any year since 1888.

In September, 1902, there was a stringency in the money

market in New York, and Secretary Shaw, who succeeded Gage in the Treasury Department, made unprecedented efforts to relieve the banks. In doing this he resorted not only to the usual expedients, such as the anticipation of interest on outstanding bonds, the purchase of bonds for the sinking fund at abnormally high premiums, and the deposit of government funds in national banks, but added others entirely novel. For example, he permitted the acceptance, as security for deposits, of certain state and municipal bonds, provided, however, that the government bonds thus released should be used to take out additional note circulation; and to make the arrangement more acceptable, banks were relieved from keeping any reserve against federal deposits. The banks willingly took advantage of the first offer, and within a few weeks the bonds of five states and seventeen cities, amounting to $20,000,000, were deposited for security; and by these means the note circulation was increased to $18,000,000. Permission to except government deposits from the customary reserve requirements was not, however, regarded so favorably, and the New York clearing house association of banks promptly refused to make use of it.

In August, 1903, there were signs of another autumnal stringency due to the call for money to move the crops. Secretary Shaw then announced that he would transfer to the banks internal revenue receipts which had already been deposited in the Treasury. As the Constitution provides that "no money shall be drawn from the Treasury but in consequence of appropriations made by law," many thought that such a transfer could not be made on the responsibility of the secretary alone, and that this administrative action was consequently illegal. Previous deposits had been made by officials without first passing into the Treasury. The Treasury Department, however, held that banks which served as depositaries were in reality a part of the Treasury, and that the transfer of a special form of revenue which could be "segregated" was simply a change of place from one part of the Treasury to another. In the following year the policy of relief was extended to admit railway bonds to the list of acceptable securities against deposits. In 1906 still another method of assistance was devised by helping the banks to import gold: government deposits were made in banks equal to actual engagements of gold for importation, upon pledge of satisfactory collateral. These advances were regarded as temporary loans to relieve a financial stringency to be repaid when the gold arrived. In this way about $50,000,000 was brought from abroad, and the operation was repeated in September of the same year. According to Secretary Shaw this policy at least demonstrated that the United States was in a position to influence effectually international financial conditions.

The development of the depositary system is seen in the following table which shows the number of depositary banks and the amount of deposits:

	No. of depositary banks	Deposits (millions)		No. of depositary banks	Deposits (millions)
1900	442	$93	1908	1436	$148
1901	448	93	1909	1414	60
1902	577	117	1910	1380	41
1903	713	140	1911	1362	36
1904	842	104	1912	1353	38
1905	837	65	1913	1535	70
1906	928	81	1914	1584	77
1907	1255	167	1915	1491	79

204. National Banks.

Under the act of 1900 a national bank could be organized with a capital of $25,000 in a town with a population not exceeding 3000. Circulation was increased to the full face value of bonds deposited so long as they stood at par or above par, and, if the new two per cent refunding bonds provided for under the act were deposited to secure circulation, the tax on circulation was reduced to one-half per cent per annum. The privileges thus granted led to a marked increase in the establishment of banking institutions and to an enlarged circulation. The number of national banks increased from 3595 in 1899 to 7492 in 1913; state and private banks were converted into national institutions, and many new banks were organized. The extension of the national system was especially rapid in the South and West on account of the reduction in the requirement as to minimum capitalization. Of the new organizations, nearly one-half had a capital of but $25,000. The circulation nearly trebled between 1900 and 1911, increasing from $254,000,000 to $759,000,000, or an annual average of nearly $40,000,000. The inflation was steady; notwithstanding the seasonal variations in commercial demands for money, contraction rarely occurred and then only in trifling amounts. The act of 1900 undoubtedly increased the credit medium of the country, and to this Secretary Shaw added pressure during the first part of the period by endeavoring to persuade banks to enlarge their circulation. Little, however, was done to facilitate the retirement of notes, and the monetary system showed marked inflation. A further consequence of the extension of the national system was the absorption by national banks of federal bonds. In 1900 these institutions owned $245,000,000 of United States bonds; in 1913, this increased to $741,000,000, or three-fourths of the total interest-bearing debt.

By 1906 an agitation for a reform of the banking system was again under way, primarily to secure elasticity in the circulation. Plans were proposed by the American Bankers' Association and the New York Chamber of Commerce. Though differing in details, they proposed that national banks be empowered to issue credit notes in addition to the bond secured notes, to be taxed at varying rates according to the amounts taken out, and that all restrictions on retirement of notes be removed. It was, however, impossible at that time to agree on any plan, due largely to the fear of an inflation which would encourage speculative credit undertakings, and Congress contented itself in 1907 (March 4) with the passage of an act whereby the monthly retirement of notes was extended from $3,000,000 to $9,000,000. At the same time the acceptance of securities other than United States bonds in pledge for deposits was specifically authorized by statute.

205. Panic of 1907.

In October, 1907, business was brought to a standstill by a panic, in some ways the most spectacular the country has ever witnessed. Many reasons have been assigned in explanation of this disaster. New York was the center of the crisis. Vast railway and industrial properties absorbed an enormous amount of capital, it being estimated that at least $500,000,000 had been borrowed in Europe, and that $300,000,000 of deposits of interior banks had been placed at the disposition of New York city financial institutions. Violent speculation beginning in 1906 made heavy demands upon banks; discount rates rose to an abnormally high point; banks showed deficits in reserves; gold was imported, and the Treasury increased its deposits in banks. Thus by the beginning of 1907, the resources of financial institutions were strained and a partial liquidation took place. Railroads, however, had already committed themselves to large expenditures and were forced to raise funds by the sale of short-time notes at higher rates of interest instead of by the usual method of long-term bonds. Even the city of New York was embarrassed in placing a new issue of municipal bonds. Abroad there were abundant evidences of difficulty, extending to Egypt, Japan, and Chili. The national banking system had also been weakened by the growth of trust companies which had extended their business from that of trusteeship to commercial banking. Comparatively unrestricted by law, they had engaged in operations far beyond the limit of conservative practice, and in particular did not protect their deposits by adequate reserves. On October 22 the Knickerbocker Trust Company of New York city failed to meet its obligations and this was quickly followed by failures of other trust companies. Banks which had intimate relations with these institutions were in turn involved. The country banks sought in vain to recall their deposits and for a time there were almost no monetary payments except through clearing-house exchanges.

206. Aldrich-Vreeland Act of 1908.

The panic naturally gave great impetus to the discussion of the currency problem, and many currency bills were promptly presented in Congress. These involved plans for a central bank, for legalizing notes issued by clearing-house associations, and for an emergency circulation as in the plan of 1907. The outcome was the passage of the Aldrich-Vreeland Act, May 30, 1908. This provided for the issue of credit notes by individual banks upon the deposit of other than government bonds; or through National Currency Associations upon the pledge of commercial paper, such issues to be taxed at the rate of five per cent for the first month, with an additional tax of one per cent for each succeeding month until ten per cent is reached. The act also authorized the payment of interest upon government deposits at not less than one per cent per annum, and exempted banks from keeping a reserve against such deposits.

The plan for the establishment of National Currency Associations as agencies for an emergency circulation was not, however, regarded as a satisfactory solution of existing defects; and the act expired by limitation in 1914. Owing to the commercial disturbances in that year, it was temporarily continued and for several months did good service in affording credits in a period of emergency, while the new federal reserve system was being established.

Of importance in 1908 was the authorization of the appointment of a Monetary Commission composed of members of Congress, to report future legislation. This commission under the chairmanship of Senator Aldrich devoted three years to investigation of recommended plans, and published a valuable series of documents upon banking methods in this and foreign countries. In 1912 it submitted a plan to Congress. In brief, this provided for the establishment of a Reserve Association of the United States, chartered by the federal government, to act as the fiscal agent of the government, and to hold its deposits. Its banking powers were limited to dealings with banks and trust companies and to operations in foreign exchange. For banks it might re-discount commercial paper and purchase acceptances, thus extending to local banks the resources of a strong national institution. National banks were no longer to take out further circulation on bonds, the plan providing for giving ultimately to the Reserve Association the sole power of note issue. In order to avoid objections which might be made to the establishment of a central bank dominating all local institutions it was proposed that district associations should be formed, each of which within its own sphere had a certain degree of independence.

207. The Payne-Aldrich Tariff of 1909.

In 1908 the desire for a change in the tariff became more marked. Eleven years had passed since the Dingley law was enacted; many rates were out of harmony with existing industrial conditions, and the conviction was growing, particularly in the Middle West, that the tariff fostered trusts and monopolies which were exercising a larger and larger power in the commercial and financial development of the country. The Republican party in its convention for the nomination of a President recognized this sentiment, and although its platform declared in favor of such duties "as will equal the difference between the cost of production at home and abroad, together with a reasonable profit to American industries," it was generally understood that if successful in the election, the party would promptly make a reduction in rates. This conviction was strengthened by the speeches of Mr. Taft, the nominee for

President, who frequently referred with approval to "revision downward."

The Republicans elected their candidate as well as a large majority in the House of Representatives. A special session of Congress was promptly called in March, 1909, for the sole purpose of framing a new tariff. The oft-repeated struggle of affected interests immediately took place. In the House extended hearings were held, but no serious effort was made to determine the real differences in cost of production between this country and abroad. The bill of the House Committee on Ways and Means under the chairmanship of Mr. Payne of New York did not make many radical changes; it proposed reductions in iron and steel, and the removal of duties on certain raw materials, as iron ore, coal, lumber, and hides. On the other hand, a few rates were raised. The wool and woolen rates under schedule K of the Dingley tariff were untouched, notwithstanding the protests of consumers and of manufacturers who used carded wool and desired lower rates on the raw material. The measure was not so favorably received in the Senate. The senators from Wisconsin, Minnesota, Iowa, and Nebraska fought for a more consistent reduction, but were unable to move the Finance Committee under the leadership of Senator Aldrich. Even the trifling concessions of the House bill were disapproved; duties on iron, coal, and hides were demanded, and the rate on lumber increased above the House proposal. More significant were the increases in the cotton and hosiery schedules. When the bill reached the Conference Committee President Taft endeavored to secure reductions, but even executive pressure was of little avail. The most important result was free hides. Seven Republican senators voted against the bill including those from Minnesota and Iowa.

Under this act reciprocity was abandoned and a policy of retaliation endorsed through the adoption of the maximum and minimum principle. Rates on goods coming from countries which discriminated against the United States might be increased, by order of the President, twenty-five per cent of the value of the goods imported. Through efforts of the Administration all causes of complaints were removed, and the minimum rates went into effect April 1, 1910. In order to carry out the provisions of the maximum and minimum clause, the President was authorized to employ the aid of experts, organized through the establishment of a Tariff Board, which made an energetic effort to collect data in regard to cost of production at home and abroad. Although there was opposition to the perpetuation of such a board on the ground that it encroached upon the prerogatives of Congress in the framing of revenue measures, there was a general hope that this new branch of administrative service might, as far as the collection of exact data is concerned, tend to take the tariff out of politics, or at least to afford a substantial basis for the necessary adjustments which must necessarily be made as industrial conditions change.

The Democrats, however, who soon obtained control of the House, opposed its continuance. The board made several valuable reports, but in June, 1912, was denied further support.

Although reciprocity was slighted by the tariff act, President Taft showed an eager interest to secure reciprocity with Canada; a preliminary agreement was signed January 21, 1911. It provided for free trade in certain food products, lessened the rates on others, and reduced duties on manufactured goods. There was a long struggle in Congress; even Republicans denounced it as a betrayal of the principle of protection. The farmers in the Northwest who had received little relief by the tariff act claimed that they were being singled out for sacrifice, — to pay high duties on the manufactured goods which they purchased, and be denied protection on the goods which they produce. The bill passed the House by a vote of 221 to 93, the majority of the Republicans voting against it. In the Senate the contest was renewed, but with the same result. The decision of Canada, however, was adverse and the effort to mitigate the rigors of a high protective tariff by reciprocal agreement failed.

208. Corporation Tax.

The Payne-Aldrich tariff act also authorized a special excise tax of one per cent on incomes above $5,000 of all corporations organized for profit. The adverse decision in 1895 in regard to the unconstitutionality of a general income tax had disappointed many followers of both the political parties, and there was a general desire to add an income tax, if only partial in its application, to the revenue resources of the government. Moreover the growing hostility towards trusts and large corporations gave the proposal popular support. It was opposed on the ground that the taxation of corporations belonged primarily to the states; that it discriminated against the corporate form of enterprise in favor of the partnership; that it introduced inquisitorial examination of the accounts of corporations; and that being a direct tax it was unconstitutional. The Supreme Court, however, sustained the constitutionality of the measure. The revenue from this source is classified with internal revenue; the proceeds until 1914, when this tax was merged into the income tax, were as follows:

1910	$20,960,000	1912	$28,583,000
1911	33,512,000	1913	35,006,000

209. Financing the Panama Canal.

In 1904 payment for the purchase of the Panama Canal was made, — $40,000,000 to the Panama Canal Company in France and $10,000,000 to the government of Panama. These large transfers were made by dealers in foreign exchange without disturbing the money market or requiring the shipment of any gold from this country. The Treasury transferred deposits from banks outside of New York to those within that city; a single draft for $40,000,000 which was settled through the clearing house was paid to a banking house and the proceeds were at once deposited by the banking house in New York banks. The foreign credit was then liquidated through gradual purchase of foreign exchange. To meet the cost of constructing the canal, treasury surpluses were used and money was borrowed by the sale of bonds.

The total expenditures for this great public undertaking, between 1904 and 1916, amounted to $400,000,000, for which approximately a third came from borrowings. The first sales of bonds were made at two per cent interest, but in 1909, owing to the objection to increasing the volume of bonds which would not be attractive to the private investor, authority was given for the issue of bonds at three per cent. A further departure in the policy of federal borrowing was made by the Act of March 3, 1911, which excluded subsequent issues of Panama Canal bonds from being used as a basis of national bank circulation.

210. Postal Savings Banks.

In 1910 (June 25) Congress authorized the establishment of a postal savings bank system. While the primary object of this is to encourage thrift and to afford depositors a safe place for the keeping of their savings, it may become a serviceable agency in providing the government with a market for bonds. Five per cent of the deposits are to be kept as a reserve fund in the Treasury of the United States; the management is authorized at its discretion to invest thirty per cent in government securities; and the President may direct, when public interest demands, the investment of all the deposits in such securities. In the course of time, as these funds accumulate, the Treasury may have at its disposal resources to draw upon without resorting to usual loaning operations. In 1916 deposits amounted to over $80,000,000 made by 600,000 depositors.

211. Underwood Tariff, 1913.

The tariff of 1909 had a short life. There was much disappointment over its outcome; the cost of living continued to increase; trusts and large corporations appeared to be controlling prices with the firmer grip of monopoly; and the consumer felt that he had been sacrificed to the interest of the producer. The Republicans were beaten in the congressional elections of 1910 in very much the same way as they were after the enactment of the McKinley tariff twenty years earlier. The new Democratic House passed several tariff bills by which rates were reduced, particularly on cottons and woollens, and the free list was enlarged. Though favorably acted upon by the Senate, these bills were vetoed by the President on the ground that action should be delayed pending the investigation of the Tariff Board, and that the bills were loosely drawn.

The Democrats, however, in 1912, achieved a sweeping victory and secured full possession of both the executive and legislative branches of government. A special session of Congress to meet in early April, 1913, was promptly called and at once a tariff measure was introduced by Representative Oscar F. Underwood of Alabama, chairman of the Committee on Ways and Means. The committee had at hand the bills which had been vetoed. Hearings were held even before the party came into power on March 4. The bill was reported back to the House, accompanied by a report in which an effort was made to formulate a principle on which tariff schedules might be logically based. The committee condemned the cost-of-production theory for which the Republicans had endeavored to derive merit in framing the tariff of 1909, and the use of which justified the establishment of the Tariff Board. To base a tariff on cost of production, it asserted, was erroneous, because (1) it was difficult to get accurate data, and (2) the data gathered from efficient establishments differed greatly from those obtai from inefficient.

As a substitute the committee prop l the competitive-tariff theory. Rates should be fixed at a point where foreign competition may be effective, thereby preventing the growth of monopoly. In the words of President Wilson, "the object of the tariff duties henceforth laid must be effective competition, the whetting of American wits by contest with the wits of the rest of the world."

The original Underwood bill proposed reductions in all of the fourteen schedules, reducing the general average, calculated on an ad valorem basis, from 40.1 to 29.6 per cent. The most marked reduction proposed was in Schedule K (Wool and Manufactures of), from 56 to 18⅛ per cent. The free list was extended, notably by the addition of sugar and wool. The House loyally supported its committee, passing the measure by the vote of 281 to 139. In the Senate there was decided opposition to free wool and sugar, but for once compromising tactics failed. The bill in its original essentials became law October 3.

The distinguishing characteristics of the Underwood tariff are: (1) Elimination of specific and compound duties; ad valorem duties prevail. (2) Extension of free list. Among the articles so included are meats, cattle, sheep, eggs, fish, potatoes, wheat, sugar, wool, steel rails, agricultural implements and machinery, lumber, wood pulp, coal, and leather. In order to lessen a possible loss to the Louisiana sugar planters and Western beet sugar producers, the entire duty on sugar is not removed until May, 1916. (3) Reduction in rates on many manufactured products, especially woollens, cottons, linens, jute goods, earthenware, and glassware. The elaborate and complicated system of compensatory duties in the woollen schedule is swept away.

212. The Income Tax.

When Congress enacted the corporation tax in 1909, it also proposed an amendment to the Constitution whereby Congress shall have power to levy taxes on all kinds of income, freed from restriction as to apportionment among the States. This amendment was adopted by the necessary three-fourths of the States barely in time to enable the Democrats to utilize this revenue agency to make good the losses expected under the Tariff Act. Making sugar free meant the sacrifice of over $50,000,000 of revenue annually; and the total deficit under the Underwood tariff was estimated at nearly $70,000,000. The Underwood Act, therefore, carried with it the imposition of a tax upon net personal income in excess of $3000, or $4000 in case of a married couple.

Besides the normal tax of one per cent upon incomes in excess of $3000 (or $4000 for married couple) an additional tax (surtax) was imposed upon parts of net income, as follows:

Amount	Per cent
$20,000 to $50,000	1
50,000 " 75,000	2
75,000 " 100,000	3
100,000 " 250,000	4
250,000 " 500,000	5
500,000 " any excess	6

A married man with a net income of $5000 thus paid a tax of $10; with an income of $20,000, $160; and with an income of $500,000, $25,020.

In computing net income, certain deductions are allowed, as: (1) necessary expenses of carrying on business, but not including personal or living expenses; (2) interest on indebtedness; (3) taxes; (4) losses not compensated by insurance; (5) worthless debts; (6) reasonable allowance for depreciation; (7) dividends of corporations which pay the one per cent tax; and (8) income upon which the tax has been collected at the source.

This law adopts the principle of collection-at-the-source, it being estimated that at least two-thirds of the income would be so reached. All persons or corporations paying to other persons income in the form of rent, interest, and salaries in excess of $3000 must deduct the one per cent tax and pay it over to the collector. Individuals liable to the tax are obliged also to make full returns, including data as to exemptions and the amounts withheld at the source.

The final imposition of this tax, though long discussed and probably expected, created much irritation. The law was not clear on many points; there were no administrative rulings to fall back upon; individual accounts often had not been kept in such a form as to admit a clear statement of actual net income; and in the East particularly there was protest that the new tax was sectional and class legislation. The tax was not as productive as anticipated. In 1914, the yield was $28,000,000; in 1915, $41,000,000, and in 1916, $68,000,000. Of this last amount more than $12,000,000 was paid as the additional tax (surtax) on incomes in excess of $500,000. There were 336,652 returns; 120 paid on incomes of $1,000,000 and over, and of these 74 resided in the state of New York, 16 in Illinois, and 10 in Pennsylvania. New York furnished 55,008, or about one-seventh, of all the income of taxpayers; Pennsylvania, 25,494; Illinois, 23,215; Massachusetts, 15,478, and California, 14,055.

213. The Federal Reserve Act of 1913.

Notwithstanding the general dissatisfaction with the banking system, the plan of the National Monetary Commission (see page 483) made little headway. There was suspicion of its authorship; its sponsor was a partisan Republican leader and generally regarded as favorable to the strong financial interests of Wall Street. Every effort was made to convince the public of the merits of the plan, but for a time little progress was made.

After the elections the Democratic leaders determined upon a settlement of the currency problem; and the House and Senate committees, under the chairmanship of Glass of Virginia and Owen of Oklahoma, respectively, devoted themselves to the preparation of a bill. The ground had been broken by the educational campaign of the promoters of the Aldrich plan;

popular interest had been awakened by wide discussion; and the Democratic party made banking reform a part of its constructive program. The result was the Federal Reserve Act enacted Dec. 23, 1913, after a year of prolonged hearings and serious deliberation. In many of its banking operations and fundamental features it is similar to the Aldrich plan: the organization of the system, however, is vitally different. Democratic principle demanded (1) that the new centralized system be brought under greater control of the government, and (2) that there be a sufficient amount of decentralization to prevent a "money trust" or single powerful financial group from dominating the field of banking credit. With these ends in view, the central committee of seven known as the Federal Reserve Board, instead of being elected as in the Aldrich plan by the member banks entering into the system, is appointed by the President; and secondly, instead of one central reserve association or bank, which should carry reserves of the member banks, the act provides that the country be divided into districts, at least eight and not more than twelve, in each of which a federal reserve bank shall be established to which the member banks within the given district shall be related.

In the organization of this new system there are three divisions. (1) At the top is the Federal Reserve Board, composed of seven members, including the secretary of the treasury and the comptroller of the currency, ex-officio, and five others appointed by the President. This board has its office at Washington. (2) The actual banking machinery is in the hands of federal reserve banks and member banks. In each of the twelve districts there is a federal reserve bank. The cities in which these are located are: Boston, New York, Philadelphia, Cleveland, Richmond, Atlanta, Chicago, St. Louis, Minneapolis, Kansas City, Dallas, San Francisco. These federal reserve banks do not engage in banking operations with private individuals; they are banks for banks; their capital is subscribed by banks in their respective districts;

and two-thirds of the management of each is elected by the local member banks. They receive deposits, hold reserves, and also make rediscounts and clear checks, for member banks. They also may hold the deposits of the government. (3) All national banks must join the system, and state institutions may, upon approval of the Reserve Board, become members without surrendering their state charters. The capital for the twelve federal reserve banks is subscribed by the member banks; their earnings in excess of six per cent are to go to the government as a franchise tax, to build up the gold reserve or to be applied to the retirement of United States bonds. These reserve banks must retain reserves against deposits of member banks and also against notes issued by them to member banks. The notes so issued must be secured by commercial paper accepted for rediscount or by gold.

As the reserves carried by member banks, in the twelve federal reserve banks, are less than those required under the old national banking system; and as notes may be issued by the rediscount of commercial paper, it was believed that the note-issue would henceforth respond to commercial needs, thus ridding our monetary system of the hard-and-fast characteristics of a bond-secured currency. This expectation, however, was in a large measure defeated when the nation entered the Great War, and the reserve banks were called upon to rediscount notes secured by government obligations.

Of importance to national finance is the plan for refunding the United States bonds. After 1915 the Federal Reserve Board was given power to direct reserve banks to purchase at par, not to exceed $25,000,000 in any one year, two per cent bonds used to secure circulation; and when so purchased, the circulation of the national banks would be retired. By this and other provisions it was hoped that the bond-secured circulation might be eliminated in the course of twenty years. Of more immediate importance is the transfer of government deposits from the national banks to the federal reserve banks, particularly in the federal reserve cities. A single bank in New York City thus lost $4,000,000 of government deposits.

On June 30, 1916, the total bank holdings of government funds amounted to $157,000,000, of which $113,000,000 was held by the federal reserve banks (see p. 479).

214. Receipts and Expenditures, 1902-1916.

By years the receipts from 1902 to 1916 were as follows:

	Customs	Internal revenue	Other	Total net ordinary
1902	$254,445,000	$271,880,000	$36,153,000	$562,478,000
1903	284,480,000	230,810,00	45,107,000	560,397,000
1904	261,275,000	232,904,000	46,538,000	539,717,000
1905	261,799,000	234,096,000	48,711,000	544,606,000
1906	300,252,000	249,150,000	45,316,000	594,718,000
1907	332,233,000	269,667,000	61,226,000	663,126,000
1908	286,113,000	251,711,000	63,237,000	601,061,000
1909	300,712,000	246,213,000	56,664,000	603,589,000
1910	333,683,000	289,934,000	51,895,000	675,512,000
1911	314,497,000	322,529,000	64,346,000	701,372,000
1912	311,322,000	321,612,000	58,845,000	691,778,000
1913	318,891,000	344,417,000	60,803,000	724,111,000
1914	292,320,000	380,041,000	62,312,000	734,673,000
1915	209,787,000	415,670,000	72,454,000	697,911,000
1916	213,186,000	512,702,000	53,777,000	779,665,000

Expenditures by years, 1902–1916, were as follows:

	War	Navy	Pensions	Interest on debt	Indians	Miscellaneous	Total
1902	$112,272,000	$67,803,000	$138,489,000	$29,108,000	$10,050,000	$113,469,000	$471,191,000
1903	118,620,000	82,618,000	138,426,000	28,556,000	12,935,000	124,934,000	506,089,000
1904	115,035,000	102,956,000	142,559,000	24,646,000	10,438,000	136,602,000	532,238,000
1905	122,175,000	117,550,000	141,774,000	24,591,000	14,236,000	143,034,000	563,360,000
1906	117,947,000	110,474,000	141,035,000	24,309,000	12,747,000	142,984,000	549,405,000
1907	122,576,000	97,128,000	139,310,000	24,481,000	15,164,000	153,046,000	551,705,000
1908	137,747,000	118,037,000	153,982,000	21,426,000	14,580,000	175,420,000	621,102,000
1909	161,067,000	115,546,000	161,710,000	21,804,000	15,695,000	186,502,000	662,324,000
1910	155,912,000	123,174,000	160,696,000	21,343,000	18,504,000	180,076,000	659,705,000
1911	160,136,000	119,938,000	157,981,000	21,311,000	20,934,000	173,838,000	654,138,000
1912	148,795,000	135,592,000	153,590,000	22,616,000	20,135,000	173,825,000	654,554,000
1913	160,387,000	133,268,000	175,085,000	22,899,000	20,306,000	170,830,000	682,771,000
1914	173,523,000	139,682,000	173,440,000	22,864,000	20,215,000	170,530,000	700,254,000
1915	172,973,000	141,836,000	164,388,000	22,903,000	22,130,000	207,170,000	731,400,000
1916	164,636,000	155,029,000	159,302,000	22,900,000	17,570,000	204,039,000	724,493,000

In addition there was spent, during this period, on account of the Panama Canal, $400,000,000. The foregoing table includes the postal deficiencies; in 1909 this amounted to $19,501,000, but in 1911, for the first time since 1884, this was converted into a slight surplus.

From the beginning of the twentieth century, expenditures by the War and Navy Departments rapidly increased. In part this was due to the new demands created in protecting the new colonial possessions, and in part to the more intimate participation of the United States in world politics and the conviction that the integrity and dignity of the government can be maintained in the face of increasing international rivalries only by a generous provision for defense. The government is also extending its activity in many new directions. Of special importance are the expenditures for the Department of Agriculture. Between 1841 down to and including the year 1900, the total sum appropriated for agricultural purposes was $45,000,000, while in the opening decade of this century it reached double the sum, or $90,000,000. In a single year this branch of public service now calls for $30,000,000. New services have been undertaken, as food and meat inspection, the reclamation of arid lands, and the construction of the Panama Canal; the forest service has been extended; salaries with the increased cost of living have been raised; new public buildings, especially in Washington, have been constructed; the work of the Interstate Commerce Commission has been enlarged; the Census Bureau placed on a permanent basis; new departments of cabinet rank, as those of Commerce and of Labor, have been established.

A comparison of ordinary receipts and expenditures is shown in the following table in millions of dollars.

	Receipts			Expenditures	Surplus	Deficit
	Taxes	Other	Total			
1902	$526.3	$36.2	$562.4	$471.2	$91.3	
1903	515.3	45.1	560.4	506.1	54.3	
1904	494.2	46.5	540.6	532.2	8.4	
1905	459.9	48.4	544.3	563.3		$19.0
1906	549.4	45.3	594.7	549.4	45.3	
1907	601.9	61.2	663.1	551.7	111.4	
1908	537.8	63.2	601.1	621.1		20.0
1909	546.9	56.7	603.6	662.3		58.7
1910	623.6	51.9	675.5	659.7	15.8	
1911	637.0	64.3	701.3	654.1	47.2	
1912	632.9	58.8	691.8	654.6	37.2	
1913	663.3	60.8	724.1	682.8	41.4	
1914	672.4	62.3	734.7	700.3	34.4	
1915	625.5	72.5	697.9	731.4		33.5
1916	725.9	53.8	779.7	724.5	55.2	

This table does not include postal accounts or the financing of the Panama Canal.

During this period, there was little change in public indebtedness, the slight increase being due to the construction of the Panama Canal. The total debt, less cash in the Treasury, for the years 1902–1916, was as follows in millions of dollars:

1902	$969.5	1910	$1046.4
1903	925.0	1911	1015.8
1904	967.2	1912	1027.6
1905	989.9	1913	1028.6
1906	964.4	1914	1027.3
1907	878.6	1915	1090.1
1908	938.1	1916	989.2
1909	1023.9		

Nearly three-fourths, $721,000,000, of the total interest-bearing debt in 1916 bore interest at the low rate of two per cent. A detailed table showing the composition of the debt will be found on the following page.

PUBLIC DEBT 1902–1916[1]

(Millions of Dollars)

	1902	1903	1904	1905	1906	1907	1908	1909	1910	1911	1912	1913	1914	1915	1916
4% loans of 1907: refunding and redemption	$233	$173	$157	$157	$117	$36									
Loan of 1904: 5%	19	19													
Loan of 1925: 4%	135	119	119	119	119	119	$119	$119	$119	$119	$119	$119	$118	$118	$118
Spanish War Loan, 1908–18: 3%	98	83	77	77	64	64	64	64	64	64	64	64	64	64	64
Consols of 1930: 2%	446	520	543	543	596	646	646	646	646	646	636	646	645	646	636
Panama Canal Loan: 2-3%						30	55	85	85	87	135	135	135	135	134
Legal-tender notes	347	347	347	347	347	347	347	347	347	347	347	347	347	347	347
Gold certificates	347	409	494	518	560	678	820	853	863	995	1040	1087	1081	1218	1730
Silver certificates	454	465	471	465	478	476	474	484	489	464	482	484	491	493	499
Treasury notes of 1890	30	19	13	9	7	6	5	4	4	3	3	3	2	2	2
National bank-notes (redemption account)	42	40	36	32	43	48	73	29	28	33	25	22	15	19	52
Other	8	8	9	8	8	8	25[2]	10	9	9	9	11	13	16	22
Total	$2159	$2203	$2264	$2275	$2337	$2457	$2627	$2640	$2653	$2766	$2868	$2916	$2912	$3058	$3609
Cash in treasury[3]	1189	1278	1297	1285	1373	1579	1689	1616	1606	1750	1841	1888	1885	1968	2620
Debt less cash	$970	$925	$967	$990	$964	$879	$938	$1024	$1046	$1016	$1028	$1029	$1027	$1090	$989

[1] In continuation of table on page 473.
[2] Includes $14,000,000, Certificate of indebtedness.
[3] In large part held in pledge against the gold certificates.

CHAPTER XXII.

THE GREAT WAR.

215. References.

TAXATION: E. R. A. Seligman, *The War Revenue Act*, in *Pol. Sci. Quar.*, XXXIII (1918), 1–37; E. D. Durand, *Taxation versus Bond Issues for Financing the War*, in *Jour. Pol. Econ.*, XXV (1917), 888–916; R. G. Blakey, *The New Revenue Act*, in *Amer. Econ. Review*, VI (1916); 837–850; R. G. Blakey, *The War Revenue Act of 1917*, in *Amer. Econ. Review*, VII (1917), 951–815; R. M. Haig, *Revenue Act of 1918*, in *Pol. Sci. Quar.*, XXXIV (1919), 369–391; R. G. and G. C. Blakey, *The Revenue Act of 1918*, in *Amer. Econ. Review*, IX (1919), 213–243; C. C. Plehn, *War Profits and Excess Profits Taxes*, in *Amer. Econ. Review*, X (1920), 283–298; R. G. Blakey, *The Revenue Act of 1921*, in *Amer. Econ. Review*, XII (1922), 78–108; T. S. Adams, *Should the Excess Profits Tax Be Repealed*, in *Quar. Jour. of Econ.*, XXXV (1921), 363–393; T. S. Adams, *Fundamental Problems of Federal Income Taxation*, in *Quar. Jour. of Econ.*, XXXV (1921), 527–556; T. S. Adams, *The Concentration of Taxes Upon Wealth and Business*, in *Bankers Mag.*, XCIV (1917), 514–519; E. R. A. Seligman, *The War Revenue Acts*, in *Essays in Taxation* (1921), 679–716; T. S. Adams, *Federal Taxes Upon Income and Excess Profits*, in *Amer. Econ. Review, Supplement*, VIII (1918), 18–35, with discussion, 36–54; R. H. Montgomery, *Income Tax Procedure, 1918* (and succeeding editions); *The New Revenue Bill*, in *Hearings, June 7–Aug. 15, 1918, before the House Committee on Ways and Means.*

LOANS: J. H. Hollander, *Certificates of Indebtedness in our War Financing*, in *Jour. of Pol. Econ.*, XXVI (1918), 901–908; J. H. Hall, *War Borrowings. A Study of Transfer Certificates Indebtedness of the United States* (1919); C. J. Bullock, *Financing the War*, in *Quar. Jour. of Econ.*, XXXI (1917), 357–379; E. R. A. Seligman, *The Cost of the War and How It Was Met*, in *Amer. Econ. Review*, IX (1919), 739–770; F. F. Anderson, *Fundamental Factors in War Finance*, in *Jour. of Pol. Econ.*, XXV (1917), 857–887; H. Secrist, *Fundamentals of War Finance*, in *Bull. Nat. Tax. Assoc.*, III (1917), 26–33; E. R. A. Seligman, *Loans versus Taxes in War Finance*, in *Essays in Taxation* (1921), 717–249; also *The Cost of the War and How It Was Met*, 750–782; E. L. Bogart, *War Costs and Their Financing* (1920); *Financial Mobilization for War*,

(University of Chicago Press, 1918); *Financing the War*, in *Annals Amer. Acad. of Pol. and Soc. Sci.*, LXXV (Jan., 1918); A. B. Hepburn, *Financing the War* (1918); C. C. Plehn, *Substance and Shadow in War Finance*, in *Amer. Econ. Review*, VIII (1918), 564–578.

BUDGET SYSTEM: C. W. Collins, *The National Budget System and American Finance* (1917); W. F. Willoughby, *The Good National Budget Bill (with Text of Bill)*, in *Nat. Municipal Review*, VIII (1919), 360–365; *Establishment of a National Budget System*, in *Hearings before Select Committee of the House of Representatives* (1919).

EXPENDITURES: *National Expenditures and Public Economy*, in *Proceedings of Acad. of Pol. Sci., of N. Y.*, IX (1921), No. 3; *Taxation and Public Expenditures*, in *Annals of Amer. Acad. of Pol. and Soc. Sci.*, XCV (1921), No. 184; E. L. Bogart, *Direct and Indirect Costs of the Great World War* (1919), 161–182.

FEDERAL RESERVE SYSTEM: H. P. Willis, *What the Federal Reserve System Has Done*, in *Amer. Econ. Review*, VII (1917), 269–288; *The Federal Reserve System — Its Purpose and Work*, in *Annals of Amer. Acad. of Pol. and Soc. Sci.*, XCIX (1922), 188; H. P. Willis, *The Federal Reserve*, 297–312; H. P. Willis and G. W. Edwards, *Banking and Business*, 440–477; D. R. Dewey and M. J. Shugrue, *Banking and Credit*, 331–341, 350–352; *Annual Report of the Federal Reserve Board.*

216. Revenues Affected by European War.

The war which overwhelmed Europe in August, 1914, seriously affected the finances of the national government. Commerce was disorganized; imports were checked; and customs duties declined. Congress acted promptly but cautiously, without a full realization of the ultimate needs. The revenue act, enacted October 22, 1914, increased the duties on fermented liquors, imposed special taxes upon bankers and brokers, reintroduced stamp taxes and made other slight changes in the internal revenue schedules. This would yield $54,000,000; and, as it was believed the emergency was but temporary, the act was to expire at the end of 1915. The yield of these two taxes nearly met expectations, but this was not enough to offset the final losses of the year. The spread of prohibition cut into the revenue from distilled and fermented liquors, and customs duties fell off $83,000,000. The fiscal year 1915 consequently saw a deficit of over $30,000,000.

The need of more generous appropriations for the army and

navy and for national defense, even if the United States did not enter the conflict, was recognized by the administration, and on June 3, 1916, the national defense law was enacted, calling for largely increased expenditures. The sending of troops to the Mexican border in the summer of 1916 and forthcoming outlays by the new Shipping Board also had to be provided for.

217. Revenue Act of September 8, 1916.

To meet these heavy expenditures Congress voted (Dec. 17 1915) to extend the revenue act of 1914; to retain the duty on sugar, which under the Underwood act was to be free; and for additional relief, new taxes were levied under the revenue act of September 8, 1916. The significant features of this measure are as follows:

(1) The income tax was increased by making the normal rate on individuals and corporations two instead of one per cent, and the graduated surtax rates on incomes of $80,000 and over were raised. For incomes of $2,000,000 and over, the surtax rate was advanced from 6 to 13 per cent. (2) A progressive tax on inheritances was introduced, ranging from one per cent on amounts in excess of $50,000 to ten per cent on amounts in excess of $5,000,000. There was some opposition as the separate states were beginning to utilize this fiscal aid, but the plea of emergency prevailed. Three times previously, in 1797–1802, in 1862–1870, and in 1898–1902, an inheritance tax has been levied, but abandoned when the emergency was over. (3) A temporary excise tax of 12½ per cent on the net profits of manufacturers of munitions was levied. (4) A tariff commission was once more established. In accepting this administrative agency, the Democratic party abandoned the opposition which it had formerly shown. The duties of the commission are confined to investigation of the administration and the fiscal and industrial effects of the customs laws of the United States, and their relation to federal revenues and the industries of the country. The commission is composed of six members, serving for twelve years. The appointment of

Professor F. W. Taussig as chairman of the Commission gave assurance that the work of this board would not be affected by partisan political influences.

A further step in preparation for emergency was taken March 3, 1917, by the passage of an act to provide a special fund for military and naval purposes. By this law, revenue was to be derived from an excess-profits tax and an increase of the inheritance tax, graduated from $1\frac{1}{2}$ to 15 per cent. The excess-profits tax was 8 per cent on the amount by which the net income of a corporation or partnership exceeded $5,000 and 8 per cent of the actual capital invested.

The new taxes proved fruitful — the treasury budget suddenly expanded; ordinary receipts rose from $777,000,000 in 1916 to $1,123,000,000 in 1917, an increase of 44 per cent. For this gain the income tax was largely responsible, yielding $360,000,000 as compared with $125,000,000 in 1916.

218. Entry into War; Liberty Loans.

The decision of the United States to enter into the European War against Germany immediately imposed financial tasks of the greatest magnitude. In comparison, all previous revenue and loaning measures appear insignificant. War was declared April 6, 1917; eighteen days later, on April 24, Congress authorized the issue of $5,000,000,000 bonds at a rate of interest not exceeding $3\frac{1}{2}$ per cent. It was not, however, intended at the time to borrow this full amount. Expert advisors varied as to the amount which could be sold and absorbed; some indeed doubted if more than $500,000,000 could be borrowed under a single loan. The Treasury, however, decided to call for $2,000,000,000, under what is known as the First Liberty Loan of 1917. The bonds mature in thirty years but are redeemable in fifteen years at the option of the government; they are exempt from all taxation except inheritance or estate taxes imposed by the federal government.

To secure the sale of these bonds a direct appeal was made to the entire population. Under the supervising agency of the federal reserve banks, Liberty loan committees were established throughout the country. "Bankers, business men, bond houses, newspapers, press associations, and citizens generally co-operated in a great movement that vibrated with energy and patriotism and swept the country from coast to coast in the greatest bond-selling campaign ever launched by any nation." To the surprise even of the treasury department the subscriptions amounted to $3,035,000,000, or nearly 52 per cent more than the amount offered. More than four million subscriptions were made.

A Second Liberty loan was offered on October 1, amounting to $3,000,000,000. The rate of interest was raised to 4 per cent, but the exemption from federal taxes was not so generous. They are subject to federal inheritance taxes and also to income surtaxes and excess profits taxes. Again there was oversubscription, the total amounting to $4,618,000,000, an excess of 54 per cent of the bonds offered. The organization of committees was perfected; popular appeal was made more effective; and the total number of subscriptions was more than twice as great as that of the first loan.

Anticipating the sale of bonds was the issue of short-term certificates running as a rule for a period of one year. For the sale of these certificates, reliance was placed upon the federal reserve banks. As a fiscal agency in a time of emergency, the federal reserve system more than justified its establishment. In need of immediate funds, even before bonds could be sold, the treasury department sold certificates by a systematic allotment to the reserve banks which in turn distributed them largely to member banks. The latter then sold them to their customers. By these agencies, the government was able to avoid recourse to the issue of treasury notes and avoided many of the embarrassments which characterized the financing of the Civil War.

The service of the federal reserve banks went even farther than the making of temporary loans to the government. They made it possible for purchasers of Liberty bonds to borrow on easy terms. A preferential rate of discount was established for rediscount of notes of member banks, secured by government obligations. A member bank could loan to its customer on the collateral of a government bond or treasury certificate, in full assurance that the note would be rediscounted by its reserve bank. As the rediscount rate was no greater than the interest on the government obligation, it was possible for a purchaser of a bond to secure funds, by pledging it as collateral with his bank which in turn rediscounted the note with the federal reserve bank. Without this agency it would have been impossible to secure the widespread and generous subscriptions to bonds which has been noted.

219. War Revenue Act of October 3, 1917.

The financing of tax measures requires greater deliberation than the passage of loan acts. Particularly was this true in 1917; the past revenue experience of the United States was entirely inadequate to furnish a basis for future legislation to meet the enormous tasks which confronted the government. The war was to be fought over-seas and it was well-nigh impossible to estimate its probable cost. In December, 1917, when the country had been eight months at war, McAdoo, Secretary of the Treasury, laid down the estimates for the fiscal year, 1918, as over $10,000,000,000 for the war and navy departments, and $6,000,000,000 for loans to foreign governments. Fortunately the income tax was already in operation as a result of the sixteenth amendment, and it was natural therefore that in seeking for increased revenue, chief reliance should be put upon this new financial support.

The war revenue act, which was approved October 3, 1917, related wholly to internal revenue duties, including an excess-profits tax and the income tax upon individuals and corporations. Old rates were increased and new taxes added. The excess-profits tax authorized in March was repealed and the munitions tax was lowered from 12½ to 10 per cent. The total internal revenue duties collected in the fiscal year ending June 30, 1917, was $909,000,000; and it was estimated that the new act would provide $3,400,000,000, an increase of two and a half billion dollars.

The principal items to provide this unprecedented tax levy were estimated as follows: excess-profits tax, $100,000,000; income tax, $851,000,000; transportation taxes, $157,000,000; distilled spirits, $140,000,000. These four items thus accounted for four-fifths of the expected gain. Additional duties were placed upon fermented liquors, wines, tobacco; and new taxes on insurance, sale of automobiles, musical instruments, jewelry, sporting goods, cameras and moving picture films, cosmetics, toilet articles, medicines, and chewing gum. The act also included taxes on admissions to amusements and dues to clubs; war stamp taxes; and additional rates on inheritances, graduated from 2 to 25 per cent. Postal rates were also increased.

To secure the additional revenue from the income tax, the normal tax was raised from 2 to 4 per cent; exemption was lowered to $1000 for unmarried, and $2000 for married persons; and the surtaxes were greatly increased: first, by making them effective on incomes over $5000 instead of over $20,000; and second, by changing the graduated scale from 1 to 13 to 1 to 63. Incomes of $2,000,000 and over paid a total rate of 67 per cent. As Professor Seligman, in commenting upon this legislation, says: "This is the highwater mark thus far reached in the history of taxation. Never before, in the annals of civilization, has an attempt been made to take as much as two-thirds of a man's income by taxation . . . The American scale is an eloquent testimony to the fact, not only that large fortunes are far more numerous here than abroad, but also that there is greater appreciation of the democratic principles of fiscal justice."

The excess-profits tax was practically a new tax. It was imposed upon the profits of all business which showed a profit in excess of the period 1911 to 1914. Deductions ranging from 7 to 9 per cent of the capital were allowed. The tax was graduated according to the excess profit: 20 per cent on the excess up to 15 per cent; 35 per cent on the excess from 15 to 20 per cent; 35 per cent on the excess from 20 to 25 per cent; 45 per cent on the excess from 25 to 33 per cent; and 60 per cent on the excess over 33 per cent.

220. Third and Fourth Liberty Loans, 1918.

Notwithstanding the heavy taxes imposed by the war revenue act of 1917, it was soon necessary to seek further loans. The Third Liberty loan was offered in April, 1918, calling for $3,000,000,000. Owing to the speeding-up of business, caused by the demand for war materials, the market rate of interest on loanable funds had increased since the placing of the earlier Liberty loans, and these bonds were now quoted below par. It was therefore decided to offer 4¼ per cent on the new loan. Again there was over-subscription, the total amounting to $4,177,000,000. A Fourth Liberty loan quickly followed in September of the same year, calling for $6,000,000,000. Supply still exceeded demand, and subscriptions were received for nearly $7,000,000,000. The rate on this loan was 4¼ per cent. In order to make this loan more attractive to investors it was provided that interest on $30,000 of these bonds held by one person was exempt from surtaxes until two years after the close of the war. Further compensating exemptions were also granted to holders of Second and Third Liberty loans.

In the placing of these loans, renewed efforts were made to arouse patriotic coöperation. There was a War Loan Organization with a speaker's bureau and a publicity bureau engaged in the preparation and distribution of posters, buttons, flags, and advertising copy. Liberty days were designated by presidential proclamation to arouse enthusiasm in the several campaigns; and it was estimated that two million men and women devoted themselves to the work of distributing bonds.

221. Need of Additional Tax Revenues.

From the beginning of the war there was widespread discussion as to the relative proportions which taxation and borrowing should bear to provide means for the enormous appropriations. Some indeed advocated a policy of "pay as you go" and even proposed a conscription of wealth, if necessary, in order to meet the war costs. Others favored a more equal division between taxes and loans. These views, however, did not prevail. There was fear of "frightening capital" and arousing popular discontent which would retard the progress of military and naval plans. Although no exact ratio was formally adopted, there slowly developed an accepted conviction that taxation should provide at least one-third of the cost of the war. The four Liberty loans represented a new debt of nearly 16 billion dollars. For the fiscal year, 1918–1919, expenditures were estimated at 24 billion dollars. If taxation bore its share, it was obvious that the revenue act of 1917 must be revised. In the summer of 1918, a revenue bill of 8 billion dollars was proposed; congressional action, however, was deliberate, and the armistice in November was signed while the bill was under discussion. Reductions in proposed rates were immediately made and the estimated yield reduced from 8 to 6 billions. Finally on February 24, 1919, the bill was enacted; although passed in 1919, the law is known as the revenue act of 1918.

Few important new taxes were introduced by this measure; old rates were revised and many increased. It was estimated that four-fifths of the 6 billions would be derived from income and excess-profits taxes. The law was retroactive, covering incomes and excess-profits for the year 1918, and slightly lower rates were fixed for subsequent years. The following table shows the rates of normal tax imposed by the act of 1918 as compared with previous laws:

Amount of Net Income	Act of 1913	Act of 1916	Act of 1917	Act of 1918	
				1918	1919
$1000–$2000	exempt	exempt	2[1]	6[1]	4[1]
2000– 3000	exempt	exempt	2	6	4
3000– 4000	1	2	4[2]	6	4
4000– 5000	1	2	4	6	4
Over $5000	1	2	4	12	8

[1] Applicable only to income of single persons or of married persons not living with wife or husband.

[2] For heads of families and married persons the rate was only 2 per cent.

Graduated surtax rates on net incomes of $8000 and over were increased; for example, on $8000, from 2 to 3 per cent; on $50,000, from 12 to 24 per cent; on $100,000, from 27 to 52 per cent; on $500,000, from 50 to 64 per cent; on $2,000,000 and over, from 63 to 65 per cent. The income tax of corporations for 1918 was fixed at 12 per cent, and for subsequent years at 10 per cent. Although there was opposition to the excess-profits tax, on account of its burden upon business enterprise, its influence in increasing the cost of living, and the technical difficulties in calculating the excess to be taxed, it was retained. A general sales tax was suggested, but this was regarded as too radical and novel a substitute for a duty already incorporated in the revenue system. Moreover, large fortunes had been acquired by manufactures of war material and there was a strong demand that these gains be shared by the government.

222. The War Debt.

A further loan was necessary to reinforce the revenue act of 1918. In May, 1919, the Victory loan of $4,500,000,000 was offered. This was in two series of notes, one tax-exempt, except for inheritance and estate taxes, at $3\frac{3}{4}$ per cent; and the other, subject to surtaxes and excess-profits taxes, at $4\frac{3}{4}$ per cent. As there was expectation that revenue would soon exceed expenditure and that before no long period funds could be borrowed at a lower rate, the Victory notes ran for but a short period, maturing in 1923 and redeemable in 1922. For a fifth time, the loan was oversubscribed.

The use of short-term certificates of indebtedness, both in anticipation of the Liberty loans and in anticipation of income and excess-profits taxes, was continued on a huge scale throughout the war and subsequently in the financial policy of reconstruction. Between April 6, 1917 and October 31, 1921, 51 billions were issued; 21 billions were issued in anticipation of loans; 11 billions in anticipation of taxes; and 19 billions for special purposes. In October, 1921, about 2 billions of unmatured certificates were outstanding, thus constituting a large floating debt which must be funded.

Of no little importance as a factor in popularizing investment in government securities throughout the war was the sale of thrift and war savings stamps. The thrift stamp was issued in denominations of 25 cents, and the savings stamp in denomination of $5. Although the proceeds of sales of certificates of so small amount could not be large as compared with Liberty loans, their use cultivated thrift and often led to investment in bonds of small denominations. Under the direction of National War-Savings Committee, appointed by the Secretary of the Treasury, state, county, city, and town committees were appointed throughout the country. The gospel of thrift was vigorously preached. Thousands of war-savings societies were formed; and savings-certificates placed on sale at every post-office. Introduced in December, 1917, this agency secured in less than a year the sale of $834,000,000 war-savings and thrift stamps, having a maturity value of over a billion dollars. The thrift stamp costing 25 cents was redeemable for the same sum, but the war-savings stamp, maturing in 1923 was purchasable at from $4.12 to $4.23 according to the month in which it was bought. Thrift stamps could be used in the purchase of certificates.

So successful was this movement that at the close of the war it was decided to organize the work on a more permanent basis under the supervision of a Treasury director of savings. War-savings certificates of larger denominations, $100 and $1000, known as treasury savings certificates, were authorized, thus meeting the needs of investors with larger resources.

The public debt reached its maximum, approximately 25 billion dollars, in 1919, as compared with a little over one billion at the beginning of the war.

223. Cost of the War.

It is impossible as yet to estimate the cost of the war, even apart from interest on debt, pensions and other permanent charges which war always leaves in its wake. Exclusive of debt operations and postal disbursements from postal revenues, the total expenditures of the government, from April 6, 1917 to October 31, 1919, by which time the over-seas troops had been returned, was over $35,413,000,000; of this total, $11,280,000,000, or nearly 32 per cent, was met by taxes and other minor ordinary receipts. The expenditures, given above, include $9,406,000,000 loaned to foreign countries. If this be subtracted, the disbursements for the purposes of the American government, during the war period under consideration, was $26,007,000,000; and on that basis the proportion met out of tax receipts and revenues other than borrowed money was over 43 per cent.

224. Cost of Government after the War.

After the war it was difficult to reduce expenditures. War liabilities had to be met and the cost of government increased with the universal higher cost of living. For the fiscal year 1920, expenditures were nearly $6,500,000,000; and for 1921, over $5,500,000,000. It was believed that for 1922, this might be cut to $4,000,000,000. To secure greater economy in governmental administration a budget system was authorized in 1921. By this it was believed that several hundred millions might be saved. But the cost of government will undoubtedly be threefold or more than it was in 1917. The interest on the public debt alone will approximate a billion dollars, nearly as much as the entire cost of the government before the war.

The burden which the nation must assume was necessarily heavy. The situation was thus summed up by Mellon, Secretary of the Treasury, in his report of 1921: "The increase in population, the enlargement of government functions, the addition of new agencies, the interest on the public debt, and the expenditures indispensable in connection with the disabled veterans of the war make it manifest that the ordinary expenses of the government for some years to come will probably be several times those for pre-war years."

While no one expected that taxes would return to the pre-war rates, there was a general expectation and demand that they be reduced. The new and high taxes had been on the whole cheerfully borne during the war, but the need of their retention was not so clearly seen. The inadequacy of the old pre-war sources of revenue is seen in the following table comparing the three pre-war years, 1913–1915, with the two after-war years, 1920–1921 (in millions of dollars).

		Internal Revenue										Total Ordinary	
	Customs	Tobacco	Spirits and liquor	Incomes, individual and corporation	Transportation, etc.	Estate	Special, sales, luxuries, etc.	Stamps	Admissions and dues	Miscellaneous	Total internal revenue	Receipts	Disbursements
1913	319	77	230	35	...	...	...	...	...	2	344	724	725
1914	292	80	226	71	...	...	...	...	...	2	380	734	735
1915	210	80	224	80	...	...	...	23	...	8	416	696	761
1920	324	296	140	4050	289	104	319	88	82	40	5408	6695	6482
1921	308	255	83	3310	302	154	282	76	96	38	4595	5625	5538

225. Revenue Act of 1921.

The demand for a new tax bill was urgent; the Republican party which came into power in March, 1921 had pledged itself to a revision of the revenue system; the industrial depression which succeeded the abnormal and speculative activity, culminating in the early part of 1920; and the deep-seated opposition to the taxation of capital as represented in the high surtaxes or the income tax and in the excess-profits tax, all combined to force Congress to legislate. Congress was summoned in special session in April, 1921. An emergency tariff bill was first considered and not until mid-summer was the revenue bill introduced. The conflicting currents of opinion noted above gave rise to a long struggle, resulting finally in the revenue act of 1921, approved November 23. As a basis for legislation Congress had before it the following recommendations of Secretary Mellon (April 30 and August 4, 1921):

(1) The repeal of the excess-profits tax;
(2) As compensation for this loss, the increase of the corporation tax;
(3) Reduction of combined normal and surtaxes upon incomes to 40 per cent for 1921 and 33 per cent thereafter;
(4) Repeal of certain minor luxury taxes, popularly known as "nuisance" taxes, as on fountain drinks;
(5) Imposition of new stamp taxes, or a license tax on the use of automobiles;
(6) Reduction of transportation taxes;
(7) Increase of first-class postage, which had been reduced after the war, from 3 to 2 cents;
(8) Increase in tobacco taxes.

Expenditures for 1922 at first were estimated at $4,566,000,000, but later when the new budget bureau began its investigations, a slight reduction was made in the probable needs of the government. Although there was a popular hope that taxation might be greatly lowered, Congress had no disillusion on this point. The difficulty was to revise and meet popular expectation in some small degree, at least. On the one side it was argued that taxes should be laid upon wealth, both upon that which had been accumulated and that which was being earned in large amounts. High surtaxes in income were therefore advocated, and some in this group would retain the excess-profits tax. It was stated in the minority report of the Senate Finance Committee that 180 corporations, making annually from $5,000,000 up to $300,000,000 and over, had a net income of over $2,500,000,000, on which they paid only $203,000,000 income tax and $848,000,000 excess-profits taxes. Tax returns showed that all corporations in the United States between January 1, 1916 and July, 1921, made net profits of $47,000,000,000, and that after paying all federal taxes, income, excess-profits, and war taxes, they had a clear profit of $38,000,000,000, of which more than half was made by about a thousand corporations. The proposal to increase the corporation tax to make good some of the loss, occasioned by the repeal of the excess-profits tax, was attacked on the ground that it would bear more heavily upon the smaller and weaker corporations. The Republican party, however, had practically pledged itself to repeal the excess-profits tax, and there was abundant proof that its productivity was diminishing. The enormous profits of the war period were vanishing; business was depressed; and the internal revenue bureau was involved in endless disputes in the collection of the tax. The tax was repealed and the corporation income tax increased from 10 to 12½ per cent.

The attempt to lower the surtax rates on income was not so successful. Notwithstanding the plea that the high rates retarded the creation of new capital, diverted old capital from productive industry into tax-exempt securities, destroyed incentive, and interfered with the freedom of business, the Senate finance committee was unable to carry its recommendation that the maximum surtax be reduced from 65 to 32 per cent. A group of Republican senators from western states, forming what was known as the "agricultural bloc," joined the Democrats in opposing the marked reduction. Finally, 50 per cent was adopted as a maximum on net income in excess of $200,000, and surtaxes on lower incomes were also reduced.

The only other important change affecting the yield of revenue was the repeal of the transportation tax and certain excise duties. Again and again during the debate efforts were made to substitute a sales tax as a substitute for most of the schedules in the tax bill. This was advocated because of its simplicity and economy of administration as compared with the irritating difficulties of interpreting the revenue laws. The substitute was favored by a Republican senator from New England on the ground that it would "strike down the vicious principle of graduated taxation which appears in the pending tax bill, and which is but a modern legislative adaption of the communistic doctrine of Karl Marx." On the whole the act of 1921 did not greatly change the revenue system, the income tax upon individuals and corporations still remaining the chief fiscal support of the government.

226. Federal Reserve System.

We have seen that the adoption of the sixteenth amendment to the Constitution made it possible for the government to tap new sources of revenue by taxation. The recent organization of the federal reserve banking system also made it possible to borrow billions of dollars quickly with a minimum of disturbance to the money market. Since its establishment in 1914, the reserve system had developed slowly; its service was confined almost entirely to banks. The twelve reserve institutions held a portion of the reserves of member banks and had begun to rediscount commercial paper, but the demand for this was not great. A small volume of federal reserve notes had been issued and filtered into general circulation, but the new system thus far had made but little impression on the business community. After the declaration of war in April, 1917, reserve banks were called upon to act on a large scale as the fiscal agency of the government, and in this duty they performed notable service in supporting the financial operations of the war. Reference has already been made to the rediscounting of notes of member banks secured by collateral of war obligations on favorable terms, and the aid this rendered in securing prompt subscription and payment by individual investors. The federal reserve banks handled all details connected with the sale, allotment, distribution, and redemption of treasury certificates of indebtedness; they received subscriptions to the several Liberty loans; effected the exchanges and conversions of bonds; and paid and canceled coupons of war securities as they fell due. They established foreign branches and arranged reciprocal accounts in foreign countries, which facilitated the financial transactions between the United States and her European allies. By an amendment to the reserve act in 1917, member banks were required to keep all their reserve balances with the federal reserve banks; this strengthened their position and gave them control of the monetary gold of the country. Indirectly, this fortified the credit of the government, for the government and the banks worked in close coöperation in financial plans.

In 1920 (act of May 29) the subtreasuries existing since 1846 were abolished and their duties were transferred to the treasurer of the United States, the mints, and the federal reserve banks. This did away with the embarrassments caused by the holding of idle funds in non-banking institutions.

227. Receipts and Expenditures, 1917–1921.

By years the receipts from 1917 to 1921 were as follows:

Year	Customs	Internal revenue	Other	Total net ordinary
1917	$225,962,000	$809,366,000	$82,846,000	$1,118,174,000
1918	182,759,000	3,696,043,000	295,208,000	4,174,011,000
1919	183,429,000	3,840,231,000	623,944,000	4,647,604,000
1920	323,537,000	5,399,149,000	972,689,000	6,695,375,000
1921	308,025,000	4,579,974,000	684,604,000	5,572,603,000

The increased figures in the column "Other" were in part due to interest on loans to foreign governments which was paid in 1918 and 1919; to discount on bonds purchased; and to sales of government supplies.

Expenditures by years, 1917–1921, were as follows:

Year	War	Navy	Pensions	Interest on Debt	Indians	Miscellaneous	Total
1917	$440,277,000	$2,257,166,000	$160,318,000	$24,742,000	$30,598,000	1,153,530,000	$2,066,779,000
1918	5,684,349,000	1,368,643,000	181,138,000	197,527,000	30,888,000	6,309,734,000	13,768,899,000
1919	9,253,059,000	2,009,272,000	221,615,000	615,867,000	34,593,000	6,805,059,000	18,039,532,000
1920	1,094,832,000	629,893,000	213,344,000	1,024,024,000	40,517,000	3,131,104,000	6,135,714,000
1921	557,169,000	644,279,000	260,611,000	996,677,000	41,471,000	1,820,623,000	4,322,210,000

The foregoing table does not include postal deficiencies; these were slight, except in 1921, when it amounted to $130,000,000. Under "Miscellaneous" are included, for the years 1917–1919, $9,102,000,000 expended in purchase of obligations of foreign governments; in 1917, $25,000,000 for purchase of Danish West Indies; in 1917–1919, $171,000,000 in subscriptions to federal land banks and purchase of farm loan bonds. In 1920, $350,000,000 was paid out to liquidate the wheat guarantee fund which the wheat-growers had been promised during the price-fixing period of the war and $689,000,000 on account of the federal control of railroads. In 1919, $1,866,000,000 was disbursed to the United States Shipping Board and in 1920, $467,000,000. Apart from the large sums paid out to defray the expenses of war operations, expenditures were greater because of the higher price level. Materials cost more and salaries were increased to meet the higher cost of living.

CHAPTER XXIII.

LEGISLATION AND ADMINISTRATION

228. References.

APPROPRIATIONS: *Finance Report*, 1894, pp. lxvii, 837, 838 (specific and permanent); J. A. Garfield, *Works*, II, 1-19 (Jan. 23, 1872), 740-753 (1879); E. D. Adams, *The Control of the Purse of the U. S.*, in *Kansas Univ. Quarterly*, April, 1894; J. Sherman, *Recollections*, I, 154; Bolles, III, 227-240, 536-560; H. C. Adams, *Finance*, 121-132, 150-153, 157-160; F. J. Goodnow, *Comparative Administrative Law*, II, 291-295; W. M. Daniels, *Public Finance*, 348-359; L. G. McConachie, *Congressional Committees*, 175-185, 233, 373-387; A. B. Hart, *Practical Essays on American Government*, 206-232 (river and harbor bill; see note p. 232); E. R. Johnson, *Appropriations for River and Harbor Bills*, in *Annals Amer. Acad.*, II, 782-811; R. Ogden, *The Rationale of Congressional Extravagance*, in *Yale Review*, VI, 37-49; E. I. Renick, *Control of National Expenditures*, in *Pol. Sci. Quar.*, VI (1891), 248-281; N. H. Thompson, *Control of National Expenditures*, in *Pol. Sci. Quar.*, VII (1892), 467-482; H. J. Ford, *The Cost of our National Government* (1910); C. J. Bullock, *The Growth of Federal Expenditures*, in *Pol. Sci. Quar.*, XVIII (1903), 97-111; W. H. Glasson, *The National Pension System as applied to the Civil War and the War with Spain*, in *Ann. Amer. Acad. Pol. and Soc. Sci.*, (1902); C. A. Beard, *Readings in American Government and Politics* (1909), 338-342; P. S. Reinsch, *Readings in American Federal Government* (1909), 301-361.

TREASURY DEPARTMENT: *Report of the Select Committee of the U. S. Senate*, 50th Cong., 1st Sess., Senate Report, No. 507, 1888. Vols. I-III; see especially I, 4-25, 130-133, 145-159, 235-238; II, 1-474 (treats particularly of accounting); L. J. Gage, *Organization of Treasury Department*, in *Cosmopolitan*, XXV (1898), 355; R. Mayo, *The Treasury Department* (Washington, 1847); H. C. Adams, *Finance*, 193-201; C. C. Plehn, *Public Finance*, 334-339; F. A. Cleveland, *Funds and their Uses*, 195-208 (the maintenance of the reserve).

CUSTOMS ADMINISTRATION: *Finance Report*, 1890, pp. xxxii-xxxvii; 1891, pp. xxxviii-xlii; 1892, pp. xxxvii-xxxix; 1893, p. xli (expense); 1894, pp. xxxix, 959, 962-966 (expense); 1895, pp. 737-738 (undervaluation); 1898, pp. xliv-xlv, 868-876 (appraisement); *Reports of Board of Appraisers*, published annually in *Finance Report*, 1892-1898; now separately; *Hearings on Administrative Customs Laws before the Committee on Ways and Means* (Washington, 1896); *Report of the Secretary of the*

Treasury on Collection of Duties, in *Finance Report*, 1885, Vol. II; *ditto*, 1886, Vol. II; J. D. Goss, *The History of the Tariff Administration in the U. S.*, in *Columbia College Studies in History, etc.*, I. No. 2; F. J. Goodnow, *The Collection of Duties in the U. S.*, in *Pol. Sci. Quar.*, I (1886) 36–44; E. J. Shriver, *How Customs Duties Work*, in *Pol. Sci. Quar.*, II (1887), 265–273; Bolles, II, 486–501; III, 489–522; C. S. Hamlin, *The Customs Administrative Act*, in *No. Amer. Rev.*, Vol. 158, pp. 222–230; W. C. Ford, *Official Tariff Comparisons*, in *Pol. Sci. Quar.*, XIII (1890), 273–285; *Yale Review*, I, 233–235 (tariff statistics).

Custody of the Public Funds: *Finance Report*, 1900, p. xxviii; D. Kinley, *Independent Treasury System*, chs. 6–7; J. B. Phillips, *Methods of Keeping the Public Money of the U. S.* (pp. 160), in *Pub. Mich. Pol. Sci. Assn.*, IV, No. 3 (Dec., 1900); *Letter from the Secretary of the Treasury*, Jan. 10, 1900, 56th Cong., 1st Sess., H. R., Doc. 264 (pages 348); J. Sherman, *Recollections*, II, 798; H. C. Adams, *Finance*, 214–218; W M. Daniels, *Public Finance*, 322–324; G. E. Roberts, *Forum*, XXIX (1900), 1–14; C. A. Conant, *The Treasury and the Money Market*, in *Review of Reviews*, XXI (1900), 202–205; E. B. Patton, *Secretary Shaw and Precedents as to Control over the Money Market*, in *Journal of Political Economy*, XV (1907), 65–87.

Accounting: *Finance Report*, 1894, pp. lxvi, 737, 836–837 (comptroller); 1895, p. 587 (audit); 1896, pp. 676–678 (comptroller); R. B. Bowler, *Decisions of the First Comptroller of the Treasury*, 1893–1894; *Decisions of the Comptroller of the Treasury*, I–VIII, 1896–1902; *Report of a Committee of the Senate on the Books and Methods of Accounting in the Treasury Department* (Washington, 1880); see also *Report of Senate Committee*, 1888, under "Treasury Department;" *Report of Dockery Commission* (Washington, 1893); Bolles, II, 567–575; III, 523–535; *Treasury Statement*, in *Bankers' Magazine*, LVIII (1899), 717–719; *Yale Review*, IX (1900), 3 (debt statement); *Quarterly Journal of Economics*, I (1887), 357 (inaccurate debt statement). *The Accounting System of the U. S.* (Treasury document, 1911.)

229. Initiative in Tariff Bills.

The Constitution clearly provides that "all bills for raising revenue shall originate in the House of Representatives, but the Senate may propose or concur with amendments as on other bills." In spite of this limitation, the Senate exercises a powerful influence over revenue legislation, and sometimes has taken the initiative in shaping the details of a tariff measure. The tariff bill of 1820 passed the House, and failed by but one vote in the Senate; and the House woollens bill of 1827 was defeated in the Senate by the casting vote of the vice-president. In 1828 the Senate changed the House bill in a most important particular, by making the duties on woollens ad valorem instead of specific. In 1833 the agitation in South Carolina led Senator Clay to introduce into the Senate a still more radical method of procedure in the bill known later as the Compromise Tariff measure. When objection was made that the Senate had no constitutional power to take the initiative, it was explained that the bill did not propose to raise duties but to reduce them, and since the measure was intended for protection and not for revenue, it came out of the category of revenue measures. A discussion was consequently permitted in the Senate, but after a full debate the same bill was introduced into the House, there passed, sent to the Senate, and finally became a law.

A similar attempt to assert the independence of the Senate was made in 1843, when a bill was introduced by Senator McDuffie of South Carolina, to revive the tariff act of 1833, in place of the existing tariff of 1842. After a prolonged debate running over weeks, the Senate agreed almost unanimously that such a measure could not originate in that body. Although this distinct claim has not been revived over a tariff bill, the Senate has interpreted its powers to amend in a most generous spirit. In 1867, for example, it substituted as an amendment to the House bill the tariff measure which had been prepared by David A. Wells, the special commissioner of revenue, but the bill in this form failed to find approval in the House. Again in 1871 the Senate took great liberties with a House measure; this was less than four lines in length, and was confined simply to the repealing of the tariff on tea and coffee. The Senate substituted as an amendment, a bill of twenty printed pages, containing a general revision, reduction, and repeal, not only of customs duties, but also of internal revenue taxes. As might be presumed, a protest was raised in the House, and on this point Garfield a year later in the House of Representatives spoke as follows:[1] —

[1] *Works*, i, 699.

"It is clear to my mind that the Senate's power to amend is limited to the subject-matter of the bill. That limit is natural, is definite, and can be clearly shown. If there had been no precedent in the case, I should say that a House bill relating solely to revenue on salt could not be amended by adding to it clauses raising revenue on textile fabrics, but that all the amendments of the Senate should relate to the duty on salt. To admit that the Senate can take a House bill consisting of two lines, relating specifically and solely to a single article, and can draft upon that bill in the name of an amendment a whole system of tariff and internal taxation, is to say that they may exploit all the meaning out of the clause of the Constitution which we are considering, and may rob the House of the last vestige of its rights under that clause."

Notwithstanding these protests the Senate succeeded in enlarging the scope of the tax bill framed in 1872. In 1883 the Senate followed a similar procedure, and added to an internal revenue bill which had passed the House, the tariff recommendations submitted by the "Tariff Commission," propositions which were entirely alien to the original import of the House bill. Once more, in 1888, the Senate which was at that time Republican, deliberately and independently framed a tariff measure to offset the Democratic Mills bill prepared in the House; and the Senate bill served as the basis of the tariff act of 1890. The Senate in 1894 also recast the Wilson bill so radically that its revenue reform principles were hardly recognizable; nevertheless, through political stress, the House was forced to accept most of the amendments of the upper chamber. In 1897 the Senate finance committee met, even before Congress assembled, and drew up a tariff bill, the principles of which were expressed in 872 amendments to the House bill, though not all of these were adopted after conference.

These illustrations are sufficient to show that practice has worn away any constitutional limitations which may have originally been intended in the disposal of tariff bills; the

Senate has virtually assumed a leadership in shaping the revenue legislation of Congress. The Senate committee of finance by its hearings and deliberations has acquired as important a position in tariff legislation as the House committee on ways and means.

On at least one occasion the executive branch has prepared tariffs; this was the Walker bill of 1846, substantially drawn up by the secretary of the treasury; Secretary Dallas also had a large part in the preparation of the tariff of 1816. The presidential power of veto, however, has rarely been exercised in connection with a tariff bill. The notable exceptions are the two vetoes of President Tyler in 1842; his objections, however, applied not to the revenue clauses of the bill, but to the provision for the distribution of the proceeds from sales of public lands. In 1869 President Johnson vetoed a minor tariff bill, providing for an increase of duties on imports of copper. In 1894 President Cleveland showed disapproval of the Wilson tariff by refusing to sign the measure.

The preparation of a tariff bill is a long and complicated task, for not only must considerations of revenue, but the adjustment of protection to industries, be taken into account. This often excites prolonged contest, both between the high and low tariff men, and between friends of particular industries. The framing of a revenue bill is undertaken in the House by the committee on ways and means; a sub-committee, composed entirely of members of the controlling political party, is appointed to draft the schedules, and its work is frequently accompanied by extended hearings, when manufacturers and other business men present the claims of their respective industries for legislative favor. As the tariff is treated as a political measure, the minority of the committee is given no share whatever in this preliminary work and may have no knowledge of the schedules to be finally reported to the House; the minority usually submits a dissenting report, necessarily vague and general in character, which can be little more than a party pronunciamento. After

THE HISTORY OF THE WOOL SCHEDULE, 1897

	THE DINGLEY BILL AS IT LEFT THE HOUSE (MCKINLEY LAW RATES)	AS IT WAS REPORTED TO THE SENATE	AS IT WAS APPROVED BY THE SENATE	AS IT WAS REPORTED BY THE CONFERREES, AND SIGNED BY THE PRESIDENT
Wools, Hair, etc. Class 1, unwashed .	11 c. per lb.	8 c. per lb.	10 c. per. lb.	11 c. per lb.
washed . .	22 c. "	16 c. "	20 c. "	22 c. "
scoured . .	33 c. "	24 c. "	30 c. "	33 c. "
" 2, unwashed .	12 c. "	9 c. "	11 c. "	12 c. "
washed . .	12 c. "	9 c. "	11 c. "	12 c. "
scoured . .	36 c. per lb.	27 c. per lb.	33 c. "	36 c. per lb.
" 3, . . (BY THE WILSON LAW ALL WOOLS WERE FREE)	32 per cent. ad valorem, if valued at less than 13 c. per lb. If valued at more than 13 c. per lb., 50 per cent. ad valorem.	4 c. per lb., if valued at less than 10 c. per lb.; 7 c. per lb., if valued at more than 10 c. per lb.	4 c. per lb., if valued at 10 c. or less per lb.; 7 c. per lb., if valued at more than 10 c. per lb.; if imported in condition to spin or card, or if not containing more than 8 per cent. of dirt and foreign substances, three times the regular rates.	4 c. per lb., if valued at not more than 12 c. per lb.; 7 c. per lb., if valued at more than 12 c. per lb.; if imported in condition to spin or card, or if noc containing more than 8 per cent. of dirt and foreign substances, three times the regular rates.

debate and passage in the House, the bill goes to the Senate where it is referred to the committee on finance. This committee may undertake its consideration *ab initio*, or it may summarily set the bill aside for new plans which have been informally determined upon. In either case the House bill when it re-emerges from the committee is hardly recognizable. The Senate permits the offering of amendments, and many of them pass. If the bill then goes through the Senate, the next step is the designation of a joint committee of conference of the two Houses. This committee has of late years been the place for the actual conflict of forces; theoretically it considers only points of disagreement; in practice it strikes out some non-contentious matter and inserts new quarrels. Hence, the bill, when it once more comes to the House, is a compromise measure and represents no harmonious principle. This roundabout method, with no one guiding mind behind it, makes errors unavoidable, and so exhausting is the task of enacting a tariff law that the dominant political party is naturally indisposed to alter or amend the measure, even for the purpose of removing inconsistencies, for fear that the whole question of tariff revision may be reopened. As an example of the vicissitudes of tariff legislation the illustration of the changes made in the wool schedules in 1897 is given on the opposite page.

230. Appropriation Bills.

In an earlier discussion in this book, it was shown that the constitutional restrictions on appropriation of money for public needs are not intended to cramp Congress to a narrow range of action and hence practices have grown up which on the whole are not conducive to a well-balanced system of finance. The only constitutional limit on appropriation is that no vote for the support of the army shall last more than two years. Appropriations are made under three different forms: "permanent specific appropriations," "permanent," and "annual." In theory the great bulk of appropriations are annual in accordance with the principle of popular government that the people shall have a firm grip on its purse. In practice, however, large expenditures are made outside of this annual provision, by permanent specific appropriations, as for river and harbors, fortifications and public buildings, which remain available until the money is spent. The reason for this is clear: continuing construction work cannot be subjected to the fortunes of legislative procedure, but when once made must be so pledged that they can be drawn upon as the necessities of engineering work demand. Permanent appropriations are those which do not require the periodic sanction of Congress; once voted, they are annually paid until the law authorizing the expenditure is repealed. In this class are included the appropriations for the sinking fund of the public debt, annual interest charges, the support of the customs service, and the salaries of judicial officers. For the fundamental operations of government, permanency is needed for administrative stability; this principle applies particularly to the public debt: public credit must be relieved from the uncertainties of annual legislative debate. Permanent appropriations, however, breed abuses, because the items of expenditure are not periodically subjected to the scrutiny of Congress. For lack of discussion, for example, the administration of the customs has at times developed absurdities, entailed unnecessary expense, and given poor service. Custom houses have been kept up at ports no longer of commercial importance, and the payment of officials by fees instead of by salaries has been continued long after the best interests of the government demanded their discontinuance.

It has been held by sound authority that the fixing of any salary due to the establishment by law of a branch of administration may be regarded in the light of a permanent annual appropriation; and that "in time of conflict between Congress and the president, it is very probable that the president would conduct the government and would have salaries paid without annual appropriations, and be able to do so successfully."[1]

[1] Goodnow, *Comparative Constitutional Law*, vol. ii, p. 285.

It is estimated that one-half of the current expenses of the government, exclusive of pensions and salaries, is beyond the reach of any particular Congress, except by positive legislative action of a repealing character, requiring the assent of the president, unless overruled by a two-thirds vote of Congress. A committee of the Fifty-Second Congress found that there were 185 separate statutes taking money from the treasury in the form of permanent appropriations.

Congress has frequently attempted to attach general legislation to an appropriation bill by riders or ingenious qualifications and restrictions which are alien to its real purpose. A familiar example is the Wilmot Proviso of 1846, which was an amendment to an appropriation bill, prohibiting slavery in territory that might be acquired with the money appropriated. An interesting controversy was that of a rider to the army appropriation bill in the House of Representatives in 1879; the Democrats were in control of the House from 1875 until 1881, and in 1877 they secured a majority in the Senate, though the presidency was in the hands of the Republicans. In 1878, they made an urgent effort to change the election laws: a single bill for that purpose, if passed, would have been vetoed by the president, but the same end was sought indirectly by adding sections to the army appropriation bill and by affixing amendments to the legislative, executive, and judicial appropriation bill. President Hayes set himself to defeat the scheme, vetoed the two appropriation bills, and summoned Congress to meet in special session in May, 1879. The army appropriation bill was then again reported with the so-called political sections. The Republican debaters could not deny that riders had been previously attached to bills; they urged, however, that provisions so extreme as those under discussion were a departure from the practice of Congress, and that the contest was simply an attempt to force the president and the minority out of their constitutional right of disagreement, under penalty of stopping supplies. They also made a distinction between an ordinary rider, when both branches of Congress and the presidency were of the same political party, and riders put on by a hostile majority. As Mr. Hawley of Connecticut said: "It was as if there were a special train taking a party to Baltimore by the last train of the week, and some friends wished to crowd in with their baggage, which ought not to be taken on passenger trains, but must go then or never. Rather than have them left, we consent. That is quite different from an attack of road agents, who pull up the rails saying, 'the train will not go unless you take us and all our crew and our burglarious implements.'" The Democrats replied that while in ordinary cases the putting of general legislation upon appropriation bills was inconvenient and injudicious, it was desirable at times: "It should not be used as the daily bread in legislation, but was the medicine of the Constitution and proper to purge away the diseases of the body politic. When vicious laws which impair the liberty of the people, are firmly fastened upon the statute books the House is bound to say that it will appropriate no money to give effect to such laws until and except they are repealed." The Democrats were obliged to yield, and the integrity of appropriation bills to this extent was protected.

The Constitution says nothing about which House shall prepare appropriation bills; as a matter of fact, the initiative has almost without interruption been taken by the lower House, until this procedure has come to be looked upon as a part of the unwritten constitution. In January, 1856, complaint was made that the House habitually delayed the transmission of the appropriation bills to the Senate until the last days of the session, when there was no opportunity for proper consideration. A Senator complained that it was the practice to appropriate the peoples' money at the dead hour of midnight, instead of in the face of day, and that within a very short time a naval appropriation bill for eight millions of dollars had been passed in the Senate without even being read. The charge was true: the bill passed on the night of the 4th of March,[1] the last day of the session, and under the plea of pressure the bill was voted simply by title. It was consequently proposed that a division of labor be made, whereby the House should undertake the preparation of a portion of the appropriation bills, leaving the Senate to prepare others; and then in the middle of the session make an exchange of bills. In opposition, it was urged that the practice of seventy years should be respected, and that there should be no encroachment on the privileges of the House. In accordance with its resolution, the Senate did prepare and pass appropriation bills for the repairs of fortifications and for invalid pensions; but these measures were treated by the House of Representatives with some contempt, and laid on the table. The effort to change the custom of the government proved to be ineffectual, and now for many years the House has retained the privilege of initiating the preparation of supply bills.

The most serious defect in the plan of appropriation is the scattering of responsibility in the preparation of the budget. Our form of government lacks not only controlling unity of action in finance by legislative and executive branches, but in Congress itself a distribution of functions tends to prevent any harmonious system. Until 1865 the House committee on ways and means had charge of all appropriation bills with a few important exceptions; hence the responsibility of originating plans of revenue and supply were centred in the same committee. In 1865, the enormous amount of legislative work occasioned by the Civil War caused the framing of appropriation bills to be taken away from the committee on ways and means, and intrusted to a new committee on appropriations. In 1879 and 1885 a further cleavage was made by distributing the fourteen appropriation bills to eight different committees, thus absolutely preventing any system for judiciously apportioning the total outgo. This distribution was put in practice

[1] *Congressional Globe,* Feb. 7, 1856, 34th Cong., 1st Sess., Part I, 1855–1856, p. 379. See also Garfield, *Works*, i, 694.

on the ground that it would secure an earlier and consequently more intelligent consideration of appropriation measures, an expectation not confirmed by experience. The efforts of each committee to assert its individual importance at the expense of others, and to secure, irrespective of the best general interest of the country, as large a share as possible of the total appropriation, has led to extravagance and even to improvidence. The principles of popular government in the United States are against giving to the executive much influence in the preparation of bills of supply; the secretary of the treasury enjoys the formal privilege of submitting to the House of Representatives a "Book of Estimates" which contains the estimate of the needs of the several departments, and which are not always respected by either of the two Houses. These memoranda find their way to the several committees dealing with appropriation bills, and form a useful body of information, but have no binding force.

If there has been a loss in unity of preparation, there has been a definiteness in the designation of the objects of supplies. Appropriations must be specific. In 1789 there was but one appropriation bill, thirteen lines in length, containing four items relating to civil expenses, military expenses, payment of the public debt and pensions. Not only has the number of bills increased, until there are now fourteen, but the law requires that each section of a bill shall contain as nearly as may be a single proposition for enactment. Definiteness of control has also been emphasized by the passage of laws forbidding the transfer by the executive of any appropriation from one object to another, even if within the same branch of service.

231. Collection of Revenue.

The collection of the revenue is divided between two branches of the treasury department, — one for customs duties, and the other for internal revenue taxes. The internal revenue service is organized into a separate bureau under a commissioner of internal revenue, but the local customs officials report directly to the secretary of the treasury. The country is divided into customs districts, in each of which there is at least one port of entry, where are stationed the principal officer of the district, the collector of customs, assisted by subordinate grades of officials, appraisers, including in a few offices a naval officer and surveyors, and in all offices inspectors, special agents, etc. If commercial needs demand it, other ports of delivery are designated within the district, and at these subordinate officials are stationed. The largest port of entry is New York city, through which flows two-thirds of the whole foreign commerce of the United States. More than 8000 persons are employed in the collection of the customs duties; and the annual expense of collecting this class of revenue is about three per cent of the receipts. There are 49 districts, the number having been cut in 1913 from more than a hundred. As foreign commerce became insignificant in many of the ports which were important a century ago when the districting was established, the expense of administration became excessive in many districts, exceeding the revenue collected. Every attempt, however, to deprive a State of an established administrative district with its attendant political prerogatives, for years met with local opposition which was instantly reflected in Congress.

The method of entering an importation of foreign goods, including the appraisement and payment of duties, has gone through many variations, but is now briefly as follows: The initial step is the authentication of an invoice of the goods by the American consular officer in the district from which the foreign goods are exported to this country; the certificate must state the market or wholesale price in the country of export; and the consular authentication is made in triplicate, one for the shipper to be used in making entry at the American port, one is transmitted to the collector of the port of entry, and the other is filed in the consul's office. The invoice is more than a formal declaration of value; it must contain a description of the merchandise, with its cost, discounts, charges, etc. Armed with this certificate, upon arrival of the goods, the importer makes an entry; he submits a description with the rates of duty which he considers applicable and pays into the custom house the gross amount thus computed: an immediate delivery of the goods is then granted, the government retaining one package in every ten as a sample. These packages are sent to the public stores or appraisers' warehouses for examination: if the appraisement does not agree with the valuation made, a re-settlement is ordered, and if the proper valuation has not been declared by the importer, whether through ignorance or fault, severe penalties may be incurred. An excessive valuation by the shipper is never lowered, but an undervaluation is punished under the present law by the imposition of an additional duty of one per cent. upon the appraised value for each one per cent. that the appraisers' value exceeds that declared in the entry. Opportunity is given to the importer who does not wish to use his goods at once, to deposit them under bond in a warehouse for not more than three years, and to defer the payment of the duties until withdrawal.

The principal difficulty in the administration of the customs for many years lay in the persistent practice of undervaluation. Some of the efforts to check this evil have already been discussed, but the difficulty long remained and has not yet entirely disappeared. The trouble was aggravated by the habit of consigning goods by foreign firms to agents in America, so that the buyer and the seller were practically the same, and could agree on any valuation that pleased them. In 1885 Secretary Manning asserted that very extensive frauds were due to this agency system; a foreign manufacturer would refuse to sell goods to other buyers, and then insist that no manufactured articles similar to those consigned to this country were sold in his market, and hence that there could be no market value at that place in the sense intended by law. Repeated decisions of the courts adverse to such juggling with the plain intent of the law did not put an end to frauds.

Ingenious methods have been devised to evade the customs: for example, when coverings came in free, articles of small value were enclosed in valuable coverings; sugar was artificially colored so as to imitate standards which entered at lower rates of duty. One method was that of fictitious invoices: articles were shipped by an agent of the American buyer in Paris to his agent in New York with a fictitious and fraudulent invoice; the buyer often persuading himself that he, as a passive recipient, was free from wrong or illegal behavior. Even among honest merchants, the administration of the tariff since the Civil War has been puzzling, because of the increasing complexity in the schedules and consequent inequalities in classification and valuation. Where no open fraud was intended, there was great opportunity for entries which would defeat the express purpose of the tariff acts, especially in the confusion created by the varying classification between "worsted" and "woollens," goods which, as far as use was concerned, were becoming more and more identical. In 1886 it was stated that 90 per cent. of the silk importations were as a rule undervalued; and so great were the apparent difficulties of securing an equal and just administration of the law, that the Democratic secretary of the treasury, representing a party generally standing for ad valorem rather than specific duties, recommended specific duties on silks. Much litigation grew out of the frequent changes in classification; and suits were entered much more rapidly than the courts could dispose of them.

A special effort was made in 1885 to remedy some of these evils and simplify the administration, and a bill originally drawn by Secretary Manning became the basis of the so-called McKinley administrative act of 1890. The stringency of the provisions to prevent fraud was increased: additional penalties were provided for undervaluation, and the number of general appraisers was increased in order to correct inequalities in the appraisement at different ports. The appraisers were organized into boards or courts for the prompt settlement of questions of appeal. On a simple question of value, a board of three general appraisers is a tribunal of last resort, and this simple device has greatly expedited the customs business. A further appeal to the Court of Customs Appeals lies only in case of alleged illegal action or irregular procedure by the government officials in arriving at the valuation. On the equally important question of classification, another board of general appraisers acts as a judicial court, but in cases of this character, there is the right of appeal to the federal courts either by the importer or by the government.

The administration of the internal revenue service does not at present involve many special difficulties, for questions of valuation and classification are easy to settle. Great and notorious frauds and scandals did spring up from the operations of the Whiskey Ring, especially in the years 1872–1875, and high government officials were involved, but these were instances of bribery and defiance of law, and the corrupt practices are to be interpreted as one of the symptoms of a debased tone of business and political life, rather than as a defect in the revenue system. At present the illicit distillation of whiskey is for the most part confined to the mountain districts of the South, where moonshiners operate on a small scale. The system has now been so long established that attempts to evade the tax, by illicit distillation or fraudulent packages, are rare. Under the jurisdiction of the commissioner of internal revenue are 63 district collectors, and a force of special agents who watch distilleries and ferret out frauds.

232. Custody of the Public Funds.

Until 1920 the moneys of the government were kept in the treasury at Washington and in sub-treasuries at Baltimore, Boston, Chicago, Cincinnati, New Orleans, New York, Philadelphia, St. Louis, and San Francisco. Each sub-treasury was in charge of an assistant treasurer of the United States. At times other offices, as mints or assay offices, were designated as depositories. In addition, a portion of the public funds might be kept on deposit in national banks which had been designated as depositories; for security, "the secretary of the treasury shall require of the associations thus designated satisfactory security by the deposit of United States bonds and otherwise." In October, 1902, Secretary Shaw accepted municipal and State bonds as well as federal securities in order to place with banks more of the government funds than they would otherwise have been able to take. In recent years the relation of the treasury to the money market has occasioned much perplexity. Large sums are accumulated in the treasury and thus withdrawn from the money market; the periods of large receipts and large payments do not correspond. The disturbance of the money market occurs even when the annual budget is well balanced, but much more so when the annual receipts greatly exceed the expenditures and create the serious and special problem of dealing with a surplus.

This subject has been investigated at length by Mr. David Kinley in his work on "The Independent Treasury of the United States": he shows that the regular absorption and disbursement of money, particularly at the sub-treasury in New York, necessarily affects the volume of circulation, and that this in turn influences prices; the spasmodic variation in prices is then felt in speculation. More than this, the irregular operations of the treasury affect the amount of credit which the banks can offer to their customers. If the bank reserve is cut into by steady withdrawals for payment of customs duties or other government obligations, and there is no corresponding deposit, loans must be reduced and business contracted. The independent treasury system has provided for the safety of public funds, and has helped to furnish a safe currency; but it does not allow enough elasticity in the circulating medium, and by its operations exposes business to the alternating arbitrary contractions and expansions of the currency. The treasury really engages in the banking business, though it lacks many of the powers of protecting its funds which the banks possess; it must issue and redeem treasury notes, and must maintain a gold reserve; it is also called upon to relieve the money market whenever stringency occurs, either to move the crops in the autumn, or because of unusual activity in business.

The surplus funds which accumulate in the treasury can be turned back into commercial currents in four ways: increased expenditures; increase of deposits in banks as far as these funds are derived from internal revenue; prepayment of interest on bonds, and the purchase of bonds in the open market. Expenditures suggested by an overflowing treasury are not likely to be wise. The deposit of public moneys in banks invites criticism because of the suspicion that particular banks are favored, and also because such deposits may become a basis for speculative opportunity to the detriment of legitimate business; the prepayment of interest is only a temporary alleviation; while the purchase of bonds necessitates the payments of premiums, generally highest when the treasury most needs to unload. Under the new Federal Reserve Act, a reserve bank might accept government deposits; and in the larger cities, at least, it was evident that these institutions would become the chief depositories of government funds. This was formally accomplished by the Act of 1920. The advantages of exclusive government custody are: safety, complete control, divorce of the treasury from speculative movements in the money market, and absence of political favoritism; but with all these benefits, such a system has had to face the serious injury caused by the derangement of the money market through the withdrawal of large sums.

Beginning with 1913, an important change was introduced in order to make treasury funds more available for the money market. All receipts, not only from internal revenue duties, but also from customs, could be placed at once in depositary banks to the credit of the government. All government checks might likewise be paid at any depository.

221. The Mint.

From the simple institution authorized in 1792, the coinage office of the government has grown to a large business enterprise. Coinage is now carried on at three mints, — Philadelphia, San Francisco, and Denver. The coinage executed in the fiscal year 1900 exceeded that of any previous year, amounting to over one hundred and eighty-four million pieces, valued at $141,351,960. Each mint is in charge of a superintendent, and is divided into the melter and refiner's department, the coiner's department, and the assayer's department. Government assay offices at New York, Carson, Salt Lake City, Helena, Boise, Charlotte, New Orleans, Deadwood, and Seattle serve a commercial purpose by determining the fineness of gold and silver deposited by private individuals; they assay, melt, and stamp bar specie. At the assay offices, as well as at the mints, deposits of gold and silver bullion may be made by private individuals for conversion into bars of standard weight, which are more useful than coin in making large shipments, particularly to foreign countries. Each of the mints, and also the assay office at New York, possesses a refinery for the parting and refining of bullion. In 1913 the earnings of the refineries amounted to $365,000; the total expenditures for the entire mint service were $1,172,000. Since 1873 there has been no seigniorage on gold, but on subsidiary and minor coins the profits have been large, and the seigniorage on silver since 1878, including dollars coined under the Bland-Allison and the Sherman Acts, in 1910, amounted to $160,000,000.

234. Supervision of Banks.

Until the passage of the Federal Reserve Act of 1913 the treasury department had entire administrative responsibility over national banks: first, in chartering them under acts of Congress; second, by printing and issuing circulating notes for the banks; third, by examining the condition of the banks in order to determine whether they comply with the provisions of the national banking act as to reserves, indebtedness, loans, etc.; fourth, by assuming charge of any banking institution which becomes insolvent; and fifth, by the collection of the taxes imposed upon banks. Most of these duties are undertaken by a special bureau in charge of the comptroller of the currency; a part of the work, as the custody of bonds deposited and the collection of the tax on circulation, is performed by the treasurer of the United States.

In addition to the more administrative duties, the comptroller is required by law to make an annual report to Congress in regard to the condition of banks, and also to suggest amendments to the national banking laws by which the system may be improved, and the security of holders of notes and other creditors be increased. As the monetary question has been a subject of first importance since the Civil War period, the public interest in the recommendations and discussions of the comptroller have been usually second only to that given to the reports of the secretary of the treasury.

No bank can begin business until the articles of association have been submitted to the comptroller and approved by him; the government is not only interested in the fulfilment of the conditions as to paying in of capital and deposit of bonds, but in recent years has endeavored to make judicial inquiry whether there be a commercial need for a bank in the place named. Since the beginning of the system in 1863, 10,918 banks have been organized, of which 7608 were in operation in 1916. For many years, in particular after the panic of 1893, the number of banks annually organized was small, — in some years less than the number surrendering their charters. In 1900, however, owing to the more liberal privileges granted by the Currency Law, the number of charters greatly increased. Banking corporations under State charters, trust companies, and private firms still do a large amount of commercial banking, it being estimated that there are about 20,000 private and State banks of deposit and discount. The official control by the government after the bank has once begun operations is not complete. Each bank is obliged to make to the comptroller five reports annually on forms prescribed by him, and must make special reports whenever called upon; it must also promptly report the amount of every dividend voted, and all earnings in excess of such dividend. National bank examiners are appointed who have power under the comptroller to make, without notice, a thorough personal examination into the affairs of a bank. Though this supervision has been in the main wholesome and efficient, a large number of failures is evidence to the incompetency of bank officials, to the neglect of bank directors to heed warnings of examiners, and to the making of loans over the security of which the comptroller has no jurisdiction. From the adoption of the system to Oct. 31, 1916, 579 national banks failed and were placed in the hands of receivers selected by the government. These failures have rarely been disastrous, since the note-holders are always safeguarded, and depositors and other creditors of failed banks have received, on the average, three-fourths of their claims.

235. Accounting System.

The accounting system established by Hamilton served the treasury efficiently for more than a century. As the annual payments of the government grew into the hundreds of millions of dollars, and bureaus and officials multiplied, the settlement of accounts by the old methods became complicated, and exasperating delays were frequent. In 1894 a change was introduced, whereby the system of audit was simplified and the number of comptrollers reduced to one. This results in the saving of much red tape: the settlement of accounts by the auditor is conclusive unless an appeal be taken to the comptroller; or the comptroller on his own motion, independently of any request, may make a revision; in either case his revision is final. The autocratic power of the comptroller still continues great, as was notably shown in the refusal of Comptroller Bowler in 1895 to pay the sugar bounties, even after the warrants had been drawn by the secretary of the treasury upon the treasurer of the United States; he yielded only to a decision of the Supreme Court. The secretary of the treasury reports to the House of Representatives a statement of all expenditures, which are referred to standing committees on expenditures, and by them examined. The entire system of accounting is one of publicity and checks. The principal defect in the publication of the accounts is the lack of clear classification of expenditures. Some improvement has been made in the "Statistical Abstract" by the publication of detailed groupings, but it is difficult to harmonize the figures here given with those found in the "Finance Reports."

236. Public Debt Statement.

The condition of the treasury is daily exhibited in what is known as the Treasury statement, prepared and issued under the direction of the treasurer. In addition there is also a monthly public debt statement. Unfortunately frequent changes in the form have served to obscure the real amount of public indebtedness. A few examples will illustrate this: For 1869 the debt was reported at four different amounts: —

Finance Report, 1869, p. 29	$2,656,603,000
Monthly debt statement, July 1, 1869 . .	2,645,170,000
Finance Report, 1870 (June 30, 1869), p. 25.	2,588,452,000
Finance Report, 1870, by the Register, p. 276	2,489,002,000

These several statements were afterwards explained by the secretary of the treasury as follows:[1] —

The first is a statement of the amount of the principal of the United States securities and Pacific Railroad bonds, issued under various acts of Congress.

The second is a statement of the principal of the outstand-

[1] *Bankers' Magazine*, 1872–1873, p. 467.

ing debt, including the accrued interest thereon, with the Pacific Railroad bonds excluded.

The third shows the outstanding principal of this debt with the sinking fund deducted, in accordance with the act of Congress of July 14, 1870, and exclusive of the Pacific Railroad bonds.

The fourth is a statement of the net debt of the United States — principal and accrued interest — with the cash in the treasury deducted.

In 1885 a radical change was made in the form of the debt statement by Secretary Manning. The Pacific Railroad bonds, heretofore excluded on the ground that the debt thus represented was covered by a mortgage, were counted in as a liability; accrued interest was made a liability; and fractional silver which was not legal tender was ruled out as an asset. The apparent total of the interest-bearing debt was thereby increased from $1,196,000,000 to $1,260,000,000. While the new debt statement was clearer than the old one in distinguishing the character of the several liabilities, the changes referred to led to absurd results, as when over $5,000,000 of fractional silver was exchanged for gold certificates, that is, a non-asset was exchanged for an asset. The new form did not continue long; in 1890 the national bank-note redemption fund was transferred from a liability to an asset; and in 1891 the Pacific Railroad bonds and accrued interest were once more excluded from the liabilities.

The use of certificate forms of money has also created confusion. Gold, silver, and United States notes deposited in the treasury against certificates have been treated as assets, and the certificates issued have been considered as part of the liabilities or indebtedness of the government. As the issue of certificates increased with the coinage of silver, the "cash in the treasury" piled up enormously; and this of course must be subtracted from the gross debt, in order to arrive at the true indebtedness. In the table of "outstanding principal of the public debt" published annually in the "Finance Report," an attempt has been made to guard against misinterpretation, as, for example, "Finance Report," 1900, page xcix, it is explained that between 1873 and 1884 certificates of deposit are included in the debt, though offset by notes held on deposit. Since 1884 certificates of all kinds "held in the treasurer's cash" are excluded, but the balance of certificates, i.e., those in circulation, are included. To arrive at a true statement, the volume of the silver, gold, and currency held in trust against the certificates in circulation must be known. Pacific Railroad bonds are also included in the table referred to. According to this presentation, the debt in 1900 was $2,101,000,000. On page xcviii the debt, however, is given as $2,137,000,000; on page ci, "cash in the treasury" is reported as $1,029,000,000, leaving a net debt, July 1, of $1,108,000,000. The kinds of money which make up the cash balance in the treasury, and the amount set aside for the agency account, are stated (for June 30) in the treasurer's report of 1900, on page 42. This table further indicates the portion of the "cash in the treasury," which is an "available balance." Upon the passage of the Currency Act in 1900, the daily treasury statement was much improved, making a clearer presentation of the trust funds of the government and the balance available for current needs. Other changes were made in 1913 and 1915.[1]

237. Miscellaneous Treasury Bureaus.

For many years several bureaus which have little to do with finance were under the jurisdiction of the treasury department, as, the marine hospital service, steamboat inspection, lighthouses, life-saving, immigration, coast and geodetic survey. Political convenience is the only explanation of these administrative anomalies. Some of these bureaus deal with commercial questions, and as no department of commerce has yet been organized, they are placed under the department nearest akin. Upon the creation of a new executive department of commerce and labor in 1903, changes were made which secure a more harmonious management of public affairs.

[1] See *Finance Report, 1915*, pp. 41–43.

In the course of the narrative, attention has been directed to a few of the more notable secretaries of the treasury. In the Appendix, a list of all the secretaries from 1789 until the present time is given. While a number of the men who have served in this office have not been leaders in public affairs, the list, as a whole, represents a roll of political intelligence and integrity. In the past quarter of a century there has been a greater disposition to select for secretary of the treasury some one equipped with special training in private finance, but it cannot be said that these have stood conspicuously above those selected from political life. This speaks well for the general stability of the fiscal system and is evidence that the treasury administration is not vitally dependent upon the personality of the secretary.

The subject of treasury administration cannot be left without an expression of congratulation over the experience of the United States in this field of governmental activity. There are many discouraging chapters in the history of local and State finance; democracy has too frequently turned aside from the straight path of honor and integrity, but the record of national finance may well give satisfaction. At times there has been a lack of courage both on the part of Congress and of the treasury; on occasion there has been stupid blundering, but treasury scandals have been few; extravagance has rarely been degraded into corruption. In every emergency the country has regained its courage and acquired the intelligence necessary to maintain its financial reputation at a high mark. When it is remembered that under our system of government, finance is not regarded as a profession, that few of the secretaries of the treasury have had any special training in commerce or banking, that the departmental heads are commonly chosen on account of political service, and that the rapid growth of governmental business makes enormous strains upon the civil service, the results are more than satisfactory.

APPENDIX

I

Amounts collected on some of the principal classes of commodities imported, 1880–1913 (millions of dollars).

	Fruits and nuts	Spirits, wines, malt liquors	Sugar, etc.	To-bacco	Cotton, manu-factures of	Silk, manu-factures of	Wool, manu-factures of	Wool, raw	Fibers, flax, hemp, jute, manu-factures of	Chem-icals, etc.	Earthen, stone, and china ware	Glass, manu-factures of	Iron and steel, manu-factures of	Leather, manu-factures of	Total
1880	3.4	6.2	42.2	4.7	10.0	18.6	21.9	7.4	9.7	4.1	2.4	2.8	23.2	3.4	182.4
1885	3.7	7.2	52.2	7.4	10.9	14.0	24.3	3.2	9.1	3.8	2.7	3.7	12.0	2.9	177.3
1890	3.9	8.5	55.2	13.3	11.7	18.9	37.4	5.5	11.9	5.0	4.0	4.2	15.4	3.8	225.3
1891	4.3	9.5	32.5	16.2	14.8	19.4	34.9	6.6	10.1	4.7	4.7	4.5	18.3	4.1	215.8
1892	3.1	8.8		10.2	16.4	17.0	34.3	7.8	11.0	4.5	5.0	5.3	16.5	4.5	173.0
1893	3.8	9.2	.2	14.8	19.0	20.3	36.5	8.1	11.3	4.8	5.4	5.0	21.9	5.2	198.4
1894	2.8	6.9	.3	13.7	12.2	12.8	19.1	2.1	7.3	3.4	3.9	3.5	14.1	3.2	128.9
1895	2.7	6.9	15.6	14.9	15.7	14.7	20.7	.2	7.2	4.0	3.2	3.1	11.6	3.6	147.9
1896	2.6	6.7	29.9	14.9	14.8	12.5	23.1		6.6	4.0	3.6	2.9	10.1	3.4	156.1
1897	3.0	8.0	41.3	21.0	16.3	12.4	22.7		7.7	3.8	3.6	2.6	6.6	3.3	171.8
1898	4.3	5.7	29.5	9.9	14.6	12.2	10.2	2.4	8.5	4.8	3.6	2.1	5.8	3.7	144.3
1899	5.3	7.1	61.6	10.6	17.7	13.5	13.3	4.0	10.6	5.4	4.5	2.5	5.1	4.0	200.9
1900	5.2	8.4	57.7	14.4	22.0	15.8	14.3	7.4	12.8	6.3	5.0	2.8	7.8	4.6	228.4
1901	4.5	9.1	63.0	16.7	21.8	14.2	13.4	8.1	12.6	5.6	5.5	2.7	7.0	4.1	232.6
1902	5.5	10.1	53.0	18.8	24.5	17.3	15.5	10.8	14.8	6.4	5.7	3.5	10.5	4.1	250.6
1903	5.7	11.2	63.6	21.9	27.8	19.3	17.6	11.6	15.5	6.6	6.2	4.3	16.9	4.0	279.8
1904	6.2	11.6	58.2	21.2	26.3	16.6	16.3	10.9	15.6	6.4	7.0	3.9	9.7	4.0	257.3
1905	5.8	12.1	51.4	22.7	26.6	17.0	16.5	16.5	15.8	6.4	6.8	3.3	8.4	4.0	257.9
1906	6.6	13.5	52.6	23.9	33.3	17.4	20.2	17.8	18.9	6.8	7.5	3.8	9.8	5.1	293.6
1907	7.0	15.8	60.3	26.1	39.0	20.2	20.0	16.6	22.1	7.5	8.0	3.9	12.3	6.1	329.1
1908	7.7	14.7	50.2	22.2	34.6	16.5	17.4	11.4	18.2	6.7	7.7	3.3	9.3	4.5	282.3
1909	6.2	15.7	56.4	23.3	33.1	16.2	16.3	17.1	18.1	7.4	5.9	2.6	8.2	5.0	294.4
1910	8.4	17.6	53.1	24.1	38.1	17.7	20.8	21.1	21.9	7.2	6.5	3.3	12.4	5.3	326.3
1911	8.0	16.7	52.8	26.2	35.8	16.8	16.5	12.5	20.5	7.2	6.7	3.7	10.2	4.8	309.6
1912	8.4	16.8	50.9	25.6	35.3	14.1	12.6	14.5	22.3	7.0	5.9	3.0	8.8	4.8	304.6

The figures in the above table are taken from the "Statistical Abstract, 1893," pp. 32–35; and "Statistical Abstract, 1913," p. 468. It is also to be observed that the total in the above table includes some classes not found in previous columns, and does not agree with the figures for customs receipts as found in the "Finance Report."

II.

Secretaries of the Treasury, 1789 to 1921.

Name	Whence Appointed	Date of Commission	Expiration of Service
Alexander Hamilton	New York	Sept. 11, 1789	Jan. 31, 1795
Oliver Wolcott, Jr.	Connecticut	Feb. 2, 1795	Dec. 31, 1800
Samuel Dexter	Massachusetts	Jan. 1, 1801	May 6, 1801
Albert Gallatin	Pennsylvania	May 14, 1801	Apr. 20, 1813
George W. Campbell	Tennessee	Feb. 9, 1814	Sept. 26, 1814
Alexander J. Dallas	Pennsylvania	Oct. 6, 1814	Oct. 21, 1816
William H. Crawford	Georgia	Oct. 22, 1816	Mar. 3, 1825
Richard Rush	Pennsylvania	Mar. 7, 1825	Mar. 3, 1829
Samuel D. Ingham	Pennsylvania	Mar. 6, 1829	June 20. 1831
Louis McLane	Delaware	Aug. 8, 1831	May 29, 1833
William J. Duane	Pennsylvania	May 29, 1833	Sept. 23, 1833
Roger B. Taney	Maryland	Sept. 23, 1833	June 24, 1834
Levi Woodbury	New Hampshire	June 27, 1834	Mar. 4, 1841
Thomas Ewing	Ohio	Mar. 5, 1841	Sept. 11, 1841
Walter Forward	Pennsylvania	Sept. 13, 1841	Feb. 28, 1843
John C. Spencer	New York	Mar. 3, 1843	May 2, 1844
George M. Bibb	Kentucky	June 15, 1844	Mar. 7, 1845
Robert J. Walker	Mississippi	Mar. 6, 1845	Mar. 5, 1849
William M. Meredith	Pennsylvania	Mar. 8, 1849	July 22, 1850
Thomas Corwin	Ohio	July 23, 1850	Mar. 7, 1853
James Guthrie	Kentucky	Mar. 7, 1853	Mar. 6, 1857
Howell Cobb	Georgia	Mar. 6, 1857	Dec. 8, 1860
Philip F. Thomas	Maryland	Dec. 12, 1860	Jan. 14, 1861
John A. Dix	New York	Jan. 11, 1861	Mar. 6, 1861
Salmon P. Chase	Ohio	Mar. 7, 1861	June 30, 1864
Wm. P. Fessenden	Maine	July 1, 1864	Mar. 3, 1865
Hugh McCulloch	Indiana	Mar. 7, 1865	Mar. 4, 1869
George S. Boutwell	Massachusetts	Mar. 11, 1869	Mar. 16, 1873
Wm. A. Richardson	Massachusetts	Mar. 17, 1873	June 2, 1874
Benj. H. Bristow	Kentucky	June 2, 1874	June 20, 1876
Lot M. Morrill	Maine	June 21, 1876	Mar. 9, 1877
John Sherman	Ohio	Mar. 9, 1877	Mar. 3, 1881
William Windom	Minnesota	Mar. 5, 1881	Nov. 13, 1881
Charles J. Folger	New York	Nov. 14, 1881	Sept. 4, 1884
Walter Q. Gresham	Indiana	Sept. 24, 1884	Oct. 19, 1884

Name	Whence Appointed	Date of Commission	Expiration of Service
Hugh McCulloch	Indiana	Oct. 31, 1884	Mar. 6, 1885
Daniel Manning	New York	Mar. 7, 1885	Mar. 31, 1887
Charles S. Fairchild	New York	Apr. 1, 1887	Mar. 4, 1889
William Windom	Minnesota	Mar. 6, 1889	Jan. 29, 1891
Charles Foster	Ohio	Feb. 25, 1891	Mar. 6, 1893
John G. Carlisle	Kentucky	Mar. 7, 1893	Mar. 5, 1897
Lyman J. Gage	Illinois	Mar. 6, 1897	Jan. 31, 1902
Leslie M. Shaw	Iowa	Feb. 1, 1902	Mar. 4, 1907
George B. Cortelyou	New York	Mar. 4, 1907	Mar. 4, 1909
Franklin MacVeagh	Illinois	Mar. 4, 1909	Mar. 4, 1913
William G. McAdoo	New York	Mar. 6, 1913	Dec. 15, 1918
Carter Glass	Virginia	Dec. 16, 1918	Feb. 1, 1920
David F. Houston	Missouri	Feb. 2, 1920	Mar. 3, 1921
Andrew W. Mellon	Pennsylvania	Mar. 4, 1921	

INDEX

Printed in Dunstable, United Kingdom

91221342R00358